Physiological Psychology Dictionary

A Reference Guide for Students and Professionals

GEORGE S. GROSSER

American International College

CAROL S. SPAFFORD

American International College

McGraw-Hill, Inc.

New York   St. Louis   San Francisco   Auckland   Bogotá   Caracas   Lisbon
London   Madrid   Mexico City   Milan   Montreal   New Delhi
San Juan   Singapore   Sydney   Tokyo   Toronto

PHYSIOLOGICAL PSYCHOLOGY DICTIONARY
A Reference Guide for Students and Professionals

This book is printed on acid-free paper.

2 3 4 5 6 7 8 9 0   DOC/DOC   9 9 8 7 6 5

ISBN 0-07-059860-6

The editor was Beth Kaufman;
the production supervisor was Phil Galea.
R. R. Donnelley & Sons Company was printer and binder.

Library of Congress Cataloging-in-Publication Data is available: LC Card #94-18010

About the Authors

D r. George S. Grosser and Dr. Carol S. Spafford are teaching associate professors in the School of Psychology and Education at American International College. Dr. Grosser earned a doctorate in experimental physiological psychology from Boston University and Dr. Spafford in educational psychology from American International College. Their research interests include exploring the nature and causes of learning disabilities and the means for enhancing the quality of diagnostic procedures in the field. Drs. Grosser and Spafford are in the process of publishing a research and resource guide on the subject of dyslexia. The authors can be contacted at American International College, Box 60, 1000 State Street, Springfield, MA, 01109-3189.

Preface

Dictionaries, according to Merriam-Webster's Third New International Dictionary, are reference books alphabetically arranged along with information about word forms, pronunciations, functions, etymologies, meanings, and syntactical and idiomatic word usage. Typically, dictionaries are alphabetical reference guides of extensive vocabulary listings. In our experiences with undergraduate, graduate, and doctoral psychology, education, and science students, we have found that traditional dictionaries and glossaries are incomplete in providing a "mind's-eye" picture of a multitude of physiology and related psychology terms which are advanced in the field. Terminology is frequently presented in education, science, and psychology college classes that is easily pronounceable but more difficult to understand, such as "the Hawthorne effect," "learning disabilities," "memory," and "depression." Many such terms can be related in terms of physiological and psychological implications. The term "learning disabilities" is an excellent example.

Learning disabilities have been defined as being "constitutional in origin," characterized by "social misperception." There you have it--physiology and psychology intertwined, interjoined, interconnected, interwoven, interlaced, interlapped, interlayered, and . . .OK OK. You've got the message. For terms that appear to have just physiological or just psychological roots, (e.g.,"neurotransmitter" and "personality disorder"), one need only look down the road of experience to find connections between such terms. In the present instance, it is now well known that certain neurotransmitters can cause personality disorders such as depression and mania. These connections are difficult to make via traditional dictionaries or book glossaries. We have provided some refinement of appropriate terminology necessary for a more in-depth understanding of several terms related to physiology and psychology and some relationships between the two. Relationships sometimes lead to theories or paradigms that put forth important postulates or hypotheses. Ordinarily, dictionaries do not lend themselves to these higher-order connections. A case in point would be "Alzheimer's disease." "Alzheimer's disease" is defined in Merriam-Webster's Third New International Dictionary as "senile dementia occurring at an early age." Characteristic symptoms and possible causes are not mentioned, since such material would be inappropriate for such a reference source. Certainly the physiological relationships to the psychology of the mind cannot be presented in a dictionary format. Particularly poignant would be the social-medical patterns of children with neurologically based syndromes whereby diminished cognitive and behavioral responses follow the progressive nature of the diseases (e.g., Friedreich's ataxia, Von Recklinghausen's disease, and Lesch-Nyhan syndrome).

The jargon of physiological psychology many times requires two- and three-word terminology entries, so that most dictionaries would exclude such entries (e.g., "sustained visual pathway," "affective personality disorder," "sweep test," and "elimination diet"). Even though a term such as "Snellen chart" will be found in Webster's Dictionary, it is difficult to determine exactly what a Snellen chart looks like or its relationship to the terms "20/20 vision" and "visual acuity." For most readers, a standard Merriam-Webster's definition might suffice. Even simple definitions are often difficult to abstract from dictionaries or glossaries. Take the word "stereopsis," for example. We define "stereopsis" as "seeing the world stereoscopically, that is, in three dimensions." Merriam-Webster's Third New International Dictionary necessarily defines "stereopsis" as "stereoscopic vision; capacity for depth perception." One then must define "stereoscopic vision" which reads, "characterized by stereoscopy." Finally, "stereoscopy" leads one to the understanding that stereopsis is related to "the seeing of objects in three dimensions." One entry versus three entries for the college student is adequate, time-efficient, and easy to follow. The key for all entries is to present the "lingo" of physiological psychology in "down-to-earth" terminology. You will find several difficult-to-find definitions, such as "orthomolecular," "gene mapping," "sham lesion," "postural rehabilitation," "scotopic sensitivity syndrome," "phantom limb," and so on presented in "laypersons'" terms. Even "easy-to-find" definitions for words such as "memory" are further refined for the student who needs a more detailed physiological and/or psychological explanation. That's where we bring in "flashbulb memory," "autobiographical memory," "echoic memory," and "iconic memory." You will also find listed measures of memory and ways to improve your memory skills! These various foci on memory are not found in most glossaries or dictionaries.

Then there are the words that take on special meanings in a particular science so that their regular dictionary definition fails to convey the meaning that the scientific writer intends. Take the word "arachnoid," which implies spidery things. In neuroanatomy, the arachnoid is the middle of three membranes surrounding the brain. It is called the arachnoid because it is made up of cross-hatched fibers that resemble a web made by an outdoor spider (not the familiar cobweb, by the way). Another example is the word "confabulate," which, the regular dictionary tells us, means "to confer with other people in a group," what one might call "chit-chat." In neuropsychology, to confabulate is to exhibit a pathological symptom, namely, to make up stories and believe in them as if they were true. This occurs in Korsakoff's syndrome, where the patient has severe memory losses but cannot acknowledge that any loss of memory has occurred.

This reference guide will assist the reader when encountering duplicate or overlapping terms in "commonsensible terms." For example, you might have found it difficult in psychology classes to differentiate among such terms as "antisocial," "asocial," "psychopathic," and "sociopathic." That's because these are terms which characterize one type of disorder and are one and the same. Only a reference guide such as this one could help you "unmuddy" these "muddied" waters. It is critical for the college student to go beyond the elements of dictionary entries such as word forms, pronunciations, functions, and syntactical and idiomatic word usage to focus more upon meanings and relationships within the fields of psychology and physiology. This work does exclude the fields of education and other fields, inasmuch as our focus is directed toward the physiological psychology realms. These fields have a technical jargon and terminology that cannot be easily defined or understood within the context of traditional reference materials. You might enjoy reading some of this reference material to learn more about the world of physiological psychology. You may be surprised to learn that horseradish is more than a food enhancer; horseradish peroxidase can be valuable to science! The study of physiological psychology might satisfy your curiosity about such questions as . . .Why are we called warm-blooded animals, and what is the only warm-blooded fish (being warm-blooded is an exceptional talent for a fish to have)? What causes aggression to erupt? Where in the body are the hammer, anvil, and stirrup? Who are the trichotillomanics? When do unconditioned responses occur? What makes some responses "conditioned"? How can physical things such as drugs cause changes in immaterial abstractions such as minds and feelings? Why is grandma's glass of milk the key to insomnia treatment? What is the difference between a night terror disorder and a nightmare disorder? What makes some of the axons in a sensory nerve running from a sense organ to the brain carry nerve impulse away from the brain and out to the sense receptors? Did they get lost, or what? Check out the entries for "centrifugal bipolar cells" and the "olivocochlear bundle" to find out! What are the best years of our lives for smelling the world of odors that surrounds us all the time? And is it true that learning can improve when humor is injected into the content?

Readers who enjoy playing "trivia" might relish the challenge of finding the answers to the following questions: If the cerebral cortex were pressed flat as a pancake, how many inches would it stretch out to the left and right sides? And what would its total area be? On another subject, what animals are able to see ultraviolet "light," which humans cannot? And what kind of animal sees infrared "light," that humans feel as heat but cannot see? In still another area: What structure of the brain has the Greek word for "bridal chamber" as its name? What structure of the brain looks like two footballs side by side? What brain structure is named with the Greek word for "seahorse"? And what brain structure is named after the Latin word for "almond"? What in the brain are the "blobs" and "interblobs," and where can they be found? What are the X0, XXX, XXY and XYY disorders? What are the physiological changes involved in the emotion of love, and what are the five types of love one can experience? Better yet, what causes gooseflesh or goosebumps when you are in love? (Don't you love those questions?) Finally, does IQ diminish with age or after using this dictionary? Speaking of using this dictionary, the reader will find the following suggestions helpful when looking for information or a given word:

1. *The Main Entry.* The main entry is entered in bold-face letters flush with the left-hand margin in alphabetical order by letter. Words preceded by numbers (e.g., "6-hydroxydopamine") will be listed alphabetically by the initial letter.

2. *Pronunciation.* The 1987 Random House Pronunciation Guide found in the Random House Dictionary was used to prepare easily understood phonetic equivalents of more difficult to pronounce entries.

3. *The Etymology.* The pronunciation guide (when applicable) is sometimes followed by the etymological meanings in parentheses which may tell what language and form it came from or the relevant English-language derivative. Occasionally, such information is imbedded in the definitions.

4. *Cross-References.* The meaning of many terms can be enhanced by cross-references that expand the meaning of the main entry. Cross-references appear in bold-face letters within the definition itself or at the end of the definition, preceded by the phrase "See also."

5. *Topical Information.* If the reader is looking for a particular topic such as "emotion," a general definition will be given, along with several references for a more in-depth understanding of the subject (e.g., "aggression," biofeedback," and "psychophysiology."

6. *Alternative Names.* Many scientific and psychological terms are known by more than one name. This dictionary cross-references such terms as neurohypophysis/posterior pituitary gland and hammer/malleus. Proper nouns are also cross-referenced; usually they refer to dis-

eases or conditions (e.g., Sturge-Weber syndrome is also known as Sturge-Kalischer disease, Parks-Weber-Dimitri disease, Sturge-Weber-Dimitri disease, and Sturge-Weber-Krabbe disease).

7. *Subtypes.* Some definitions contain overviews of general areas (e.g., phobias) with specific subtypes listed under the topic (e.g., acrophobia, agoraphobia, arachnophobia, astrophobia, and so on) and often cross-referenced.

8. *Key Words.* Words critical to the understanding of a definition are sometimes underlined in order to emphasize essential phrases or words.

9. *Pronunciation Key.* The pronunciation key for this dictionary is based on the key used by Random House in their 2nd 1987 edition.

a	bat	ēr	ear	j	just	ô	ball raw	t͟h	that
ā	paid	f	foot	k	make	oi	oil	u	sun
â(r)	air	g	beg	l	law bottle (bot'l)	oo / o͞o	book fool	û(r)	burn
ä	father	h	hear	m	him	ou	loud	v	river
b	back	hw	which	n	now button (but'n)	p	stop	w	away
ch	teacher	i	big	ng	sing	r	near red	y	yes
d	bed	ī	bite	o	pot	s	miss	z	zoo
e	red			ō	no	sh	shoe	zh	treasure
ē	seat					t	ten	ə	about (the reduced sound of the "a")
						th	thin	R	rouge (fr.)

( ) optional e.g., "n(y)oo" ′ primary stress ″ secondary stress

Your own "orienting response" toward this reference guide when learning, preparing for exams, or writing a paper will, we hope, result in many happy "episodic" or "flashbulb" memories. Our flashbulb memories (which occur in increased amounts in social situations) involve definitions such as that of "oxytocin," as well as those of a couple of terms we'll introduce now - "friend at court" (one who acts on behalf of another) or just plain "friend" (one who likes and respects another in a mutually pleasurable relationship in which loyalty and "a helping hand" prevail). For those friends who assisted us in the preparations of this manuscript, we acknowledge their assistance with the highest regard, respect, and gratitude: first and foremost - Jane Vaicunas, our contact at McGraw-Hill Publishing who moved this project from the status of a hope to that of a reality. We also thank demon book agent Mike Fried, our initial contact with McGraw-Hill. American International College colleagues who provided support and assistance include President Harry Courniotes (who is the "raphe" that holds the parts of A.I.C. together), Richard Bedard, Henry Benjamin, Dr. Bernie Berenson, Susan Blackington, Maria Cahillane, John Coleman, Dr. Ann Courtney, Judy Dumont, Dr. Austin Flint, Betty Gandy-Tobin, Margarite Genest, Richard Hansen, Annette Krzyzek, Manisha Lalwani, Dr. Royce Layman, Michelle LaVallee, Lena Lefebvre, Dean Charles Maher, Leticia Matos, Debbie McCarthy, Mildred McKenna, Lee Mitchell, Pauline Mortenson, Lisa Basile Nettis, Madelyn Orozco, Beth Peckham, Beatrice Pires, Eileen Pisarski, Liza Quirk, Mary Saltus, Miriam Santiago, Kathy Sullivan, Karyn Taber, Tina Toohey, Aleyda Torres, Dean Gerry Weaver, Ryan Wells, and Naomi White. Finally, we extend our appreciation to some friends in the field who reviewed various drafts of the manuscript: Dr. Carol Batt, Sacred Heart University; Dr. Barbara Dautrich; Dr. Yoshito Kawahara, San Diego Mesa College; Dr. Susan P. Luek, Millersville University; Dr. Allen Schneider, Swarthmore College; and Dr. Gus Pesce spent numerous hours reviewing our work, and their constructive comments were always insightful and encouraging.

We would be remiss not to give special recognition to five individuals. Beth Jones and Marie Stevens were invaluable resources who were responsible for dealing with the fine details, editing, proofing, and correspondence regarding this manuscript. Michelle Hervieux, Matt Pappathan, and Cathy Meadows were also great assets when researching those "hard-to-find" resources. Cathy Meadows expertly "pounded the pavement" researching articles at several libraries (can you believe she asked to be assigned to us?). Matt always "came through" with those resources we couldn't find.

At McGraw-Hill Publishing, a number of people deserve our undying gratitude as they guided us to final completion of this project. Beth Kaufman with kindly, firm "hand on the tiller," kept us on course. She was ALWAYS available for consultation and assistance. Naomi Sofer was responsible for creating the outstanding appearance of the printed text. She was most accommodating and helpful when needed. Mike Clark was responsible for the smooth trafficking of the manuscript, and Fred Burns was responsible for the meticulous, accurate, and thorough copy editing. Any errors that remain in the text are the sole responsibility of the authors.

The authors would like to give special acknowledgment to C. Ammons, M. Caretas, J. Michael Harrison, P. Harrison, G. W. Hynd, A.M. Lassek, B. Miller, G. Pavlidis, J. Perez, J. Potter, H. Roazen, M. R. Rosenzweig, R. Tremble, and J. Voress who indirectly had a special and positive impact on the content of this text. These practitioners in the field of physiological/ psychology generously imparted their knowledge and expertise during some formative years.

We would like to acknowledge the indispensable assistance of our friend and colleague, linguist Judith Speckels. Assisted by Cristin Carpenter, Ms. Speckels provided the pronunciation guide for the terms in this dictionary. Judy not only assisted us in meeting deadlines, but finished a doctoral dissertation as well. We're proud of her! Cristin and Judy's hard work and efforts are gratefully acknowledged. Finally, we must thank our family members Eleanor Grosser; Irene, Kenny, and Richard Spafford; and all of the Sullivans (especially Richard and Carol) for their never-ending support and love. The **key** contributions of **Ken Spafford** and **George Sullivan** allowed us to move forward during all phases of this project. They're the best!!! Thanks to all!!! and

Welcome to physiological psychology!

P. S.

We are submitting to our readers an. . .

AUTHORS' CHALLENGE

We, the authors, conscientiously are concerned with keeping this resource guide both useful and accurate. Our interest is to recommence our re-edition of this resource with recollectable replenishments and refreshing refinements that will rejuvenate this work with renewed effort rededicated to the resurgence of readability in our rather recherche research area. We hope that our next edition will contain relevant additions to our lexicon through submissions from you, the readers. We will gratefully acknowledge any and all contributions of new entries and their definitions in the preface to our second edition. Please send prospective contributions to either author at Box 2512, Springfield, MA 01101-2512.

The Authors.

A

AAC. Augmentative and Alternative Communication. See: augmentative communication; alternative communication.

Abduction. The movement of an arm or leg to the side and/or away from the body. See also: **adduction**.

Abducens (ab dōōs′enz) **nerve**. The sixth cranial nerve. It innervates the external rectus muscle that would pull the eye to one side, for a sidelong glance, for example. See also: **cranial nerves.**

Aberration (ab″ə rā′shən). [1] A deviation from what is considered normal or average. Neural aberrations can result in disabilities or disorders. [2] Uneven refraction of light by the lens of the eye.

Ablatio penis (a blā′shē ō pē′nis). The destruction of the penis as, for example, by an accidental injury.

Ablatio placentae (a blā′shē ō plə sen′tē) (also called **abruptio placentae**). The premature detachment of an otherwise-normally-positioned placenta (after the 20th week of gestation). There is a risk involved for both the mother and the fetus.

Ablatio retinae (a blā′shē ō ret′i nē″). Detachment of the retina.

Ablation (a blā′shən). One of the three major techniques used to analyze the relations between the central nervous system and behavior, the other two being stimulation and recording. The ablation method uses the logic of subtraction. Delete a part of the brain or spinal cord and note what part of the organism's repertoire of behavioral abilities or skills is now missing. This method cannot be used alone in attempting to account for a particular skill or activity, primarily because the brain will reorganize itself after an injury and can partially make up for the lost material.

Abnormal behavior. Socially unconventional and unacceptable behaviors which create discomfort in other individuals or disruption in the society. The abnormal behavior is often shown in maladaptive responses to others. It is usually an expression of an abnormal personality, i.e., a total maladjustment to one's life circumstances. See also: **DSM IV**; **personality.**

Abnormality. Any behavioral/mental/emotional state leading to poor adjustment to the social environment, to poor health, or to personal distress.

Absolute refractory (ri frak′t(ə)rē) **period**. A time period of one-half millisecond after the onset of a nerve impulse during which no stimulus, however strong, can begin a new nerve impulse in the axon. The significance of this fact is that there is a ceiling (i.e., an upper limit) on the number of nerve impulses that can occur in an axon during a given time. This limit is approximately 1,000 impulses per second. See also: **all-or-none law**; **relative refractory period**.

Absolute threshold. The minimum intensity of stimulating energy needed to produce the detection of the presence of the stimulus. An example of a measurement of the absolute threshold is the taste of 1 gram of salt dissolved in 500 liters of distilled water; the salt taste can just barely be detected when the salt solution is that weak. That dilution level is the absolute threshold for salt taste. Due to fluctuations of human sensory thresholds, the experience has to be repeated several times, with the average concentration of the solution that is just detected (e.g., with salt detected in half of the trials) being taken as the measure of the absolute threshold. See also: **psychophysics**.

Absorption spectrum. A kind of graphic display produced from shining a white light on a test substance and recording the wavelengths of light that fail to pass through the substance (i.e., are absorbed by it). This is often used in the quantitative chemical analysis of unknown substances, because each chemical element absorbs its own unique set of light frequencies. The graphic record comes in the form of absorption lines. The test substance selectively absorbs only some of the light, so that there are gaps in the graph of the wavelengths of light arranged by size (i.e., the light spectrum). These gaps are indicated by vertical black lines.

Absorptive phase. That phase of the eating-fasting cycle that comes directly after the consumption of a meal. In the absorption phase, the fat and glucose are removed from the blood by the cells of the body so that they may be burned as fuel. Any excess fat is stored in the lipocytes (fat cells) in the form of triglyceride. Due to the action of the hormone insulin, excess sugar is converted to glycogen (animal starch) and stored in the liver. See also: **fasting phase; glucose; glycogen; hunger; insulin; lipocytes; triglyceride.**

Academic achievement. The accomplished level of functioning in a particular subject (e.g., physiology) or skill (e.g., ability to infer causation).

Accommodation. [1] In Piaget's theory, the modification of existing cognitive patterns. One's cognitive schemes are changed to accommodate new experiences or information. [2] The reflexive bulging of the lens in order to focus on objects that have come closer to the observer. See also: **accommodation reflex.**

Accommodation reflex. The bulging of the human lens so that near objects are thrown into sharp focus. This is accomplished by the **ciliary muscle.** The ciliary muscle receives parasympathetic nervous system commands from the Edinger-Westphal nucleus, which is part of the **superior colliculus** of the midbrain. See also: **ciliary muscles; refraction; midbrain; superior colliculus.**

Accumbens (ə kum'bənz). A nucleus (collection of neuron cell bodies) in a forebrain structure, the septum, which is part of the limbic system (see definition). The accumbens receives messages from the midbrain's ventral tegmental area (from dopamine-releasing neurons), and, via glutamate-releasing neurons, from the frontal lobe of the cerebral cortex as well as the limbic system's amygdala and hippocampus. The axons of the accumbens go to a part of the basal ganglia (see definition), the ventral globus pallidus, releasing the inhibitory neurotransmitter GABA to receptor sites on neuron membranes of the globus pallidus. Behaviorally, the accumbens may be involved in circuits dealing with aggression, pleasure, and cognition. Clinically, it may be connected with a psychosis, viz., schizophrenia. The pathway including the ventral tegmental area and the nucleus accumbens is called the mesocorticolimbic dopamine system. It is to be distinguished from the longer-known (and more studied) nigrostriatal dopamine system (dopaminergic axons arising from neurons in the

midbrain's substantia nigra and running to the corpus striatum, which is one of the basal ganglia). Drugs that relieve schizophrenic symptoms by suppressing dopamine activity in general (e.g., haloperidol) eventually produce a motor disorder (tardive dyskinesia) which is similar to Parkinson's disease. The drug clozapine opposes dopamine activity only in the mesocorticolimbic system, thus acting against schizophrenia without risking the development of tardive dyskinesia. See also: **clozapine; haloperidol; neuroleptic drug.**

Acetaldehyde. A toxic chemical produced during the metabolism of ethyl alcohol or alcohol. Enzymes in the liver metabolize the alcohol and change it to acetaldehyde. Prolonged use of alcohol causes acetaldehyde to initiate cirrhosis of the liver. See also: **acetaldehyde dehydrogenase; alcohol.**

Acetaldehyde dehydrogenase (as˝ə tal'də hĭd dē˝hī dro'jin ās). An enzyme that changes acetaldehyde to acetic acid (as in ethyl alcohol or drinking alcohol). Individuals vary in their levels of acetaldehyde dehydrogenase, which directly impact their tolerance for alcohol consumption. Approximately 50% of some Asian groups have low amounts of acetaldehyde dehydrogenase and feel ill after ingesting alcohol or feel an intense flushing in the face. Adequate amounts of this enzyme are needed to metabolize alcohol. The drug Antabuse is used to treat individuals with alcohol problems (as a treatment of last resort) and actually decreases one's level of acetaldehyde dehydrogenase. In turn, one's craving for alcohol is decreased as alcohol ingestion now causes nausea and sickness. Even shampoos with alcohol have to be avoided when an individual is taking Antabuse treatment. See also: **alcohol; Antabuse.**

Acetic acid. A chemical that the body uses as a source of energy.

Acetylcholine (ə set˝əl kō' lēn˝,-sēt˝, as˝ə til˝-). The most prevalent of the neurotransmitters and the first one to be discovered. Acetylcholine (ACh) in the peripheral nervous system plays a role in both the parasympathetic and the somatic nervous system components. Parasympathetic axons release ACh at muscarinic receptors on the smooth muscles and glands. The muscarinic action of ACh can be blocked by the drug atropine. Somatic nervous system axons release ACh at nicotinic receptors on the striate ("voluntary") muscles. The nicotinic action of ACh can be blocked by the drug curare. In the central nervous system, ACh is released in widespread areas. High levels of ACh activity have been observed in actively functioning areas of the brain. One of the correlates of Alzheimer's disease is reduced ACh activity in the cerebral cortex. ACh is apparently important both for our survival and for our higher intellectual functions.

Acetylcholinesterase (ə sēt″ əl kō″ li nes′ tə rās) (AChE). The enzyme that breaks up acetylcholine (ACh) from the synapse after the message has been sent. Clearing the synapse is like clearing a calculator after having performed a given mathematical procedure. Leaving the answer to a preceding problem in the window would allow that number to add in with the numbers used in attempting to solve another, different problem. This essential synapse-clearing role can be disturbed by certain chemicals known as anticholinesterase agents which are more familiar to the general public as "nerve gas." Nerve gas prevents the clearing away of ACh from its synapses and causes the over-activity of ACh circuits in the nervous system. This is particularly dangerous to life in the case of the muscarinic (smooth muscle and gland) ACh receptors. The victims of a nerve gas attack may be killed by the overactivity of their own salivary and mucous glands, for example. When soldiers are expected to be facing an opponent armed with nerve gas, they are provided with atropine which blocks the muscarinic receptors and thus prevents their overactivity.

ACh. See **acetylcholine.**

AChE. See **acetylcholinesterase.**

Achieved role. A social role one has obtained voluntarily such that of being a spouse, teacher, church leader, and so on. See also: **ascribed role.**

Achievement discrepancy. A measurable difference between one's innate intellectual talents (e.g., IQ) and one's academic performance (as measured by achievement tests). Learning disabilities are manifest in discrepancies between IQ scores and actual reading/language/math performance(s).

Achievement motive. The psychological need to attain success experiences or achievements, and/or to complete goal-directed activities successfully.

Achievement test. A test intended to measure a person's rate of learning acquisition regarding a particular subject area. For example, a math achievement test might measure a person's learned problem solving technique and/or ability to perform math computations.

Achromatic (ā″krō mat′ik) colors. Black, white, and gray. See also: **opponent-process theory of color vision.**

ACID profile. A profile is a distribution of subtest scores for complex test such as the Wechsler Intelligence Scales (the WAIS, WISC, and WPPSI). Male dyslexics are said to have lower scores on four particular subtests than on any of the other six; these four are Arithmetic, Coding, Information, and Digit Span, an acrostic for which is ACID.

Acoustic (ə kōō′stik) aids. Mechanical devices or assists for hearing-impaired individuals (e.g., hearing aids). Any method permitting an individual to hear with greater accuracy or sensitivity (i.e., hearing aids).

Acoustic (ə kōō′stik) nerve, cochlear (kok′lē ər) nerve or **auditory nerve.** The auditory component of the auditory vestibular nerve, the eighth cranial nerve. The acoustic nerve's cell bodies are bipolar cells in the spiral ganglion, which is near the inner ear. Its axons travel for the most part in the eighth cranial nerve, but separately come to their end in either the ipsilateral dorsal or ventral cochlear nucleus of the medulla. See also: **auditory vestibular nerve; bipolar neuron; cranial nerves; ganglion; ipsilateral; medulla; nucleus (part of the gray matter).**

Acquired dyslexia (dis lek′sē ə). A reading disability due to brain damage. This is in contrast with **developmental dyslexia** (see definition).

Acquired immune deficiency syndrome (AIDS). A fatal sexually transmitted disease which is caused by one of the HIV group of viruses. It destroys the body's immune system. No cure has been discovered as of this writing. It should be noted that some individuals may be affected by the HIV virus without succumbing to full-blown AIDS.

Acquisition. A stage of learning (e.g., in conditioning) during which responses are acquired (e.g., in classical conditioning, through the pairing of conditioned stimuli with unconditioned stimuli). In rote learning of verbal material, the acquisition stage would involve the memorizing of listed items.

Acrophobia (ak″rə fō′bē ə). Fear of heights. See also: **phobias**.

Across-fiber pattern theory. A theory of how aspects of stimuli are encoded by sensory neurons. This is the view that each receptor responds to a wide range of stimuli and contributes to the perception of every stimulus that affects the sensory system.

ACTH. The abbreviation for **adrenocorticotropic hormone**. See also: **adrenocorticotropic hormone**.

Action component. That part of one's attitude(s) which govern actions toward the object(s) of the attitude(s).

Action potential. A transitory negative voltage moving along the outer surface of the axon membrane, the action potential is the physical basis of the nerve impulse. Each axon leaves the cell body at an axon hillock which is affected by graded potentials (both excitatory and inhibitory). Whenever there is sufficient net excitory potential at the axon hillock, the spike potential begins and automatically moves down the axon. There is a momentary change of the voltage of the outer surface of the cell membrane from +70 mV to -50 mV; alternatively, we could just as correctly say that the voltage of the inner surface of the membrane changes from -70 mV to +50 V (all voltage measurements are relative). This is the actual action potential. All action potentials are approximately equal in size and shape (i.e., amplitude) within a given neuron under normal conditions; this fact is known as the all-or-none law. The transmission of the action potential down the axon is known as the propagation of the action potential. See also: **all-or-none law**.

Activating effect. The temporary effect of a hormone on behavior (only while the hormone is present).

Activation. The degree of arousal experienced when stimuli are presented.

Activation-synthesis theory. This is Hobson's theory that dreams result from subcortical nerve impulses randomly stimulating portions of the visual area of the cerebral cortex. The stimulated cortex in turn produces the sometimes bizarre sequence of events we call "dreaming."

Active sleep. See: **REM sleep**.

Active transport. The transfer of chemicals (e.g., potassium and sodium ions) across semipermeable cell membranes with the expenditure of energy from adenosine triphosphate (ATP). This can be contrasted to passive diffusion. See also: **adenosine triphosphate**.

Activity level. See: **circadian rhythms**.

Activity theory. The theory of aging which presumes that the best psychological adjustments to aging occur among individuals who remain mentally and physically active.

Actor. The person or animal whose behaviors are under study.

Acuity. That aspect of vision which involves the sharp resolution of images.

Acupuncture (ak′yōō pungk″chər). The insertion and rotation of needles into the skin at any of various places on the body in order to alleviate pain. The place stimulated by the acupuncture needles may be quite far from the painful area being influenced. The practice comes from ancient Chinese medicine. Although the pain relief has been said to be a placebo effect, physiological psychologists attribute the analgesia to the release in the brain of endorphins and enkephalins, the body's own opiates. The anti-opiate drug naloxone restores the pain, supporting the opiate-release theory and casting doubt on the placebo view.

Acute. Refers to the sudden onset of a symptom (e.g., a kidney stone or an appendicitis attack). In physiological research, the phrase acute preparation may refer to an animal under general anesthesia with its brain exposed so that an electrode may be applied to various places on the brain's surface. See also: **chronic**.

Adaptation. An organism's adjustment to prolonged stimulation of a sense organ by lowering the response level to that stimulation. For example, working in a fish market for a day lowers an individual's sensitivity to the odor of fish.

Adaptation level. The average level of stimulation at which an organism adapts. This applies to various environmental situations. For example, the level of cold that forces a Floridian to shiver would not stimulate this reflex in an Alaskan.

Adaptive behaviors. Responses of organisms to various environmental stimuli which allow for survival and successful adaptation to the environment.

Adaptive fitness. The set of behavioral and anatomical characteristics of a species that affect its ability to survive and reproduce.

Adaptive reflexes. Inborn reflexes which are not under our conscious control. Newborns, for example, have a number of adaptive reflexes, which include grasping, sucking, and the Moro reflexes.

ADD. See **attention-deficit disorder.**

ADHD. See **attention-deficit disorder with hyperactivity.**

Addiction. A strong compulsive need, usually for ingestion of a given drug. In the case of drug addiction, there is usually the buildup of tolerance (whereby the individual must ingest more and more of the drug in order to obtain the same effect), strong behavioral dependence (involving the directing of great efforts toward obtaining a supply of the drug), and withdrawal symptoms (the appearance of illness and suffering when the individual abruptly stops taking the drug).

Addictive drugs. Drugs that produce physical and/or psychological dependence on the part of the user. Additionally, withdrawal symptoms are encountered when the user ceases drug intake. Furthermore, tolerance mechanisms are initiated which force the user to take greater and greater amounts (dosage levels) of the drug in order to obtain the same desired effects of the drug.

Addition. A disorder of articulation in which a speaker inserts one or more sounds that do not belong in the words being pronounced. See also: **articulation disorder.**

Additive color mixing. The process of combining lights of different colors in order to create new hues. The principle here is that the two (or more) lights are reflected together from the same object. For example, if the two wavelengths are those of red and green light, the result is yellow light (since the wavelength of yellow is midway between those of red and green). Additive mixing of light waves produces the perception of the intermediate color. If all the light waves are focused together on the same object, the object would reflect white light (the combination of all

the wavelengths of light). Note how these two examples work very differently for **subtractive color mixing** (see definition).

Adduction. The movement of an arm or leg inwardly and/or toward the body. See also: **abduction.**

Adenohypophysis (ad″ə nō hī pof′i sis). A name for the anterior portion of the pituitary gland, the master gland of the endocrine system.

Adenosine (ə den′ə sin, ə dē′nə-,-sēn′) **triphosphate** (trī fos′fāt) **(ATP).** The chemical that provides the chemical energy for the endothermic (i.e., energy-consuming) chemical reactions for the body's metabolic processes. Adenosine in ATP is attached to a linear string of phosphate (PO_4) groups, the third and last of which is linked to the main group by a high-energy phosphate bond. To draw from the energy bank, all that is required is the conversion of the molecule to adenosine diphosphate (ADP) by releasing the third phosphate, as this also releases the needed chemical energy. The ATP energy reserve is stored in the organelles known as the **mitochondria** (see definition).

Adiadochokinesia. The inability to make rapid alternating movements. This may reflect cerebellar disease. See also: **dysdiadochokinesia.**

Adipsia. A lack of drinking.

Adjustment Disorder. Emotional dysfunction caused by stressors within the range of common experience. Anxiety and physical symptoms surface in adjustment disorders.

Adolescence (ad″l es′əns). A socially and culturally defined period of life following childhood and preceding adulthood which is initiated at puberty.

Adrenal cortex (ə drē′nəl kôr′teks″) (plural = cortices). The outer portion of the adrenal body. The adrenal gland's cortex (i.e., "covering") is the stress-reaction organ of the endocrine gland system. The adrenal cortex releases steroid hormones into the bloodstream. The anterior pituitary gland hormone ACTH can stimulate the adrenal cortex to release cortisol, which is an example of these steroid products of the adrenal cortex. These hormones enable the body to deal with such physical forms of stress as extremes of temperature, the cutting, crushing, burning, or freezing of body tissues, the onset of infection, the ingestion of a poisonous substance, and so on. These individual threats to health and welfare are called stressors. The adrenal cortex and its stress reaction are not to be confused with the adrenal medulla and its emergency reaction, although the latter may kick-start the stress reaction to get it going. See also: **adrenocorticotrophic hormone; anterior pituitary; endocrine system; steroid hormones.**

Adrenal (ə drē′nəl) **glands.** (meaning = near the kidney). Shaped like inverted cones, these two glands, one on top of each kidney, each consist of an inner core, the adrenal medulla, and an outer covering, the adrenal cortex, which produce several types of hormones including epinephrine (adrenaline), sex hormones, and others that regulate the concentration of minerals in the body and sugar in the blood. See also: **adrenal cortex; adrenal medulla.**

Adrenal medulla (ə drē′nəl mə də′lə). The inner core of the adrenal gland. The adrenal medulla releases hormones (see definition) such as norepinephrine, epinephrine, and dopamine. They supplement the activity of the sympathetic nervous system in mediating the organism's "fight-or-flight" emergency reaction. The relative amounts of epinephrine (adrenaline) and norepinephrine that are released may account for the differences between fleeing and fighting behaviors. With fear, more epinephrine is secreted than norepinephrine; with anger, the reverse occurs. Epinephrine causes an increase in the heart rate and initiates hormone actions that result in making available a greater supply of glucose for the skeletal muscles and the brain. Norepinephrine raises the blood pressure and signals the anterior pituitary to release the hormone ACTH. ACTH in turn affects the adrenal cortex. This activity is the alarm and mobilization phase of the stress reaction known as the general adaptation syndrome. See also: **adrenal cortex; adrenocorticotrophic hormone; alarm and mobilization stage; anterior pituitary; endocrine system; epinephrine; general adaptation syndrome; norepinephrine; stress.**

Adrenaline (ə dren′əl in). See **epinephrine.**

Adrenergic. An adjective referring to axons that release the neurotransmitter epinephrine (adrenaline) at their terminals. See also: **epinephrine; neuromodulator.**

Adrenocorticotropic (ə drē ″nō kôr ″ti kō trop′ik, -trō′pik) **hormone (ACTH).** A hormone released by the anterior pituitary or master gland. When, after traveling in the bloodstream, ACTH reaches the adrenal cortex, it stimulates that organ to release steroid hormones. Adrenal cortex steroid hormones serve to counteract the effects of stressors (agents of stress) such as extreme temperatures, toxins, infectious agents such as viruses and bacteria, and tissue damage. See also: **adrenal cortex; general adaptation syndrome; stress.**

Adrenogenital syndrome (ə drē″nō jen′i təl). A disorder involving the release of the adrenal cortex hormone cortisol which causes elevated levels of androgens (male hormones). This leads to the masculinization of genetic females. See also: **adrenal cortex; cortisol.**

Adventitiously deaf. The condition of someone who was born with hearing, but, through disease or injury, has lost hearing.

Advocate. One who aggressively pursues improved and appropriate services for a person (or persons) with disabilities.

Affect. The subjective side of an emotion or feeling. The emotional responses or feelings which have physiological aspects. For example, reacting to a painful blow with aggressive rage, or feeling content and happy when stroked with a soft, light touch.

Affectional needs. Emotional needs which include the needs to be loved and respected.

Affective attack. One form of attack behavior, which can be elicited by electrical stimulation of the hypothalamus or the amygdala. In the case of a cat, the animal bares its teeth, arches its back, screeches, and makes lunging motions. In some cases, the electrical stimulus may cause only the ferocious and threatening expression without an attack taking place. See also: **aggression; amygdala; hypothalamus.**

Affective disorders. Disorders related to two opposing emotions--depression and elation or mania. According to the DSM-III-R, there are two major affective disorders: bipolar disorder (see definition) and major depression (see definition). A person with a bipolar disorder, or manic depression, has alternating episodes of mania and depression that can last for weeks or months; there are periods of normality, however. Long-lasting depression that can be considered severe without mania is also known as major depression.

Affective personality disorder. A disorder characterized by three types of mood disturbances: (1) an intense anxiety that surfaces with all new encounters, (2) a chronic depressive state, and (3) cyclothymic episodes, or excessive mood swings, over long periods of time.

Affective psychosis (ə fek′tiv sī kō′sis). Any major mood disorder which involves psychotic symptoms.

Afferent (af′ər ent) (from Latin "ad-" = "toward"; "fero" = "I carry"). Afferent neurons carry messages toward the central nervous system and are therefore sensory. The antonym is **efferent** (see definition).

Afferent (af′ər ent) **neuron.** A neuron that has an afferent axon which carries neural messages into a structure. See also: **axon.**

Afferent (af′ər ent) **nerves.** Nerves that carry impulses from sense receptors toward the central nervous system. See also: **afferent; central nervous system; receptors.**

Affiliation motive. The psychological need to associate with other people.

Afterimage. A strictly sensory effect which involves the prolonged visual stimulation of a stationary eye. When the eye is shifted to a white wall or white piece of paper, an afterimage appears. Wherever the eyes move, the afterimage will follow.

Ageism (ā′jiz əm). The discrimination against or mistreatment of individuals based on their age.

Agenesis (ā jen′ə sis) **of the corpus** (kôr′pus) **callosum** (kə lō′sum). A congenital defect in brain development wherein the great commissure connecting the right and left cerebral hemispheres is absent. This condition, other things being equal, would be expected to disclose important facts about the separate functions of each of the two hemispheres. Unfortunately, this hope is defeated by the great flexibility of the brain, particularly its ability to reorganize itself. Each hemisphere in an individual without a corpus callosum seems to possess an unusually high endowment of the skills normally expected to be exclusive to the opposite hemisphere. See also: **cerebral cortex; commissure; corpus callosum.**

Ageusia (ə gyōō′zē ə). Taste blindness or taste insensitivity.

Aggregate field. The entire area of all the receptive fields of the neurons in a particular column of the visual cortex. Since the complex cells in the column, those in cortical layers II, III, V, and VI, have wider receptive fields than the simple cells (found in layer IV), the limits of their receptive fields decide the extent of the aggregate field for the cell column. See also: **column; occipital lobe; primary visual cortex; visual cortex.**

Aggregation. Cell alignment taking place during embryonic development when the various body organs are being formed.

Aggression. Behavior directed toward harming another individual; or the emotional state that consists of negative feelings (such as hate) and involves the intention to commit harm. Aggressive behavior has a physiological basis and has been categorized in several schemas. Some of the efforts at classification are rooted in physiological explanations. There is a fear-induced type of aggression wherein the organism lashes out in response to a real or perceived threat. Involving the expression of aggression against other members of the same species, intermale aggression features the taking up of a threat posture by presenting the side of one's body to an intruder; if the latter remains, the body is used to shove against the intruder. Should the intruder animal shove back, the resident animal whirls in preparation to bite the intruder's neck. Both fear-induced and inter-male aggression involve the activity of the preoptic nucleus of the hypothalamus and the amygdaloid nucleus. Fear-induced aggressive behavior also involves the ventral medial nucleus of the hypothalamus and the periaqueductal gray matter of the midbrain. Intermale aggression makes use of the ventral portion of the midbrain tegmentum. Some have linked an excess of the male hormone testosterone with male social aggression, although this remains controversial. A predatory type of aggression (which is called a quiet-biting attack) is characterized by the organism's stalking potential victims, seeking to injure or kill. This is related to the activity of the lateral hypothalamus and the amygdaloid nucleus. The septum, the medial accumbens, the medial hypothalamus, and the raphe nuclei have been implicated in the inhibition of defensive and predatory aggression. See also: **accumbens; affective attack; amygdaloid nucleus; central gray matter; lateral hypothalamus; predatory aggression; ventral tegmental area.**

Aggression cues. Stimuli which tend to evoke or elicit aggressive responses. For example, Berkowitz has obtained evidence that the presence of a weapon raises the probability of aggressive behavior in a given situation.

Agnosia (ag nō′zhə). Cognitive disturbances, usually resulting from brain injury, that involve the inability to correctly perceive the meaning of stimuli, such as words, objects, or other visual stimuli. The diagnosis does not apply to those with major sensory handicaps such as blindness.

Agonist (ag′ə nist). Usually, a chemical that mimics a chemical neurotransmitter by occupying its receptor sites in neuron cell membranes. Some would also apply the term to those chemicals that act as metabolic precursors for the cellular synthesis of neurotransmitters. In this second sense of the term, it would be correct to call l-DOPA a dopamine agonist, since dopamine is synthesized from l-DOPA. See also: **antagonist.**

Agoraphobia (ag″ə rə fō′bē ə). An anxiety disorder which involves the abnormal fear of being in public places. The individual with agoraphobia usually fears the development of a particular symptom, such as heart pains or the loss of control of the bladder or bowels. The fear develops in such situations as being in a crowd, crossing a bridge, standing in line, or traveling in a public conveyance. Agoraphobia is different from social phobia, in which the person is afraid of public embarrassment rather than developing a given physical symptom. See also: **panic disorder; phobia; social phobia.**

Agrammatism (ā gram′ə tiz″əm). Difficulty in using proper grammar structures frequently seen in individuals with Broca's aphasia. Such patients tend to drop articles and auxiliary verbs.

Agraphia (ā graf′ē ə). The inability to write due to difficulties with spelling. Acquired agraphia is a result of damage to a portion of the cerebral cortex.

Ailurophobia (ī loo″rə fō′bē ə) Excessive and irrational fear of cats. See also: **phobias.**

Air conduction test. A hearing test in which test tone stimuli are pure tones (one frequency only) presented via earphones.

Akinetic seizure. A seizure involving an absence or infrequency of muscular movement; the muscles of the limbs may have either too much or too little tone to permit movement. See also: **seizure.**

Alarm and mobilization stage. This is the first part of what Hans Selye has described as a general adaptation syndrome or stress reaction. During this stage, the body releases an adrenal cortical hormone which assists the organism in maintaining health and/or normality. This stage is succeeded by the second stage, that of resistance. See also: **general adaptation syndrome; stress.**

Alcohol or ethyl alcohol. Alcohol is defined as the most common depressant. In small amounts, it can cause a release of tension and feelings of happiness. In larger doses, this depressant produces emotional symptoms, physical ill effects (e.g., liver damage), loss of physical coordination, impaired memory, and in some cases a loss of consciousness. Alcohol is really ethyl alcohol, which is metabolized in the body into acetaldehyde, which in turn is changed to acetic acid. The rate of change or conversion of acetaldehyde to acetic acid is governed by the enzyme acetaldehyde dehydrogenase. See also: **acetaldehyde; acetaldehyde dehydrogenase; acetic acid.**

Alcoholism. This is a disease of excessive alcohol consumption which may lead to **Korsakoff's Syndrome** (see definition) or relatively mild cognitive impairment which would have to be detected via neuropsychological testing. Chronic alcoholism may lead to enlargement of the brain ventricles (which are fluid-filled cavities inside the central nervous system) and widening of the cerebral sulci. The increased width in sulci implies that cortical atrophy has occurred. This in turn means that there has been a loss of dendritic branches and dendritic spines. This results in a great reduction in the number of functioning interneural synapses. Therefore, the brain is functioning at a lower cognitive level than before. This nerve degeneration is permanent and is reflected in a diminished IQ. For example, individuals with chronic alcoholism have difficulty with some performance tasks on IQ tests and certain memory tests. Type 1 alcoholism involves a genetic predisposition to drink together with a triggering situation such as being in an environment in which heavy drinking is occurring, or being subjected to peer pressure to have a drink or two. Type 2 alcoholism involves a strong genetic disposition that is influential regardless of the environmental conditions. Type 2 alcoholism is more prevalent in males than in females.

Aldosterone. That hormone of the adrenal cortex which causes the kidneys to retain sodium while they are forming urine from the venous blood. It is released from the adrenal cortex in response to the kidney hormone, angiotensin II. See also: **adrenal cortex; angiotensin II.**

Alexia (ə lek′sē ə). The total inability to read despite having adequate vision. The individual can copy the letters of words but cannot read or decode them as symbols for meanings.

Algorithm (al′ gə rith″əm). A strategic routine used to solve a problem.

Allele (ə lēl′). The particular form of a gene that calls for a particular way for a hereditary trait to be expressed. For example, there is a gene for eye color, and one form of that gene, the b allele, is the allele that codes for blue eyes, while another, the B allele, codes for brown eyes.

Allergen (al′ər jin). A type of antigen that causes a hypersensitive allergy state and usually affects the eyes (red and swollen), nose, and bronchi. Common allergens include pollens, certain drugs, dust, dyes, some chemicals in foods, certain foods, spores, animal dander and hair, and blood serum.

Allergies. A hypersensitive reaction of the body's system to some antigen or foreign substance. Antigens that actually induce allergic reactions are called allergens. Common allergens are pollens, animal dander, certain drugs, dust (which the authors accumulated in their homes during the final stages of this project), dyes, some chemicals in foods, and certain foods. An unexplained peculiarity of schizophrenics is that they seldom have allergies. It is thought by some researchers that individuals with learning disabilities suffer more from allergies than the general population, although this finding is controversial. See also: **allergen; antigen.**

All-or-none-law or **all-or-none principle**. A basic premise related to action potentials in cells. This principle states that the size and shape of an action potential within a cell are independent of the intensity of the initiating stimulus. Thus this principle is the defining characteristic of a true nerve impulse, as opposed to a graded and decremental type of voltage change on a neuron's membrane. If the neuron is stimulated (depolarized) strongly enough to send out a nerve impulse, no stronger stimulation can further increase the strength of the impulse. If the stimulus is only weakly depolarizing, it may not suffice to start a nerve impulse, and the axon will remain at rest. The axon, therefore, is either at rest or it is conducting a full-strength nerve impulse; there is no in-between. An analogy is the relation between the force applied to the trigger of a gun and the speed of the bullet fired from that gun. Let us say it takes 5 pounds of pulling force to fire the gun. Pulling the trigger with 4.75 pounds of force has no effect. Pulling the trigger with 5 pounds of force fires the gun. Pulling the trigger with 10 pounds of force also fires the gun; the gunshot is equally strong as the result of a 5-pound or a 10-pound pull. This is because the potential energy for the gunshot is not in the trigger but in the gunpowder. Returning to the nerve impulse, the potential energy for the impulse is not in the stimulating event but in the voltage difference across the axon membrane at one place on the axon after another. See also: **action potential.**

Alpha adrenergic (ad″rə nûr′jik) **receptors**. A group of receptor sites that receive such adrenergic neurotransmitters as epinephrine and/or norepinephrine. These receptor sites are found on nerve cell membranes (as autoreceptors) and on membranes of the smooth muscles that line the blood vessels. The alpha receptors are excitatory for these smooth muscles, causing the blood vessels to constrict, thus raising the blood pressure. See also: **beta adrenergic receptors; epinephrine; norepinephrine.**

Alpha cells. Some of the islet cells of the islets of Langerhans, the endocrine glands that are attached to the pancreas. The hormone released by the alpha cells is glucagon, which causes the conversion of liver-stored glycogen (animal starch) into glucose (blood sugar), thereby increasing the level of blood sugar. Epinephrine, a hormone released by the adrenal medulla gland, is thought to be the activating factor in glucagon release. See also: **adrenal medulla; beta cells;**

emergency reaction; epinephrine.

Alpha efferents (ef'ər ents). Efferent (motor) nerves that run to the extrafusal (regular) muscle fibers. See also: **extrafusal fiber; gamma efferents; intrafusal fiber; muscle spindle.**

Alpha feto-protein. A type of protein found in the blood stream of immature mammals. It binds with estrogen, preventing it from leaving the bloodstream and entering brain cells or other organs that are developing during this time. This actually has a feminizing effect (the shutting-out of estrogen); any steroid hormone getting into the developing brain cells will have a masculinizing influence--yes, even, the female hormone, estrogen! See also: **estrogen; testosterone.**

Alpha male. The dominant male animal in a colony. This sort of social role is part of the group living observed in many species of birds and mammals. One example would be the alpha wolf in a pack of wolves or the alpha male in a herd of sea elephants. The alpha male gets to service all the nubile females of his group. It will take a younger, tougher, and better-fighting male to displace him. See also: **aggression; comparative psychology; ethology; polygamy.**

Alpha rhythm. Rhythmic changes of voltage recorded in an electroencephalogram, with a frequency of 8 to 13 cycles per second. Of human brain rhythms, alpha waves tend to be relatively high in amplitude (voltage) and relatively low in frequency (HVLF). They can be obtained most easily when the subject is awake, resting with eyes closed. See also: **electroencephalogram.**

Alpha waves. See **alpha rhythm.**

Alphabetic strategy. Frith refers to a conceptual scheme of reading development with four distinct stages. Stage 2 involves acquisition of alphabetic strategies or a knowledge of phonology which allows the reader to decode words phonetically.

Altered states of consciousness (ASC). Ways of behaving that are different in major ways from ordinary waking activity. Some altered states are quite natural; some are artificial. Examples of natural altered states include sleep, dreaming, daydreaming, and night terrors. Artificially induced altered states may result from sensory deprivation, ingestion of hallucinogenic drugs, hypnotism, or meditation. See also: **waking consciousness.**

Alternative communication. Systems of communicating that are taught to children who are unable to speak intelligibly. See also: **AAC; augmentative communication.**

Altricial (al trish'əl). The tendency, in some species of birds, for the newly hatched fledglings to be very dependent on parental care. The opposite term is **precocial** (see definition).

Alzheimer's (älts'hī mərz) **disease.** One of the three dementia diseases, involving a progressive decline in cognitive abilities. Alzheimer's disease is the most prevalent of the three, affecting 65% of all dementia sufferers. Alzheimer's disease is marked by a loss of neurons in the cortex and the hippocampus portion of the limbic system. This results in the shrinkage of much of the cortex with the exception of the visual cortex. Brain abnormalities that occur as a result of Alzheimer's disease are neurofibrillary tangles; neuritic plaques which interfere with neural transmitting; and a decreased production of ACh, the neurotransmitter acetylcholine. Statistical analyses of Alzheimer's families have shown that children of Alzheimer's parents have a one-in-four chance of developing the disorder by the age of 90. This fact should not sound an alarm, since most people die before the age of 90. Possible causes include the abnormal-protein theory, which posits that a toxic form of amyloid protein material (beta amyloid) may cause the brain damage; genetic predisposition; and a blood-flow model. The amyloid hypothesis is based on the observation that clumps of beta amyloid appear next to dead neurons in brain specimens taken from deceased Alzheimer's patients. Some studies have actually linked Alzheimer's disease to chromosome 21, with other studies pointing to other genetic defects. There is no current consensus to validate any one causal theory, and it should be noted that there is no sound evidence to validate a causal connection between aluminum ingestion and Alzheimer's disease. See also: **amyloid plaques; chromosome 21 trisomy; neuritic plaques; neurofibrillary tangles.**

Amacrine (am'ə krīn) **cells.** Neurons located in the retina in the region of the synapses between the bipolar cells and the ganglion cells. These neurons are not included directly in the pathway from the retina to the brain but are situated at right angles to that pathway. The amacrine cells have no axons and therefore do not conduct true nerve impulses. Instead, graded potentials drift along the fibers of these neurons. See also: **axon; bipolar neuron; ganglion cells; graded potentials; nerve impulse; retina.**

Amaurosis (am″ô rō′sis). A loss of vision, which is not accompanied by damage to the eyes. Amaurosis may be due to any of a number of factors, including kidney disease, epileptic seizures, birth defects, atrophy of the optic nerve or more central parts of the visual nervous system, insufficient blood flow to the eyes, a transient attack resembling migraine, a reflexive result of irritation at another part of the body, and ingestion of a toxic substance.

Amaurotic (am″ə rot′ ik) **familial idiocy.** Any of several diseases presenting as symptoms dementia, impaired vision, and inability to metabolize lipids.

Ambiguous stimuli. Stimuli or patterns of stimuli which allow for more than one perceptual organization or interpretation.

Ambivalence. Mixed responses to identical stimuli which could include positive and/or negative feelings, attraction and/or repulsion, and so on. See also: **approach-avoidance conflict.**

Amblyopia ex anopsia. The deterioration of vision in one eye resulting from the underutilization of that eye.

Ambulation. The ability to move around from place to place.

Amentia. [1] Congenital mental retardation, with the individual having an intelligence quotient below 70. [2] A mental disorder, typified by confusion, semi-consciousness, and disorientation.

American Sign Language. The standard system of hand gestures used by hearing-impaired and deaf individuals in order to communicate.

Amimia (ə mim′ē ə). A loss of the ability to use gestures or signs in communication.

Amine (ə mēn′). An organic chemical compound that contains a nitrogen atom to which two hydrogen atoms are attached. That group of three atoms is called an amine radical and is symbolized as "-NH₂". Many neurotransmitters are amines. Amines are unable to penetrate the blood-brain barrier, so that ingestion or injection

of an amine cannot deliver it to neurons of the spinal cord or the brain.

Amino acid. An organic chemical compound containing both the amine radical (-NH₂) and the organic acid (i.e., carboxyl) radical (-COOH). Amino acids are used in metabolism as the building blocks of proteins, peptides and polypeptides. A peptide contains two or more amino acids. Large peptides having 10 or more peptide components are called polypeptides. Complex chains of different kinds of peptides are called proteins. Many of the neurotransmitters, such as the glutamates, the aspartates, GABA, and glycine, are of the amino acid type.

Amnesia. A psychological memory disorder which involves the forgetting of past experiences, people, or events which can be stressful. Specific amnesia involves forgetting specific episodes or periods of time, while total amnesia involves forgetting one's entire past history.

Amniocentesis (am″nē ō sen tē′sis). A test done during pregnancy that reveals many inherited traits of the fetus. A small amount of the amniotic fluid is extracted and the chromosomes are examined. The gender of the newborn will be predicted as well as the risk of various genetic defects. See also: **chorionic villus sampling.**

Amotivational syndrome. The chronic lack of motivation that can result from long-term drug abuse. An often-cited example is the chronic marijuana smoker who is believed by many to be unconcerned with success and unable to put forth much effort. After all, for people addicted to much harder drugs, the motivation level is hardly likely to be a major issue; they've got bigger problems than that! See the following entry, for example.

Amphetamine (am fet′ə mēn, -min) **psychosis.** A psychotic mental state induced by the abuse of amphetamines. The hallucinations involved tend to be auditory rather than visual; hence the psychosis resembles acute schizophrenia more than it does the psychotic state produced by ingesting LSD.

Amphetamines (am fet′ə mēnz, -minz). The class of synthetic drugs such as benzedrine which have stimulating effects on the central nervous system. These stimulants produce initial feelings of euphoria, tending to activate the neurons of the sympathetic nervous system. Afterward, however, these feelings are followed by sadness and depression.

Amplitude. The intensity or magnitude of an energy wave. The amplitude of a sound wave is the main determinant of how loud a sound is. The physical basis for high amplitude in a sound wave is the intense compression of air molecules. This is what takes place when a thunderclap is produced, for example. Low-intensity sounds may become very difficult for aging individuals to detect. A way to make hearing easier for some elderly or hard-of-hearing people is to use high-frequency sounds, which do not require as much amplification as lower-frequency sounds.

Amygdala (ə mig'də lə). Another name for the amygdaloid nucleus. The word means "almond" in Latin. See also: **amygdaloid nucleus.**

Amygdaloid nucleus (ə mig'də loid″ nŏŏ'klē əs, nyŏŏ-). An almond-shaped nucleus (collection of neuronal cell bodies) in the telencephalon (see definitions of **nucleus** [part of the gray matter], **cell body,** and **telencephalon**). This nucleus is sometimes counted as one of the basal ganglia. It is also considered to be part of the limbic system. The amygdaloid nucleus (also called the amygdala, which means "almond" in Latin) has interacting connections with areas of the hypothalamus in relation to the regulation of aggressive behavior. It may also have a role in memory, involving the association of stored information from various modes of sensory input.

Amyloid plaques (am'ə loid″ plaks). These are clumps of the protein beta amyloid that encircle remnants of degenerated nerve cells, resulting in impaired neural transmission. Alzheimer's sufferers frequently exhibit these plaques. According to some theorists, the amyloid protein is toxic to neurons and causes the disease. See also: **Alzheimer's disease; neuritic plaques; neurofibrillary tangles.**

Amyotrophic lateral sclerosis (ALS) (also called **Lou Gehrig's disease**) (ā″mī ə trof'ik lat'ər əl skli rō'sis, -trō'fik). A disease leading to gradually increasing weakness and paralysis. There is damage both to central neurons running down the spinal cord to the ventral horn cells of the spinal cord and to the peripheral motor neurons running from the ventral horn cells to the striped muscles. See **efferent; ventral horn; ventral root.**

Anabolic steroids (an ″ə bol'ik ster'oidz ″, stēr'-). Steroid hormones (including the male sex hormone, testosterone) that stimulate the anabolism (buildup) of body parts. Indiscriminate use of these hormones could produce undesirable side effects. Such side effects in women include the appearance of facial hair, clitoral hypertrophy, etc. patterns of maleness. See also: **testosterone.**

Anabolism (ə nab'ə liz ″əm). The metabolic buildup of the body. Anabolism is the growth and repair aspect of metabolism. The opposite, breaking-down type of metabolism is **catabolism.** See also: **anabolic steroids; catabolism; opponent-process theory of color vision.**

Analgesic (an'əl jē'zik). A substance that relieves pain.

Anandamide (ə nan'də mīd″). A chemical neurotransmitter that settles into receptor sites that accommodate THC (tetrahydrocannabinol), the active principle of marijuana. Most of the receptor sites are found in the hippocampus and the substantia nigra, while there are no signs of any such sites in the pons or the medulla. See also: **marijuana; THC.**

Anankastic (an″an kas'tik) **personality disorder** or **compulsive personality disorder**. A disorder which is marked by perfectionist behaviors, overly conscientious attention to rules and procedures, a preoccupation with efficiency and work, and an inability to express warm emotions. This disorder is seen more often in men than in women.

Androgen (an'drō jən″) **insensitivity.** An inherited failure of the male embryo to develop male genitals. See also: **testicular feminization.**

Androgenital (an″dro jen'i təl) **syndrome**. A disorder in which the adrenal glands produce excess amounts of androgens. This syndrome can cause masculinizing of the developing female fetus.

Androgens (an'drō jenz″). The male sex hormones. These are steroid hormones released by the testes, the male gonads. One of these hormones is testosterone, which is responsible for the male pattern of asymmetry in the cerebral cortex of the brain, with the left hemisphere becoming larger than the right. See also: **androstenedione; testosterone.**

Androgyny (androj'i nē). Literally, the combination of male and female identities in one person. In current usage, the term refers to the natural presence of both male and female traits in a person. One's culture will determine acceptable masculine and feminine behaviors.

Androstenedione (an˝drō stēn'dē ōn˝, -stēn ˝dī'ōn˝) (**AD**). An androgen which causes the growth of pubic and axillary (i.e., underarm) hair in females at the time of puberty. See also: **androgens**; **puberty**.

Anesthetics. Drugs that block sensory input to one part of the body. For example, Novocain, a <u>local anesthetic</u>, can be used to anesthetize the mouth for dental work. The Novocain attaches to the sodium gates of axons and prevents sodium ions from entering neurons, thus blocking nerve transmission to that part of the body. A <u>general anesthetic</u> (e.g., ether) opens potassium gates in neurons with a resultant increased flow of potassium ions out of the neuron. The cell is now is a state of hyperpolarization decreasing the probability of an action potential. The nervous system now becomes immune to outside stimulation because few neurons are available to fire action potentials. This situation would be important for individuals in surgery. See also: **action potential**; **hyperpolarization**.

Aneurysm (an'yoo riz˝əm) (or **aneurism**) ("aneurysma" = "widening" in Greek). An abnormal, local dilation of an artery. The arterial wall swells in balloon-like fashion and loses its elasticity. The swelling must be surgically removed.

Angiography (an˝ jē og' rə fē). The taking of a series of X-rays of the brain following the injection of a radio-opaque dye into a cerebral artery. This will allow the inspection of the brain's circulatory system to see if there are any breaks or obstructions in it. A single X-ray picture taken by this method is an <u>angiogram</u>. The displacement of a cerebral blood vessel because of mechanical pressure from a brain tumor would be revealed by this technique.

Angiotensin II. A hormone from the kidneys that causes the blood pressure to increase. Angiotensin II plays a key role in hypovolemic thirst. Its release is caused by a decline in blood pressure sensed by the baroceptors, blood pressure sensors in the walls of the larger blood vessels.

The enzyme renin is released by the kidneys. Renin affects the chemistry of angiotensin I, an inactive chemical, causing it to be converted to the hormone, angiotensin II. Injection of angiotensin II into areas of the hypothalamus adjacent to the third ventricle can generate hypovolemic thirst, resulting in increased drinking. Angiotensin II also stimulates the production and secretion of <u>alsosterone</u>, a hormone of the adrenal cortex involved in the regulation of the metabolism of sodium, potassium, and chloride. See also: **hypovolemic thirst**; **intracellular thirst**; **volemic thirst**.

Angular gyrus (plural = gyri). An L-shaped gyrus (outward fold of gray matter) in the parietal lobe of the cerebral cortex, near the junction of that lobe with the occipital and temporal lobes. In most people, the left angular gyrus is thought to play a role in the reading process. It is conveniently near the visual and the auditory projection areas of the cortex.

Anion (an'ī ən). An ion is an atom or group of atoms bearing an electrical charge. An anion is a negatively charged ion of at least -1, because it has at least one more negatively charged electron than the number of positively charged protons. Important examples of anions in nerve physiology are chloride and also the heavy, organic anions within the axoplasm.

Anisomycin (an ī˝sō mī'sin, an ī˝-). A drug that inhibits protein synthesis. It will block the memory of a trained rat for the location of an electric shock but will not interfere with the rat's memory of an odor that serves as a guide to food.

Anomalous trichromats (ə nom'ə ləs trī˝ krō mats˝). Persons who are not as severely color blind as dichromats. Anomalous trichromats have deficiencies in sensitivity to some wavelengths of light.

Anomia (ə nō'mē ə). Word-finding difficulties frequently seen in individuals with Broca's aphasia or with conduction aphasia.

Anorexia (an˝ə rek'sē ə) **nervosa**. An abnormal eating pattern, usually exhibited by young women with an intense dread of obesity, that results in dangerously low caloric intake. It results in extreme weight loss and involves an inaccurate body image; the patient perceives herself as fat when she is quite slender. The condition can be fatal, because the patient may refuse to eat even the minimum amount required for survival.

Anorgasmia (an″ôr gaz′mē ə). The inability of a woman to achieve orgasm during sexual activity. There are two types of anorgasmia: (1) primary organic dysfunction, which involves the failure ever to have experienced orgasm, and (2) secondary orgasmic dysfunction, in which a woman can achieve orgasm but only under the right circumstances. The latter may well be a normal type of female sexual behavior.

Anosmia (an oz′mē ə). Lacking the sense of smell, perhaps due to disease of or injury to the olfactory nerves. A complete loss of the sense of smell can cause people to lose interest in food and even lower sexual desire. There is some danger involved, since an anosmic individual cannot smell food spoilage.

ANOVA. A statistical test of the impact of two or more independent variables (causal factors) on a behavioral measure or dependent variable; analysis of variance.

Anoxia (an ok′sē ə) or **asphyxia** (az fik′sē ə). The deprivation of blood-borne oxygen for the tissues to an extent that prevents normal tissue functions. The central nervous system, and particularly the neocortex, is extremely vulnerable to asphyxia-caused damage.

Antabuse (an′tə byo͞os″). The trade name of the drug disulfiram, which is used as an aversive stimulus to cause alcoholics extreme nausea after ingesting alcohol. This treatment is used as a last resort. Antabuse actually changes the way one's body metabolizes alcohol by decreasing the body's level of acetaldehyde dehydrogenase. See also: **acetaldehyde dehydrogenase; aversive therapy.**

Antagonist (an tag′ə nist). [1] A chemical substance that blocks the actions of a neurotransmitter, often by blocking the receptor sites on the postsynaptic neuron's cell membrane. The neuroleptic drugs given to schizophrenics (such as haloperidol or clozapine) are antagonists of dopamine, the neurotransmitter that is believed to be overworking in the forebrains of schizophrenics. See also: **agonist.** [2] A muscle working in opposition to another muscle. For example, the biceps and the triceps work in opposite ways, so that each is the antagonist of the other.

Antagonistic muscles. See **antagonist** [2].

Anterior. Toward the front or at the front end.

The side of a part of the body which is the side where the organism's face may be found.

Anterior chamber. The small forward extension of the eyeball in front of the lens and iris, which contains mostly the colorless fluid known as the aqueous humor.

Anterior commissure. A commissure is a group of axons linking a part of the left side of the brain to its mirror-image on the right. The anterior commissure links the rostral parts of the temporal lobes of the cerebral cortex as well as portions of the limbic system. See also: **anterior; cerebral cortex; commissure; limbic system; rostral; temporal lobe.**

Anterior pituitary (pi to͞o′i ter″ē) **gland**. Also called the adenohypophysis and the master gland, this is the front part or lobe of the pituitary gland. Its work is regulated in part by hormones arriving to it in the bloodstream. In turn, the anterior pituitary releases hormones of its own, called tropic hormones, that regulate most of the other endocrine glands. This fact is what earns the anterior pituitary its designation as the master gland. It should be regarded as a "first among equals" rather than a "master", however. The anterior pituitary also produces the growth hormone, which controls the extent and the pace of bodily growth and development. See also: **endocrine system; growth hormone; pituitary gland.**

Anterograde amnesia (an′tə rō grad″). Literally, forward-going lack of memory. There is an inability to recall events after there has been damage to the brain. New learning fails to be stored. This type of memory loss can result from a degenerative disease such as Korsakoff's syndrome or from electroconvulsive shock (ECS) treatments.

Anterograde axonal (an′tə rō grad″ ak′sən l, ak son′l, ak sō′nəl) **transport**. The transport of materials (such as chemicals or synaptic vesicles) down the axon to the terminal boutons.

Anterograde (an′tə rō grad″) **degeneration**. See: **Wallerian degeneration.** See also: **retrograde degeneration.**

Anterograde (an′tə rō grad″) **tracing technique**. The term "anterograde" means that one is tracing something in a forward direction, and, when neurons are the scene of the action, that means from the cell body, along the axon, toward the telodendria. Neuroscientists often have to learn the route taken by long axons and have used various methods, the **histological techniques**, to accomplish that. In anterograde tracing, the method called **autoradiography** is the most used. A radioactive atom is added to a glucose-based compound; not to glucose itself, because glucose is metabolized too quickly by the nerve cells. A commonly used kind of radioactive atom is that of tritium, the kind of hydrogen atom that has an atomic weight of 3 (the normal atomic weight of hydrogen is just 1). This tritiated glucose product travels down the axon. At various times after injection, different test animals (subjects) are sacrificed (killed). The brain of each animal is removed and photographic chemicals are applied. The result is that the radiation, wherever it has traveled, will expose the negative, thus taking its own picture (i.e., producing an autoradiogram). Inspection of the series of photographs taken of the brain tissue will therefore readily show where the radiation ended, and that is where the traced axons normally go; mission accomplished! The opposite of anterograde tracing is retrograde tracing. For an example of that, see **horseradish peroxidase**. In that technique, the tracer chemical enters the axon at the terminal end and travels back along the axon until it reaches the cell body. See also: **histological techniques**.

Anterograde (an'tə rō grād˝) **transneuronal degeneration.** The destruction of a neuron due to the degeneration of other neurons whose axons have synaptic endings on the first neuron's receptor sites. This kind of neuronal destruction would require that the neuron have no remaining intact inputs. Transneuronal degeneration is, accordingly, a very rare occurrence. See also: **retrograde degeneration; Wallerian degeneration.**

Anterolateral system or anterolateral pathway. A collective name for the **lateral spinothalamic tract** and the **ventral spinothalamic tract**. These two tracts are part of the **somatosensory system**. The lateral spinothalamic tract carries nerve impulses (produced originally by pain and temperature sensations) to the thalamus of the brain, traveling within the **lateral funiculus** of the spinal cord. The ventral spinothalamic tract carries light touch sensory messages to the

thalamus and travels within the **ventral funiculus** of the spinal cord. In each case, the axons arise from neurons in the **dorsal horns** of the spinal cord's **gray butterfly**. In each case, the axons cross the midline as soon as they leave their cell bodies, so that they travel rostrad (toward the brain) on the **contralateral** side of the spinal cord (i.e., the side opposite from the side of the body that had been stimulated). These two tracts therefore contrast sharply with the deep-pressure-sense tracts, namely the gracile and cuneate tracts, because they stay on the same side as the one stimulated, i.e., the **ipsilateral** side. The gracile and cuneate tracts are called the **dorsal columns**, because they travel in the **dorsal funiculus.** Their use of the ipsilateral side of the cord seems to contrast them with the so-called anterolateral pathway. But don't give up on the dorsal column pathway, dear reader. After a synapse takes place, the **next** axon in line crosses over to the opposite, contralateral, side. This crossover just happens in the brain's medulla, instead of down in the spinal cord. See definitions of terms in bold type. See also: **cuneate tract; medulla; spinal cord; spinoreticular tract; thalamus**.

Anthropomorphic fallacy (an˝thrə pə môr'fik, -thrō˝ pō˝-) or **anthropomorphism** (an˝thrə pə mor'fiz əm). Error(s) of reasoning in which one attributes human thoughts, behaviors, or emotions to nonhuman animals.

Antianxiety drugs. Chemicals that when ingested relieve anxiety. Valium (which is the trade name for diazepam) is one example of such a drug.

Antibody. A protein, shaped like the letter Y, which is produced by the B cells that develop in the bone marrow. Antibodies fit onto the antigen portion of a microorganism, either weakening it or setting it up for later destruction. See also: **antigen; B cell.**

Antidepressants or **antidepressant drugs**. Chemicals that when ingested relieve clinical depression. This category includes the tricyclic antidepressants and the MAO-inhibitors. These two groups have different mechanisms of action but both increase the levels of norepinephrine and serotonin (two chemical neurotransmitters) in the higher parts of the brain such as the cerebral cortex and the limbic system. The drug Prozac (the trade name of fluoxetine) is one example of an antidepressant.

Antidiuretic (ant″i dī (y)ə ret′ik, an″tĭ″-) **hormone** (**ADH**). A hormone manufactured by the supraoptic nucleus of the hypothalamus and sent to the neurohypophysis (the posterior pituitary gland), whence it is released into the bloodstream. At the kidneys, ADH causes the reabsorption of water from the urine, slowing down the formation of urine and allowing the body to maximize its retention of water. The intake of ethyl alcohol interferes with the activity of ADH. A deficiency of ADH leads to excessive urination and increased water drinking (polydypsia). These symptoms make up the condition known as diabetes insipidus. ADH is also known as vasopressin; it was earlier thought that these were two different hormones. In its role as "vasopressin," ADH causes the constriction of smooth muscles lining the walls of the arterioles and capillaries, thereby raising the blood pressure in the peripheral parts of the body. See also: **diabetes insipidus; endocrine system; neurohypophysis; pituitary gland; polypeptide; posterior pituitary; supraoptic nucleus.**

Antidromic (ant″i drom′ik, an″tĭ″-). The direction of a nerve impulse traveling from the point of stimulation on the axon toward the cell body. This only happens during laboratory investigations; in life, a nerve impulse starts in a modified part of the cell body, called the axon hillock, which is located at the very beginning of the axon. The natural direction of travel for the nerve impulse, which is from the cell body down the axon to the end brush, is called the dromic (or orthodromic) direction. See also: **dipole; dromic; nerve impulse.**

Antigen. [1] A protein found on the surface of a microorganism. An antigen stimulates the immune system of the host organism to manufacture and release antibodies. [2] A foreign substance (e.g., dust, pollen, certain foods, dyes, and certain drugs) that stimulates an immune response of the body by stimulating lymphocytes to produce antibodies. See also: **antibody.**

Antihypnotic drugs. Drugs that reduce sleeping. The amphetamines would be an example of a class of anti-hypnotic drugs.

Antipsychotics or **antipsychotic drugs.** Drugs used to alleviate psychotic symptoms, particularly the so-called positive symptoms of schizo-

phrenia. Chlorpromazine is one example of such a drug. What most antipsychotics have in common is their tendency to reduce the activity of the neurotransmitter dopamine indiscriminately, wherever dopamine synapses occur in the cerebral cortex and parts of the limbic system. The long-term use of these drugs has led to the development of a motor disorder called tardive dyskinesia. A new drug, clozapine, may provide therapeutic effects without leading to tardive dyskinesia because of its selective action upon just one dopamine-using neural pathway.

Antipyretic (ant″i pī ret′ik, an″tĭ″-). An agent that works against fever. Examples include phenacetin, quinine, and aspirin. They dilute the blood, which lowers body temperature, and widen the skin capillaries, which increases the rate of perspiration. Cold baths and ice packs would also do the trick.

Anti-Rh gamma globulin. A protein antibody which is administered to an Rh-negative mother soon after she has given birth to an Rh-positive infant (or, possibly, following the abortion of an Rh-positive fetus). This prevents disease from occurring due to incompatibility of blood type between mother and infant.

Antisocial, asocial, psychopathic, or **sociopathic personality disorder.** This disorder is known by many names and is characterized by chronic and ongoing antisocial behavior. The antisocial individual cannot function successfully to any satisfactory degree, to the point where holding a job is just about impossible. Other personality deficits include irresponsible and callous behavior, impulsiveness, lack of conscience, criminal types of behavior, poor interpersonal functioning, aggressiveness, deviant sexual behavior, and so on. Frequently, these individuals are at high risk for suicide, alcohol and drug abuse, and accidental death. Childhood evidence of the problem is usually observed before the individual has reached the age of 15 (see **conduct disorder**). See also: **generalized anxiety disorders.**

Anvil (also called **incus**). The second of a chain of three tiny bones (ossicles) in the middle ear. The anvil receives sound vibrations from the first ossicle, the hammer, and passes them on to the third tiny bone, the stirrup.

Anxiety. An intense fear or dread with no apparent real-life justification, characterized by irritability, attention problems, and restlessness. Anxiety should be differentiated from true fears, which are apparently triggered by real-life events (e.g., a true fear is that a two-year-old will be hit by a car if crossing a street without adult supervision). Anxiety is a symptom in many psychological disorders such as obsessive-compulsion neurosis and schizophrenia. Anxiety is the primary symptom of all phobias. Physical symptoms include tightness in the throat, sweating, shortness of breath, abdominal problems, dizziness, and trembling.

Anxiety disorder. A form of neurosis (a relatively mild emotional disorder) involving the chronic experience of anxiety in the absence of stimuli that might account for it. That is, there are no fearsome things close by but the patient is fearful anyway. It is considered an illness when the pathology is so extreme that the person cannot live a normal life.

Anxiety reduction hypothesis. An explanation of the self-defeating avoidance responses of anxious individuals which emphasizes the psychological relief obtained from avoiding the anxiety-provoking situation(s).

Anxiolytic (ang″zē ō lit′ik, angk″sē ō-). Tending to diminish the level of anxiety. Either drugs or psychotherapeutic measures could be anxiolytic.

Aphagia (ə fā′jē ə, -jə). A refusal to eat. The cause might be the bilateral (left and right) destruction of the lateral hypothalamus.

Aphasia (ə fā′zhə, zē ə). A disturbance in the production and/or comprehension of speech caused by lesions to the cerebral cortex.

Aplysia californica (the sea slug or sea hare). A marine mollusc (described as a sea snail) that has served as a model system for studies of the basic neural circuits underlying operant and respondent conditioning as well as such simpler forms of learning as habituation and sensitization. See also: **conditioned reflex; habituation; model systems approach; operant conditioning; sensitization.**

Apnea (ap′nē ə). Interrupted breathing. Sleep apnea is thought to be one possible cause of sudden infant death syndrome (SIDS), See also: **sleep; sleep apnea; sudden infant death syndrome.**

Apparent distance hypothesis. The explanation of

the moon illusion which states that the moon at the horizon appears more distant than the moon at the zenith of the night sky because there are more depth cues near the horizon for the individual to interpret.

Applied behavior analysis. An approach to teaching and behavior management that involves the use of behavior observation, the separate charting of the number of occasions that each of several different behaviors occurs, task analysis, the systematic planning of a sequence of teaching procedures, the application of those procedures, the scheduling of appropriate reinforcement, and the monitoring of student behavior change. See also: **behavior modification.**

Applied research. A scientific study undertaken in order to solve presented problems of a practical nature.

Approach-approach conflict. The situation whereby an organism must choose between two desirable or positive alternatives.

Approach-avoidance conflict. The situation in which the organism has conflicting tendencies to approach or to withdraw from the same person or object. See also: **ambivalence.**

Apraxia (ə prak′sē ə, ā prak′-). An inability to carry out intended movements despite the absence of paralysis, due to damage to the cerebral cortex. Although the apraxic patient is unable to carry out voluntary muscle movements, there is no paralysis evident. The variety of apraxia one has depends on where in the brain the injury is located. This is often a hard sign of damage to an area of the brain. See also: **constructional apraxia; hard signs; limb apraxia.**

Aptitude test. A test intended to predict the examinee's ability for a given type of work or academic area.

Aqueous (ā′kwē əs, ak′wē-) **humor.** The colorless fluid which fills the anterior chamber of the eye. It is apparently identical to the cerebrospinal fluid that fills the ventricles of the brain as well as the rest of the lumen, that is, the internal opening of the brain and spinal cord.

Arachnoid (ə rak′noid) **membrane.** The middle of three membranes, the meninges (the singular is "meninx"), that surround the central nervous system. The arachnoid is a thin sheet of collagen, a kind of connective tissue. It is constructed of criss-crossed fibers, reminding one of an outdoor spider's web, the kind of web observed in hedges, <u>not</u> a cobweb. The arachnoid and the still finer membrane below it together make up the <u>leptomeninx</u>, which means "thin membrane." The arachnoid membrane is the middle one of the three, situated between the outermost <u>dura mater</u> and the innermost <u>pia mater</u> (so, the "maters" are the bread slices and the arachnoid is the meat of the sandwich). The arachnoid is fine enough to follow the outer boundaries of the gyri (ridges) of the cerebral cortex but is too thick to get down into the sulci (grooves). Between the arachnoid and the thin membrane below it is the subarachnoid space, which contains cerebrospinal fluid. Above the arachnoid and below the first membrane is the subdural space, which contains venous blood. See also: **dura mater; pia mater.**

Arachnoid (ə rak′noid) **villi**. Projections from the arachnoid membrane into the subdural space (a space filled with venous blood below the dura mater). Spent cerebrospinal fluid (CSF) is passed from the subarachnoid space (a space below the arachnoid filled with CSF) by means of these villi into the venous blood. See also: **arachnoid; cerebrospinal fluid.**

Arachnophobia (ə rak′nə fō″bē ə). Fear of spiders. See also: **phobias.**

Architectural barrier. A condition present in the physical environment of a disabled person which prevents that person from moving about or from using a facility.

Architectural psychology. The study of the effects buildings have on behavior(s) and the design of such buildings using behavioral principles.

Arcuate fasciculus. An arching bundle of axons in the white matter of the cerebral cortex. The cell bodies that give off the axons are to be found in Wernicke's area, the part of the hearing area in the left temporal lobe that is specialized for understanding spoken language. The axons run rostrad to the frontal lobe where they terminate in Broca's area for motor speech. This fasciculus (tract) provides the basis for acquiring the language of one's cultural group, since the heard words (Wernicke's area-activity) serve to program the word-forming controls (Broca's area-activity). When the arcuate fasciculus is severed in an adult, the result is often <u>conduction aphasia</u>. See also: **Broca's area; conduction apha-**

sia; **Wernicke's area.**

Aromatization hypothesis. This is the view that perinatal estrogen (a female sex hormone) is an aromatized (changed chemically to an aromatic form) product of perinatal testosterone. The hypothesis states that it is that chemical structure, the aromatic one, that allows <u>estrogen</u> to get into the brain cells and <u>masculinize</u> them. If this seems paradoxical, remember: the hormone-neutral brain is feminine. In computerese, the "default" state of the brain is female (nothing derogatory is intended by the use of the word "default"--it just means the natural, basic state). So any effect of a steroid hormone, even a female sex hormone, does a masculinizing job on brain cells. To be specific for those who know some basic organic chemistry, a steroid has three hexagonal rings and one pentagonal ring of carbon atoms. There is only one double bond (it's in the first hexagon) between any two adjoining carbon atoms in the molecules of cortisol, corticosterone, testosterone, and progesterone. But estradiol has three double bonds (they alternate with single bonds), so that the first hexagon has the benzene or phenyl ring, which is the hallmark of aromatic compounds. Therefore, changing any of the other steroid hormones mentioned here into estradiol would be an act of aromatization.

Arousal. The overall level of excitation generated at any given time in an organism.

Arousal theory. A theory of motivation put forth by Berlyne and others to the effect that we strive for some optimal level of arousal. All motives, according to this view, do not aim at drive reduction. When drive levels are very high, we will try to lower them; however, when things are very quiet and "nothing much is happening," arousal theory predicts that we will seek increased drive and greater amounts of tension.

Arteriosclerosis (är tēr ″ē ō skli rō′sis) ("sklerosis" = "hardening" in Greek). A pathological thickening and/or hardening of the wall of an artery. Tobacco use, lack of exercise, emotional problems, and Type A behavior are all considered potential causes.

Arthritis. An inflamed condition of the joints, leading to pain and stiffness.

Arthrogryposis (är″thrō gri pō′sis). The fixation of a joint in a flexed or curved position, brought on by one of any of a number of congenital factors affecting the spinal cord, connective tissues, or musculature.

Articulation. The movements of the vocal cords and other mouth and throat structures in the production of speech sounds.

Articulation disorder. A communication disorder that may involve any one or more of the following: substitutions, omissions, additions, and/or distortions of speech sounds.

Articulatory-graphomotor dyscoordination problem (är tik′yə lə tôr′ē-graf ō mō″tər dis″kō ôr di nā′shən). This is a dyslexic subtype described by Denckla as language-based with problems centered in the speech and motor areas; specifically, the dyslexic has problems in blending sounds and in coordinating writing skills.

Artificial intelligence. Activity by a sophisticated computer program that is analogous to the working of a human brain. The term also refers to a field of study, the designing of artificial intelligence programs.

ASC. See **altered states of consciousness.**

Ascending reticular arousal system (ARAS). The midbrain portion of the reticular formation, the ARAS sends messages to nonspecific relay nuclei within the thalamus. Impulses from these nuclei are directed to all parts of the cerebral hemispheres. This input is necessary for arousal, alerting, and wakefulness. Loss of the ARAS leaves the organism in a deep coma, even with all the pathways for the individual senses (vision, hearing, touch, temperature, and pain) left intact.

Ascribed role. A social role one obtains by dictum, since these roles are not under the control of the individual. Being male versus female, a child, or an inmate of an institution for the retarded or the emotionally disordered, is not under one's own control. See also: **achieved role.**

Asocial personality disorder. See: **antisocial personality disorder.**

Asomatognosia (ə sō″mə tog nō′zhə). The inability to recognize the parts of one's own body.

Aspartate. A type of amino acid found throughout the body which is also used as a synaptic transmitter.

Asperger's disorder. A set of rigid, stereotyped patterns of social behavior that does not involve cognitive or oral expressive language skills. According to the DSM-IV, two of the following four conditions must be present for this diagnosis to be made: (1) impoverished age-appropriate peer relationships, (2) an inability to display happiness at other people's good fortune, (3) an inability to maintain adequate nonlinguistic behaviors (e.g., eye contact, normal facial expression, and normal body gestures), and (4) a lack of social reciprocity.

Asphyxia (az fik′sē ə). The impairment (or complete absence) of the exchange of oxygen for carbon dioxide in respiration. This results in an excessive, toxic buildup of carbon dioxide content in the blood.

Aspiration method. A technique for making a brain lesion in an experimental animal. The surgeon fits a hose over the vacuum extension of a laboratory water faucet and attaches a hypodermic needle to the other end of the hose. When the water is turned on, a vacuum is created at the side extension and that condition applies to the hose also. The surgeon can now place the tip of the needle against an exposed bit of brain and suck away ("aspirate") as much of the tissue as his plan requires. This technique is too crude for most modern research, which involves the use of the stereotaxic instrument to place small lesions in precise locations in the brain. The aspiration equipment doesn't work as well in a stereotaxic as an electrode or a fine cannula. We won't knock it, though, because some of Karl Lashley's best work on the relation of the brain to problem-solving was done using the aspiration method. See also: **stereotaxic instrument.**

A/S ratio. An index introduced by Donald Hebb as an estimate of the comparative intelligence of mammalian species. The amount of brain volume devoted to "association" functions (i.e., brain areas that are neither the origins of outgoing motor pathways nor the terminals of incoming sensory pathways) is divided by the amount of brain volume that is "sensorimotor" (either the ends of sensory pathways or the beginnings of motor pathways). The larger this quotient, presumably, the brighter the animal. Hebb's reasoning was that intelligent brain activity must take place between the strictly perceptual processes and the response-initiating activities. See also: **encephalization quotient (EQ); progres-**

sion index.

Assessment. An evaluation or measurement device or system. Psychological assessments could assess behavioral responses, cognitive functioning, or emotional well-being. Physiological assessments could look at general or specific neurological functioning.

Assimilation. The application of new situations or stimuli to existing mental patterns or schemas.

Assistive technology. Any services or devices used to assist disabled persons in improving their functioning. Various stages of technical development may be involved. See also: **prosthesis; Automated Learning Device.**

Association. A band of axons in the central nervous system linking a structure A on one side of the body's midline to another structure B on that side of the midline, on the same level. An example would be the arcuate fasciculus which links the posterior receptive speech area (Wernicke's area in the temporal lobe of the left cerebral cortex) to the anterior motor speech area (Broca's area in the frontal lobe of the left cortex). The association is a "vertical connection" (see explanation under **projection**), but it differs from a projection because it is fully contained within one level (specifically, the cerebral cortex level) of the central nervous system and includes no synaptic breaks in the continuity of its component axons.

Association cortex. All areas of the cerebral cortex that are not immediately related to sensory reception or to motor activation.

Assumption of modularity. The hypothesis that cognition (e.g., thought processes) is based on the assembly of very specific neural modules, with each subsystem performing its own special function.

Astereognosis (ā″ster ē og nō′sis). An inability to identify objects through the use of the sense of touch, despite the absence of any impairment of the touch sense. This alleged symptom is a controversial one, since the only observed cases of failure to identify objects by touch have been accompanied by damage to the touch-sense nerve pathways or to the projection areas for touch in the cerebral cortex.

Asthenic (as then′ik) **personality disorder** or **dependent personality disorder**. A disorder wherein the individual lacks the normal amount of initiative and energy needed to function adequately in both a personal and social sense. This is a passive-dependent type of individual who must rely on others for decision making.

Asthma. Labored, sometimes spasmodic breathing involving constriction of the bronchial tubes and the accumulation of thick fluids in the air passages of the lungs. This chronic condition involves sporadic attacks of wheezing, coughing, and shortness of breath. Asthma can be caused by allergic reactions to allergen substances (e.g., dust) (extrinsic asthma), a malfunctioning of the autonomic nervous system, an infection (e.g., a cold) in individuals with sensitive bronchi (e.g., intrinsic asthma), an intense and especially psychologically stressful situation in individuals with sensitive bronchi (e.g., a physiology exam with terms you don't understand), and weather conditions (e.g., a change in humidity) in individuals with sensitive bronchi. Prevention is aimed at determining the triggering substances or situations that induce asthmatic reactions and avoiding exposure to them in the future. Approximately 40% of childhood asthmatics improve after puberty with another 40% worsening. See also: **allergen.**

Astigmatism (ə stig′mə tiz″əm). A defect in the shape of the cornea, lens, or eye as a whole which causes some aspects of the visual field to be out of focus.

Astraphobia (as″trə fō′bē ə). An irrational fear of thunder or lightning. See also: **phobias.**

Astrocytes (as′trō sīts″) or **astroglia** (as trog′lē ə, as″trə glī ə) (from Latin "aster" = "star"). A star-shaped kind of neuroglial cell of the central nervous system. The astrocytes have a number of functions. First, they provide mechanical support for neurons and help keep each of the various nuclei (collections of gray matter) and tracts (bundles of white matter) in their particular size and shape. Second, when there are damaged myelin and shredded nerve tissue present following an injury, astrocytes act as phagocytes, ingesting the waste material. Third, after damaged neurons in the brain or spinal cord have been cleaned away by phagocytosis, the astrocytes multiply and fill in the empty space. A patch of astrocytes with no neurons in it would be a glial scar. The forming of the glial scar is called gliosis. Fourth, the end feet of astrocytes anchored around small blood vessels screen chemicals in the blood before those chemicals can enter the cytoplasm of the astrocyte. The chemicals taken from the blood go to the rays of the astrocyte and then enter neurons through nerve cell membranes. This mechanism keeps chemicals of certain types, such as amines, from entering neurons; it is called the blood-brain barrier. See also: **blood-brain barrier; neuroglia; radial glia.**

Ataxia (ə tak′sē ə). A loss of the ability to direct and control the pace of muscular movements. The continuous flow of motor information from the senses of light touch and deep pressure is needed for the maintenance of balance and coordination in walking. People who have had congenitally caused degeneration of the dorsal funiculi in the spinal cord (i.e., the white matter containing the dorsal and cuneate tracts which carry touch sense information to the brain) lose their position sense and have to walk with staggering, reeling, and shuffling, with the legs spread apart. That condition is known as **Friedreich's ataxia.** In advanced cases of the venereal disease syphilis, the syphilis bacteria attack the dorsal roots (where the touch sense nerves enter the central nervous system). This results in ataxia, along with other symptoms; the condition is known as **tabes dorsalis.**

Athetosis (ath″ə tō′sis). A condition involving slow, uncoordinated, and involuntary movements of the extremities. These movements are termed athetoid movements. See also: **chorea; Parkinson's disease.**

Atonia. A condition of lack of muscle tone. This can be pathological, as when the muscle has to be contracted in order to carry out an action but the atonia prevents it.

Atresia (ə trē′zhə). The absence of an external auditory canal of the outer ear. This condition can result in hearing problems.

Atrophy. The reduction in size of a part of the body through inactivity or disuse.

Atropine. An antagonist of muscarine. Atropine blocks the muscarinic receptor sites of acetylcholine (ACh). These receptor sites are utilized in the parasympathetic nervous system actions of ACh on smooth muscles and glands. When a pre-surgical patient undergoes general anesthesia, the anesthetist will administer atropine as

well as the general anesthetic. This is to make sure that mucous and/or salivary secretions cannot drown the patient in his/her own body fluids while he/she is unconscious and, therefore, unable to use voluntary muscles to clear the airways. Atropine is provided to soldiers when nerve gas may be used on them. Nerve gas blocks the enzyme acetylcholinesterase (AChE) (which normally clears away ACh from its synapses), and the most devastating effect of overactive ACh is the muscarinic action on the salivary-and mucous-secreting cells.

Attention. An orientating response toward (a) given stimulus or stimuli. This response plays a role in selecting which stimuli that are received momentarily in the sensory register are preserved for retention in the relatively more stable short-term memory (STM).

Attentional overload. The anxiety-producing situation caused when sensory stimulation makes excessive demands on attention.

Attention deficit disorder (ADD). The inability to attend to the same stimulus for a long time interval. This can, but need not always, be accompanied by restlessness and impulsive actions. The existence of such a syndrome without the hyperactivity is currently under suspicion. For the time being, it is designated as "undifferentiated attention- deficit disorder." With regard to attention deficit specifically, the following behavior patterns should be observed: (1) difficulty in following directions, (2) difficulty in sustaining attention during both academic and play activities, (3) making frequent careless errors in school and work activities, and (4) having an inability to listen. See also: **attention-deficit with hyperactivity disorder.**

Attention-deficit with hyperactivity disorder (ADHD). The inability to attend to the same stimulus for a long time interval which is accompanied by impulsiveness and hyperactivity. Contrary to popular belief, not all learning disabled children have ADHD. To be diagnosed, this childhood disorder should have persisted for at least six months and should interfere with normal adaptive functioning. For a diagnosis of hyperactivity/impulsivity, several of the following behavior patterns should be noted: (1) blurting out answers to questions before the questions have been fully expressed, (2) having trouble waiting in line or for one's turn to come during games, (3) running around and/or climbing when these actions are inappropriate, (4) jumping out of a seat when being seated is required, and (5) fidgeting and squirming. Persons with ADHD are further classified as predominantly inattentive, predominantly hyperactive/impulsive, or being of the combined type. See also: **attention deficit disorder**.

Attitude. An attitude is a relatively fixed way of thinking, feeling, and acting toward a person, situation, or thing. It is a learned tendency to respond to particular stimuli (the objects of the attitude) in certain ways, to harbor feelings consistent with those responses, and to hold opinions that make the responses and feelings seem reasonable.

Attitude Scale. An assessment scale which looks at collective attitude statements by respondents.

Attractivity. An aspect of female mammalian sexual behavior in which the female elicits sexual advances from males. See also: **estrus; proceptivity; receptivity.**

Attribution. The cognitive process of assigning causation to environmental events. In emotion, attribution is the process of attributing perceived arousal to particular stimuli.

Aubert-Foerster law (ō bâʀ′-fər′stər). The size, in visual angle, at which a letter becomes just recognized varies directly with its distance from the center of the retina, measured in degrees of visual angle from the fixation point. The law is said to be true for values of eccentricity from 2 to 40 angular degrees. At an eccentricity greater than the one at which the letter is just recognized, the probability of correct identification of the letter falls sharply.

Audiogram (ô′dē ō gram″). A table or graph showing the sound level in decibels that is just detectable at each of several sound frequencies. For example, threshold hearing levels might be represented for pure tones of 125, 250, 500, 1,000, 2,000, 4,000, and 8,000 cycles per second respectively. These measurements are taken separately for each of the two ears. The testing device used is called an <u>audiometer</u>. It is possible to test separately with air-conducted and bone-conducted sounds. An air-conducted sound is provided by an earphone. A bone-conducted sound is provided by applying a tuning fork di-

rectly to the mastoid bone. When the ear responds well (has low thresholds) to bone-conducted tone stimuli but poorly (showing high thresholds) to air-conducted tone stimuli, the ear in question has conduction deafness (outer ear or middle ear disorder).

Audiologist. A specialist in the assessment and remediation of auditory disorders.

Audiology. The science of hearing disorders, their assessment, and their remediation.

Auditory agnosia (ag nō′zhə). The inability to identify nonverbal sounds, although the patient has no identified sensory deficits or intellectual problems.

Auditory analysis. The ability of an individual to isolate, and separately respond to, the components of an auditory signal. See also: **hearing; sound**.

Auditory area. The site on the temporal cortices where auditory information is received and interpreted. See also: **auditory cortex.**

Auditory canal. An opening in the outer ear which leads to the eardrum. Sound vibrations in air travel along the auditory canal until they arrive at the eardrum.

Auditory cortex. The part of the cerebral cortex that must be preserved if we are to have perfect hearing, it is the terminal of the auditory neural pathway which arises from the inner ear. The auditory cortex is found in the posterior part of the superior temporal gyrus of the temporal lobe. The Brodmann numbers used to label this portion of the cerebral cortex are 41 and 42. The left auditory cortex receives its messages mostly from the right ear and "hears from" the left ear to a somewhat lesser extent. Similarly, the right auditory cortex monitors mainly the left ear. See also: **cerebral cortex; temporal lobe.**

Auditory discrimination. The ability to detect differences among different sounds.

Auditory dyslexia (dis lek′sē ə). This is a type of dyslexia first described in detail by Myklebust in 1978, which is characterized by the individual's inability to integrate auditory information or to make the connection between phonemes and graphemes.

Auditory figure-ground perception. The ability to detect a particular sound or word when that sound is embedded in a set of other sounds occurring simultaneously.

Auditory integration. The ability to associate a sound (or combination of sounds) with other kinds of experience.

Auditory-linguistic dyslexia (dis lek′sē ə). This is a type of dyslexia which many researchers, including your authors, believe to be caused by neurological dysfunctioning in some language center in the cerebral cortex.

Auditory nerve. See: **acoustic nerve**; **auditory vestibular nerve.**

Auditory ossicles. See: **ossicles.**

Auditory processing. The use of auditory stimuli in identifying and giving meaning to units of language.

Auditory radiation. The bundle of axons sent from the medial geniculate nucleus of the thalamus to the auditory cortex, Brodmann's areas 41 and 42 of the temporal lobe's superior temporal gyrus. These axons have to pass through the constricted internal capsule at the level of the basal ganglia, but, above that level, they can spread out toward the various regions of the auditory cortex, which gives them a radiating or spraying appearance. See also: **auditory cortex; hearing; internal capsule; medial geniculate nucleus.**

Auditory training. Procedures for teaching the hard-of-hearing or deaf how to make good use of what hearing abilities they possess. Auditory training usually involves assisting the individual in developing an awareness of sound, an ability to make gross discriminations among environmental speech stimuli, and an ability to distinguish among various speech sounds.

Auditory vestibular (ves tib′yə lər) **nerve.** The eighth of the 12 pairs of cranial nerves, it carries information from the sense organs of the inner ear for two senses, hearing and balance. The nerve communicates with cochlear nuclei and vestibular nuclei in the medulla of the brain. See also: **cranial nerves.**

Auditory-visual integration. The ability to combine sounds and visual symbols in the cognition of phonetic symbols or other test stimuli with both sight and sound components.

Augmentative communication. A set of techniques for supplementing speech during communication (e.g., pointing to pictures, gesturing, or writing). See also: **AAC; alternative communication.**

Aura. A modification of consciousness just before the onset of an epileptic seizure. The individual may experience unusual colors, hear odd sounds, smell strange odors, and so on.

Auricle (ôr′i kəl) (also called the **pinna**). The outer visible ear which is the least important part of the ear involved in hearing. Sound is transmitted through the auricle to the external auditory canal and then to the tympanic membrane or eardrum.

Authenticity. In therapy, the reference to the ability of the therapist to be in tune or honest with his or her feelings or attitudes.

Autism (ô′tiz″əm). The word implies severe isolation of the individual. In this severe developmental disorder, the infant (and later, the child) cannot react with the appropriate emotional responses to the actions of others. The autistic child has severely restricted language abilities. As a result of these two essential features of this syndrome, autism presents great problems to special educators.

Autobiographical memory. Memory for events from one's own life and a form of long-term memory.

Autokinetic effect or **autokinetic illusion.** The apparent movement of a stationary pinpoint of light seen by an observer seated in a darkened room, although no movement actually occurs. This happens because the observer has no cues relating to the distance or size of the light source. See also: **illusion; phi phenomenon; stroboscopic motion.**

Automated Learning Device (ALD). Any communications or recording device adapted for use by a disabled person. Such devices may include special appliances, added battery-powered components, and so forth.

Autonomic (ô″tə nom′ik) **nervous system (ANS)** or **autonomic division.** That autonomic (autonomic = self-regulating) part of the peripheral nervous system which links the central nervous system to the internal organs of the body, such as the heart, stomach, and intestines. The ANS is critical to the maintenance of such necessary body functions as digestion, breathing, and heart rate. The two branches of the autonomic nervous system are the sympathetic division and the parasympathetic division. Both are directly involved in our emotional states. Generally, the function of the sympathetic division is to arouse the body, while, generally, the parasympathetic works to relax the body. Both systems may be working at the same time, but usually one of them is more active than the other. Often the successful activity of one branch requires the noninterference of the other. Neural mechanisms are present that lead to the inhibition of one of the two branches when the other must be activated. This relationship between the sympathetic and the parasympathetic systems is known as reciprocal inhibition. The arousal effects of the sympathetic nervous system, taken collectively, are labeled the "emergency reaction" (or "fight or flight"). The components of the emergency reaction include the diversion of blood from the viscera to the skeletal muscles and the brain; increased heart rate and blood pressure; rapid breathing; perspiration at the forehead, the palms, and the soles; and suppression of digestion and elimination. Biofeedback techniques have been used successfully to control such autonomic functions or malfunctions as high blood pressure, migraine headaches, and too rapid or too slow a heart rate. The nerve endings of the sympathetic nervous system release the neurotransmitter norepinephrine at the smooth muscles or glands that they contact. The nerve endings of the parasympathetic division release acetylcholine at the smooth muscles and glands with which they communicate. See also: **biofeedback; parasympathetic nervous system; peripheral nervous system; sympathetic nervous system.**

Autoradiographic tracing. See **autoradiography**.

Autoradiography (ô″tō rā″dē og′rə fē). A diagnostic procedure involving the injection of a radioactive chemical (often a radioactive amino acid such as proline) into the brain. The chemical is transported along axons to the terminal boutons of axon end brushes. Since the traceable chemical begins at the cell body and then moves down the action until arriving at the telodendria, the method can be termed an anterograde tracing technique. Autoradiography permits the mapping of the distribution of the radioactivity afterward, by the use of photographic materials that register luminant energy. See also: **anterograde tracing technique.**

Autoreceptors (ô″tō ri sep″tərz). Receptor sites on the presynaptic membrane of a synaptic bouton that respond to the very transmitter released from that bouton. The function of these receptor sites may be to regulate the rate of release of the neurotransmitter. See also: **receptor sites; synaptic bouton.**

Autosomal (ô″tə sō′məl) **disorders**. These are disorders resulting from genetic aberrations, but not of the sex (i.e., X or Y) chromosomes. There are autosomal dominant disorders (e.g., Huntington's chorea) and autosomal recessive disorders (e.g., phenylketonuria and Friedreich's ataxia). These disorders can be devastating for growth and development. See also: **Friedreich's ataxia; Huntington's chorea; phenylketonuria.**

Autosomal (ô″tə sō′məl) **gene**. A gene on any one of the chromosomes other than the sex chromosomes, i.e., X and Y.

Autosomal (ô″tə sō′məl) **recessive trait**. A trait or characteristic (e.g., eye color) that originates from a chromosome other than a sex chromosome. In order for this trait to be expressed, two recessive genes must be paired. For example, the color blue is recessive: Blue eyes occur only after the individual receives a recessive gene from each parent. On the other hand, brown eyes (which are dominant) can result from one dominant (brown) gene and one recessive (blue) gene. The recessive gene in this instance cannot be expressed.

Autotransplantation. The transplanting of (a) body part(s) to a different location in the same body. For example, veins have been taken from the patient's leg to replace clogged coronary arteries.

Average evoked response (AER) (also called **average evoked potential (AEP)** or **evoked response technique**). While a subject is undergoing an EEG examination, the same stimulus is presented on a number of occasions. Computer analysis allows the electrical potentials obtained from each electrode to be averaged, allowing a valley or peak to emerge that might not be apparent during a single observation. The canceling out of random errors is assumed to result from the process of averaging; hence the averaged data are regarded as more reliable than a single, unrepeated recording.

Aversion therapy. Suppression or undesirable behaviors or responses (e.g., smoking, drinking, gambling, hiccups, sneezing, stuttering, hair pulling, and maladaptive sexual responses) by associating the unwanted behaviors with aversive stimuli which could be painful or uncomfortable. Rapid smoking and Antabuse therapies are considered aversive therapies and are typically used as last resorts. See also: **Antabuse; rapid smoking.**

Aversive conditioning. A type of operant conditioning in which the correct response is reinforced by the removal of an unwanted object or situation (a so-called aversive stimulus). If the object is a primary (unconditioned) aversive stimulus, the aversive conditioning is considered to be escape training. If the removed object is aversive only because of previous pairings with an aversive stimulus (so that the object is a secondary or conditioned aversive stimulus), the aversive conditioning is defined as avoidance training, since the primary aversive event has been prevented from occurring.

AVID profile. Female dyslexics have been hypothesized by Spafford to do more poorly on four subtests of the Wechsler Intelligence Scales (the WAIS, WISC, and WPPSI) than on the six other subtests. These four subtests are Arithmetic, Vocabulary, Information, and Digit Span, for which AVID is an acrostic.

Avoidance-avoidance conflict. An unpleasant circumstance which requires one to make a choice between two negative and mutually undesirable alternatives.

Avoidance learning. Learning that is initiated in order to avoid painful or unpleasant stimuli. See also: **aversive conditioning.**

Avoidant personality disorder. A type of personality disorder wherein the individual is overly sensitive to criticism and will avoid interpersonal contact for fear of rejection by others. This type of individual is preoccupied with social rejection.

AVP$_{4-9}$. A metabolic product of the hormone vasopressin. AVP$_{4-9}$ is even more effective than vasopressin in heightening the memory of senile persons. It seems to accomplish this by raising the individual's attention to dominant cues in the environment.

Axillary hair. The hair of the armpit or axilla. The appearance of underarm hair at puberty is due to androgens in both males and females. See also: **androstenedione.**

Axoaxonic synapses (ak″sō ak son′ik sin′ap sēz). There are two major types of these synapses. [1] The first one is the type of neuron circuit referred to as presynaptic inhibition. In this type of arrangement, the synaptic bouton at the end of the axon of one neuron (let's call it A) may form a synaptic connection with the end branch leading to the synaptic bouton of another neuron (B). In order to understand the functional significance of this type of synapse, we must examine the involvement of the postsynaptic neuron (C), the membrane of which is across the synaptic cleft from the presynaptic membrane of neuron B. The synapse from B to C is an excitatory one, so that if neuron A is resting, B can depolarize (i.e., excite) neuron C. This situation changes when and if neuron A is active. The axoaxonic synapse between neurons A and B is an excitatory one in that the membrane of B is depolarized, but the depolarization is only partial. The synaptic bouton of neuron B does not release its full supply of neurotransmitter into the synaptic cleft, and the lesser amount of neurotransmitter that does get released is deactivated. When the impulse in the axon of cell B comes along, the synaptic bouton cannot provide enough of the excitatory neurotransmitter to depolarize neuron C. Functionally (effectively) the neuron is inhibited, even without activating any specific inhibitory synapse. The inhibitory process just described is called presynaptic inhibition. This is inhibition by excitation; it can be likened to the deliberate lighting of a small brush fire in order to consume inflammable material, thereby preventing the spread of a raging forest fire. [2] The presence of autoreceptors on the presynaptic membrane of a terminal bouton allows the neurotransmitter released from that bouton to affect the rate at which the bouton releases more molecules of the neurotransmitter. This effect on the release rate is most likely to be inhibitory, so that the process is self-limiting, a form of negative feedback. See also: **autoreceptor; presynaptic inhibition; receptor site; synapse.**

Axodendritic synapses (ak″sō den drit′ik sin′ap sēz). Axon terminals forming synaptic connections with dendrites. Many synapses are of this type. Often, budlike outgrowths from the dendrites meet the synaptic boutons. These little extensions from the dendrites are called **dendritic spines**, and the synapses in which they appear are called **dendritic spine synapses** (see definitions). See also: **axosomatic synapses**.

Axon (ak′son). A fiber-like outgrowth from the cell body of a neuron that is cylindrical (i.e., has a constant diameter) until the very end, when it breaks up into numerous small branches, the <u>telodendria</u> (see definition). The axon carries the nerve impulse, and, since it may stretch out as far as three feet, it can be considered the "sending fiber" of the neuron. The axon ends very close to either other neurons or to effectors (viz., muscle fibers or gland cells). These targeted cells "receive" the neuron's "message." The axon can be as narrow as two-tenths of one-millionth of a meter, so it is too small an object to be seen by the unaided eye. Each neuron has only one axon, at most.

Axon collateral (ak′son kə lat′ər əl). A side branch of an axon. This structural feature allows the neuron to contact target neurons in a part of the brain different from that reached by the direct route followed by the main part of the axon. A collateral retains the cylindrical form of the axon. In pyramidal cells, especially the giant ones called Betz cells, there may be <u>recurrent collaterals</u>. A recurrent collateral feeds information to the neuron's own dendrites. In the case of a pyramidal cell, the axon leaves the cell body at the base of the pyramid and a collateral rises up past the cell body to contact an apical dendrite, which is a dendrite coming from the peak or apex of the pyramid-shaped cell body. The point of a cell's having a recurrent collateral? Probably inhibition, in order to limit the time that the cell is actively sending nerve impulses along its axon. See also: **axon; Betz cell**.

Axon hillock (ak′son hil′ək). The small knob on the cell body of a neuron from which the axon arises. The cytoplasm of the axon hillock, like the axon cytoplasm, lacks Nissl granules and is much clearer than the cytoplasm of the rest of the neuron. Under natural conditions, the nerve impulse is initiated at the axon hillock. It is here that the "votes are counted", so to speak. The EPSPs would be like votes to fire an impulse and the IPSPs are analogous to votes against sending the nerve impulse. If the EPSP margin is favorable and is large enough, the action potentials begins. See also: **excitatory post synaptic potential (EPSP); inhibitory post synaptic potential (IPSP)**.

Axonal (ak′sən l, ak son′l, ak sō′nəl) **transport**. Usually, the transport of chemical substances, such as neurotransmitters, and even small objects (the synaptic vesicles) down the axon from the cell body toward the telodendria, i.e., <u>anterograde</u> axonaltransport. It should not be overlooked that excess bits of presynaptic membrane are sent back via the axon from the telodendria toward the cell body, this process being called <u>retrograde</u> axonal transport.

Axoplasm (ak′sō plaz″əm). The cytoplasm of the axon (as well as the axon hillock). The axoplasm is much clearer than the rest of the cytoplasm of the neuron. It is lacking in Nissl substance, that is, the rough endoplasmic reticulum, which is typically found in neuron cell bodies. See also: **axon; axon hillock; cytoplasm; Nissl substance**.

Axosomatic synapses (ak″sō sō mat′ik sin′ap sēz). Axon endings forming synaptic connections with sites on the membrane surrounding the cell body (soma) of a receiving neuron. Many synapses are of this type. Axosomatic synapses usually are inhibitory synapses because they are very near the axon hillock. Positioning an excitatory synapse too close to an axon hillock would prevent the inhibition of the neuron; by the time an inhibitory message arrived from, say, an axodendritic synapse, it would be too late, as the axon would already be firing the nerve impulse triggered at the axon hillock. See also: **axodendritic synapses**.

Axotomy. The severing of an axon.

B

Babbling. The repetition by young children of speech utterances, including vowel and consonant sounds, in a meaningless language

Babinski (bə bin′skē) **reflex.** The reflex initiated by a stimulus to the sole of the foot of a human infant. The toes fan while the big toe points upward. This will be exhibited in an adult after damage to the motor area of the cerebral cortex instead of the normal <u>plantar reflex</u>. The Babinski reflex found in an adult is one example of a <u>hard sign</u> of central nervous system dysfunction in a neurological examination.

Background stressors. The irritations that occur in everyday life (such as misplacing one's keys or the eyeglasses) that are capable of enhancing the severity of stress-related disorders, although, in and of themselves, they do not cause such disorders.

Backward masking. Presenting interfering stimuli very quickly after the showing of meaningful stimuli. This requires at least a two-field tachistoscope. When the subject has trouble reporting the meaningful stimuli, the failure is attributable to a memory processing deficiency. This procedure has also been referred to as <u>metacontrast</u>. See also: **forward masking; masking (in visual research); tachistoscope.**

Bacterial meningitis (bak tēr′ē əl   men″in jī′tis). A bacterial inflammation in the membranes of the brain or spinal cord.

Balanced placebo design. A plan of research involving four groups of subjects. Two of the groups are told to expect to receive a given treatment; the other two groups do not get this instruction. Half of the subjects in each of the above groups get the actual treatment, while half get the placebo control treatment. See also: **placebo; subject.**

Bait shyness. An unwillingness on the part of animals to consume or eat certain foods which is caused by a taste aversion.

Ballistic movement. A movement that, once begun, cannot be controlled further. Once the rubber hammer taps the patellar tendon just below the knee, for example, the kicking response is launched and is automatically carried out to completion.

Barbiturates (bär bich′ər its, -ə rāts″). The main group of depressant drugs (aside from ethyl alcohol), barbiturates are commonly referred to as "downers." They have various kinds of activity: Some are anticonvulsants, some are tranquilizers, and almost all are sedatives. They are prescribed to relieve insomnia; they are also used in cases of epilepsy or arthritis. Phenobarbital, pentothal, and nembutal are examples of barbiturates. They are highly addictive. When they are abused along with ethyl alcohol, barbiturates can be life-threatening. See also: **psychoactive drugs; sedatives.**

Barnum effect. This is a tendency to believe general personal descriptions. It accounts for the ready acceptance by individuals of horoscopes or "fortunes."

Baroceptors. These are pressure receptors located in the heart and in the walls of the larger arteries. They respond to elevation or to depression in the local blood volume. The baroceptors and angiotensin II have a synergistic effect on hypovolemic thirst. When both are present, their combined effect on thirst is greater than twice the effect of each one by itself. See also: **angiotensin II; synergy.**

Barrier-free facility. A facility or building designed to accommodate individuals with physical disabilities. Disabled individuals can move freely throughout the structure without architectural barriers to impede mobility.

Barrier motor-skill task. A task given to monkeys in psychological laboratory research. The animal is allowed to earn a fragile breadstick, provided that the monkey is able to maneuver it around obstacles arranged in a maze-like pattern.

Basal age. The lowest age level (on the original form of the Stanford-Binet test of general intelligence) at which the individual is able to perform all tasks and answer all questions. The usual score reported from such tests is the <u>mental age</u>. See also: **ceiling age; mental age.**

Basal blood insulin level. The insulin level in the blood following an overnight fast.

Basal forebrain region. The area of the forebrain just rostral to the hypothalamus.

Basal ganglia (bā′səl   gang′glē ə). A part of the

gray matter of the telencephalon or cerebrum of the brain. These are more appropriately called nuclei rather than ganglia, since they are part of the brain [See the definitions of **ganglion** and **nucleus (part of the gray matter.)**]. They include the amygdala, the caudate nucleus, the globus pallidus, the putamen, and the claustrum. In general, these structures are related to the control of posture and movement, that is, striped muscle activity. They have connections with nuclear masses in the midbrain, such as the red nucleus, the substantia nigra, the subthalamic nucleus, and the ventral tegmental area. Some writers include these four nuclei among the basal ganglia, even though they are not in the cerebrum.

Basal metabolism. The rate of energy consumption when the body is in a completely rested state.

Baseline data. Data taken on the subject of a research study before the planned treatment is administered. The baseline data may be compared with data taken after the treatment is given in order to discover whether or not the treatment has had any effect.

Base rate. The usual rate at which events occur over time or the probability of an event occurring at a certain threshold. See **operant level** for a particular example.

Basic or **pure research**. The scientific study of matters without attention or regard for the immediate or future applications. This is research undertaken for the sake of research.

Basic suggestion effect. This involves a tendency of hypnotized individuals to carry out suggestions as if they were involuntary.

Basilar membrane. A membrane running the length of the cochlea in the inner ear. It serves as the floor of the organ of Corti, in which the auditory hair cells (the receptor cells for sound) are located. The basilar membrane is connected to the oval window, which receives sound waves from the middle ear. The basilar membrane in turn vibrates, but in a selective way. The basilar membrane is narrowest at the oval window, and gradually widens as it extends toward its inner edge at the helicotrema, the center of the cochlea. Thus, the membrane will vibrate in resonance with high pitched sounds (20,000 cycles per second) at the oval window end, where it is

the narrowest; resonant vibrations will get lower and lower for successive areas of the basilar membrane as the membrane goes farther along toward the other end, the helicotrema (the "end of the helix"). The lowest vibrations to which a part of the membrane will resonate are about 4,000 cycles per second. See also: **cochlea; inner ear; place coding; place-resonance theory of hearing**.

B cell. A type of leukocyte (white blood corpuscle) that develops in the bone marrow and that generates antibodies. See also: **antibody; antigen**.

BEAM (brain electrical activity mapping). A computerized technique for integrating EEG data from all over the cerebral cortex. This permits researchers to produce a detailed map of the active and inactive areas of the cortex during various tasks or at rest. The technique was developed by Dr. Frank Duffy and associates.

Before-and-after design. An experimental design in which the same subjects get both the experimental and the control treatments. It is referred to as "using the subject as her or his own control." The design avoids the risk of intertreatment variability due to individual differences between control and experimental subjects. It is open to order effects, e.g., it might make a difference whether the experimental treatment is applied first or second. For example, when someone bumps into you and says "Pardon me" is not the same as someone accosting you, saying "pardon me", and then bumping into you. See also: **between-subject design**.

Behavior checklist. A list of various behaviors that characterize some group of children. The children in a school may be observed systematically and the frequency of each behavior on the checklist noted for each child. The data are used to help decide whether a child should be referred for special services.

Behavior disorder. A nonstandard pattern of action that deviates from accepted social norms, that continues to occur over a long time period, and that occurs with either high intensity, high frequency, or both.

Behavior genetics. A field of study that is concerned with the hereditary bases for the behavior of organisms.

Behavioral assessment. Scoring the behavior of an individual by direct observation, along with self-evaluation and interviews. Making a behavioral assessment implies the avoidance of subjective scoring; indirect assessment, depth interviewing, and interpretation are not used.

Behavioral excesses. Behaviors that exhibit too much intensity, frequency, or duration or that occur at untimely occasions, provided that the social acceptability of the intensity, and so on, are close to zero.

Behavioral medicine. The study of behavioral factors in the treatment of illnesses. This is the area of medicine that deals with the effects on people's health of such habits as smoking, drinking alcoholic beverages, experiencing psychological stress, and engaging in physical exercise.

Behavioral model. The assumption that behavior disorders are the result of inappropriate learning; this leads readily to the assumption that an appropriate environmental intervention can effectively teach the appropriate behavior.

Behavioral neuroscience. See: **physiological psychology.**

Behavioral paradigm (par'ə dīm ″, -dim). A unitary set of procedures used in the systematic study of a given type of behavior. Staying with the paradigm allows researchers to introduce independent variables one at a time and compare the relative effects of these variables on the behavior tested.

Behavioral personality theory. Models of personality theory which embody the observation of behaviors, stimuli, and responses as well as their impact on learning and personality.

Behavioral risk factors. These are behaviors which increase the chance(s) of injury or disease or that shorten life expectancy (e.g., smoking).

Behavioral setting. An environmental area whose use is well defined, such as your physiology or psychology classes.

Behaviorism. That school of psychology which deals with the study of overt, observable behaviors in a number of settings, as well as responses to such behaviors.

Behavior modification. The use of conditioning techniques (classical conditioning or operant conditioning, whichever is appropriate) to reduce a maladaptive, abnormal behavior and/or train the organism in a skilled, well-adapted mode of behaving.

Belief component. The attitudinal belief system of an individual which impacts behaviors toward, or attitudes about, the object(s) of those attitude(s).

Bell-Magendie (bel'-mə″zhän dē') **law.** The observation that the ventral roots of the spinal nerves transmit motor commands to the muscles while the dorsal roots of the spinal nerves transmit sensory impulses from peripheral sense receptors to the central nervous system. In sum: dorsal = sensory, ventral = motor, or "DS/VM" (remember that!).

Benign. An adjective that can be applied to a tumor if it can be removed without leaving traces behind that can lead to the growth of another tumor. If the tumor cannot be removed cleanly, and it seems to be growing uncontrollably, the term applied would be malignant.

Benzodiazepine (ben″zō dī az′ə pēn″). A class of antianxiety drugs. The best known of them is diazepam, which is known by its trade name of Valium. See also: **anxiolytic.**

Beta adrenergic (ad″rə nûr′jik) **receptors.** A class of receptor sites for an adrenergic neurotransmitter (norepinephrine and/or epinephrine) on nerve cell membranes (such as autoreceptors), on the membrane surrounding the heart, or on membranes surrounding the smooth muscles of the lungs and intestines. The adrenergic neurotransmitter is excitatory for the heart muscle but has inhibitory action at the intestines and the lungs, which lets them relax.

Beta cells. The cells of the islets of Langerhans (the endocrine organs attached to the pancreas) that release insulin as their hormone. Insulin leads to the removal of glucose (blood sugar) from the bloodstream and its conversion to glycogen (animal starch) which is stored in the liver. See also: **diabetes mellitus; endocrine system; hormones.**

Beta endorphins (en dôr′finz). Natural brain chemicals which are similar in structure to synthetic morphine and which possess powerful pain-reducing qualities.

Beta waves. Electroencephalogram records that fluctuate rapidly, so that the frequency is high (14 Hertz or more). Since the change from positive to negative and vice versa is so rapid, the EEG cannot reach a high value of negative or positive voltage. Beta waves are therefore described as low voltage, high frequency (LVHF) waves. See also: **BEAM; electroencephalogram.**

Between-subject design. An experimental design in which the available subjects are randomly assigned either to the group getting the experimental treatment or to the group getting the control treatment. If the number of subjects is large enough and the original pool of subjects includes various types of individuals, the two groups will very likely be equated for any biological or psychological trait that is normally distributed. See also: **before-and after design.**

Betz (bets) cell. A giant, pyramid-shaped type of neuron found in the fifth cortical layer, particularly in Brodmann's area 4, the primary motor cortex. The axons of these cells constitute the pyramidal motor tract. Area 4 is where the corticospinal tract (the pyramidal motor tract) originates. See also: **Brodmann numbering system; cerebral cortex; frontal lobe; pyramidal motor tract.**

Bezold-Brücke phenomenon (bets′ôld-broo͞o′ke). The hues of most visual stimuli change as illumination increases. Red, yellow, and green show diminished saturation but no hue change when the illuminance is raised. However, yellowish-red and yellowish-green both look more yellow when highly illuminated, and bluish-red and bluish-green appear more blue when highly illuminated.

Bilateral medial temporal lobectomy (lō bek′tə mē). The removal of medial (i.e., midline-side) parts of the right and left temporal lobes, including the left and right amygdala and hippocampus. This was done to Dr. Brenda Milner's widely publicized patient, "H. M.", and led to the establishment of the memory-consolidation concept. The anterograde amnesia in H. M. strangely persisted, leading to the conclusion that his difficulty was the total inability to consolidate short-term memory (STM) into long-term memory (LTM). H. M.'s memories from his pre-operation life were intact. See also: **consolidation; hippocampus; long-term memory; long-term potentiation; short-term memory.**

Bimodal distribution. A frequency distribution that deviates from the bell-shaped form of the normal curve. In a frequency distribution, the X-axis shows the value of the score or measurement while the Y-axis shows the number of individuals obtaining each score. The score with the highest count or frequency is known as the mode, since it is the most fashionable or popular score. In the normal curve, the mean score is also the mode. Sometimes a distribution is obtained in which two far-apart scores are tied for the highest frequency, that is, there are two modes. The curve drawn for this distribution looks like the outline of a two-humped camel. Neither mode is close to the center of the distribution, as defined by the mean or the median. The mode is these distributions is not an acceptable indication of the distribution's central value. See also: **normal curve.**

Binaural cue. A cue to a sound's location which requires the cooperative activity of the two ears. See also: **monaural cue; sound localization; superior olivary nucleus.**

Binocular. Receiving visual cues or inputs from both eyes.

Binocular depth cues. These are depth cues which function only when both eyes are being used. The most important of these cues is **retinal disparity** (see definition).

Binocular disparity (also called **binocular parallax** or **retinal disparity**). See: **retinal disparity.**

Binocular parallax. (bī nok′yoo lər, bi- par′ə laks″) See: **retinal disparity.**

Binocular vision. Viewing a target with both eyes at the same time. This requires the nervous system to integrate the two sets of visual impulses into a single complex perception.

Biochemical abnormalities. Various chemicals such as hormones and enzymes are present in the body in certain quantities. Other chemicals, metabolic breakdown products, may be found in the body as well. If the quantity of chemical(s) is unusually high or unusually low, this indicates pathology, and physical or chemical pathology sometimes involves the mind, the emotions, and behavior (psychopathology).

Biochemistry. A specialty within the science of biology, the science of life. Biochemistry is concerned with the attempt to account for biological functions by reference to chemical activity. The applications of biochemistry have improved our knowledge of nutrition, nerve physiology, genetics, medicine, pharmacology, endocrinology, and agriculture. Synonymous terms are "biological chemistry" and "physiological chemistry."

Biofeedback. This is the providing of a visual and/or auditory signal that allows an individual to follow the variations of one of his or her physiological functions (e.g., respiratory rate, blood pressure, finger temperature, EEG, muscle tension, or galvanic skin response). The individual is required to try to change that physiological variable, using the signal as a guide, but without being given specific advice as to how to do it. Such training, surprisingly, will often result in successful learning. Biofeedback is controversial because its results are spotty, sometimes successful, sometimes failing, and it is not clear why it is not more consistently effective. In the case of one uncomfortable symptom, it is the only known therapy: in Raynaud's disease, where the hands turn blue and the fingers are very cold. More conventional medical treatment for Raynaud's disease has never been successful, so that finger temperature biofeedback seems to be the only available treatment method. Certain forms of neuromuscular dysfunction, such as torticollis (in which the patient presents a bizarre appearance, having the head pressed against one shoulder), are hard to treat by conventional medical techniques and may be alleviated by biofeedback training in muscle relaxation. Biofeedback also has been used to treat such disorders as peptic ulcers, asthma, and migraine headaches. Musicians just before a concert and athletes just before competing use biofeedback to relieve preperformance stress. A major drawback to the use of biofeedback is the amount of time required to produce an effective improvement, such as reduced heart rate. The technique requires much dedication and disciplined effort on the part of the individual. See also: **Raynaud's disease; torticollis.**

Biological aging. The physiological changes which accompany increasing age and alter physical and/or psychological functioning.

Biological biasing effect. The hypothesized effect(s) that prenatal exposure to male or female hormones has on the development of the body and later behavior patterns.

Biological chemistry. See: **biochemistry.**

Biological clock. An internal time control for regulating rhythmic behaviors, such as waking, sleeping, and dreaming. See also: **biorhythms;**

suprachiasmatic nucleus; Zeitgeber.

Biological constraints (on learning). Due to innate arrangements of the nervous system, certain modes of learning can be extremely difficult for the members of a given species of animal. For example, attempts to train raccoons to carry objects over moderate distances (with food reinforcement provided for correct responding) will run afoul of the animal's inborn tendency to try to wash and clean such food-related objects.

Biological model or **biological perspective**. The attempt to account for human and animal behavior by referring to the biological functions of the species. A variant of this is the medical model, which would explain emotional/behavioral/mental disorders according to the genetic and/or physiological aberrations of the patient.

Biological motion. The visual perception of moving people or of other living organisms in motion.

Biological predisposition. The presumed hereditary readiness of an individual to acquire such variables as language, diseases, and character traits.

Biological psychiatry. The study of the biological bases of psychiatric disorders, with emphasis on drug treatments for the correction of metabolic irregularities in brain or endocrine system functioning.

Biological psychology. See: **physiological psychology**.

Biologically based psychotherapy. The treatment of emotional/mental/behavioral disorders by such medical modes as prescribed drugs or psychosurgery.

Biophysical model. The assumption that behavior disorders or learning disabilities are due to central nervous system dysfunction. The cause may be a brain lesion, an endocrine irregularity, or a genetic defect. This leads to the assumption that the best corrective would be a prevention or correction of the biological problem. See also: **biological model.**

Biophysics. A specialty within the science of biology, the science of life. Biophysics is concerned with the physics of living matter. Any development within physical science that adds to the ability to make discoveries about living organisms and their tissues and organs would illustrate how biophysics contributes to the furtherance of biology in general. For example, electron microscopy has revealed important details about the makeup of body cells and of synapses, the points of contact between adjoining nerve cells.

Biopsychology. See: **physiological psychology**.

Biorhythms. Periodic increases and decreases of behaviors and/or physiological functions that are controlled by internal or biological clocks. See also: **biological clock; suprachiasmatic nucleus; Zeitgeber**.

Bipolar affective disorder. A severe mood disorder in which the parent alternately experiences deep depressions and manic heights of euphoria. See also: **bipolar disorder**.

Bipolar cell. See: **bipolar neuron**.

Bipolar cell layer. A layer of bipolar neurons in any part of the nervous system. The second-order neurons in the retina constitute such a layer. The first-order cells are the rods and cones, the receptors, which are modified neurons. The third-order neurons are the large ganglion cells, which give off the axons making up the optic nerve. See also: **retina; bipolar neuron**.

Bipolar depression (bi = two; polar = poles or extremes). A condition in which depressed episodes alternate with episodes of mania. This is also called manic depression. See also: **bipolar affective disorder; bipolar disorder; clinical depression; depression (major); mania; manic depressive disorder; mood disorder.**

Bipolar disorder or **bipolar manic-depressive disorder**. A genetically inherited disorder which is also known as manic depression. An individual with a bipolar disorder has alternating episodes of mania (elation) and depression which can last for weeks or months. Intervening periods of time are marked by relative normality. The risk for developing this disorder is 0.7 % in both men and women. The onset of this disorder usually occurs after age 30. See also: **bipolar affective disorder; bipolar depression.**

Bipolar neuron. The most easily taught shape of the neuron and the most often pictured in elementary textbooks, but the rarest neuron type of all. The bipolar neuron has one dendrite and one axon. The two fibers meet the cell body at directly opposite locations (reminding one of the Earth's North and South poles), hence the term "bipolar." Some bipolar cells are of miniature size and occur in the olfactory mucous membrane and in the retina. In these tiny bipolar cells, both fibers are "dendrites," in that neither fiber carries a true nerve impulse, but carries, rather, the variable-strength graded and decremental potentials typical of the membranes of the cell body and dendrites of neurons. Almost always, bipolar neurons are sensory in function. Retinal bipolar cells are second in the pathway leading up to the brain.

Birth injury. Any injury or damage which occurs to the fetus during delivery.

Birth order. The ordinal number of the individual child's time of birth within the family, as in: first-born, middle- born, only child, last-born, and so on.

Bisexuality. The tendency to be sexually attracted by members of either sex.

Bizarre delusions. The unrealistic and fantastic beliefs of some schizophrenic patients. These would be counted among the positive symptoms of schizophrenia. There are delusions of being controlled, or of being persecuted, or of grandeur. See also: **schizophrenia; schizophrenics.**

Blind or **Blindness**. A visual disability, where visual acuity is 20/200 in the better eye with the best possible correction. Alternatively, one is blind if the visual field subtends a visual angle of no more than 20 degrees. The blind need to be provided with Braille materials and with tactile and auditory aids in their education. See also: **Braille**.

Blindsight. The phenomenon whereby a person can locate an object by vision and reach for it successfully while being unaware that he or she is able to see. This type of vision requires an intact pair of superior colliculi (see **superior colliculus**). Awareness of vision is lost when visual area 1 (Brodmann area 17) in the occipital lobe of the cerebral cortex is damaged (see **visual cortex**). Patients showing blindsight express the belief that they are "only guessing."

Blind spot. An area of the retina which is free of any and all visual receptors. It is the place from which the optic nerve emerges on its way to the main part of the brain.

Blobs. Areas within a sublayer of the cerebral cortex that are part of the "sustained" visual pathway. The fourth layer of the cerebral cortex in Brodmann's area 17, visual area V1, is subdivided into sublayers IVa, IVb, and IVc. Sublayer IVc is further subdivided into parts IVc-alpha and IVc-beta. The parvocellular (i.e., small-celled) layers of the lateral geniculate nucleus of the thalamus send axons toward sublayer IVc-beta of area V1 of the cortex. When the layers of the cortex are stained with cytochrome oxidase, some portions of sublayer Ivc-beta absorb the stain, while other parts fail to absorb it. The neuroanatomist M. Wong-Riley, observing these blotchy areas of stained and unstained tissue under the microscope, named the stained parts "blobs" and the unstained portions "interblobs." The "blobs" respond differentially to visual information about hue, whereas the "interblobs" fail to discriminate colors but respond to fine differences in detail. The neurons in the blobs send axons to thin dark stripes of area 18 (visual area V2) while neurons in the interblobs send axons to pale stripes of area V2. The dark stripes are formed by the absorption of cytochrome oxidase stain while the pale stripes occur because the tissue in those areas fails to absorb cytochrome oxidase. See also: **cerebral cortex; interblobs; lateral geniculate nucleus; sustained visual pathway.**

Block-tapping memory span test. A kind of digit-span test in non-verbal form. The examiner taps a series of times, with short or long breaks between taps, and the subject then must repeat the pattern by his own tapping. The test resembles the game of "Simon", which uses musical sounds rather than taps. See also: **Corsi's test.**

Blocking. A learning phenomenon in which the pairing of one neutral stimulus to an unconditioned stimulus interferes with the learning of an association between a second neutral stimulus and the same unconditioned stimulus. For example, having learned that a buzzer is a signal of coming electrical shock, the organism may fail to learn that a light is also a signal for an impending shock.

Blood. The fluid circulating through the heart, the arteries, and the veins which contains the basic fluid component, the plasma, as well as individual cells (the red and white corpuscles) and also various chemicals, platelets, and fat globules. The blood in the arteries carries nourishment and oxygen to the tissues of the body and the blood in the veins removes waste products and

carbon dioxide from the tissues. The blood gets rid of carbon dioxide by travelling to the lungs, where it picks up oxygen. The blood gets around the entire circulatory system every 20 seconds. See also: **blood-brain barrier.**

Blood-brain barrier. A physiological screening mechanism that prevents many kinds of chemicals from entering brain and spinal cord neurons from the arterial blood. The end feet of astrocytes encircle arterioles (the smallest branches of arteries), and the astrocyte membrane either passes or denies passage to chemicals that move out of the arterial wall. In turn, the astrocyte contacts a number of neurons by means of its ray-like extensions. The blood-brain barrier is especially efficient at screening out monoamines (i.e., chemicals containing the $-NH_2$ group). This is why injection of a chemical neurotransmitter (usually a monoamine) will have little or no effect on the workings of the brain. The barrier will allow amino acids to pass, however, and the brain neurons' metabolism can manufacture the appropriate monoamine from an amino acid. Thus, for example, l-DOPA (an amino acid) can be injected so that the brain cells can generate the related chemical neurotransmitter, dopamine. See also: **astrocytes.**

Blood-flow receptors. Sense-receptors in the kidneys that monitor the rate of blood flowing through those organs. If the blood-flow reading is low enough, specialized cells in the kidneys will release the enzyme **renin.** What renin does is to convert the inactive chemical **angiotensin I** into the active hormone **angiotensin II.** Angiotensin II causes blood vessels to constrict, stimulates the release of **aldosterone,** and initiates the hypovolemic thirst processes. See also: **aldosterone; angiotensin II; hypovolemic thirst; volemic thirst.**

Blueprint hypothesis. A hypothesis purported to account for the precise placement of various kinds of neurons throughout the brain. It holds that the developing nervous system provides chemical and mechanical trails that act as guides for growing axons so that collections of axons (tracts) will be properly positioned. See also: **radial glia.**

Blunted affect. The failure of a schizophrenic patient to react with the appropriate emotions either to world events or to interpersonal reactions. This would be considered one of the negative symptoms of schizophrenia. See also: **schizophrenia; schizophrenics.**

B memory cell. A modified type of B cell that immunizes the body against further attacks by an antigen that has already been resisted. This type of cell is produced from a regular B cell by helper T cells from the thymus gland. See also: **antigen; B cell; helper T cell; T cell.**

Body (of corpus callosum). The middle part of the corpus callosum, which lies on a relatively straight line between the front end of the corpus callosum, the genu, and the rear part of the corpus callosum, the splenium. The body of the corpus callosum is in a position to connect the left and right anterior parts of the temporal lobes, the posterior parts of the left and right frontal lobes, and the anterior parts of the left and right parietal lobes of the cerebral cortex. See also: **cerebral cortex; corpus callosum.**

Body language. The communication of messages by gestures and mannerisms, without speaking.

Bone conduction test. A hearing test that measures the performance of the inner ear, bypassing the outer and middle ears. The sound vibrations are passed by the bones of the skull directly to the cochlea.

Bottom-up processing. The organization of perceptual stimuli beginning with low-level features. See also: **top-down processing.**

Bottom-up reading models. These models consider oral and written language processing to consist of a series of steps that begin with detection of auditory and visual stimuli.

Boutons (boo tonz′). The relatively large, swollen tips of the end-branches (telodendria) of axons. The bouton's membrane is the presynaptic membrane that contacts the postsynaptic membrane of another neuron in order to relay a message form one neuron to another. See also: **excitatory post synaptic potential; inhibitory post synaptic potential; synaptic bouton; synaptic cleft; synaptic vesicles.**

Boxing. A defensive behavior on the part of an rat attacked by another rat (as in intermale aggression, e.g.) in which the animal stands up on its hind legs and makes rapid batting gestures at the other combatant with its forelegs.

Bradycardia (brad ′′i kärd′ē ə, brād ′′-) (in Greek, "bradys" = "slow "and "kardia" = "heart"). A slow heartbeat, defined as less than 60 beats a minute. See also: **tachycardia.**

Braille (brāl) . A method for allowing blind people to "read" devised by the Frenchman, Louis Braille (1809-1852). A system of raised dots is used with blind individuals so that they can read with their fingers. Quadrangular cells contain from one to six dots in different arrangements which indicate different letters and symbols.

Braille Embosser (or **braillewriter**). A printer resembling a typewriter that produces writing in braille form. See also: **Braille.**

Brain. The three major parts of the brain are the hindbrain, midbrain, and forebrain.

Brain-derived neurotrophic (n(y)oo ′′rō trof′ik, trō′fik) **factor.** A chemical promoting the growth of a set of acetylcholine-releasing neural axons. These axons are found in the olfactory areas (rhinencephalon), the cerebral cortex, and in parts of the limbic system (the amygdala and the hippocampus). See also: **nerve growth factor.**

Brain modules. Separate units of the brain, each of which deals with specific tasks. These are simultaneously activated during the parallel processing of incoming sensory data. For example, one brain circuit handles the information on the movement of a visual stimulus, another deals with the colors of the stimulus, and still another with the shape of the stimulus. See also: **parallel processing.**

Brain scan. The use of various techniques for obtaining an image of the activity of the various areas of the brain without the need for cutting the membranes surrounding the brain or even for opening the skull. Such techniques include the CAT scan, the PET scan, MRI imaging, and rCBF (regional cerebral blood flow), among others. Even the venerable electroencephalogram (EEG) can, by computer enhancement, be made to yield a view of activity levels in various brain areas (through BEAM, which stands for "brain electrical activity mapping").

Brain stem. The portion of the brain which is directly attached to the spinal cord and enlarges only gradually, so that the stem-like appearance of the spinal cord remains. The reticular formation runs through all three parts of the brain stem. The brain stem is involved in several lower-level functions, including breathing, digestion, and sleep-wake cycles. The brain stem includes the medulla, pons, and midbrain.

Brain stem reticular formation. A brain structure with patches of interspersed white matter and gray matter that runs continuously through the medulla, the pons, and the midbrain. The latter three structures comprise the brain stem. The midbrain portion of the reticular formation is responsible for the arousal and awakening of the organism. See also: **ascending reticular arousal system; brain stem.**

Brain structure abnormalities. The cerebral cortex of the human brain can vary in structure from one person to another. Sometimes the variation is so extreme that it leads to unusual brain functioning and, almost always, to a learning disability.

Brainwashing. The forced intrusion of attitudes upon a captive audience for less than honorable reasons. The allegation of brainwashing in the Korean war prompted research on sensory deprivation, which was believed to be one of the major techniques of would-be brainwashers. See also: **sensory deprivation.**

Brand image. This is the psychological image or emotional response of consumers to various products.

Breathiness. A speech sound due to air running past the vocal cords without making them vibrate. When the cords fail to vibrate, the resulting speech is like a whisper.

Breech presentation. This refers to the abnormal position of a fetus during delivery with the buttocks positioned toward the cervix. It is a common abnormality of delivery, one that may result in anoxia due to a straining or pinching of the umbilical cord.

Bregma. A position on the skull where the parietal and frontal bones meet. It is used as a landmark in planning an operation on the brain.

Brightness. The subjectively perceived intensity of light reflecting from a surface.

Brightness constancy. See: **light constancy.**

British system. A system used in some of the western European countries for treating drug addicts. The drugs are given to the addicts by prescription. The assumption is that the addict's condition is basically an illness, rather than a crime.

Broadband neurons. Visual nervous system neurons (such as retinal ganglion cells or lateral geniculate nucleus neurons) that respond to a broad range of wavelengths of light, the light stimuli affecting all three types of cones. These neurons cannot be part of the color recognition machinery, since selectivity in responding to hue would be needed.

Broca's aphasia (brō′kăz″, brō′kəz ə fā′zhə). A speech production deficiency resulting from lesions to Broca's area wherein nonfluent, laborious speech occurs. Individuals with Broca's aphasia frequently experience difficulties with articulation, anomia, and agrammatism, but what they intend to say can usually be grasped.

Broca's (brō′kăz″, brō′kəz) **area.** The area (usually in the left hemisphere) of the cerebral cortex which is involved in the production of speech sounds. It is Brodmann's area 44, at the ventral ends of Brodmann's areas 4 and 6, in the frontal lobe. Often, Broca's area is described as being in the "third frontal convolution", which is to say that it is in the third gyrus in from the front edge of the cortex. Damage restricted to Broca's area and not involving the rest of the brain would result in Broca's aphasia. See also: **Broca's aphasia; Brodmann numbering system; cerebral cortex; frontal lobe.**

Brodmann (brod′mən) **numbering system.** A procedure for identifying separate functional areas of the cerebral cortex. The system assigns a numeral for a given area of the cortex. The number is changed, and a new area is designated, when the arrangement of neuron cell bodies and of axons in the six layers of the cortex is changed. For example, Brodmann's area 4, the pyramidal motor cortex, has a prominent fifth layer with a large number of Betz cells. In other cortical areas, this layer is much decreased in prominence. The Brodmann numbers are applied to the lateral and to the medial surfaces of the cortex. They run from area 1 to area 50. Other numbering systems have been proposed and choosing among them is somewhat arbitrary, but the Brodmann system is perhaps the easiest to become familiar with and to get into the habit of using. See also: **cerebral cortex.**

Brown adipose (ad′i pōs) **tissue.** Adipose tissue in general is a kind of connective tissue which contains fat cells. Brown adipose tissue also contains mitochondria, those organelles which provide ATP, the basic substance for chemical energy in the body's metabolic processes. Brown adipose tissue provides an animal with extra metabolic efficiency, so that the calories from recent meals are burned more rapidly and completely when enough brown adipose tissue is on hand. Without brown adipose tissue, the extra calories are converted to fat and the animal becomes more obese. The presence of brown adipose tissue can make up for the lack of exercise, because it is another way to get rid of excess calories.

Brown–Séquard syndrome. The symptoms that ensue from a unilateral severing of the spinal cord. Some of the ascending and descending neural pathways are crossed and some uncrossed, so that some of the symptoms will be ipsilateral (same side) and some contralateral (opposite side). The contralateral losses would involve pain and temperature (since these afferents cross the midline as soon as they reach the spinal cord), while ipsilateral losses involve the touch and kinesthetic senses. Patients can walk again a few days after the injury, because the efferents to the striate muscles are bilateral, that is, motor fibers to both legs run down one side of the spinal cord.

Buerger's (bûr′gərz) **disease.** A disease induced by the excessive intake of nicotine, which constricts the flow of blood to the legs and can result in gangrene and the amputation of the leg. See also: **infarction; ischemia; necrosis.**

Bulimia or **bulimia nervosa** (byo͞o lim′ē ə, bo͞o-). An eating disorder which features alternate overeating and self-induced vomiting, the binge-and-purge cycle. Psychological/psychiatric counseling is recommended. In extreme cases, hospitalization may be necessary so that the individual receives life-sustaining nutrients.

Buphthalmos (bo͞of thal′məs, byo͞of-) or **buphthalmia** (bo͞of thal′mē ə, byo͞of-). An infantile glaucoma involving an enlargement of the eyeball, and, particularly, a distension of the cornea. In some cases, the disease stops spontaneously, but sometimes it continues to progress until blindness occurs.

Burnout. A state of physical and psychological exhaustion, usually job-related, which often produces feelings of inadequacy, anxiety, and isolation, as well as lowered productivity. Afflicted persons are frequently (1) fatigued, tense, and prone to physical complaints, and (2) depersonalized in the sense of being detached from others. Frequently there are feelings (3) of being used and (4) of reduced personal accomplishment(s).

Buttons. See **boutons**.

Butyrophenones (byo͞o ″tir ō fē′nōnz, -fə nōnz′). A category of psychoactive drugs with neuroleptic activity. The best known of these drugs is haloperidol (Haldol), which is used to control acute schizophrenia. The butyrophenones block the dopamine receptor sites on postsynaptic cell membranes and interfere with the release of dopamine from presynaptic cell membranes. See also: **dopamine; neuroleptic drug; neurotransmitter; psychoactive drugs; receptor sites; schizophrenia.**

C

CA1 subfield. An area of the hippocampus, containing a layer of pyramidal cells. The axons from CA1 run in the fornix, but only as far as the septum; they do not travel past the septum toward the hypothalamus. See also: **fornix; fimbria; septum; hippocampus; limbic system.**

Cafeteria diet. A choice of various foods offered to experimental animals. The study of animal food preferences provides important clues to the mechanisms of hunger and satiation in humans. See also: **hunger.**

Caffeine (ka fēn′). A stimulant, which may be somewhat addictive, that is found chiefly in coffee but also occurs in other foods and beverages such as chocolate, tea, and colas.

Caffeine intoxication. Excessive consumption of caffeine in coffee or other beverages, such as soft drinks. This excessive consumption is defined as being over 250 milligrams a day (i.e., the caffeine in three cups of brewed coffee). The symptoms include nervousness, a flushed appearance, insomnia, excessive muscle movements, restlessness, and muscle twitching.

Cajal (kä häl′, kə-) **stain**. A procedure in which tissue from the central nervous system is immersed in several chemicals, including silver nitrate. An obvious difference from the Golgi technique is that, in the Cajal procedure, no osmium salt is used. The silver ions are reduced to metallic silver, tending to be deposited on the axons and dendrites of neurons while avoiding the neuron cell bodies. The fibers are stained brown or, occasionally, orange. Since the procedure requires the impregnation of the entire block of tissue, it is only afterward that the tissue is cut into serial sections by microtome. The tissue slices are mounted on glass microscope slides. This may permit the researcher to follow the course of an axon from the cell body to the synapse. The nervous system is so complex, however, that more ingenious methods are sometimes required. See also: **Golgi stain; horseradish peroxidase.**

Calcarine (kal′ kə rīn, -rēn) **cortex**. ("calcarine" = shaped like a spur, from the Latin "calcar", spur). The area of the cerebral cortex on the dorsal and ventral sides of the calcarine fissure.

This is the primary visual area of the occipital lobe, and is the medial part of Brodmann's area 17 (visual area V1). See also: **calcarine fissure; cuneus; geniculocalcarine tract; lingual gyrus.**

Calcarine (kal′kə rīn,-rēn) **fissure** or **calcarine sulcus** (sul′kus, sool′-). A horizontal groove observable on the medial (midline) surface of the occipital lobe of the occipital cortex. Its rostral end is at the parieto-occipital fissure, which separates the occipital lobe from the more rostral remainder of the cerebral cortex. At its posterior end, the calcarine fissure runs all the way to the back of the brain. The portion of the occipital lobe dorsal to the calcarine fissure is a large, wedge-shaped gyrus called the cuneus. The portion of the occipital lobe ventral to the fissure is vertically compressed, but stretched out from front to back (rostro-caudally), so that it looks like a tongue. This is also a gyrus, namely, the lingual gyrus. The areas of the two gyri adjacent to the calcarine fissure constitute the primary visual area V1, and are referred to as the calacarine cortex. This is the primary visual projection area. See also: **calcarine cortex; geniculo-calacarine tract.**

Calpain (kal″ pān′). A protein found in some dendritic spine synapses. Utilization of such a synapse results in the removal of the calpain and a consequent facilitation of the synapse, so that, in the future, even a mild stimulus can activate it. This, according to Lynch and Baudry, makes possible the physical embodiment of learning, without the necessity of assembling new proteins. Calpain plays a role in an interesting hypothesis (of Lynch and Baudry) regarding the formation of long-term memory following long-term potentiation (LTP). This electrical reactivity change in the hippocampus (a part of the brain involved in the consolidation of short-term memory into long-term memory) results in increases of the calcium ion around the active synapses. The increased concentration of this ion activates calpain, which attacks the cell membrane of the postsynaptic neuron. The breakdown of the local cell membrane allows the postsynaptic neuron to shoot out a new dendritic spine. Thus a new memory structure is not the result of a slow growth process, but rather is the result of "uncorking" a previously "stopped-up" synapse, all set up and ready to operate. In this way, new functional connections between neurons are formed without requiring time for tissue growth. See also: **consolidation; Hebbian synapse; hippocampus; long-term memory; long-term potentiation; short-term memory.**

Cannabis sativa. The botanical name for the hemp plant. In addition to providing the basic raw material for making rope, this plant also provides humans with marijuana. To slightly alter the famous words of former heavyweight champion Muhammad Ali, the cannabis plant provides "Rope AND Dope!" See also: **anandamide**.

Cannon-Bard theory of emotion. The view that emotional reflexive actions and emotional awareness are aroused simultaneously by the appropriate stimulus. Theoretically, the afferent neural messages are routed simultaneously to the motor areas of the cerebral cortex and hypothalamus (for immediate action) and also to the limbic system and the prefrontal areas of the two cortical hemispheres (for rapid cognitive assessment and evaluation of the situation). See also: **emotion**.

Cannula. A thin tube (or, perhaps, a hypodermic needle) implanted in a part of the body in order to introduce or to extract chemicals. For example, an intraventricular cannula could extract samples of cerebrospinal fluid (CSF) or introduce saline solution into the CSF. See also: **cerebral ventricles; cerebrospinal fluid (CSF); lumen; stimulation method.**

Capsaicin (kap sā'i sin). A chemical that causes neurons which contain the Substance P neurotransmitter (for pain messages) to release it quickly. See also: **Substance P**.

Carbohydrates. Any organic chemicals with the basic formula of $C_x(H_2O)_y$--where C is the "carbo-" part, and the H_2O (water) is the "-hydrate." Edible carbohydrates include the sugars and starches. Other carbohydrates (cellulose) are not digested, but provide fiber or bulk, which assists the efficiency of the process of digestion.

Carboline (kär'bə lēn˝). A type of chemical compound that binds to the same receptor sites on nerve cell membranes as do the benzodiazepines. Some carbolines have an excitatory effect on these receptors, but others have an inhibitory effect. The receptor sites involved are believed to interact with receptor sites for the neurotransmitter GABA.

Cardiac muscle. The musculature of the heart. It has a striped appearance, somewhat like skeletal muscle. The cardiac muscle fibers are frequently fused together at the sides, so that they work as a unit. The parasympathetic nervous system slows down (inhibits) the activity of these muscles while the sympathetic nervous system speeds up (excites) their activity. But the control mechanism of cardiac muscle is not identical to that of smooth muscle; there is also an added control system provided by the cardiac muscle fibers themselves, namely, the atrioventricular node (a natural pacemaker) and the Purkinje fibers. See also: **parasympathetic nervous system; Purkinje fibers; skeletal muscle; smooth muscle; sympathetic nervous system.**

Carnivore (kär'ni vôr). An animal that eats only meat (i.e., the tissues of other animals). Most members of the cat family are carnivores; so are sharks.

Carousel apparatus. An apparatus used for the sleep deprivation of laboratory rats. The animal is kept on a turntable above a tankful of cold water. When the animal shows signs of falling asleep, the turntable begins to spin, forcing the animal to walk for at least six full seconds. The result is that the rat loses more than 7/8 of its sleep. Control rats were forced to do the same amount of walking, but at random times. Almost all the sleep deprived rats either drowned or suffered severe weakening. Autopsies on the experimental rats revealed both stomach ulcers and enlarged adrenal glands. See also: **sleep; stress.**

Case study. A type of research which involves the gathering of much information about one person. Methods such as personal interviewing, individual testing, and gathering personal documents and official records may be used.

Castration. The surgical removal of the gonads (the testes or ovaries).

Cataplexy (kat'ə plek˝sē). A type of disorder whereby the individual experiences a sudden and acute loss of muscle tone. This is often a symptom of the sleep disorder called narcolepsy.

Cataract. The clouding of the lens of the eye, which progresses gradually until the lens becomes opaque.

Catatonia (kat ə tō'nē ə). A disorder usually considered to be a subtype of schizophrenia. The individual is semiconscious, unresponsive to social stimulation, and sometimes exhibits a "waxy flexibility" of the limbs (i.e., an examiner can bend the patient's arm or leg into a new position). The passive pattern may be interrupted by a spasmodic outburst of violent, even frenzied, motor activity. See also: **catatonic schizophrenia**.

Catatonic schizophrenia (kat ə ton'ik skit sə frē'nē ə, -fren'ē ə). A type of schizophrenia characterized by rigid motor behavior. These schizophrenic patients are mute, immobile, and passive for extensive periods of time. Their behavior is robot-like. See also: **catatonia**.

Catecholamines (kat″i kō' lə mēnz″). A "family group" of chemical neurotransmitters, hormones, amino acids, and drugs. The chemical neurotransmitters in the catechol group that are active in the central nervous system include dopamine (DA), norepinephrine (norEp), and, possibly epinephrine (Ep). In the peripheral nervous system, norepinephrine is released by sympathetic nervous system axons onto targeted smooth muscles and glands. Peripherally, norepinephrine communicates with two types of postsynaptic membrane receptors, the alpha and beta receptors. The catecholamines released by the adrenal medulla gland include epinephrine, norepinephrine, and, possibly dopamine. The amino acids (which are ingested as components of our protein foods) are metabolically built into the structural parts of the body, including the chemical neurotransmitters. The catechol amine category of amino acids includes phenylalanine and tyrosine. Catecholamines are also found among hallucinogenic drugs. Mescaline is an example of a drug that is both a catecholamine and a hallucinogen. Sometimes, functional categories may overlap. The drug l-DOPA is a catecholamine and an amino acid (although not a constituent of proteins in our diet); it is used to treat the neuromuscular disorder known as Parkinson's disease or Parkinsonism.

Catechol-O-methyltransferase. See **COMT**.

Catharsis (kə thär'sis). This is the theory that instinctual aggression is steadily built up and stored in the nervous system until an occasion arises that will permit the behavioral expression of that aggression. This theory of aggression has little empirical support.

Cation (kat'ī″on). An ion is an atom or group of atoms bearing a positive or negative electrical charge. A cation is an ion with a positive charge of +1 or higher. Important cations in neural and synaptic physiology are sodium, potassium, and calcium.

CAT scan. Acrostic for computerized axial tomography, which implies computer-regulated cutting, in series, along an axis. This is a type of X-ray whereby beams of radiation pass through a particular body location under study from a variety of angles. This results in a two-dimensional picture that resembles a horizontal slice of the body region studied.

Caudal (kôd'l) (from Latin "cauda" = "tail"). Toward the tail of an animal. The antonym of "caudal" is "rostral" or "cranial." In a four-legged creature, or quadruped, the tail is in back, so that caudal structures are posterior structures. In the case of bipedal humans, the "tail," being opposite the "head," would be at the bottom, hence, in bipeds, the toes, for example, are both caudal and inferior. There is an important exception to this usage. The human brain is treated like a quadruped body part, with "caudal" meaning the same thing as "posterior." This is because the central nervous system makes a right angle bend where the spinal cord merges with the brain, so that the brain is directed toward the front of the animal. The eyes and nose, which are attached to the front of the brain, are thus able to keep track of the world directly in front of the organism. This realignment also means that, for the human brain, the rostral parts are anterior.

Caudate (kô'dāt″) **nucleus**. The word "caudate" means tail-shaped. The caudate is one of the basal ganglia. It is concerned with motor coordination and, along with other basal ganglia, receives dopaminergic axons from the substantia nigra of the midbrain. The caudate, putamen, and globus pallidus, along with axons crossing between the caudate and the other two, comprise the corpus striatum.

Ceiling age. The age level (on the original form of the Stanford-Binet Intelligence Test) above which the individual fails to answer any question or perform any task. The usual score from such a test is the individual's mental age. See also: **basal age; mental age**.

Ceiling effect. A restricted range of questions on a test which prohibits an individual from demonstrating his or her "true ability levels or potential."

Cell adhesion molecule (CAM). A glycoprotein located on the surfaces of cells that guides growing axons toward their proper synapses during the development of the brain.

Cell body (or **perikaryon** or **soma**). The major part of a neuron (in both mass and volume), the cell body, or soma, of the neuron is the part that closely resembles a generalized animal body cell. The nucleus is centrally located within the cell body. Voltage changes can occur on the membrane of the cell body; these would be of the graded and decremental type, such as occur on the membranes of dendrites. Only the axon membrane can exhibit the all-or-none type of voltage change that is the hallmark of a true nerve impulse.

Cellular dehydration. A reduction in the fluid volume within the cells. See also: **osmotic thirst**.

Center (of a receptive field). The innermost circle of the receptive field of a retinal bipolar or ganglion cell. In the case of the bipolar neurons, a stimulus from the center of a bipolar cell's receptive field occurs when a message is passed from the receptor directly to that bipolar cell. See also: **receptive field; surround**.

Central. Toward the inner center or core of a solid object. The "central" nervous system is an example. The antonym of "central" is peripheral. The words "central" and "medial" are not synonyms. While the stomach is both central and medial, the nose and the navel are both medial, although neither one is central.

Central auditory disorder. When the peripheral hearing apparatusis intact and there is damage to auditory brain areas, patients have problems with auditory discrimination and comprehension, auditory learning, and language development. The loss of the ability to perceive the sequence of a series of sounds follows damage to the auditory cortex.

Central canal. A narrow portion of the lumen, or the hollow center within the central nervous system. The central canal runs through the spinal cord and the caudal half of the medulla. Like the rest of the lumen, it is filled with cerebrospinal fluid. See also: **cerebrospinal fluid; lumen**.

Central core. The innermost part of the brain, or "old brain," that serves the most elementary, life-sustaining behaviors such as eating and sleeping. This is part of the three-part (triune) model of the brain put forth by Paul MacLean. He refers to this central core as the "reptilian brain" because all vertebrates, from the least to the most-evolved, have this part of the brain in common.

Central gray matter or **periaqueductal** (per″ē ak″wə duk′təl) **gray matter**. A circular region of the midbrain that is central (removed from the midbrain's outer surface) and medial (at the boundary between the left and right midbrain). It surrounds a small canal (filled with cerebrospinal fluid) called the cerebral aqueduct or aqueduct of Sylvius. The central gray is the terminal of a local CNS pathway that services the pain sense, viz., the spinotectal tract. It is also part of several pathways that are activated in aggressive behavior. The reflexes that unsheathe a cat's claws and that cause its back to arch or its hairs to stand on end (piloerection) may be employed in several different types of aggression; Graham suggests that the central gray matter seems to be a "tool box" for use in any emotional behavior pattern that might require those reflexes as a part of the total activity. See also: **aggression**.

Central nervous system (CNS). The brain and the spinal cord as a whole.

Central nervous system disorders. These are diseases and/or conditions which adversely affect the brain and/or spinal cord.

Central sensorimotor programs. Patterns of activity that are represented schematically within the sensorimotor nervous system. Activation of some of these programs in the right order can generate a particular complex behavior.

Central sulcus or **fissure of Rolando**. A large groove running down the outside of either cerebral hemisphere, forming a natural boundary between the frontal lobe (anterior to the sulcus) and the parietal lobe (posterior to the sulcus). The central sulcus approaches the temporal lobe but does not quite reach it. A gray matter convolution in the frontal lobe just anterior to the central sulcus forms the precentral gyrus and constitutes the primary motor cortex, Brodmann's area 4. A similar convolution in the parietal lobe also runs next to the central sulcus. It is called the postcentral gyrus and accounts for Brodmann areas 1, 2, and 3. The postcentral gyrus is the primary projection area for the general body senses of touch, pressure, pain, temperature, and kinesthesis. See also: **Brodmann numbering system; cerebral cortex; fissure; frontal lobe; parietal lobe; sulcus.**

Central tendency. A measurement specifying the most typical or representative measurement of a set. Examples of measures of central tendency include the mean, the median, and the mode. See also: **mean; median; mode.**

Centrifugal (sen trif′yoo gəl, -trif′i gəl) bipolar cells. Neurons in the retina positioned among the bipolar cells that receive information from the visual receptors (i.e., the rods and cones) and send information to the ganglion cells that give forth optic nerve axons. The centrifugal bipolar cells, however, receive efferent messages <u>from</u> the brain and relay them <u>to</u> the receptors! The function of these "wrong-way" messages might be to adjust up or down the threshold of the receptors. See also: **bipolar neuron; retina.**

Cephalad (sef′ə lad). Toward the head or toward the front end of the body; in a rostral direction.

Cephalic phase. The metabolic phase that comes late in the fasting period, just before a meal is to be ingested. The body is prepared for the food that is about to be taken. The cephalic phase is triggered by the sight and smell of ready-to-eat food. See also: **absorption phase; fasting phase.**

Cephalocaudal (sef″ə lō kôd′l) principle. The rule for the embryological development of a vertebrate organism which states that parts of the body at the head (cephalic) end will grow and develop much more faster than parts at the opposite, or tail (caudal) end. Intermediate parts would develop at intermediate rates, with the rate of growth for a given part depending on the relative distance of that part from the head and tail ends.

Cerebellar cortex (ser″ə bel′ər kôr′teks). The gray outer surface of the cerebellum. It exchanges messages with the cerebellar nuclei

(masses of gray matter in the heart of the interior white matter) and midbrain areas such as the red nucleus. See also: **cerebellum; midbrain; red nucleus.**

Cerebellar vestibular dysmetria (ser″ə bel′ər ves tib′yə lər dis mē′trē ə, -met′rē ə). A hypothetical malfunctioning of the neural pathway going from the vestibular sense organs through the cerebellum toward the cerebral cortex and toward the midbrain areas that control the external muscles of the eyes. As a result of this disorder, sensory messages reach the cortex much too quickly, producing a feeling much like vertigo.

Cerebellar vestibular (ser″ə bel′ər ves tib′yə lər) malfunction. The vestibular senses control the balance of the head, and, indirectly, the body. They help line up the eye muscles and to make allowances for changes in head position while we look at our surroundings. The cerebellum is a part of the brain that is involved in this eye-muscle process. One theorist holds that dyslexia is due to a malfunction of the cerebellar vestibular eye-muscle control system.

Cerebellum (ser″ə bel′um). A part of the hindbrain which receives inputs from most of the external senses (touch, vision, hearing) and the vestibular senses, it is responsible for coordinated posture and movement. It controls sensory-motor integration, and parts of it participate in the conditioning of striate muscle responses.

Cerebral commissures. Tracts connecting between left and right cerebral hemispheres on the same rostral-caudal level. If they ran from one level to another, they would be decussations, not commissures. The corpus callosum is the largest cerebral commissure, since it links the two cerebral hemispheres. There are also smaller commissures, such as the anterior commissure and the hippocampal commissure. See also: **commissure; decussation.**

Cerebral cortex or cerebral hemispheres. The most highly developed and newly evolved part of the brain in vertebrate animals. It controls the highest levels of cognitive processing. The word "cortex" means "(tree) bark" in Latin. The outer surface of the cortex consists of gray matter. In humans, it takes up half of the brain. Again in humans, the cortex surrounds the remainder of the brain, so that a view of the uncut brain will almost entirely be one of the cerebral cortex. The cortex consists of two nearly symmetrical hemispheres. It is divided into a set of sensory receiving areas [called projection areas; see the definition of **projection (in neuroanatomy)**], a set of motor-control areas, and areas where information is synthesized and organized (so-called association areas). The cerebral cortex is about 2 millimeters thick and has a surface area of 1.5 square meters. If spread open and smoothed out, the cortex would stretch for 18 inches to the left and to the right side. Most of the cortex is the most recently evolved part of the brain, the neocortex. The neocortex has six layers, numbered I through VI from outermost to innermost: I, the molecular layer, has very few nerve cell bodies being filled mostly with nerve fibers; II, the external granular layer, is peppered with small neuron cell bodies (Sensory areas feature thick, well-developed granular layers.); III, the pyramidal layer (neurons with pyramidal cell bodies that give off dendrites at the apex and at the corners of the base); IV, the internal granular layer; V, the giant pyramidal layer [featuring very large pyramidal cells; the area giving rise to the pyramidal motor tract (Brodmann area 4, the precentral gyrus in the frontal lobe) has an especially prominent layer V]; and VI, the fusiform layer (where fusiform means "spindle-shaped"; some of the neuron cell bodies in this cell layer are fusiform). A mnemonic device for remembering these six layers begins with the image of a city experiencing a widespread electrical blackout before the invention of circuit breakers. In those days householders would short out a burned-out fuse by inserting a penny in the fuse box. Therefore, there were "Many Extra Pennies in Giant Fuse boxes." This is an acrostic-plus device, with "M" standing for molecular, "Ext" for external granular, "P" for pyramidal, "in" for internal granular, "Giant" for giant pyramidal, and "Fus" for fusiform. The old cortex's cingular gyrus, visible on the medial surface of each hemisphere, has only three layers. The cerebral cortex takes up a greater percentage of the total brain in the human species than in any other. The cortex is responsible for the specifically human side of our animal existence. Some countries have adopted, as their official criterion for an individual's death, the

complete cessation of electrical activity in the cerebral cortex.

Cerebral ischemia. A blockage of the flow of blood to a given part of the brain. Since brain cells are extremely dependent on the glucose and oxygen supplied by the bloodstream, the neurons in the ischemic region may die off before therapy can be done. See also: **ischemia; infarction; necrosis.**

Cerebral palsy (also known as **Little's disease**). A movement disability (palsy = paralysis) due to developmental defects or to a trauma to the brain at the time of birth. The symptoms are usually bilateral, symmetric, and nonprogressive.

Cerebral ventricles (ser'ə brəl,   sə rē'brəl ven'tri kəlz) Four large openings in the brain. Each of these cavities contains **cerebrospinal fluid** (see definition). There is a continuous opening in the central nervous system known as the lumen. More familiar versions of a lumen would be (1) the hollow center of the gastrointestinal tract and (2) the continuous open route of the blood vessels. The two largest ventricles are contained, one each, in the left and the right cerebral cortex. They are called the lateral ventricles or ventricles I and II. Each is connected by a very thin opening (the interventricular foramen of Monro) to the third ventricle, which is in the diencephalon. The third ventricle has the dorsal hypothalamus as its floor and the thalamus as its walls. Among the structures that form the roof of the third ventricle (and the top of the diencephalon as well) is the **pineal gland** (see definition). The lumen constricts again after the third ventricle: running through the midbrain is the narrow cerebral aqueduct (or aqueduct of Sylvius). On reaching the pons, the lumen expands into the diamond-shaped fourth ventricle, half of which is located in the rostral half of the medulla. Posterior to the fourth ventricle, the lumen constricts into the narrow central canal, which remains the central canal in the spinal cord.

Cerebrospinal (ser″ə brō spī′nəl, sə rē″brō-) **fluid** (CSF). The colorless fluid in the ventricles (hollows) of the brain and in the rest of the lumen of the brain and spinal cord. This fluid serves to nourish and cushion the brain. It can be sampled as an aid in diagnosis. Measurements such as bacterial count, quantitative chemical analysis, and fluid pressure readings are taken. When the circulation of this fluid is blocked (usually by an obstruction of the foramen of Monro), it accumulates in the fore-brain (telencephalon), with the head enlarging so much that the skull's bones fail to knit together. Often, the victim of this condition is unable to have a fully developed cerebral cortex. The condition is called **hydrocephalus** ("water on the brain") and it is often accompanied by mental retardation. See also: **cerebral ventricles**.

Cerebrovascular (ser″ə brō vas′kyə lər, sə rē ″brō-) **accident**. See: **stroke**.

Cerebrum (ser′ə brum, sə rē′brum). See **telen-cephalon**.

Cerumen (si roo′ men). Another name for earwax. Excessive buildup of cerumen can result in hearing loss. The wax is secreted by glands in the skin lin-ing the outer two-thirds of the auditory canal.

Cerveau isolé (sâr vō′ ē″sō lā′). A preparation, studied by Bremer, which is produced by severing the brain stem between the inferior and the superior colliculi. This leaves the cortex and diencephalon rostral to (above) the cut and the brain stem and hindbrain caudal to (below) the cut. Bremer re-corded the EEGs from cerveau isolé cats and found no signs of normal waking activity; only the delta waves of deep sleep appeared on the record. There were no eye movements, and the pupils of the eyes were constricted. The term "cerveau isolé" means "isolated cerebral cortex" in French. For the pos-tural results of such surgery, see **decerebrate rigid-ity**. See also: **encéphale isole**.

Cervical (sûr′vi kəl). Pertaining to the neck. There are eight cervical spinal nerves and 7 cervical ver-tebrae. See also: **spinal cord**.

Channels. Lines of communication carrying both verbal and nonverbal information simultaneously. The nonverbal messages may include facial ex-pressions, body gestures, even eye focusing (i.e., meeting or avoiding someone else's eyes), and speech quality.

Cheese effect. A reference to the large surge of blood pressure that takes place when people who have been maintained on an MAO-inhibiting anti-depressant drug take in large amounts of tyramine-rich foods, such as cheese. Tyramine is a metabolite of the amino acid tyrosine, and tyramine is metabo-lized in turn into the catechol amine neurotransmit-ters (dopamine, norepinephrine, and epinephrine). The necessary oxidation of the monoamine is not

performed (due to the drug's inhibitory action on the MAO enzyme), and our cheese-loving friend may experience headache, irregular heartbeat, hy-pertension, or even cerebral hemorrhage. So, be sure to avoid cheese with any MAO-inhibiting an-tidepressant drugs.

Chelation (kē lā′shən) **therapy**. A proven medical treatment which involves reduction of toxic levels of lead in the blood.

Chemically gated ion channels. First of all, chan-nels are tuned passageways running through a neu-ron's semi-permeable membrane and serving for the movement of a particular ion (e.g., chloride chan-nels or sodium ion channels). Some chemical neu-rotransmitters specifically open (or, in other cases, close) particular ion channels. This could lead di-rectly to an EPSP (if the outer surface of the mem-brane is given a more-negative voltage), or to an IPSP (if the positive voltage becomes even more strongly positive).

Chemoaffinity hypothesis. The hypothesis that, during the development of the nervous system, the postsynaptic surface is tagged with a specific chemical label that attracts a particular axon to it. See also: **blueprint hypothesis**.

Chemotherapy (kē″mō ther′ə pē). The treatment of a behavioral problem with drugs. For example, Ritalin may be given to ADHD children to control their hyperactivity and allow them to relax enough to be instructed in the classroom.

Chest physiotherapy. A type of physical therapy applied to the chest area.

Chiasma (kī az′mə) or (optic) **chiasm** (kī′az″ əm). A formation similar to the Greek letter chi, which is shaped like our letter X. In neuroanatomy, the de-cussation of two bundles of myelinated axons would present this appearance. The entry point for the op-tic nerves into the brain, on the ventral surface of the hypothalamus, is called the optic chiasm or op-tic chiasma. See also: **decussation; optic chiasma.**

Child abuse. Accidental and/or non-accidental trauma (physical, psychological, and/or sexual) to a child which can cause psychological stress, disor-ders, and other disabilities. Individuals witnessing child abuse have a legal and moral obligation to re-port this problem to a responsible individual or agency that can help the child.

Child neglect. Depriving a child of physical, social, psychological, or cognitive factors which are impor-tant to the child's emotional, social, and psychological well-being and growth. Such neglect can have long-lasting and harmful psychological and physical effects. Individuals witnessing child neglect have a moral and legal obligation to report this problem to a responsible individual or agency that can help the child.

Chill phase. The first phase of fever. The patient acts as if he or she is cold, despite having a normal body temperature.

Chimeric (kī mir′ik, ki-) **faces** (The term "chimeric" comes from the monster in Greek mythology called the Chimera, which had various body parts from different kinds of animals.). Visual stimuli consisting of composites of two half-faces (left and right halves of different faces). These stimuli are used in research with split-brain patients. They are flashed tachistoscopically to the subject so that each half-face is presented to each visual field (i.e., one half-face to the left visual field and one to the right). The subject is then shown an array of different faces. Sometimes the subject is asked to say which face she or he saw; on other occasions, the subject is asked to point to the face just seen. See also: **split-brain surgery; tachistoscope**.

Chiropractic (kī′rō prak′tik) **intervention**. Therapeutic activity initiated by a professional chiropractor.

Chlamydia (klə mid′ē ə). A sexually transmitted disease that, in women, may lead to pelvic inflammation and even sterility and can produce, in men, pain during urination as well as discharge from the penis.

Chlordiazepoxide. An anxiolytic drug. Its trade name is Librium. See also: **anxiolytic; psychoactive drugs**.

Chlorolabe (klôr′ə lāb). One of the three varieties of the photopigment iodopsin. Iodopsin is found in the cones of the retina. Chlorolabe is most sensitive to the color green (i.e., to wavelengths in the middle of the visible light spectrum). See also: **cyanolabe; erythrolabe; trichromatic theory of color vision**.

Chlorpromazine (klôr prō′mə zēn″). A neuroleptic drug of the phenothiazine family. Chlorpromazine helps control the positive symptoms of schizophrenia. Chlorpromazine blocks the receptor sites on postsynaptic cell membranes for catecholamines (e.g., norepinephrine and dopamine) and blocks the release of catecholamines from presynaptic cell membranes. See also: **butyrophenones; dopamine; neurotransmitter; norepinephrine; psychoactive drugs; receptor sites; schizophrenia; synapse**.

Cholecystokinin (kō″li sis″tə kī′nin) **(CCK)**. CCK is both a hormone and a neurotransmitter. As a hormone, it is released from the duodenum (first part of the small intestine) after ingested food reaches that part of the gastrointestinal tract. The hormone gives a satiety signal to receptors in the brain, leading to the cessation of eating. In the brain, it is released along with dopamine (DA) into the corpus striatum (the terminal of the nigrostriatal dopamine pathway) and the nucleus accumbens (a terminal of the mesocorticolimbic dopamine pathway). It seems to curtail the release of DA at the terminals in those parts of the brain, acting much like a neuroleptic drug. However, CCK seems to amplify and enhance the motor effects of DA. See also: **dopamine**.

Choline (kō′lēn″). A dietary component (found in, e.g., egg yolk) that is used in the production of the neurotransmitter acetylcholine (ACh). After ACh is broken down in the synapse by the enzyme AChE, choline, one of the breakdown products, is reuptaken past the presynaptic membrane. After such reuptake, it can be reused to make more Ach. See also: **acetylcholine**.

Cholinergic. An adjective referring to axons that release the neurotransmitter acetylcholine at their terminals. See also: **acetylcholine; neurotransmitter**.

Chorda tympani. One of the branches of the facial nerve, cranial nerve VII. The chorda tympani supplies efferent impulses to two of the salivary glands, the submandibular and sublingual glands. It also receives afferent impulses from the anterior two-thirds of the tongue, carrying all the sweet and some of the salty and sour taste messages.

Chorea (kə rē′ə). A disorder of the nervous system primarily affecting young people. The main symptom is a rapid, involuntary twitching of the muscles. See also: **athetosis; Huntington's chorea; Sydenham's chorea**.

Chorionic villus (kō″rē on′ik vil′əs, kôr″ē-) **sampling**. A procedure for diagnosis of the prenatal fetus. A 30-milligram sample is collected from the chorion around the fetal placenta. A catheter is inserted through the uterus by way of the vagina. This technique is less invasive than amniocentesis, which requires breaking the uterine wall in order to obtain the sample. Chorionic villus samples may be taken safely in the first 8 to 12 weeks of pregnancy.

See also: **amniocentesis.**

Choroid (kôr'oid). The coating of the eyeball just internal to the sclera. It is opaque and houses blood vessels that nourish and sustain the rest of the eye.

Choroidoretinal degeneration. A deterioration of the choroid and retina of the eye.

Chromaffin (krō'maf in) **cells.** Cells of the adrenal medulla gland that release hormones. See also: **adrenal medulla; catecholamines.**

Chromatic adaptation. A visual phenomenon in which prolonged exposure to stimulation with yellow light produces the experience of blue (on looking at a white background) and prolonged stimulation with green light leads to the experience of red (on looking at a white background). The resulting experiences are called negative afterimages. See also: **afterimage; trichromatic theory of color vision.**

Chromatic colors. The hues; colors that correspond to particular wavelengths of light. They include red, orange, yellow, green, blue, indigo, and violet. See also: **achromatic colors.**

Chromatin (krō'mə tin) (Also known as the **Nissl substance** or **Nissl granule**). These granules consist of ribonucleic acid (RNA) and are found in the cytoplasm of neuronal cell bodies. RNA in the cytoplasm of other cells is bound with the ribosomes, except when, in the form of transfer RNA, it is involved in attaching to amino acid molecules during protein construction. Nissl substance or chromatin is also referred to as the "rough endoplasmic reticulum." A function for this "free" RNA in the neurons has not been pinned down. Is it, perhaps, modified by experience, instead of by DNA? See **chromatolysis; Nissl stain; Nissl substance.**

Chromatolysis (krō"mə tol'i sis). Two changes in the appearance of a neuron cell body taking place after the axon has been cut. First, the chromatin begins to disappear. Second, the nucleus migrates to the edge of the cell body. If the degeneration of the neuron is halted (which usually happens in the peripheral nervous system, but not in the central nervous system), these changes are reversed (during the process of regeneration): The chromatin reappears and the cell nucleus migrates back to the center of the cell body. See also: **retrograde degeneration.**

Chromosomal abnormalities (krō"mə sō'məl). These are defects or damages caused to the chromosomes which can result in a number of debilitating disorders or conditions. See also: **Down's Syndrome.**

Chromosome (krō'mə sōm") **21 trisomy** (trī'sō mē). A genetic defect that leads to the infant's possessing three, rather than two, of chromosome number 21. This condition produces Down's syndrome and tends to produce Alzheimer's disease when the individual is past the age of 40. See also: **Alzheimer's disease; Down's syndrome.**

Chromosomes. Ribbon-like structures found within the nucleus of an animal cell. They occur in pairs, one member of a pair coming from the father and one from the mother. Each species has its own characteristic number of chromosomes, the diploid number. The hereditary information for the individual is found in the DNA molecules located on chromosomes. Each DNA molecule is specialized for the control of its own specific hereditary trait. Such a molecule is commonly known as a gene.

Chronaxie (krō'nak sē, kron' ak-). A time measurement representing the sensitivity of a single neuron, an entire nerve, or other tissue. It is obtained by plotting a graph called the strength-duration curve. The X-axis (abscissa) represents the length of time that an electric stimulus is applied to the tested tissue. The Y-axis (ordinate) represents the electrical strength in volts that is required to cause a nerve impulse in the tested tissue for each of the presentation times covered by the X-axis. If the time is very short, then clearly a very high strength of stimulating current will be required. The function curves downward from left to right, but at the right end it levels off. This is because there has to be a minimum strength of stimulation even if the stimulation time is unlimited. The value of current strength for that level stretch at the end of the strength-duration curve is called the rheobase (i.e., the threshold value of the current). One can move to the left along the function to find any value of current greater than the rheobase. Finding the value that equals twice the rheobase, one can find the required time of stimulation needed to cause a nerve impulse. That time value (the one that causes an impulse when the stimulation has a strength of 2 times the rheobase) is called the chronaxie. The value of the chronaxie is used to describe the sensitivity of the tested tissue. See also: **strength-duration curve; rheobase.**

Chronic. Refers to the gradual development of a symptom over along duration, for example, chronic heart disease or chronic appendicitis. In physiological research, a <u>chronic preparation</u> refers to an animal which is in the waking state and which has an electrode permanently embedded in a given location in its brain. See also: **acute.**

Chronobiology (kronˮō bī olʹə jē). The branch of biology concerned with circadian rhythms or functions that operate on temporal cycles.

Chronological age. This is the individual's physical age (the "real" age in years since birth). Chronological age is a factor in the original formula (devised by Wilhelm Stern) for the calculation of the intelligence quotient or IQ, viz., IQ = (mental age / chronological age) X 100.

Chunk. A grouping of bits of information (usually, a meaningful grouping that makes an intelligible object) that can be saved as a unit of the short-term memory (STM).

Ciliary body (silʹē er ē). The structure that includes the ciliary muscles and the ciliary processes. See also: **ciliary muscles; ciliary processes.**

Ciliary muscles (silʹē er ē). These muscles can apply pulling forces to the flexible human lens, causing accommodation. See also: **accommodation reflex.**

Ciliary processes. The part of the ciliary body that releases the aqueous humor into the eye's anterior chamber. See also: **anterior chamber; aqueous humor; ciliary body.**

Cinefluoroscopy (sinˮə floo rosʹkə pē). X-ray motion pictures.

Cingulate (singʹgyoo litˮ, -lātˮ) **cortex** or **cingulate gyrus** (from Latin "cingulum" = "belt"). A long gyrus of the "old" cerebral cortex visible only on the medial surface of the cortex (i.e., within the longitudinal fissure separating the cortical hemispheres). It lies superior to and almost surrounds the corpus callosum; hence the reference to a belt in the term. Electrical stimulation of this gyrus has brought on uncontrollable tics and bursts of profanity, similar to the symptoms of patients with Tourette's syndrome. Injury to this gyrus in experimental rats interferes with their ability to learn an avoidance behavior [running over a short hurdle to reach the safe (nonshock) half of a shuttle box].

Circadian (sər kāʹdē ən, sûrˮkə dēʹən) **rhythms** or **cycles.** The daily (24-hour) cycles of many of our physiological functions. Literally, "circa diem" means "around the day." Among these cyclic functions are metabolic activities, levels of alertness,

sleeping/waking, temperature, blood pressure, and hormone levels in the blood. The suprachiasmatic nucleus (SCN) of the hypothalamus appears to be crucial for the ability to maintain these rhythmic functions (e.g., urinary potassium excretion, REM/slow-wave sleep/waking, and the ups and downs of body temperature). Levels of the hormone epinephrine are greatest early in the day and lowest at midnight. This hormone is related to excitability. See also: **suprachiasmatic nucleus; ultradian rhythms; Zeitgeber.**

Circadian rhythm sleep disorder. A sleep disturbance resulting from a disruption of the sleep-wake cycle due to environmental factors (e.g., working nights). The individual shows social or occupational anxiety due to this upset of the sleep-wake cycle. See also: **sleep disorders.**

Circannual (sər kanʹ yoo wəl) **rhythms** (Latin for "around the year"). Annual cycles in some species of animals include hibernation, estivation, and sexual arousal. These cycles may have evolved by matching the creature's activity with periods of food availability (based, in turn, on the cyclic functions of plant life, for instance). Sexual activity seems to fit into a circannual cycle, since more children are conceived in the months of April and October than at other times.

Circular muscles. Smooth muscles arranged around the edge of the pupil, so that, when they contract, the pupil is constricted. This action is known as the pupillary reflex. See also: **pupillary reflex; radial muscles.**

Cirrhosis (from Greek "kirrhos" = "gold-colored," and "osis" = "condition"). A chronic disease of the liver with widespread and varied damage. It may result from dietary deficiency, infections, or toxins. About one-fifth of all chronic alcoholics develop cirrhosis.

Cisternas. Irregularly-shaped organelles that are found within the synaptic vesicles. Their cytoplasm carries an available supply of chemical neurotransmitter. See also: **neurotransmitter; synaptic vesicles.**

Classical conditioning. A basic form of learning initially studied in a scientific way by Ivan Pavlov. A previously neutral stimulus is paired with an unconditioned stimulus that automatically elicits a reflexive response. As a result, the once neutral stimulus comes to elicit that response. This form of conditioning is also known as Pavlovian conditioning, stimulus substitution, and respondent conditioning.

Claustrophobia (klôs″trə fō′bē ə). Fear of closed spaces. See also: **phobias.**

Cleft palate. A cleft in the upper lip and/or palate due to a failure of the sides of the lip or the palate to come together during fetal development. The result is an articulation disorder. Speech will be excessively nasal and excessively breathy. See also: **breathiness.**

Clinical depression. A mood disorder so disabling that it requires medical intervention. Other types of depression may be annoying impediments to life without reaching the levels of intensity and severity that would qualify them as clinical. See also: **depression (major).**

Clinical psychology. An applied specialty of psychology which deals with the diagnosis and treatment of behavior/mental/emotional disorders. The clinical psychologist uses tests and clinical interviews as her or his principal diagnostic techniques. Most clinical psychologists are restricted to either psychotherapy or behavior therapy in treating their patients. Psychiatrists, who are medical specialists, are additionally able to use psychosurgery, to prescribe drugs, and to administer electroconvulsive shock therapy. In most states, psychologists are prevented by law from using the latter three methods of therapy.

Clitoris (klit′ər is). The much smaller analog in the female of the male penis. The clitoris has high tactile sensitivity.

Cloacal (klō ā′kəl). Another name for "pelvic." The hip joints have been hypothesized to take part in cloacal reflexes that control alignment of the head.

Clomipramine (klō mip′rə mēn). A drug used to treat individuals with obsessive-compulsive disorder or people with trichotillomania. Clomipramine prevents the reuptake of serotonin from synaptic clefts through the presynaptic membrane, making serotonin available for the restimulation of serotonin-fitting receptor sites on postsynaptic membranes. This would suggest the hypotheses that obsessive-compulsive problems are due to a shortage of brain serotonin and that trichotillomanics suffer from a shortage of brain serotonin. See also: **anankastic personality disorder; obsessive-compulsive neurosis; psychoactive drugs; serotonin; trichotillomania.**

Clonic. See **phasic**, the synonym. See also: **myo-clonus.**

Clonic phase ("klonos" = "turmoil" in Greek). The second phase of an epileptic grand mal seizure, beginning after the first phase, the tonic phase, runs out. This start of the clonic phase occurs about 15 seconds after the onset of the seizure. the muscles start quivering, then begin to jerk convulsively. The tongue may be bitten. The eyes roll uncontrollably. Profuse sweating and salivation are visible. The muscles relax 30 seconds after the onset of the clonic phase. The patient then falls asleep for 15 minutes. See also: **epilepsy; grand mal seizure; tonic phase.**

Closed-caption. A communication system for hearing-impaired individuals which provides subtitles that are translated into dialogue on the screen itself.

Clozapine (klō′zə pēn). An antischizophrenia drug (i.e., a neuroleptic) that lowers the level of dopamine in the accumbens nucleus but not in the corpus striatum. This selectivity allows the antischizophrenic function to be separated from the risk of developing a motor disorder, tardive dyskinesia, that arises when the corpus striatum (which is ordinarily activated by dopamine) is chronically depressed. For this reason, clozapine is expected to become the drug of choice in preference to haloperidol, which affects both dopamine pathways. See also: **accumbens; antipsychotics; corpus striatum; dopamine; haloperidol; neuroleptic.**

Club foot. A congenital deformity in which the foot is turned downward and inward at the ankle.

Cluster analysis. This is a variety of factor analysis which uses the intercorrelations among a group of variables to sort out which variables seem to belong together (i.e., to the same cluster) and which do not.

CNS. See: **central nervous system.**

Coca paste. A paste prepared by processing the dried leaves of the coca shrub. This is treated with hydrochloric acid to produce one form of the drug cocaine, namely cocaine hydrochloride.

Cocaine (kō kān′, kō′kān). An addictive stimulant drug that works by blocking the reuptake from the synapse of such monoamine neurotransmitters as norepinephrine and serotonin. The sympathetic nervous system (SNS) is aroused. The over-activity of these transmitters and the SNS results in an elevated mood, along with alertness and self-confidence. Unfortunately, the abuse of this drug eventually results in mental and physical deterioration.

Cocaine hydrochloride. A form of cocaine. Extracted from **coca paste**, it acts as a strong anesthetic and stimulant.

Cocaine psychosis. Psychotic behavior shown by an individual bingeing on cocaine. The symptoms resemble those of schizophrenia. See also: **amphetamine psychosis**.

Cocaine spree. A binge (wild, uncontrolled, and unending consumption) on cocaine. See also: **cocaine psychosis**.

Cochlea (kok′lē ə) ("cochlea" = "snail" in Greek). The snail-shaped inner ear organ of hearing. The organ consists of coiled tubes that give it a snail-like appearance (the human cochlea taking two and one-half turns). The receptors for hearing are the inner and outer hair cells set into the organ of Corti. In turn, the organ of Corti is seated on the basilar membrane, which begins at the oval window and follows the turns of the cochlea. Sound vibrations are picked up by the cochlea at the oval window. After the vibrations have been processed by the organ of Corti, they exit the cochlea at the round window. See also: **basilar membrane; inner ear; organ of Corti.**

Cochlear (kok′lē ər) **implant**. A device consisting of several microelectrodes that is implanted in the inner ear of a nerve- deaf individual. Each electrode is attached to a small speaker tuned to a limited range of sound frequencies. Sounds are converted by the implant into stimuli for auditory nerve fibers. See also: **acoustic nerve; auditory vestibular nerve; cochlea; nerve deafness.**

Cochlear nuclei (kok′lē ər nōo′klē ī″, nyōo′-). These are two groups of cell bodies in the medulla (namely, the dorsal and ventral cochlear nuclei) reached by the axons of the acoustic nerve, the auditory branch of the auditory vestibular nerve (the eighth cranial nerve). There is one of each of these nuclei on either side of the medulla. The cochlear nuclei receive ipsilateral inputs from the ear on the same side, that is, the left acoustic nerve reaches the left dorsal and ventral cochlear nuclei. See also: **acoustic nerve; auditory vestibular nerve; cranial nerves; ipsilateral; medulla.**

Cocktail-party phenomenon. The ability to monitor different conversations going on around us, so that we focus on (and participate in) one conversation, while keeping track of the flow of another.

Cocontraction. The condition of the two members of an antagonistic muscle-pair, under most circum-

stances. For example, when we are standing still, both the flexor and the extensor muscles of our legs have high levels of muscle tone, even though neither type is overtly contracting. See also: **antagonist**.

Codeine. An alkaloid compound obtainable from opium or morphine. Codeine is an effective cough-suppressant. It also has analgesic (pain-killing) and hypnotic (sleep-inducing) properties, like the other opiates. An overdose of codeine can be life-threatening.

Code switching. The ability to modify one's language according to the audience and the situation. For example, we typically compliment a younger child with such positive remarks as "good boy/girl," "nice job, honey," and so on. With adults we tend to use a more expanded vocabulary and more complex terminology, such as in "I appreciate your efforts."

Coding. The formation of energy and/or material patterns in time or space into vehicles for carrying intended meanings (e.g., framing the words of a spoken sentence). See also: **decoding; encoding.**

Codon. A set of three nucleotide bases on the DNA molecule; these three together are the code for one particular amino acid. Codons are the basis for the ability of a DNA molecule to control the assembly of peptides and proteins from the various amino acids.

Coexistence. The presence of two different neurotransmitters (usually one is a peptide and the other is not a peptide) within the same neuron. See also: **Dale's Law.**

Cognition. The entire group of the higher mental activities; that is, all behaviors involving the acquisition. storage, retrieval, and application of knowledge.

Cognitive appraisal. The recognition of a threatening part of the environment, along with an evaluation of the type of threat involved, the defensive activity required, the resources on hand for defensive action, and the preparation of an appropriate strategic plan to deal with the threat.

Cognitive-arousal theory of emotion. According to this view, an emotion must be triggered by activation of the sympathetic nervous system and/or the adrenal medulla gland (physiological arousal). This is not enough, however, because the appropriate mood needs to be defined. That defining is an evaluation performed by the cerebral cortex. Once the situation has been labeled, the full emotion has taken shape. This view was first stated by Schachter and Singer. A discussant has relabeled it the "juke box theory of emotion." The physiological arousal is analogous to inserting a quarter into the coin slot of a juke box. The machine is primed, but no song is being played. The customer then pushes a letter-number combination, designating the choice of song. That procedure is analogous to defining the situation so that, for example, joy will be felt instead of fear, anger, or some other emotion. See also: **emotion**.

Cognitive behavior modification. An approach to behavior therapy involving cognitive functions such as thinking and attitude change. Motives and habits are altered by combining response-reinforcement contingency schedules with such cognitive strategies as self-monitoring, self-evaluation, and self-reflection.

Cognitive-behavioral approach. A school of psychotherapy in which the goal of therapy is to correct patients' faulty cognitions about their world and themselves. In addition to attempting to modify behavior (as in traditional behavior therapy), the cognitive-behavioral therapist seeks to change the patient's way of thinking.

Cognitive bias. A consistent way of thinking that may be generally productive, but which can lead to incorrect decisions, poor judgments, and faulty inferences in the event that the person fails to perceive that this mode of thinking is not suitable for every circumstance. For example, an individual who judges that people with "shifty eyes" are dishonest exhibits a cognitive bias.

Cognitive development. The process of gradually changing one's understanding of the environment as one grows older and gains experience.

Cognitive-developmental theory. A theory of gender development which holds that the child's own thinking process is the major determiner of the development of the child's gender typing.

Cognitive dissonance. Leon Festinger's conception of attitudinal change which views pressure to change attitudes as analogous to physiological drives such as hunger or thirst. When one's responses and/or cognitions are inconsistent with one's attitude, a high level of discomfort is experienced and there is a strong motive to relive the tension.

Cognitive learning. A type of knowledge acquisition that requires conscious reasoning processes rather than either operant or respondent conditioning. Cognitive learning takes place in stages beginning with the encoding of basic elements (or component skills, if a procedure is to be acquired). Then, as a result of rehearsal (or practice), the knowledge is entered into long-term memory. Finally, the knowledge is available for automatic recitation (or, in the case of a skill, the correct performance is automatically executed).

Cognitive neuropsychology. The study of the neural structures and functions that underlie cognitive processes. These are inferred from the systematic analysis of the cognitive impairments of brain-damaged research subjects.

Cognitive reappraisal. A problem-solving strategy intended to reduce stress by internal mental rearrangements, for example, altering one's own level of aspiration. See also: **level of aspiration; stress** .

Cognitive theories of motivation. Theories that attempt to account for motivation by appealing to the individual's thoughts and expectations. These theories differentiate between extrinsic motivation (the influence of rewards and punishments) and intrinsic motivation (the pleasure inherent in performing a task).

Cognitive therapy. An attempt to treat psychological disorders by teaching individuals to change their ways of thinking about personal relationships and stressful situations. Cognitive therapy helps the patient identify erroneous patterns of thinking and correct them in order to reduce the level of stress. Two specific types of cognitive therapy are **rational-emotive therapy** and **stress-inoculation therapy** (see definitions).

Cohort. The population of those persons who were born during the same period of time. The time-span used is optional; it could be defined, for example, as a decade, as a span of five years, as two years, or as a year.

Colchicine (kol'chi sēn, kol'ki-, -sin). An alkaloid that has a number of uses in medicine and in physiological and genetics laboratories. This compound has been found useful in treating gout. It can induce the doubling of chromosomes in cell nuclei. Colchicine interferes with the axonal transport of chemical materials from the nerve cell cytoplasm to the various parts of the axon and the axon endings. The axon has a clear cytoplasm, the axoplasm, and depends on the mechanism of axonal flow for growth and repair; the axon endings usually receive their supply of neurotransmitter by this means.

Cold-blooded organisms. See **poikilotherms**.

Collaborative consultation. The cooperative interaction between a child's regular classroom teacher and the child's special education teacher to solve the child's educational problems. Specialists such as speech/language therapists, school psychologists, audiologists, and optometrists may also be involved in the consultation, whenever appropriate.

Collateral. See **axon collateral**.

Collateral sprouting. After an injured axon has degenerated, neighboring healthy axons send out processes (i.e., sprouts) to establish synapses on the receptor sites that were formerly serviced by the terminals of the now-degenerated axon.

Collicular-pulvinar pathway. A visual neural tract from the superior colliculus of the midbrain to the pulvinar (a nuclear mass of gray matter in the thalamus). This tract services the visual function of spatial localization. See also: **blindsight; depth perception; sound localization; superior colliculus**.

Colloids. Glue-like substances in a solvent that fail to go into solution, remaining in suspension with the molecules dispersed evenly throughout the solvent. Colloids cannot pass through semi-permeable cell-membranes, as their molecules are too large. A colloid in the follicles of the thyroid gland holds the thyroid hormones.

Color blindness. The lack of ability to recognize some color(s) of the visible spectrum. This is a genetic disorder wherein some individuals lack the short-wavelength, medium wave-length, or long-wavelength cones, or have low numbers of cones, or have defective cones. There are many types of color blindness. A common form is red-green color blindness, wherein people have difficulty differentiating between the colors red and green. Either the red colors or the green ones appear to look a grayish-yellow, depending on whether the individual is a protanope or a deuteranope. In red-green color blindness, there is a gene alteration in the coding for the opsins in either the medium- or the long-wavelength cones. The particular recessive genes involved are located on the X chromosome (a sex chromosome). Approximately 8% of males are red-green color blind, but only 1% of all females are. See also: **chromosomes; genes; opsin; protanopia; deuteranopia.**

Color constancy. The ability to identify correctly the color of an object even when looking through colored lenses or filters. Color constancy, like light constancy, size constancy, or shape constancy, enables us to keep track of objects even when they move closer or farther, turn sideways, move into shadows or under colored lights, and so on. These constancy abilities are not inborn but are acquired with experience. Our color constancy ability depends on the integrity of a part of the visual cortex, area V4, which corresponds to Brodmann's area 19 (the outer rim of the occipital lobe). See also: **light(ness) constancy; occipital lobe; visual cortex**.

Color vision. The ability to discriminate among the wavelengths of visual stimuli. The perception of color involves the assessment of a light stimulus on three different dimensions. The first dimension is hue, the identity of the color as red, yellow, orange, green, or whatever. Hue is primarily related to the wavelength of the light stimulus: Longer waves are seen as red and shorter ones as violet, with other hues corresponding to intermediate lengths of waves. A second dimension is brightness, which is chiefly correlated with the intensity (strength) of the light stimulus. The third dimension is known as saturation. Saturation refers to the freedom of the light stimulus from the admixture of wavelengths other than the principal one. A well-saturated color is one that looks quite pure, because the stimulus presents only one wavelength of light energy to the retina. A poorly saturated color, on the other hand, involves a mixture of wavelengths. An example is pink, which could be called whitish red; pink is a badly-saturated red. The average human being is able to discriminate among about 300,000 different colors. Three theories have been put forth which try to account for how some neurons create the experience of color. These theories are: (1) the trichromatic (Young-Helmholz) theory, (2) the opponent-process theory, and (3) the retinex theory. See also: **chlorolabe; cones; cyanolabe; erythrolabe; opponent process theory of color vision; photopigments; retinex theory of color vision; trichromatic theory of color vision.**

Column. [1] A column of neurons in the cerebral cortex, perpendicular to the cortical surface. The neurons in the same column all have similar properties. In the visual cortex, for instance, they are all responsive to the same particular aspect of a visual stimulus. [2] A collection of myelin-covered axons in the spinal cord.

Commissure (kom′i shoor″). A band of myelinated axons which cross the midline "horizontally," that is, from structure A on the left side to the mirror-image structure A on the right side (e.g., the commissure of the superior colliculus runs between the left and the right superior colliculus). The largest of all the commissures is the corpus callosum, which runs between the left and right cerebral hemispheres.

Commissurotomy. The severing of the cerebral commissures. See also: **cerebral commissures; corpus callosum; split-brain surgery.**

Communication. The act or process of receiving or transmitting language messages. Normal communication involves adequate neurological functioning of involved cerebral areas and a "normal" psychological state. Certainly an individual in a state of depression or severe stress will in all likelihood evidence impaired communication ability.

Communication disorder. The inability of an individual to express his or her own needs or wishes. The futile attempts to do this can be accompanied by signs of severe distress.

Community psychology approach. An approach to psychotherapy that is aimed at preventing psychological disorders as well as providing for psychotherapy in community mental health centers.

Comorbidity. The incidence (number of cases in a specified population) that one disease syndrome appears together with a second syndrome. For example, ADHD with aggressiveness may have a high comorbidity with conduct disorder. See also: **morbidity; incidence.**

Comparative psychology. A specialty in psychology concerned with the behaviors of non-human species. Comparative psychologists have similar interests to those of ethologists. The difference is more a matter of background training than subject matter. Most ethologists are trained in zoology, the biology of animals. They set up experiments in natural settings, based on their observations of the animals in the wild. Comparative psychologists are more likely to use laboratory techniques, due to their training in experimental psychology.

Complementary colors. Pairs of colors that, when added to one another in a 50-50 combination, produce white. Each spectral color has its particular complementary. One example of a complementary pair is red and blue-green.

Completion. A phenomenon observed in patients with lesions of the primary visual cortex. Such a patient has a blind spot in the visual field corresponding to the location of the brain injury, since there is a kind of retinotopic map on the brain (i.e., point in visual field to corresponding point on visual brain). When viewing a figure that partly falls on the "blinded" part of the retina, the patient "fills in" the missing piece, making up for the missing visual information. Thus, the patient completes an incomplete picture. Completion also takes place in uninjured persons during monocular vision. When the figure's image is formed on the "blind spot" where the optic nerve leaves the retina, the subject will resort to completion. See also: **scotoma; blind spot.**

Complex cell. A cell of the visual cortex (in Brodmann's area 18) that responds optimally to line or edge stimuli of a particular slant anywhere within the aggregate receptive field for the cell column that includes that cell. See also: **aggregate field; column; feature detectors; receptive field; simple cell; visual cortex.**

Complex partial seizures. A seizure of any kind involves the disordered activity of a large number of brain neurons. This activity is readily seen in the electroencephalogram (EEG). In a complex partial seizure, consciousness is not totally lost, but the person feels that he/she is in a semi-conscious state. Automatic behavior sequences are reeled off, such as taking on a bizarre pose, fooling with buttons, smacking the lips, repeating a phrase, etc. Some believe that this syndrome is due to abnormal discharges from the temporal lobes. See also: **seizure; grand mal seizure; petit mal seizure; epilepsy.**

Component theory. See **trichromatic theory of color vision.**

Componential intelligence. According to Sternberg, the part of general intelligence that involves the components of the thinking process. Componential intelligence consists of three processes: (1) metacomponents, dealing with the planning for and the awareness of the reasoning activity; (2) performance components; and (3) knowledge-acquisition components. See also: **triarchic theory of intelligence.**

Compulsion. A recurring behavioral tendency to repeat an act that even the performing individual agrees is unreasonable, for example, repetitious hand-washing or doorknob-checking. See also:

anankastic personality disorder.

Compulsive personality disorder. See: **anankastic personality disorder.**

Computer xerophthalmia (zēr″of thal′mē ə). A dryness of the eyes, involving redness and soreness, that afflicts people who work for hours at a personal computer. When staring at the monitor, they fail to blink at the normal rate. Ordinarily, blinking supplies the needed moisture to the cornea of the eye. In order to avoid this problem, take hourly breaks or remember to blink purposefully every few minutes.

Computerized Axial Tomography (ak′sē əl tə mog′rə fē′). See: **CAT scan.**

COMT (catechol-O-methyltransferase) (kat′i kôl - ō- meth″əl trans′ fər ās″) An enzyme that breaks down catecholamine neurotransmitters (dopamine or norepinephrine) in the synaptic cleft. Not all of the neurotransmitter molecules will be affected by COMT, so the remaining molecules are reuptaken past the presynaptic membrane into the synaptic bouton from which they were released earlier. The tricyclic antidepressant drugs block the activity of COMT. See also: **enzyme; MAO; neurotransmitter; synapse; synaptic bouton; synaptic cleft; tricyclic antidepressants.**

Concept. A category of things, events, or abstract ideas that share common properties. Whenever we group things together on the basis of some similarity among them, we are using a concept.

Concordance. This simply means "agreement." In physiological psychology, twins can be concordant for a trait (e.g., brown eyes) if both have the trait. The same twins can be concordant for blue eyes because neither has the trait.

Concordance rate. The frequency with which two persons (in a given category, such as a pair of identical twins) manifest the same condition (e.g., schizophrenia).

Concordant trait. A trait seen in both members of a pair of research subjects. The two subjects may be identical twins, for example. The trait might be a physical feature such as blond hair, but it may also be a disposition toward a form of mental disorder. See also: **biological predisposition.**

Concurrent validity. The size of the correlation between a group of persons' scores on a test and the scores they achieve on a currently given criterion measurement. A test having high concurrent validity may be useful as an easy-to-administer substitute for a laborious criterion measurement.

Concussion. An effect of a blow to the head, when there is no external bleeding and no massive internal damage, but there is an impairment of consciousness. At least I think so...just how many fingers <u>are</u> those?

Conditioned compensatory responses. Responses elicited by the stimuli associated with drug intake. These responses are opposite to the effects of the drug and help develop tolerance to the drug. See also: **opponent-process theory of drug withdrawal symptoms.**

Conditioned defensive burying. A research paradigm in which the subject is trained to react to an aversive stimulus by burying the object that puts it forth.

Conditioned place-preference test. A test of a laboratory animal's preferences for locations in which it has previously experienced drug effects.

Conditioned reflex. A reflex that has to be acquired by learning because it is not programmed by the genetic makeup of the organism. A conditioned reflex is usually acquired by the association of the stimulus destined to become the initiator of the conditioned reflex with a stimulus that is already the initiator of a reflex, because the latter reflex is an unconditioned one. For example, a dog's automatic salivating to the sound of a bell is a conditioned reflex. It was acquired by the dog when the animal experienced pairings of the bell with meat in the mouth. The meat in the mouth is another stimulus, and, more specifically, the stimulus with an unconditioned reflexive link to the response of salivating.

Conditioned response (CR). A response that is elicited by a conditioned stimulus as the result of Pavlovian (classical)conditioning, for example, salivating at the ringing of a bell.

Conditioned stimulus (CS). A previously neutral stimulus (i.e., one that neither elicited nor reinforced the response prior to the training) that has come to elicit a conditioned response after classical conditioning has taken place. An example of a CS would be the ringing of a bell that elicits a conditioned salivation response.

Conditioned taste aversion. A learned avoidance of a taste because one has previously experienced that taste to come before illness or nausea.

Conditioning, classical. See: **classical conditioning.**

Conditioning, operant. See: **operant conditioning.**

Conduct disorder. A syndrome, usually appearing before the age of 15, involving constant disregard for the rights of others and rejection of social norms. Physical aggression against others is often manifested, along with disruptiveness, negativism, defiance of authority, disrespectfulness, and irresponsibility. After the individual reaches the age of 18, provided the conduct disorder was evident before age 15, the syndrome is essentially renamed antisocial personality disorder. See also: **antisocial personality disorder; oppositional defiant disorder**.

Conduction aphasia (kən duk'shən ə fā'zhə). A language deficit resulting from damage to the arcuate fasciculus, which is a bundle of axons running from Wernicke's area to Broca's area. Unlike a person with Broca's aphasia, the person with conduction aphasia articulates speech well. The person may have some problem with comprehending heard language, but not as badly as someone with Wernicke's aphasia. The patient with conduction aphasia is unable to repeat phrases correctly and may have trouble finding words (i.e., anomia). Some researchers doubt that damage to the arcuate fasciculus leads to permanent aphasia at all. See also: **aphasia; arcuate fasciculus**.

Conductive deafness or middle ear deafness. A loss of hearing due to damage to a part of the middle ear. The middle ear is needed for the conduction of sound waves from the outer ear to the cochlea. Conductive deafness may result from birth complications, infections, or tumors. Since the cochlea and auditory nerve are intact, the individual with conductive deafness can detect sounds that bypass the middle ear; the individual is able to hear his or her own voice. A hearing aid can be helpful because it sets up vibrations in the bones of the skull to compensate for the disabled small bones (ossicles) in the middle ear. See also: **hearing; middle ear; ossicles**.

Conductive hearing loss. Hearing impairments which result from the interference with sound transmission along the conductive pathway of the ear. Conductive losses usually result from problems of the outer and/or middle ear.

Cones. Visual receptor cells found in the retina; specifically, the only visual receptors to be found in the fovea. They come in three subvarieties, each maximally sensitive to a different color (blue, red, or green). They enable us to perceive color differences and to perform the fine detail analysis involved in such activities as reading.

Confabulate (kən fab'yoo lāt). To tell a falsehood and believe it to be true. This is one of the symptoms of patients with Korsakoff's syndrome. It enables the patient to remain unaware of his or her losses of memory. See also: **Korsakoff's syndrome**.

Confounding variable. In experimental research, any variable that is not equivalent for all conditions or treatments, but which was not planned to be one of the experiment's independent variables. See also: **experiment; independent variable**.

Congenital. Refers to a condition present at birth. The cause of the condition might be hereditary, prenatal, or perinatal.

Congenital aural atresia (kən jen'i təl ôr'əl ə trē'zhə). A condition at birth which involves a malformed or absent external auditory canal.

Congenital condition. A condition present at birth. It may be due to heredity or to the prenatal environment.

Congenital cytomegalovirus (CMV) (kən jen'i təl sī"tō meg"ə lō vī'rus). A frequently occurring congenital virus among newborns which can result in hearing loss.

Congenital heart diseases. Heart conditions or problems existing at birth in either the structure or functioning of the heart.

Congenitally deaf. The condition of being born deaf. See also: **adventitiously deaf**.

Congenital rubella. Contraction of the German-measles virus by a fetus from the mother during pregnancy. A variety of problems can ensue, including mental retardation, blindness, hearing loss, and learning problems.

Congenital syphilis. Syphilis which is transmitted from a pregnant mother to her unborn child. This is a serious condition and can cause stillbirths and spontaneous abortions.

Congestive heart failure. Heart failure which is due to an unnatural accumulation of fluids near the heart which interferes with the normal functioning of the heart.

Conjugate eye movement. The coordinated movement of both eyes in the same direction and to the same extent.

Conjugate reinforcement technique. A system for investigating the memory of an infant. A ribbon is tied around the baby's ankle at one end, while the other end of the ribbon is tied to a mobile, so that a kicking movement makes the mobile jiggle around. Memory is tested by disassembling the setup after the child has shown learning and restoring the setup a number of days later, in order to see whether or not the child will immediately kick the foot tied to the mobile. See also: **operant conditioning; positive reinforcement.**

Conjunctiva (kon˝jungk tī′və). The thin transparent mucous membrane lining the eyelid and covering the cornea.

Consolidation. The establishment of a pathway in the brain on the basis of a temporary neural circuit. Consolidation is hypothesized to be the process by which short-term memory is converted to long-term memory. See also: **calpain; hippocampus; long-term memory; long-term potentiation; short-term memory.**

Constructional apraxia (kən struk′shən əl   ə prak′sē ə, ā-). The specific loss of the ability to draw or construct objects in three-dimensional space. This results from injury to the right parietal lobe. See also: **apraxia; parietal lobe.**

Construct validity. The quality of a test indicating that the behavior or ability being measured is a well-established, genuine trait or behavioral tendency. Ingredients for making a favorable decision on a test's construct validity include proving that it has high content validity, high internal reliability, and significant correlations, some positive and some negative, with other tests and measurements as appropriate. No one correlation study can give a test high construct validity. Rather, it has to be inferred from a number of supportive research findings. Factor analysis (as well as other, similar techniques) is often employed in the service of construct validity. Age-differentiation validity is a type of construct validity that shows the degree to which test scores show increases or decreases with age increases or decreases (e.g., some groups have been shown to evidence IQ increases with age). See also: **validity.**

Consulting teacher. A teacher who is qualified to provide assistance or support for students with disorders or disabilities (e.g., resource room specialist, speech therapist, or occupational therapist).

Consultive services. Services provided to individuals with disorders or disabilities, by qualified staff or professionals, in order to improve the social, psychological, medical, and academic well-being of those individuals.

Content validity. A sophisticated version of face validity, requiring that the tasks assigned to the examinee should be an adequate sample of the skill or behavior that the test is meant to measure. The content validity of a test is the extent to which it includes items that are relevant to the behavior of interest. Furthermore, a sufficiently large number of relevant items should be included so that the behavior is adequately sampled. The decision as to whether a test has high content validity must be made by someone who is an expert in the skill or activity which is being measured. See also: **validity.**

Contextual intelligence. The intelligence shown in one's adjustment to everyday life; "street smarts." Both this category of intelligence and componential intelligence have been suggested by Sternberg. See also: **componential intelligence; triarchic theory of intelligence**.

Continuity-stages question, the. As children grow older, does their repertory of skills and abilities increase steadily, or do they arrive at a stage where their inventory of cognitive skills becomes qualitatively different from the skills of children at earlier stages of development? Piaget is famed for his stage theory of cognitive growth; Kohlberg has posited a stage theory of moral development; and Erikson has presented a stage theory of the development of personality.

Continuous reinforcement schedule. In operant conditioning, the reinforcement of every single correct operant response. See also: **operant conditioning; partial reinforcement schedule.**

Contracoup injury. A contusion occurring on the side of the brain opposite to the side that was struck by a blow. See also: **contusion.**

Contralateral. Across the body's midline. A contralateral reflex, for example, might involve a stimulus to the left side producing a response from muscles on the right side. Contralateral connections may be formed by commissures or decussations. In the brain's visual pathway, the lateral geniculate nucleus (LGN) has three layers that receive their inputs from the eye on the opposite side, that is, LGN layers 1, 4, and 6 are contralateral layers. See also: **commissure; decussation; ipsilateral.**

Contralateral neglect. A disturbance of the patient's ability to respond to stimulation (visual, auditory, and somatosensory) of one side of the body as the result of an injury to the brain of the opposite side.

Usually, it involves the neglect of the left side of the body and damage to the parietal lobe of the right cerebral hemisphere. See also: **parietal lobe; somatosensory system; unilateral neglect.**

Contrast enhancement. The enhancement of black-white contrast at edges between light and dark areas. this enhancement is the result of lateral inhibition. See also: **lateral inhibition; Mach bands.**

Contrast X-ray techniques. X-ray techniques involving the injection of a radio-opaque substance. See also: **angiography.**

Control-question technique. The operator of a lie-detector polygraph obtains the suspect's psychophysiological responses (galvanic skin response, heart rate, blood pressure, and skin temperature) to relevant questions as well as to a group of control (i.e., neutral) questions. The responses to the two sets of questions are then compared.

Contusion. An injury in which the skin is not broken, but in which there is internal bleeding. This will often show up as a bruise. See also: **contracoup injury.**

Convergence (kən vûr′jens). The movement of the eyes toward one another (and the midline of the body) made when a viewed object comes nearer to the observer. The visual stimuli that cause the convergence response constitute a binocular cue for depth perception. See also: **depth perception.**

Convergent semantic production (kən vûr′jent si man′tik). This term is frequently attributed to Wiig and her associates who have identified reading-disabled children who exhibit convergent semantic word production problems, namely, difficulty in retrieving words stored in long-term memory.

Convergent thinking. A form of thinking in which the individual stays focused on one plan, working toward the one correct solution of a problem. The convergent thinker assumes that there are only a very limited set of approaches to use in solving a problem. This form of reasoning can be contrasted with divergent thinking. See also: **divergent thinking.**

Converging operations. The attempt to solve a scientific problem by using several different research methods in order to arrive at the one solution that can fit with all the data. For example, a physiological psychologist might use the ablation, stimulation, and recording methods to investigate the relationship of a part of the brain to one type of behavior.

Convulsions. Seizures that involve overt muscular twitches. Muscular contractions and relaxations alternate with one another. See also: **seizure; grand mal seizure.**

Coprophilia (kop″rō fil′ē ə). A type of paraphilia in which the individual obtains sexual pleasure from feces. See also: **paraphilias.**

Copulation. Sexual congress; carnal knowledge; sexual intercourse.

Cornea (kôr′nē ə). The transparent, forward extension of the sclera, which both admits and refracts incoming light.

Corollary discharge (kôr′ə ler″ē). A hypothetical set of nerve impulses sent from the motor cortex to another part of the brain, possibly a sensory area, simultaneously with the direct movement command. The information is supposedly used to permit the individual to correct for his or her own movements when performing a skilled act, for example, throwing a javelin while running.

Coronal. See: **frontal.**

Corpus callosum (kôr′pus kə lō′sum). The large band of axons connecting the left hemisphere of the cerebral cortex with the right hemisphere across the longitudinal fissure. The corpus callosum is the largest commissure in the central nervous system. There are about 800,000 axons in this thick bundle of nerve fibers. See also: **body; cerebral cortex; commissure; genu; splenium; split-brain surgery.**

Corpus striatum (kôr′pus strī ā′tum). A set of structures in the forebrain, below the cerebral cortex, that belong to the basal ganglia. The caudate nucleus is separated from two other nuclei, the globus pallidus and the putamen, by the white matter that makes up the internal capsule. The internal capsule contains axons going in both directions between the thalamus and the cerebral cortex. The three parts of the corpus striatum send axons across the internal capsule in order to communicate among themselves. These crossing axons provide a striped appearance for this region, hence the name "corpus striatum," which means "striped body."

Correlation. A statistical technique used to determine how strongly one variable tends to change in agreement with another. Correlation refers to the extent to which scores on one variable change in the same direction as do scores on another variable. This tendency for two variables to agree with each other can be measured in order to obtain an index of agreement called the <u>correlation coefficient</u>. If the highest scores on the two variables are obtained by person A, the next-highest scores on the two variables are obtained by person B, and so on down the line, this would be a perfect positive correlation. The value of the correlation coefficient would be +1.00. If the highest score on one variable and the lowest score on the other variable are obtained by person A and the next-highest score on one variable and the next-lowest score on the other variable are obtained by person B, and so on, down the line, the correlation would be a perfect negative one. The value of the correlation coefficient would be -1.00. If subjects' scores on one variable are completely unrelated to their scores on the other variable, the correlation coefficient would be 0.00. The numerical size of the coefficient indicates the strength of the tendency for the two variables to agree or disagree. The closer the correlation coefficient to a plus or minus 1.00, the stronger the relationship. The algebraic sign (+ or -) shows the quality or direction of the tendency for the two variables to agree, that is, high scores going with high scores show a positive correlation while high scores going with low scores indicate a negative correlation. Correlations are rarely perfect in psychology or medicine, but they allow predictions to be made and can provide useful information. For example, there is a known correlation between cigarette smoking and cancer, which provides a reason for trying to prevent some individuals from smoking too much. Moreover, if you square the correlation coefficient (r X r), the percentage of variance accounted by the correlation is determined. For example, the correlation between IQ and college grade point average (GPA) is 0.5. Accordingly, 0.5 X 0.5 = 25% of the variance for a GPA can be accounted for by IQ. Other factors also help to account for GPA, thereby eliminating the possibility of inferring causation. See also: **scatter diagram**.

Correlational research. Research done in order to determine whether or not two variables change their values together. In this type of research, behavior may be observed naturalistically, since subjects cannot be assigned to different groups each getting different treatments.

Corsi's Block-Tapping Test. This test is set up by spreading a set of blocks irregurlarly over a tabletop. The tester taps a sequence of blocks. The subject must try to repeat the sequence. The task is analogous to the popular game of "Simon Says." Subjects who have damage to part of the right temporal lobe and the right hippocampus are impaired on this test. They can do well on a repeated-digits test, however. See also: **double dissociation technique**; **Hebb's recurring-digits test**.

Corticospinal tract. See: **pyramidal tract**.

Cortisol. A steroid hormone of the adrenal cortex. It leads to an increased blood sugar level and an increased metabolic rate.

Counseling psychology. A specialty in psychology emphasizing diagnosis and treatment of behavior problems. The clients of counseling psychologists do not have problems as severe as do those of clinical psychologists. Some counseling psychologists further specialize; they may do marriage counseling, vocational counseling, or school or college counseling work with students having any of a variety of adjustment problems.

Counterconditioning. A way of training an individual to give up a well-learned response (i.e., break a bad habit) not by extinction of the conditioned reflex but rather by conditioning the stimulus to produce a different response. See also: **classical conditioning; conditioned reflex; conditioned response; conditioned stimulus; extinction**.

Counterregulation. An eating pattern shown by some dieters. After eating a food high in calories, the individual continues to eat greedily and lustily, throwing calorie-counting aside. See also: **bulimia**.

Counter theory model. A view of deviant child behavior that rejects the concept of disordered behavior. Emphasis is on advocacy for the child's needs and the delivery of effective services. This is to be done in a context that rejects the contrast between approved ("normal") and disapproved ("abnormal") behavior.

Crack. The free-base form of cocaine, usually ingested by smoking it in a pipe. Crack can lead to fatal heart attacks in a number of first-time users.

Cranial. See: **rostral**.

Cranial nerves. Part of the interface between the central and the peripheral nervous systems, the cranial nerves (along with the spinal nerves) belong to the peripheral nervous system but either begin or end in the CNS. The cranial nerves are connected to the brain. Some of them are mainly sensory in function, some chiefly motor, and still others contain some subgroups of axons that are sensory and other subgroups that are motor. The cranial nerves are arranged in pairs, one member of each pair covering the left side of the body and the other the right. There are 12 pairs of cranial nerves, numbered from the rostral end to the caudal, as follows (Sensory nerves are designated "s", motor nerves "m", and mixed sensory and motor nerves "b" for "both."): I. olfactory, s; II. optic, s; III. oculomotor, m; IV. trochlear, m; V. trigeminal, b; VI. abducens, m; VII. facial, b; VIII. auditory vestibular, s; IX. glossopharyngeal, b; X. vagus, b; XI. spinal accessory, m; and XII. hypoglossal, m. The names of the cranial nerves can be brought to mind by the mnemonic device "Olaf Opdyke okays trouble trip aboard fast auto; Gloria vigorously spins hips." The functional designations "sensory," "motor," or "both" can be recalled in identical order with the following mnemonic device: "Some say, marry money", but my brother says, "Bad business, marry money."

Creativity. A quality of problem-solving behavior in which the attempted solution is unexpected, unusual, and has a good chance of being successful. It is also the ability to produce novel ideas or works (e.g., poems, novels, scientific hypotheses, musical compositions, or works of art). Some psychologists believe that creativity is a distinct type of intelligence. Creative persons may be so involved in their areas of talent that their normal social interactions are reduced to a minimum. Creative persons tend to have high IQs, but the converse is not true. Some people with high IQs are low in creativity. Creative people are more subject to extremes of mood than other people; their greatest productivity occurs during their mood peaks.

Cretinism (krē'ti niz″əm). A condition involving retarded physical and intellectual growth due to the absence of thyroxin, a hormone of the thyroid gland, from birth. Early detection of the condition can allow the individual to be put on a thyroxin-maintenance regime and achieve normal development.

Creutzfeldt-Jakob's disease (kroits'felt yä'kôps). One of the dementias, this is perhaps the most merciful. It takes a rapid course, moving from stupor to coma and then to death. Even though memory loss is a prominent symptom at disease onset, further losses are evident each day. The disease process involves damage both to the cerebral hemispheres and to subcortical areas. See also: **Alzheimer's disease; dementia.**

Criterion-referenced tests (CRTs). These tests are meant to check the extent to which a given reading program's objectives are being met. They tend to measure specific skills, unlike the norm-referenced tests (NRTs), which usually measure general areas of skill. CRTs are intended to be used with an absolute standard of successful achievement, while NRTs relate performance to that of the norm group.

Criterion-referenced validity. Any measure of validity that involves the calculation of a correlation coefficient between the test score and some other, independent criterion which represents the actual skill or behavior being measured. Both the test and the criterion must be measurable, unbiased, and relevant to the behavior being tested. If the criterion measure is made at the same time that the test is administered, the test's concurrent validity is being determined. If the criterion measure is made some time after the test has been administered, the test's predictive validity is being assessed. See also: **validity.**

Critical period. A stage of behavioral development during which exposure to stimulation allows a specific response to be appropriately shaped. This is necessary if the normal expression of that response is to occur. For example, if the eyes have been blindfolded throughout the critical period, the individual will later have severely impaired vision. See also: **ethology; sensitive period.**

Cross-cuing. A strategy developed by split-brain patients after participating in numerous experiments involving the independent stimulation of their left and right visual fields. A reaction to a visual stimulus in one half-field may produce a somatosensory stimulus to both hemispheres. That stimulus may inform the non-stimulated hemisphere about the nature of the visual stimulus that was not reported to that hemisphere. As a result, the subject responds correctly, even when the optic and visual-neural conditions seem to make it impossible to do so. Think of this as another triumph of mind over matter!

Cross-section. A cut which is perpendicular to the long axis of the body; the cut would be either through the waist or parallel to such a slice. Cross-sectional views of the central nervous system are often inspected under a microscope. Often a continuous front-to-back series of cross-sections is examined. The cross-section taken through the body of a biped (such as a human) would be a horizontal section. In the case of a quadruped, the cross-section is identical with a frontal section. A synonym for "cross-section" is "transverse section."

Cross-sectional research. A research technique whereby people of different ages are measured on the same date. See also: **cross-sequential research; longitudinal research.**

Cross-sequential research. A technique for doing research that involves a combination of the cross-sectional and longitudinal research methods. People in different age groups are measured at the same time and restudied at several later dates as well. See also: **cross-sectional research; longitudinal research.**

Cross-tolerance. The buildup of tolerance for one drug due to the ingestion of a different drug. This usually happens with two drugs in the same major category of psychological activity. For instance, abuse of a barbiturate drug may increase the tolerance for ethyl alcohol, or vice versa. This is because alcohol and barbiturates are both depressants. See also: **psychoactive drugs; sedatives.**

Cryogenic blockade. The temporary stoppage of nerve-impulse propagation by the application of a cryoprobe (a very cold needle).

Crystallized (kris′tə līzd) **intelligence.** A general ability that includes learned skills, for example, verbal facility. Crystallized intelligence is the sum of those aspects of intelligence that are the result of experience and training, including specific information, vocabulary, skills, and strategies for problem solving. This sort of intelligence will keep on growing throughout one's life. See also: **fluid intelligence.**

Cued speech. This is a method of communication used with the hearing-impaired which combines hand signals with lip-reading. The hand gestures cue the individual to words and word-parts not easily identified by lip-reading.

Cultural-familial retardation. Mental retardation that can be traced to environmental causes. The environment in question may be impoverished economically, socially, and/or psychologically.

Culture. The socialization process which reflects life patterns in such areas as language, marriage customs, sex roles, entertainment, and rewards and punishments. The impact of culture can be seen in the different ways societies treat the mentally ill. When such disorders are perceived as biologically based, treatments and behaviors tend to reflect this

perspective. Societies that lack such diagnostic sophistication and have a low tolerance level for mentally ill individuals may use social isolation or punishment when dealing with them.

Culture-fair IQ test. An intelligence test that does not favor (due to differences in experience and social background) the members of the majority over the members of ethnic, racial, and/or religious minority groups.

Cuneate (kyo͞o′nē āt″) ("cuneate" = wedge-shaped) **nucleus.** A collection of nerve cell bodies in the medulla, the hindmost part of the brain. The axons of the cuneate tract arrive at this nucleus carrying information from the general body sense of deep pressure. The cuneate nucleus is located in the superior (dorsal) portion of the caudal (back) half of the medulla and, like the gracile nucleus beside it, creates a visible ridge on the outer surface of the medulla. In turn, the cell bodies of the neurons in the cuneate nucleus send out axons that join the medial lemniscus, a tract that leads to the posterior ventral nucleus of the thalamus (PVNT). From there, nerve impulses are sent by way of the internal capsule to the somatosensory cortex, Brodmann's areas 1, 2, and 3, which comprise the postcentral gyrus of the parietal lobe of the cerebral cortex. See also: **dorsal funiculus; medial lemniscus; medulla; parietal lobe; somatosensory system.**

Cuneate (kyo͞o′nē āt″) ("cuneate" = wedge-shaped) **tract** (also known as the **fasciculus cuneatus**). A collection of axons in the dorsal funiculus of the spinal cord. These carry nerve impulses from the neurons of the dorsal horn of the gray butterfly. In turn, the spinal nerves that have arrived at those dorsal horn cells carry nerve impulses from the receptors for deep pressure. Receptors for this sense are located throughout the body. Deep pressure is one of the general body senses. Sensory messages from the upper torso and the upper extremities fill in the dorsal funiculus from the lateral side, pushing the other deep pressure sensory tract of the dorsal funiculus, the gracile tract, toward the midline. Therefore, the lower segments of the spinal cord, the coccygeal, sacral, and lumbar segments, contain dorsal funiculi filled entirely with the gracile tracts. The cuneate tract appears only at the start of the thoracic segments of the cord, and it becomes progressively larger at higher levels of the cord. The axons of the cuneate tract terminate in the cuneate nucleus of the medulla. See also: **cuneate**

nucleus; dorsal funiculus; gracile tract; gray butterfly; somatosensory system.

Cuneus (kyoo′nē us) ("cuneus" is Latin for "wedge"). A wedge-shaped gyrus of the occipital lobe observable only in a midline (medial) view. It is dorsal to the calcarine fissure, and occupies the larger share of the occipitalobe's medial surface. Along with the lingual gyrus (the tongue-shaped gyrus ventral to the calcarine fissure), the more ventral part of the cuneus makes up the calcarine cortex, which is the primary visual projection area of the cerebral cortex. See also: **calcarine cortex; calcarine fissure; lingual gyrus; occipital lobe; striate cortex; visual cortex.**

Cyanolabe (sī an′ō lāb″). One of the three types of iodopsin, the photopigment found in those visual receptors called **cones.** Cyanolabe is most sensitive to blue light (i.e., the shortest wavelengths of visible light). See also: **chlorolabe; erythrolabe; trichromatic theory of color vision.**

Cyanosis (sī″ə nō′sis). A blue discoloration of the skin due to insufficient blood circulating to that part of the body. The blue areas will be below normal in temperature. Cyanosis of the fingers is a symptom of Raynaud's disease. See also: **Raynaud's disease.**

Cyclic AMP (cyclic adenosine monophosphate) (cAMP) (sī klik, sik′lik, ə den′ ō sēn″, -ə sin mon″ō fos′fāt″). A chemical produced in a postsynaptic neuron after the neuron has been stimulated by a neuromodulator, for example, epinephrine. The cAMP serves as a "second signal system" (or "second messenger"), the first signal being the arrival of the neuromodulator. The cAMP alters the permeability of the cell membrane to specific ions (either Na+, K+, or Cl-) thus promoting either de-polarization (an excitatory change) or hyperpolarization (an inhibitory change) of the cell membrane. The effect of this "second signal system" is longer lasting than that of an ordinary neurotransmitter, but not as powerful. A mnemonic device you might use (keeping in mind that epinephrine is a good example of a neuromodulator that gets cAMP going) is this: "Eppie N. Efron goes to cAMP!" See also: **neuromodulator; second messenger; volume transmission theory.**

Cystic fibrosis (sis′tik fī brō′sis). A chronic hereditary disorder involving the lungs, the pancreas, or both. If the lungs are affected, the exchange of the blood's oxygen and carbon dioxide contents does not take place efficiently. If the pancreas is involved, the nutrition processes are impaired.

Cytochrome oxidase. An enzyme found in very high concentrations in the color-discriminating neurons of the visual cortex. See also: **blobs.**

Cytomegalic (sī′tō me gal′ik) **inclusion.** A disease condition, of variable severity, especially likely to occur in infants, resulting from infection by the cytomegalovirus (CMV). There many be a latent infection, activated in later life by pregnancy, immunosuppression therapy, and/or blood transfusions. See also: **cytomegalovirus.**

Cytomegalovirus (CMV) (sī′tō meg″ə lō vī′rus). One of a group of viruses of the herpes type. CMVs are species-specific. The human CMV infects the salivary glands and can cause the cytomegalic inclusion disease. See also: **cytomegalic inclusion.**

Cytoplasm (sī′tō plaz″əm). One of the three major parts of a body cell. The main bulk and volume of the cell is the cytoplasm (a watery solution). See also: **axoplasm.**

D

Dale's law. This is the principle, recently modified, that all the axon endings of a neuron must release the same neurotransmitter. As now modified, the principle is that the same combination of neurotransmitters is released at each axon ending of the neuron. The reason for the change is that one neurotransmitter is often released along with another neurotransmitter, usually a peptide, from the same synaptic boutons.

Dark adaptation. An increase in sensitivity to light that takes place after one has been in darkness for several minutes. The eyes are able to adapt to prolonged darkness by increasingly growing more and more sensitive to faint lights. This adaptation requires two discontinuous stages. The initial stage of dark adaptation is due to the recovery of the photopigments by the less sensitive retinal cones. The latter stage of dark adaptation is attributable to the rebuilding of rhodopsin, the photopigment of the very sensitive rods. See also: **light adaptation**.

Daydream. A shifting of attention from external stimuli to one's private imagination.

Deaf-blindness. A disorder which involves a substantial loss of hearing and vision.

Deafferent (dē af'ər ent). To remove the neural inputs to a given part of the body. For example, in research on motor activity, investigators have severed the dorsal roots to partially deafferent the spinal cord. See also: **deafferentation; dorsal root**.

Deafferentation (dē af″ər en tā'shən). The removal of sensory input. One example would be the cutting of the dorsal roots of some spinal nerves in order to deprive the spinal cord of any input from the general body-sense receptors connected to the severed axons in those roots. See also: **Bell-Magendie law**.

Deafness. The condition of not hearing sounds at or above certain intensity levels. A deaf individual is not able to process language through audition with or without the use of hearing aids.

Debriefing. A procedure followed by psychological experimenters in keeping with ethical principles. If these experimenters had employed human subjects who were given false instructions or untrue explanations of their roles in the re-

search, the psychologists will tell the full story (the true purpose of the study, the nature of any deception used on them, and a correct description of how they were treated during the research) to these subjects after the experiment has been completed. That final explanation is the debriefing.

Decay. The process by which a memory trace is degraded spontaneously after a lapse of time. A good example of memory decay would be the forgetting of foreign language vocabulary after a time lapse because it is not used. It is not decay if the memory is altered by other processes such as motivation or the interference of other memory traces.

Decerebrate rigidity (dē ser'ə brit). A postural syndrome resulting from severing the midbrain between the inferior colliculi and the superior colliculi. The extensor muscles contract to an abnormal extent, leaving the limbs chronically extended. See also: **cerveau isolé**.

Decibel. The decibel is one tenth of a **Bel** (named for Alexander Graham Bell). It is a unit of measurement of the loudness of sound. Normal conversation occurs at about 65 decibels (Db). Exposure to sounds over 85 Db over a protracted period of time can be damaging to hearing. The louder forms of rock music can reach 110 Db; this is why teenagers are warned by their parents that they may be ruining their hearing. Those rock musicians who wear earplugs while performing are no dummies. Ordinarily, a musician wants to get auditory information about her or his own performance, but that is not worth losing one's hearing. See also: **cochlea; hearing; inner ear; nerve deafness**.

Decision-commitment. One portion of the Sternberg triangular theory of love, decision-commitment has two aspects: (1) the short-term aspect, the decision to love someone, and (2) the long-term aspect, the commitment to remain in love with that someone. See also: **triangular theory of love**.

Declarative memory. A component of long-term memory, declarative memory is the storage of specific facts (as distinct from memories that belong to skills, which would be procedural memory). This kind of memory is readily lost in amnesia cases, as opposed to procedural memory, which tends to resist being lost. See also: **long-term memory; procedural memory**.

Decoding. The conversion of energy fluctuations or shape differences (produced in coding) into any meaningful form (logical, verbal, or mathematical, for example). See also: **coding; encoding**.

Decremental potentials (dek″rə men′təl). Voltage changes occurring on the membranes of the dendrite or cell body of the neuron, but not on the axon, decremental potentials grow weaker and weaker the farther they spread along the cell membrane. See also: **graded potentials**.

Decussation (dē″kə sā′shən). A band of axons crossing the midline diagonally. A structure A on the left is connected to a structure B on the right. Since the central nervous system (in the global sense) is bilaterally symmetrical, the structure A' on the right will be linked to the structure B' on the left. The total decussation will therefore be shaped like an X. The letter X in the English alphabet resembles the letter "chi" in the Greek alphabet. The best-known decussation in the human central nervous system involves the axons of the left retina's nasal half going to the right half of the brain and the right retina's nasal half going to the left side of the brain. That particular decussation is called the optic chiasma. The word "chiasma" signifies the formation of the letter "chi." See also: **chiasma; great motor decussation; great sensory decussation.**

Deductive reasoning. Thought processes directed from general principles to specific situations.

Deep dyslexia. Deep, or phonic, dyslexia is described as an inability to decode words from phonic-based principles. The dyslexic relies instead on the whole-word approach, with meaning substitutions frequently seen in oral reading miscues (e.g., "humor" is pronounced as "happy"). As with surface dyslexia, deep dyslexia is thought to result from neurological damage.

Deep sleep. A term that has become ambiguous. Some sleep researchers use the term "deep sleep" to refer to REM sleep, while others use it for stage-4 (slow-wave) sleep. See also: **REM sleep; sleep; Stage 1 sleep (ascending); stage 4 sleep**.

Deep structure. The logical and meaningful makeup of a statement that may be expressed in the surface structure in one or another set of words and in either the passive or the active voice. The particular expression (including the words used and active or passive construction) is the surface structure. The distinction between these two types of sentence structure is made by the school of psycholinguistics and its originator, Noam Chomsky. Psycholinguistic theory holds that deep structure is universal, common to all human tongues. Languages are thought to differ only in the surface structures they use. See also: **psycholinguistics; surface structure; universal grammar**.

Defeminizing. Tending to suppress or disrupt feminine characteristics. See also: **adrenogenital syndrome; diethylstilbestrol (DES)**.

Defense mechanism. An attempt to cope with stressful circumstances by adjusting one's own cognitive structures, that is, by rearranging one's way of thinking and/or altering one's beliefs. The individual is only partially, if at all, aware that this procedure is being used. The defense mechanisms were first described by the founder of psychoanalysis, Sigmund Freud. At the center of these various techniques, and involved in all of them, is repression, the selective forgetting of unacceptable memories because they are too shameful or anxiety-provoking to retain. Also see the definitions for each of the individual defense mechanisms: **repression; denial; displacement; identification; intellectualization; projection (in the psychology of personality); rationalization; reaction formation; sublimation.** See also: **stress**.

Defensive aggression. Attacking behavior that occurs in response to the perception of threat.

Defervescence phase. The terminal phase of fever. The temperature set point returns to normal. See also: **chill phase; set point**.

Deindividuation. A lowering of self-awareness resulting from participation in a crowd. As part of either a mob or an organized grouping of persons, the individual loses some of his or her restraint and becomes more willing to act aggressively and do harm to others.

Delacato system. The method of treatment of learning disabilities devised by Delacato and Doman. A key point is the reeducation from the ground up of the individual's patterns of basic locomotion.

Delayed alternation task. A task requiring the subject to alternate between two responses (e.g., turning left and turning right) with a delay inserted between consecutive trials. Delayed alternation is impaired with frontal lobe damage.

Delayed matching-to-sample task. A task in which the subject is first shown one object (i.e., the "sample") and after an interval is given a choice between two objects, one of which is the sample. Selecting the sample results in a reward but selecting the other object goes unrewarded. If new objects are used for each trial, monkeys with damage to the prefrontal cortex have little trouble with the task. However, if the same two objects are used on each trial (a procedure called recurring-items delayed matching-to-sample), monkeys with prefrontal lesions have great difficulty with the task. See also: **delayed nonmatching-to-sample task; frontal lobe; recurring-items delayed matching-to-sample task.**

Delayed nonmatching-to-sample task. A task in which the subject is shown one object (i.e., the "sample") and later is presented with two objects (one of which is the sample). The subject is required to select the other object, not the sample, in order to obtain a reward. Selection of the sample is not rewarded. Monkeys with hippocampal lesions will be impaired at this task, and even more impaired with lesions in both the hippocampus and the amygdala. See also: **delayed matching-to-sample task; hippocampus; amygdaloid nucleus.**

Delirium tremens (DTs). A part of the withdrawal syndrome in alcohol addiction (alcoholism). The DTs involve delusions (false beliefs), hallucinations (abnormal misperceptions), and agitated behavior. See also: **alcohol; alcoholism.**

Delta-9-THC. Tetrahydrocannabinol of the delta-nine form. It is the main psychoactive ingredient in marijuana.

Delta sleep (or **slow-wave sleep**). The portion of sleep in which delta waves may be observed in the EEG (electroencephalogram). Stage 3 sleep has delta waves taking up from 10% to 49% of the record. Stage 4 sleep shows an EEG with over 50% delta waves. See also: **delta waves; electroencephalogram (EEG); sleep; slow-wave sleep**.

Delta sleep-inducing peptide (DSIP). See **Factor**

S.

Delta waves. The slowest rhythms to be observed in the electroencephaloric recording of the activity of the human brain. The range of frequency is from 1/2 a cycle per second to 4 cycles per second. How can there be only a half a cycle per second? That means it requires two full seconds to have the wave form return to the same value of voltage, completing the cycle of voltage changes. These EEG frequencies are observed only in delta sleep, never in waking. The delta waves are the kind of wave referred to in the term "slow-wave sleep." See also: **delta sleep; electroencephalogram; slow-wave sleep**.

Delusion. A false belief held without regard for the evidence. Having delusions is one of the positive symptoms of acute schizophrenia.

Demasculinizing. Tending to suppress or disrupt male characteristics. See also: **androgen insensitivity**.

Dementia (di men′shə, -shē ə, -chə). A pathological decline in mental ability, due to a disease process. There are three such diseases: **Alzheimer's disease, Pick's disease,** and **Creutzfeldt-Jakob's disease**. See also the definition of each.

Dendrite (den′drīt) (from Greek "dendron" = "tree"). A fiber-like outgrowth from the cell body of a neuron. In most cases, the neuron gives off numerous dendrites. Dendrites are tree-like in appearance in two ways: (1) They are tapering in shape, being widest where they leave the cell body and narrowing continuously from there. (2) They give off branches that are tapered in shape, being widest at the original dendrite that gives rise to them. In turn, the branches, too, give off branches. Even those branches are considered to be dendrites. Dendrites are called the receiving fibers of the neuron, because information reaching them from the axon endings of other neurons is funneled toward the cell body. Dendrites do not carry true nerve impulses, but there are voltage changes that spread along their surfaces. Such voltage changes are known as graded and decremental potentials. Unlike the nerve impulse, these voltages can vary in strength (hence, "graded") and weaken the farther they spread (hence, "decremental").

Dendritic spine (den drit′ik). A small, bud-like outgrowth from a dendrite that meets the synaptic bouton from another neuron. See also: **axodendritic synapse.**

Dendritic spine apparatus. Material observed by the electron microscope only inside the dendritic spines of neurons in the cerebral cortex and hippocampus. Another point about dendritic spines in these two brain areas is that they can arise when impulses travel over incoming pathways and, on the other hand, can disappear (from disuse) when no impulses reach them.

Dendritic spine synapse. A synapse in which the postsynaptic membrane is the membrane surrounding a dendritic spine. See also: **axodendritic synapses; dendritic spine.**

Dendritic zone. The sense receptors and their attached small incoming branches of the single nerve fiber (axon) of a unipolar neuron (in Bodian's terminology). See also: **unipolar neuron.**

Denial. One of the defense mechanisms identified by psychoanalyst Sigmund Freud. The individual acts as if a certain past event never happened or as if a present threat does not exist. This obviously can be life-threatening, especially if the threat is a serious one. There is a version of this defense in folklore; it is the myth that a threatened ostrich will bury its head in the sand until the danger blows over. If this myth were true, ostriches would have been extinct years ago! Denial has some relationship to the symptoms of schizophrenia. For one thing, there is a great discrepancy between the emotion shown by the patient and that warranted by the actual circumstances. The buildup of a delusional system (a coherent set of false beliefs) in paranoid schizophrenia can happen more readily if denial of real conditions has already taken place. See also: **defense mechanism.**

2-deoxyglucose (2-DG). A substance very much like glucose. Like glucose it is taken up by active neurons. But it stays in those neurons much longer than glucose does, because the neurons cannot metabolize 2-DG as they do glucose. This makes the compound ideal for autoradiography. A radioactive atom is added to the 2-DG molecule and the atoms can be detected by photographic techniques. See also: **autoradiography.**

Dependent personality disorder. See: **asthenic personality disorder.**

Dependent variable. In experimental research, the "effect" of the cause-and-effect relationship or the result of a manipulated independent variable.

Depolarization (dē pō″lər i zā′shən). A voltage change on the membrane of a nerve cell that lowers the external positive voltage (and, of course, the internal negative voltage). For example, the negative voltage of the cell membrane's interior surface may be reduced from -70 millivolts to -55 millivolts. This kind of change tends to excite the neuron, that is, to lower the resistance against the neuron sending a nerve impulse down the axon. See also: **excitatory post-synaptic potential; nerve impulse.**

Depolarization (dē pō″lər i zā′shən) **blockade.** A decrease in impulse frequency occurring in a neuron following a prolonged period of neural firing.

Deprenyl (dep′rə nəl). A drug that not only controls the symptoms of Parkinson's disease (which *l*-DOPA does), it slows the progression of the disease as well. Deprenyl inhibits the action of an enzyme, monoamine oxidase B, that creates a toxic substance which destroys the substantia nigra. The integrity of the substantia nigra is essential for smooth neuromuscular performance. The enzyme converts an otherwise harmless chemical into the toxin. See also: **catecholamines; *l*-DOPA; enzyme; Parkinson's disease.**

Depressants. Drugs that depress mood and lower the activity level. See also: **alcohol; barbiturates; psychoactive drugs.**

Depression. A condition of melancholy, sad feeling, low motivation, and loss of efficiency that can vary quite widely in severity. More than half of all Americans report that they or some member of their family has had a recent episode of depression. About 10% are depressed at least once a week. Those at the greatest risk are widows, members of minority groups, young people, and those with low earnings. A smaller number suffer the more severe type of condition, known as major depression. See also: **depression (major).**

Depression (major). A common disorder that exists without the presence of mania and is characterized by melancholia, mood swings, loss of appetite (sometimes) and weight (sometimes), constipation (sometimes), and loss of interest in sex (sometimes). Episodes of major depression occur in about 140 men per 100,000 and 4,000 women per 100,000. The rates for major depression increase in men with age but peak in women between the ages of 35 and 45. Both psychological and biochemical causes come to bear. It appears that there is a faulty regulation of the release of one or more amines at synapses in the brain where nerve impulses are generated. A deficiency in the amines results in depression and an excess, mania. Norepinephrine, dopamine, and 5-hydroxytryptamine are the suspected culprits. Many severely depressed individuals have been found to exhibit low levels of the adrenal cortex steroid hormones such as cortisol. Treatment includes antidepressant drugs (which include MAO-inhibiting drugs, tricyclics, and such serotonin-activity enhancing drugs as Prozac), behavior modification, psychotherapy, and cognitive behavior modification. Social factors also contribute to major depression and include poverty, lack of job and education opportunities, and loss of a loved one. See also: **clinical depression**.

Depth perception. This is the perceptual ability to discriminate distances directly in front of the observer. The image projected on the eye's retina is a curved, two-dimensional one. Such an image, in and of itself, does not present enough information for such accurate discrimination. That information is provided by a number of cues. Most of the depth cues are pictorial or monocular; they require the use of only one eye, because they are present in the details of the image. The monocular depth cues include degree of shading, interposition (nearer objects block out part of the view of farther ones), relative height (more distant things seem to be higher up), relative retinal size (the farther away the object is, the smaller its image will be on the retina), and texture differences (the small details of nearer objects are coarse-grained, while those of faraway objects are fine pinpoints of light and darkness). The term "perspective" covers a number of these; "aerial" perspective refers to the blue and hazy look of faraway hills while "linear" perspective refers to the greater height in the visual field and the smaller relative size of far-off objects. More related to physiology are the binocular depth cues of convergence and retinal disparity. As an object comes closer to the observer, the eyes must be rotated inward (i.e., toward the nose) in

order to keep the object in focus. This is the convergence reflex. Feedback from receptors in the tendons of the external eye muscles reports the orientation of the eyes to the brain. The length of the line of sight from either eye to the object is roughly proportional to its distance from the observer. The major cue to visual depth is a second binocular cue, retinal disparity, which is also called binocular parallax or binocular disparity. The images on the two retinae are different from one another, due to the different positions of the left and right eyes. Alternately wink with each eye and you can confirm this for yourself. The magnocellular (or transient) visual neural pathway deals with the binocular cues to depth, among other things. See also: **retinal disparity; transient visual pathway.**

Dermatome. An area of skin innervated by the dorsal root axons of a particular spinal nerve. Each spinal nerve monitors the somatosensory stimulation affecting its own particular dermatome. See also: **Bell-Magendie Law; dorsal roots; somatosensory system; spinal nerves; unipolar neuron.**

Desensitization techniques (dē sen ″si ti zā′shən). The gradual approach to a stimulus which elicits great fear or a phobic anxiety while maintaining a relaxed state. Almost everyone has fears (e.g., heights, snakes) and can be desensitized by following three steps: (1) make a list of fear-provoking actions involving the phobia, ranked from least to most disturbing; (2) learn relaxation techniques; and (3) gradually perform the actions on the list in the order from least disturbing to most disturbing. For example, a fear of heights (acrophobia) can be approached by (1) standing on a chair until there is no anxiety, (2) then standing on a small step ladder until there is no anxiety, (3) then looking down a flight of stairs until there is no anxiety, and so on.

Detoxified addicts. Former drug addicts who have none of the drug in their system and who are no longer experiencing withdrawal symptoms. See also: **alcoholism; drug tolerance; opponent-process theory of drug withdrawal symptoms.**

Deuteranopia (doo″tər ə nō′pē ə, dyoo″-). A form of color blindness (dichromatism) in which the individual cannot distinguish red from green. Green objects look black and red ones look yellow to a deuteranope. This is probably due to the inactivity of the cones that normally respond to green wavelengths. Note: there is another type of red-green color blindness called **protanopia** (see definition).

Developmental approach. This is an approach in which the researcher or professional considers developmental issues for particular age ranges as important to issues of assessment and remediation. Piaget is probably the best-known developmental psychologist; he describes cognitive development in terms of developmental stages.

Developmental dyslexia. A reading disability that is unexpected, due to the absence of cultural deprivation, a physiological syndrome, or a low intelligence level, any of which might have served to account for it.

Developmental neurobiology. A specialty in neuroscience. It is concerned with the study of the growth and development of the nervous system.

Deviant. This term refers to behaviors which are unacceptable in terms of the social mores and rules governing a society. Deviant behavior(s) prevent individuals from successfully adapting to the environment and establishing good interpersonal relationships.

Deviation IQ score. A way of calculating an individual's IQ that allows it to be compared mathematically with other people's IQ scores. Standardized IQ tests have the same mean (100) and standard deviation (usually 15 or 16) for test takers of all ages. This approach involves the use of the mean and standard deviation in relation to the normal (Gaussian) curve. It has superseded the earlier method of comparing the person's mental and chronological ages with each other.

Dextrals ("dexter" = "right" [side] in Latin). Right-handed persons; right-handers.

Diabetes insipidus (dī″ə bē′tēz in sip′i dus) ("Diabetes" means "flows through" in Greek). Excessive urination due to an inadequate supply of the hormone ADH (the antidiuretic hormone), which is normally released by the posterior pituitary gland. To prevent water loss, the individual drinks great amounts of water.

Diabetes mellitus (dī″ə bē′tēz mel′i tus, mə lī′tus). Sometimes called sugar diabetes, this condition is caused by low levels of the hormone insulin, which is secreted by the beta cells of the pancreas. The shortage of insulin leads to the buildup of high blood sugar levels; the amount of glucose in the blood can soar to three times the normal value. Nevertheless, little of this glucose can enter the cells of the body. Patients consume more food than normally because their cells are starved for fuel. Diabetics even lose weight because so much glucose is excreted without having been used. The treatment calls for a low-glucose diet along with daily injections of insulin. See also: **insulin; pancreas.**

Diaschisis (dī as′ki sis). [1] A decrease in the activity of healthy neurons because they have lost a portion of their input (due to damage to the neurons that had supplied axon endings to their synapses). Diaschisis is also a hypothetical concept, since it implies that, following brain injury, function is lost not only from the area destroyed but also (temporarily) from related regions. The functions lost from the related areas will, of course, return after some time. The word means, literally, "to shock thoroughly" in Greek, referring to the lowered activity of undamaged neurons. The cause of diaschisis, as stated earlier, is the reduction of input because the neurons that had been providing input have been destroyed. This diaschisis effect is similar to spinal shock, in which partial spinal cord damage serves (at first) to produce total loss of function in spinal levels below that of the injury, including even the (temporary) loss of spinal reflexes that require no connections with higher parts of the central nervous system. [2] Alteration of the functioning of a part of the brain as the result of disturbance or injury to some distant part of the central nervous system. Diaschisis in this sense may refer to a temporary cognitive impairment as the result of a brain injury, even if the damage is done to an area that is not usually involved in cognition.

Diazepam (dī az′ə pam) **binding inhibitor (DBI).** A brain protein that binds to the receptor sites on nerve cell membranes that accept the benzodiazepines. DBI blocks the action of the benzodiazepine drugs on behavior. See also: **benzodiazepine; carboline.**

Dichhaptic stimulation (dī kap′tik). Presentation of a pair of different-shaped objects, one to the left hand and one to the right. The subject is asked to identify, by touch alone, what he or she is holding.

Dichotic listening (dī kot'ik). A form of auditory test in which the sound message incoming via the left earphone is different from the sound information arriving at the right earphone. Usually, the subject is asked to report, as fully as possible, what he or she is hearing.

Dichromats (dī'krō mats"). These are color-blind individuals who seem to be lacking the specialized retinal receptors for one of the three primary colors, viz., red, green, or blue. Some are red-green blind; others, more rare, are yellow-blue blind. See also: **deuteranopia; protanopia; tritanopia.**

Diencephalon (dī " en sef'ə lon ") (from the Greek "di" = between and "enkephalon" = "brain"; the word "enkephalon" was formed from "en" = "within" and "kephalon" = "the head"). The part of the brain just below and in back of the telencephalon. The diencephalon is the posterior part of the forebrain. The two main parts of the diencephalon are the thalamus and the hypothalamus. The diencephalon is above and in front of the midbrain, so it is <u>between</u> the telencephalon (which includes the cerebral cortex) and the rest of the central nervous system, hence the use of the prefix "di" meaning "between." The third ventricle, a hollow area filled with cerebrospinal fluid, has the thalamus for its walls and the hypothalamus for its floor. See also: **cerebral ventricles; hypothalamus; telencephalon; thalamus.**

Diethylstilbestrol (dī eth"əl stil bes'trôl) **(DES).** A synthetic hormone that mimics estrogen. It has been administered in order to prevent miscarriages, but DES can produce masculinizing effects on the infant female that are comparable to the influence of testosterone, which is a male hormone.

Difference threshold. The smallest recognizable difference between two similar stimuli, such as two lights or two sounds. The difference threshold is also called the <u>just noticeable</u> <u>difference</u> or <u>j n d</u>.

Differential adhesion hypothesis. A hypothesis about the fetal development of the brain. The neural crest cells migrate through tissues by following pathways to which they have a tendency to adhere. This view might have been inspired by the way Velcro works, with the loops on one side and the hooks on the other.

Differentiation. The formation of the axons and dendrites that confer a specific shape on a given neuron. This is the specific case for neurons; "differentiation" is usually used as a general term for the formation of specialized cells from the generalized, undifferentiated body cells of the embryo.

Diffusion. The tendency for dissolved ions or molecules to move from areas in the solution where they are highly concentrated to areas where they are in lower concentration. Diffusion will be completed when the dissolved material is evenly distributed throughout the entire solution. See also: **ion concentration gradient.**

Digestion. The process of food absorption. The food is broken down chemically by digestive enzymes and absorbed into the bloodstream from the gastrointestinal tract.

Digit span. A test of short-term memory capacity. The examiner reads off a string of one-digit numbers, which the subject is required to repeat verbatim. The digit span subtest is incorporated into the Wechsler intelligence tests as part of the measurement of the Verbal IQ. See also: **ACID profile; AVID profile; Wechsler Intelligence Scales; short-term memory (STM).**

Digit span + 1 test. If, in taking the digit span task, the subject correctly repeats a string of digits, the examiner asks for that same series again plus one added digit at the end of the string. See also: **digit span.**

Digital grasp. Grasping an object with the fingers (digits) only, rather than using the whole hand.

Digitized speech. The recording of speech in a digitimized format which is useful for electronic communications and computers.

Dihydrotestosterone. An androgen that cannot be aromatized, i.e., converted to estradiol (a form of the female hormone, estrogen). Testosterone is converted to estrogen or aromatized in the development of the brain. See also: **aromatization; estrogen; testosterone.**

Diphthong. A speech sound involving the combining of two vowels in the same syllable.

Diplophonia (dip"lō fō'nē ə). Producing speech sounds with two different tones at once. Sometimes, this can be prevented by clearing one's throat of mucus or saliva. At other times, however, it may be a sign of physical injury to the vocal cords.

Dipole (dī′pōl″). A double circle (i.e., two circles that touch one another) of flowing positive ions. The dipole travels in both the dromic and the antidromic direction (toward the end brush and toward the cell body, respectively) along the axon during a nerve impulse. The central flow of ions is composed of the sodium ions that have entered a gate in the axon membrane when the membrane was stimulated. Potassium ions are repelled from the entering sodium because like charges repel one another. Both kinds of ions are positively charged. The back of the dipole is composed of potassium ions filling in a negatively charged part of the membrane exterior, thus returning it to its earlier positive charge. The front edge of the dipole is made up of potassium ions thrust against the membrane from inside and providing a new gate for the entry of more sodium ions. What has been the front end of the dipole now becomes the middle of it. Hence, the nerve impulse has moved along the axon by the length of the diameter of one circle. This keeps on repeating itself until the nerve impulse has rolled all the way to the end of the axon. After the impulse is completed, the positive charge on the outside has been restored and the neuron is electrically at the resting potential. It is still not in position to fire off another impulse, though, because the sodium and potassium ions are out of position, with too many potassium ions outside the membrane and too many sodium ions inside the membrane. See also: **depolarization; nerve impulse; polarization; resting potential; sodium-potassium pump.**

Dipsogen. A substance that induces thirst and/or drinking behavior.

Directed synapses. Those synapses in which the presynaptic membranes are in close proximity to the receptor sites on the postsynaptic membrane. At these synapses, the synaptic transmission model of information processing (the "dry" model) is the appropriate one. See also: **information processing; synapse.**

Disability. A loss of the ability to function normally in either the physical (e.g., cerebral palsy) or cognitive (e.g., dyslexia, a learning disability) realms. Disabilities interfere with normal growth and development. Although the term "disability" is used synonymously with "dysfunction" and

"disorder," it is a more specific reference to a problem.

Disabled. An individual who has a disability or disabilities. See also: **disability.**

Discrepancy analysis. Following the measurement of a number of abilities that a student might have, the profile of high and low scores on all these abilities is examined. If one of the scores is so low that the student is expected to be unable to participate in some activity, the teacher records the type and level of assistance that the student will need and the materials and methods needed to implement that special training.

Discriminated Pavlovian conditioning. A classical (Pavlovian) conditioning procedure in which conventional training trials (with the conditioned stimulus presented just before the unconditioned stimulus) are interspersed with presentations of a stimulus strongly resembling the conditioned stimulus (but which is never followed by a presentation of the unconditioned stimulus). The conditioned response will originally be made to both the conditioned stimulus and its look-alike (or sound-alike, or smell-alike, or whatever) because of the natural stimulus generalization process. The subject soon learns to respond to the conditioned stimulus and to withhold responding to the generalized stimulus. See also: **classical conditioning; stimulus discrimination; stimulus generalization.**

Discriminative stimulus. A stimulus in the presence of which a learned response is reinforced (during **operant conditioning**); in the absence of that stimulus, the same response is not reinforced. The discriminative stimulus is said to "set the occasion for responding." An example of a discriminative stimulus would be approaching a red traffic light, which sets the occasion for a driver to step on his or her brake pedal. See also: **operant conditioning; stimulus discrimination; stimulus generalization.**

Disfluency. A speech problem marked by hesitations, prolongations, and repetitions. Many refer to this as stuttering.

Dishabituation. The removal of habituation by stimulation. Another term for dishabituation would be sensitization. The sudden release of responding (mediated by an added novel stimulus) to a repeated regular, but not behaviorally significant, stimulus to which the subject has been habituated (i.e., the subject was no longer re-sponding to the familiar stimulus at the time of the dishabituation). Sudden loud noises are great choices as dishabituating stimuli; they tend to make us "jumpy", ready to react to any old stimulus that we would have ignored a moment before. See also: **habituation; sensitization.**

Disinhibition (dis″in i bi′shən). The active proc-ess of removing inhibition.

Disorder. A disturbance of or difficulty in normal functioning in the psychological (e.g., neurosis), social (e.g., conduct disorder), academic (e.g., learning disorder), or cognitive (e.g., amnesia) realms. One may evidence a disorder(s) in one or more of the mentioned areas. A disorder such as dyslexia, which is a specific type of learning disorder, is called a disability. See also: **disabil-ity.**

Disordered. An adjective describing an individual who has (a) disorder(s).

Disorganized schizophrenia. A variety of schizo-phrenia in which the patient's chief symptoms are incoherence, silliness, inappropriate emo-tional responding, and speaking in jumbled phrases (word salad), but without well-patterned delusions. This condition was once called he-bephrenia.

Displacement. One of the defense mechanisms identified by the psychoanalyst Sigmund Freud. An emotional reaction (such as fear or anger) appropriate for one object in the environment is irrationally switched to another, otherwise ir-relevant, object. For example, if one is angered by a powerful, large individual, one might dis-place the angry feelings on a weak, small target. Displacement of fear is considered to be the dy-namic cause of phobias. An example of this would be a boy, who, instead of expressing fear of his domineering father, exhibits fear of horses instead. See also: **defense mechanism.**

Dissociative disorder (di sō′sē ā″tiv, -shē-, -ə tiv). A category of neurotic behavior problems involving sudden changes of consciousness, per-sonal identity, or motor activity. Dissociations may involve sensory or motor losses (as in hys-teria) or dramatic personality changes (as in multiple personality disorder).

Distal (from Latin "distans" = "far off"). Toward the extremities (e.g., the fingers or toes), far off the midline of the body. Alternatively, the term means away from the point of origin or attach-ment of a body part. The antonym of "distal" is "proximal."

Distal segment. After an axon is severed, one part, the proximal part, remains attached to the cell body at the end opposite to the cut. The other segment, which is the distal segment, is the one that is still attached to the telodendria and the synaptic boutons. The terms "proximal" and "distal", in the context of a severed axon, refer to location relative to the cell body. All other pos-sible meanings, e. g., relative to the body's midline, are irrelevant, in this context. The axon undergoes one kind of degeneration (anterograde or Wallerian) in the distal segment and another kind (retrograde degeneration) in the proximal segment. See also: **retrograde degeneration; Wallerian degeneration.**

Distension. The filling up of the stomach or intes-tines. This is a satiation cue, telling the individ-ual to stop eating. Impulses arrive at the brain over neurons stimulated by the distension of the stomach and small intestine, increasing the sa-tiety stimulation received by the brain. See also: **cholecystokinin.**

Distortion. A disorder of articulation in which the correct sound is replaced by a sound that is alien to the language being used. See also: **articula-tion disorder.**

Diuretic. A process that steps up the production of urine and the rate of urination. The application of cold to an area of the skin has a diuretic ef-fect; so does drinking large amounts of fluid. In addition, some drugs can be termed diuretics be-cause they have such activity. Caffeine is an ex-ample of a diuretic.

Diurnal. Daily. "Diurnal" is the antonym of "nocturnal."

Divergent thinking. A flexible style of thinking that involves originality and creativity. The in-dividual using this mode of reasoning will con-sider several solutions to a problem. The oppo-site form of reasoning is called convergent thinking. See also: **convergent thinking.**

Dizygotic twins. Fraternal twins. Twins that de-velop from two different zygotes (fertilized eggs). Unlike the case with identical twins, it is possible for fraternal twins to be of two different sexes. See also: **fraternal twins.**

DMPEA (dimethoxyphenylethylamine) (dī″me

thok″sē fen″əl eth'əl ə mēn″, -fēn″-). A compound discovered in the urine of schizophrenic patients. As a memory aid, think of "D.M. Pee" as the
compound from urine. When purified and ingested
by a normal subject, DMPEA can produce hallucinations. The compound is a catecholamine and
closely resembles the natural hallucinogen mescaline in its chemical structure.

Dominant gene. The form of the gene (allele) for a
given trait that overrides the other form of the gene
in an individual with one allele of each type. Such
an individual is heterozygous for the trait in question. The other allele, the one that takes a back seat
to the dominant one, is called the recessive gene. In
the example of eye color, a person having an allele
for brown and an allele for blue will have brown
eyes, because the brown allele is the dominant gene.
See also: **allele; heterozygous; recessive gene.**

DNA (Deoxyribonucleic acid) (dē ok″sē rī′bō noo
klē′ik). This is the basic blueprint for our human
existence and constitutes the make-up of our 46
chromosomes. Approximately 50,000 to 100,000
genes are located on these chromosomes.

Dominant hemisphere. A term for the cortical
hemisphere (a) related to the dominant arm and leg
and (b) including Broca's area (for motor speech),
Wernicke's area (for speech reception), and the
larger-sized planum temporale (of the left and right
plana). In most persons, including almost all the
right-handers, the dominant hemisphere is the left
hemisphere, which receives most of the sensations
from the right side of the body, visual information
from the right visual field, most of its auditory input
from the right ear, provides most of the motor
commands to the muscles of the right side, and
houses the main language areas. In some persons,
including less than half of all left-handers, the
dominant hemisphere is the right one. In a few persons, neither hemisphere is clearly dominant. See
also: **hemisphere asymmetry; hemispheric dominance.**

l-**DOPA.** A drug that has been of great help to patients with Parkinson's disease. It is a precursor of
the chemical neurotransmitter dopamine (DA). DA
is not available to the telencephalic basal ganglia of
the patient's brain, due to the deterioration of the
midbrain's substantia nigra, whose axons normally
release DA at their synapses with the forebrain basal ganglia. Dopamine, being an amine, cannot
cross the blood-brain barrier. DOPA, which has an
amino acid structure, is able to cross the blood-
brain barrier. Once in the brain, the DOPA is
picked up by forebrain neurons and metabolized
into the needed dopamine. This medication stops
the further progress of Parkinsonism, but cannot reverse it. See also: **basal ganglia; blood-brain barrier; dopamine; Parkinson's disease; substantia
nigra.**

Dopamine (dō′pə mēn″) **(DA).** One of the
catecholamine chemical neurotransmitters. It is
simpler in structure than either norepinephrine or
epinephrine and therefore dopamine is a preliminary stage, a precursor, in the preparation of these
other catecholamines. A shortage of dopamine in
the basal ganglia leads to the neuromuscular disease Parkinsonism. It is hypothesized that an excess
of brain dopamine leads to the psychosis known as
schizophrenia. The receptor sites for dopamine are
not all of the same functional type; the dopamine
receptors come in four varieties, imaginatively labeled D_1, D_2, D_3, and D_4.

Dopamine hypothesis (dō′pə mēn″). This is the
hypothesis that overactivity of dopamine in the
cerebral cortex and basal ganglia leads to schizophrenia. The effectiveness of haloperidol in controlling the positive symptoms of acute schizophrenia (delusions and hallucinations) is supportive
of this view, because this drug lowers the level of
dopamine activity in the brain. Another argument
for the hypothesis is the occasional appearance of
schizophrenic symptoms in patients with Parkinsonism who have been given the drug *l*-DOPA,
which is a precursor of dopamine; the possibility is
that the drug was too successful, not only supplying
dopamine in quantities sufficient to alleviate the
symptoms of Parkinsonism but overdoing it enough
to generate the delusions and hallucinations of
schizophrenia. Still more evidence comes from the
unusually high numbers of dopamine receptor sites
identified in the brains of deceased schizophrenia
patients.

Dopaminergic or **dopinergic.** An adjective referring
to axons that release the neurotransmitter dopamine
at their terminals. See also: **dopamine; neurotransmitter.**

Dorsal (dôr′səl). Toward the anatomical back. The
shoulder blades are always dorsal structures,
whether the animal in question is a biped
(two-legged, like an ape or a human being) or a
quadruped (four-legged). The antonym of dorsal is

ventral. A dorsal structure can be considered <u>posterior</u>, in the case of a biped, or <u>superior,</u> in the case of a quadruped. A human's shoulders are behind (posterior to) the rest of the body; a dog's shoulders are above (superior to) most of the rest of its body. A special and very important exception is the human brain. Where the brain comes out of the spinal cord, the central nervous system takes a right angle bend forward, so the biped brain is oriented in space the same way as the quadruped brain. This permits the eyes and nostrils to be directed to the environment in front of the creature. Consequently, in the case of the human brain, the word "dorsal" is usually synonymous with the word "superior."

Dorsal-column medial-lemniscus system. The sensory pathway carrying deep pressure (i.e., touch from below the epidermis or top skin layer) sensory messages. Stimulation affects deep-pressure-sensitive endings of some unipolar neurons. Impulses travel past the dorsal root ganglion and reach cell bodies in the dorsal horn of the gray butterfly. The axon of the dorsal horn neuron ascends in the dorsal funiculus of the spinal cord's white matter with either the gracile or the cuneate tract. These tracts (the dorsal columns) terminate in the gracile and cuneate nuclei in the posterior half of the medulla, the lowermost (hindmost) part of the brain. The axons from the cell bodies in those two nuclei sweep across the midline (forming the great sensory decussation) and run through the pons and the midbrain, with synaptic endings at the posterior ventral nucleus of the thalamus (PVNT). That tract from the gracile and cuneate nuclei to the PVNT is called the medial lemniscus. The axons that arise from cell bodies in the PVNT pass through the internal capsule and radiate to the postcentral gyrus, the most rostral portion of the parietal lobe. The postcentral gyrus includes Brodmann's areas 1, 2, and 3; it is the projection area for all the somesthetic senses (deep pressure, light touch, pain, warmth, cold, and kinesthesis). See also: **Brodmann numbering system; cuneate nucleus; cuneate tract; dorsal columns; dorsal funiculus; dorsal horn; dorsal root ganglion; gracile nucleus; gracile tract; gray butterfly; lemniscus; medial lemniscus; parietal lobe; posterior ventral nucleus of the thalamus; somatosensory system; somesthesia.**

Dorsal column nuclei. See: **gracile nucleus** and **cuneate nucleus.**

Dorsal columns (also called the **posterior columns**). The two large tracts of the dorsal funiculus of the spinal cord (namely the <u>gracile</u> and <u>cuneate</u> tracts) which carry somatosensory messages from the <u>dorsal horns</u> of the spinal cord's <u>gray butterfly</u> to the <u>gracile</u> and <u>cuneate</u> nuclei of the <u>medulla.</u> Ultimately, the information arrives at the <u>postcentral gyrus</u> of the <u>parietal lobe</u> of the <u>cerebral cortex.</u> See also: **cuneate nucleus; cuneate tract; dorsal funiculus; dorsal horn; gracile nucleus; gracile tract; gray butterfly; somatosensory system; spinal cord.**

Dorsal funiculus (dôr′səl fə nik′ yoo lus, fyoo-) ("funiculus" = little cable from Latin "funis" = "cable"). One of three major collections of white matter (i.e., myelin-covered axons) visible in cross-sections of the spinal cord. In the lower segments of the spinal cord, the dorsal funiculus carries only one tract, the gracile tract, which reports the deep pressure sensations of the lower trunk and lower extremities. Throughout the upper segments of the spinal cord (the thoracic and cervical segments), the cuneate tract fills in the lateral portion of the dorsal funiculus, with the gracile tract left to the medial side of the funiculus. The cuneate tract supplies deep pressure sensory information from the upper torso and upper extremities. The two tracts together are known as the dorsal or the posterior columns. See also: **cuneate tract; dorsal columns; dorsal horn; gracile tract; somatosensory system; spinal cord.**

Dorsal horn. The horn-like extensions of the centrally located gray matter of the spinal cord (one on the left side, one on the right) that point toward the dorsal surface of the cord. At some points the dorsal horns actually contact the outer surface of the cord. The dorsal horns receive the incoming axons of the dorsal roots of spinal nerves.

Dorsal root. The dorsal fork of a spinal nerve. The fibers of unipolar neurons flow to a dorsal point of entry in the spinal cord at each of the 31 levels known as the spinal cord segments. These are incoming (sensory) fibers that are cylindrical, like axons, and carry nerve impulses, like axons. Their cell bodies contact these fibers at only one point, so that the neurons are of the <u>unipolar</u> variety. The same fiber now flowing past the cell body becomes a conventional axon with synapses, in most cases, within the dorsal horn of the gray butterfly, although a few continue through into the ventral horn before coming to a synapse. The cluster of cell bodies at a given segment is the **dorsal root ganglion** (see definition) for that segment. See also: **gray butterfly.**

Dorsal root ganglion (gang′glē ən). Cluster of cell bodies of the peripheral nervous system found just outside the spinal cord at each of the cord's 31 segments. There would be two per spinal cord segment since the spinal nerves occur in left and right pairs, and the spinal cord is bilaterally symmetrical. These cell bodies are parts of unipolar neurons carrying somatosensory information into the central nervous system.

Dorsolateral corticospinal tract. See **dorsolateral tract.**

Dorsolateral corticorubrospinal pathway (the "rubro" is from the Latin "ruber" which = "red"). A neural pathway of the motor control system, which involves two tracts. The first tract consists of axons running from the basal ganglia and widespread areas of the cerebral cortex to the red nucleus of the midbrain; this is the corticorubral tract. The corticorubral tract axons make synaptic connections with the neurons in the red nucleus. From the red nucleus, axons decussate (i.e., run across the midline) and travel all the way to the spinal cord, continuing (in the lateral funiculus of the spinal cord white matter) to the ventral horn cells of the spinal cord's gray butterfly. This second tract is the rubrospinal tract. The ventral horn motoneurons, in turn, send axons to the muscles. See also: **basal ganglia; extrapyramidal motor fibers; gray butterfly; lateral funiculus; midbrain; motoneurons; red nucleus; ventral horn.**

Dorsolateral (dôr″sō lat′ər əl) **tract**. The crossed or decussated continuation of the pyramidal tract in the spinal cord. These axons are concerned with the control of the extremities, that is, the toes and fingers. See also: **decussation; pyramidal tract; spinal cord.**

Dorsomedial thalamus. A set of nerve cell bodies located in the superior and near-midline portion of the thalamus. Damage to this region has been linked to the type of memory loss that occurs in Korsakoff's syndrome. See also: **Korsakoff's syndrome.**

Double-barreled micropipette. A micropipette is a very fine tube used to analyze small amounts of fluid. A double-barreled micropipette consists of two coupled micropipettes and is used in microion-

tophoretic analysis of tissues. See also: **microiontophoretic.**

Double bind. A problematic situation in which a person is given two different, and logically inconsistent, messages from an authority figure. This is theoretically a developmental trap that could lead the individual into a mental disorder, such as schizophrenia.

Double-blind control. A research technique in which (1) the subject is not informed as to whether he or she is getting the experimental or the control treatment, and (2) the experimenter who scores the dependent variable (i.e., the subject's behavior) is also unaware of whether the subject is receiving the experimental or the control treatment.

Double dissociation technique. A control procedure used in planned experimental ablation studies or in neuropsychological testing research on brain-damaged human patients. The idea is to include subjects having one of two kinds of brain injury; they are tested on two kinds of behavior, with one behavior hypothesized to be impaired by the first type of brain damage and the second behavior hypothesized to be disrupted by the second type of brain damage. If both hypothesized outcomes are found, with no cross-over (i.e., no disrupted behavior resulting from the hypothetically nonrelated damage), both hypotheses gain more credibility than they would have had the results been obtained from two separate studies. For example, with some human subjects suffering right hemispheric damage and others having injuries to the left hemisphere, an experimenter assigns all the subjects two tasks: (1) counting all the blocks in a two-dimensional drawing of an irregular pile of blocks and (2) reading a passage from an unfamiliar piece of written material. If only the right-hemisphere-damaged subjects show impairment of block counting, and only the left-hemisphere-damaged subjects show impaired reading performance, the double dissociation has been established. See also: **Corsi's Block-Tapping Test; Hebb's Recurring-Digits Test.**

Down's syndrome. A disorder resulting from a genetic abnormality which involves having an extra chromosome added to the 21st pair. This genetic problem occurs in about 1 out of 700 live births, with older mothers being at higher risk. This syndrome was originally described by Down in 1866; Down termed the condition "mongolism" because he thought the facial features of individuals with the syndrome indicated a "throwback" to the "more primitive" mongolian race. The original terminology was, clearly, racist. As a result, the name of the disorder has been changed to honor its discoverer. Chromosome 21 (We normally have 23 pairs of chromosomes.) is where the relevant gene, beta-APP, is located (see **chromosome 21 trisomy**). Physical characteristics such as round faces and small folds of skin along the inner edges of the eyes distinguish individuals with Down's syndrome. Individuals with Down's syndrome also develop **senile plaques** and **neurofibrillary tangles** (see definitions) in their 40s and 50s. Excessive amyloid protein deposits begin accumulating during the teen years; these are a forerunner of the plaques and tangles to follow. Senile **dementia** similar to that occurring in **Alzheimer's disease** (see definitions) may well accompany these plaques and tangles. Many Down's syndrome individuals are retarded, although not all of them are. The retardation is usually mild. These individuals tend to have cheerful dispositions.

Drive theory or **drive-reduction theory**. The belief that organisms are motivated to behave in certain ways because certain needs arise that require action to maintain balanced, regular conditions within the body. The arousal of need-reducing behavior is called a drive. When the organism is deprived of a needed substance, such as food, its behavior is directed toward the obtaining of food in order to reduce that state of need. When the goal is food, the drive to perform this goal-oriented behavior is called hunger. Many motivation theorists believe that not all our motives are restricted to drives that reflect physiological needs. See also: **hunger drive; motivation; need.**

Dromic (drō'mik) or **orthodromic**. The direction of flow of a nerve impulse down the axon toward the end brush at the tip of the axon. If an axon is stimulated in the middle, the resulting nerve impulse will travel in the natural (dromic) direction and also toward the cell body, the antidromic direction. See also: **antidromic; dipole; nerve impulse.**

Drug metabolism. The chemical process by which the molecules of an active drug are altered into nonactive chemical products. Such metabolic actions take place in the body cells generally and in the liver in particular. The liver, as a matter of note, does the general detoxification work of the body. See also: **drug tolerance.**

Drug self-administration paradigm. An experimental set-up in which an animal performs an operant response (e.g., pressing a lever in a Skinner box) to receive small injections of a drug as positive reinforcements. The drug is administered through a chronically implanted hypodermic. See also: **chronic; operant conditioning; positive reinforcement.**

Drug therapy. The treatment of emotional/ behavioral/ mental disorders by prescribed drugs.

Drug tolerance. A decreased reaction to a drug after the drug has been in continuous use. Tolerance mechanisms are found in individual cells and in the liver as well. See also: **opponent process theory of drug-withdrawal symptoms.**

DSM III and **DSM-III-R**. Respectively, the third edition and the revised third edition of the Diagnostic and Statistical Manual of Mental Disorders published by the American Psychiatric Association; the DSM-III-R is the more recent version. Both versions are similar, with the DSM-III-R reflecting more accurately specific clinical syndromes in order to provide a more valid and reliable differential diagnosis. For example, in the DSM-III-R, a new measure called the Global Assessment of Functioning (GAF) Scale assesses current mental health functioning on a continuum. A total of more than 200 disorders in 17 categories are described, with each disorder given specific descriptive criteria. Causality is not assumed in these descriptions, so that practitioners in the field can use this system regardless of a specific theoretical approach. The DSM-III-R includes five separate axes of evaluation. Axis I covers clinical mental/ behavioral/ emotional syndromes plus what are referred to as "V codes," namely, conditions relevant to diagnosis or treatment that are not attributable to a mental disorder. Axis II deals with developmental and personality factors. Axis III is concerned with physical disorders. Axis IV reflects psychosocial stressors. Axis V has to do with the global assessment of functioning. The following shows how the five axes are used in arriving at a full evaluation of a patient: Axis I. Schizophrenia, undifferentiated, chronic with acute exacerbation. Axis II. Borderline intellectual functioning. Axis III. Late effects of viral encephalitis. Axis IV. Psychosocial stressor: death of mother; severity rating 5 (acute event). Axis V. Current GAF = 28; highest GAF during preceding year was 40. The GAF is a rating scale that runs from 1 (a very serious threat to others and/or a strong risk of suicide) to 90 (minimal problems of adjustment). In this particular example, the rating of 40 is still low enough to indicate that the patient has very serious problems of social adjustment and is probably unable to keep friends or hold a job.

DSM-IV. This is the fourth edition of the American Psychiatric Association's Diagnostic and Statistical Manual of Mental Disorders. This manual is a clinical guide to the classification of mental disorders which is based on five axes: (1) Axis I. Clinical Disorders; (2) Axis II. Personality Disturbances, (3) Axis III. General Medical Problems, (4) Axis IV. Environmental and Psychological/Social Interaction Problems, and (5) Axis V. Overall Global Functioning.

Dualism. The position taken on the mind-brain problem that there are two separate kinds of reality, the mental and the material. See also: **double-aspect theory; interactionism; mind-brain problem; monism; pineal gland; psychophysical parallelism.**

Dual-center assumption. The concept that the control of food-related behavior depends on two centers: a hunger center, which turns eating activity on, and a satiety center, which sends out commands to stop eating. The prime candidate for the hunger center seems to be the lateral hypothalamus and the best bet for the satiety center would seem to be the ventral medial nucleus of the hypothalamus (VMNH). See also: **hunger; lateral hypothalamus; ventromedial hypothalamus.**

Dual-opponent color cells. Neurons (of the visual neural pathway) that respond to one color in the center of their receptive field and to the complementary color in the surround of their receptive field. See also: **center (of receptive field); complementary colors; opponent-process theory of color vision; receptive field; surround.**

Dual-route models. Explanatory models that account for cognitive functioning by the activity of two different neural pathways. See also: **cognitive neuropsychology.**

Duodenal (dōo͞ō dē′nəl, dōo od′ə nəl). Pertaining to the duodenum, which is the first part of the small intestine, the part which is attached to the stomach. It is through the duodenal wall that the bloodstream receives most of the glucose and the amino acids that it absorbs. One of the hormones released from the duodenum is cholecystokinin

(CCK), which seems to signal satiation and cause reduced eating in the organism. Cholecystokinin is also released by some neurons in the brain as a neurotransmitter. See also: **cholecystokinin; distension.**

Duplexity (or duplicity) theory. The theory (originated by von Kries in the 1890s) that there are two kinds of visual receptors (i.e., the rods and the cones), each related to a different visual system. The rods and their pathway operate under scotopic conditions (dim light), whereas the cones and their neural connections are active in photopic conditions (bright daylight). See also: **cones; rods.**

Dura mater (dōo͞′rə mā′tər, dyōo͞′rə). The outermost of the three membranes (meninges) that surround the brain and spinal cord. The name literally means "hard mother" (remember that!), although the "mater" here is intended to mean something like "matrix" or "material." The dura mater is white, tough, and leathery. It fits around the brain like a skullcap. Below the dura mater is the subdural space, which contains venous blood. A head injury rupturing the dura is called a subdural hematoma, in which excessive blood pressure compresses the brain to such an extent that the ventricles are displaced.

Dyadic relationship. A relationship between two individuals.

Dynamic assessment. A technique for the combination of assessment with instruction. The student's readiness to learn a subject matter is assessed and the testing is supplemented with instruction in the relevant academic area. This approach is recommended for students with nonmainstream cultural backgrounds.

Dynamic phase. The first phase of the hyperphagia (overeating to obesity) process resulting form the bilateral destruction of the ventromedial hypothalamus in laboratory animals. A hyperphagic rat will overeat until his weight reaches three times the normal. A rat that would normally weigh 1.5 pounds will gain weight until reaching 4.5 pounds. That period of rapid weight-gain is the dynamic phase. The dynamic phase ends when the new (3 X normal) set point is reached. After this, the animal settles into the static phase of hyperphagia, eating enough to maintain, but not increase, its weight. See also: **hypothalamic hyperphagia; set point; static phase; ventromedial hypothalamus.**

Dynamic contraction. Increased tone in a muscle

sufficient to cause the muscle to contract, shortening its length, and thus move a part of the body. In addition to this phasic increase in muscle tone (resulting in movement), there is also the kind of increased muscle tone that increases the supporting value of the limbs, a tonic increase in muscle tone, as described in the definition of cocontraction. See also: **cocontraction; phasic; tonic.**

Dysarthria (dis är'thrē ə). A speech disorder resulting from an impairment of either the peripheral or the central nervous system.

Dyscalculia (dis˝kal kyoo'lē ə). A difficulty in performing arithmetic tasks such that the individual's performance is well below the standard expected of her or him on the basis of IQ, age level, or grade level.

Dysdiadochokinesia (dis˝dī ad˝ō kō ki nē' zē ə, -zhə). The impairment of the ability to make rapid alternating motions such as those used in hand clapping. It may result from damage to the cerebellum. See also: **adiadochokinesia.**

Dyseidesia (dis˝ī dē zhə, -zē ə). The inability to recognize complex visual stimuli. This is considered by some to be a subtype of dyslexia. See also: **dyslexia; dysphonesia.**

Dyseidetic dyslexia (dis˝ī det'ik dis lek'sē ə). The inability to read words visually.

Dysgraphia (dis graf'ē ə). The relative inability to write based on extreme spelling disability which is due not to observable brain damage but to a developmental, probably genetic, condition.

Dyslexia (dis lek'sē ə). An inability to read which is inappropriate to the individual's level of general intelligence. In other words, there is a discrepancy between an individual's innate abilities (i.e., as measured by IQ tests) and reading/language performance. Dyslexia is thought to: (1) co-occur with social (e.g., more negative interactions with others) and behavioral (e.g., attention deficits) difficulties; (2) last a lifetime, with residual symptoms in adulthood after successful interventions (e.g., spelling problems, reduced reading rate, etc.); (3) be caused by some type of neurological dysfunctioning; (4) be genetically based or "run" in families; (5) involve different subtypes, with your authors favoring a visual-dysphonetic subtype, an auditory-linguistic subtype, and a mixed subtype (i.e., with visual/auditory-language deficiencies); and (6) require specific educational strategies and interventions as well as assistance from other professionals when needed (e.g., medical, psychological, etc.). See also: **alexia; auditory dyslexia; dyseidesia; dyseidetic dyslexia; dysnemkinesia; dysphonesia; dysphonetic-dyseidetic dyslexia; dysphonetic dyslexia; linguistic deficiency dyslexic subtype; visual dyslexia; visual-dysphonetic dyslexic.**

Dysnemkinesia (dis nem'ki nē˝zē ə, -zhə). The third of Christiansen, Griffin, and Wesson's subtypes of dyslexia, involving eye-movement disorders. Their first two subtypes are Boder's **dysphonesia** and **dyseidesia** (see definitions).

Dysphasia (dis fā'zhə, -zē ə). A developmental syndrome identified by P. Tallal. It is defined as a specific dysfunction in the development of speech and language which involves: an auditory temporal-processing deficit; a visual temporal-processing deficit that is spontaneously resolved in later childhood; and a strong positive relationship between the extent of the auditory temporal-processing difficulty and the extent of receptive language (i.e., the ability to listen to words and decode verbal sounds) impairment. The latter suggests that there may be an overlap, even a convergence, of the dysphasic population and the population of dyslexic persons. See also: **aphasia; dyslexia.**

Dysphonesia (dis˝fō nē'zhə, -zē ə). The inability to learn the phonic elements for which visual symbols stand. Some consider this a subtype of **dyslexia** (see definition).

Dysphonetic dyslexia (dis˝fō net'ik dis lek'sē ə). The inability to read words by using appropriate grapheme-phoneme conversions.

Dysphonetic-dyseidetic dyslexia (dis˝fō net'ik-dis ˝ī det'ik dis lek'sē ə). The type of dyslexia which is a combination in one person of two types, the dysphonetic and the dyseidetic. This is also called the "mixed" form of dyslexia. See also: **dyseidesia; dysphonesia.**

Dyspnea (disp nē'ə, disp'nē ə). Difficulty in breathing, hunger for air, gasping. In extreme cases, there may be cyanosis (bluish discoloration of the skin).

Dyssomnia. A term used for sleep disorders in general. See also: **apnea; circadian rhythm sleep disorder; hypersomnia; insomnia; narcolepsy; sleep disorders.**

Dysthymic disorder (dis thī'mik). A depressive neurosis. This disorder frequently occurs with other neurotic symptoms, such as phobia, anxiety, or hypochondria. A dysthymic disorder is diagnosed if an external cause can be found; the person exhibits a disproportionate or prolonged depressive reaction to a distressful experience(s). Dysthymia will continue even after removal of the causal factor(s). The mood depression is chronic, lasting two or more years, but it is not as profoundly low as that which typifies major depression.

E

Eardrum (also called the **tympanic membrane**). The cone-shaped, elastic piece of skin in the auditory canal that covers the entrance to the middle ear. The tympanic membrane acts like the diaphragm of a microphone; its vibrations copy the vibrations of the air molecules in the auditory canal that are alternately compressed and spaced-out in the sound waves. See also: **hearing; outer ear.**

Early intervention. Services intended for the development and well-being of infants and young children whenever those children appear to be at risk for, or are exhibiting, developmental delays and/or disabilities. See also: **developmental dyslexia; disability.**

Echoic memory (e kō′ik). Auditory sensory memory. This type of memory involves auditory stimuli, whereby sounds seem to echo (thus the name) in one's head for up to 2 seconds. One can usually store about five items in echoic memory as compared to nine or ten items in iconic (visual) memory. See also: **encoding; engram; iconic memory; linguistic coding; memory trace; motor code.**

Echolalia (ek″ō lā′lē ə). Imitation of the speech sounds of others.

Ecological inventory. A strategy for individualizing instruction by identifying the specific abilities required for a child to function independently in her or his present and future environments.

Ecological model. A model to account for behavior problems and learning disabilities that assumes they are the product of the child's interaction with other persons in the child's social environment.

Ectoderm. The fertilized egg, or zygote, forms three layers of cells, an outer, a middle, and an innermost layer. The outer layer, the ectoderm, later develops into the skin, the nerve cells, and almost all of the neuroglia, with the sole exception being the microglia.

Ectotherms (ek′tō thûrmz). Animals (e.g., insects, fish, and reptiles) that receive most of their body heat from the environment. They are known as cold-blooded or poikilothermic animals.

Edema. The excess buildup of serous (watery) fluid in one of the body tissues or cavities.

Edge detector. A neuron in the visual system that responds to visual stimuli with sharp contours or edges between areas with different colors or black and white. In the frog, for example, the ganglion cells of the retina do the edge detecting. In that animal, there are moving edge detectors and also sustained contrast detectors (for stationary edges).

Educable mentally retarded (EMR). A term applied to the mildly mentally retarded, emphasizing their ability to profit from instruction in basic academic subjects, such as reading, mathematics, and science. Vocational training is usually possible. Independent living in adulthood is also possible. The IQ range for this category of persons is 50 to 70. See also: **mild mental retardation.**

Efferent (ef′ər ent) (from Latin "ex" = "out from"; "ferent" = "carrying"). Motor. Efferent neurons carry messages out from the brain and/or spinal cord to the muscles and/or glands. Hence, efferent neurons are motor neurons. The antonym of "efferent" is "afferent." To keep straight the difference between "afferent" and "efferent," remember that the efferent fibers go to the muscles and glands, which are the body's effectors. See also: **afferent.**

Ego-dystonic homosexuality. The pathological type of homosexuality. The individual has extreme anxiety and shame about his or her sexual orientation. Without this disturbed sense of self, mere homosexuality is not considered to be pathological. See also: **homosexuality.**

Eidetic imagery (ī det′ik). Also known as photographic memory, this occurs when the person can retain a visual image clear enough to be scanned mentally and retained in memory for longer than 30 seconds. The individual with this ability can reconstruct a complex picture in full detail. For example, a painting of a crowd scene can be shown to a subject for one minute and then turned over. The subject is then asked to describe the painting as fully as possible. Individuals with this ability achieve remarkable accuracy in such tasks. This ability is found mostly in children; it is estimated that 8 out of 100 children possess eidetic imagery.

Ejaculation (i jak″yo͞o lā′shən). The expulsion of sperm from the penis.

Electroconvulsive shock (ECS). See: **electroconvulsive therapy (ECT).**

Electroconvulsive therapy (ECT) (i lek″trō kən vul′siv). The treatment of mental disorders by administering an electric current to the patient's head; the shock is applied either bilaterally (to both cerebral hemispheres) or unilaterally (to one hemisphere). A mild electric current, but strong enough to cause a seizure (a loss of consciousness) is sent across the head from one ear to the other for 1/25th of a second. ECT will at times produce convulsions and temporary comas. Inasmuch as the current can destroy brain cells, this treatment is controversial. It is to be used only when medication and behavioral therapies have been attempted and have proven unsuccessful.

Electrocardiogram (ECG or EKG). A recording of the increases and decreases of voltage from the cardiac muscles. See also: **cardiac muscle.**

Electroencephalogram (EEG) (i lek″trō en sef′ə lə gram″). The record of voltage changes measured from the surface of the cerebral cortex. Electrodes placed on shaven positions of the scalp each record the summed electrical potentials (i.e., voltages) of numerous neurons. Each electrode is wired to the electromagnetic control mechanisms of a separate pen on a polygraph (which is a multiple-pen recorder). The evaluation of EEG data from children is complicated by the fact that, during development, variations between EEG records at different stages of growth are to be expected. EEG output can be affected by illness or by metabolic irregularities. Despite such limitations, the EEG is a useful tool for evaluating adults and children with psychiatric complaints, suspected epilepsy, brain trauma, or convulsive disorder. The EEG is a vital tool with comatose patients; it measures the presence or absence of "brain death" in such cases. See also: **BEAM.**

Electromyogram (EMG). A measure of the electrical activity (in the form of voltage increases and decreases) of the skeletal muscles. Recording electrodes are placed on the targeted muscle and on a neutral (ground) object. High levels of muscle tone recorded from skeletal muscles are called muscle action potentials (MAPs).

Electrooculogram (EOG). A measure of eye movements. Electrodes are usually placed lateral to the eyes. These can reveal rapid eye movements (REMs) and slow eye movements (SEMs). See also: **REM sleep.**

Elimination diet. A diet intended to eliminate toxic chemicals from the dieter's body. The Feingold diet is an example, or perhaps the model, for this concept.

Embolism. A plug, usually consisting of clotted blood, that forms in a larger blood vessel but can be washed into a narrower vessel where it blocks the passage of the bloodstream.

Embryo (em′brē ō). The developing human organism from the fifth through the fortieth day after conception.

Emergency reaction. The name given by American physiologist W. Cannon to the complex set of smooth muscle and glandular responses of the sympathetic nervous system to an external danger. Sweating palms, for example, have their value to a primate organism, helping it to grasp vines and swing away from a threat. As another example, diversion of blood to the brain and skeletal muscles helps the organism make strong running or fighting responses. Cannon also spoke of this complex response as the "fight-or-flight" response. See also: **autonomic nervous system; sympathetic nervous system.**

Emergent property position. An answer to the mind-body or mind-brain problem which can go along with either a monism or a dualism, depending on the details of the position taken by the theorist. The emergent property view holds that mind is the result of the complex organization of matter. Given the right kind of complex organization of material things, a functioning mind may emerge. This is analogous to the appearance of water (a liquid) from the combination of hydrogen and oxygen (two gases). The end-product of this mixture is not foreshadowed by the properties of the unmixed ingredients. The more or less straightforward version of the emergent-property position is that of Henri-Louis Bergson, in whose hands the position was a kind of dualism. The physiological psychologist M. Gazzaniga, however, has combined the emergent-property view with a type of interactionism. After mind emerges from the complexity of the brain, mind and matter then can (and do) interact. Since the existence of a physical brain is an absolute prerequisite for the appearance of a mind, in this view, Gazzaniga regards his position as a kind of <u>materialistic monism</u>. See also: **dualism; interactionism; materialism; mind-brain problem; monism.**

Emergent stage 1 EEG. See: **electroencephalogram; stage 1 sleep (ascending).**

Emmetropic (em˝ə trop′ik) **eye.** A normal eye. The kind of eye that is focused so that the image of a visual stimulus falls on the retina. See also: **hypermetropia; myopia.**

Emotion. A complex condition of a behaving organism. There are four elements to the concept of emotion: (1) adaptive behaviors, (2) physiological changes, (3) emotional expressions, and (4) subjective emotional feelings. In the case of humans, one of the identifying features of emotion is the subjective experience of pleasantness or unpleasantness. For lower animals, as a substitute for this criterion, one could observe the tendency of the organism to engage in "approach," "withdrawal," or "aggressive" behavior. Of course, it is also possible to use these behavior categories in judging the activities of humans. Body language and facial expressions constitute a second means of identifying an emotional state. The participation of the autonomic nervous system is a third indicator of emotion: The activity of the sympathetic nervous system, including higher levels of catecholamines (epinephrine, norepinephrine, or dopamine), is dominant in the expression of the negative emotions such as "fight" or "flight," while the parasympathetic nervous system is dominant in expressing positive states such as pleasure or satisfaction. The pioneer experimental psychologist W. Wundt insisted on three subjective dimensions for the scoring of emotions: Pleasantness-unpleasantness was supplemented by two others, namely, tension-relaxation, and excitement-calm. Titchener, Wundt's student, reduced tension and excitement to unpleasantness, and relaxation and calm to pleasantness. Our ordinary language contains references to the physiological aspects of our emotions: "The very sight of you makes my heart beat faster"; "My hair stood on end"; "I'm quivering with rage." In psychosomatic (stress-related) illnesses, emotions are linked with the condition of a part of the body; for example, heart attacks, high blood pressure, gastric or duodenal ulcers, colitis, asthma, allergies, and even death following a curse from a voodoo witch doctor can all be results of negative (fear or anger) emotions. The pioneer American psychologist W. James, noting the dogmatic remarks of the Danish physiologist C. Lange that emotion is only a physiological response, stated the paradoxical theory that subjective emotions are caused by reactive behaviors, instead of vice versa. An example of the James-Lange theory in action would be, "I see a bear, I run away, I am afraid." The popular song writers of earlier days apparently adopted the James-Lange theory of emotion, since they advised us to "let a smile be your umbrella on a rainy, rainy day" and "direct your feet to the sunny side of the street." Their implication was that acting happy when we are depressed will relieve the depression. The controversial method of psychotherapy known as <u>biofeedback</u> requires the individual to monitor a physiological condition (which may be muscular tension, EEG reading, finger temperature, breathing rate, or galvanic skin response) by means of a clearly audible or visible stimulus and to attempt, subjectively, to cause the readings to change. The American forensic psychologist L. Keeler developed the polygraph (commonly called the lie detector), which measures blood pressure, galvanic skin response, rate of respiration, and heart rate. The assumption of polygraphy is that lying and/or evasiveness will reveal themselves through such sympathetic nervous system responses as elevated blood pressure, sweating of the palms, rapid and shallow breathing, and a fast, perhaps irregular, heartbeat. The reader will notice that the negative emotions (fear, anger, aggression, anxiety) and the behaviors associated with them seem to have been studied in greater detail than the positive emotions (pleasure, satisfaction, love). This is partly because the sympathetic nervous system operates as a complex whole, having an organized pattern of reaction that takes in the entire body, whereas parasympathetic responses take place separately, often affecting one organ at a time. Since, as indicated earlier, the negative emotions are handled by the sympathetic nervous system, they are easier to investigate than the positive emotions. Brain areas involved in the processing of emotion include parts of the hypothalamus and the limbic system. The limbic system communicates with the hypothalamus via the two mammillary bodies at the base of the hypothalamus. Rage reactions have been the most extensively studied in relation to brain areas. See also: **aggression; biofeedback; psychophysiology.**

Empathy. The sharing of the experience of another person's feelings, which makes one more likely to behave with sympathy and understanding toward that person.

Encéphale isolé (än″sef äl′ ē zō lā′). A preparation, studied by Bremer, produced by severing the CNS between the spinal cord and the medulla. Taking the EEG of encéphale isolé cats, Bremer observed what looked like a normal sleep-wake cycle. The term "encéphale isolé" means "isolated brain" in French. See also: **cerveau isolé.**

Encephalitis. An inflammation of the brain, either caused by a viral disease that attacks the brain directly or existing as the aftereffect of other infectious conditions, such as rubella, influenza, measles, chickenpox, or cowpox.

Encephalization (en sef″ə li zā′shən). An evolutionary trend observed in vertebrates in which more advanced organisms require more and more brain tissue. This is because functions that are carried on by reflex action in simpler animals become more complex and require more complex control. Within the brain, there is a similar trend for functions to be shifted from being controlled by the endocrine system and lower parts of the brain to being regulated by the cerebral cortex (and, implicitly, becoming subject to environmental influences and learning processes). This second, more specialized trend has been termed "encephalization" by some authors; it is also called "corticalization" or "encorticalization." See also: **encephalization quotient; ovariectomy; progression index.**

Encephalization quotient (EQ). A ratio devised by Jerison and used to estimate the relative intelligence of various animal species. It is the ratio of brain size to the expected brain size (expected on the basis of the animal's body size). The typical mammal, the cat, is assigned an EQ of 1.0. On that scale, the EQ of a rat is 0.4, a chimpanzee's is 2.48, a dolphin's is 6.0, and a human's is 6.3. See also: **A/S ratio; progression index.**

Encoding. Framing the words of a spoken phrase or sentence. See also: **coding; decoding; echoic memory; engram; iconic memory; linguistic code; memory trace; motor code.**

Encoding specificity principle. The memory principle which states that memory retrieval is best when the retrieval context, that is, the environment in which memory is tested, is most like the encoding context, that is, the environment in which the learning had occurred. This especially applies to infants tested by the conjugate reinforcement technique, when changes in the pattern on the bedding in the crib can greatly impair the baby's memory (as measured by the number of days after which the learning can be retrieved). See also: **conjugate reinforcement technique; state-dependent learning.**

Encopresis (en kō prē′sis). A lack of bowel control due to incomplete toilet training rather than to disease or injury.

End bulb. See: **synaptic bouton.**

End plate. A modified region of the membrane around a muscle bundle that is reached by the axon endings of a motor nerve. It is similar to the postsynaptic membrane at a synapse.

End plate potential. A voltage change that initiates muscle contraction. Following the arrival of a nerve impulse in the axon of a motor neuron, neurotransmitter molecules from the axon terminals arrive at receptor sites on the end plate. The end plate is analogous to the postsynaptic membrane at a synapse. If the synaptic activity is strong enough, an end plate potential develops which is analogous to the voltage change that initiates a nerve impulse. As a consequence, the muscle bundle contracts. See also: **end plate; receptor sites; synapse.**

Endocrine system (en′dō krin, -krēn, -krīn) ("endocrine" = "to secrete within" in Greek). The endocrine glands are the ductless glands that release hormones into the bloodstream. They are closely related to the autonomic nervous system and are strongly linked to the regulation of the emotions. The pituitary gland is the most dominant gland (the so-called master gland) in this system. The list of endocrine glands, in order from the top to the bottom, is as follows: (1) the **pineal gland**, (2) the **pituitary**

gland, (3) the **thyroid gland**, (4) the **parathyroid glands**, (5) the **adrenal glands**, (6) the islets of Langerhans (**alpha cells** and **beta cells**) in the pancreas, and (7) the **gonads** (see definitions). See also: **autonomic nervous system; negative feedback; peripheral nervous system.**

Endoderm. One of the three "germ layers" formed in the earliest growth of the fertilized egg, or zygote. There is an outermost layer, an intermediate layer, and an internal layer. The endoderm is the innermost layer. It will develop later into the internal organs known as the viscera.

Endogenous. This term applies to chemicals produced within the body by metabolic processes.

Endogenous opiates (en dojʹə nəs ōʹpē its). Neurotransmitters that activate opiate receptors in the brain. Chemically, they are peptides. There are two major groups of endogenous opiates, namely, the **enkephalins** and the **endorphins** (see definitions). The endogenous opiates relieve pain. The paradoxical ability of acupuncture to relieve pain has been hypothesized to be due to the release of these peptides in response to the widespread, mild pain stimulation from the acupuncture needles.

Endogenous pyrogens. Substances that can induce fever that are produced by the body and its own metabolic processes.

Endogenous sleep factors. Sleep-inducing factors produced by the body's own metabolism. See also: **delta-sleep inducing peptide; Factor S.**

Endorphins (en dôrʹfinz). The term is derived from "endogenous morphines." Endorphins comprise one of the two major types of endogenous opiates. These are brain-produced morphine-like peptides that activate opiate receptors. Like the drug morphine, the endorphins relieve pain. Their receptor sites on postsynaptic membranes can be blocked by the drug naloxone, which is known to counter the action of opiates.

Endotherms (enʹdō thûrmz). Animals (i.e., the mammals and birds) whose internal metabolic processes regulate the temperature of the body and maintain it in an acceptable range. They are also known as warm-blooded animals or homoiotherms. Humans (among endotherms) go even further. Through their behavior, they modify the external environmental temperature (e.g., by operating furnaces or air conditioners). Accordingly, the human species is the one best

adapted to a great variety of environmental conditions and the one best able to settle the greater part of the planet Earth.

Engram (enʹgram) (also called a **memory trace**). The physical representation of a learned bit of information. The basic unit of information that exists in memory. It may be functional (e.g., nerve impulses traveling between particular neurons) or structural (e.g., a physical change taking place at some synapse. See also: **echoic memory; encoding; Hebbian synapse; iconic memory; linguistic code; long-term potentiation; memory trace; motor code.**

Enkephalins (en kefʹə linz). One of the two major groups of endogenous opiates. Enkephalins and endorphins are endogenous opiates, peptide neurotransmitters released by the brain that activate opiate receptors in the brain and serve, as do opiate drugs, to relieve pain. Enkephalins, more precisely, have a chain of five amino acids per molecule.

Entrainment (en trānʹment). The process of synchronizing a biological rhythm (e.g., circadian or ultradian) with a recurring environmental stimulus. The result is the matching of circadian rhythms to the actual day-night cycle experienced by the organism. The entrainment function seems to take place in the suprachiasmatic nucleus (SCN) of the hypothalamus. Some of the optic nerve fibers run to the SCN, apparently "reporting the time of day." The process of generating the rhythm is hypothesized to be the manufacture of protein by the neurons of the SCN. When the proteins are at a low level, the metabolic activity of generating them is speeded up. When the supply of protein becomes large enough, the manufacturing process slows down. Researchers have shown that the SCN is very active during the daylight hours but inactive during the night. Another related process is the synthesis of the hormone melatonin in the pineal gland. The highest levels of melatonin are present at night (or in darkness). A neural pathway runs from the eye to the pineal gland. This suggests that the level of light in the environment acts as a Zeitgeber (German for "time-giver"). See also: **circadian rhythms; melatonin; suprachiasmatic nucleus; Zeitgeber.**

Enuresis (en‴yoo rēʹsis). A lack of bladder control. A number of pathological factors can produce it. A normal child can be expected to learn bladder continence before the age of 2.

Environment. Those influences on behavior that are to be found in the world around the individual. The environment is the sum of all external stimuli. Conversely, a stimulus is a unit of the environment. Environmental factors include one's family, one's neighborhood, one's school, the cultural milieu, the climate, and so on.

Enzyme. A catalyst in the body's metabolic reactions. All catalysts, including enzymes, enter into chemical reactions but emerge from them without being consumed or changed. Meanwhile, they promote the chemical reactions, which might not even take place in their absence. Enzyme activity is needed in the body because so many chemicals coexist in proximity to one another. An enzyme can select which of the many materials should react with one another. The names of most enzymes end in the suffix "-ase." See also: **acetylcholinesterase; COMT; MAO.**

Epidemiology. The study of all the conditions that affect the spread of a given disease throughout the population.

Epilepsy. A condition involving periodic spells of abnormal brain activity. There may be motor or sensory symptoms. Consciousness may be lost. Occasionally, the patient exhibits convulsions. The word "seizure" may be applied to any epilepsy attack, whether or not there are any convulsions. Epilepsy is second only to stroke as the most common form of neurological disease. See also: **generalized seizure; grand mal seizure; petit mal seizure.**

Epileptic aura. A set of changes of consciousness (sounds and colors being hallucinated) that foreshadows the onset of an epileptic seizure of the grand mal type. See also: **grand mal seizure.**

Epinephrine (ep″i nef′rin, -rēn). Also called adrenalin, epinephrine is a hormone released by the adrenal medulla. It is one of the catechol amines, and its molecule resembles those of dopamine and norepinephrine. In the nervous system, epinephrine is released at some axon terminals; it then acts as a metabolic neurotransmitter (a neuromodulator), activating the second messenger system.

Epiphenomenalism (ep″ē fə nom′in əl iz″əm). A type of answer to the mind-body problem, which basically amounts to an endorsement of materialistic monism combined with a reason for the appearance of conscious phenomena. Consciousness is held to be a non-functional by-product of neural activity. When using an electric razor, hairs are cut and the razor makes a humming sound. The humming is an inessential accompaniment of the work of the electric razor. A soundless electric razor, other things being equal, would cut the hairs equally well. Mental phenomena are regarded, in this view, as essentially useless adjuncts of physical activity, analogous to the hum of that electric razor. See also: **materialism; mind-brain problem; monism.**

Episodic drives. These are drives that occur in distinct episodes. Pain, for example, is an episodic drive; it is activated only when there is damage to the tissues of the body.

Episodic memories. Memories of one's own personal experiences. These are the most easily lost in most types of amnesia.

Epistemology (i pis″tə mol′ə jē). That branch of philosophy which is concerned with the basis of knowledge, how knowledge works, and the relationship between knowledge and reality. See also: **double-aspect theory; mind-brain problem; philosophical behaviorism; psychophysical parallelism.**

Equipotentiality (ē″kwi pə ten chē al′ i tē, ek″wi-). The hypothesis that, after damage to the cerebral cortex, the remaining parts of the cortex are able to assume the functions of the lost tissue. This view was stated by Lashley and derived from his maze-learning studies with rats. It appeared to be correct only because he investigated complex behaviors, ones that involved the probable use of various sense organs and muscle groups.

Equivocal signs. See: **soft signs.**

Erectile disorder or **erectile failure** (i rek′ til, -tīl). An inability of a male individual to achieve or to maintain an erection of the penis during sexual intercourse and/or the lack of sexual thrill. For this diagnosis to be made, the problem should <u>not</u> occur <u>only</u> during psychotic or severely depressed episodes. Psychological factors such as fear of ridicule, fear of causing pregnancy, concern about adequacy of performance, and so on may play a causal role. See also: **primary erectile dysfunction; secondary erectile**

dysfunction.

Erogenous zones (i roj'ə nəs). Those parts of the body that, when stimulated tactually, are most likely to promote the arousal of sexual desire.

Erotic (i rot'ik). Sexually arousing.

Erratic eye movements. Normal eye movements in reading, including fixations and saccades, have been observed by some researchers. Many dyslexics have different sorts of eye movements, including regressions and reversals. These abnormal events have been used as the basis for dyslexic subtyping by some investigators.

Erythrolabe. One of three variants of the cone photopigment iodopsin. Erythrolabe is most responsive to red light, i.e., to the longer waves of the spectrum of visible light. See also: **chlorolabe; cyanolabe; trichromatic theory of color vision.**

Escape conditioning. That form of aversive conditioning in which the correct response discontinues the aversive stimulation. See also: **aversive conditioning.**

Esophageal (i sof″ə jē′əl, es″o fa′jē əl). Pertaining to the esophagus, which is the tube in the gastrointestinal tract that runs from the mouth to the stomach.

Essential hypertension. High blood pressure which is attributable to severe psychological stress.

Estradiol (es″trə dī ′ôl). The most common of the estrogens. See also: **estrogen.**

Estrogen. A group of steroid hormones released by the ovaries, the female gonads. More specifically, estrogen is released from the follicle, a body built up around the ovum. The development of the follicle, and thus the increased released of estrogen, is stimulated by FSH, a hormone of the anterior pituitary gland.

Estrous cycle (es′trəs). The cycle of alternating increases and decreases in the secretion of the two female hormones, estrogen and progesterone. The time duration of the cycle varies with species. It is only four days in the case of rats and guinea pigs, but is monthly in the human female. See more under the definition of **estrus.**

Estrus (es′trus). In the female, a stage of sexual receptivity ("heat") that appears when the **estrous cycle** (see definition) has produced a mature egg awaiting fertilization by a male. At the peak of estrus, estrogen is at a relatively low level in the bloodstream, while the level of progesterone is extremely high. In monkeys, apes, and humans, the cyclic, endocrine regulation of sexual activity is almost entirely replaced by learned behavior patterns that are dependent upon the cerebral cortex of the brain. The estrous cycle in these species controls fertility only, not sexual receptivity.

Ethology (e thol′ə jē) ("ethos" = "behavior" in Greek). The experimental study of the behavior of higher animals (birds and mammals) under natural conditions. See also: **fixed action pattern; internal releasing mechanism; motor program.**

Ethyl alcohol (eth′əl al′kə hôl). This is the type of alcohol found in beverages that people consume. Other forms of alcohol, such as methyl alcohol and isopropyl alcohol, are too toxic for consumption. See also: **alcohol.**

Etiology. The cause(s) and origin(s) of a particular condition or disease process.

Eustachian (yo͞o stā′shən, -stā′kē ən) **tube.** An open air passage linking the middle ear to the nasopharynx, the air passage between the nose and the throat.

Event-related potential (ERP). A modification of the EEG during which a peak or valley of positive or negative voltage is recorded during a specified activity. For example, the subject may be trained to expect a given stimulus a certain number of seconds after a preceding stimulus. In such a case, a large positive wave occurs, 300 milliseconds after the onset of the first, "get ready," stimulus. ERPs differ from ordinary evoked potentials in that they are not simple reactions to stimulation. ERPs, some hope, are clues to the physiological basis in the brain of such higher mental processes as attention. See also: **electroencephalogram; evoked potentials.**

Evoked potentials (EPs). These can be thought of as electroencephalogram records that are time-locked to a specific stimulus. The term covers any change in the EEG resulting from an auditory, somatosensory, or visual stimulus. EPs assist the exploration of the functional integrity of afferent neural pathways. They are affected by neurological, gender, and developmental factors. They are not influenced by higher cognitive processes; those processes are much more likely to affect <u>event-related potentials (ERPs)</u>. See also: **electroencephalogram; event-related potential.**

Evoked-response audiometry. A technique used to measure changes in brain-wave activity by using the electroencephalogram. This technique is expensive, and results are difficult to interpret.

Exceptional children. Any children who vary from average mental, physical, or behavioral characteristics to such an extent that they require special schooling, special training, or other special treatment. The category includes those who are mentally retarded, those who are learning-disabled, those with emotional or behavioral disorders, as well as those who are highly intelligent and gifted.

Excitatory postsynaptic potential (EPSP). A graded and decremental electrical potential that is set up in the postsynaptic membrane of a message-receiving neuron's dendrite or cell body at a synapse, provided that it is depolarizing. If the voltage change is a depolarization (i.e., a decrease in the positive charge on the outside of the membrane), the effect is excitatory, in that the likelihood of a nerve impulse being initiated in the postsynaptic neuron is increased. Such depolarizing voltage changes may be due to the infiltration of positively charged sodium ions into the cytoplasm of that neuron. EPSPs (and IPSPs) are subject to temporal and spatial summation. See also: **decremental potentials; graded potentials; inhibitory post-synaptic potentials; spatial summation; temporal summation.**

Excitatory synapse. A kind of synapse in which an excitatory effect is produced in the receiving (or postsynaptic) neuron, due to the release of a chemical neurotransmitter from the sending (or presynaptic) neuron that depolarizes (excites) a receptor site on the receiving neuron's cell membrane. See also: **depolarization; excitatory postsynaptic potential; synapse.**

Excitement phase. According to Masters and Johnson, the period during which the individual is made ready for sexual activity. The male's penis and the female's clitoris become erect, due to being engorged with blood in the sponge-like erectile tissues. In females, the vagina is lubricated and a sexual flush may be seen in the skin of the throat and chest.

Exclusionary definition. Defining a concept or condition by what the concept or condition is not. For example, the term dyslexia is frequently defined by researchers as to what it is not. It cannot include individuals with below average IQ, primary emotional disturbance, primary sensory disorders, cultural disadvantage, and so on.

Exhaustion phase. This is the third stage of what Selye has described as a general adaptation syndrome. During this stage, the organism has failed to adapt to an environmental stressor, resulting in physical and/or mental disorder or disease. For example, when an individual experiences a winter cold and does not succeed in fighting it off, more serious respiratory ailments might ensue.

Exhibitionism. The obtaining of sexual gratification by exposing one's genitalia to strangers. This behavior has to be habitual if there is to be a diagnosis of pathology.

Exocrine glands. Glands with ducts that secrete their products to places in the body that are located near the gland. This is in contrast to the endocrine (ductless) glands that release hormones into the bloodstream.

Exocytosis (ek ″sō sī tō′sis). The release of chemicals from cells into the extracellular fluid. One example would be the release from an axon terminal of a chemical neurotransmitter into the synaptic cleft.

Exogenous (ek soj′ə nəs). Coming from outside the body. This is the opposite of the term "endogenous."

Experiential intelligence. The type of intelligence exhibited by people while performing either (1) tasks with which they have hardly any experience at all or (2) tasks with which they have a great deal of experience. See also: **triarchic theory of intelligence.**

Experiment. The research procedure that best enables the investigator to draw inferences about cause and effect relations. The variable that may cause a change in some behavior is set at various values; this is the independent variable. The behavioral measure that may or may not show changes related to the values of the independent variable is called the dependent variable. Factors that could affect the dependent variable (other than the independent variable) must be held constant or otherwise controlled.

Experimental allergic encephalomyelitis. A laboratory model of the disease multiple sclerosis. It is induced in test animals by injecting them with the lipid myelin plus a stimulant to the immune system, which results in the destruction of the animal's own myelin. See also: **multiple sclerosis; myelin.**

Explicit memory. That type of memory which involves the deliberate effort to recall or to recognize something. It is the type of memory tested by objective or subjective examinations.

Explosive personality disorder. A disorder wherein the individual will "fly into a rage" that is beyond a normal reaction to provocation. Temper tantrums, physical assaults, and emotional outbursts will occur with even the slightest frustration or anxiety.

Expressive language. The ability to produce meaningful communications in oral, written, or signed form.

Extended scale scores (ESSs). These allow a group's development in reading to be followed for several years on one continuous scale of measurement. Like normal curve equivalents (NCEs), the ESSs are arranged in equal sized steps so that they may be added up and averaged.

Extensor. A muscle that, when it contracts, thrusts a limb out from the body. One example of an extensor is the triceps of the upper arm. Another example is the quadriceps femoris, the muscle that contracts during a knee-jerk reflex.

External auditory canal. See: **auditory canal.**

External otitis (ō tī′tis). An infection of the skin of the external auditory canal, also known as swimmer's ear.

Exteroceptors (ek″stə rō sep′tərz). The sense receptors that are directed at, and monitor, the external environment. Such receptors include distance receptors (the eyes, ears and nose) as well as the sense organs for taste, touch, and exteroceptive pain (i.e., pain felt on the skin or the cornea). See also: **interoceptors; proprioceptors.**

Extinction. The process of reversing the behavioral effect of conditioning. In the case of Pavlovian conditioning, the continued stimulus is repeatedly presented alone, with the unconditioned stimulus no longer being presented. Gradually, the conditioned response is made less and less often. In the case of operant conditioning, the response may continue to occur, but no reinforcement will be provided. As a result, the rate of responding will decline to the operant level, the rate that prevailed before the response was being reinforced.

Extracellular (ek″strə sel′yoo lər) **fluid** or **interstitial** (in″tər stish′əl) **fluid.** The fluid that circulates between and around the body cells. It is separated from the cells' cytoplasm by the semipermeable membranes that surround the cells.

Extracellular (ek″strə sel′yoo lər) **thirst.** See: **volemic thirst.**

Extrafusal ("extra" = "outside of", "fusal" = the spindle) (ek″strə fyoo′zəl) **fiber.** A muscle fiber is an individual muscle cell. Regular skeletal muscle fibers, outside of the muscle spindle sense organ, are designated the extrafusal fibers; they do the work of moving the body parts. See also: **intrafusal fiber; muscle spindle organ.**

Extrapunitive. Having the tendency to blame others for everything that goes wrong. See also: **intropunitive.**

Extrapyramidal disorder. The disruption of movements due to damage to a part of the extrapyramidal motor system. Examples are Parkinson's disease and Huntington's disease. See also: **basal ganglia; extrapyramidal motor fibers; Huntington's chorea; Parkinson's disease; premotor cortex; supplementary motor cortex.**

Extrapyramidal motor fibers. The local route from the cerebral cortex to the muscles. Axons arising from cell bodies in Brodmann's area 6 of the cerebral cortex (and other cortical areas also) travel to structures in the brain stem and the basal ganglia. After a number of synaptic connections, these pathways finally send axons to the ventral horn motoneurons, which in turn relay axons to the muscles. See also: **Brodmann numbering system; cerebral cortex; frontal lobe; motoneuron; motor cortex; ventral horn.**

Extrasensory perception (ESP). Perception without the need for prior stimulation of any sense organ. This is an ability that is claimed for some people, who are said to have the gift of "psi," which refers to powers of perception that go beyond the normal range of the senses. There are various types of ESP: (1) clairvoyance, the knowledge of events that could not be witnessed by the individual because of great distances between the knower and the event, or physical barriers between the knower and the known; (2) telepathy, the ability to know what another person is thinking or feeling, despite the absence of spoken or written evidence of those thoughts or feelings; (3) precognition, the ability to predict accurately future events; and (4) telekinesis or psychokinesis, the ability to use mental force to move or alter physical objects (e.g., to bend spoons or keys by just thinking). Parapsychology is the term for the study of these phenomena. The validity of parapsychology as an area of science, as well as the reality of any ESP phenomena, has often been effectively challenged by skeptical investigators, who include philosophers, psychologists, journalists, and professional magicians. See also: **absolute threshold; subliminal perception.**

Extrinsic reward. Rewarding an operant response by providing a reinforcement that is not inherently linked to the activity itself (e.g., a food pellet given to a rat after the rat has pressed the lever in a Skinner box is an extrinsic reward). See also: **intrinsic motivation; reinforcement**.

Extrovert. According to Jung, an extrovert is an outward going individual who chooses to emphasize socializing with others as opposed to focusing on inner reflections or experiences. See also: **introvert.**

Eye-patch treatment. The radical solution for dyslexia proposed by Stein and his associates. Since the dyslexic has basic problems coordinating the visual axes of the two eyes, according to these investigators, let them simply use one eye!

Eye-voice span (EVS). The horizontal range in vision (scored by the number of words) that the reader can report beyond the last word read aloud during oral reading.

F

Face validity. The apparent appropriateness of the test items for assessing the behavior or ability being tested, in the estimation of someone who knows about this behavior or ability. This is not considered to be a sound basis for evaluating the usefulness of a test, but it has great acceptance among laypersons who have not been trained in the theory of testing.

Facial feedback hypothesis. The concept that emotional experiences and their labels are determined by the facial expressions that accompany them. Having the facial muscles arranged in a given type of expression provides muscle-sense information to the brain that leads to an emotion consistent with that expression.

Facial nerve. The seventh pair of cranial nerves, the facial is a mixed (i.e., motor and sensory) nerve. On the sensory side, taste sensations from the anterior two-thirds of the tongue are carried in a subset of facial nerve axons known as the chorda tympani (does this have to do with good musical taste?). The muscles of facial expression, on the motor side, receive facial nerve axons sent to them from the facial nerve nucleus. This nucleus in turn receives impulses from the pyramidal tract. The facial nerve as part of the parasympathetic nervous system activates two of the salivary glands, contributing to the onset of salivation. See also: **cranial nerves**.

Facilitative Learning or **Facilitative Communications**. A support system provided by a teacher or aide to a disabled student (handicapped by paralysis, cerebral palsy, or autism) to help with the physical motions of the student's hand in order to allow the student to write or make expressive movements. The helper may hold the student's hand, wrist, or arm in providing this physical support. The response must not be made by the helper, who only facilitates the student's attempt to express herself/himself.

Factor analysis. A statistical method that reduces a large number of trait names to a manageable few by combining related traits into larger units. Correlation coefficients are obtained among the tests of the numerous traits. A group of traits with high positive correlations among them is formed into a single factor.

Factor S (may or may not be the same thing as the delta-sleep inducing peptide [DSIP]). A small glycopeptide that has been extracted from the nervous system and the bloodstream of sleeping animals. When injected into a waking animal, Factor S will induce slow-wave (delta) sleep. See also: **slow-wave sleep; delta sleep.**

Fading. The gradual removal of stimuli such as letters or prompts during the instruction process. This gradually increases the difficulty of the task. The goal of this technique is for the learner to acquire the ability to produce the material independently.

Fallopian (fə lō′pē ən) **tubes**. The ducts in the female body leading from the ovaries to the uterus. The egg cell or ovum is formed in the ovary and, after fertilization, the egg (now a zygote) must travel through the Fallopian tube to the uterus. See also: **ovaries; zygote.**

False transmitter. A chemical having a molecular structure similar to a given neurotransmitter. Such a chemical can bind to the receptor sites for that neurotransmitter and block them, thus preventing the neurotransmitter from acting in its normal manner.

Familial retardation. This refers to instances of mental retardation found in several members of the same family but with no signs of a biological cause for the retardation.

Family dynamics. The social forces at work in that microcosm of society, the nuclear family (parents and their children).

Family therapy. A type of psychotherapy used to improve the psychological well-being of an individual within the context of that person's family. Lines of communication are opened among the family members in order to facilitate more positive interactions than those that prevailed before the start of the therapy. Each family member is encouraged to identify and help satisfy the needs of other family members. The goal is to have the family function as a cohesive, whole unit.

Far-field potentials. Electroencephalographic voltages recorded from a place on the scalp far removed from their source in the brain. Such voltages will necessarily be somewhat attenuated. See also: **electroencephalogram.**

Fasciculation (fa sik″yoo lā′shən). In neural development, the tendency for growing axons to follow paths used by earlier-growing axons. See also: **fasciculus.**

Fasciculus (fa sik′yoo lus) or **tract**. A bundle of

axons in the central nervous system. The word comes from the Latin "fascis," meaning "bundle." A bundle of rods with diagonal ties and two ax-heads coming out of the top was the symbol of ancient Rome. When the dictator Mussolini tried to revive for Italy the ancient glory of Rome, he named his own political movement "fascism," adopting the "fascis" as the political symbol for his party. The added particle "-culus" is a diminutive ("small-making") adjectival change to the word, making it mean "small bundle." The word "fasciculus" is used interchangeably with the word "tract." The pyramidal tract, for example, is the pathway from the motor cortex (the precentral gyrus) down the rest of the brain and the spinal cord to the ventral part of the gray matter of the spinal cord, the ventral horns of the gray butterfly. Another example: The gracile and cuneate tracts (or fasciculus gracilis and fasciculus cuneatus) carry impulses up the spinal cord to two nuclei of the medulla [being the first CNS part of the pathway headed toward the somatosensory cortex (the postcentral gyrus)].

Fast-twitch muscle. A kind of striped muscle that delivers contractions with the greatest power and speed, at the price of having little or no resistance to fatigue. These are the white muscles, which are not provided with muscle hemoglobin or fat. These things are present in the red muscles (the "dark meat" in poultry) and confer stamina. See also: **slow-twitch muscle.**

Fasting phase. The metabolic phase of the organism hours after the ingestion of the last previous meal. The triglycerides that have been stored in the lipocytes (fat cells) of the adipose tissue are chemically changed into fatty acids and glycerol. The hormone glucagon plays a part in these changes. The glycerol travels to the liver, where it is converted to glucose. This glucose is now released into the bloodstream, where it can be accepted and utilized by the body cells. The fasting phase alternates with the absorption phase. See also: **absorption phase; fatty acid; glucagon; glucose; lipocytes.**

Fatty acid. A fatty acid is just an organic acid, meaning it has a chain of carbon atoms and a carboxyl (COOH) group. Unsaturated (meaning some of the links between carbon atoms are either double- or triple-bonds instead of the single bonds seen in saturated fats) fatty acids are necessary diet supplements which can be found in foods such as

vegetable oils and olives. Acetic acid is an example of a saturated fatty acid. Fatty acids are not soluble in water, which prevents them from being directly absorbed from the intestines. Fatty acids must combine with bile before they can be absorbed by the red blood cells. The blood plasma can then carry these fatty acids to the various body organs.

Feature analysis. The perception of a complex stimulus such as an object or a scene by consideration of the separate elements of the stimulus. Neurons in the cerebral cortex are selectively sensitive to particular features such as lines with 30-degree slants. See also: **feature detectors.**

Feature detectors. Cortical neurons that are selectively sensitive to lines of a given slant, to a particular width, to motion in a given direction, and so on are examples of feature detectors. See also: **feature analysis.**

Feingold diet. A diet prescribed for hyperactive individuals. It includes foods free of artificial coloring and artificial flavorings. Although research has shown positive outcomes only for a small percentage (10%) of hyperactive children, there does seem to be evidence for physiological ill effects from certain food additives. For example, red dye #3 has been reported to alter the permeability of neural membranes.

Female sexual arousal disorder. A failure of a female individual to arrive at or maintain the lubrication and swelling of the vagina during sexual activity or the lack of subjective sexual thrill during the sex act. If this diagnosis is to be made, such failures should <u>not</u> occur <u>only</u> during psychotic or severely depressed episodes. See also: **primary orgasmic dysfunction; secondary orgasmic dysfunction.**

Feminizing. The production or the enhancement of female characteristics, due to an increased supply of estrogens relative to the supply of androgens. See also: **androgens; estrogens.**

Fetal alcohol syndrome. The occurrence of mental retardation and physical problems in a newborn infant as the result of the mother's abuse of alcohol during pregnancy. The danger point is estimated to be the daily consumption of 89 milliliters of ethyl alcohol (about 3 ounces). The safest way is for the pregnant mother to avoid drinking alcoholic beverages altogether. The possible symptoms of this condition include: mental retardation (the level of which can vary from one baby to another), hyperactivity, lowered alertness, motor difficulties, heart defects, low birth weight, and facial abnormalities.

Fetishism (fet′ish iz əm). A psychosexual behavior pattern involving sexual arousal by contact with physical objects such as shoes, underwear, or bathroom articles, or with sexually irrelevant body parts such as the feet.

Fetus. An unborn infant that is mature enough to look like a human being. This stage of development is reached at the ninth week of pregnancy (i.e., during the third month).

Fever. An increased body temperature resulting from bodily defenses against infection or injury.

Fictional finalism. The setting of a goal by an individual so that the goal can guide that her or his behavior, even if the goal is never actually attained.

"Fight-or-flight" reaction. See: **emergency reaction.**

Fimbria (fim′brē ə). A band of axons in the limbic system that follows the medial surface of the hippocampus. Carrying nerve impulses from the hippocampus, the fimbria branches off from the **fornix** (see definition) and runs toward the septum. See also: **hippocampus; limbic system; septum.**

Fine motor skills. The use of small muscles (particularly those of the fingers) for manipulating objects, reaching, and grasping. These skills may be applied to mechanical puzzles, drawing, rotating and stacking cubes, and so on. See also: **gross motor skills.**

First-night phenomenon. The sleep problems affecting the typical human volunteer subject during the first few nights in the sleep laboratory.

Fissure. A groove (sulcus) in the cerebral cortex or the cerebellum which is unusually long and deep. The largest of the fissures is the longitudinal fissure, which separates the left and right hemispheres of the cerebral cortex. Another fissure of importance is the lateral fissure (or fissure of Sylvius), which separates the temporal lobe of the cortex from the frontal and parietal lobes; the temporal lobe is ventral to that fissure, while the other two are dorsal to it. A transitional groove, which qualifies as either a sulcus or a fissure, is the one that runs down the side of the cortex, separating the frontal lobe (in front) from the parietal lobe (which is caudal to the fissure). This fissure is called the fissure of Rolando and is also known as the central sulcus. See also: **cerebral cortex; sulcus.**

Fixation. A brief stoppage of eye movement after a saccade. See also: **saccade.**

Fixed action pattern. A motor program, specific to a species of animals, that develops almost automatically as the animal matures in a species-normal environment. An example is the circling routine a dog goes through before it lies down. Ethologists, who scientifically study the behavior of animals in their natural environments, have examined many of these motor programs. See also: **ethology; motor program.**

Fixed interval schedule of reinforcement. A schedule arranging for the reinforcement of some correct responses made by an organism, but not all of them. In a fixed interval schedule, a given time interval must expire after reinforcement has occurred before another response can be reinforced. For example, with a fixed interval of 30″ (FI30″), the organism must wait 30 seconds before the response is given reinforcement. Responses made earlier than that will not be followed by reinforcement. See also: **schedules of reinforcement.**

Fixed ratio schedule of reinforcement. A schedule arranging for partial reinforcement of correct responses made by an organism, such that every "nth" response results in reinforcement while all other responses are not reinforced. The term "fixed ratio" refers to the ratio of the number of responses made before the reinforcement is given to 1, the reinforced response. For example, a fixed ratio of 5 (FR5) means that five responses are made before reinforcement is provided. See also: **schedules of reinforcement.**

Flashbulb memory. Long-term memory (-ies) for emotionally charged events that occurred at a particular time. For example, remembering where you were when President John F. Kennedy was shot is an example of flashbulb memory.

Flat affect. An emotionless display with little indication of either positive or negative feelings. A person with flat affect frequently speaks in a monotone voice and shows little facial expression. Schizophrenics are known to display flat affect.

Flavor. The perceptual experience from eating or drinking, which results from the combination of the two chemical senses of taste and smell.

Flexion reflex. The quick withdrawal of a limb or finger after a strong, painful stimulus is applied to the receptors. For example, touching a hot stove leads to a rapid bending of the finger, the wrist, the elbow, and the shoulder away from the pain stimulus. The organization of this elementary form of behavior involves two reflex arcs: The first of these reflex arcs requires a minimum of only two neurons, namely, an afferent neuron (to send nerve impulses into the spinal cord's dorsal horn), and a motor neuron sending an axon out the ventral root along a spinal nerve to the flexor muscle. The second reflex arc requires three neurons, the afferent neuron, an inhibitory interneuron traveling to the dorsal horn cell (the third neuron) which normally sends tone-maintaining impulses to the extensor muscle antagonistic to the flexor. The second circuit is required so that flexion can take place without resistance. See also: **dorsal horn; extensor; flexor; interneuron; reflex arc; unconditioned reflex; ventral horn; ventral root.**

Flexor. A muscle that causes a limb to flex, that is, to bend toward the midline of the body. An example would be the biceps muscle of the upper arm.

Floor effect. The insensitivity of a test (or other measurement tool) to differences among very low scores. This may impair the validity of the test as a measure of different types or levels of mental retardation and/or severe learning disabilities.

Fluid intelligence. The kind of intelligence that does not result from training or experience. This type of intelligence involves the ability to handle novel problems and situations. This kind of ability reaches a peak during the teens and declines gradually thereafter. See also: **crystallized intelligence.**

Fluoxetine (floo ok′sə tēn). The generic name for the antidepressant drug now sold under the name Prozac. See also: **antidepressants.**

Fluvoxamine (floo vok′sə mēn). A drug that blocks the reuptake by the presynaptic neuron of the neurotransmitter serotonin (5-HT). This results in extra 5-HT activity, because the 5-HT molecules can continue working in the synaptic cleft. The drug helps alleviate obsessive-compulsive symptoms, suggesting that the obsessive-compulsive disorder is due to the underactivity of 5-HT in the brain. See also: **clomipramine; obsessive-compulsive neurosis; serotonin.**

Follicle (fol′i kəl). The group of cells formed around the ovum as the ovum begins to grow within the ovary. See also: **follicle-stimulating hormone (FSH).**

Follicle-stimulating hormone (FSH). A hormone released by the anterior pituitary or master gland. FSH stimulates the ovaries to release estrogen. It also leads to the development of a body of cells, a follicle, around the ovum just as the ovum itself begins to develop. In males, FSH causes the testes to produce sperm cells. See also: **luteinizing hormone (LH).**

Forebrain (also called the prosencephalon; pro = front, encephalon = brain). The forebrain consists of the **telencephalon** and the **diencephalon**. The telencephalon includes the **cerebral cortex** (the cerebral hemispheres or neocortex), the **rhinencephalon**, which is the old cortex or "smell brain", most of the **limbic system**, and most of the **basal ganglia**. The diencephalon includes the **thalamus** and the **hypothalamus** (See definitions).

Forgetting. See **theories of forgetting.**

Formal tests. These tests, usually standardized, include specified tasks and procedures that must be adhered to very strictly, so that the test results can be comparable to those from other administrations of the test.

Fornix (fôr′niks) (from Latin "fornix" = "arch"). An arch-shaped bundle of axons running ventrally from the dorsal anterior hippocampus to the posterior hypothalamus, the fornix constitutes the major source of input to the hypothalamus as well as the major outlet for information leaving the hippocampus. Injury to the fornix has caused experimental animals to overeat (i.e., to demonstrate hyperphagia); this helps to demonstrate that the hypothalamus is not so much a "satiety center" as a part of a "satiety pathway" traveling through a large portion of the entire brain. See also: **fimbria; hippocampus; hypothalamic hyperphagia; hypothalamus.**

Forward masking. Presenting the interfering stimuli shortly before the target stimulus by means of a two-field tachistoscope. See also: **backward masking; masking; tachistoscope.**

Fourier (foo Rē ā′) **analysis.** The dissection of a complex wave of physical energy into its simple sine wave components (each individual sine wave having just one wavelength). Usually this is done with particular interest in the amplitude (or power) that each component sine wave has in the complex wave being analyzed. The original work was done on sound waves. An interesting use of the method, BEAM, or brain electrical activity mapping, sorts out the various EEG rhythms (such as alpha, beta, etc.) in order to use the electroencephalogram in mapping out brain regions of high and low activity.

See also: **BEAM; harmonics**.

Fovea (fō′vē ə). A centrally placed small part of the retina which is indented so as to maximize the placement of cones along its surface. The fovea contains about 40,000 cones and has no rods.

Fragile X syndrome or **Fra (X) syndrome**. The second most common genetic factor in mental retardation (the first being chromosome 21 trisomy, which leads to Down's syndrome). Unlike a normal X chromosome, the fragile X has a loosely attached terminal segment that can easily break away. In people with a fragile X chromosome, the loosely attached segment snaps off in some cells, but not in others. In females, there are seldom any fragile X effects, because a female in all probability has a normal X chromosome along with the fragile one. A male whose only X chromosome is fragile will suffer from the effects of fragile X. In 1 male of every 1,000 births, there will be mental retardation due to a fragile X chromosome. A fragile X chromosome has been observed in many autistic children (most of whom are male). See also: **autism; sex chromosome abnormalities**.

Fraternal twins or **dizygotic twins**. Fraternal twins are the products of two separate fertilizations. Two different ova are each penetrated by a sperm cell. The similarity of the genes of the two resulting zygotes is comparable to that of ordinary siblings conceived at different times. Fraternal twins have an equal chance of being of the same gender or of different genders. About 12 out of every 1,000 births are of fraternal twins. See also: **identical twins**.

Free fatty acids. The chemical products released from stored fat during the fasting phase. These, along with glucose, are a source of energy for the body. See also: **fasting phase**.

Free nerve endings. Unspecialized receptors (at the position where dendrites would be in most neurons) of unipolar neurons supplying the skin. Pain and temperature stimuli stimulate these receptors, sending afferent nerve impulses toward the spinal cord or the brain. See also: **exteroceptors; unipolar neuron**.

Free-running period. The amount of time required to complete one cycle of a free-running rhythm.

Free-running rhythm. A circadian rhythm that is independent of environmental cues (e.g., the amount of sunlight). See also: **circadian rhythms**.

Frequency. the number of complete vibrations of an energy wave occurring over a fixed period of time

(e.g., one second). Frequency is usually measured in Hertz (Hz), the number of complete cycles within each second. See also: **Fourier analysis; Hertz; sound**.

Frequency theory of hearing. Also called the telephone theory, this view holds that the perception of auditory pitch is made possible by the direct coding of the number of cycles per second in the sound wave (or the matching number of vibrations of the basilar membrane) as the number of impulses per second in the auditory nerve. Currently this view is considered to be correct for low frequency sounds, especially those between 20 and 100 cycles per second (cps). The existence of the absolute refractory period impairs the ability of this mechanism to track sound frequencies higher than 1,000 c.p.s. Other mechanisms account for the perception of the higher pitches above 1,000 c.p.s. See also: **basilar membrane; telephone theory of hearing; volley theory of hearing**.

Friedreich's ataxia (frēd′rī shəz ə tak′sē ə). An autosomal recessive disorder involving progressive neuromuscular degeneration. The symptoms include ataxia, nystagmus, general weakness, and scoliosis. Individuals with this disease cannot walk by adulthood; the average life span is halved. Among the psychological symptoms are decreased speed in processing information, limited attention, and memory deficits. See also: **autosomal disorders**.

Frontal or **coronal** (kôr′ə nəl, kə rō′nəl). One of the three planes of sectioning for the microtome slicing of central nervous system tissues in the preparation of slides for microanatomic study. Each of these planes is perpendicular to the other two. A frontal or coronal cut separates the body into front and back parts. The frontal section permits the observer to see the tissue from directly in front of it. In the case of a four-legged creature, the frontal cut might yield an anterior or rostral portion including the head, upper trunk, and forelimbs, and a posterior (caudal) portion containing the lower trunk, hind limbs, and tail. For such a quadruped, the frontal cut is also a transverse section or cross-section, which is perpendicular to the long axis of the "body tube."

Frontal eye fields. A part of the frontal lobe (including the posterior portion of Brodmann's area 8) just forward of the premotor cortex. Activity in this region can affect eye movements. See also:

Brodmann numbering system; cerebral cortex; frontal lobe; premotor cortex.

Frontal lobe. That portion of the cerebral cortex that includes the motor cortex, which controls voluntary movement; the most rostral (i.e., "frontal") of the four lobes of the cerebral cortex. The very front portion of the frontal lobe is the <u>prefrontal area</u>, which has been associated with anxiety and foresight. The prefrontal area has been assigned the Brodmann numbers 8, 9, 10, and 11. The posterior portion of the frontal lobe, backing into the boundary of this lobe with its neighbor, the parietal lobe, is the precentral gyrus. This gyrus is the beginning of a motor pathway with very long axons called the pyramidal motor tract. The boundary between the frontal and parietal lobes is a long, deep groove known as the central sulcus or the fissure of Rolando. The Brodmann number for the precentral gyrus is 4. Just anterior (or rostral) to area 4 is area 6, from which arise many short-axon paths toward the muscles. If the pyramidal tract is the "express train" of our motor control system, then the short-axon, many-stopover route from area 6 can be regarded as the "local." Ventral to both areas 4 and 6 is area 44, Broca's area for the motor control of speech. The left hemisphere's area 44, in most people, is needed for the ability to form speech sounds and to speak grammatically, using all the "helping" words such as conjunctions and prepositions. The right hemisphere's area 44 plays a role in prosody, the loudness and tone of the speech sounds. The boundary of the ventral side of the frontal lobe is the <u>lateral fissure</u> or <u>fissure of Sylvius</u>. Ventral to that fissure lies the temporal lobe.

Frontal operculum (ō pûr′kyoo̅ lum) ("operculum" = "cover"). An area of the frontal cortex, which seems to turn inward, providing a cover for interior parts of the cortex, such as the insula. The frontal operculum is another name for Broca's area for motor speech.

Frotteurism (frä tyoor iz əm). The obtaining of sexual gratification by rubbing oneself against another person without that person's consent. This can occur on crowded sidewalks or in public transportation vehicles at busy times. For a diagnosis of pathology, this behavior (called <u>frottage</u>) must be habitual.

Frustration. A source of stress due to the failure to achieve a specific goal or to a general lack of success in life.

Fugue (fyoo̅g). A psychological disorder marked by (1) sudden departure from one's home or job, (2) assumption of a new identity, and (3) amnesia of one's past identity.

Function. A type of action that a person may take in order to satisfy a need. Human functions include: existence, body alignment, recreation, communication, adaptation to the environment, and so on.

Functional curriculum. A set of academic courses intended to teach those skills that are age-appropriate for the student and that the student will be able to apply immediately. See also: **ecological inventory; function.**

Functional fixedness. The failure to find the solution to a problem based on an inability to find a novel use for a familiar object. A classic example is the problem of mounting a candle on a wall in an upright position, using a box of kitchen matches, thumbtacks, and the candle itself. The solution calls for tacking an end-piece of the inside of the match box to the wall, so that the object sticks out into the room. Now that the box, having been emptied, is usable as a shelf, light the candle and drip some hot wax onto the surface of the box. Then stand the candle onto the surface of the box. Many will fail because they will not see the new way to think of a match box that the solution requires.

Functional hearing loss. A loss of hearing that cannot be accounted for by physical damage to the hearing apparatus or to the nervous system. The loss is attributed to psychological factors.

Functional learning handicap. A learning problem arising from the difficulty that a student has in functioning within her or his present social environment.

Functional retardation. Mental retardation attributable to environmental events that have shaped, and are presently helping to support, retarded behavior.

Functional tolerance. Drug tolerance due to a lowered reactivity of the nervous system to the drug. See also: **tolerance.**

Funiculus (fə nik′yoo̅ lus, fyoo-) ("funis" = cable or cord in Latin; the ending "culus" is a diminutive, making it smaller; literally a funiculus is a "little cable"). One of the three main groupings of white matter on either side of the spinal cord. The cross section of the spinal cord shows a gray butterfly or gray H, with the outflung butterfly wings (or the vertical lines of the H) separating the parts of the white matter into three main groups; the midline serves as another border and so does the outer edge of the spinal cord. Between the dorsal horn and the midline, abutting the dorsal edge of the spinal cord, there is the dorsal funiculus. Between the dorsal and the ventral horns and adjacent to the outside edge of the spinal cord, there is the lateral funicu-

lus. Finally, between the ventral horn and the midline, and abutting the ventral edge of the spinal cord, there is the ventral funiculus. See also: **gray butterfly; dorsal funciculus; dorsal horn; lateral funiculus; ventral horn; ventral funiculus; spinal cord.**

G

GABA (gamma-aminobutyric (gam′ə ə mē″nō byo͞o tēr′ik) **acid)** or **GAMA**. The neurotransmitter GABA is found in the in the brain. Its action at all the synapses that it affects is inhibitory. It permits chloride ions, which are negatively charged, to cross the cell membrane into the neuron, making the interior even more negative than before, that is, hyperpolarizing the neuron. See also: **glutamate; glycine.**

GABAA receptor complex. A receptor site for the inhibitory neurotransmitter GABA accompanied by a variety of other receptor sites. Chemicals binding with the other receptors either assist or impede the action of the GABA molecule. These complex chemical interactions around GABA$_A$ sites help determine the level of anxiety or ease an individual experiences. See also: **GABA; receptor sites.**

Galactosemia (gə lak″tō sē′mē ə). A genetically caused inability to metabolize the simple sugar galactose into glucose, the sugar utilized by the body cells.

Galvanic skin response (GSR). A measure of the electrical conductivity of the skin. When a measured drop in electrical resistance is found on the skin, this indicates that perspiration is occurring. Normally, the GSR is taken from the palm of the hand. Perspiration there, as well as on the forehead and on the soles of the feet, results from activity of the "fight-or-flight" reaction of the sympathetic nervous system (SNS). The GSR therefore indicates emotional arousal (as indicated by the SNS activity). It is one of the four components of L. Keeler's original "lie detector." See also: **emergency reaction; sympathetic nervous system.**

GAMA. See: **GABA.**

Gametic potential (gə met′ik). The gametes are the sperm cells and egg cells (ova) provided by fathers and mothers, respectively. Each parent supplies half the genetic material for the fertilized egg, which becomes the offspring. In most species, the male contributes many more sperm cells than the female does ova during reproductive behavior. This is quantified as greater gametic potential for males. Another implication of this difference is that male gametes have to compete among themselves for the relatively fewer female gametes. See also: **natural selection; phylogeny.**

Gamma-aminobutyric acid. See: **GABA.**

Gamma efferents (gam′ə ef′ər ents). Motor neurons that communicate to the tiny intrafusal fibers located within muscle spindle sense organs. These signals lead to the adjustment of the level of muscle tone in the entire muscle, including the regular extrafusal muscle fibers, because the intrafusal fibers signal stretch (the opposite of contraction) receptors located inside the muscle spindle. The central nervous system reacts to stretch messages by sending impulses via alpha efferents to extrafusal fibers, causing them to contract. Contraction is a continuous variable; a muscle may have muscle tone without contracting enough to move its part of the body.

Ganglion (gang′glē ən). A collection of neuron cell bodies, usually in the peripheral nervous system (i.e., outside of the brain and spinal cord). The one exception would be the basal ganglia, which are parts of the brain ventral to the cerebral hemispheres. Additionally, the brain has been called (in jest, with tongue in cheek) the great cerebral ganglion.

Ganglion cells. The cell bodies of these retinal neurons are quite large. The axon of each ganglion cell is an optic nerve fiber. The light stimulus affects the receptor cells, i.e., the rods and cones. Rods and cones in turn communicate with retinal bipolar cells. These in their turn communicate with the retinal ganglion cells. Most axons of these cells (i.e., most of the optic nerve fibers) terminate in the lateral geniculate nucleus (LGN) of the thalamus.

Ganglioside (gang′glē ō sīd). A chemical that has a molecular structure consisting of a combination of fat and carbohydrate.

Gap junctions. Synapses in which the communication does not occur by the diffusion of a chemical neurotransmitter but rather by the induction of a voltage change in the receiving neuron by the electrical field of the sending neuron. Few synapses employ this electrical mode of transmission.

Gastric fistula (gas′trik fis′ choo lə, -tyoo lə). A traumatic opening in the stomach wall or, possibly, a surgically caused opening in the stomach of an experimental animal. Observation of blood flow in the exposed stomach lining has enabled psychiatrists and clinical psychologists to observe the effects of "fight" (anger) and of "flight" (fear) situations. The surgically imposed gastric fistula has been used in studies of the effects of food and/or water deprivation on experimental animals. It allows the researcher to reduce the deprivation level at will by the direct placement of food or water into the stomach via the gastric fistula.

Gastrointestinal tract. The food-absorbing passageway. The gastrointestinal (GI) tract starts at the mouth and includes the esophagus, the stomach, and the duodenum as well as the remainder of the small intestine. It also includes the colon (the large intestine) and the rectum, coming to an end at the anus.

Gate control theory of pain. The theory that pain messages to the brain travel along two pathways, one of which is capable of blocking the other. The brain area where such blocking occurs is the "gate", the location of which has not yet been determined. This theory can account for such phenomena as the damping of dental pain by sounds presented over earphones worn by the patient (the idea being that nonpain stimuli also have access to the pain-blocking pathway), the ability of acupuncture to dampen pain experience, the increase in the perception of pain after damage to the tissues that must contain the pain receptors (the idea here being that the gate for pain is thereby opened), and so on. Data indicate that large nerve fibers are the ones that cause the closing of the gate, while small ones open the gate. This is parallel to the subjective experience of sharp, "bright" pain lasting only for a brief moment (presumably because it is carried over the large-fiber pain pathway) while slow, "dull" aching never seems to go away (presumably because this experience is reported by the small, unmyelinated axons).

Gaze-contingent paradigm. A method for measuring the span of perception. It involves the alteration of a display of text which the subject is in the process of reading. The measuring system works by altering more and more letters (beginning at the periphery of gaze and working inward) in order to see when the person's reading pattern falters. Previous span-of-perception measures (before the introduction of this refinement) produced relatively unreliable measurements.

GE (grade equivalent). A kind of score that places a student's test performance in the grade grouping that it best matches. A GE score of 4.7 means the kind of performance expected from the average fourth-grader after seven months of the school year.

GE differences do not occur in equal steps; therefore they should never be averaged.

Generator potential. Following transduction, a voltage change in a sensory receptor cell capable of initiating nerve impulses in the afferent neuron connected to that receptor.

Gender constancy. The concept that an individual's gender is unchanged despite any alterations of outward appearance.

Gender roles. Social expectations regarding appropriate dress, behaviors, jobs, and so on of males and females.

Gene mapping. A technique which allows researchers to locate specific areas on chromosomes of disease-causing genes. The goal is to determine how specific genes direct the synthesis of particular proteins, with such efforts many times leading to prevention, cures, or treatments for specific diseases. For example, gene mapping led to the discovery that the cystic fibrosis gene was mapped to a small portion of chromosome 7. With that knowledge, it is now possible for prenatal detection of this disease with 99% accuracy. It is also possible to determine whether or not an unaffected member of a family carries the gene for cystic fibrosis.

General adaptation syndrome (GAS). A model of stress which describes personally stressful situations in 3 stages: (1) the alarm and mobilization phase, (2) the resistance phase, and (3) the exhaustion phase. See also: **alarm and mobilization phase; exhaustion phase; resistance phase.**

General paresis (pə rē'sis, per'i sis) ("paresis" refers to paralysis, and is related to the Greek word for "letting fall"). The syndrome resulting from the infection of the brain by the bacterial parasite for syphylis (The brain is not attacked until from five to fifteen years after the original, genital infection. Insanity and intellectual deterioration accompany the paralysis.

General senses. Those senses having receptors scattered all over the body, instead of having them located in specialized sense organs of the head. The general senses are collectively referred to as **somesthesia** (see definition). See also: **somatosensory system; somesthetic; somesthetic area.**

Generalization. The carry-over of a learned behavior to a situation other than the one in which the learning had taken place.

Generalized anxiety disorders. Disorders characterized by long- lasting tension. Individuals with generalized anxiety disorder cannot pinpoint a specific culprit. Physical symptoms in such disorders include dizziness, nausea, muscle twitches, and so on.

Generalized seizure. A type of brain seizure involving a loss of muscle control and a loss of consciousness. The term "generalized" implies that the brain as a whole is involved. Examples of such seizures are the grand mal and petit mal seizures characteristic of epilepsy. See also: **epilepsy; grand mal seizure; petit mal seizure.**

Genes. The units of heredity, as well as the building blocks of heredity. The genes are located, in humans, on 23 pairs of chromosomes in the nuclei of cells. Genes are molecules of the nucleic acid, DNA, and occupy horizontal strips on the chromosomes in the nuclei of animal cells. DNA is a molecule that replicates itself. This is what enables a parent to pass hereditary material along to the offspring. Each particular gene has its own specific location on its chromosome. Genetic research plays an important role in our understanding of diseases. Genetic abnormalities are studied not only for their own sake, but also because they provide clues to the processes at work in heredity. Autosomal disorders, for example, are disorders that have been linked to a specific one of the 22 autosomes. [The other chromosome pair would be the sex chromosomes (X and Y or two X, in the male and the female, respectively).] Conditions related to the X chromosome are known as sex-linked traits. For example, color blindness, male-pattern baldness, and hemophilia are all sex-linked disorders. Of particular importance in genetic research is the furthering of our knowledge of cancer causes, especially those forms which run in families such as colon, breast, and lung cancer. In 1986, for example, scientists isolated and cloned the gene responsible for retinoblastoma, which is a rare and sometimes fatal childhood eye cancer. See also: **autosomal disorders; chromosomes; DNA.**

Genetic drift. Once different subgroups of an animal species become isolated from one another, there are no chances for the sharing of genetic materials among them. Each group must separately adapt to its own environment. The separated gene pools of these groups gradually come to be more and more different. If, at the same time, environmental changes take place, the rate of genetic drift will be accelerated. See also: **natural selection;**

phylogeny.

Genetic subtype. A type of dyslexia which is marked by a strong familial link where reading problems tend to "run in families." Bannatyne suggests that this group displays a WISC-R subtest profile pattern of Spatial > Conceptual> Sequential. Spatial = Picture Completion + Block Design + Object Assembly; Conceptual = Similarities + Vocabulary + Comprehension; Sequential = Arithmetic + Coding + Digit Span. The sign ">" indicates that the score on the left of the sign was greater than the score to the right of the sign.). DeFries and Decker refer to a genetic subtype which is characterized by spatial representation and reasoning deficits instigated by visual-perceptual problems.

Geniculocalcarine (je nik′yo͞o lō kal′kə rīn, -rēn) **tract** (also known as the optic radiation). The group of axons that travels from the lateral geniculate nucleus to the primary visual area of the cerebral cortex, the area on either side of the horizontally-positioned calcarine fissure (visible on the medial surface of the occipital lobe). See also: **calcarine cortex; calcarine fissure; lateral geniculate nucleus; visual cortex.**

Genital herpes. An incurable disease of the genitalia whereby a virus causes the spread of blisters and sores.

Genital warts. A sexually transmitted disease involving the appearance of warts around the genitalia.

Genitalia (jen″i tā′lē ə, -tāl′yə) or **genitals.** The reproductive organs, including the gonads and the penis or clitoris.

Genome. The entire set of genes (determiners of heredity) possessed by an individual.

Genu (jē′no͞o) ("knee", in Latin). The front (anterior) end of the corpus callosum. The genu is in a position to link the anterior parts of the left and right frontal lobes of the cerebral cortex, as well as the left and right parts of the anterior portions of the limbic system (e.g., the cingulate gyrus of the "old cortex"). See also: **corpus callosum; cingulate gyrus; cerebral cortex.**

Gerontology. The study of the elderly. Approximately 25% of the disabilities of the elderly are medical; 75% are the result of social, political, or cultural factors. Contrary to popular opinion, there is only a very small decline in IQ with aging. The cognitive disorders that attack the elderly are not universal, and they may be attributed to unfortunate heredity in many cases. See also: **Alzheimer's disease; Creutzfeldt-Jakob's disease; Pick's disease; senility.**

Gerstmann's syndrome. A controversial cluster of four symptoms which some consider to be one of the subtypes of dyslexia. The four symptoms of this supposed syndrome are dyscalculia, right and left perception problems, finger agnosia (the inability to identify which finger has been stimulated), and dysgraphia.

Gestalt (gə shtält′, -shtôlt′, -stält′, -stôlt′) **psychology** (from German "Gestalt" = "organized whole; pattern; configuration"). The school of thought that accounts for perception by appeal to the organization of whole stimulation patterns rather than the summation of many simple stimulus components of a sensation. The Gestalt psychologists adopted as their slogan the axiom that "the whole is greater than the sum of its parts." Gestalt psychologists have discovered such laws of perceptual organization as similarity, proximity, closure, and figure versus ground.

Gestalt (gə shtält′, -shtôlt′, -stält′, -stôlt′) **therapy.** A type of psychotherapy that aims for the integration of the patient's feelings, cognitions, and actions into an organized whole.

Giftedness. A combination of a superior general intelligence(with the IQ being generally greater than 130) with talents in more specialized areas, such as leadership, creativity, artistic or musical ability, and high aptitudes for either or both gross and fine motor skills (e.g., athletics). Giftedness is thought by most psychologists to be genetically inherited.

Glabrous (glā′brəs) **skin.** Hairless skin, such as the skin of the palms and the soles.

Glaucoma (glô kō′mə, glou-). A vision disorder involving the buildup of excessive fluid pressure in the eyeball to the point that visual acuity is lost.

Glia (glī′ə, glē′ə) (from Greek "glia" = "glue") or **Glial cells.** See: **neuroglia.**

Global amnesia. An amnesia for information received from all the sense modalities.

Global aphasia (ə fā′zhə, -zē ə). The elimination of almost all language ability. See also: **aphasia.**

Global dyslexia (dis lek′sē ə) **subtype.** Weller and Strawser have identified a global or mixed dyslexic subtype which they define as characterized by a dysfunctioning in language and visual-perceptual realms. Denckla has described a global language disorder with several noted problems in language as

a result of some type of right hemispheric involvement.

Global retardation. Profound and widespread learning difficulty, as opposed to having a specific difficulty with one subject such as reading or mathematics.

Globus pallidus (glō′bus pal′i dus) ("pale globe" in Latin). A nucleus (collection of nerve cell bodies), one of the basal ganglia of the forebrain. It is bounded on three sides by another nucleus belonging to the basal ganglia, namely, the putamen. The combination of the two has the aspect of a lens, so the two together have been termed the lentiform nucleus. The lentiform nucleus is on the opposite side of a band of white matter (i.e., the internal capsule) from the caudate nucleus, another of the basal ganglia. These three nuclei (globus pallidus, putamen, and caudate) comprise the corpus striatum. See also: **caudate nucleus; corpus striatum; internal capsule.**

Glossopharyngeal nerve (glos″ō fə rin′j(ē) əl). The ninth pair of cranial nerves, the glossopharyngeal is of mixed function (sensory and motor). On the sensory side, it reports taste sensations from the posterior third of the tongue. The motor fibers innervate the throat musculature. The glossopharyngeal nerve is involved in both salivation and swallowing responses. See also: **cranial nerves.**

Glucagon (gloo′kə gon). The hormone released by the alpha cells of the islets of Langerhans, the endocrine glands attached to the pancreas. Glucagon causes a buildup of blood sugar (glucose) by stimulating the conversion of the glycogen (animal starch) stored in the liver and the release of the resulting glucose into the bloodstream. Glucagon also promotes the utilization of free fatty acids by the body during the fasting period.

Gluconeogenesis (gloo″kō nē″ō jen′ə sis). The synthesis of glucose from the breakdown of the body's own tissues. This drastic procedure is followed only during acute starvation.

Glucoreceptors (gloo″kō ri sep′tərz). Nerve cells in the hypothalamus that are stimulated by increased glucose levels in the blood. They are hypothesized to send "satiation messages" leading to the animal to stop feeding. See also: **ventromedial hypothalamus (VMN).**

Glucose. A monosaccharide (i.e., simple sugar) nutrient that provides energy to the body cells. This is the form of nutriment which is carried by the arterial blood to the cells.

Glucostatic theory. The theory that the onset of the hunger drive and the satiation of that drive are primarily due to the fall and rise, respectively, of glucose levels in the blood.

Glucostats (glōō'kō stats˝). Also known as glucoreceptors, these are neurons that respond to glucose levels in the blood supply. See also: **glucoreceptors.**

Glutamate (glōō'tə māt). Chemically related to glutamic acid, glutamates are the neurotransmitters of the brain that are always excitatory. Glutamate synapses in the hippocampus play an important role in the consolidation of short-term memory into long-term memory through the process known as long-term potentiation. See also: **hippocampus; learning; long-term memory; long-term potentiation; neurotransmitter; short-term memory.**

Glycine (glī'sēn). A neurotransmitter that occurs in the spinal cord which is inhibitory at all of its synapses. See also: **GABA.**

Glycogen (glī'kō jen˝). The animal starch stored in the liver as a glucose reserve. When the need for extra blood sugar arises, the hormone glucagon stimulates the liver to metabolize glycogen into glucose (blood sugar) and release the glucose into the bloodstream.

Glycoprotein (glī˝kō prō'tēn). A type of peptide hormone made up of a chain of amino acids connected to a carbohydrate. See also: **cell adhesion molecule.**

Glycosuria (glī˝kō soor'ē ə, -kōs yoo rē' ə). The presence of glucose in the urine. It may be due to diabetes mellitus or other factors, such as rapid ingestion of carbohydrates, severe anxiety, the dysfunctioning of the anterior pituitary gland or the kidney, or the administration of a drug such as phloridzin.

Gold thioglucose (thī˝ō glōō'kōs˝). A selective toxin, that kills the neurons serving as glucoreceptors. It does so by using the glucose end of the molecule to enter them and the gold and sulphur portion to poison them. Animals treated with this chemical will develop hypothalamic hyperphagia. See also: **glucostatic hypothesis; hypothalamic hyperphagia; ventromedial hypothalamus.**

Golgi (gôl'jē) **apparatus** or **Golgi complex.** A set of membranes in the cytoplasm that wraps itself around chemicals released by secretory cells. In neurons, this structure manufactures the synaptic vesicles.

Golgi (gôl'jē) **stain.** A procedure in which tissue from the central nervous system is immersed first in osmium tetroxide and potassium dichromate and then in silver nitrate. The silver nitrate is taken up, seemingly at random, by a few neurons (less than 1 in every 100). The silver ions are reduced and metallic silver is deposited, as in a photographic negative. The entire neuron, the fibers and the cell body, is stained dark brown, rendering it clearly visible. Due to its unpredictability, this staining technique has earned the nickname "the capricious Golgi."

Golgi (gôl'jē) **tendon organ.** A kinesthetic sense organ in the tendons. The tendons are the attachments, composed of connective tissue, between the skeletal muscles and the bones. The Golgi tendon organs respond to increases in muscle tone, whether or not the muscle actually contracts. If a muscle contraction is not accompanied by a change in tone, the Golgi tendon organ will not respond. See also: **kinesthesis.**

Gonadotropin-releasing hormone. One of two releasing hormones prepared in the hypothalamus that are relayed to the anterior pituitary gland. There, the gonadotropin-releasing hormone controls the release of either of the two gonadotropic hormones, LH and FSH.

Gonadotropins. FSH, the follicle-stimulating hormone and LH, the luteinizing hormone. These are the released by the anterior pituitary, the master gland, to control the output from the ovaries of progesterone (from the corpus luteum) and of estradiol (from the ovaries during the period when the follicle surrounds the ovum). The gonadotropins have effects on the testes also. FSH promotes sperm production while LH accelerates the release of testosterone.

Gonads. Essentially, the reproductive organs. Gonads are the endocrine glands which serve as the sex glands. The male sex glands are testes and the female, ovaries. The testes produce testosterone, while the ovaries produce estrogen and progesterone. All three of these hormones are steroid hormones. The gonads play a major role in reproduction and sexual development. See also: **endocrine system; estrogen; progesterone; steroid hormones; testosterone.**

Gonorrhea (gon ə rē'ə). A sexually transmitted disease which is caused by a bacterial infection that infects the genital membranes.

Goodness-of-fit. A psychological concept which states that an individual's personality usually matches the expectations, behavior of mentors, opportunities, and so on of significant others (especially family members).

Gooseflesh or **goosebumps** or **goose pimples**. A reaction on hairless skin which is similar to the erection of the hairs on hairy skin (piloerection), due to activity of the sympathetic nervous system (SNS). This response is a throwback to our evolutionary forebears, who had hair all over their bodies. The erection of the hairs provided an insulating layer of warm air, protecting the creature from excessive heat loss. On a cold morning, stepping barefoot from your bed onto a deep pile rug feels nicer than stepping onto the plain wooden floor for much the same reason. Species such as porcupines have evolved extra-stiff hairs for defensive purposes. Why not? The SNS will work in any emergency situation, whether it is exposure to excessive cold or threat from a predator. In either case, the object is to erect the hairs. See also: **emergency reaction; sympathetic nervous system.**

Gower's sign. One of the characteristic symptoms of the Duchenne type of muscular dystrophy. After a child has been sitting, the child must first use his or her hands to grab the knees and pull upward, then must use the hands the same way on the thighs, thus "walking up the leg" in order to rise to a standing position. The need to do this is due to the weakening of the thigh, stomach, and back muscles due to the disease. Gower's sign would qualify as a "hard" neurological sign, a clear-cut symptom of physical damage. See also: **hard signs.**

Gracile (gras'il, -īl ˝) **nucleus** ("gracile" means gracefully slender, in English). A collection of nerve cell bodies in the medulla, which receives the axon endings of gracile tract fibers, bearing information about the deep pressure sensations of the lower extremities and the lower trunk. In turn, the gracile nucleus releases axons from its own cell bodies that comprise the medial lemniscus, which travels to the posterior ventral nucleus of the thalamus, the PVNT for short. See also: **cuneate nucleus; cuneate tract; gracile tract; medial lemniscus; medulla; somatosensory system.**

Gracile (gras'il, -īl˝) **tract** or **fasciculus gracilis** (fa sik'yoo lus gras'il is). A collection of axons receiving inputs from unipolar neurons, which act as spinal nerve afferent fibers, receiving deep-

pressure-sense information from the lower trunk and lower extremities. In the coccygeal, sacral, and lumbar (lowermost) segments of the spinal cord, the gracile tract takes up the entire dorsal funiculus of the spinal cord's white matter (i.e., about one-third of the cord's white matter). At the caudal boundary of the thoracic segments (i.e., segments T-12, T-11, etc.), the deep-pressure messages from the upper trunk enter the dorsal funiculus at the lateral edge. As more and more of the upper segments of the body "report in", a new, wedge-shaped tract emerges, namely, the cuneate tract. The gracile tract is now seen (in spinal-cord cross-sections as long and narrow, squeezed into the medial part of the dorsal funiculus; this shape, in the upper cord segments, is responsible for the descriptive name "gracile." See also: **cuneate nucleus; cuneate tract; dorsal funiculus; gracile nucleus; posterior ventral nucleus of the thalamus; somatosensory system.**

Graded potentials. Voltage changes occurring on the membranes of the dendrite or cell body of the neuron, but not on the axon, graded potentials may vary in strength. If a local area of the membrane is near a number of active synapses, it should have a stronger voltage (i.e., an electrical potential of a greater amplitude) than an area affected by only one active synapse. See also: **decremental potentials; excitatory post-synaptic potential; inhibitory post-synaptic potential; spatial summation; temporal summation.**

Graded response. A response the size of which is proportional to the strength of the stimulus that evoked it.

Grammatical rules. The rules specifying how words and word groups are assembled in a language. These rules specify the placement of nouns and verbs and the rules for indicating verb tenses, noun cases, pronoun gender, and so on. See also: **syntax.**

Grand mal seizure. A generalized brain seizure (occurring in epilepsy) that takes place in two phases. Losses of consciousness and of balance are involved. The seizure begins with a tonic phase, during which the muscles contract, resulting in a stiffness of the limbs. The tonic phase lasts for 1 or 2 minutes. It is followed by the clonic phase, which involves jerky movements of the limbs. This is followed by relaxation. Finally, the clonic phase ends in sleep. See also: **epilepsy; generalized seizure; petit mal seizure.**

Granule cell layer. A layer of neuron cell bodies in the dentate gyrus of the hippocampus.

Grapheme (graf′ēm). The smallest component of written language that can represent a phoneme, which is a consonant or vowel sound.

Grapheme-phoneme (graf′ēm-fō′nēm″) **matching** or **correspondence.** The pairing of graphemes with the sound units that they represent.

Graphemic-lexical (grə fē′mik-lek′si kəl) **reading disorder.** A reading disability which is attributable to a difficulty in decoding the meanings of graphemes.

Grasp reflex. A reflex observed in babies in which the hand closes into a fist when an object (such as the finger of an adult) is placed on the hand. While the more mature child shows a different kind of grasp reflex, with the opposable thumb closing over the fingers, an infant will close all five fingers together.

Gray butterfly. The centrally located gray matter within the spinal cord. The four extensions, or horns (left dorsal, right dorsal, left ventral, and right ventral), of this gray matter give it the outline of a butterfly. It is also called the gray H.

Gray H. See: **gray butterfly.**

Gray matter. An area of the central nervous system consisting mostly of the cell bodies of neurons. The "gray" is a dirty pale yellow; it has been likened to the color of raw macaroni. It is due to the color of nerve tissue itself. See also: **white matter.**

Great motor decussation (dē″kə sā′shən). The word "decussation" refers to a bundle of axons crossing the midline of the body (other than commissural axons). The "motor decussation" involves the main motor pathway, the pyramidal tract. As the pyramidal motor tract (or corticospinal tract) arrives at the caudal part of the medulla, near the start of the spinal cord, most of its axons cross to the other side of the midline and continue running caudally down the contralateral side of the spinal cord. The crossed axons, which are in the majority, now comprise the dorsolateral tract, which is also known as the lateral corticospinal tract. They are concerned with control of the muscles of the extremities, the arms, hands, fingers, legs, feet, and toes. The uncrossed axons, running caudad but on the ipsilateral side, constitute the ventromedial tract, also known as the ventral corticospinal tract. They deal with movements of the trunk. See also: **decussation; dorsolateral tract; medulla; py-**ramidal tract; spinal cord; ventromedial tract.

Great sensory decussation (dē″kə sā′shən). The word "decussation" can refer to any band of axons that crosses the midline of the body, so long as it is not a commissure. The body of axons referred to as being involved in a "sensory" decussation is the medial lemniscus, which is part of the sensory pathway for deep pressure. The lemnisci cross the midline higher (more rostrally) than do the pyramidal tract axons involved in the great motor decussation. The messages of the pressure sense travel ipsilaterally in the spinal cord, but after they reach the relay stations in the medulla called the gracile and cuneate nuclei, the messages cross over in axons of the lateral lemniscus and continue running rostrally on the contralateral side to their destination in the thalamus, the posterior ventral nucleus (PVNT). See also: **cuneate nucleus; decussation; gracile nucleus; great motor decussation; lemniscus; medial lemniscus; medulla; posterior ventral nucleus of the thalamus; thalamus.**

Grosser-Spafford anomalous receptor hypothesis. The hypothesis that the peripheral retinal vision of some individuals with dyslexia is more cone-like (photopic) and less rod-like (scotopic) than the visual performance of the peripheral retinae of normal-reading observers. The hypothesis is supported by the fact that (a) visual dyslexics are able to identify the color of peripherally-positioned objects that appear to be colorless to normal readers and by (b) the higher brightness thresholds shown (for the peripheral retina) by dyslexics than those exhibited by normal readers. See also: **Spafford-Grosser lower peripheral brightness sensitivity hypothesis.**

Grosser-Spafford reduced contrast sensitivity hypothesis. The hypothesis that, for visual brightness ratings ranging from 3 to 12 cycles per degree in spatial frequency, the contrast sensitivity of normal readers is superior to those of visual-dysphonetic dyslexics.

Gross motor skills. The use of large muscles for such activities as climbing, swimming, running, or walking. See also: **fine motor skills.**

Group therapy. That form of psychotherapy in which two or more individuals meet with a counseling psychologist or clinical psychologist in order to discuss, examine, and ameliorate emotional/behavioral disorders. See also: **psychotherapy.**

Growth cone. The bud-like structure at the tip of a growing nerve fiber. The direction of growth is believed to be controlled by the chemical interaction between the growth cone and its environment.

Growth hormone (GH). A hormone released by the anterior pituitary gland, the master gland of the endocrine system. The growth hormone is also known as somatotropin or as the somatotropic hormone (STH). It controls the amount and the timing of the growth and development of the body. It is secreted during the onset of sleep. Too little STH leads to pituitary dwarfism; too much, to giantism. Excessive STH after childhood growth has been established leads to an enlargement of the bones of the head, distorting the facial features, a condition called acromegaly. Release of STH can be inhibited by the action of somatostatin, a hormone released by the posterior pituitary gland. STH is also responsible for the pubertal growth spurt. See also: **anterior pituitary gland; endocrine system; hormones; pituitary gland; somatostatin.**

Growth spurt. A rapid increase in height and weight occurring in late childhood. The average age at which boys undergo the growth spurt is 12-1/2, while, for girls, the typical age for the growth spurt is 10-1/2.

Guide dogs. Commonly known as "Seeing-Eye Dogs", these large dogs are trained to help blind people walk safely in public streets and in office buildings. As an extra dividend, the dog provides the blind person with companionship.

Guilty-knowledge technique. A procedure employed with the lie detector to measure physiological responses (breathing rate, blood pressure, heart rate, and galvanic skin response) of a suspect to stimuli that should be meaningful only to the guilty party.

Gustatory nucleus. A nucleus (collection of neuron cell bodies) in the medulla. Afferent neurons for the sense of taste terminate in the gustatory nucleus.

Gyrus (jī′rus) [plural = **gyri** (jī′rī″)]. An outward convolution or fold of brain tissue. The cerebellum and the cerebral cortex exhibit numerous examples of gyri; hence these two parts of the brain present a very wrinkled appearance. The gyri are separated from one another by inward-going grooves known as sulci (singular = sulcus).

H

Habitual pitch. The pitch one uses the most frequently when speaking. A discrepancy between a person's optimal pitch and that person's habitual pitch is one criterion for the diagnosis of a pitch disorder, which is one kind of voice disorder. See also: **optimal pitch; voice disorder.**

Habituation. The gradual reduction of a response after it has been repeatedly elicited by moderate unconditioned stimuli. The modification of neural circuits underlying this process has been studied in the sea slug Aplysia californica. See also: **Aplysia californica; dishabituation; model systems approach; sensitization.**

Hair cells. The receptors in our inner ears necessary for hearing. The hair cells are located in the basilar membrane of the cochlea. The sense of balance, also located in the inner ear, likewise uses hair cells for its receptors. See also: **inner ear; organ of Corti; otolith organs; vestibular senses.**

Hair color. A small number of researchers have linked melanin, which is involved in determining one's hair color, to the development of motor dominance. More specifically, when left- handedness is paired with blondness, the person is claimed to be at greater risk for dyslexia as well as for immune disorders.

Hair mineral analysis. A technique used to detect excess mineral traces such as lead, cadmium, aluminum, arsenic, and mercury, which have been linked by a few researchers to learning disabilities.

Hair-follicle receptors. Receptors, consisting of net-like formations wrapped around the base of the hair follicles, found near the bases of the roots of the hair. These receptors are at the dendritic ends of some of the unipolar neurons. They respond to movements of the hair, because the hair presses like a lever against a part of the net surrounding the follicle. This indicates the direction of the touching force that had been applied to the hair. Such receptors are not found in glabrous skin. See also: **glabrous skin; unipolar neurons.**

Hallucinations (hə loo̅˝si nā′shənz). False perceptions that are unrelated to sensory information. Hallucinations are not to be confused with illusions, which are false perceptions that can be accounted for by reference to sensory information. Hallucinations are the products of abnormal brain activity, the action of hallucinogenic (also called psychotogenic) drugs, or the state of dreaming.

Hallucinogens (hə loo̅′sin ə jenz˝) or **hallucinogenic drugs** or **psychotogenic drugs** or **psychedelic drugs.** Drugs that lead to drastic changes of perception, so that the objects of perception are separate from physical reality. The most potent of the hallucinogens is LSD-25 (lysergic acid diethylamide).

Haloperidol (hal˝ō per′i dôl). A widely used neuroleptic (i.e., antischizophrenia drug) belonging to the group of drugs called **butyrophenones.** Haloperidol is known by the trade name of Haldol. It blocks the action of the neurotransmitter dopamine, but not that of another catecholamine transmitter, norepinephrine. Unfortunately, lifelong administration of this drug to institutionalized schizophrenia patients often produces a neuromuscular disorder, tardive dyskinesia. See also: **clozapine; dopamine; neuroleptic drugs.**

Halstead-Reitan (hôl′sted-rī′tan) **Battery** (of neuropsychological tests). A set of ten or more tests intended to detect injury to the cerebral cortex. These include: One of the Wechsler intelligence scales (the WAIS, WISC, or WPPSI), a category test, a critical flicker-fusion test, a tactile-performance test (specifically, the Seguin-Goddard Form Board), a rhythm test (a part of the Seashore Test of Musical Talent), a speech-sounds perception test, a finger oscillation test, a time sense test, the Minnesota Multiphasic Personality Inventory (MMPI), a trail-making test, and an aphasia screening test. The battery has its limitations; some researchers could not use it to discriminate schizophrenic patients from brain-damaged individuals. See also: **Luria-Nebraska Neuropsychological Battery**.

Hammer or **malleus.** The first of the three tiny bones (ossicles) of the middle ear, the hammer receives sound vibrations from the eardrum (tympanic membrane) and passes them on to the second auditory ossicle, the anvil or incus. See also: **anvil; stapes.**

Handedness. The specification of the dominant hand, as in right- handedness, left-handedness, or ambidexterity (neither hand dominating).

Handicap. A problem that a person who is disabled has in adjusting to the environment (e.g., someone who is confined to a wheelchair being unable to use a staircase or a revolving door).

Hard-of-hearing. Individuals with hearing losses that can be corrected at least to the extent that some language via audition can be heard and processed.

Hard signs. Obvious indications of nerve damage/brain damage observed in a neurological examination. Examples are pathological reflexes, abnormal EEGs, abnormal audiograms, unilateral movement disturbances, and one-sided loss of function on the part of one or more of the 12 cranial nerves. Hard signs are to be contrasted with **soft signs** (see definition).

Harmonics. [1] The science of musical sounds. [2] Overtones. A harmonic or overtone is a note that is fainter and higher than a note played on a musical instrument. It is a whole-numbered multiple (an integer multiple) of the basic note, which is called the fundamental. The set of harmonics that accompanies the fundamental note provides the timbre of the instrument's sound. Each musical instrument has its own timbre, by which its playing can be recognized. See also: **Fourier analysis; timbre.**

Harrison Narcotics Act. A United States Act passed in 1914 that renders illegal the sale and use of cocaine, opium, and morphine.

Harshness. A roughness of speech due to a mixture of sound frequencies; harshness may be due to psychological stress or to organic causes such as a tumor on the vocal cords. See also: **frequency; timbre; voice disorder.**

Hashish. The processed resin of cannabis; hashish is a more powerful source of delta-hydrocannabinol than marijuana.

Hawthorne effect. The impact of a treatment variable that unexpectedly produces the same effect, such as improved performance, whether the variable is increased or decreased. The real reason for the improved performance is not the treatment factor as such, but the awareness of the research subjects that they are under the eyes of prestigious supervisors, professionals, or the like. Most of the time, when these other factors are controlled, the treatment in question would be ineffective. The Hawthorne effect is named after the industrial electric plant in which it was first discovered.

Health psychology. That field of psychology which deals with the relationships among psychological variables and physical disorders. This area of applied psychology is concerned with the improvement of health, the prevention of illness, the diagnosis and treatment of disease, and rehabilitation strategies.

Hearing. The auditory sense. It is stimulated by sound waves that arrive at the eardrum (tympanic membrane). The pinna, or auricle, of the outer ear collects sound waves and directs them into the auditory canal. The sound waves then cause matching vibrations in the eardrum. In turn, these eardrum vibrations are passed on to a series of small bones (ossicles) in the middle ear (the hammer or malleus, the anvil or incus, and the stirrup or stapes). The stapes relays the vibrations to the oval window, a membrane at the entrance to the cochlea of the inner ear. The cochlea consists of a set of fluid-filled canals separated by membranes. The basilar membrane varies in width, so that the part of it which goes into sympathetic vibration is the one that resonates with the incoming sound wave. The higher the sound frequency, the narrower will be the part of the basilar membrane that vibrates. The organ of Corti, which is set into the basilar membrane, contains the inner and outer hair cells, which are the hearing receptors. The hair cells provide a generator potential, a change in voltage, when their hairs are bent in the fluid around the basilar membrane. This signal is passed onto neurons of the cochlear nerve, the auditory branch of the auditory vestibular nerve. Thus the hair cells are providing transduction, a change from mechanical energy to the forms of energy useful to neurons, namely, electrical and chemical energy. The frailty of the hearing mechanism is demonstrated by the ease with which hearing losses occur. Millions suffer some form of deafness. Diseases, infections, birth complications, and prolonged exposure to loud sounds can all cause permanent damage. Conductive deafness involves middle ear problems, whereas nerve deafness results from damage to the cochlea or to the auditory nerve. See also:

amplitude; auditory vestibular nerve; basilar membrane; conductive deafness; hearing, theories of; inner ear; middle ear; nerve deafness; ossicles; outer ear; receptors; transduction.

Hearing aid. An electronic sound amplification device inserted into the auditory canal or worn on the side piece of one's eyeglasses. A hearing aid can assist someone with conduction deafness but is useless in nerve deafness. See also: **hearing; sound.**

Hearing loss. Problems in hearing classified by the anatomical location of the problem. There are three major types of hearing loss: (1) conductive (generated from either the outer ear or the conductive pathway to the middle ear, or both); (2) sensorineural (generated from the inner ear); and (3) mixed losses (a combination of conductive and sensorineural losses). Slight hearing losses indicate a 27-40 decibel (dB) loss; mild, a 41-55 dB loss; marked, a 56-70 dB loss; severe, a 71-90 dB loss; and extreme, over 91 dB loss.

Hearing, theories of. The two chief attempts to account for pitch discrimination are the place or resonance theory and the frequency or telephone theory. These two views have balanced strengths and weaknesses: place/resonance theory accounts for high pitches but not low ones, whereas frequency/telephone theory explains the perception of low tones but fails to account for high ones. A third viewpoint, the volley theory, offers a modified form of the telephone theory to cover the middle frequencies that cannot be explained by either place or frequency theory alone. Georg von Békésy stitched the three theories together into a complete account of our full range of hearing. See also: **frequency theory of hearing; place-resonance theory of hearing; telephone theory of hearing; volley theory of hearing.**

Heart. The organ which Aristotle thought was responsible for our mental and emotional processes. Aristotle regarded the brain as a cooling device for the blood, which in turn passed the cooler temperature on to the rest of the body. This ancient connection between the heart and emotional/intellectual functions has survived in our language, as in the expressions "hard-hearted," "warm-hearted," "half-hearted," and

"heartless." It has also survived in the practice of using stylized heart shapes in Valentine's Day cards. It is reflected, too, in the belief of some fanatical bigots that recipients of an implanted artificial heart have ceased to qualify as human beings.

Hebbian synapse (heb'ē ən sin'aps). A synapse that becomes functional only after it has had the presynaptic neuron leading to its neuron fire a nerve impulse and its own neuron fire an impulse shortly thereafter. See also: **calpain; long-term potentiation; synapse.**

Hebb's Recurring-Digits Test. Nine digits are read aloud by the examiner, and subjects attempt to repeat them. Few will recall nine correctly, due to the limitations of short-term memory. Twenty-three more sets of digits are given, but, unknown to the subjects, every third set is a repeat of the first. Normal subjects gradually learn this repeating set. People with damage to the left temporal lobe and the underlying left hippocampus are impaired on this task. See also: **Corsi's Block-Tapping Test; double dissociation technique.**

Helper T cell. Some of the T cell leukocytes (white blood corpuscles) that come from the thymus stimulate the B cell leukocytes (from the bone marrow) to form B memory cells, which in turn immunize the body from further attack by a microorganism that has entered the body in the recent past. See also: **B cell; B memory cell; T cell.**

Helping-hand phenomenon. In a split-brain patient, the part of the brain controlling one hand "knows" the correct hand-response. In a particular situation, the patient may be required to use the hand controlled by the other half-cortex, the one that "does not know" the correct hand-response. Experienced split brain-patients have learned to use the "knowing" hand to guide the other hand so that the response is carried out successfully.

Hematoma (hē″mə tō′mə). A discoloration and swelling due to a subcutaneous tearing of the wall of a blood vessel, commonly known as a "bruise."

Hemianopia (hem″ē ə nō′pē ə) or **hemianopsia.** Blindness for one half of the field of vision. In hemianopia, each eye sees half of what it would normally see. This occurs because the <u>na-</u>

sal half-retina projects its sensations to the <u>opposite</u> side of the brain (e.g., left nasal retina communicates to the right brain) and the <u>temporal</u> half-retina projects to the brain on the <u>same</u> side (e.g., left temporal retina communicates to the left brain). [Use as a mnemonic device the nonsense word "nots" (nasal = opposite; temporal = same).] Therefore, damage to one side of the brain results in the loss of an entire half of the visual field. For example, loss of the right visual cortex leads to blindness for the left visual field (which sends light rays onto the nasal half of the left retina and the temporal half of the right retina). This example is called homonymous hemianopia of the left visual field. Note that damage to one eye (or one optic nerve), while it does cut the visual field down to half, does <u>not</u> qualify as hemianopia by the present definition. See also: **quadrantanopia.**

Hemiplegia (hem˝i plē′jē ə, -jə). A paralysis of the muscles on one side of the body.

Hemisphere asymmetry. Recent discoveries about the human cerebral cortex show that the right and left hemispheres have anatomical differences. Some individuals, said by some researchers to be left-handers and/or dyslexics, have what seems to be an abnormal degree of anatomical similarity between the left and right hemispheres.

Hemispherectomy (hem˝is fēr ek′tə mē). The surgical ablation of an entire cerebral hemisphere. This operation may be dictated by severe epileptic disorder of the hemisphere in question. It would be expected that many behavioral losses would be incurred in the absence of half of the entire cerebral cortex. However, since the brain has the ability to reorganize itself after damage, and the removed hemisphere has already undergone a long period of impairment, most of the important functions of that hemisphere are already being carried out by the remaining, intact hemisphere, even prior to the surgery.

Hemispheric dominance. The ability of one of the two cerebral hemispheres, usually the left one, to control the dominant side of the body (usually the right) as well as the production and reception of language. The concept of hemispheric dominance was introduced by Marc Dax in 1836.

Hemophilia (hē˝mō fil′ē ə, hem˝ə-, hē˝mō fē′lyə). A sex-linked hereditary disease (i.e., the gene for the disease is recessive and is found on the X chromosome) involving the inability of the blood to clot. See also: **chromosomes; genes**.

Hemophobia (hē˝mō fō′bē ə, hem˝ə-). Irrational and uncontrollable fear of blood. See also: **phobias**.

Hepatic-portal system. A part of the cardiovascular system that carries various nutrients absorbed from the gastrointestinal tract to the liver.

Herbivore ((h)ûr′bi vôr). An animal that eats only plants. Examples are cattle, sheep, deer, and elephants.

Heritability. A statistical index of the extent to which some physical or personality characteristic can be traced to differences in heredity rather than to environmental factors.

Hermaphrodite (hûr maf′rə dīt˝) (from Hermaphroditus, who was the son of Hermes and Aphrodite in Greek mythology). An individual having some female and some male body parts. A true hermaphrodite is rarely seen; such an individual has one testis and one ovary. Most hermaphroditic individuals are referred to as pseudohermaphrodites. See also: **pseudohermaphrodite**.

Heroin. An opiate, that is, a drug that depresses activity but promotes pleasant feelings. It is prepared from opium, which is obtained from the opium poppy. Heroin is very addictive: (1) It produces both physical and psychological dependence. (2) It leads to tolerance effects whereby more and more of the drug must be taken to produce the same effects. (3) Ceasing to take the drug results in painful withdrawal symptoms.

Hertz (Hz). Cycles per second. These are the units of frequency for an energy wave, such as a sound wave. The number of Hertz is the main determinant of how high or low a pitch is. A double bass generates a sound of 50 Hz in frequency. The high notes of a piano provide frequencies of about 5,000 Hz. The wavelength of an energy wave is inversely proportional to its frequency, that is, the higher the frequency, the shorter the wave length. Even the changes of voltage seen in an electroencephalogram, the EEG waves, are measured in Hertz. See also: **BEAM; Fourier analysis**.

Heschl's gyrus. A fold of gray matter found at the posterior end of the superior temporal gyrus of the cerebral cortex. Heschl's gyrus contains the Brodmann areas 41 and 42. It is, therefore, the site of the primary auditory cortex. See also: **auditory area; auditory cortex; gyrus; hearing.**

Heterogeneity (het″ər ō̄ je nē′i tē) **of symptomatologies.** Terminology frequently associated with dyslexia is so diverse that this population cannot be defined by one set of criteria. However, there appear to be subgroups within this diversity containing similar within-group symptoms, with between-group differences distinct enough to warrant subcategorization classifications. No one subtyping system has been consensually accepted to date.

Heterosexual. Being sexually attracted to one or more of the opposite sex.

Heterozygous. Having two opposed genetic influences for a given hereditary trait. For example, one might have the blue allele and the brown allele of the gene for eye color. The blue allele is the recessive gene, while the brown is the dominant one. This individual will have brown eyes. See also: **allele; dominant gene; recessive gene.**

Heuristic. Strategies that assist in simplifying the problem-solving process. One example of a heuristic would be to memorize acronyms when studying for physiology exams (such as that given in the definition for **hemianopia**).

5-HIAA (5-hydroxyindoleacetic acid) (hī drok″sē in″dōl ə sē′tik as′id). A metabolite of serotonin (5-HT). The level of activity of 5-HT synapses can be monitored indirectly by measuring levels of 5-HIAA in the blood, the urine, and/or the cerebrospinal fluid. The amount of 5-HT released and resynthesized by presynaptic (5-HT-releasing) neurons (i.e., the 5-HT turnover) is proportional to the levels of 5-HIAA found in the body fluids. The smaller the level of 5-HIAA measured, the lower is the 5-HT turnover. See also: **indole amines; serotonin; turnover.**

Higher-order conditioning. A type of respondent (classical) conditioning in which a neutral stimulus is paired with a well-established conditioned stimulus. The latter takes the place of the unconditioned stimulus in ordinary respondent conditioning.

Hindbrain. The hindmost (most caudal) of the three main divisions of the brain. The hindbrain includes the medulla, the cerebellum, and the pons. The alternate name for the hindbrain is the rhombencephalon, a name implying a rhombic shape. That shape is mostly due to the medulla oblongata, to give the medulla's seldom-used full name. The rhombencephalon includes the metencephalon (the cerebellum and pons) and the myelencephalon (the medulla).

Hippocampal slice preparations. Slices of the living hippocampus taken from a laboratory animal's brain and kept functional in a special sort of saline solution. The purpose is to stimulate them and recorded electrical responses from them.

Hippocampus (hip″ō kam′pus). A part of the limbic system below the cerebral hemispheres. The word means "seahorse", which is what this collection of gray matter resembles. The hippocampus is essential for the consolidation of short-term memory into long-term memory. Bilateral removal of the hippocampus leads to the quick forgetting of material learned after the injury, although the patient retains the memories of pre-injury learning. The physiological basis of learning is believed to be the process known as long-term potentiation, which is known to occur in cells of the hippocampus.

Histofluorescence (his″tō floo res′əns, -flô-) **technique.** If monoamines are exposed to formalin vapor before being incorporated into the brain, brain slices can be put under fluorescent light. The formalin-treated momoamines will glow, thus revealing their location.

Histological techniques. A set of procedures used in preparing brain or spinal cord materials for microscopic study. The tissue is fixed or frozen in order to harden it. The fixative is usually a chemical solution containing alcohol or formalin. The hardened tissue is embedded in paraffin wax or celloidin. The wax or celloidin block is then thinly sliced into serial sections (which may vary in thickness from 10 to 64 microns, depending on the nature of the research) by a cutting device known as a microtome. The waxy slices are attached to glass slides by albumen. The wax is cleared by repeated baths of alcohol and water mixtures, with every consecutive bath being more diluted, until a final bath with distilled water is used. At this point, a chemical stain (e.g., a Nissl stain such as methylene blue) may be provided, although some methods involve whole-block impregnation which is done earlier, after hardening and before embedding. Very thin glass cover slips are attached to the slides over the tissue sections, using Canada balsam, which is a clear adhesive. The slides are then ready to be examined by microscope.

Histrionic personality disorder (his″trē on′ik). A disorder which is seen more often in women than in men and is characterized by attention-seeking behaviors, an inordinate craving of excitement and daring, highly reactive and excitable behavior, and excessive feelings of dependency.

HIV. Human immune deficiency virus. This virus attacks the body's immune system and is transmitted via sexual contact, blood transfusions, or injection using contaminated needles. The virus invades white blood cells called T-helper lymphocytes. See also: **sexually transmitted diseases**.

Hoarseness. A coarse and rough speech quality. This is often the result of using the vocal cords too much, as in cheering or yelling. Laryngitis, a swelling of the larynx or voice box, may be involved. If hoarseness persists for longer than a few days, medical help should be obtained. See also: **harshness; voice disorder.**

Homeostasis (hō ″mē ō stā′sis)(from Greek "homeo" = "the same"; "stasis" = "standing" or "staying"). This is the name of the ability of warm-blooded animals (i.e., birds and mammals) to regulate their internal environment. Homeostasis is the ability of the body of higher animals to maintain bodily functions within acceptable limits, a dynamic equilibrium. One example is the maintenance of body temperature at normal values despite extreme variation of temperature in the external environment. Another example is the maintenance of the blood glucose at a normal level in the blood supply (80 to 130 milligrams per 100 milliliters) with the assistance of the hormone insulin (which lowers the glucose level) and the hormone glucagon (which raises the glucose level). Other body functions subject to homeostasis include the pH (acidity-level) of the blood and blood pressure. Behaving animals are able to take direction from their physiological drives, such as hunger, thirst, and sex to supplement their internal homeostatic reflexes in the maintenance of equilibrium. See

also: **endotherms; homoiotherms.**

Homeothermic (hō″mē ō thûr mik). See **endotherms; homoiotherms**.

Homogeneity (hō ″mō je nē′i tē, -nā′i tē) of subtypes. This is a concept promulgated by Ellis who believes that a multidimensional model of dyslexics is preferable to models that cluster dyslexics into discrete subtypes.

Homoiotherms (hō moi′ə thûrmz). A classification of animals (i.e., mammals and birds) based on the organism's maintenance of a relatively constant internal body temperature despite fluctuations in the temperature of the environment. Humans are provided with reflexes that permit cooling or warming, permitting us to make appropriate adjustments to the environmental temperature. When it is warm outside, responses such as increased respiration, perspiration, and the dilation of peripheral blood vessels help the body cool off. In a cool environment, responses such as shivering, peripheral vasoconstriction, piloerection, and the release of thyroxin from the thyroid gland warm up the body, the former three by conserving body heat and the last one by increasing heat production. Homoiotherms are also called warm-blooded animals. See also: **endotherms; homeostasis.**

Homologous animal model. A disorder in laboratory animals that follows the same course as a disease process in human beings.

Homosexuality. The condition of preferring sex with partners of the same gender rather than the opposite one. It is considered pathological only if the condition is coupled with feelings of self-doubt and a disturbed concept of one's own identity. The origin of many, if not most, cases of homosexuality is genetic, according to recent research findings. See also: **ego-dystonic homosexuality.**

Homozygous. Having two identical genetic influences (both parents contributing genes with the same allele). With two alleles for a recessive trait, that trait can be expressed. For example, in the case of eye color, brown is dominant over blue. If the individual inherits the blue-color allele from both parents, the individual will have blue eyes. It is possible for the individual to be homozygous for the dominant trait as well. Getting the brown-color allele from both parents makes the individual homozygous for brown eyes. The issue of dominance versus recessiveness arises only for an individual who is heterozygous for the trait in question. See also: **allele; dominant gene; heterozygous; recessive gene.**

Hoover cane. The long white cane, with the lowest six inches being bright red, typically carried by blind persons when they are walking on public streets. Motorists must stop for a person with such a cane until the person has crossed the street safely.

Horizontal. One of the three reference planes (each being at right angles to the other two) for slicing central nervous system tissues to prepare them for microscopic study. The horizontal plane runs parallel to the floor or ceiling. This plane would show brain structures as if viewed from above. A horizontal cut would separate a four-legged creature into a dorsal part, containing, for example, the shoulder blades and ears, and a ventral part, containing, for example, the belly and the four limbs. A horizontal cut would sever a human being at, say, the waist, separating the upper (head end = rostral) and lower (tail end = caudal) parts of the body. A sweeping slash by a long and wide sword wielded by a powerful warrior would do the trick. In the case of the two-legged, upright creature (such as a human), the horizontal cut is perpendicular to the long axis of the "body tube," which qualifies the cut as a transverse section or cross-section.

Horizontal cells. Some neurons lie perpendicular to the main receptor-to-brain pathway in the retina. One group of these is the horizontal cells, which lie alongside the synapses between the visual receptors (rods and cones) and the bipolar cells. When a message is sent from cones to a horizontal cell and then to a bipolar cell, the bipolar cell responds to information about a light stimulus in the surround portion of its receptive field.

Hormones. Chemicals that are released by the glands of the endocrine system. These chemicals travel via the bloodstream to the parts of the body where they perform their specific actions. The shape of the hormone's molecule fits into the shape of a receptor site in the receiving organ; this enables the hormone to leave the bloodstream and go to work at its proper site of action. This shape-coding process is called the lock-and-key recognition system. See also: **endocrine system; polypeptide; steroid hormones.**

Horseradish peroxidase (pə rok′si dās″) **(HRP).** An enzyme found in the roots of the horseradish plant that is useful in tracing pathways of axons traveling through the brain. HRP enters an axon after passage through the axon terminals (i.e., penetrating the presynaptic membranes) and is transported along the axon to the cell body of the neuron. Subsequent addition of other chemicals results in the selective staining of those neurons that have absorbed the HRP. This can tell us which nerve cell bodies are connected to the axon terminals getting the HRP treatment.

Hue. The color of a visual stimulus. Hue is determined by the different wavelengths of light.

Humanistic personality theory. Any psychological theory of personality which assumes that people have fundamentally good qualities (i.e., all people are basically good) and that these qualities can be used to realize our true potentials.

Humanistic psychology. The school of psychology which emphasizes the importance of nonverbal experiences (e.g., feelings) and altered states of consciousness.

Humor. A funny and amusing quality of some speech, singing, activity, or written work. Research has shown that people improve their ability to solve problems after experiencing humorous situations. Further research indicates that, when college students hear lectures with humor integrated into the content, they remember the academic material in the lectures more easily. The television industry knows this relationship very well; find out how much you would have to pay to purchase 1 minute of advertising time during a popular situation comedy. Advertisers well know that people will remember ad messages delivered during such programs, and they have bid up the cost of the ad time accordingly.

Hunger drive. One of the primary drives, the hunger drive is a consequence of the body's physiological need for food. At least one of the two sides of the lateral hypothalamus must be intact if the organism is going to begin seeking food and eating it. Activation of the lateral hypothalamus causes the release of digestive juices into the stomach and of the hormone insulin into the bloodstream. The insulin causes a drop in blood glucose levels, because the glucose is converted into fat or into animal starch (glycogen). This, in effect, puts the food supply into storage; hence the organism will be forced to take in more food in the attempt to rebuild glucose levels. Some researchers have attributed the development of the drive to the underactivity of the glucostats, the receptors that measure the level of glucose in the bloodstream. The glucostatic theory holds that, when glucose levels are low enough, the brain receives signals from the glucostats and responds by causing hunger pangs in the stomach. Satiation mechanisms exist that work to end the hunger drive, making the organism stop eating or seeking food. The glucostatic theory accounts for satiation by the activation of the glucostats in the ventromedial nucleus of the hypothalamus (VMNH), which sense the presence of sufficient glucose in the bloodstream and send a "stop-eating" message to the brain. The lateral hypothalamus (LH) houses the low-glucose sensors, so that its activity can initiate eating behavior (still according to the glucostatic theory). In any event, an animal with bilateral damage to the LH will refuse to eat and requires forced feeding to be kept alive. Other theories point to temperature factors (the thermostatic theory) or to the level of fat in the blood (the lipostatic theory). Environmental stimuli such as odors, the sight of food, emotional situations, and the social setting can also have an influence on the hunger drive. See also: **lateral hypothalamus; primary drive**.

Hunter's syndrome. A sex-linked hereditary disorder (due to a recessive gene on the X chromosome). There is a lack of an enzyme that is needed to break down complex carbohydrates. This leads to a buildup in the system of polysaccharides, with ensuing facial dysgenesis, skeletal deformities, and mental retardation. This serious disease usually results in death before the age of 21. The disease can be detected in a prenatal examination. As of this writing, little can be done by way of treatment.

Huntington's chorea or **Huntington's disease**. This is an autosomal dominant disorder that can be detected by genetic screening. Due to dysfunctioning of the basal ganglia (particularly the forebrain structures called the caudate nucleus,

putamen, and globus pallidus), this motor disorder starts out with a facial tic. Henceforward, other body parts are also involved in tremor. Talking, walking, and other voluntary actions become difficult, then impossible. Speech will be dysfluent and irregular. Some mental symptoms are also evident when the condition is fully expressed. These include impaired memory, depressed mood, paranoid delusions, profound dementia, and hallucinations. The condition is latent until middle age, first appearing between the ages of 30 and 50. The cause is a single dominant gene (which has been found on an autosome identified as chromosome number 4); hence half of a victim's children should inherit the disease.

H-Y antigen. A protein that stimulates the cells of the medullary part of the embryonic gonads to multiply and develop into the testes.

Hydrocephalus (hī″drō sef′ə lus) (from Greek "hydro" = "water"; "cephalus" = "head"). A condition due to blockage of the circulation of the cerebrospinal fluid. The lateral ventricles (open spaces deep within the cerebral hemispheres) are each connected by a narrow passage, the foramen of Monro, to the third ventricle. An obstruction (e.g., a tumor) or a congenital malformation may block the passage sufficiently to prevent the escape of the fluid during fetal development. The fluid builds up and presses the cortex so much that it evens out the folds (the gyri). The result is that the cortex is enlarged in volume, but its surface area is reduced, meaning that the cortex has fewer neurons than it would have had under normal growth conditions. Most cases of hydrocephalus involve mental retardation. The condition can be corrected at birth by surgically inserting a bypass (known as a shunt) to allow the fluid to be drained off either into the esophagus or into the third ventricle. See also: **cerebral ventricles; cerebrospinal fluid**.

6-hydroxydopamine (hī drok″sē dō′pə mēn) (**6-OHDA**). A chemical that, when injected into a region of the brain, selectively damages dopamine-releasing and nor-epinephrine-releasing neurons, but spares other neurons. This property of 6-OHDA makes the chemical a valuable research tool to reveal the contribution of dopamine-releasing and/or nor-epinephrine-releasing neurons in a given kind of behavior. See also: **dopamine; norepinephrine.**

5-hydroxytryptamine (hī drok″sē trip′tə mēn) **(5-HT).** The neurotransmitter better known as serotonin. Its precursor is 5-hydroxytryptophan, which is an amino acid that is produced by a metabolic change of the dietary amino acid tryptophan. After it crosses the blood-brain barrier (BBB), the 5-hydroxytryptophan is metabolically converted into 5-hydroxytryptamine. This two-step metabolic conversion is required, since amino acids are able to cross the BBB, while amines cannot do so. See also: **5-hydroxytryptophan.**

5-hydroxytryptophan (hī drok″sē trip′tə fan). An amino acid that is able to cross the blood-brain barrier, 5-hydroxytryptophan is a precursor (a chemical forerunner) of the neurotransmitter serotonin (5-HT). The arrival of this chemical in brain neurons enables them to manufacture and release the 5-HT. 5-HT, which is a monoamine, cannot cross the blood-brain barrier. See also: **blood-brain barrier; 5-hydroxytryptamine; serotonin; tryptophan.**

Hyperactivity. A condition of some learning-disabled children. The hyperactive child is noisy, active, and difficult to control in the classroom. These children are famous for their paradoxical response to stimulant drugs, which seem to calm them down instead of exciting them further. See also: **attention-deficit hyperactivity disorder.**

Hypercomplex cell. A kind of feature-detecting neuron in the visual cortex (in Brodmann's area 18 and 19). Like simple cells and complex cells, hypercomplex cells are optimally sensitive to a line or edge stimulus, each responding to a particular slant of the stimulus. The receptive fields of these neurons are linear stimuli on the surface of the retina. Like complex cells, hypercomplex cells are not restricted to just one small retinal location, which means they can follow the movement of a line or edge with the orientation for which they are tuned. Unlike complex cells, though, hypercomplex cells are "end-stopped", i.e., the length of the line is cut off by neural inhibition. Different hypercomplex cells are specialized for sensitivity to particular lengths of linear stimuli as well as particular slants. Moreover, there is a subset of hypercomplex

cells that responds to two different orientations of lines; these are capable of being specialized to respond to particular angles. See also: **complex cells; edge detectors; feature detectors; receptive field; simple cells; visual cortex.**

Hyperglycemia (hī″pûr glī sē′mē ə). Blood levels of glucose above the normal range. The condition can lead to the destruction of the body tissues (e.g., blindness resulting from diabetes mellitus). See also: **diabetes mellitus.**

Hyperinsulinemia (hī″pûr in″soo li nē′mē ə). A condition in which excessive insulin is released into the blood, causing hypoglycemia, an insufficiency of blood glucose.

Hyperlexia (hī″pûr lek′sē ə). A paradoxical ability to read very accurately, with excellent mastery of phonics, on the part of a low-intelligence individual. The hyperlexic individual will often fail to understand what he or she is reading so clearly.

Hypermetropia (hī″pûr me trō′pē ə). An inability to see nearby things clearly; also called farsightedness and hyperopia.

Hyperopia (hī″pûr ō′pē ə). See: **hypermetropia.**

Hyperphagia (hī″pûr fā′jē ə, -jə) (from Greek "hyper" = "over" and "phagia" = "eating"). Overeating.

Hyperpolarization (hī″pûr pō″lər i zā′shən). A voltage change on the membrane of a nerve cell that raises the external positive voltage. For example, the voltage may be raised from +80 millivolts to +90 millivolts. This kind of change tends to inhibit the neuron, that is, to cause resistance against the neuron sending a nerve impulse down the axon. See also: **inhibitory postsynaptic potential; inhibitory synapse.**

Hypersomnia (hī″pûr som′nē ə). Excessive sleepiness, not due to medication, which lasts longer than one month, with episodic sleep occurring during the day.

Hypertension. Chronic high blood pressure.

Hypertonic (hī″pûr ton′ik) **fluid.** The extracellular fluid when it has a higher concentration of dissolved substances than does the cytoplasm of the body's cells. This results in a tendency for the cells to lose water. See also: **osmotic thirst.**

Hypertonicity (hī″pûr tō nis′i tē). An excessively high state of muscle tone in which the muscles are too tense and tight.

Hyperventilation (hī″pûr ven″ti lā′shən).

Breathing more deeply or quickly than necessary. This is a symptom of panic or anxiety. Prolonged hyperventilation lowers blood carbon dioxide so much that anything leading to a slight increase in blood CO_2 creates a high percentage increase, causing a sharp increase in sympathetic nervous system activity. Control of this symptom, whether it results from physical or psychological therapy, can promote health in such a patient.

Hypnagogic (hip˝nə goj′ik, -gō′jik) **hallucinations**. Bizarre, dreamlike perceptions that accompany the onset of sleep when a sleep attack occurs in narcolepsy. See also: **narcolepsy; sleep; sleep disorders.**

Hypnosis (hip nō′sis). An altered state of consciousness involving suggestibility and leading to surprising feats of strength and endurance, remarkable levels of anesthesia, and equally startling failures to recall the instructions that account for one's own behaviors. It seems to involve a narrowing of one's consciousness such that it is tightly focused on a limited set of objects; this is referred to as "being in a trance." The explanation of hypnosis is as much a matter of contention among psychologists today as it has been since it appeared (in the guise of "mesmerism") around 1774. The technique has been successful in relieving some hysterical disorders, and it has been effective in helping people give up addictive behaviors such as smoking.

Hypnotic drugs. Drugs that induce or encourage sleeping.

Hypochondriasis (hī˝pō kən drī′ə sis). A neurotic disorder manifested by constant complaints of illness that cannot be confirmed by objective medical examination, exaggerated descriptions of aches and pains, and fear of poor health.

Hypoglossal nerve (hī˝pə glos′əl, -glôs′-). The twelfth pair of cranial nerves; a motor nerve that sends messages to the musculature of the tongue. The functions of speaking and licking are thereby controlled by this one nerve. See also: **cranial nerves.**

Hypoglycemia (hī˝pō glī sē′mē ə). A blood sugar deficiency caused by over activity of the beta cells of the pancreas. Too much insulin is being secreted, so that the body is short of the needed amount of glucose (blood sugar). Symptoms include hunger, weakness, inability to maintain one's posture, double vision, and, in severe cases, coma and death. See also: **diabetes mellitus; hyperinsulemia; insulin.**

Hypothalamic hyperphagia (hī˝pō thə lam′ik hī ˝pûr fā′jē ə, -jə). An overeating syndrome observed in experimental animals after damage to the left and the right ventral medial nucleus of the hypothalamus (VMNH). The animal, on recovery from surgery, is allowed to eat without restrictions. Ordinarily, the animal with total VMNH damage will go through a <u>dynamic</u> phase (lasting about 3 weeks) during which its weight reaches triple the starting value. Afterward, the hyperphagia (over-eating) is only <u>static</u>, i.e., the weight is not increased further, but is maintained at three times normal.

Hypothalamopituitary (hī˝pō thal˝ə mō pi tōo′i ter˝ē) **portal system.** A network of blood vessels connecting the neurosecretory cells of the hypothalamus to the anterior pituitary. The hormones have to be transported along the infundibulum, which is the stalk connecting the hypothalamus to the pituitary body.

Hypothalamus (hī˝pō thal′ə mus). The part of the brain which is located ventral to (below) the thalamus and controls the autonomic nervous system. Such behaviors as eating, drinking, fighting, fleeing, and sexual activity are controlled by the hypothalamus.

Hypothermia (hī˝pō thûr′mē ə). A condition of cold stress whereby the temperature of a human's body falls below 35 degrees Celsius, or 95 degrees Fahrenheit.

Hypothesis (hī poth′ə sis). A good educated guess. Hypotheses are tentative explanations of what you expect to happen based on certain conditions; that is, they are suggested cause-and-effect relationships. Testable hypotheses are stated in such a way that one can confirm or disconfirm the truth or falsity of their basic premises. Hypotheses not only predict relationships between independent and dependent variables, they also help to explain them.

Hypotonic (hī˝pō ton′ik) **fluid.** The extracellular fluid when it has less of a concentration of dissolved materials than the cells of the body have. The fluid is more dilute than the cells, so there is a tendency for water molecules to be lost by the fluid to the cells. Excessive water in the cells may cause them to rupture.

Hypotonicity (hī″pō tō nis′ i tē). A flaccid state of the muscles in which muscle tone is so low that the muscles are unable to resist stretch or to maintain any level of contraction.

Hypovolemia (hī″pō vō lē′mē ə). Reduced blood volume.

Hypovolemic thirst (hī″pō vō lē′mik) also called **extracellular thirst** or **volemic thirst**. A need for water intake (coupled with a behavioral drive toward water ingestion) that stems from decreased blood volume. The neurons responsible for this kind of thirst motivation are located near the third ventricle. Also involved is a hormone, angiotensin II, that is a metabolic product of the kidney hormone renin. See also: **angiotensin II; osmotic thirst; renin; volemic thirst**.

Hypoxia (hip ok′sē ə, hī″pok′-). A shortage of oxygen in the blood.

I

Iatrogenic (ī a″trō jen′ik) **disorder** (from the Greek "iatros", "physician" and "genic", "producing"). A disorder resulting from an attempt to give therapy to the patient.

Iconic (ī kon′ik) **memory**. Visual sensory memory. Our iconic memories can hold between nine and ten items as opposed to approximately five items we can store in echoic (auditory) memory. Typically visual stimuli remain in iconic memory for less than half a second after the stimuli have been removed. Most physiologists believe that iconic memory involves more than receptor functions; that is, higher-level visual processing. See also: **echoic memory; encoding; engram; linguistic coding; memory trace; motor code.**

Identical or **monozygotic** (mon″ō zī got′ik) **twins**. Twins having the same genes because their birth has resulted from a single fertilized egg, or zygote. The zygote splits into two identical cells, with each daughter cell having exactly the same genome (set of genes) as the other. If these two were each to split in the same manner again, identical quadruplets would result. Identical twins have to be of the same sex. Out of every thousand births, there are about four sets of identical twins. See also: **fraternal twins.**

Identification. One of the Freudian defense mechanisms. One protects oneself from anxieties and painful feelings by taking on the characteristics of someone else who is stronger and better-equipped. Children often resort to identification and it may be part of the natural process of gaining maturity and confidence. In pathological extreme cases of this defense, paranoid schizophrenics may believe themselves to be incarnations of great military conquerors or godlike figures. See also: **defense mechanism.**

Idiopathic. Pertaining to disease conditions that have no apparent cause and seem to have originated spontaneously.

Idiot savant. A retarded, mentally handicapped, or autistic person who displays exceptional talent or ability in a single special area. Some idiot savants play a musical instrument with great ability; others may perform amazing feats of rapid and accurate calculation.

Image. A cognitive representation of a sensory experience.

Imagery. The formation of mental images based on past sensations. Imagery may result from such processes as memory, dreaming, hypnosis, meditation, drug effects, and imagination.

Imaginal coding. The storage of information in memory according to its visual features (as opposed to a linguistic code that would use names, for example).

Immune system. The bodily system which protects the body from viruses, bacteria, and other dangers to health. The major active body parts or materials that participate in immunity are (1) antibodies, which are usually produced in reaction to a vaccination, and/or (2) the body cells themselves, reacting against the antigens, which include red blood cells, pollen, transplanted tissue, or even the patient's own tissues.

Immunohistochemistry (i ″myōō nō his ″tō kem′is trē) - (from Latin "immunis" = "safe"; Greek "histos" = "tissue"; the term implies that the immune system is used for a chemical analysis of body tissues). A method of using the immune system to help label the tissues of an animal specimen. To search for the serotonin receptors distributed throughout the brain, for example, the protein from such a receptor site would be injected into an animal, forcing its body to form antibodies against that protein. The antibodies are collected, chemically bonded to dye molecules, and injected into another animal. The antibodies (along with the attached dye) will bond to the serotonin receptor sites anywhere in that second animal's brain. Slides prepared from that brain will reveal the location of all the serotonin receptors.

Impairment. A condition involving a loss of normal functioning which is due to an injury or a disease that has brought about some tissue damage.

Impedance (im pē′ dans) **audiometer**. A measuring device that tests the functioning of the middle ear and the stapedial reflex. This reflex is a response of the stapedius muscle to pure-tone sound stimuli. See also: **middle ear; stapedius; stapes.**

Implicit memory. Memory for information that one did not intentionally commit to memory or information that is unintentionally retrieved (e.g., suddenly remembering that you have a dinner date).

Implosive (im plō′siv) **therapy.** A therapeutic technique for removal of an undesired fear response by flooding the patient with fearful imagery until she or he realizes that one can endure the situation and respond constructively to it.

Impotence (im′pə təns). The inability of a male to have an erection of the penis.

Imprinting. A rapid kind of learning, which takes place in a single trial. The stimulus that is to be imprinted must be presented to the learner at a particular age (usually measured in hours or days). The required age range is called the critical period or sensitive period. Once the stimulus has been experienced, its effect is supposedly stamped in for good, which is why this kind of learning is called imprinting. The acquisition of the species-specific song by male songbirds is one example of imprinting. In species that depend on imprinting, if the sensitive period expires with the young male never having heard the song, the bird, when mature, will never be able to replicate it.

In vivo voltammetry. The measurement of changes in the concentration in the extracellular fluid of specific chemicals using the tip of an electrode to detect changes in current flow as the voltage of the electrode's charge is gradually raised.

Incentive properties. The pleasure expected from the consumption of an object such as a food.

Incidence. An estimate of the number of individuals in the population who exhibit a given condition at some point during their lives. See also: **prevalence; morbidity; comorbidity.**

Incomplete pictures test. A memory test of the ability to identify fragmented versions of pictures that were shown to the subject at an earlier time.

Incus (ing′kus). See **anvil.**

Independent variable. In experimental research, the "cause" of a cause-and-effect relationship; the variable that the experimenters manipulate.

Indole amines (in′dōl ″ ə mēnz′) or **indolamines.** A group of chemicals, the members of which may be chemical neurotransmitters, amino acids, or hallucinogenic drugs. The chemical neurotransmitter known as serotonin [chemically named 5-hydroxytryptamine

(5-HT)] is of importance in our sleeping-dreaming-waking cycle and to our degree of elation or depression. It is metabolically constructed from the amino-acid indole amine, tryptophan. Other indole amines are known to be hallucinogenic. The best known is lysergic acid diethylamide (LSD). Other hallucinogenic indole amines are psilocin and psilocybin.

Induction. The influence of a developing cell's local environment on the course of that cell's development. For example, the mesoderm can induce changes in the neighboring neural plate.

Infant amnesia. The loss of memory for events occurring before age 5.

Infantile autism. A behavioral/mental disorder of children and young adults that begins before the age of 2-1/2 years. It involves a lack of responsiveness to social stimuli, very poor language ability, and bizarre behavior.

Infarct. A diseased area of an organ consisting of dead cells due to an infarction. See also: **infarction; ischemia; necrosis.**

Infarction. A necrosis (tissue death) due to an interruption of the blood supply to the tissue involved. See also: **ischemia; necrosis.**

Inferential statistics. Statistical procedures that determine whether or not the researcher is justified in generalizing the outcome of an experiment done with small groups of subjects (i.e., samples) to the entire population(s) from which the samples were drawn. A finding (from statistical inference) that the result of an experiment could easily be due to chance requires that the researcher should not make a general statement on the basis of that study alone. If the result is given an acceptably low probability (the lower the better, but five chances out of 100 is often considered the highest acceptable probability) that it is due to chance, then the result may be generalized to the entire population. In that case, the result is considered "statistically significant."

Inferior. Under or below; or at the bottom end.

Inferior colliculus (kə lik′yoo lus) ("collus" = hill in Latin;"-icul-" is a diminutive, a "make-it-smaller" particle). One of two (a left and a right) hill-shaped bumps on the roof of the midbrain, lying below and behind the superior colliculi. The inferior colliculus is a nucleus that serves as a way-station to the auditory cortex. It is in the main line of the neural pathway from the cochlear nuclei of the medulla to the auditory region in the temporal lobe of the cerebral cortex. Impulses from the inferior colliculus travel to the medial geniculate nucleus of the thalamus. The medial geniculate nucleus in turn sends axons to the auditory cortex (Brodmann areas 41 and 42 of the temporal lobe). See also: **auditory area; auditory cortex; hearing; medial geniculate nucleus; midbrain; superior colliculus.**

Inferotemporal (in ˝fə rō tem′pər əl) **cortex.** The cortex of the inferior temporal lobe. It is involved in the analysis of visual forms.

Infiltrating tumor. A tumor that grows into and through the tissues that surround it.

Informal assessment. Supplementing the standardized formal tests that can be given to a group of examinees are such other measures as observations, teacher-made classroom tests, sample behavior situations, anecdotal records, checklists, and so on.

Information processing. The brain processes information by means of a complex network of interconnected neurons, using a number of communication pathways. There are two major conceptions of how this happens. The synaptic transmission theory holds that the flow of information follows electrochemical nerve impulses down axons and the flow of neurotransmitter chemicals across synaptic clefts to immediately neighboring neurons. The volume transmission theory postulates that some information can spread far in the extracellular fluid between widely spaced neurons, as the neurotransmitters from sending neurons find receptor sites suitable for themselves on the membranes of receiving neurons. This allows information to be chemically diffused for fairly long distances. We can think of these two theories as "dry" and "wet" models, respectively. The linear flow along axons described in the synaptic transmission model qualifies that one as the "dry" model, and the concept of the extracellular fluid as an information conduit makes the volume transmission model the "wet" one.

Information-processing model. The theoretical representation (i.e., modeling) of perception, learning, cognition, and/or reading as equivalent to the computerized handling of information, with input, data, processing, and output functions serving as models for the brain's cognitive

activities.

Infundibulum (in˝fun dib′yoo lum). See: **pituitary stalk.**

Inhibited ejaculation (i jak˝yoo lā′shən). The inability of a male individual to ejaculate when he attempts to do so.

Inhibited sexual desire. The condition of having a highly restrained motivation toward sexual activity or even the lack of such motivation.

Inhibitory factors. Chemicals released from the hypothalamus that regulate anterior pituitary hormones by blocking their release.

Inhibitory postsynaptic potential (IPSP). A graded and decremental positive electrical potential on the membrane of the receiving, or postsynaptic, neuron at a synapse. By adding to the resting amount of positive voltage on the outside of the cell membrane (or, the equivalent, adding to the negative charge on the cytoplasm within the cell), this voltage change makes it more difficult for the neuron to initiate a nerve impulse. It may involve the infiltration of negative chloride ions into the cytoplasm or the escape from the cytoplasm of positive potassium ions. See also: **excitatory post-synaptic potential; hyperpolarization; inhibitory synapse; nerve impulse; resting potential.**

Inhibitory synapse (in hib′i tôr˝ē sin′aps˝). A synapse in the nervous system which produces an inhibitory effect on the receiving neuron, due to the release of a neurotransmitter that hyperpolarizes (inhibits) a receptor site on the receiving neuron's cell membrane. See also: **hyperpolarization; inhibitory postsynaptic potential.**

Initial stage 1 EEG. The stage of sleep that occurs at sleep onset. Unlike the later stage 1 periods, it is not associated with dreaming or with rapid eye movements. it is also called "descending stage 1" because the later episodes of stage 1 follow a previous stage 2, as the stages figuratively ascend the stairway from stage 4 to stage 1. See also: **sleep; stage 1 sleep (descending).**

Inner ear. The fluid-filled cavity which is often called the labyrinth because of its complex functions and parts. The inner ear is divided into two sections: the cochlea (responsible for converting mechanical sound waves to electrical impulses via the cochlear nerve) and the vestibular mechanism (responsible for our sense of balance). After the cochlear nerve is stimulated and electrical impulses are relayed to the auditory cortex, sound is heard.

Innumeracy (i nōō'mûr ə sē″). The inability of an individual to deal readily with number concepts or to understand how random probability works.

Insanity. A legal term which denotes the condition of an individual who is not legally responsible for his/her actions. Such an individual may be committed to a mental hospital rather than to a penitentiary.

Inside-out pattern of cortical development. The deepest layers of the cortex are the first to be formed. The outer layers must be formed by neuroblasts (or very young neurons) traveling through already-formed cortex to their eventual locations.

Insight. [1] A psychoanalytic term which indicates one's awareness of inner drives or unconscious conflicts that are causing distress or psychological problems. Psychoanalytic sessions involve free association, transference, and dream analysis, all of which focus on developing insight. [2] A Gestalt psychology term for the sudden awareness of the solution to a complex problem, based on the mental assembling of the elements of the problem that had earlier seemed to be unrelated or whose interrelationships had been misunderstood. Some Gestaltists speak of such a sudden understanding as the "Aha!"-experience.

Insight therapy. A type of psychotherapy focused on the individual's obtaining an understanding of her or his own motives and actions in order to improve well-being. See also: **psychotherapy.**

Insomnia (in som'nē ə). An inability to go to sleep and/or to stay asleep that persists over a period of several days and nights. This disorder affects 30% of all adults. There may be trouble with falling asleep, waking up too early, waking up in the middle of the night, or any combination of these. Sedatives (even if prescribed) lower the quality of sleep, especially reducing both stage 4 sleep and REM sleep, which are the two most valuable phases of sleep. There may also be a drug tolerance aspect, with higher dosages needed to maintain the same effect. The amino acid tryptophan (which is metabolized into the transmitter serotonin) has been found to help people fall asleep; it is found in milk, chicken, cheese, soybeans, and cashews. It will also help the insomniac to reduce the intake of caffeine and ethyl alcohol and stop using tobacco. As a cautionary note, pills of pure tryptophan seem to be toxic as of this writing. See also: **barbiturates; REM sleep; sedatives; serotonin; sleep; stage 4 sleep; tryptophan.**

Instrumental conditioning. See: **operant conditioning.**

Insulin. A hormone that is secreted by the beta cells (one of two types of islet cells) in the pancreas. Insulin assists in converting blood glucose into a starch in the form of glycogen to be stored in the liver. It also helps convert fatty compounds in the blood to a form that permits them to be stored in the liver. Insulin deficiencies result in the condition of diabetes mellitus, in which there is an excess of glucose in the blood. Excessive insulin activity, on the other hand, leads to a shortage of glucose in the blood (i.e., hypoglycemia). See also: **diabetes mellitus; hyperglycemia; hypoglycemia.**

Integrated Learning System (ILS). A computer software system in which several computers are arranged in a network. The computer network incorporates instructional tools for teachers and instructional software.

Integration. The combination of several signals into a consolidated, unitary signal.

Intellectual ability. A broad spectrum of cognitive abilities, including memory, reasoning, and comprehension.

Intellectualization. A defense mechanism identified by Sigmund Freud. This involves avoidance, not having to face one's own feelings by developing a superficial type of insight into one's inner problems. There is a rational and well-thought-out analysis of oneself and one's own motives, but feelings are buried and are covered by logical thinking. See also: **defense mechanism.**

Intelligence quotient (IQ). A global intelligence score which is based on performance (usually verbal and perceptual areas are measured) on an intelligence test. The IQ is purported to measure the test taker's global ability to adapt effectively to the environment. It supposedly reflects such cognitive variables as memory, problem-solving ability, reasoning, judgment, and so on. After the age of 6, someone's IQ is relatively stable, unless there are complications from illness, drug or alcohol abuse, or brain trauma. Generally, an IQ score in the range of 90 to 110 is considered to fall in the average range of performance. Lower scores generally mean that there are general intellectual lags or areas of mental deficit. Higher scores, especially those above 120, indicate giftedness or superior intellectual functioning. The distribution of IQ scores in the population is represented by a normal, bell-shaped curve: IQs above 130, considered "very superior," are manifested by 2.2% of the population; 120-129, "superior," 6.7%; 110-119, "bright average," 16.1%; 90-109, "average," 50%; 80-89, "low average," 16.1%; 70-79, "borderline," 6.7%; and below 70%, "mentally retarded," 2.2%. An individual's IQ is thought to be affected by genetic factors and also depends on education, maturity, and experience. There are two types of intelligence, as indicated by typical measurements. First, there is verbal intelligence, which involves the size of one's vocabulary, the extent of the general information one has, the ability to solve arithmetic problems, and so on. The second type is performance intelligence, which deals with the ability to solve complex visual puzzles, to solve jigsaw puzzles, to find the missing detail in a picture, and so on. There is some criticism to the effect that minorities sometimes evidence lower-than-average IQ scores because questions on these tests reflect "white middle-class" standards. However, the better IQ tests are still considered a good barometer of intellectual functioning and potential in our society. The word "quotient" refers to the earliest way of measuring intelligence, in which the person's mental-age score (MA) was divided by the person's actual chronological age (CA) and the resulting quotient was multiplied by 100. Today the IQ of 100 is the population mean of a normally distributed collection of test scores; in early tests, such as the Stanford-Binet, an IQ of 100 meant that the person's mental age was the same as that person's chronological age.

Interactionism. A position taken on the mind-brain problem to the effect that mental phenomena can affect physical events and physical happenings can make a difference in what happens in consciousness. Originally, interactionism was a form of dualism, the idea that the mind and the brain are separate entities. This view was espoused by the French philosopher Descartes, who suggested that the physical effects of sensory stimulation could be registered as mental sensations at the tiny, centrally located pineal body (a small gland attached to the roof of the brain's thalamus). Furthermore, Descartes theorized, one's wishes and desires could affect the workings of the arms and legs (thereby, allowing voluntary behavior to occur) by exerting force on the pineal body. Later interactionist views were not expressed systematically and consistently until recently. Physiological psychologist M. Gazzaniga combined interactionism with the emergent-property point of view. The complexity of the brain's structure enables the mind to emerge (just as, when the gases hydrogen and oxygen combine, the liquid, water, emerges). Once the mind has emerged, it interacts with the brain so that physical events can change thoughts and thoughts can change the flow of chemical neurotransmitters and the spread of nerve impulses. Gazzaniga considers his view a variety of materialistic monism, because mind can not exist without the necessary physical organization of matter that leads to its emergence. See also: **dualism; emergent property position; materialism; mind-brain problem; monism; pineal gland.**

Interactive reading models. These models stress the simultaneous information processing of verbal data at high or low levels, using both bottom-up and top-down channels of information flow.

Interblobs. A part of the sustained visual pathway to be found in sublayer IVc-beta of area 17 of the cerebral cortex (area V1, the first visual area). M. Wong-Riley, after having applied the stain cytochrome oxidase to tissue of the visual cortex, noted that sublayer IVc-beta had blotches of stained tissue surrounded by patches of unstained tissue; she called the former the blobs and the latter the interblobs. The blobs project (i.e., send axons) into thin, dark stripes of area 18 (area V2, the second visual area), while interblobs project to the pale stripes of area V2. The blob-thin, dark-stripe pathway provides for color discrimination; whereas, the interblob-pale stripe pathway, which is color-insensitive, provides fine-detail visual information. See also:

blobs; sustained visual pathway.

Interference. Forgetting in memory due to conflicting or co-occurring information that interferes with remembering. There is proactive interference, which refers to old memories interfering with new memories. When a child learns a second language (e.g., Latin), the first-language vocabulary and grammar (e.g., English) can produce proactive interference or failure to recall second-language vocabulary or grammar (i.e., Latin). The opposite is true with retroactive interference or new memories interfering with older memories. Using the same example, second-language acquisition (i.e., Latin) can interfere with the recall of primary-language vocabulary and grammar (i.e., English).

Interindividual differences. The ability differences observed among different students. This is commonly referred to as individual differences.

Internal capsule. A compact bundle of white matter which contains (a) all the axons carrying messages from the cerebral cortex to all parts of the nervous system below the telencephalon, including the axons of the pyramidal motor tract and extrapyramidal axons, and (b) all inputs to the cerebral cortex from the thalamus, including the optic radiation, the auditory radiation, etc. After the internal capsule fibers rise past the corpus striatum, they fan out so that each part of the overlying cortex receives the appropriate inputs. This fanning-out or radiating look is the reason why the axons feeding some of the primary sensory areas of the cortex are called "radiation fibers." See also: **cerebral cortex; corpus striatum; optic radiation; pyramidal tract; thalamus.**

Internal desynchronization (dē sing ″krə ni zā′shən). A complication of the circadian rhythms that results when two free-running circadian rhythms (each responsible for a different process) begin to operate on different schedules. See also: **circadian rhythms or cycles; free-running rhythm.**

Internal releasing mechanism (IRM). The simultaneous triggering of a series of reflexive actions by the appropriate environmental stimuli. These stimuli are the supposed releasers, while the mechanism itself is an organization of a part of the brain. Researchers in the field of ethology have investigated many examples of IRMs. The psychotherapist H. Levinson regards the brain's programming of seasickness after the rapid inflow of visual messages into the cerebral cortex as one example of an IRM, which he has used in accounting for (a) dyslexia and (b) panic reactions. See also: **ethology.**

International 10/20 system of electrode placement. A system for controlling the placement of 19 electrodes on the scalp for recording an EEG (electroencephalogram). Seven electrodes are placed in an arc over the front edge of the head, over the frontal bone of the skull, and, therefore, over the frontal lobe of the cerebral cortex; one of them is on the midline of the body. Five electrodes (one of which is on the midline) are placed in line between the two ears; the two outermost are over the temporal lobe, while the other three are designated "central"; the middle one is over the midline of the body. Farther back, five more electrodes are positioned in a gently-curved line; the outer two of these are also over the temporal lobes, while the inner three are over the parietal lobes; the middle electrode of these three is over the midline. Finally, four electrode sites go around the back edge of the head. Of these, the outermost two have already been mentioned, since they correspond to the two posterior temporal lobe locations given with the "gentle arc", described above, containing the three parietal lobe placements. The inner two sites on the back rim of the head are placements of electrodes over the occipital lobes. The three midline electrodes are labeled "z," for zero distance away from the midline. Even numbers designate placements over the right hemisphere and odd numbers indicate sites positioned over the left hemisphere. This 10/20 scheme helps to assure standardization of research procedures using EEG data. See also: **electroencephalogram.**

Interneuron. A neuron which is neither sensory [afferent (i.e., attached to a sense receptor)] nor motor [efferent (i.e., attached to a muscle or gland cell)]. Most neurons are "in between" (hence, "inter-") the motor and the sensory ends of the nervous system. All the in-between or interneurons belong to the central nervous system, in sharp contrast to the neurons at the starting points or the terminals of the sensory and motor pathways, the afferent and efferent neurons, respectively. All afferent and efferent neurons belong to the peripheral nervous system.

Internode. A distance along the axon between consecutive nodes of the myelin sheath [see definitions of **myelin; node (of Ranvier)**]. An internode is one millimeter (i.e., 1/1000th of 1 meter) long. It corresponds to the length of an oligodendrocyte (in the central nervous system) or a Schwann cell (in the peripheral nervous system).

Interoceptors. Sense receptors directed at the internal environment, monitoring carbon dioxide levels in the blood, blood glucose level, blood pressure, temperature, blood volume, etc.

Interpersonal skills. Clusters of skills which are enabling in a social sense. One's own physical well-being impacts to a great extent on the quality of one's interpersonal skills. Berenson offers interpersonal models for skills building in human resource development.

Interpositus nucleus. A nucleus in the midst of the white matter within the cerebellum. R. F. Thompson and colleagues found that this nucleus is essential for the performance of a respondent-conditioned eyeblink response in the rabbit. See also: **classical conditioning; cerebellum.**

Intersex. See: **pseudohermaphrodite.**

Interstitial (in″tər stish′əl) **fluid**. See: **extracellular fluid.**

Intimacy. A feeling of close connectedness that prevails in a loving relationship. It includes the desire to maintain and enhance the welfare of the loved one, the sharing of happiness with the loved one, high esteem for the loved one, reciprocal emotional support with the loved one, and considering the loved one a part of one's own life. See also: **triangular theory of love.**

Intracellular (in″trə sel′yoo lər) **thirst**. Normally, there are two kinds of thirst, intracellular and volemic, and water deprivation arouses them both at the same time. An experimenter named Gilman in 1937 injected a test subject with a hypertonic salt solution. This leads to the depletion of water in the cells without reducing the volume of water in the extracellular fluid around the cells. The sodium and chloride ions do not pass the cell membrane into the cells, accumulating in enough quantity in the fluid around the cells to set up osmotic pressure. The only way for the

osmotic pressure to be returned to equilibrium (osmolality = osmotic neutrality) is for water molecules to move from the cell across the semipermeable cell membrane to the extracellular fluid, diluting that fluid. Meanwhile, however, the cells have been depleted of water. The same effect is produced by salty potato chips, pretzels, or peanuts (no wonder your neighborhood bartender is so generous with these "munchables"!). See also: **volemic thirst.**

Intracranial self-stimulation (ICS). The repeated pressing of a lever in a Skinner box by an animal with an electrode chronically implanted in a reinforcing area of the brain, reinforced by the delivery of brief electrical pulses to the brain via the electrode.

Intrafusal (in″trə fyoo′zəl) **fiber**. A small muscle fiber, too weak to contribute to moving a part of the body, which is found inside the muscle spindle sense organ. When regular (extrafusal) muscle fibers contract, the intrafusal fibers also contract. When extrafusal fibers are stretched, so are the intrafusal fibers. Stretched intrafusal fibers stimulate afferent nerve endings within the muscle spindle. These nerve endings send impulses to the spinal cord and, by reflex action, nerve impulses are sent along motor nerves to the extrafusal fibers, maintaining muscle tone. The stretch reflexes (those utilizing intrafusal fibers and the stretch receptors to which they connect) include the knee-jerk reflex which is often tested during medical examinations. The central nervous system is enabled to reset the required tone in a muscle by sending impulses via special motor neurons, the gamma efferents, to the intrafusal fibers within that muscle. See also: **extrafusal fiber; gamma efferents; kinesthesis; muscle spindle; stretch reflex.**

Intragastric feeding. A preparation of an animal with a tube implanted into its upper gastrointestinal tract, permitting the animal to press a lever reinforced by the delivery of food directly into the stomach.

Intraindividual differences. Measured differences between or among two or more ability scores of the same individual, that is, differences within students.

Intramuscularly (IM). Refers to injection of a chemical into a muscle.

Intraperitoneally (IP). Refers to injection of a

chemical into the abdomen (i.e., past the peritoneum, the lining of the abdomen).

Intravenously (IV). Refers to injection of a chemical into a vein.

Intrinsic motivation. Motivation being the directing force and energizing factor in behavior, intrinsic motivation spurs on the individual to perform actions that make him or her feel more competent, able, self-determined, and satisfied.

Intromission. The thrusting of the penis into the vagina.

Intropunitive (in″trō pyoō′ni tiv). Tending to punish oneself, to feel guilty or ashamed, when one's efforts are frustrated.

Introvert. According to Jung, individuals who focus more on their own inner feelings and thoughts than those of others. Introverts tend to like solitude and lack confidence in social situations. See also: **extrovert.**

Inverted image. The upside-down image formed by reflected light refracted by the cornea and lens on the surface of the retina.

Ion. An atom or group of atoms that has an electrical charge, positive or negative. Positive ions, such as those of metallic elements, are called cations while negative ions are called anions.

Ion channels. Passages or gates in a neuron's cell membrane that are opened to a particular ion (or to certain ions); the opening of an ion channel is followed by either a depolarization (excitatory voltage change) or a hyperpolarization (inhibitory voltage change) of the neuron.

Ion concentration gradient. A force generated by the difference between the concentration of a dissolved ion, for example, the sodium ion (Na^+) in a watery solution on one side of a semipermeable membrane (such as the axon membrane) from the concentration of that ion in the watery solution on the opposite side of the membrane. There is a pressure for the ions in the solution in which they are more concentrated to flow into the other solution. This pressure or force is referred to as the ion concentration gradient. Its strength is proportional to the difference be-

tween the two concentrations. See also: **diffusion; resting potential.**

Iproniazid (ī″prə nī′ə zid). An antidepressant drug, originally used against tuberculosis. It is an MAO-inhibitor. See also: **MAO-inhibitors.**

Ipsilateral (ip′si lat″ər əl). On the same side of the body. An ipsilateral reflex has the response being made by a muscle on the same side as the part of the body that had been stimulated. Ipsilateral neural connections can be of two varieties, namely, associations and projections. Some layers of the lateral geniculate nucleus (which is in the retina-to-brain neural pathway) receive their inputs from the eye on the same side; these are layers 2, 3, and 5, the ipsilateral layers. See also: **contralateral.**

Iris. The forward extension of the choroid, it contains the pigmentation that gives someone's eyes their distinctive blue, brown, or other color. The iris acts like a diaphragm, controlling the size of the pupil.

Ischemia (is kē mē ə). A local, temporary shortage of blood due to an obstruction of the circulation into the affected body part.

Islands of memory. Memories for isolated past events that took place during longer periods the rest of which have been forgotten.

Isolation. The separation of subgroups of a species by physical barriers, for example, mountain ranges or oceans. See also: **genetic drift; natural selection; phylogeny.**

Isometric contraction. The contraction of a muscle that increases its pulling force without changing the muscle's length.

Isomorphic animal model. A disease condition artificially produced in a laboratory animal to resemble a human disorder.

Isotonic (ī″sō ton′ik) **fluid.** The condition in which the concentration of substances dissolved in the extracellular fluid is equal to (i.e., isotonic with) the concentration of solutes within the body cells. This is the normal condition supported by the body's homeostatic functioning. See also: **homeostasis; osmolality.**

J

James-Lange theory of emotion. The view that an emotional experience does not take place until physiological responding to the emotion-provoking stimulus has taken place. "I see a bear--I run away--I am afraid. " That sentence is a succinct statement of the James-Lange theory in action. The idea is that physiological events cause emotions, not the reverse. Physiologically, the implication of this view is that the cerebral cortex has to wait in order to process not only information about the emotion stimulus but also information about the initial reactions to that stimulus before it can decide on an emotion. See also: **Cannon-Bard theory of emotion; cognitive-arousal theory of emotion.**

Jet lag. The result of having the Zeitgebers controlling one's circadian rhythms become accelerated when taking an airplane flight from east to west or become decelerated when one flies from west to east. See also: **circadian rhythms or cycles; Zeitgeber.**

Just noticeable difference (jnd). Another name for the difference threshold. See: **difference threshold.**

Juvenile delinquency. A term for deviant behavior among children and adolescents which derives its meaning from legal criteria rather than from the sociology or psychology of the child.

Juvenile rheumatoid arthritis (rōo′mə toid är thrī′tis). A chronic disorder observed in school-age children; the symptoms include fatigue, stiffness, and pain in the joints.

K

Kainic acid (kī′nik). A chemical that, when injected into a region of the brain, will destroy local nerve cell bodies but will spare axons passing through (i.e., fibers of passage). This chemical is a useful research tool for following up experiments which have revealed that damage to a given brain area affects a behavior. Such experiments lead to the question, "Did the injury have an effect because local neurons were destroyed or just because passing axons were severed?" Follow-up work with kainic acid can settle such issues.

Kamin effect. A memory phenomenon observed in testing rats in a standard avoidance-learning apparatus, the shuttle-box. The box has a floor of metal grids; the two halves of the floor are separately connected to a source of electricity. When one half-grid is electrified, the animal must run over a dividing hurdle to the other half of the shuttle-box. This is escape training, but by providing a light and/or a sound signal that comes on a few seconds before the shock, the experimenter can commence avoidance training. The animal must now change ends of the box before the shock begins; when the animal crosses the barrier, the signal turns off and the shock does not turn on. After some training, the rats are tested for their memory of the avoidance lesson: Some are tested 1 minute after the last training trial, some 30 minutes after, some 1 hour after, some 6 hours after, some 1 day after, and some 20 days after the last trial. The animals succeed in remembering to avoid at the 1-minute, 30-minute, 1-day, and 20-day marks, but they forget after 1 or 6 hours. This strange dip in the avoidance response versus time curve is called the Kamin effect. Apparently the earlier tests allow the rat to use a relatively "short-term" memory trace, and the longer delays let the rat use its "long-term" memory; during the 1- and the 6-hour post training time span, although the short-term memory is in the process of being consolidated into its long-term form, it is unavailable for use in guiding ongoing activities.

K complexes. Large, biphasic EEG waves that are observed during stage 2 sleep. See also: **stage 2 sleep.**

Kennard principle. The concept that, for a given amount of injury to the cerebral cortex, behavioral functions tend to be spared more in infantile animals than in fully grown ones. The presumed reason is that undamaged parts of the brain can become reorganized to take over some of the functions of the damaged cortical areas. This principle seems to hold in some circumstances, but to be the opposite from the truth in others. The Kennard principle may be generally true for language development, but particular skills, such as syntax, may be permanently damaged after brain lesions suffered in infancy. Although the right hemisphere can take over control of language after damage to the left one, a price has to be paid: Visuospatial functioning becomes impaired.

Ketones. Carbon compounds in which one carbon atom is attached to two other carbon atoms and has a double-bond attachment to an oxygen atom. Ketones can be the breakdown products of fatty acids and can serve as a source of energy when the supply of blood glucose is low.

Kimura Box Test. An objective test for apraxia.

Kindling. A phenomenon observed after repetition of low-intensity electrical stimulations to the same site in the brain. After a few stimulations, a small and localized tremor occurs. After each later stimulation, a larger area of the body goes into convulsions. Finally, after hundreds of stimulations, the animal shows spontaneous convulsing, "spontaneous" in that no stimulation precedes the seizure. This has proven a useful model of epilepsy. For example, the drug diphenylhydantoin (Dilantin) reduces convulsions kindled by stimulation of the cerebral cortex but not those due to amygdaloid stimulation; whereas, the drug diazepam (Valium) blocks amygdaloid-originated convulsions and not those due to cortical stimulation. This means that epileptic humans ought to differ in their responses to drug treatment, depending on the location of the epileptic focus in the brain.

Kinesthesis (kin″es thē′sis). The sensation of movement. Kinesthetic receptors are located in the muscles, tendons, and joints. Kinesthesis is one of two proprioceptive senses, with the vestibular senses being the other. The muscle spindle organ (a modified muscle bundle) reports on the state of contraction of the entire muscle bundle of which it is a part. The length of a muscle is an indicator of how relaxed a muscle is; the more tone in the muscle, the more it contracts. The sense receptors in each joint send afferent nerve impulses at rates proportional to the number of angular degrees at which the joint is turned. From joint receptor information, the central nervous system can construct a body image with the relative positions of all the limbs identified. Kinesthetic sensations are among the few that do not enter into awareness; we process kinesthetic information, but we are not conscious of doing so. See also: **gamma efferents.**

Kinesthetic approach. A technique of instruction that uses the sensations from the student's muscles, tendons, and joints as well as her or his movement sensations.

Kinship genetics. The more closely related two individuals are, the more alike their genetic makeup. Therefore, behavior that defends one's own close relatives also defends one's own genetic material. See also: **natural selection; phylogeny; relative adaptive fitness.**

Kleptomania (klep″tō mā′nē ə). An impulse control disorder in which the individual habitually steals for personal pleasure.

Klismaphilia (klis″mə fil′ē ə). A type of paraphilia whereby the individual derives sexual enjoyment from taking enemas. See also: **paraphilias.**

Klüver-Bucy (klōo′ver-byōo′sē) **syndrome**. After bilateral removal of the temporal lobes of the cerebral cortex and possible incidental lesions to underlying parts of the limbic system, Klüver and Bucy noted in their monkey subjects five novel kinds of behavior: (1) Orality, a tendency to sniff objects and bring these objects to the mouth. (2) Hypermetamorphosis, the touching and rubbing of moisture patches or pictures on the walls or floor and the picking up of small objects for oral examination over and over again. (3) Psychic blindness, the inability to interpret the meaning of seen objects, with the experimental monkey even demonstrating curiosity about the tongue of a snake. (4) Excessive taming, a kind of flatness of emotion and an absence of normal rage behavior. (5) Excessive and indiscriminate sexuality, often disregarding gender and species. A human case of this syndrome was reported following a severe viral attack that destroyed areas of both temporal lobes.

Korsakoff's (kôr′sə kôfs″) **syndrome**. A disorder of the brain involving memory losses and visual hallucinations. The immediate cause is nutritional, a lack of vitamin B_1 (thiamin), which is needed for the proper utilization of oxygen and glucose by central nervous system neurons. Damage appears in the mammillary bodies on the ventral surface of the hypothalamus and other parts of the diencephalon and limbic system. Patients suffer from both anterograde amnesia (forgetting learning they have just acquired) and retrograde amnesia (forgetting events from their past lives). They profess a lack of awareness of their memory problems, which they "cover up" by confabulation, using made-up stories as if they are true reports of past events. These patients also tend to exhibit apathy, an indifference to ongoing activity. The most usual reason for the nutritional problem is alcoholism. The consumption of the "empty calories" in ethyl alcohol prevents normal hunger from being aroused, hence the vitamin B_1 deprivation. See also: **dorsomedial thalamus; mammillary bodies.**

K-P (Kaiser-Permanente diet) (kī′zər pûr″mə nen′tā″). A diet recommended by a few practitioners which eliminates synthetic food colors and natural salicylates in order to remedy learning disabilities and behavior problems.

Kuru (kōo′rōo). A condition caused by a slow-acting virus that attacks the brain. The disease strikes more women than men and more children than adults. The brain degenerates rapidly. Symptoms of kuru include trembling, paralysis of the limbs, and early death.

Kurzweil Reading Machine. A machine that is capable of converting written matter into spoken English. The user has to be thoroughly trained in order to benefit from the machine, so it is best used by older students and/or adults.

Kyphosis (kī fō′sis). A condition in which the shoulders have a rounded appearance, with a backward convexity of the spine. This postural problem can lead to medical difficulties. It may be due to poor posture or to such disorders as arthritis or rickets. It is also known as humpback or spinal curvature.

L

Labeled-line theory. The theory of sensory perception which holds that each receptor responds to a very restricted range of stimulation and is provided with a direct line to a specific location in the brain which provides for the meaningful perception of the stimulus. For example, a red-light-sensing cone in the eye sends the first of a chain of neural messages that ends up at a "red"-interpretation area in the cerebral cortex. This view has historical antecedents, one of which is Helmholtz's place-resonance theory of hearing and the other of which is Müller's law of specific nerve energies. The opposite view is the across-fiber pattern theory of sensory coding. See also: **across-fiber pattern theory; law of specific nerve energies; place coding.**

Labyrinthine (lab˝i rin′thin˝, -thēn˝) **sense organs.** A labyrinth is a maze; in the cavity in the skull that houses the inner ear is a complex arrangement of tunnels, the labyrinth. Within the labyrinth are the three semicircular canals and the two vestibular sacs, the utricle and the saccule. The semicircular canals sense rotary accelerations (spins) in space, since they cover the three dimensions of: up-down, right-left, and forward-back. The utricle monitors horizontal linear accelerations, for example, accelerating in an automobile. The saccule covers vertical linear accelerations, for example, riding an elevator in a skyscraper office building. See also: **saccule; semicircular canals; utricle; vestibular organs.**

Lactase (lak′tās). The enzyme necessary for the metabolism of the milk sugar, lactose.

Lactose (lak′tōs). The type of sugar found in milk. It is a disaccharide (a compound sugar made up of two simpler sugars) and can be broken down into the monosaccharides (simple sugars) glucose and galactose.

Lamina (plural = laminae). A layer of cells. For example, the six cell layers of the human cerebral cortex are referred to as laminae.

Language. A system of symbols shared by the persons within a social group with which they can communicate among themselves. See also: **pragmatics; semantics; syntax.**

Language-based deficiency. A language-based deficiency refers to problems centered in the verbal realm and includes articulatory-motor difficulties, poor listening comprehension, limited vocabulary, problems with verbal expression, difficulties with verbal fluency, dysphonemic-sequencing disorders, problems with verbal organization, poor blending of phonemes, verbal organization problems, and so on. The problems described by researchers in the language area vary widely, depending on the researcher's perspective, factors studied, and adherence to a particular philosophy or school of thought.

Language deficit. Deficits in language skills which could be due to central nervous system dysfunctioning, lesions, brain injury, chemical imbalances, or learning disabilities.

Language lateralization. The concept of unihemispheric control of speech production and speech interpretation. Specifically, the left hemisphere of the cerebral cortex is the dominant one (in nearly all right-handers and even in the majority of left-handers) for major speech and language functions.

Lanugo hair (la nyoo′gō). A fine, downy hair that appears on the skin of fetuses and may also develop in individuals with anorexia nervosa. See also: **anorexia nervosa.**

Large-print books or **large-type books.** Books printed in an enlarged typeface. The print is clear and the letters are widely spaced. These are for the use of visually impaired persons. See also: **talking books.**

Laryngectomy (lar˝in jek′tə mē). The surgical removal of the larynx.

Laryngitis (lar˝in jī′tis). Inflammation of the larynx.

Larynx (lar′ingks). The organ at the upper end of the trachea or windpipe. It consists of cartilage, muscle, and an elastic membrane. Included in the musculature of the larynx are the two vocal cords, which are separated by a slit known as the glottis.

Laser cane. A cane that uses emitted laser-light beams to identify obstacles, in order to help blind people travel in safety. It emits three infrared beams, one up, one down, and one forward. When the beam is reflected from an object between 5 and 12 feet away, a sound signal is produced as a warning to the user. See also; **guide dogs; Hoover cane.**

Latent learning. Learning in the absence of immediate reinforcement of a correct response. It occurs when incorrect behavior (and, occasionally, correct behavior) takes place. Learning is demonstrated at a later time, however, when reinforcement is made available after correct responding. The time that has passed between the time of the learning and the time when the correct behavior appears consistently is a latency period, hence the name.

Lateral. To the side. The word is an antonym of "medial." The adjective "lateral" may be converted to an adverb by changing the terminal "l" to a "d," as in "laterad." The "lateral" pass in football does not go forward (in front of the line of scrimmage), but sideways. The lateral geniculate body is toward the outside part of the brain; it is to be distinguished from the medial geniculate body, which is closer to the body's midline. Hands and feet are examples of lateral parts of the anatomy.

Lateral attack. The mode of attack used by a dominant male rat against an intruding male rat. The dominant rat rams the other rat sideways, reminiscent of car-chase scenes in movie thrillers in which one driver attempts to force the other off the road. See also: **aggression.**

Lateral corticospinal (kôr″ti kō spī′nəl) **tract**. See: **dorsolateral tract.**

Lateral fissure. A long, deep groove on the side of the cerebral cortex, the lateral fissure is the main boundary line between the temporal lobe, which lies ventral (inferior) to it, and the frontal and parietal lobes, which are dorsal (superior) to it. Another name for the lateral fissure is the fissure of Sylvius. See also: **cerebral cortex.**

Lateral funiculus (fə nik′yoŏ lus, fyoo-) (funiculus = small cable). One of the three major bundles of white matter to be seen on either side of a cross-section of the spinal cord. Several tracts (bundles of axons) run through the lateral funiculus, some going rostrad toward the upper cord segments or to the brain, others going caudad toward lower cord segments. An example of a tract (in the lateral funiculus) going in the rostral direction is the lateral spinothalamic tract which conducts nerve impulses reporting pain and/or temperature sensations to the posterior

ventral nucleus of the thalamus (PVNT). A tract of the lateral funiculus that runs caudad would be the dorsolateral tract which carries contralateral motor commands to the extremities (i.e., the limbs and the digits). See also: **funiculus; spinal cord; dorsolateral tract; lateral spinothalamic tract.**

Lateral geniculate (je nik′yoŏ lit) **nucleus** ("geniculate" = "knee-shaped"; "genu" = "knee" in Latin). The word "nucleus" here refers to a large grouping of nerve cell bodies within the brain. The lateral geniculate nucleus (LGN) is that nucleus in the thalamus which is reached by the great majority of the axons in the optic nerve. This nucleus relays messages from the eye to the visual areas of the cerebral cortex.

Lateral hypothalamus (hī″pō thal′ə mus) **(LH)**. A part of the hypothalamus of the brain that, if damaged bilaterally (i.e., on both sides of the brain), will lead to the cessation of eating and drinking behaviors. Such an organism must be kept alive by forced feeding. This behavioral function was formerly interpreted to mean that the lateral hypothalamus is the "feeding" or "hunger" "center." The lateral hypothalamus is also important in quiet biting (non-affective) aggressive behavior. See also: **hypothalamus; predatory aggression.**

Lateral inhibition. In the compound eye of an invertebrate, the term refers to an inhibition against responding in one ommatidium (facet) of a compound eye caused by light stimulation of a nearby ommatidium. The inhibition of the one ommatidium is indicated by a recording electrode on the sensory nerve fiber from the ommatidium. There are three laws of lateral inhibition, stated by Ratliff. The area law states that the more of an area (i.e., the more ommatidia) of a compound eye that is illuminated, the greater will be the inhibition of the tested ommatidium. The intensity law states that the stronger the illumination of a nearby ommatidium, the more the inhibition of the tested ommatidium. The proximity law states that the strength of the inhibition in a tested ommatidium depends on the distance from it to another illuminated ommatidium; ommatidia more than two ommatidium-widths away do not inhibit the tested ommatidium at all. These three laws apply to the vertebrate eye, if one simply substitutes for the word "ommatidium" a "small set of visual receptor cells."

Lateralization. [1] The determination that a given behavior function depends specifically on a particular cortical hemisphere, for example, the left hemisphere. [2] The extent of the division of functions between the left and right sides of the forebrain.

Lateral lemniscus (lem nis'kus). A tract of axons (which, in cross-section, is oval or lens-like in appearance, rather than circular, as most tracts are). The lateral lemnsicus is part of the auditory neural pathway from the ear to the auditory cortex. It carries nerve impulses from the superior olivary nucleus (of the border region between the medulla and the pons) to the nucleus of the lateral lemniscus in the inferior colliculus of the midbrain. See also: **axon; hearing; lemniscus; medulla; pons; superior olivary nucleus; tract.**

Lateral masking. An individual letter within a horizontal string of letters is harder to identify than a single letter positioned at the same eccentricity (i.e., degrees of visual angle from the point of fixation). This lateral masking effect is weakened for letter strings that are relatively close to the fixation point. The effect can also be weakened by increasing the space between the letters in the string. See also: **Aubert-Foerster law; lateral inhibition.**

Lateral plexus. The network of nerve connections that allow for lateral interactions, such as lateral inhibition, in the compound eye of the horseshoe crab, Limulus polyphemus.

Lateral preoptic (prē″op′tik) **area.** A region of the hypothalamus on which osmotic thirst depends. Its neurons have osmoreceptors (sensors for change in osmotic pressure). See also: **osmotic thirst.**

Lateral spinothalamic (spī″nō thə lam′ik) **tract.** A bundle of axons running through the spinal cord and the brain stem. The spinal cord section of this tract runs rostrad through the lateral funiculus. The lateral spinothalamic arises from neurons of the dorsal horns of the gray butterfly of the spinal cord. Almost immediately after the axons leave the dorsal horn cells, they cross the midline, so they ascend to higher levels of the CNS in the contralateral lateral funiculus. The axon terminals reach some of the neurons in the posterior ventral nucleus of the thalamus (PVNT). The lateral spinothalamic tract carries information about pain and temperature (as well as some messages from the sense of touch) and is part of the somatosensory system. See also: **brain stem; contralateral; dorsal horn; gray butterfly; lateral funiculus; posterior ventral nucleus of the thalamus; somatosensory system.**

Law of specific nerve energies. A doctrine stated by Johannes Müller in the early nineteenth century to the effect that each sense modality used a specific quality of nerve impulse in its afferent nerves, so that the brain could sort out sensory information according to the radically different qualities of nerve energy it was receiving. Moreover, within a modality, detailed resolution of the information was dependent on more subtle qualitative distinctions, so that, for example, you could tell the difference between something touching your index finger and something touching your middle finger by the quality (the "indexity" or the "middleness") of the touch message that arrives at the brain. Why was this "spendthrift law" taken seriously? (It was spendthrift because it postulated many qualitatively different kinds of nerve stimulation, violating the principle of "parsimonious explanation" valued by scientists.) It had an audience because it seemed to be the only way to explain certain puzzling facts about perception, for example: (1) the **phantom limb** (see definition), and (2) **phosphenes**. This doctrine was reworked into a more reasonable version by Helmholtz, who offered the **place-resonance theory of hearing** in the middle of the nineteenth century. A still more modern version is today's **labeled-line theory** (see definitions).

Lazy eye. See: **amblyopia ex anopsia.**

l-DOPA (levo-dihydroxyphenylalanine). The immediate precursor of dopamine; l-DOPA is a non-dietary amino acid.

Leaky-barrel model. One of the models for the representation of the set point in the regulation of body fat. It is an alternative to older set-point models.

Learned helplessness. The learned belief that no strategy can save one from a stressful environment. This phenomenon results from multiple experiences of failure. It has been hypothesized by M. Seligman to be the basis of clinical depression.

Learned-inattention theory of schizophrenia. The concept that schizophrenic persons have learned not to respond to social stimuli and to attend, instead, to stimuli that are unrelated to ordinary human relationships.

Learning. A relatively permanent change(s) in behavior or knowledge which is due to environmental experiences. Learning is the process by which we acquire knowledge and skills that help us adapt to the environment. It may be implicit (when there is no conscious effort to learn and it is simply a by-product of experience; sometimes this is called incidental learning in order to contrast it with intentional learning) or explicit (when there is a deliberate effort to learn; intentional learning). Even the development of the brain during infancy partly depends on environmental stimulation. Explicit learning requires the integrity of the temporal lobe of the cerebral cortex, whereas implicit learning takes place at any synapse involved in reflexive behavior. Hebb's rule has set the stage for a physiological theory of learning: "When an axon of one neuron repeatedly participates in the firing of a second (postsynaptic) neuron, a growth process and/or metabolic change takes place in one or both neurons such that the ability of the first neuron to cause the second to fire is increased." Kandel and Tauc, based on empirical research on learning in the sea snail Aplysia californica, added a second rule as a supplementary alternative to Hebb's: "The synaptic connection between two neurons can be strengthened even without the activity of the postsynaptic neuron provided that a third neuron, a modulatory neuron, repeatedly enhances the release of an excitatory neurotransmitter from the axon terminals of the first, presynaptic, neuron." Later research work has confirmed that both mechanisms occur.

Learning disability. A disorder involving one or more of the psychological processes required for understanding, or for using, either written or spoken language. The individual may be handicapped by the decreased ability to listen, speak, think, spell, read, write, or do mathematical operations. There is a discrepancy between an individual's innate abilities (e.g., IQ) and actual academic performance. Learning disabilities are thought to (1) persist for a lifetime, (2) be caused

by some type of neurological dysfunctioning, (3) have correlating symptoms or behaviors (e.g., social misperceptiveness and attention deficits with or without hyperactivity), (4) warrant specialized educational and other professional interventions, and (5) cause psychological distress related to learning and social problems which results in depressed self-esteem, lowered self-confidence, more negative interactions with others, and an external locus of control (i.e., attributing problems or situations to external influences as opposed to internal factors).

Learning theory (of language acquisition). The belief that the principles of operant and respondent conditioning can fully account for the development of language behavior in human individuals.

Least-restrictive environment. The principle expressed in PL94- 142 (in 1990 renamed IDEA, or the Individuals with Disabilities Education Act) that promises disabled persons the right to full education in an environment as like a regular classroom as possible. Any limits on such an environment must be justified as being required due to the specific handicap(s) of the person concerned. See also: **mainstreaming.**

Legally blind. Visual acuity of 20/200 (normal = 20/20) or less in the better eye even with corrective lenses. This term can also refer to the narrowing of the field of vision to an angular distance of no greater than 20 degrees.

Lemniscus (lem nis'kus) or **fillet.** A tract or fasciculus which is flattened in cross-section, because most of the component axons are side by side with fewer axons to be found above and below the center of the bundle. One example is the medial lemniscus, which continues the somatosensory pathway after the gracile and cuneate tracts have reached their synaptic endings at nuclei in the medulla. The medial lemniscus crosses over, so that sensations from the right side of the body reach the left side of the brain and vice versa. The cross-over fibers of the medial lemniscus constitute the "great sensory decussation." (See **decussation.**) Another example is the lateral lemniscus, which is part of the auditory pathway from the inner ear through the medulla.

Lens. A structure in the eye which is directly behind the iris and the pupil. The lens bends light rays to a point(s) on the retina where further visual processing occurs.

Lentiform (len′ti fôrm) (from Latin "lentiform" = "lens-shaped") **nucleus**. The combination of the globus pallidus and the putamen, which are two of the basal ganglia. The globus pallidus is the smaller of the two and is closely surrounded, on three sides, by the putamen. See also: **basal ganglia; corpus striatum; globus pallidus; putamen.**

Lesch-Nyhan syndrome (lesh nī′hən sin′drōm). Hereditary hyperuricemia, a disorder of metabolism involving progressive mental retardation along with self-mutilating behaviors. Death usually occurs, by renal failure, before adulthood. Although medical interventions offer little promise, behavioral approaches have been successfully used to reduce the self-mutilating behaviors.

Lesion (lē′zhən). An injury or wound of the brain.

Leu-enkephalin (loo″en kef′ə lin). A chain of five amino acids (i.e., a peptide) that is thought to function as a pain-relieving neurotransmitter.

Leukocyte (loo′kə sīt ″). A white blood cell (white corpuscle) that is found in any of several forms, namely, the **macrophage**, the **T cell**, the **B cell**, and the **natural killer cell** (see definitions).

Level of aspiration. The verbalized (at least internally) statement of the level of skill or achievement one intends to reach in performing any action that requires some proficiency or ability. A high level of aspiration commits the individual to become one of the leading performers of the skilled action involved, a moderate level of aspiration is simply a decision to do well but not to try for stardom at the task in question, and a low level of aspiration is simply a hope to keep on doing as well as one has been doing, without expecting any great improvement. See also: **cognitive reappraisal.**

Lexical procedure. A system for reading aloud according to the stored information, acquired through earlier learning, about the pronunciation of certain printed or written words.

LH. See: **luteinizing hormone.**

Life expectancy. The number of years that the average person lives. On the average, American males live to age 73 and females, to age 81.

Keeping socially and economically active after retirement, not smoking, not consuming food or alcohol to excess, and keeping one's weight down all contribute to prolongation of life expectancy.

Lifesaver motor-skill task. A learning task in which a monkey is trained to thread a "Life-Saver" candy (a round candy with a hole in the center) along a bent metal rod.

Light adaptation. The loss of reactivity to very dim light exhibited by an eye that has been exposed to strong light. See also: **dark adaptation.**

Light(ness) constancy or **brightness constancy**. The phenomenon whereby an object appears to stay at the same level of lightness even when the amount of light falling on the object changes. Maintaining light constancy is an acquired ability that enables the individual to keep track of objects in the environment.

Limb apraxia (ə prak′sē ə, ā prak′-). A type of inability to carry out an intended movement that involves either (1) performing movements in the wrong order, (2) making an incorrect movement with the correct part of the body, or (3) using the wrong part of the body to perform a movement. Injury to the corpus callosum leads to the inability to use the left hand to make a movement requested by spoken words (callosal apraxia). When neural control is lost over a limb, say, on the right side, due to damage to the left cerebral cortex, there may also be an apraxia of the limb on the left side, controlled by the undamaged right cortex (sympathetic apraxia). Lesions in the left parietal lobe of the cerebral cortex may produce bilateral apraxia, involving the limbs on both sides of the body (left parietal apraxia). See also: **apraxia; constructional apraxia; corpus callosum; parietal lobe.**

Limbic system ("limbus" = "border" in Latin). Several structures in the brain including the **hippocampus**, the **amygdala**, the **cingulate cortex**, the **hypothalamus**, the **fimbria**, the **fornix**, the **mammillothalamic tract**, and the **accumbens** nucleus which assist in regulating emotions, memory, and higher-level thought processes (see definitions). These telencephalic tracts and nuclei serve as a border zone between the cerebral cortex and the diencephalon of the brain.

Limulus. The horseshoe crab, Limulus polyphemus. An invertebrate animal with a compound eye made up of several facets each serving as a basic, miniature eye. The study of the visual nervous system of this animal allowed Hartline to discover the on-responses and the off-responses of the neurons in the visual pathway. Further research allowed Hartline's student, Ratliff, to discover the principles of lateral inhibition. Extensions of their work to the vertebrate visual system led to the discovery of the circular receptive fields of retinal ganglion cells. See also: **lateral inhibition; Ratliff's Laws of Lateral Inhibition; ommatidium.**

Linear circuitry. The arrangement of neurons in a single line so that each nerve cell in the line receives information only from its predecessor and passes information only to its successor.

Linear perspective. A monocular cue to visual depth (i.e., front-to-back distance) by which nearby objects look larger than faraway objects. Furthermore, the nearby objects are also apparently more widely-separated than faraway things.

Lingual gyrus (from Latin "lingual" = "tongue-shaped"). A gyrus of the occipital lobe of the cerebral cortex, visible on the midline or medial surface of the cortex. It is the more ventral of only two gyri that comprise the medial aspect of the occipital lobe. Its dorsal border is the **calcarine fissure**. Dorsal to this fissure is the wedge-shaped **cuneus**, which is the second gyrus of the occipital lobe's medial aspect. The lingual gyrus and the more ventral part of the cuneus make up the **calcarine cortex**, which is the primary visual area, at which the nerve endings of the **geniculocalacarine tract** terminate (see definitions). See also: **striate cortex; visual cortex.**

Linguistic coding. The storage of information in memory based on language (rather than on sensations, e.g.). See also: **echoic memory; encoding; engram; iconic memory; memory trace; motor code.**

Linguistic deficiency dyslexic subtype (LDD). This is a dyslexic subtype proposed by Spafford and Grosser which is typified by language-based deficiencies.

Linguistic functioning. The ability to use language in communicating with others.

Linguistic relativity hypothesis. The theory put forth by Whorf that the language of a cultural group shapes that group's perceptions and cognitions about the world.

Linguistics. The scientific study of language, including speech sounds, syntax (the rules of grammar), and semantics (the meanings of words). See also: **psycholinguistics.**

Lipectomy (lip ek′tə me). The removal of body fat by surgery.

Lipid. A fatty substance that will dissolve in an organic solvent, such as benzene or ether, but will not dissolve in water. Lipids form the basis for neuron cell membranes. The cell membrane has been depicted as a bimolecular leaflet. Each molecule has a water-soluble head (consisting of a protein, which is compatible with water) and a water-rejecting tail (consisting of lipid). The head part faces a watery solution (either the cell's cytoplasm or the extracellular fluid that exists between cells), while the fatty tail faces another fatty tail in the interior of the cell membrane. Lipids are the major constituent of myelin. See also: **lipoprotein.**

Lipocytes (lip′ə sīts). The fat cells. Digested fats are chemically converted to triglycerides and stored in the fat cells of adipose tissue, during the absorption phase (directly after a meal). The adipose tissue is a form of connective tissue modified to include the fat cells. In the following, fasting phase, the hormone glucagon induces the release of fat, in the chemical form of free fatty acids and glycerol. The glycerol is sent to the liver, converted to glucose and released into the bloodstream. See also: **absorption phase; fasting phase; glucagon.**

Lipogenesis (lip″ō jen′ə sis). The formation of the body's lipids or fats.

Lipolysis (li pol′i sis). The breakdown of the body's lipids (fats).

Lipoprotein (lip″ō prō′tēn). A compound which is part **lipid** and part **protein** (see definitions). A pair of lipoprotein molecules, each having its water-seeking head projecting outward to the nearby fluid and its lipid parts (which are fatty and water-repelling) meeting one another, comprises the bimolecular leaflet which constitutes the cell membrane of a neuron. One "head" (of the lipoprotein pair) contacts the extracellular fluid; the other head meets the neuron's cytoplasm (for the axon, this head meets the axoplasm). With this arrangement, the watery heads may be exposed on one side of the membrane while, just opposite, the heads could be blocked off. This would permit ions from one solution to have the first opportunity to cross the membrane and get to the other watery fluid, as in the opening of a one-way gate, an ion channel. Multiple layers of lipoproteins comprise the myelin sheaths of myelinated axons.

Lipostatic theory. The theory that eating is controlled by lipid receptors that read an oversupply of lipids in the blood in relation to a "normal-value" set-point for fat content.

Lipreading. The use of visual cues (especially by hearing-impaired individuals) from the movements of the lips to understand what is being said. This technique needs to be distinguished from **speechreading** (see definition) which is a more comprehensive assessment of spoken messages.

Lithium (lith′ē əm). An element similar in its chemical activity to sodium and potassium. Drugs containing the lithium cation (lithium carbonate, e.g.) have been useful in treating both mania and depression. Since it is effective against either kind of mood disorder, it should not be surprising that lithium does not affect the availability of norepinephrine or serotonin at synapses. Instead, it does its work on the second messenger system, blocking the production of the second messenger, phosphoinositide.

Lobectomy (lō bek′tə me). The removal of a lobe (or the greater part of a lobe) from the brain.

Lobotomy (lō bot′ə mē) or **prefrontal lobotomy**. Literally, "lobe-cutting." In the 1930s and 1940s, a faddish operation was performed on many mental patients in which the prefrontal areas [Brodmann areas 8, 9, 10, and 11 on the very front (rostral) rim of the frontal lobe of the cerebral cortex] were surgically isolated from the rest of the brain. The procedure was done to alleviate (1) intractable pain that would not respond to analgesic drugs, (2) persistent debilitating anxiety, and (3) any neurotic or psychotic problem that failed to respond either to psychotherapy or to drug treatment. Eventually the operation lost popularity as the view became prevalent that this treatment was nonspecific and too extensive.

Localization. The determination of a function's specific dependence on a given area of the brain.

Local norms. The statistical description of test scores taken by students in a given community or small area of the nation. These allow for the comparison of a student's scores with those of others in a similar geographic setting.

Locus coeruleus (lō′kus kə roo′lē us). A blueish-hued nucleus of the pons that sends axons toward the cerebral hemispheres that are norepinephrinergic (i.e., they release norepinephrine at their axon endings). One function of the locus coeruleus is to impose REM sleep on the organism after a preliminary interval of slow-wave sleep has taken place.

Locus of control. The subjective conception that our destiny is under a type of control, which by some people is felt to be internal and by others external. The locus of control is the place where one's own behavior is felt to be controlled. Having an <u>external locus of control</u> is to consider one's fate to be dominated by outside factors, while having an <u>internal locus of control</u> is to have the confident feeling that one's own decisions, along with hard work and skill, can be effective in deciding the future. Individuals with an external locus of control blame others for their own personal and occupational problems. Many learning-disabled individuals have been found to display an external locus of control.

Logographic strategy. This first stage in Frith's conceptual scheme of reading development involves reading by the "look- and-say" method as opposed to using a phonetic approach.

Longitudinal method. A long-term research method of analysis whereby individuals are tested and retested at various intervals in order to assess change (e.g., due to experimental conditions) over time. See also: **longitudinal research.**

Longitudinal research. A term for the research tactic of investigating the behavior of the same subjects over a long period. See also: **longitudinal method.**

Long-term memory (LTM). Information storage for more than 30 seconds of time. An item or event is more likely to be recorded in long-term memory if it is relevant to the individual or the individual's experience (= self-reference effect). Retrieval or recall is more likely in long-term memory if the retrieval context resembles the encoding context (= encoding specificity principle). Different types of long-term memory processes are cited in the literature. Some examples include autobiographical memory, or memory for events in one's own life; flashbulb memory, or memory for a particularly emotionally charged event or time; retrospective memory; or memory for previously learned information; and prospective memory, or our "work-list" memory (remembering what to do). The physiological activity in the hippocampus that results in the formation of LTM is **long-term potentiation** (see definition). See also: **memory.**

Long-term potentiation (LTP). A physiological process involving the modification of synapses that resembles the process of learning and that may be one of the physiological bases for learning. The process begins with a presynaptic neuron receiving a barrage of high-frequency electrical stimuli, preferably at different synapses. This results in greater responsiveness of the post-synaptic neuron to low-intensity stimulation of the presynaptic neuron, an effect that last for several days. The receptor sites that are most effective for LTP are one variety of those keyed to the neurotransmitter known as glutamate, namely, the NMDA type. Once the NMDA receptors are activated, the other glutamate receptors (kainate and quisqualate) are facilitated. The result is that after LTP, nerve impulses take place that would not have been excited previously under the same conditions. LTP takes place in the hippocampus, which has been identified as the brain structure needed for the consolidation of short-term into long-term memory. The experimental blocking of NMDA receptor sites has been found to prevent learning (see **hippocampus; learning; memory**). Furthermore, after the LTP of hippocampal neurons, extra synaptic terminals appear.

Lordosis (lôr dō′sis). In humans, an abnormal anterior convexity of the spine. This inward curvature of the spine could lead to a swaybacked appearance and a protruding abdomen. In quadrupeds (four-legged mammals), the female in estrus exhibits lordosis, making her genitalia easily accessible to the male. Not only does the female animal arch her back, but she thrusts her tail to one side, making room for the penis.

Lordosis quotient. The proportion of the total mountings of the female animal that result in lordosis.

Loss-of-control syndrome. Bursts of firing by masses of neurons in the temporal lobe of the cerebral cortex and the amygdaloid nucleus of the limbic system may be accompanied by intense emotional arousal and uncontrollable violence. It is this type of epileptic seizure that has created interest in the Mark-Ervin operation, which directs a strong direct current toward a small portion of the amygdala; this is a modern example of psychosurgery. See **amygdaloid nucleus; psychosurgery; temporal lobe.**

Lou Gehrig's (lŏŏ gâr′igz) **disease.** See: **amyotrophic lateral sclerosis.**

Love. One of the more intense emotions. Love appears to involve different levels of (1) intimacy, (2) passion, and (3) commitment, depending on the particular relationships and individuals involved (e.g., parent, spouse, child, friend, or lover). Love can have a number of physiological correlates, such as a pounding heart, "butterflies" in the stomach, trembling, restlessness, dryness of the throat and mouth, and perspiration. These reactions are due to the autonomic nervous system, mostly to its sympathetic division. There are five kinds of love, as follows: (1) romantic love, which combines high levels of passion and intimacy with little commitment, at least in the beginning; (2) fatuous love, which involves deep commitments made quickly, on the basis of passion; (3) infatuation, a superficial, although passionate, form of love, with no commitment intended at first; (4) companionate love, which involves a deep attachment based on mutual respect, friendship, and shared interests; and (5) consummate love, which occurs only in particularly special relationships, with passion, commitment, and emotional closeness present on both sides. See also: **autonomic nervous system.**

Lower-layer IV neurons. Neurons of the fourth layer, the internal granular layer, of the occipital lobes striate cortex that receive signals from the lateral geniculate nucleus. See also: **cerebral cortex; lateral geniculate nucleus; occipital lobe; visual cortex.**

LQ (laterality quotient). A statistical measure devised by Keefe and Swinney to indicate whether, and to what extent, one hemisphere is to be regarded as dominant. It is derived from observations of the perception of tachistoscopically flashed visual stimuli to either visual field and from reported observations of sound stimuli presented in a dichotic listening format. A negative LQ indicates that the right hemisphere is dominant, while a positive LQ indicates that the left hemisphere is dominant. An LQ score is also provided by the Edinburgh Laterality Questionnaire.

L-type dyslexia. The condition of a dyslexic whose reading problems are primarily linguistic, according to Bakker and Licht. The L-type dyslexic uses the left hemisphere prematurely, never having learned to identify the shapes of letters and letter groups well enough for the reading task to be done efficiently. The person reads quickly but makes many errors in word identification.

Lucid dreaming. Dreaming while the sleeper is aware of dreaming the content. The sleeper can voluntarily change the course of the dreamed events.

Lumen (loo'mən). The hollow center of the central nervous system. It is filled with cerebrospinal fluid. Some parts of the lumen are wide open; they are called the cerebral ventricles. Other parts of the lumen are quite narrow. See also: **cerebral ventricles; cerebrospinal fluid.**

Luria-Nebraska Neuropsychological Battery. A series of tests intended to objectify and standardize the examination procedure of the Soviet neuroscientist A. R. Luria. Most neuropsychologists find this battery to be less satisfactory than using Luria's subjective assessment techniques. See also: **Halstead-Reitan battery.**

Luteinizing (loo'tē i nīz"ing) **hormone** (LH). A hormone released from the anterior pituitary gland that stimulates the ovary to release the egg (the ovum). When fertilization occurs, LH prepares the wall of the uterus for the implantation of the fertilized egg (the zygote). LH also causes the ovary to release progesterone. In males, LH causes the release of androgens from the testes. The name "luteinizing" comes from the fact that, after the follicle has released the ovum, the rest of the follicle forms the corpus luteum ("yellow body"), which releases the progesterone. A more appropriate name for this hormone in males is the interstitial-cell stimulating hormone (ICSH), because LH acts on the interstitial cells of the testes to stimulate the production and release of testosterone. See also: **anterior pituitary gland; endocrine glands; hormone; progesterone; steroid hormone.**

Lymphocytes (lim'fə sīts). Antibody-producing blood cells that develop in the bone marrow. The lymphocytes are the chief contributors to the immune system. See also: **B cell; T cell.**

Lysergic (lī sûr'jik) **acid diethylamide** (dī eth"i ləm īd, dī eth' əl ə mīd") **(LSD).** Perhaps the most powerful of the hallucinogenic drugs. LSD is chemically similar to the neurotransmitter serotonin in that both are indole amines. It is believed that LSD mimics serotonin at some synapses and blocks the action of serotonin at other synapses. Since serotonin is the deep sleep neurotransmitter, it is quite possible that LSD produces dream hallucinations (due to its serotonin-mimicking action) while preventing sleep (due to its serotonin-blocking action). Accordingly, the user experiences waking hallucinations.

M

Mach bands (named after physicist/philosopher/ pre-Gestalt psychologist Ernst Mach, whose name is also used for airplane speeds, as in, e.g., "Mach two", twice the speed of sound). In the perception of edges between, say, a very light gray (almost white) patch on a very dark gray (almost black) background, a thin strip of light gray at the edge is perceived as brighter than the interior of the whitish patch and a thin strip of dark gray near the edge is perceived as darker than the rest of the blackish area. These strips are the Mach bands; one of them is, in the words of detergent ads, "whiter than white", while the other is "blacker than black." Ratliff has provided a physiological explanation for them. The interior of the grayish white patch stimulates visual receptors uniformly, so any small part of it will provide fewer nerve impulses per second than it would have done had it been surrounded by darkness. This is because of lateral inhibition from surrounding areas that are also stimulated. But, now, consider a small part of the light gray at the edge, alongside the dark gray. This small bit of light gray will get much less lateral inhibition from its darkish neighbor than from the rest of the light gray area nearby. The same applies to all other parts of the light gray at the edge. Since they have less inhibition, they will cause the retinal neurons covering them to fire off a higher rate of nerve impulses than the impulse-rate representing the greater part of the light patch. Thus the perception of the whitish edge is enhanced. What about the physiology of the blacker-than-black band? This requires the premise that, even from dark gray or black stimuli, a spontaneous series of nerve impulses are sent from the eye to the brain. In the vast interior of the blackish region, there is no lateral inhibition, and this spontaneous flow of nerve impulses is at its maximum. At the edge with the whitish patch, though, small regions of the dark gray undergo inhibition from whitish-gray neighboring regions, and the rate of spontaneously-fired nerve impulses is reduced, hence, "blacker than black." See also: **lateral inhibition; Ratliff's laws of lateral inhibition.**

Macrophage (mak'rə fāj″). A variety of leukocyte that engulfs and destroys microorganisms invading the body. The macrophage displays the microorganism's antigen, helping other leukocytes participate in the immune response. See also: **antigen; leukocyte**.

Macula (mak'yoo lə). A mostly cone-filled central region of the retina which includes the fovea. "Macula" means "stain" in Latin; the macula is yellowish, since it is packed with red and green pigmented cone endings; the addition of red and green lights produces a yellow hue. See also: **fovea; macular; macular sparing; cones; additive color mixing.**

Macular (mak' yoo lər). Refers to a mostly cone-filled region of the retina that surrounds the fovea, namely, the macula.

Macular sparing. Refers to the fact that damage to the visual cortex often leaves unimpaired the ability to see images falling on the macula, the central portion of the retina. See also: **macula.**

Magnetic resonance imaging (MRI). See MRI.

Magnetoencephalography (mag nē″tō en sef″ə log'rə fē) **(MEG)**. A technique for mapping the brain which allows observers to monitor the responses of areas of the brain to stimuli such as a pleasing touch. Magnetic fields around the brain become modified one-tenth of a second after a stimulus is presented. See also: **MRI.**

Magnocellular (mag ″nō sel'yoo lər) (from Latin "magnum" = "large"). The larger ganglion cells of the retina as well as the large-sized neurons of the two most ventral layers of the lateral geniculate nucleus (LGN). The large-sized retinal ganglion cells, the Y cells, send their axons (which are optic nerve fibers) to large-sized LGN cells. This magnocellular system is believed by some to be identical with the transient visual pathway. See also: **transient visual pathway; Y cells**.

Magnocellular (mag ″nō sel'yoo lər) **nucleus** (also called the **basal nucleus of Meynert**). A collection of nerve cell bodies in the "old" cerebral cortex just rostral to the hypothalamus. The axons of the neurons that are gathered into Meynert's basal nucleus run to the neocortex, where they release the neurotransmitter acetylcholine (ACh). Alzheimer's disease is associated with a shortage of ACh in the neocortex and also with destruction of the magnocellular nucleus.

Mainstreaming. The approach to the education of children with learning disabilities which involves assigning them to regular classrooms and affording them the opportunity for social relationships with others their own age. Supportive educational services are provided as needed for these students. See also: **least-restrictive environment**.

Maintenance rehearsal. The repetition of information held in short-term memory with no attempt at interpretation or elaboration. This will tend to enhance the recall of the physical appearance or sound of the stimulus, but not the meaning of it.

Major depression. See: **clinical depression; depression (major)**.

Male climacteric (klī mak'tər ik, klī mak ter'ik). Change(s) experienced by middle-aged men, including decreased sex drive and decreased fertility.

Malignant. Refers to the type of tumor that continues to spread through the body even after it is surgically removed.

Malleus (mal'ē us) ("hammer" in Latin). See: **hammer**.

Mammillary bodies. Two nuclei at the base of the hypothalamus. The mammillary bodies are a part of the limbic system. They bulge outward from the surface of the brain, which explains the name; "mammillary" is derived from the Latin word for "breasts." Damage to these structures is one aspect of Korsakoff's syndrome; the memory losses of Korsakoff's patients are attributed in part to damage to the mammillary bodies. Nevertheless, some patients with damage to these structures have shown no loss of memory. See also: **Korsakoff's syndrome; mammillothalamic tract**.

Mammillothalamic tract. A bundle of nerve fibers carrying impulses from the mammillary bodies of the hypothalamus to the thalamus. See also: **hypothalamus; mammillary bodies; thalamus**.

MANCOVA. A MANOVA with one factor held constant by statistical treatment instead of by experimental control; that factor would normally "covary" with one of the dependent variables. Multiple analysis of covariance. See also: **ANOVA; MANOVA**.

Mania. A hyperactive condition with heightened euphoria and impaired judgment; the extreme positive type of mood disorder and the opposite of depression, which is the extreme negative mood. See also: **manic-depressive disorder; mood disorders**.

Manic-depressive disorder. The bipolar variety of mood disorder, in which the patient swings between the extremes of mania and depression. See also: **depression (major); mania; mood disorders**.

MANOVA. A statistical test of the impact of two or more causal factors (independent variables) on two or more behavioral measures (dependent variables). The multiple analysis of variance. See also: **ANOVA; MANCOVA**.

Manscan (mental activity network scanner). The combined use of the EEG with the MRI to snap a fresh picture of brain activity (showing active and idle areas) every 4 milliseconds. The EEG points number 124, instead of the conventional 8 to 19.

Mantra (man'trə). In meditation, a word or syllable that the meditator is asked to attend to as fully as possible so that her or his powers of concentration are funneled narrowly onto one small target. The chant of "Om" in Tibetan Buddhism, the secret and private word in Transcendental Meditation, and the word "one" in the Relaxation Response procedure are all examples of mantras. See also: **meditation**.

Manual communication. Communicating by the use of hand signals. These signals may be natural or may be part of an elaborate system, such as the signs used in American Sign Language.

MAO (monoamine oxidase) (mon″ō am'in, -ə mēn' ok'si dās). An enzyme that breaks down a monoamine neurotransmitter's molecules after the transmitter has been reuptaken past the presynaptic membrane but before it can reach the synaptic vesicle that would insulate it from the MAO. These monoamine compounds include dopamine (DA), norepinephrine (norEp or NE), and serotonin (5-HT). See also: **MAO-inhibitors**.

MAO-inhibitors. A group of drugs used to alleviate severe chronic depression. After a monoamine neurotransmitter such as norepinephrine (norEp) has done its work at the synapse, some of the norEp molecules undergo reuptake and return to the synaptic bouton through the presynaptic membrane. In the bouton, they migrate to the synaptic vesicles, where they are stored for use when the next nerve impulse arrives. The enzyme MAO breaks up some of these norEp molecules in the bouton before they manage to arrive at the synaptic vesicles. This is a third synapse-clearing procedure, in addition to (1) the breakup of the norEp molecule in the synapse by the action of the enzyme COMT and (2) reuptake past the presynaptic membrane back into the sending neuron. The other neurotransmitters that can be affected by MAO in this manner are serotonin (5-HT) and dopamine (DA). Some neuropsychiatrists believe that depression is related to the underactivity of norEp in the cerebral cortex. This in turn may be due to a scarcity of brain norEp (or of 5-HT). The MAO- inhibitors block the action of MAO upon norEp (and/or 5-HT), leaving the presynaptic or sending neuron with an extra supply of available neurotransmitter. See also: **MAO; tricyclic antidepressants.**

Marchi (mär′kē) **stain**. A procedure for staining tissue from the central nervous system for microscopic study. This method is most effective after a part of the brain or spinal cord has been damaged during the animal's lifetime. That is because the Marchi stain picks up chemically degenerated myelin from dead nerve cells. This permits the tracking of axonal pathways, beginning at the damaged cell bodies. See also: **Cajal stain; Golgi stain; Nauta stain; Nissl stain.**

Marijuana (mar i (h)wä′nə). A very commonly used mild hallucinogen. It leads to a "reverse tolerance" reaction; that is, after a while, ingesting less of the drug produces the same effect that previously required a greater dose of the drug. See also: **THC; anandamide.**

Masculinizing. The production of, or increase of, male characteristics.

Masking (in auditory research and testing). The stimulation of one of the subject's ears with controlled noise to prevent that ear from picking up auditory stimuli being presented to the opposite ear, See also: **dichotic listening**.

Masking (in visual research). The tachistoscopic projection of meaningful stimuli and interfering stimuli so close together that the meaningful stimuli are very hard to recognize.

Matching-to-sample test. A test procedure in which the subject is required to select the test stimulus that matches an earlier-shown stimulus. A delay may be interposed between the presentation of the stimulus sample to be matched and the presentation of the test stimuli. Another test, using a very similar situation, but requiring the subject to pick the one stimulus that is different from the others, is known as the "oddity problem."

Materialism. An answer offered by some philosophers to the **mind-brain problem**. Materialism is a type of **monism**, which is the contention that there is only one kind of reality and that reality is entirely physical. Bertrand Russell and Gilbert Ryle have proposed a sophisticated version of materialism that can be termed **philosophical behaviorism**. See definitions of terms in bold type.

Maternal aggression. Aggressive behavior on the part of mother animals toward human or animal intruders who approach the young or the nest.

Matthew effect. A conception, first introduced by Keith Stanovich, intended to guide theory and diagnosis in the area of learning disability. It refers to the text in the New Testament book of Matthew which holds that the rich will get richer while the poor get poorer. The handicap of the learning-disabled (LD) child prevents him or her from learning as efficiently as the learning-able child, so that the LD child gains new information at a comparatively slow pace. This causes the LD child to fall farther and farther behind as the child grows older. As a result, many behavioral measures would be expected to reveal inferior performance by disabled learners, not because these behaviors are causally related to the disability, but only because they are by-products or artifacts of a learning deficit that becomes more and more widespread. See also: **positive feedback**.

Maturation. A systematic change in behavior with increasing age that is attributable not to learning but to the unfolding of a genetically-defined pattern of neural development. The word refers to all the aspects of behavioral development that result from growth, with special emphasis on the central nervous system. Rates of maturation will vary from one person to another. An example of behavioral maturation might be the replacement of the reflexes of infancy by more mature reflexes (e.g., the Babinski reflex is replaced by the plantar reflex; the Moro reflex is replaced by the startle reflex; grasping with all five fingers curled the same way is replaced by grasping with the thumb curled the opposite way from the four other fingers).

Mean. One of the three measures of central tendency. The mean is the arithmetic average of a group of scores. For example, the mean of the numbers 13, 14, 20, and 22 is 17.25.

Means-end analysis. A strategy of problem solving which focuses on the discrepancy between present conditions and those that would exist if the problem were to be solved. Along the way to the solution, several choice-points arise. At each choice-point, the individual repeats the comparison of the present situation with what would be the post solution state of affairs. An example might be climbing to a great height and looking at the landscape when trying to reach an area of the city by walking toward it. If the structure of a problem calls for intermediate steps that seem to increase the discrepancy between the present and projected state of affairs, means-end analysis will not be very helpful.

Measures of central tendency. See: **central tendency.**

Measures of memory. The techniques for measuring memory include (1) recall, or the reproduction of memorized information with a minimum of cues, (2) recognition, or the correct identification of previously learned material, (3) relearning material that was learned at a previous time, with a measure of savings, namely, the amount by which the second learning is easier than the original learning, and (4) priming, or the activation of memories by providing limited information associated with those memory items. See also: **memory.**

Medial. Toward the midline. The word is an antonym of "lateral." The adverbial form is "mediad." The "median" strip separates the right lane of a highway from the left. A medial section is a cut made along the median plane or midline of the part of the anatomy under examination. The nose and the navel are examples of medial parts of the anatomy. A medial section is the same thing as a midsagittal section. See also: **sagittal.**

Medial dorsal nucleus (of the thalamus). A part of the neural pathway for the olfactory sense. See

also: **mediodorsal nuclei; olfactory nerve; olfactory sense.**

Medial forebrain bundle (MFB). A bundle of axons running through the lateral hypothalamus. These axons carry nerve impulses from the hypothalamus to the septum. Electrical stimulation of this bundle produces the strongest level of positive reinforcement among all the brain locations that have been tested for such a rewarding capability. See also: **hypothalamus; positive reinforcement; self-stimulation of the brain.**

Medial geniculate (je nik'yoo lit) **nucleus.** A knee-shaped (i.e., "geniculate" is from "genu," which is Latin for "knee") nucleus in the thalamus situated just medial to the lateral geniculate nucleus. The medial geniculate nucleus is the thalamic relay nucleus for the sense of hearing, sending its axons to the auditory cortex, namely, Brodmann areas 41 and 42 of the temporal lobe. They are located in the posterior portion of the superior temporal gyrus, the dorsalmost of three horizontal folds (gyri) that make up the outer surface of the temporal lobe. See also: **auditory area; auditory cortex; Brodmann numbering system; hearing; inferior colliculus; temporal lobe; thalamus.**

Medial lemniscus (lem nis'kus). A bundle of axons that, in cross-section, prevents an oval, lens-like appearance. This is different from most tracts which have circular cross-sections. These axons arise from neurons in the gracile and cuneate nuclei of the medulla. They start to cross the midline as they travel rostrad toward higher regions of the brain. The crossing fibers of the left and right medial lemnisci make up the great sensory decussation. The medial lemniscus, therefore, contains contralateral axons (i.e., it is on the side of the brain opposite to the side of the body that provided the original stimuli. The gracile and cuneate nuclei, and their axons in the medial lemniscus, are part of the somatosensory system. The axons of the medial lemniscus terminate in the posterior ventral nucleus of the thalamus (PVNT). See also: **cuneate nucleus; gracile nucleus; lemniscus; posterior ventral nucleus of the thalamus; somatosensory system.**

Median. A measure of central tendency that is the middlemost score in an ordered distribution of scores. The median can be an actual score or, in the case of even numbers of scores, an average of the two middle scores. For example, of the scores 13, 14, 20, and 22, the median is 17.

Medical model (of abnormal behavior). Using the medical model and the theory of abnormal behavior it implies, abnormality should be attributed to bodily malfunctions, usually of the brain or endocrine system. Such medically based treatments as prescribed drugs, electroconvulsive shock, or psychosurgery would be favored by those professionals who use this model.

Mediodorsal nuclei (mēd″ē ō dôr′səl nōō′ klē ī, nyōō′-). Thalamic nuclei that, when damaged, lead to the type of memory loss associated with Korsakoff's syndrome. See also: **dorsomedial thalamus; Korsakoff's syndrome; medial dorsal nucleus.**

Meditation. Some methods of meditation focus on body movement (e.g., Zen Buddhism), while others require the meditator to be motionless and passive. Some methods require the meditator to focus on a single object; others require attending to a single word (a mantra). See also: **mantra; Relaxation Response; Transcendental Meditation**.

Medulla (oblongata) (me dōō′lə ob ″lông gä′tə, mə dul′ə). The lowest part of the brain. The medulla is a direct continuation of the central nervous system from the spinal cord. The cord is cylindrical but the medulla gradually departs from that shape, so that it has a tapering form, widening as it approaches the remainder of the brain. The medulla, being relatively long and slender, contains the origins and/or terminals of seven of the twelve pairs of cranial nerves. The medulla's integrity is necessary for such vital functions as heartbeat, blood pressure, and respiration. The gray matter within the medulla consists of nuclei (clusters of nerve cell bodies) known as the vital centers.

Megavitamins. Megadoses of vitamins. The concept of taking vitamins in doses thousands of times the size of the RDA (recommended daily allowance), is based on the orthomolecular theory that most illness is due to disordered brain or body chemistry.

Meiosis (mī ō′sis). The kind of cell division unique to the formation of gametes (reproductive cells, i.e., the sperm and egg cells). In meiosis, the usual number of chromosomes for body cells in the species (the diploid number) is halved. With the sperm cell carrying only half the species-normal chromosome number (half the diploid number = the haploid number) and the egg cell also containing only the haploid number of chromosomes, fertilization (penetration of the egg cell by the sperm cell to produce the fertilized egg cell) results in a single-celled new organism, the zygote, with the full diploid number of chromosomes. See also: **mitosis**.

Meissner's corpuscle (mīs′nərz kôr′pus əl). A kind of touch receptor found in the outermost layer of glabrous skin. See also: **glabrous.**

Melatonin (mel ə tō′nin). The hormone secreted by the pineal gland, which is an endocrine gland attached to the roof of the diencephalon. The diencephalon is the posterior portion of the forebrain; thus the pineal gland is the most rostral of the endocrine glands. Melatonin, which is produced by the metabolism of serotonin, plays a major role in regulating circadian rhythms. It prepares the body for increased activity during the day and decreased activity at night, responding to the amount of light being received by the eyes. Melatonin also helps to maintain body temperature at the normal value of 98.6 degrees Fahrenheit during the day, allowing body temperature to be somewhat lower at night. The release of melatonin is inhibited by light, presumably due to nerve connections running from the eye to the pineal gland. Melatonin may play a long-term role in addition to its once-a-day one. It suppresses the appearance of secondary sexual characteristics, keeping children juvenile. After the accumulation of 12 to 14 summers' worth of light stimulation, this holding action is finally broken down and the onset of puberty is permitted. See also: **circadian rhythms; diencephalon; endocrine system; entrainment; pineal gland; Zeitgeber.**

Membrane potential. A difference in voltage between the outer surface of a cell membrane and the inner surface of that membrane. Examples of membrane potentials for neurons would include the resting potential, the EPSP, the IPSP, and the action potentials.

Memory. Memory is an active cognitive system that receives, stores, organizes, alters, and retrieves information. If the system is working correctly, the information is retrieved in a form that is useful to the organism doing the remembering. There are three major stages involved in committing information to memory: (1) Acquisition, or encoding, involves perception of environmental stimulation; here sensory memory is initiated and involves storage of sensory information for up to 2 seconds. (2) Storage involves either short-term [= short-term memory (STM)] storage or long-term [= long-term memory (LTM)] storage of information. (3) Retrieval involves the ability to access information from either short-term or long-term storage. There are different memory models which usually incorporate sensory, STM, and LTM systems. There are also strategies one can use in order to commit information to long-term memory. See also: **long-term memory; measures of memory; mnemonics; sensory register; short-term memory.**

Memory improvement. There are a number of techniques for improving the retention of acquired information: (1) recitation; (2) rehearsal of the material during and immediately after the learning of it; (3) use of organizational techniques, such as chunking (i.e., collecting several items into one meaningful unit or "chunk"); (4) subdivision of the material into small pieces so that there is less to be learned at one time; (5) use of cues or mnemonic devices; and (6) distribution (i.e., spacing) of practice. Note that these practices are best employed at the time of acquisition of new knowledge; so, when studying, plan ahead!

Memory span. The number of items of information that can be reported after being held in short-term memory. Typically, the memory span can hold seven, give or take one or two, unrelated items. The procedure of chunking, which provides for associations among several individual items, can dramatically increase the memory span, since a chunk of items acts the same as a single isolated item. See also: **memory improvement; short-term memory.**

Memory trace. A physical or chemical change in the brain that encodes a bit of remembered information. See also: **engram; Hebbian synapse; long-term potentiation.**

Meninges (me nin′jēz) (singular = meninx). The three membranes that surround the central nervous system (CNS). The outermost meninx is the tough, leathery dura mater, which fits around the hemispheres like a skullcap and, throughout the CNS, provides an inner lining for the bony casing of the CNS, viz., the skull and the backbone. The intermediate meninx is the arachnoid, and the innermost meninx is the very fine and thin pia mater. The arachnoid and pia mater together constitute the leptomeninx ("thin membrane"). See also: **arachnoid; dura mater; pia mater.**

Meningiomas (me nin″jē ō′məs). Tumors developing between the brain membranes or meninges. See also: **meninges.**

Meningitis (men″in jī′tis). An inflammation of the three membranes (the meninges) surrounding the brain and spinal cord.

Meningocele (me ning′gō sēl″). A congenital hernia, in which the meninges (the membranes surrounding the brain and spinal cord) protrude through an opening in the skull or spinal column.

Menopause. The cessation of menstruation when a woman reaches middle age. Menopause generally occurs after the age of 40. See also: **estrous cycle.**

Menstrual cycle. The hormone-regulated monthly cycle in human females controlling follicle-formation, egg-release, buildup of the uterine wall for egg-implantation, and menstruation (which occurs when the egg has not been fertilized). See also: **estrous cycle.**

Mental age. The typical intelligence of all individuals in a given age group (usually indicated by the average test score of the age group). In early intelligence tests, such as the Stanford-Binet, performance on the test was scored as a mental age (MA). This could then be divided by the person's true, or chronological, age (CA). (The ratio would be less than 1 if the examinee performed less well than the average member of his or her age group, would equal 1 if performance was average, and would be greater than 1 if performance was above the average.) The MA/CA ratio was then multiplied by 100 to yield the Intelligence Quotient (IQ). See also: **basal age; ceiling age; intelligence quotient.**

Mental disorder. A disorder marked by social deviance and emotional turmoil. According to DSM-IV, mental disorders are associated with present distress (a painful symptom), a disability (impairment in an important area of functioning), or an increased significant risk of pain or disability. Mental disorders are considered behavioral or psychological dysfunctioning in which deviant behavior is evident.

Mental retardation. Intellectual functioning significantly below average for one's age group, accompanied by inadequate adjustment to the physical and social environment. Three essential features for this diagnosis are (1) significantly lower-than-average general intelligence, (2) significant inadequacy in social adjustment, and (3) appearance of these characteristics before the age of 18. According to the DSM-IV, mental retardation reflects low intellectual functioning (as shown by valid IQ tests) ranging from mild mental retardation (an IQ from 50 to 70) to profound mental retardation (an IQ below 20). If the diagnosis of retardation is to be made, the individual must exhibit impairment of functioning in any two (or more) of eleven behavioral areas, including communication, self-care skills, the ability to maintain a home, the ability to interact in social situations, the ability to use community resources, the ability to function independently, the possession of basic academic skills, the ability to hold a job, the ability to maintain health and safety, common sense, and the ability to enjoy leisure activities. See also: **mild mental retardation; moderate mental retardation; profound mental retardation; severe mental retardation.**

Mentalism. An answer given by some philosophers to the mind-body problem. Mentalism is a type of monism, one that says that the only reality is mental. The entire world is regarded as the content of the observer's conscious perceptions and awareness. One version of mentalism is solipsism, the view that only "I" am real and that the universe exists only in "my" consciousness. Philosopher George Berkeley's version of mentalism avoids solipsism, since he considers that the universe has a stable, unchanging presence. The reason for that stability is that the universe is a rather large, complex idea in the mind of an all-knowing God. See also: **mind-brain problem; monism.**

Merkel receptor or **Merkel's disk.** A touch receptor that maintains a response to ongoing tactile stimuli.

Mesencephalon (mez ″en sef′ə lon) (from

Greek "mes" = "middle"; "encephalon" = "brain"; "en" = "within"; "kephalon" = "head"). The midbrain.

Mesocorticolimbic system. A neural pathway originating in the ventral tegmental nucleus of the midbrain that runs to the accumbens nucleus of the limbic system. The neurotransmitter dopamine is released at the axon terminals in the accumbens. The neuroleptic drug clozapine inhibits the dopamine receptors of the accumbens but does not affect the dopamine receptors of the corpus striatum (the terminal of the nigrostraiatal pathway); this presumably allows for the treatment of schizophrenic symptoms without risking tardive dyskinesia. See also: **accumbens; clozapine; corpus striatum; dopamine; limbic system; nigrostriatal pathway; tardive dyskinesia.**

Mesolimbic dopamine pathway. The axonal pathway from the midbrain to the forebrain, with the cell bodies in the midbrain manufacturing the neurotransmitter dopamine (DA) and the axon terminals releasing DA into the forebrain. This consists of two pathways releasing DA onto two different sets of dopamine receptor-sites: (1) the nigrostriatal pathway from the substantia nigra to the corpus striatum (functionally involved in neuromuscular coordination) and (2) the mesocorticolimbic system from the ventral tegmental area to the nucleus accumbens of the septal area (the malfunction of which is more likely to be related to schizophrenia). See also: **accumbens; clozapine; corpus striatum; dopamine; mesocorticolimbic system; nigrostriatal pathway.**

Mesotelencephalic (mez″ō tel en″sə fal′ik) **dopamine system.** The pathways of dopamine-releasing axons arising in (a) the ventral tegmental area and traveling to the cerebrum, terminating in the nucleus accumbens and (b) the substantia nigra and traveling to the basal ganglia of the cerebrum. See also: **accumbens; basal ganglia; clozapine; dopamine; mesolimbic dopamine pathway; schizophrenia; tardive dyskinesia.**

Meta-analysis. A method of pooling the results of research studies by a number of different investigators, with emphasis on the size of the effect of the independent variable(s) on a particular dependent variable (response measure). The use of meta-analysis assumes that poorly designed, badly controlled studies may be safely included because random errors would average out to zero.

Metabolic tolerance. A variety of drug tolerance; in metabolic tolerance, the quantity of the drug is lowered before it arrives at its site of action in the body. See also: **tolerance.**

Metacognition (met ˝ə kog nish'ən). The awareness and understanding of one's own reasoning processes, learning styles, and problem-solving behaviors.

Metaphysics (i.e., going "beyond the science of physics"). That branch of philosophy which is concerned with defining the true nature of the universe and specifying what is meant by reality. See also: **mind-brain problem**.

Metastatic tumors. Tumors that originate in one bodily location and spread from it; surgical removal of such a tumor does not stop tumor spread. See also: **malignant.**

Methadone (meth'ə dōn˝). A newly found opiate drug that is not as addictive as other opiates. It is used to wean addicts away from dependence on opium, morphine, or heroin.

Microcephaly (mī˝krō sef'ə lē) (from Greek "micro" = "small"; "cephalo" = "head"). A cranial disorder in which the head is unusually small with a sloping forehead. Retardation results because there is insufficient room in the skull for the full growth of the cerebral cortex.

Microdialysis (mī˝krō dī al'i sis). A technique for extracting a very small amount of a chemical from a given area of the brain, or, alternatively, a technique of delivering a very small amount of a chemical to a given brain region.

Microelectrode. An electrode so small that it can be used to stimulate, or to record voltage changes in, a single neuron.

Microelectrode puller. A device that pulls very hot glass tubes into very thin hollow pipettes so that they can be used as microelectrodes.

Microglia (mī krog'lē ə) (from Greek "micro" = "small"; "glia" = "glue"). One of the varieties of central nervous system (CNS) neuroglia. Unlike other neuroglia, the microglial cells originate from the mesoderm rather than the ectoderm. When a CNS neuron is damaged and the neural and myelin tissues break up and undergo decay, the microglial cells swell up and act as phago-

cytes, ingesting the broken bits of neuron and myelin. See also: **neuroglia**.

Microiontophoresis (mī˝krō ī än˝tō fə rē' sis). A technique for measuring changes of a neuron's membrane voltage in response to chemicals applied to the membrane.

Microsleeps. Observed in sleep-deprived subjects, these are brief attacks of sleep during waking, while the subject is sitting or standing. The eyelids may droop, there is a lessening of responsiveness to stimulation, and the EEG exhibits a sleep pattern.

Microspectrophotometry (mī˝krō spek˝trō fə tom'e trē). A procedure for measuring the absorption spectrum of the photopigment of a single retinal receptor cell (rod or cone).

Microtome (mī˝krə tōm˝). A cutting instrument used on chemically fixated (and therefore hardened) brain or spinal cord material in order to prepare it for microscopic study. Literally, the word means "very small cut." Depending on the research requirements, tissues may be sliced at "thicknesses" of from 5 to 65 microns (a micron being one millionth of a meter). See also: **histological techniques; planes of sectioning**.

Microtubules (mī˝krō tōō'byōōlz). Proteins in the cell bodies and axons of neurons that are tube-shaped and make possible the transport of nutrients and metabolic products within the cell, especially from the cell nucleus out to the axon and down the axon to the terminal boutons. See also: **axonal transport.**

Midbrain or **mesencephalon**. The part of the brain that is the uppermost component of the brain stem. The midbrain has a roof known as the tectum, the outstanding features of which are four bumps or hillocks, two on the left and two on the right, the corpora quadrigemina. The front two hillocks (one left and one right) are known as the anterior or superior colliculi; they have visual functions. The hind left and right hillocks are the posterior or inferior colliculi. These belong to the auditory pathway that runs from the inner ear to the auditory cortex. Also included in the midbrain is the ascending reticular arousal system. The midbrain also contains two nuclei with pigmented cells, the red nucleus and the substantia nigra, which are part of the extrapyramidal motor system. The substantia nigra sends dopamine-releasing axons to the corpus striatum; damage to these produces neuro-muscular disorders. Above these two collections of colorful nerve cells is the tegmentum. The ventral part of the tegmentum sends dopamin-ergic axons to the accumbens nucleus of the forebrain septum; the overactivation of this pathway is thought to produce the positive symptoms of schizophrenia. Through the heart of the midbrain runs the cerebral aqueduct (or aqueduct of Sylvius). The aqueduct is a narrow part of the brain's hollow, or lumen. It carries cerebrospinal fluid from the third to the fourth ventricle. Surrounding the aqueduct is the pe-riaqueductal gray (or central gray), which is part of the neural control system for aggressive be-havior. At the very bottom of the midbrain, there is white matter. This ventralmost part of the midbrain consists of a part of the pyramidal (or corticospinal) tract, which is the direct pathway from the motor area of the cerebral cortex to the ventral horn motoneurons of the spinal cord. All in all, this tiny midbrain is quite a busy place! It contains arousal mechanisms, sleep mecha-nisms, part of the visual system, areas related to the expression of aggression, nuclei that control the eye muscles (both the smooth, internal ones and the striate, external ones), and parts of the extrapyramidal motor system.

Middle ear. The air-filled space (beginning at the eardrum, or tympanic membrane) which con-tains three tiny bones (ossicles) called the malleus (hammer), incus (anvil), and stapes (stirrup). These bones carry sound waves from the eardrum to the oval window, which connects the middle and inner ears. Two small muscles are also found in the middle ear: (1) the tensor tympani, which connects to the hammer, and (2) the stapedius, which is attached to the stirrup. These muscles dampen (tone down) the vibrat-ing of the ossicles, which would shatter them-selves if they copied very high-frequency and high-intensity sounds.

Migration. The movement of neuroblast cells (embryonic cells that are neurons-to-be) and even developing neurons toward their permanent locations in the brain. See also: **proliferation**.

Mild mental retardation. Below-average scoring on an intelligence test that falls in the 55 to 69 IQ range. Scores of 70 to 85 (sometimes labeled "dull normal") are considered to be lower than average but above the retardation range. The mildly retarded individual is able to function in-dependently. See also: **mental retardation**.

Mind-brain identity. This is one of the answers that philosophers have offered to the **mind-brain problem**. The mind-brain identity view is that the universe consists of one mental-material reality and that reality cannot be all-physical or all-conscious. This is one form of **monism**, the position that there is only one kind of reality, not two, as is argued by the proponents of **dualism**. See definitions of terms in bold type.

Mind-brain (or **mind-body**) **problem**. The mys-tery of how it is possible for physical and chemi-cal objects, such as neurons and neurotransmit-ters, to provide a basis for conscious experiences, such as feelings, sensations, emotions, thoughts, and desires. Philosophers have wrestled with this issue for centuries. In fact, there are two philo-sophical problems involved. One is the meta-physical issue of whether the real world does contain physical and mental components, and if so, how is that possible? Another is the episte-mological question, how can physical things like brains get to know about conscious experiences or how can non-physical consciousness ever at-tain knowledge of physical objects? Part of the fascination of the field of physiological psychol-ogy is that it seems to hold the promise of pro-viding at least some of the answers to specific questions that come from the mind-body issue. See also: **double-aspect theory; dualism; emergent property position; epiphenomenal-ism; interactionism; materialism; mentalism; mind-brain identity; monism; panprotopsy-chic identism; philosophical behaviorism; psychophysical parallelism.**

Minimal brain dysfunction (MBD). A condition once attributed to a category of children with learning difficulties. The term implies that the MBD child has a subtle, unidentifiable type of cerebral injury or functional defect. The term is now considered obsolete. More appropriate des-ignations used today include: learning disabili-ties (the most general term), dyslexia, and atten-tion-deficit hyperactivity disorder (ADHD).

Minimal neurological subtype. This is a dyslexic subtype described by Bannatyne. Deficits are pronounced in visual-spatial and concept forma-tion tasks.

Minimum competency tests (MCTs). Tests that set a minimum for performance in various subjects. Generally, MCTs are used to determine eligibility for promotion or graduation. They are popular with state legislatures, which believe that by mandating the use of such tests, schools are held accountable. Test authorities tend to agree that the standards used for MCTs are subjectively selected and that no single measurement should be decisive for the promotion or graduation of a student.

Minnesota Multiphasic Personality Inventory-2 (MMPI-2). An objective and standardized test used to identify and diagnose people with emotional/behavioral problems.

Minor hemisphere. An obsolete term for the right hemisphere of the cerebral cortex (which controls the left side of the body and does not contain the Broca and Wernicke speech areas) implying that the important cognitive functions are all carried out by the left (or "major") hemisphere. See also: **cerebral cortex; Broca's area; Wernicke's area.**

"Miracle berries". See: **miraculin.**

Miraculin (mi rak'yoo lin). A protein (found in "miracle berries") that, when ingested, alters the taste buds so that acids, which normally are sour to the taste, taste sweet.

Mirror-drawing test. A test in which the subject is required to draw a geometric figure (e.g., a multi-point star) while watching only the mirror-reflection of the sketch-pad.

Misperception. A lack of perception, or incorrect or incomplete perception. Learning-disabled children frequently have difficulty perceiving their social environment.

MIT Braille Embosser. A device developed at the Massachusetts Institute of Technology for helping blind students to read. The device takes printed materials and translates them into Grade 2 Braille markings. It is used with a telewriter. The materials can be requested by telephone from a computer center and will be sent by way of the telewriter in braille. Modern personal computers (microcomputers) can be provided with the capability of performing this function.

Mitochondria (mī˝tō kon'drē ə). Certain organelles (very small components) in the cytoplasm of animal cells which store adenosine triphosphate (ATP), the chemical consisting of the energy reserves for the body's metabolism. The third phosphate group (of the triphosphate) is broken away from the main ATP molecule, leaving a phosphate, ADP (adenosine diphosphate), along with released chemical energy. Think of mitochondria as the "mighty mites" of the body. See also: **adenosine triphosphate.**

Mitosis (mī tō'sis). The division of body cells as the fertilized egg gradually develops into a many-celled organism. Mitosis is asexual and is the usual form of cell reproduction throughout the body. See also: **meiosis.**

Mixed hearing loss. A hearing disorder involving both conductive and sensorineural impairment. See also: **hearing loss.**

Mixed verbal-perceptual dyslexic subtype (MVP). This dyslexic subtype, proposed by Spafford and Grosser, is typified by deficiencies in the visual-perceptual and linguistic realms.

Mnemonics (ni mon' iks). The use of a strategy to improve memory performance. Mnemonic strategies include imagery, organization, and rehearsal. If you are trying to remember what items to buy for a picnic, you might imagine (= imagery strategy) a scene of individuals eating at a picnic and visualize what they are eating in order to assist you with your supermarket purchases. If you are trying to organize (= organizational strategy) and remember the musical notes on the G clef, you could memorize the sentence "Every Good Boy Does Fine." This works for the notes on the lines (reading from bottom to top). For the notes on the spaces, again from bottom to top, spell out the word FACE. Rehearsal strategies involve the practice or repetition of material over and over until it is mastered. Have you ever repeated a sentence or studied material you want to learn aloud, in front of a mirror, or perhaps by subvocalization until you mastered it? This is the practicing of a rehearsal strategy in order to commit information to long-term memory. See also: **memory; memory improvement.**

Mnemonist (nem'on ist). An individual with highly developed memory skills. To develop such skills initially usually requires a great deal of work. One example of this skill in action: Chess masters can reconstruct complex chess positions on the board after being allowed to view them for only 5 seconds.

Mock crime procedure. A method for the study of lie detection. The interviewer is required to use lie detection techniques to examine several "suspects", one of whom has performed some unusual act (operationally defining the "crime"). See also: **lie detection.**

Mode. A measure of central tendency that is the most frequently occurring score. For example, of the scores 12, 17, 17, 18, 20, 20, and 20, the mode is 20.

Model. A presentation, which may consist of a list of assumptions, a diagram, or a three-dimensional structure, that is used to represent a theoretical approach to the subject matter of a science. The model can be a useful teaching device. The model may, additionally, assist researchers in making decisions on how best to test the theory that the model represents.

Modeling. A type of learning usually known as observational learning.

Model systems approach. The examination of simple arrangements of nerve cells that perform an elementary behavioral function. This is often done with an invertebrate animal. Examples include the study of vision in the horseshoe crab Limulus and the research on memory in the sea slug Aplysia californica. Another version of the approach is to study a particular unit of behavior even in an advanced mammal. An example of the latter is the investigation of eyelid conditioning in the rabbit. See also: **artificial intelligence.**

Moderate mental retardation. The range of intelligence represented by the IQ scores of 40 through 54 (just below the mild retardation range). Moderately retarded individuals can become productive workers. They can adapt to social life, but they usually require some supervision. See also: **mental retardation.**

Monaural (mon ôr′əl) **cue.** A cue which requires the use of only one ear for the localization of a sound.

Monism. The philosophical position that the universe consists of just one kind of reality. Monism is the more general part of the answer given by some philosophers to the mind-brain problem. They are then expected to offer a description of that one kind of reality. Basically, there are three possibilities: (1) All the universe is mental in nature. (2) All the universe is physical in nature.

(3) The universe is all of one type, being both mental and physical. See also: **materialism; mentalism; mind-body identity; mind-brain problem; philosophical behaviorism.**

Monoamine oxidase. See: **MAO.**

Monoamine oxidase inhibitors. See: **MAO-inhibitors.**

Monochromats (mon″ō krō′mats). The relatively few color-blind people who are able to see only in shades of gray, presumably because their eyes contain only rods. Most color-blind individuals are dichromats. Some individuals are only color-weak, rather than color-blind; they are called anomalous trichromats.

Monoclonal (mon″ō klō′nəl) **antibody immunohistochemistry** (i″myoo nō his″tō kem′is trē). A method of locating specific proteins in the body by the injection of labeled clones of the antibody of the targeted protein.

Monocular (mo nok′yoo lər). Receiving visual information with only one eye.

Monocular (mo nok′yoo lər) **depth cues.** Any aspects of the visual stimulus that convey cues to depth (or front-to-back distance), even when the observer uses only one eye. Such cues include patterns of shadows, interposition (of one object between the observer and the farther object), linear perspective, and aerial perspective.

Monogamy (from Greek "mono" = "one"; "gamos" = "spouse"). The formation of a breeding pair by one male and one female individual. Lifelong monogamy has been observed in some birds (e.g., geese and doves), some species of antelope, and even humans!). See also: **polygamy.**

Monoplegia (mon″ō plē′jē ə, -jə) from Greek "mono" = "one"; "plegia" = "paralysis"). The paralysis of one limb.

Monozygotic (mon″ō zī got′ik) **twins.** Identical twins. They develop from a single fertilized egg, or zygote.

Mood disorders. Disturbances of mood usually shown by the inappropriate appearance of either extreme pleasure (euphoria) or extreme misery (dysphoria). The former variety is called mania; the latter depression. Sometimes there are vigorous swings between the two extremes, with the absence of moderation; this is known as manic-depressive disorder or bipolar disorder. See also: **depression (major); mania;**

manic-depressive disorder.

Morbidity. [1] The condition of being ill. [2] The incidence (i.e., the frequency in a specified population) of a given disease or syndrome.

Moro (mô′rō) **reflex**. Named for its discoverer, Dr. Ernst Moro, this is a reflexive movement of arms, legs, face, and other body parts toward the body's midline when a sudden sound is heard. This reflex is present at birth and is frequently used to detect hearing ability with very young (or severely mentally handicapped) children. In normal children, the Moro reflex is replaced in late infancy by the startle reflex. See also: **reflex audiometry**.

Morpheme (môr′fēm). One of the smallest units of written language that can impart a meaning. One-syllable words, prefixes, and suffixes are all examples of morphemes.

Morphine. An opiate drug refined from opium poppies, and considered the main active ingredient in opium. Its medical use is for anesthesia. It is powerfully addictive. Morphine and similar drugs lead to relaxation and pleasant feelings. The symptoms created by withdrawal from such drugs are particularly unpleasant and painful.

Morris water maze. A circular featureless tank containing milky water. A rat is released in this setting and allowed to try to swim out of it to an escape platform. Even though the rat is put into the tank at different locations from one trial to the next, the animal soon learns, from spatial cues in the laboratory room, to swim directly to the exit. This device is used to test the effect on spatial orientation of various types of brain surgery or drugs.

Motherese. A language style used by adult caretakers with the children in their charge. There is a simple vocabulary, and the sentences are clearly formed. Repetition and redundancy are used. The focus of the talk is on the present situation. The rate of speaking is slow.

Motion parallax. A monocular cue to visual depth or distance, motion parallax involves the comparison of images produced before and after a movement of the head. The information yielded by this monocular cue resembles that yielded by **binocular disparity** (see definition).

Motivated forgetting. A type of memory failure due to an unpleasant experience or person. One might forget a relative's birthday due to some unpleasantries in past dealings. See also: **repression**.

Motivation. The concept of motivation refers to the factors that serve both to direct behavior and to activate responding (therefore, response choice and level of enthusiasm comprise the two main aspects of this concept). The attempt to explain human motivation goes back at least as far as the days of Plato (around 300 B.C.), who tried to probe for the reasons for various behaviors. Motivation is assumed to be a state of the individual that provides a basis for the individual's persistence in goal-directed activity. See also: **drive theory; need**.

Motoneurons. Nerve cells having their cell bodies in the ventral horn of the spinal cord's gray butterfly. The axons of these neurons run out the ventral roots of the spinal cord and join the spinal nerves. Each axon travels in the spinal nerve to the muscle bundle that it innervates. The motoneurons are those neurons that carry the motor commands from the spinal cord to the muscles. See also: **Bell-Magendie law; spinal cord; ventral root**.

Motor code. The storage of memories by means of the traces of the muscular movements employed in performing an activity or symbolically expressing an activity. See also: **echoic memory; encoding; engram; iconic memory; linguistic code; memory trace**.

Motor cortex. Those areas of the cerebral cortex from which neural pathways that travel to the muscles originate. See also: **Betz cells; cerebral cortex; extrapyramidal motor fibers; frontal lobe; pyramidal tract**.

Motor end plate. The equivalent of the receptor site on the membrane surrounding a muscle bundle at a neuromuscular junction, which is in turn analogous to a synapse between two neurons. The muscle is activated by the appropriate chemical neurotransmitter at a motor end-plate. Somatic or skeletal muscle provides motor end-plates that are nicotinic receptors for acetylcholine (ACh). Smooth muscle under the control of the sympathetic nervous system has norepinephrine-sensitive motor end-plates. Parasympathetic nervous system control is exerted at smooth muscle motor end-plates that are muscarinic receptors for ACh.

Motor homunculus (hō mung′kyə lus) [from

Latin "homunculus" ("homo" = "man"; "culus" = "little") = "dwarf"]. The map of body parts represented on the precentral gyrus of the frontal lobe (i.e., the primary motor cortex), showing which small cortical region controls movements of which part of the body. The left primary motor cortex controls the right side of the body, which is mapped upside down, i.e., the top of the precentral gyrus controls the lower leg while the bottom (ventral) end of the gyrus controls the head. See also: **cerebral cortex; primary motor cortex; somatosensory homunculus.**

Motor neurons or **efferent neurons**. Those peripheral nervous system neurons that carry impulses to the muscles and glands.

Motor pool. The entire set of motor neurons that innervate a particular muscle.

Motor program. A coordinated set of movements that are reeled off automatically by an organism. The whole set is produced as if it were a simple unitary action. The act of yawning is a motor program observed in humans. See also: **fixed action pattern**.

Motor unit. A single motor neuron together with all the muscle fibers that it innervates. Power muscles have one neuron innervating a great many muscle fibers, while fine-skill muscles have a single neuron innervating a very few muscle fibers.

MPTP. A neurotoxin that produces a disorder in primates resembling Parkinsonism.

MRI (magnetic resonance imaging). This is a technique which provides a picture(s) of living brain tissue by passing a strong but harmless magnetic field through a person's head. The MRI scanner will absorb radiation from hydrogen ions (i.e., protons), thus providing a picture of a slice of brain tissue. The application of a magnetic field and a radio wave to the head produces atomic vibrations detected as radio signals. These signals, when processed by a computer, produce a detailed view of the brain in action. Subcortical structures and bone marrow are visualized, along with the cerebral cortex. This technology permits the detection of some brain lesions, including those affecting psychological functioning, which are not found by the CAT scan. See also: **BEAM; CAT scan; Manscan; PET scan; regional cerebral blood flow; SQUID.**

Müllerian (mi ler′ē ən, myōō-) **ducts** or **Müllerian system.** Structures in the developing fetus that are precursors of mature female sex organs. See also: **Wolffian ducts**.

Müllerian-inhibiting substance. A substance released in the developing male fetus that leads to the degeneration of the precursors of the female genitalia, the Müllerian ducts.

Multimodal remediation. This generally describes remedial procedures which address more than one sensory mode. For example, lessons which introduce single letters and involve writing letters, tracing letters in sand, listening to songs about letters, and so on involve motoric, visual, auditory and tactile-kinesthetic approaches, that is, a multimodal remediation model.

Multiple causality. The concept that many factors working together are jointly the causes of a particular effect. In relation to phylogenetic evolution, the idea of multiple causality is that changes in the adaptive fitness of an animal species occur simultaneously in a number of genetic levels of potential; the individual, the group, and the population. See also: **relative adaptive fitness**.

Multiple-factor theories of intelligence. Theories that share the concept that human intelligence consists of a number of separate abilities that cannot and should not be represented by a single overall score such as an intelligence quotient (IQ).

Multiple personality disorder. A neurotic disorder that finds the patient displaying separate sets of responses, each appropriate to a different person. It is considered one of the dissociation disorders, except that, instead of memory loss, anesthesia, or paralysis, the division of the total personality is along vertical lines, with each portion of it having its own full set of memories and sensorimotor abilities. Note that this disorder should not be confused with schizophrenia, which is an error often made by movie and television authors.

Multiple sclerosis. One of the demyelinating diseases. The disease process leads to the deterioration of myelin sheaths around central nervous system axons. The result is ever-increasing numbness, weakness, incontinence, tremor, and ataxia (the loss of motor coordination). See also: **myelin**.

Multiple source/convergent circuits. A neural circuit in which several neurons send impulses to a single neuron. This is often called <u>reduction of path</u>. To avoid possible confusion on the reader's part, we are emphasizing that this is the opposite in meaning of the term <u>multiplication of path</u>. See also: **multiplication of path; reduction of path.**

Multiplication of path. The foveal cones are each connected to two bipolar neurons. This should mean that, other things being equal, 45,000 cones have their messages passed up the sensory pathway by 90,000 neurons; in this case, the multiplier would appear to be 2. Other things are not equal, though. See **center (of a receptive field)**; **horizontal cells**; **surround**. The auditory nervous system, however, does exhibit a true multiplication of path, since there are more neurons in the cochlear nerve than there are hair cell receptors in the inner ear. See also: the terms that represent the opposite situation, viz., **multiple source convergent circuits; reduction of path.**

Mumby box paradigm. One version of the delayed non-matching to sample paradigm for testing memory of experimental rats; the test items are non-recurring.

Muscarine (mus'kə rēn, -rin). Muscarine is recognized at some of the receptor sites on the membranes of postsynaptic neurons, as well as the smooth muscles and glands, for the neurotransmitter acetylcholine (ACh). Many of these receptor sites are in the peripheral nervous system, on membranes around some of the smooth muscles and glands that are activated by the parasympathetic nervous system. This muscarinic action of ACh can be blocked by the drug atropine. See also: **acetylcholine; acetylcholinesterase; motor end plate; nicotine; parasympathetic nervous system.**

Muscle spindle. A small, specialized muscle bundle that serves as a kinesthetic sense organ, the muscle spindle is to be found within a larger bundle of striped muscle. The muscle fibers of the spindle, called intrafusal fibers, are not striated all the way, as are the regular (extrafusal) muscle fibers. The motor commands to the intrafusal fibers are carried by special axons called gamma efferents. The ordinary, extrafusal muscle fibers get their commands from the alpha

efferents. The sensory endings (of afferent neurons) that are found on the spindle detect the elongation or stretch of the spindle (and, therefore, the stretch of the entire muscle bundle that includes the spindle). The gamma efferents fine tune the muscle tone of the intrafusal fibers, so that the threshold (i.e., the sensitivity setting) of the stretch reflex (which is triggered by excessive stretch) can be raised or lowered. See also: **alpha efferents; gamma efferents; intrafusal fiber; stretch reflex.**

Muscular dystrophy (mus'kyoo lər dis'trə fē). This is a disease that is inherited and is characterized by progressive muscle degeneration and weakness. There are a number of varieties of muscular dystrophy, with the Duchenne type being one of the most common and malignant. Death often occurs before age 30 due to infections or to heart failure. No known cures exist, although the prevention of obesity is helpful. Sometimes this disorder is accompanied by cognitive impairment and/or mental retardation. Psychological counseling can assist muscular dystrophy patients who are depressed, who show withdrawal symptoms after the cessation of a specific treatment, or who exhibit other behavioral/emotional side effects of the disease and/or the medical treatment for it.

Myasthenia gravis (mī″as thē'nē ə grav'is). Literally, "severe muscle weakening" in Latin. The acetylcholine (ACh) receptors on the motor end plates of the striate muscles (the nicotinic receptors) are attacked by the body's own immune system. (Hence, this is an autoimmune disorder.) Motor nerve signals ordinarily carried by ACh to these muscles are thereby blocked, and the muscles lose tone. The muscles grow progressively weaker and fatigued. One way to treat the condition has been to administer "nerve gas" drugs, anticholinesterases, since they block the action of the enzyme acetylcholinesterase (AChE) (which has the function of deactivating ACh), and so leave some ACh molecules intact at the motor end plates where they have recently been used. See also: **acetylcholine; acetylcholinesterase; nicotine.**

Myelin (mī'ə lin). A lipid substance (which means that it is soluble in such organic solvents as benzene or ether but is insoluble in water), myelin is fatty and is glistening white in color. It is wrapped sheath-like around some axons. Functionally, the presence of a myelin sheath speeds up the nerve impulse within the sheathed axon. See also: **lipid; lipoprotein; multiple sclerosis; oligodendrocytes; Schwann cells.**

Myoclonus (mī ok′lə nus). Restless muscular spasms of the limbs, especially the legs, that may disturb sleep. These are often referred to by sleep researchers as gross body movements. These spasms occur during REM sleep, in which there is a tonic (i.e., long-lasting) inhibition of the an-

tigravity muscles. Occasionally, a temporary extra inhibition will affect one member of a pair of antagonistic muscles (i.e., tonic inhibition), which leads to a twitch of the other, less inhibited muscle. Such myoclonic spasms are part of normal sleep and should not be considered alarming at all.

Myopia (mī ō′pē ə). The inability to see faraway things; also called shortsightedness or nearsightedness.

N

Naloxone (na lok'sōn). A drug that blocks the opiate receptors of brain neurons. Nalaxone can easily cross the blood-brain barrier. It blocks the analgesic (pain-killing) effects of the opiate drugs such as morphine. Nalaxone has been a valuable tool for research on the brain's own internal opiates, the enkephalins and endorphins.

Nanometer (nan'ə mē″tər) **(nm)**. A unit of linear measurement which is equal to one billionth of a meter or 10 Angstrom units.

Narcissistic (när″si sis'tik) **personality disorder**. An emotional disorder in which the patient exhibits excessive self-referencing as well as a lack of empathy for the feelings of others.

Narcolepsy (när'kō lep″sē). The sudden onset of REM sleep while the individual is awake. Such attacks of sleep can occur at any time of day, regardless of what the patient happens to be doing, although emotional excitement may trigger them. They may last from a few minutes to about half an hour. This can be dangerous because, in REM sleep, the striped muscles (including the antigravity muscles) lose practically all their tone. The person may collapse in place, and there are some places (such as the head of a staircase) where this is not advisable. EEG data show that the person falls directly into REM sleep without passing through the first four sleep stages. Stimulant drugs may lessen the frequency and the severity of narcolepsy attacks. Patients are well advised to avoid driving and/or working with machinery.

Narcotic drugs. The opiates. These drugs are highly addictive, in that they (1) produce a strong psychological dependency, (2) lead to tolerance, meaning that more and more of a narcotic drug is needed just to provide the same effect, and (3) result in very unpleasant withdrawal symptoms if a person attempts to quit using the drug "cold turkey." The term "narcotic" has a legal meaning rather than one based on the science of pharmacology.

Nasal hemiretina (nā'zəl hem″i ret'n ə). The half of the retina nearest the nose (i.e., the medial half). It sends optic nerve fibers across the midline to contralateral visual brain areas. See also: **contralateral; retina.**

Nasality (nā zal'i tē). A speech sound problem based on the lack of control on the part of the speaker of the flow of air through the mouth and the nasal cavity. When someone has a stuffy nose, the resulting speech **lacks** sufficient nasality. See also: **voice disorder.**

Nasal sound. A sound produced by blocking the oral cavity so that the sound passes through the nasal cavity.

Nativism. The theory that innate mechanisms contain the coded meanings of our perceptions so that they do not have to be learned. The rival theory, empiricism, holds that we cannot decode our sensory data until we have developed a key to their meanings by learning from experience. See also: **nature-nurture debate.**

Natural killer cell. A variety of leukocyte that destroys tumor cells and cells infected by viruses. See also: **leukocyte.**

Naturalistic observation. A scientific research method involving the careful recording of natural events while they are occurring. The researcher does not intervene to alter events.

Natural selection. The process, identified by Charles Darwin, that decides which species of animal will survive and which will undergo extinction. The competition for food, territory, and mate(s) determines which individuals will be successful (i.e., will survive long enough to leave offspring). The characteristics of these successful individuals will be passed along to succeeding generations, while traits of unsuccessful individuals will not be passed down. See also: **multiple causality; phylogeny; relative adaptive fitness.**

Nature. The term for genetically-inherited characteristics which help shape an individual's cognitions and behaviors. See also: **nature-nurture debate; nature-nurture interaction; nurture.**

Nature-nurture debate or **controversy**. A centuries-old, never-settled debate as to whether the influences of nature (heredity) or nurture (the environment) have the greater impact upon behaviors, personality, and social growth. This controversy is considered obsolete today, being superseded by the idea of nature and nurture interacting with one another. See also: **nature; nature-nurture interaction; nurture.**

Nature-nurture interaction. This is the view that

a genetic influence on one's intelligence or personality cannot be automatic or invariable, because its workings will always be occurring in some environmental context. What may be a beneficial gene for one environment may be harmful in another. For example, the gene that produces sickle cell anemia in so many American blacks also conveys some resistance against malaria, which means the gene favors survival in the context of the African rain forest. The bottom line for psychologists is that no behavior can be fully explained by attributing it to heredity or environment and leaving it there. Hebb compares cognitive ability to a field which has a given length and width; neither length nor width all by itself can account for the area. By the same token, it is absurd to say "heredity explains intelligence differences among people" or "the environment causes intelligence differences among people to develop." It always takes some heredity and some environment to make a human being's life, with its particular measure of personality and intelligence. See also: **nature; nature-nurture debate; nurture.**

Nauta (nou'tə) **stain**. A procedure for staining central nervous system tissues in preparing microscope slides. Frozen brain sections are immersed in silver pyridine, silver nitrate, and other chemicals. The reduced metallic silver settles onto degenerated nerve fibers only. This method can be used to trace both unmyelinated and myelinated axons. The older Marchi stain dyes only degenerated myelin materials, so that the Marchi method can be used to trace only myelinated axons. See also: **Cajal stain; Marchi stain; Weigert stain.**

NCEs (normal curve equivalents). These measures of performance are based on percentiles and, like percentiles, show where someone stands within the group. However, NCEs are transformed from nonadditive percentiles into a scale of units that represent equal steps of reading achievement. A difference of 6 points, for example, is the same amount of difference whether the measures are found near the middle of the scale or toward either the high or the low end of the scale. This property of the NCE s makes them suitable for averaging.

Necrophilia (nek'rō fil'ē ə). A type of paraphilia whereby the individual obtains sexual pleasure from having intercourse with dead bodies. Such persons often seek work in mortuaries. See also: **paraphilias**.

Necrosis. An area of dead tissue surrounded by healthy cells.

Need. A physiological condition which is caused by some imbalance within the body. There may be accompanying behaviors that lead to the reduction of the need. Such behavioral tendencies toward need reduction are called drives. For example, a water-deprived person will be thirsty and seek a source of water. The condition of water-deprivation is the need, and thirst is the corresponding drive. See also: **drive theory; motivation.**

Negative feedback. The mechanism by which inert matter can seemingly control itself. A good example is the case of the relationship among the neurosecretory cells of the hypothalamus, the anterior pituitary gland, and other endocrine glands such as the thyroid, the adrenal cortex, and the gonads. From the neurosecretory cells of the hypothalamus, a chemical command called a releasing hormone (e.g., TRH, the thyrotropin-releasing factor) is secreted at axon endings in the anterior pituitary. That gland releases a tropic hormone (in the present example, thyrotropin) that circulates in the bloodstream until it reaches the thyroid gland, where it is accepted by the "lock-and-key" (hormone molecule to targeted-tissue molecule fitting) setup. The thyroid secretes its hormone, thyroxin, into the bloodstream, where it goes to its sites of action in the body, speeding up the metabolic rate. Thyroxin also fits into receiving sites on the membranes of the neurosecretory cells that secrete TRH, inhibiting those cells. As a result, the action of thyroxin is self-limiting. Part of the system's output (in this instance, thyroxin hormone) is "fed back" to the source, the neurosecretory neurons. The feedback command is inhibitory (i.e., "stop what you've been doing"), hence negative. See also: **positive feedback**.

Negative reinforcement. Reinforcement in general is any event that results in the increased probability of an organism performing a given operant response. The reinforcement is called negative when the event involves the removal of a stimulus that is already present rather than the presentation of a new stimulus. When the removal of a stimulus results in an increased probability of the operant response, that stimulus is a negative reinforcer. Usually a negative reinforcer is an aversive stimulus, something that the organism would prefer to escape, avoid, or remove. Frequently, people confuse negative reinforcement with punishment, but punishment consists of the presentation of an aversive stimulus and usually results in a decreased probability of responding. See also: **negative reinforcer; operant conditioning**.

Negative reinforcer. A stimulus, usually a painful, unpleasant, or undesirable one, that can reinforce an operant action by being removed. That reinforcing effect is demonstrated by an increased probability that the organism will make that response whenever the stimulus is present. See also: **negative reinforcement; operant conditioning**.

Negative schizophrenia symptoms. The absence of a behavior that is usually observed in normally functioning individuals. For example, schizophrenics may manifest the blunting of affect, impoverished speech, and catatonia.

Neonate. A newborn human infant.

Nephrectomized (nə frek′tə mīzd). Having had a kidney removed.

Nerve. A collection of axons (and cylindrical "dendrites" of unipolar neurons) in the peripheral nervous system. Accordingly, the white matter of the peripheral nervous system resembles a set of white cables. A nerve is not the same as a neuron or nerve cell. There are no cell bodies of neurons in a nerve; instead, a nerve consists of the fibers of many neurons. It is usually comprised of myelin-sheathed axons running together in a bundle. Why call such things "tracts" in the brain or spinal cord but "nerves" in the peripheral nervous system? Because they look entirely different. When observed in peripheral parts of the body, a nerve, surrounded by muscles, connective tissue, and blood vessels, resembles a white cord that contrasts sharply with the red and brown colors around it. Within the brain or spinal cord, a component of the white matter such as a tract is surrounded by the off-white gray matter. The white matter can be differentiated, but only as a tone or shade, not as a separate, discrete rope-like thing.

Nerve cell. See: **neuron**.

Nerve deafness or **inner ear deafness**. A hearing loss due to damage to the cochlea, the hair cells, or the auditory nerve. Usually a specific range of pitch, particularly the higher pitches, is selectively impaired. Exposure to rubella, syphilis, toxins, loud rock music, factory noises, even the aging process, can lead to nerve deafness. Hearing aids may provide some relief, but the most direct intervention would be the implantation of microelectrodes into the auditory nerve or cochlea, as appropriate. Each microelectrode is attached to a miniature microphone. The best technique also involves sound filtering, so that a low-pass filter, a band-pass filter, and a high-pass filter are each connected to different microphones. A low-pass filter will pass through only the lower frequencies, a high-pass filter will allow only higher frequencies to get through, and a band-pass filter permits middle frequencies to pass while cutting out both the lowest and highest frequencies. See also: **hearing; conductive deafness**.

Nerve growth factor (NGF). Found in some areas of the nervous system, NGF is a protein issued by the postsynaptic neuron during the establishment of a synaptic connection between two neurons. Because NGF promotes the growth and survival of the presynaptic neuron's axon, it is considered a trophic factor. NGF is found in the ganglia of the sympathetic nervous system, as well as in some brain areas. See also: **brain-derived neurotrophic factor; trophic factor.**

Nerve impulse. A voltage change on the membrane of an axon that has the following characteristics: (1) The internal voltage at the site of the change dramatically shifts from negative to positive, and (2) the site of this voltage change moves steadily down the length of the entire axon, without any loss of voltage strength. This kind of electrical activity has also been termed the spike potential, the action potential, and the all-or-none voltage change. A nerve impulse maintains a constant voltage; it is neither graded nor decremental.

Nervous system. The cells, tissues, and organs that comprise the major internal communication system of the body in most animal species. Incoming messages report on environmental conditions, and outgoing messages serve as commands to react to those conditions. Between the incoming and outgoing messages, various cognitive and behavioral processes are taking place. See also: **brain; central nervous system; peripheral nervous system; spinal cord.**

Neural cell adhesion molecules. Molecules found on the surface of developing neurons that assist in the aggregation of nerve cell bodies into nuclear masses. See also: **aggregation.**

Neural crest. A structure taking form on either side of the neural tube. The neural crest later develops into the peripheral nervous system.

Neural Darwinism. Edelman has hypothesized that, during the growth and development of the nervous system, some synapses form at random and that only the synapses that turn out to be functional ones survive; the other (nonfunctional) synapses disappear. Thus the brain's neurons are involved in a "struggle for existence" which is resolved by the "survival of the fittest."

Neural folds. Some of the ectoderm of the embryo develops into neural folds that take shape around a neural groove. The groove will later develop into the neural tube. See also: **ectoderm; neural groove; neural tube**.

Neuralgia (n(y)oo ral′jə, -jē ə). A sharp, severe pain that follows the path of a nerve. It is often the result of infection(s) in the peripheral nervous system. See also: **nerve.**

Neural groove. In the embryo, the groove between the neural folds. When the neural folds join together, the neural groove develops into the neural tube.

Neural plate. A small group of cells in the embryonic ectoderm that later develops into the neural groove and the neural tube. Still later, these develop into the adult nervous system.

Neural tube. The prenatal structure of the central nervous system. The rostral part of the neural tube differentiates into the earliest forms of the brain, viz., the forebrain, midbrain, and hindbrain, and its caudal part, which remains the neural tube a while longer, is slated to develop into the spinal cord.

Neurilemma (n(y)oor″i lem′ə) or **neurolemma** (n(y)oor ″ō lem′ə). A sheath (made up of Schwann cells) that surrounds every axon in the peripheral nervous system. This sheath allows the axon to regenerate after it has been severed.

When a myelin sheath is present, the neurilemma surrounds the myelin sheath. Each Schwann cell of the sheath covers only the length of an internode, which is the distance between one node and the next of the myelin sheath in the case of a myelinated axon. Just picture a string of link sausages. The neurilemma would be analogous to the casing of the sausages, and the myelin would be analogous to the bulk of the sausages. The actual axon would be analogous to a very thin cylindrical fiber running through the entire length of the sausage string. The nodes would be where each pair of sausages is tied together. A Schwann cell interdigitates (interdigitation: picture two hands folded together and the way the fingers alternate) with another Schwann cell at a node; a chain of Schwann cells thus formed runs along the entire axon of the peripheral nervous system neuron. In the case of a myelinated axon, the neurilemma provides for the formation of the myelin sheath.

Neuritic (n(y)oo rit′ik) **plaques.** One of the characteristic hallmarks of Alzheimer's disease. Neuritic plaques are composed mainly of degenerating nerve cell processes and a material called amyloid, which is a substance deposited in tissue that has dye-binding properties. There are several different types of amyloid, and amyloid deposits can result from a number of diseases, including Down's syndrome. See also: **Alzheimer's disease; amyloid plaques; chromosome 21 trisomy; dementia; Down's syndrome; neurofibrillary tangles**.

Neuroanatomy. The scientific study of the anatomy of the nervous system.

Neuroblast (n(y)oor′ə blast″) **cells.** Embryonic cells that are slated to become neurons (i.e., nerve cells) in the mature nervous system. They migrate on the arms of the radial glia to positions in the central nervous system (CNS) where they will become particular types of neurons having their own special shapes and functions. Recent research (particularly by Walsh and Cepko) has shown, however, that it is possible for mature neurons to reposition themselves in the CNS.

Neurochemistry. The study of the chemistry of the nervous system, mainly of the neurohumors. See also: **neurohumor.**

Neuroendocrine cells. See: **neurosecretory cells.**

Neurofibrillary (n(y)o͞or″ō fī′bril ər ē) **tangles.** Bundles of protein filaments (neurofibrils) wound in helical fashion, forming a tangled web of tiny neural threads, which are frequently seen in Alzheimer's sufferers. Tangles are thought by some to be the remains of destroyed nerve cells. They also appear in middle-aged persons with Down's syndrome. See **Alzheimer's disease; amyloid plaques; chromosome 21 trisomy; dementia; Down's syndrome; neuritic plaques.**

Neurofibrils. See **neurofibrillary tangles.**

Neurofibromatosis (n(y)o͞or″ō fī brō″mə tō′sis) or **neurinomatosis** or **Von Recklinghausen's disease.** Named for the researcher who first described it in 1882, this is an inherited autosomal dominant disease (i.e., either parent can transmit it) which is characterized by tumors of the central and peripheral nervous systems and lesions of the vascular system. The name "neurinomatosis" refers to the many neuromas (benign tumors formed by the tangled, nonfunctional nerve fibers) typically exhibited in this disease.

Neuroglia (n(y)oo rog′lē ə) (also called **glial cells**). The non-neural supporting cells of the nervous system. The average glial cell is one-tenth the size of the average neuron. There are ten times as many glial cells as there are neurons in the nervous system. Since one-tenth of ten equals one, the amount of space taken up by glial cells is about equal to the space filled by neurons. There are several varieties of glial cells: Schwann cells (also called neurilemma cells), which are characteristic of the peripheral nervous system, and others which appear only in the central nervous system, viz., oligodendroglia (or oligodendrocytes); astroglia (or astrocytes); microglia; and radial glia.

Neurohormones (n(y)o͞or″ō hôr′mōnz). Hormones that affect, and/or are affected by, the nervous system.

Neurohumor (n(y)o͞or″ō hyo͞o′mər). A general term for a chemical, produced by neurons, that can excite other cells, be they neurons, muscle fibers, or gland cells. Types of neurohumors include: neurotransmitters; neuromodulators; the hormones oxytocin, vasopressin, and somatostatin, which are produced in the hypothalamus and

migrate to the posterior pituitary gland via axons; and the hormone-like releasing factors produced in the posterior hypothalamus, which are conveyed via portal veins to the anterior pituitary gland.

Neurohypophysis (n(y)o͞or″ō hī pof′i sis). A name for the posterior pituitary gland. The neurohypophysis releases the hormones oxytocin, vasopressin (which is also known as the antidiuretic hormone, ADH), and somatostatin. See also: **pituitary gland; posterior pituitary gland; somatostatin.**

Neurolemma. See **neurilemma.**

Neuroleptic (n(y)o͞or″ō lep′tik) **drug.** A drug given in order to alleviate such psychotic conditions as acute schizophrenia. Examples of neuroleptics are haloperidol, chlorpromazine, and clozapine.

Neuroleptic (n(y)o͞or″ō lep′tik) **induced acute akathisia** (ak″ə thi′zē ə). An inability to sit or to stand motionless due to the initiation of treatment by, or the increased dosage of, a neuroleptic drug. Symptoms include fidgeting of the legs, rocking back and forth, and general restlessness.

Neuroleptic-induced acute dystonia (dis tō′nē ə). Muscle spasms in the head, neck, limbs, and trunk caused by the initiation of treatment by, or the increased dosage of, a neuroleptic drug.

Neuroleptic-induced Parkinsonism. Parkinson's disease-like tremors or muscle rigidity caused by the initiation of treatment by, or the increased dosage of, neuroleptic medication. See also: **Parkinson's disease; tardive dyskinesia.**

Neurologically (n(y)o͞or″ə loj′i kəl ē) **impaired.** Having a disorder of the central nervous system.

Neurology (n(y)oo rol′ə jē). A specialty within the applied science of medicine. Neurologists are concerned with the diagnosis and treatment of diseases and injuries involving the nervous system.

Neuromodulator (n(y)o͞or″ō moj′oo lā″tər). A chemical messenger compound that is somewhat like a neurotransmitter because it is released from a sending axon's terminals. It is released from the presynaptic membrane, and it affects receptor sites on the postsynaptic membrane of receiving neurons. Also like a neurotransmitter, it functions to decrease or increase the sensitivity of receptor sites on receiving neurons to the passage of ions across the neuron membrane or to affect the sensitivity of the receiving neurons to certain neurotransmitters. But this kind of chemical does not function directly across the narrow synaptic cleft; rather, it travels a considerable distance in the extracellular fluid to the receiving neuron having the fitted receptor sites for its molecular shape. In this respect, the neuromodulator resembles a hormone; the main difference is that hormones travel in the bloodstream, while neuromodulators move by way of the extracellular fluid. A neuromodulator tends to communicate with the target neuron's second messenger system. Neuromodulators tend to be peptides, while most hormones are polypeptides. Examples of neuromodulators are the enkephalins, the endorphins, and epinephrine. Often, neuromodulators work with chemicals called second messengers, which are found inside the axoplasm of receiving neurons. The most common of these second messengers is cyclic AMP (cAMP). See also: **cyclic AMP**; **phosphoinositide**; **volume transmission theory**.

Neuromuscular junction. The functional contact point between the synaptic bouton of an efferent (motor) neuron and the motor end plate (receptor site) on the membrane surrounding a muscle or gland. The neuromuscular junction is analogous to a synapse between two neurons. See also: **motor end plate; receptor sites; synapse**.

Neuron. A nerve cell. Note that a neuron is <u>not</u> a nerve. The adult human brain is now estimated to have about 100 billion neurons (including a great many small ones that lack an axon). The older figure had been only 15 billion neurons (with the little ones not having been counted, no doubt). See also: **nerve**.

Neurophysiological approach. The study of the nervous system and its physiological functioning in order to further the understanding of an area of human behavior, such as the learning disorders.

Neurophysiology. The study of the workings of the nervous system. See also: **physiology**.

Neuropsychological measure. Any of various clinical tests, physiological examinations, and behavioral observation techniques that can provide evidence directly ("hard neurological signs") or indirectly ("soft neurological signs")

as to the amount and location of damage to the examinee's cerebral cortex. Such measures include tactile perception, rhythm, finger tapping, right-left discrimination, and tracking a visual stimulus by pointing.

Neuropsychological test. Any of a series of sensory examinations, psychomotor tests, cognitive problems, language functions, and so on, that are intended to turn up either hard or soft neurological signs that may be used in the diagnosis of an individual. See also: **Halstead-Reitan Battery; Luria-Nebraska Neuropsychological Battery**.

Neuropsychology. A specialty within applied psychology related to and allied with neurology, which is a medical specialty. The neuropsychologist is concerned with the testing of a patient's sensory abilities, cognitive functions, linguistic behavior, and motor activity. The neuropsychologist provides data to the neurologist that will assist the latter in making a diagnosis of the patient's condition.

Neuroscience. The cross-disciplinary science of all phases of the nervous system and its functions. This is a kind of supercategory that subsumes physiological psychology, neuroanatomy, neurophysiology, neuropharmacology and psychopharmacology, psychophysiology, neuropathology, and so on.

Neurosecretory (n(y)o͞orˮō si krēˊtə rē) **cells** or **neuroendocrine** (n(y)o͞orˮō enˊdō krin, -krēn, -krīn) **cells**. Some of the neurons in the hypothalamus send their axons to the anterior part of the pituitary body, which is the master gland that releases control hormones (the tropic hormones) to other endocrine glands. Instead of ordinary neurotransmitters, these axon endings release hormones called tropic-releasing hormones; hence, the hypothalamus is "commanding" the "master" gland to give certain orders to the other glands. For example, the corticotropin-releasing hormone (CRH) is the hormone released at some of these axon endings. In response, the anterior pituitary releases ACTH (adrenocortical tropic hormone) into the bloodstream. When ACTH arrives at the adrenal cortex, that gland goes into action, releasing steroid hormones such as cortisol. These hormones participate in the body's stress reaction wherever they are needed. They also circulate to the hypothalamus and activate inhibitory sites on the membranes of the neurosecretory cells. This permits the anti-stress reaction to be limited in duration and is an example of the self-control mechanism called negative feedback.

Neurosis (noo rō′sis, nyoo-). A relatively mild emotional or behavioral disorder that supposedly can be treated by psychotherapy or behavior therapy. This concept has been dropped from the DSM-III-R, the official psychiatric catalog of emotional/behavioral disorders, which, instead, lists separately the individual conditions that had formerly been classified as neuroses. This is partly because appropriate drug treatments are being discovered for some of these supposedly "functional" (i.e., nonorganic) disorders. For instance, the obsessive-compulsive disorder has been traced to a shortage of brain serotonin, which suggests that administering a chemical precursor of serotonin should be useful.

Neurotensin (n(y)ōōr″ō ten′sin). A peptide neurotransmitter which is released along with dopamine (DA) at postsynaptic membranes in the nucleus accumbens, which is one of the ends of the mesocorticolimbic dopamine pathway. Neurotensin enhances the release of DA at axon terminals in the accumbens, but it can interfere with DA activity after DA is released. Since it acts only at the accumbens and not at the corpus striatum, neurotensin has been compared to the drug clozapine. Neurotensin is therefore referred to as an endogenous neuroleptic.

Neurotransmitter. A chemical compound that is released from the presynaptic membrane surrounding the synaptic bouton following a nerve impulse in the axon that contains the bouton. The neurotransmitter crosses the narrow synaptic cleft to fit into a receptor site that matches the shape of its (the neurotransmitter's) molecular structure (like a round object fitting into a circular hole). The receptor site is located on the postsynaptic membrane around the receiving neuron. At rest, the neurotransmitter is stored in the synaptic vesicles, small containers spread around within the bouton. When the impulse arrives, the vesicles move to the presynaptic membrane and, due to the action of the calcium ion, the vesicle walls rupture, allowing the neurotransmitter to enter the extracellular fluid of the synaptic cleft. After having acted on the receptor

sites of the postsynaptic membrane, the neurotransmitter is deactivated, either by having its molecule split (due to an enzyme such as acetylcholinesterase) or by reuptake across the presynaptic membrane, and then restored to the synaptic vesicles. Some neurotransmitters are excitatory (tending to depolarize the postsynaptic membrane by lowering the positive voltage on the outside surface of the membrane), and some are inhibitory (tending to hyperpolarize the postsynaptic membrane by raising the external positive charge). In most cases, the neurotransmitter can be either excitatory or inhibitory, depending on synaptic arrangements. There is at least one neurotransmitter that is always excitatory, namely, glutamic acid. There are two neurotransmitters that are always inhibitory: glycine, which is found in the lower parts of the brain and in the spinal cord, and GABA (gamma-aminobutyric acid), which operates in the higher parts of the brain.

Neurotropic (n(y)ōōr″ō trop′ik). Those viral infections that have a special attraction toward nerve tissue.

Neutral stimulus. A stimulus that, prior to conditioning, has no effect on the response to be conditioned. In classical conditioning, neutral stimuli are made into conditioned stimuli. In operant conditioning, neutral stimuli may become conditioned reinforcers (either positive or negative) or discriminative stimuli that serve to indicate that a response can now be reinforced.

NGF. See: **nerve growth factor.**

Nicotine. Nicotine, the major drug constituent of tobacco, is accepted by some of the receptor sites for acetylcholine (ACh) on the membranes of postsynaptic neurons. The nicotinic endings in the peripheral nervous system are on striped muscle membrane, so ACh causes the movement of skeletal (striate, voluntary) muscles by activating the motor end plates on their membranes. The nicotinic action of ACh is blocked by the drug curare. See also: **acetylcholine; motor end-plate; muscarine; somatic nervous system; synapse.**

Nicotinic receptors. See: **nicotine; receptor sites.**

Nictitating (nik″ti tā′ting) **membrane**. The inner eyelid of animals such as reptiles and some mammals (e.g. rabbits).

Night blindness. Poorer-than-usual vision for

low-lighting conditions. This has been attributed to a vitamin A deficiency or to a hereditary condition. The immediate physical cause is the excessive slowness of the regeneration of the rod photochemical rhodopsin. Rhodopsin is partially deactivated in bright daylight conditions.

Nightmare disorder. Recurring nightmares taking place during REM sleep that can seriously disturb the sleep cycle. Fear or anxiety is usually shown. In the case of REM nightmares, the individual is usually able to recall the content of the bad dream. Most people may experience an average of two nightmares a month, the contents of these dreams showing little if any relation to waking activity. See also: **night terrors**.

Night terrors. A sleep disorder that involves recurring nightmares (commonly experienced by children) that take place during non-REM (NREM) sleep, which may last from 15 to 20 minutes. The sufferer experiences terror and disorganized panic. After a night terror episode, the individual awakens in a sweat and is not able to remember much of the episode. See also: **nightmare disorder**.

Nigrostriatal (nī˝grō strī āt′l) **pathway.** A neural pathway running from the substantia nigra of the midbrain to the corpus striatum of the telencephalon. This pathway releases the neurotransmitter dopamine at its terminals in the corpus striatum. It is responsible for motor coordination; depletion of the dopamine input to the corpus striatum is the main factor in Parkinson's disease. The continued use of some neuroleptic drugs to treat the positive symptoms of schizophrenia by lowering dopamine activity in the forebrain often leads to a motor disorder known as tardive dyskinesia. A new set of neuroleptics, that can reduce dopamine activity in the accumbens nucleus of the limbic system without interfering with the corpus striatum may allow the treatment of schizophrenia without incurring the risk of tardive dyskinesia. See also: **corpus striatum; neuroleptic drug; neuroleptic-induced Parkinsonism; schizophrenia; substantia nigra; tardive dyskinesia.**

Nissl (nis′əl) **stain.** A method of coloring neural cell bodies so that they may be examined under the microscope. Other material such as the neuroglia or the nerve fibers do not pick up the stain, because it selectively affects the Nissl substance (chromatin) only. See also: **chromatin; Nissl substance**.

Nissl (nis′əl) **substance** or **Nissl granules.** The rough endoplasmic reticulum of the neuron cell body's cytoplasm. It consists of ribosomes [made up of proteins and ribonucleic acid (RNA)] linked together by messenger RNA (mRNA). Since Nissl substance is acidic, it has an affinity for dyes or stains that are chemically alkaline (i.e., basic). Most of the basic stains that attach to Nissl substance impart a blue color to the cell body, as is the case with such stains as thionin, methylene blue, and toluidine blue. One of these stains, cresyl violet, colors cell bodies violet. These blue or violet dyes are known as **Nissl stains** (see definition). Slides of brain tissue can be examined microscopically for cell bodies (in mapping the brain nuclei, for example). After damage to the axon, the neuron soon loses its Nissl substance. This means that Nissl staining can identify the cell bodies that belong with a set of damaged axons, so that the procedure can be an investigative technique for the neuroanatomist. In the peripheral nervous system, neurons with damaged axons eventually recover, and the Nissl substance reappears. By sacrificing animals at various times after a lesion to a nerve or tract has been inflicted on them, the neuroanatomist can learn about the time it takes for the damaged peripheral neurons to recover. Cells other than neurons do not seem to have Nissl substance. Perhaps the need for manufacturing more protein in nerve cells is related to a mechanism for allowing experience (i.e., the environment), not just the hereditary DNA, to control the development of some of the proteins in those cells. See also: **chromatin; chromatolysis**.

NMR. See: **nuclear magnetic resonance.**

Nocturnal animals. Animals, such as bats, that stay asleep during the daytime and become active at night.

Nocturnal myoclonus. See **myoclonus.**

Node (of Ranvier). A pinching-in of the myelin sheath, so that the sheath is too narrow to block the movement of water-dissolved materials in or out of the axon membrane. A node is 1 micron (i.e., one-millionth of 1 meter) long.

Nonassociative learning. A change in behavior due to the repetition of a single stimulus (as in habituation) or the presentation of two or more stimuli that are not paired up either in time or in space.

Nondirected synapse. A synapse in which the presynaptic membrane is not located directly across a narrow gap from the postsynaptic membrane. Such synapses involve neuromodulators rather than regular neurotransmitters.

Nonhomeostatic (hō ˝mē ō stat′ik) **drive.** A drive that is independent of physical deprivation cycles or bodily needs. The sex drive is an example of a nonhomeostatic drive. See also: **homeostasis**.

Nonlexical procedure. A reading-aloud procedure that utilizes only the general rules of pronunciation.

Nonrecurring-items delayed matching to sample task. A problem-solving task in which the subject is presented with a previously unknown sample item, a period of delay, and the requirement of choosing between the same object and another unfamiliar item, with the correct choice being the newly presented item. See also: **Mumby box paradigm.**

Nonsuppurative otitis media (non sup′yər ə tiv, -sup′yə rā˝tiv ō tī′tis mē′dē ə). A middle ear problem due not to infection but rather to a disruption in functioning of the eustachian tube(s). The blood serum of the middle ear lining is sucked into the middle ear's air-filled cavity. This condition frequently results from a case of infectious otitis media. See also: **otitis media**.

Nootropics. Chemical agents that improve memory.

Noradrenergic (nôr˝ad rə nûr′jik). An adjective referring to axons that release the neurotransmitter norepinephrine (noradrenalin) at their terminals. See also: **neurotransmitter; norepinephrine.**

Norepinephrine (nôr˝ep i nef′rin, -rēn) **(norEp; NE).** One of the catecholamines, norepinephrine is a chemical neurotransmitter found in both the peripheral and the central nervous systems. It is also a hormone of the adrenal medulla gland. In the peripheral nervous system, it is released at the neuromuscular junctions of some of the smooth muscles, those activated by the sympathetic nervous system. In the peripheral system, it affects two types of receptor sites, the alpha and the beta receptors. This allows the selective

blocking of one type of norEp receptor by the administration of an appropriate drug. In the brain, norEp (most of which is released from the locus coeruleus) has arousal and mood-elevating effects. See also: **catecholamines; mood disorders; sympathetic nervous system**.

Normal curve. A typical frequency distribution for many kinds of biological and psychological measurements. The X-axis (abscissa) represents the measurement itself, starting with the lowest score on the left and increasing from left to right. The Y-axis (ordinate) shows the frequency (i.e., the number) of individuals getting each score. In a normal distribution (which is pictured by the normal curve), extremely low and extremely high measurements are very rare, so the curve rises very slowly at the left end and sinks very slowly at the right end. Average scores, on the other hand, occur very frequently. As a result of all this, the normal curve possesses certain descriptive features: (1) It is bell-shaped, with the center bulging upward (convex curvature) and the ends showing concave, sunken tails. (2) It is asymptotic to the X-axis at the left and right ends. This permits the score distribution to include one or more very extreme scores and still be considered a normal curve. (3) It is bilaterally symmetrical, the right half looking like a mirror image of the left. Data that fall into a normal distribution can be standardized; they can yield percentiles and standard scores. See also: **bimodal distribution; skewed distribution.**

Normalization. The doctrine that disabled persons should be allowed to live as nearly as possible like nondisabled persons.

Norm-referenced tests (NRTs). These are formal, standardized tests whose directions for administration must be closely followed. They should include items representing all levels of difficulty. The items should not be too similar in content, style, or vocabulary to any one particular published reading program.

Norms. A tabulation of the relationship between scores on a standardized test, on the one hand, and standard scores or percentile ranks, on the other. Such a tabulation would have resulted from the testing of a large sample of individuals of the type for whom the test is intended. The individuals making up that sample constitute the norm group, or standardization group.

NREM (en′rem″). The type of sleeping in which no rapid eye movements are taking place. This type of sleep is relatively free of dreaming.

Nuclear magnetic resonance (NMR). A noninvasive technique for taking images of the living brain, section by section. NMR measures the activity of the cerebral cortex by assessing changes in the brain of radio frequencies that interact with strong, but harmless, magnetic fields. The reactions of brain atoms to the radio frequencies are computerized to yield a visual display of the structures of the brain, producing images with very good resolution.

Nucleus (atomic). The core of an atom containing protons and neutrons. The number of protons in the nucleus, the atomic number, determines the chemical element represented by the atom in question.

Nucleus (of a body cell). One of the three major parts of an animal cell. The cell is the smallest possible unit of life. Its three components are the cell membrane, the cytoplasm, and the nucleus. In the nucleus are the chromosomes, on which are situated the genes, the units of heredity. The cell nucleus controls the metabolic activity of the entire cell.

Nucleus (part of the gray matter). A relatively large clump of neuron cell bodies in the central nervous system (i.e., in the brain or spinal cord).

Nurture. The term for an individual's experiences which affect his or her cognitions and behaviors. See also: **nature; nature-nurture debate; nature-nurture interaction.**

Nyctophobia (nik″tō fō′bē ə). Fear of darkness. See also: **phobias.**

Nystagmus (ni stag′mus). [1] A reflexive (involuntary) oscillation (rolling) of the eyes in response to rapid rotation of the body and head. The external eye muscles inserted into the eyeball are responsible for this activity. The vestibular sense organ of the inner ear is stimulated by the circular acceleration of the head. The rolling eyes help to maintain the organism's balance during the spinning, by compensating for the turns made by the head. The involuntary eye movements are steady and rhythmic. [2] Constant rhythmic, rolling eye movements observed in an organism not subjected to circular acceleration of the head may be a symptom of a neurological problem. One possible complaint might be a disease of the inner ear.

O

Obesity. The condition of pathologically overweight individuals. The condition is due to both genetic and psychological factors. One widely held theory is that obese persons are born with a greater number of fat cells than are other persons. Diet and exercise can reduce only the size of these cells but not the number of them. Eating habits formed very early in life can contribute to obesity. The social environment may add to the problem by encouraging the use of high-fat fast foods, by providing sweets as rewards for good behavior and for success in competitive activity, and by making available high-fat packaged snacks.

Object permanence. The consistent treatment of an object in the environment as real even when the object is not in view. This is developed in human infants at the age of 8 months or more. Most psychologists believe that it results from learning rather than maturation and that it is a major part of perceptual development. It is assessed by quickly dropping an opaque screen (e.g., a sheet of cardboard) between the object and the infant being tested. This test procedure is almost identical with one often used with monkeys and apes, although the research is then labeled as the "delayed reaction" experiment and considered to be part of the study of memory rather than of perception.

Observational learning. The type of learning in which the learning organism watches another organism make a response and receive reinforcement. The learner then imitates the behavior. The other organism is called a model. This kind of learning is also known as <u>modeling</u>, <u>imitation</u>, or <u>social learning</u>.

Obsessive-compulsive neurosis. A disorder typified by repetitive thoughts that the patient finds hard to ignore and by compulsively repeated actions (e.g., making hand-washing motions). This can interfere with the individual's normal life activities. This is one neurotic condition that may be caused by a brain chemistry disorder; a shortage of the neurotransmitter serotonin in the cerebral cortex may be responsible for this syndrome. See also: **anankastic personality disorder.**

Occipital (ok ″sip′i təl) **lobe**. The most caudal (posterior) of the four lobes of the cerebral cortex. It is located at the lower part of the back of the head near the nape of the neck. The occipital lobe is adjacent to the occiput, a bone of the skull. Unlike lobes of the lungs or the liver, the lobes of the cortex are not separate flaps but, rather, are comparable to the major continents of the earth. The boundaries between adjacent lobes are partly visible grooves (sulci or fissures) that cut into the gray matter but are also partly formed by imaginary borderlines. These lobes are observed only on the lateral or outside aspect of the cortex, not on the medial (midline) surface. The occipital lobe does not occupy the entire posterior area of the cerebral cortex, but only its ventral portion. Superior to the occipital lobe is the posterior portion of the parietal lobe. The occipital lobe is apparently wholly devoted to visual functioning.

Ocular (ok′yoo lər) **lock**. According to some chiropractors, the partial blocking of eye movements caused by sphenoid wing malfunction, which, they claim, is the immediate problem of dyslexics.

Oculomotor (ok″yoo lō mō′tər) **nerve**. The third pair of cranial nerves. This nerve is primarily motor, as its name clearly implies. It controls the action of four out of the six external eye muscles that are attached to each eyeball. It also has a parasympathetic component that works the iris in order to constrict the pupil, allowing this aperture to be nearly closed in a strongly illuminated area. This pupillary reflex conserves the photopigments of the visual receptors, the rods and cones. Another connection this nerve makes to the smooth muscles inside the eye is the link to the ciliary muscles, which produce the accommodation reflex of the lens. Kinesthetic sensations in the various eye muscles produce nerve impulses going toward the brain in the afferent axons of this nerve. See also: **cranial nerves**.

Oddity problem. A test situation in which the subject is presented a set of stimuli and is required to select the one stimulus that is different from the others. Another type of problem uses a similar setup, but requires the subject to select a stimulus that matches another stimulus. That type of test is called the "matching-to-sample test."

Off-center cells. Higher-order neurons in the visual neural pathway that respond to light-stimulation of the center of the receptive field by off-responses and to light-stimulation of the surround of the receptive field by on-responses. See also: **receptive field;**

center; surround.

Off-responses. Nerve impulses that come from higher-order neurons in a sensory pathway only after the stimulus is turned off. While the stimulus is present, these neurons are inhibited.

Olfactory (ol fak′t(ə)rē, ōl-) **bulb.** A bulbous, forward-pointing extension of the anterior end of the ventral forebrain. The left and right olfactory bulbs are where the axons of the two <u>olfactory nerves</u> terminate. Axons from the olfactory bulbs comprise the olfactory tract; they run to the olfactory paleocortex. See also: **forebrain; olfactory nerve; olfactory sense; olfactory tract; paleocortex.**

Olfactory mucosa (ol fak′t(ə)rē, ōl-). The mucous membrane of the upper nasal cavity, containing the olfactory receptor cells.

Olfactory (ol fak′t(ə)rē, ōl-) **nerve.** The first pair of cranial nerves, the olfactory, is concerned with olfaction, the sense of smell. The olfactory nerves run from the olfactory epithelium (where the smell-sensing receptors, the olfactory neurons, are situated) in the upper nasal cavity to the olfactory bulbs of the telencephalon. The olfactory nerves, like the optic nerves (cranial nerve pair II), are really central nervous system (CNS) tracts; if severed, their axons will degenerate completely and sensation from the damaged cells will be lost forever. True peripheral nerves, such as cranial nerves III through XII, can stop degenerating and begin to regenerate, eventually recovering their lost functions. The peripheral nervous system, unlike the CNS, has neurolemma sheaths, which are linked to the ability of the axons to regenerate themselves. See also: **central nervous system; cranial nerves; neurolemma; peripheral nervous system; telencephalon.**

Olfactory (ol fak′t(ə)rē, ōl-) **sense.** Our sense of smell. This is an important sense as it forewarns us of fire, dangerous fumes, rotten food, and so on. The sensation of smell is activated by a complex protein produced in a nasal gland. This protein combines with odorous molecules in the air streaming into the nose. The resulting chemical products activate the millions of smell receptors in the olfactory epithelium, a type of tissue found in the upper nasal cavity. It is the combination of olfaction and gustation (smell and taste) that provides for us the perception of flavor. This sense is considered to be relatively weak in human beings, in comparison with the olfactory powers of animals

such as dogs. In spite of the weak nature of olfaction, only a few molecules of a substance are needed for us to perceive the odor. The human nose contains thousands of receptors and can recognize at least 10,000 different odors. Women, particularly, are able to identify a wide range of different odors. Our greatest "smelling years" are from the age of 20 to the age of 40. One fourth of the people over 65 and half the people over 80 have lost this sense.

Olfactory (ol fak′t(ə)rē, ōl-) **tract.** A bundle of axons arising from cell bodies of neurons in the olfactory bulbs. The olfactory tract travels to a section of the <u>rhinencephalon</u> called the anterior perforated substance. See also: **olfactory bulb; rhinencephalon; tract.**

Oligodendrocytes (ol″i gō den′drə sīts) or **oligodendroglia** (ol″i gō den drog′lē ə) (from Greek "oligo" = "few"; "dendro" = "tree", "cyte" = "cell"). One of the types of central nervous system neuroglia. The oligodendrocytes form myelin sheaths around some of the axons within the brain and spinal cord by wrapping themselves around the axon. Each of the oligodendrocytes can cover only a limited length of axon, an internode. The oligodendrocytes link up to one another at the nodes along the axon, forming a chain that creates a sheath for the entire axon.

Olivocochlear (ol′i vō kōk′lē ər) **bundle.** A group of axons running from the superior olivary nucleus in the medulla to the hair cells of the cochlea. The superior olivary nucleus is one of the way stations in the auditory neural pathway from the inner ear to the auditory area of the cerebral cortex. The olivocochlear bundle seems to be headed in the wrong direction, from the brain to the hearing receptors, the hair cells. The function of these axons is to lower the sensitivity (increase the thresholds) of those receptors receiving the "wrong-way" messages. See also: **centrifugal bipolar cells; organ of Corti.**

Omission. An articulation disorder in which (a) sound(s) is (are) omitted from (a) word(s). See also: **articulation disorder.**

Ommatidium (plural, **ommatidia**). One sub-unit of the compound eye of certain invertebrates (such as lobsters, crabs, spiders, and insects). Hartline's studies of nerve impulses from a single ommatidium of the horseshoe crab, Limulus, launched a new era in the study of visual physiology. See also: **Limulus; lateral inhibition; receptive field.**

Omnivore (om′ni vôr, -vōr). An animal that will accept both plant and animal tissues as food. Examples of omnivores are human beings, some canines, some rodents, and swine.

On-center cells. Higher-order neurons of the visual nervous system that respond to light-stimulation of the center of the receptive field with on-responses and to lights striking the surround or periphery of the receptive field with off-responses. See also: **center; receptive field; surround.**

On-responses. Nerve impulses of higher-order neurons in a sensory pathway that begin when a stimulus is turned on.

Ontogeny (on toj′ə nē). The development of an individual living thing (an organism) from conception to old age.

Open-field test. Testing the behavior of an experimental animal in a large open area. For example, a very low level of mobility may indicate strong fear.

Operant. Any nonreflex response; an action that is not elicited by a stimulus but seems to be "voluntary," although, according to Skinner (who introduced the term), the rate at which the operant is performed can be explained by the organism's prior history, particularly whether the response has been followed by reinforcement and how regularly that reinforcement was given. The pairing of an operant response with reinforcement is operant conditioning.

Operant conditioning (also called **instrumental conditioning**). The conditioning of so-called voluntary behavior. The experimenter must wait for the organism to make a given voluntary response, at which time immediate reinforcement is given to the organism. After a number of response-reinforcement pairings, the rate of responding increases. This increase in the probability of the organism's making the response is, by definition, operant conditioning. See also: **operant.**

Operant level. The probability (at a given time and place) that the organism will make an operant response prior to the beginning of the conditioning or after the extinction of that response. An operant level is often taken as a baseline of measurement in research on the effects of operant conditioning.

Ophthalmologist (of˝thal mol′ə jist, op˝-). A medical doctor specializing in diseases of the eyes. See also: **optometrist.**

Opiate receptors. Receptor sites on postsynaptic neurons are shaped to accept particular neuro-transmitters. Some of these are keyed to the molecular shapes of the opiates. The discovery of opiate receptors led to the realization that the brain releases its own endogenous opiates, viz., the endorphins and the enkephalins. The activation of these receptor sites and the neurons that house them results in relief from pain.

Opiates. A category of drugs that combine some properties of depressants with some of stimulants. Opiates have relaxant and sleep-inducing effects, like depressants. They also produce elevated mood and feelings of pleasure, like stimulants. Examples of opiate drugs are opium, morphine, heroin, codeine, and methadone. The brain's chemical products, the polypeptides known as the enkephalins and endorphins, are also opiates. See also: **endogenous opiates; endorphins; enkephalins; morphine; narcotic drugs.**

Opium. The original opiate drug produced from the sap exuded by the opium poppy. It contains such psychoactive ingredients as codeine and morphine.

Opponent-process theory of color vision. Hering, who was the great rival of Helmholtz in the physiological research activities of nineteenth century German science, suggested that if chemical reactions can go in opposite directions (parts A + B combining to form the larger compound AB or compound AB being broken down into its parts A and B), each type of visual receptor could account for two colors, one color being the result of the combination reaction and the other resulting from the breakdown reaction. Moreover, the one color was likely to be the complementary color of the other. Thus we could have a set of red-or-green photoreceptors, another group of receptors sensitive to yellow or blue, and a third group reacting either to white or to black. Phenomenology (subjective experience) seemed to be consistent with this kind of thinking. The clinching argument has it that we can never sense reddish-green, greenish-red, bluish-yellow, or yellowish-blue. This would be because a red-green receptor has to be going either one way or the other; the same applies to a yellow-blue receptor. Metabolic reactions are classified into anabolism (buildup) and catabolism (breakdown). Anabolic reactions use up thermal energy (heat) in combining smaller chemical parts into larger wholes. Catabolic reactions that involve the breakdown of complex wholes into their parts also release heat. The phenomenology relates to our experience of the warm colors and the cool colors. In the case of the hypothetical red-green receptor, red is the warm color and green the cool one. The theory holds that the sensation of red is the process by which the larger compound, call it AB, breaks into A + B accompanied by the release of heat. Seeing green would feel cool because it takes in heat and results from the combining of parts A and B into compound AB. Likewise, in the second kind of receptor that Hering hypothesized, yellow is a warm color and blue is cool. Even in the case of the third, "achromatic," receptor, white is hot and black is cool. Early supporting evidence for the Hering opponent-process theory of color vision is illustrated by the phenomenon of negative afterimages. Stare at a picture of a green tree for a few minutes with a steady gaze and very few eyeblinks. Then look at a clean piece of white paper. A ghostly red tree will be seen on the plain white paper. Hering's explanation would be that the chemical reaction of anabolism has been exhausted in the set of red-green receptors receiving the image of the tree. White light may stimulate all receptors equally, but the red-green receptors can provide only one still-fresh way of responding, catabolism. The modern explanation of color vision offered by deValois and his associates transcends the retinal receptors. There are two processes in the nervous system that can be considered opposed to one another, namely excitation and inhibition. Some higher-level nerve cells in the visual pathway are excited by the cones specialized for one color and inhibited by cones specialized for another color. One kind of higher-level neuron could be designated a red +/green- neuron. It is excited when its receptive field (the relevant area of the retina of that neuron) is struck by red light, but is inhibited when its receptive field is affected by green light. Three other types of opponent-process neurons discovered by deValois and his group are green +/red -, blue +/yellow -, and yellow +/blue -. This means that trichromatic theory (the Young-Helmholtz view) can be correct at the receptor level although opponent-process action still happens, but beyond the level of the visual receptors. Moreover, the opposing processes are not anabolism and catabolism, but, rather, neuronal excitation and inhibition.

Opponent-process theory of drug-withdrawal symptoms. The key to this explanation of the appearance of withdrawal symptoms following the cessation of drug taking is the idea of biochemical tolerance mechanisms. The individual body cells (as well as the entire liver, in its own way) develop methods of neutralizing a drug that is chronically taken into the body. This is reflected in the user's need to take more and more of the drug to obtain the same effect, usually a pleasant or euphoric effect. The user then goes "cold turkey," which means that the chemical role of the drug in the body is suddenly absent. The tolerance mechanisms that have been active all along will not be readily turned off. Since their action is to counteract drug effects, they would usually be dysphoric (the opposite of euphoric, i.e., quite unpleasant). A model for this theory is the practical joke sometimes played in a game of tug-of-war in which the members of one team, on a secret prearranged signal, all let go of the rope, allowing the other team to "win" by falling over backward.

Opponent-process theory of motivation. The idea that the nervous system counteracts any departure from the midpoint of the pain-to-pleasure dimension. If a stimulus leads to a certain amount of displeasure, this is reacted to by neutralizing the displeasure and even arousing a degree of pleasure. The opponent process can be revealed by quick removal of the stimulus, which results in a rapid emotional shift to the other side of neutrality.

Oppositional defiant disorder. The display of hostility, negativism, and deviance on the part of a child. The condition, however, does not include outright physical aggression toward other people and callous disregard for their rights, which is shown by those with the more severe conduct disorder. The defiance symptoms are usually shown to those the individual knows well, rarely to strangers. The individual does not describe himself or herself as defiant, but only as making suitable responses to unreasonable demands. See also: **antisocial personality disorder; conduct disorder.**

Opsin (op'sin). The more variable of the two main components of a retinal photopigment. The opsin combines with retinal (in the 11-cis form) to make the pigment. Depending on which particular opsin it is, the resulting pigment will be sufficiently sensitive to all the wavelengths of visible light (rhodopsin), to red light (erythrolabe), to green light (chlorolabe), or to blue light (cyanolabe). See also: **retinal; retinol.**

Optacon. An optics-to-touch transducing device (converter) that copies the visual shapes of printed letters into a series of vibrations of small wire rods. The raised images of the letters may be read by the fingertips. The Optacon was developed at Stanford University. The vibratory image is presented as a configuration of 144 tactile pins. See also: **transduction**; **MIT Braille Embosser**.

Optic chiasma (op'tik kī az'mə). The X-shaped white structure marking the position at the floor of the hypothalamus where the optic nerve enters the brain. The Greek letter "chi" is shaped like the letter X, and "chiasma" means "chi-formation." In the human brain, only the optic nerve fibers from the nasal half-retinas continue across the midline to join the visual brain on the opposite side from the eye. The axons from the temporal half-retina swing back to join the visual brain on the same side as the eye from which they came.

Optic disk. Also known as the blind spot, this is the place on the eyeball from which the optic nerve leaves on its way toward the brain.

Optician (op tish'ən). A specialist in the grinding of lenses according to the prescription of an ophthalmologist or an optometrist.

Optic nerve. The second pair of cranial nerves. The optic nerve is a bundle of 1,000,000 axons traveling from the eye to the brain. The axon bundle departs from the eye at the blind spot (or optic disk), where no light receptors exist in the retina. (Such receptors would have been covered over by the gathering of the optic nerve axons.) Each of these axons is the sending fiber of a retinal ganglion cell. The optic nerve is more like a tract of the central nervous system than a peripheral nerve in several ways: (1) If cut, the optic nerve cannot repair itself, since no neurolemma is present. (2) The optic nerve, like the brain and spinal cord, is surrounded by three membranes, the pia mater, arachnoid, and dura mater. (3) At the core of the optic nerve, blood vessels run parallel to the axons. These three features also apply to the olfactory nerve, the first pair of cranial nerves. See also: **cranial nerves**.

Optic nerve fiber. An individual part of the optic nerve, which consists of 1,000,000 fibers. Each optic nerve fiber is an axon of a retinal ganglion cell.

Optic radiation. The axons that travel from the lateral geniculate nucleus to the visual cortex. These axons comprise the geniculo-calcarine tract. The optic radiation fibers, like other incoming and out-going axons, are compressed into the internal capsule at the level of the corpus striatum but fan out, or radiate, once they are clear of that level and are directly below the gray mantle of the cerebral cortex. See also: **corpus striatum; geniculo-calcarine tract; internal capsule; lateral geniculate nucleus; visual cortex.**

Optic tectum. In such lower vertebrates as amphibians, birds, and reptiles, the chief terminals of the visual neural pathway are found in the dorsal midbrain's superior colliculi. These plus the inferior colliculi make up the tectum (upper deck) of the midbrain. See also: **midbrain; tectum; superior colliculus.**

Optic tract. The continuation of the optic nerve fibers after the optic nerve has penetrated the hypothalamus at the optic chiasma. On the left side of the brain, the optic tract fibers consist of axons from the left eye's temporal half and the right eye's nasal half. This means that the left visual brain receives information from the right half of the visual world (i.e., the right visual field). Correspondingly, the right half of the brain receives visual information from the left visual field. Most of the optic tract fibers terminate in the lateral geniculate nucleus. See also: **lateral geniculate nucleus; optic chiasma; optic nerve**.

Optimal pitch. The sound that an individual produces with the least strain or effort from his or her larynx. The optimal pitch can be compared with that person's habitual pitch. If there is too great a discrepancy between the two, a pitch disorder is inferred. See also: **habitual pitch; voice disorder**.

Optometrist (op tom'ə trist). A specialist (with a doctor's degree) in the care of the eyes who is not a medical doctor. The optometrist is restricted to prescribing and fitting corrective lenses, doing screening tests for the first signs of serious visual problems, and treating optical defects by training and exercise. Only medical doctors (i.e., ophthalmologists) are legally permitted to prescribe drugs and perform surgery. See also: **ophthalmologist; optician.**

Oral-aural (ōr'əl ôr'əl). An educational approach for the deaf that emphasizes the fullest use of residual hearing ability, with speech as the main form of communication.

Oral language deficit. An oral language deficit generally refers to problems in the actual production of speech sounds or in the act of communicating information verbally.

Orchidectomy (ôr″ki dek'tə mē). The surgical removal of the testes.

Organic anxiety syndrome. Having either recurrent panic attacks or generalized anxiety that may be attributed to a physical problem. It is distinguishable from delirium, in which the patient is unable to pay attention to the environment. Either endocrine disorders or the ingestion of drugs or toxins would be the usual organic factors leading to this syndrome. See also: **organic mood syndrome.**

Organic delusional syndrome. Having systematic false beliefs, particularly delusions of persecution, that can be ascribed to a bodily condition. The abuse of amphetamines may lead to paranoid delusions that resemble those of paranoid schizophrenia. Lesions of the cerebral cortex may lead to the delusion that an arm or leg is missing. Temporal lobe epilepsy, Huntington's chorea, and the abuse of stimulant or hallucinogenic drugs may lead to organic delusions.

Organic disability. A hereditary or congenital disability involving the physical make-up of the patient's body.

Organic hallucinosis (hə lōō″si nō'sis). Having persistent or recurring hallucinations that are related to an organic factor. Delusions may be present. It is permissible for the same person to be diagnosed as having organic delusional syndrome and organic hallucinosis. The nature of the hallucinations may depend on the nature of the physical problem. Cataracts, for example, may lead to visual hallucinations, while otosclerosis may lead to auditory hallucinations.

Organic mood syndrome. Experiencing either an extremely elated or an extremely depressed mood that can be related to a physical condition. The abnormal mood must not be the product of an inability to remain attentive to the outside world, as would be the case if the patient were delirious. Hormone imbalance or the ingestion of poisons or drugs are the usual organic sources of the disturbance of mood. The condition is to be distinguished from mood disorders, such as mania or major depression, that seem to be hereditary.

Organic personality syndrome. Having a physical condition that leads to a persistent personality change involving one or more of the following: mood swings; outbursts of rage that are out of proportion to any irritant that may be present; impaired

social judgment; extreme apathy and indifference; paranoia or heightened suspiciousness. A child or adolescent with attention-deficit hyperactivity disorder (ADHD) should not be diagnosed as having organic personality syndrome; the ADHD categorization takes precedence. See also: **attention-deficit hyperactivity disorder.**

Organizing effect. The long-term effect of a hormone that is present at a certain level during a critical period of development.

Organ of Corti (kôr'tē). The inner ear structure on the cochlea's basilar membrane that serves as the organ of hearing. The auditory receptors, known as the inner and outer hair cells, are part of the organ of Corti. These receptors communicate to the dendritic endings of the cochlear nerve, which form the acoustic branch of the auditory-vestibular nerve. The receptor cells (hair cells) on the vibrating portion of the basilar membrane rub the endings of their hairs (cilia) against a second membrane just above them, the tectorial membrane. This generates an electrical response, the generator potential, in those hair cells. In this manner, the mechanical vibrations of the basilar membrane are converted (transduced) into the electrical energy of nerve impulses. Some of the nerve fibers communicate to the hair-cell receptors, presumably to readjust their sensitivity. These fibers comprise the olivocochlear bundle. See also: **basilar membrane; cochlea; generator potential; hair cells; inner ear; olivocochlear bundle.**

Orgasm phase. The stage of the human sexual response that is the peak of sexual activity. In males, the semen is expelled; in females, the vaginal muscles contract.

Orienting response. The turning of a body part (especially the head) toward a sound source. Orienting responses are frequently observed in young children in order to assess such abilities as hearing.

Orthodromic. See: **dromic.**

Orthographic (ôr'thə graf'ik) **strategy.** This is the third stage of Frith's conceptual developmental model of reading and involves matching word patterns to internalized models.

Orthomolecular (ôr″thō mə lek'yoo lər). Refers to the belief that producing the correct chemical condition of the brain and of the rest of the body is the major key to health. Orthomolecular doctrine holds that megavitamins, and often megaminerals, should be taken in order to restore (and maintain) the body's normal, healthy inner state.

Orthopedic (ôr″thō pē′dik) **disability**. A type of organic disability which involves impairment of the bones, the joints, and the muscles.

Orthoptist (ôr thop′tist). A specialist who provides eye exercises that are prescribed by an ophthamologist. See also: **ophthalmologist**; **optometrist**.

Oscillator (os′i lā ″tər). A repeated alternating movement, for example, the flapping of a wing during the flight of a bird. The scratching motions of a cat or a dog illustrate this concept. Scratching motions are alternate flexions and extensions. Their pace is not stimulus-controlled but is internally regulated by a group of spinal cord neurons.

Oscilloscope (o sil′ə skōp″). A recording device that displays voltage changes against a grid of X-Y coordinates, with the X-axis indicating time and the Y-axis indicating voltage. It consists, essentially, of a cathode ray tube with a fluorescent screen. The display is created by an electron beam (the "cathode ray") striking the phosphor to produce a dot of light. Electromagnets cause the dot to keep moving from left to right. When the dot reaches the extreme right end of the X-axis, the magnetic charges reverse instantaneously causing the dot to start from the left end again.

Osmolality (oz″mə lal′i tē). The condition of there being no osmotic pressure between body cells and extracellular fluid, which is one aspect of homeostasis. See also: **intracellular thirst**; **osmoreceptors**.

Osmoreceptors (oz″mō ri sep′tərz, -tôrs). Receptors sensitive to increased osmotic pressure (resulting from dehydration), which are found in neurons of the lateral preoptic area of the hypothalamus, as well as in the stomach, the intestine, and the portal blood vessels that communicate between the liver and the intestines. The abdominal osmoreceptors, unlike the hypothalamic ones, do not seem to be related to thirst regulation; their function is not yet understood. See also: **intracellular thirst**; **osmolality**; **osmotic thirst**.

Osmotic (oz mot′ik) **pressure**. A force due to the concentration level of a substance dissolved in one watery solution being exerted toward another water solution which is separated from the first by a semipermeable membrane. Water is drawn from the relatively hypotonic solution to the more hypertonic solution. See also: **hypertonic fluid**; **hypotonic fluid**.

Osmotic (oz mot′ik) **thirst** or **intracellular thirst**. This is a need for water intake (and a corresponding behavioral drive for ingesting water) due to there being a higher concentration of dissolved substances in the extracellular fluid than in the cells. This difference in concentration leads to the flow of water out from the cells and into the blood. This kind of thirst requires the action of the neurons in the lateral preoptic area of the hypothalamus. These neurons are osmoreceptors, that is, they sense changes in osmotic pressure: (1) When saline solution is applied to them, the animal starts to drink water. (2) When distilled water is applied to those neurons, the animal stops drinking water. See also: **hypovolemic thirst**; **intracellular thirst**; **supraoptic nucleus**; **volemic thirst**.

Ossicles (os′i kəlz) (from Latin "os" = "bone"; "-icle" is a diminutive). The three small bones lined up one after another in the middle ear. The first one in line is the hammer or malleus, which is attached to the interior surface of the tympanic membrane, which is the last part of the outer ear. Vibration of that membrane is passed on to the hammer. The hammer in turn beats upon an anvil-shaped bone, known as the anvil or incus. The base of the anvil dovetails with (is articulated with) the third small bone, the stirrup or stapes. The stapes has the oval window as its footplate; the oval window is the beginning of the inner ear. When the vibrations are both loud and high in frequency, the ossicles, other things being equal, could shatter themselves. In such a case, though, there are muscles that restrain the vibrations of the ossicles. The tensor tympani muscle, which is attached to the hammer, dampens the hammer's shaking when impulses to this muscle arrive by way of the fifth cranial nerve, the trigeminal nerve. The stapedius muscle is attached to the stirrup and dampens the shaking of that ossicle when it receives impulses from the seventh cranial nerve, the facial nerve. See also: **anvil**; **hammer**; **middle ear**; **oval window**; **stapedius**; **stapes**; **tensor tympani**; **tympanic membrane**.

Osteogenesis imperfecta (os″tē ō jen′ə sis im ″pûr fek′tə) (also called **brittle bone disease**). An inherited disorder affecting bone structure. The bones are very brittle, and there may even be some fractures prior to birth. Hearing impairments may accompany this condition.

Otitis media (ō tī′tis mē′dē ə). A middle ear infection that is fairly common. It is primarily a childhood condition that typically occurs in children under the age of 2. This is a common problem of children with Down's syndrome or cleft palates because of abnormally developed eustachian tubes.

Otolaryngologist (ō″tō lar″ing gol′ə jist). A medical doctor who specializes in disorders of the ear, nose, and throat.

Otolith (ō′tə lith″) **organs**. The sense receptors of the inner ear vestibular organ that monitor linear acceleration, as opposed to the semicircular canals that are stimulated by rotary acceleration. There are two otolith organs: the utricle, which monitors horizontal acceleration, and the saccule, which responds to vertical changes of speed. The nonsense word huvs provides a helpful mnemonic device: horizontal = utricle; vertical = saccule. See also: **labyrinthine sense organs; saccule; utricle; vestibular senses.**

Otologist (ō tol′ə jist). A medical doctor specializing in ear disorders.

Otosclerosis (ō″tō skli rō′sis). A condition of the middle ear in which bony growths at the base of the stirrup (or stapes) impede the full development of that ossicle. See also: **middle ear; ossicles; stapes.**

Otoscope (ō′tə skōp). A small light used in the visual examination of the auditory canal and the eardrum.

Outer ear. The ear has three major components: the outer ear, the middle ear, and the inner ear. Sound waves are not converted (i.e., transduced) into nerve impulses until they arrive at the inner ear. The outer ear includes the pinna, a large skin flap attached to the head that serves as a natural ear trumpet, gathering sound waves. These sound waves are funneled into an opening called the auditory canal. The end of the auditory canal is the eardrum, or tympanic membrane, which serves as the boundary between the outer ear and the middle ear. See also: **inner ear; middle ear.**

Oval window. The membrane that serves as the boundary between the middle ear and the inner ear. The stirrup (stapes), the third of the middle ear's three ossicles, is attached to the outer side of the oval window. The vibration of the stapes is conducted to the oval window. This vibration is passed on from the oval window to the basilar membrane and the fluid-filled spaces of the inner ear.

Ovariectomy (ō vâr″ē ek′tə mē). The removal of the ovaries from the female organism, which in turn removes the hormones estradiol and progesterone. In the female rat, there is a cessation of receptivity to the male. The evolutionary trend to cerebral cortical control of sexuality has already begun to appear in the male rat, however; castrated male rats retain a measure of sexual motivation. In the female monkey, ovariectomy lowers the frequency of sexual activity but does not eradicate it completely. The effect of ovariectomy on the human female's sexual activity is relatively slight. In humans of either sex, readiness for sexual behavior need not depend on hormone levels; environmental stimulation is much more important. See also: **encephalization; ovaries.**

Ovaries. The female gonads (sex glands) that secrete the hormones estradiol and progesterone. The ovaries respond to hormones from the anterior pituitary, namely, the follicle-stimulating hormone (FSH) and the luteinizing hormone (LH). The ovarian hormones initiate the development of the female secondary sexual characteristics (e.g., the emergence of the breasts). Each of the pituitary hormones takes its turn in modifying the ovary: The FSH stimulates the development of the follicle, which in turn produces estradiol. This hormone returns to the pituitary and inhibits the further release of FSH. The pituitary then secretes LH, which causes the ovary to release mature ova and stimulates the development of the corpus luteum. The corpus luteum in turn releases progesterone, which inhibits the further release of LH from the pituitary and also prepares the wall of the uterus for the implantation of the fertilized egg. This cycle of interactions between the ovaries and the anterior pituitary is called the estrous cycle or menstrual cycle. At one point in the cycle, the levels of all four hormones are low. If the ovum has been fertilized, becoming a zygote (fertilized egg cell), estradiol and progesterone levels gradually increase throughout pregnancy. When fertilization does not occur, the lining of the uterus is cast out (in the menstruation process) and the cycle begins anew. See also: **endocrine system; estrus; negative feedback.**

Ovulation (ov″yoo lā′shən). The release of an egg cell or ovum from the follicle; this is the first step in the beginning of the fertility phase of the menstrual cycle.

Ovum (plural, ova). The egg cell; the female gamete or reproductive cell which is produced by the ovary.

Oxytocin (ok″si tō′sin). A hormone, found in males

and females, which is released from the posterior lobe of the pituitary gland. Oxytocin causes the uterus to contract during childbirth. It also helps the passage of sperm cells through the uterus on their way to the ovaries. Additionally, it influences the cells in a female's mammary glands to release the flow of mother's milk immediately following par-turition (giving birth). Higher levels of oxytocin have been associated with increased sexual behavior, grooming, and positive social interactions, including positive family relationships. See also: **endocrine system; hormones; pituitary gland; posterior pituitary gland.**

P

P300 wave. A positive voltage change in the EEG (electroencephalogram) occurring 300 milliseconds after the presentation of a particular brief stimulus. The voltage change will appear provided the subject has been given a reason to expect a particular event following the stimulus. See also: **event-related potential.**

Pacinian (pä sin′ē ən) **corpuscle.** A sense receptor found in deeper layers of the skin. This encapsulated nerve ending is constructed to amplify mechanically a deep pressure stimulus so that it triggers a generator potential in the unipolar afferent neuron of which it is a part. See also: **afferent neuron; generator potential; somatosensory system; unipolar neuron.**

Pain. A physically-unpleasant experience associated with physical and psychological suffering. Harmful stimuli cause destruction or injury to tissues adjacent to nerve fibers. Chemicals are released which activate pain receptors in the skin. Such chemical mediators of pain include histamine, proteolytic enzymes, and prostaglandins. Pain thresholds are difficult to measure, because pain perception is greatly influenced by psychological factors. The gate control theory of pain holds that a neural gate (possibly located in the spinal cord) controls the pain impulses that are passed on to the brain. The theory states that pain experience is increased when the gate is opened. The large, myelinated afferent nerve fibers close the gate and prevent pain impulses from continuing on to the brain. According to the gate control theory, small, unmyelinated axons open the gate and cause pain messages to arrive at the brain. Natural opiate neuromodulators, the endorphins and enke-phalins, act in ways similar to the opiate drugs: they relieve pain. Presumably, the activation of opiate receptor sites on neural membranes leads to the closing of the pain gate. Acupuncture is gaining popularity as a method of relieving pain. The acupuncture needles may stimulate the release of endorphins and/or activate the large, myelinated afferent axons. The result would be closing the gate against the pain impulses that are directed to the brain. See also: **acupuncture; gate control theory of pain.**

Paired-associate test. A memory test involving word-pairs that a subject is given (by reading or by listening). Later the first member of each pair is presented to the subject, who is required to respond by giving the second word of the pair.

Paleocortex (pā″ lē ō kôr′teks″) (from Greek "paleo" = "old"; from Latin "cortex" = "rind"). A part of the cerebrum ventral to the cerebral cortex, which is also called the neocortex. The paleocortex includes the cingulate gyrus, as well as the hippocampus and the olfactory areas. It has only three layers, rather than the six layers characteristic of the neocortex. See also: **cerebral cortex; hippocampus; rhinencephalon; telencephalon.**

Pancreas (pan′krē əs). A large exocrine gland that releases digestive enzymes into the stomach by way of ducts. Islet cells (the islets of Langerhans) are attached to the pancreas, however, and these belong to the endocrine system. There are two types of islet cells, the alpha cells and the beta cells. The alpha cells manufacture and secrete the hormone glucagon, which converts the glycogen (animal starch) that is stored in the liver into glucose (blood sugar), thus raising the level of blood sugar. The beta cells manufacture and release the hormone insulin, which causes the conversion of glucose to glycogen and the storage of glycogen in the liver. Thus the two sets of islet cells complement one another and, between them, help to maintain a normal amount of blood sugar. Excessive insulin activity leads to hypoglycemia, which is a generally weakened state due to low blood sugar. Inadequate insulin secretion leads to diabetes mellitus, a malady involving excessive blood sugar along with a lowered supply of blood sugar to the cells of the body. See also: **diabetes mellitus; endocrine system; hyperglycemia.**

Panic attack. A sudden, intense, and unpredictable feeling(s) of fear or terror. An individual can experience physiological distress manifested by dizziness, fainting, difficulty in breathing, chest pain, sweating, stomachache, and heart palpitations. The attack usually lasts just a few minutes. These attacks can be triggered at any time without an obvious initiating stimulus or event. When the stimulus or event can be identified, the condition or disorder is called **posttraumatic stress disorder** (see definition).

Panic disorder. An anxiety disorder involving the sudden onset of emergency reactions (panic attacks) such as rapid and shallow breathing, rapid heartbeat, perspiration at the forehead and the palms of the hands, dizziness, nausea, loss of a sense of reality, depersonalization, fear of dying, fear of the loss of one's sanity, numbness, and so on. There is no particular stimulus for evoking this reaction, so it is different from a phobia. H. Levinson attributes this condition to a disorder of the cerebellum and the vestibular senses. Some panic disorders are accompanied by agoraphobia, the fear of crowds. Situations such as riding in a bus, train, or automobile, standing in line, being part of a crowd, or crossing a bridge could promote panic attacks when the agoraphobic component is present. See also: **agoraphobia; social phobia.**

Panprotopsychic identism (pan″pro″tō sī ′kik ī den′tiz əm) (from Greek "pan" = "everything", "proto" = "original", and "psychic" = "mental"). An answer that has been offered to the mind-body problem. This position assumes mind-body identity (the idea that the universe consists of one reality which is both mental and physical) and, more specifically, holds that there is a minimal degree of consciousness present in all physical things. See also: **mind-brain problem.**

Pantropic. An adjective referring to the nature of viruses that can infect the central nervous system (CNS), but which do not have a special, selective preference for CNS tissues.

Papillae (pə pil′ē). The small bumps on the tongue that contain the taste buds. See also: **taste buds.**

Parabiotic (par ″ə bī ot′ik) **preparation.** A laboratory set-up in which two organisms are forced to share the same physiological system (having a common circulation, digestion, respiratory, and elimination mechanism).

Parachlorophenylalanine (par″ə klôr″ō fen″əl al′ə nēn). See: **PCPA.**

Paradoxical heat. The simultaneous stimulation of the skin receptors by warm and cold receptors because one has touched something that is both warm and cold at the same time (e.g., a hot burner and cold adjacent metal parts of a stove).

The brain interprets the combined patterns of hot and cold receptor neuronal firings as "hot."

Paradoxical sleep. See: **REM sleep.** The "paradoxical" aspect of this sleep stage is the presence of a waking-type EEG record (low-voltage, high-frequency waves) and an active autonomic nervous system alongside a nearly-complete absence of muscle tone in the anti-gravity muscles, indicating a very deep sleep.

Parafoveal (par″ə fō′vē əl) **area.** The region of the retina that surrounds the fovea.

Paralanguage. Vocal cues other than actual spoken words that carry meaning.

Parallel fibers. A series of axons in the cerebellum running perpendicularly to the planes of the Purkinje cells. These axons provide input to the Purkinje cells. This arrangement allows the parallel fibers to activate a series of Purkinje cells, one after another. See also: **cerebellum; Purkinje cells.**

Parallel models. Explanatory models for physiological processes that involve at least two routes of activity.

Parallel play. Children playing together side by side (i.e., parallel) in identical activities but paying little or no attention to one another. This is one of the earliest stages of social interaction.

Parallel processing. The flow of information from the source to the recipient by more than one route.

Paralysis. The total inability to move a part of the body.

Paranoid personality disorder. An unjustified and intense distrust or suspicion of others. These individuals are frequently quarrelsome, litigious, and secretive. The words and actions of others are taken as aggressive or hostile acts when no such reaction is warranted.

Paranoid schizophrenic type. One of the main subtypes of schizophrenia. The paranoid schizophrenic has delusions and hallucinations relating to persecution and to exaggerated self-importance. These individuals are very mistrustful and suspicious and are hypersensitive to any type of threat. See also: **catatonic schizophrenia; disorganized schizophrenia; paranoid personality disorder; schizophrenia; undifferentiated schizophrenia.**

Paraphilias. A group of psychosexual disorders whereby individuals derive sexual gratification and pleasure from unconventional objects or experiences. Most people experience unusual sexual fantasies at some point, and this is considered normal behavior. However, the repeated, preferred, or exclusive use of nonconventional objects or experiences would be considered deviant. There are various different types of paraphilias. See also: **exhibitionism; fetishism; pedophilia; sadomasochism; transvestism; voyeurism.**

Paraplegia (par"ə plē' jē ə, -jə). Following a transection of the spinal cord, there is a loss of the ability to control the musculature of the parts of the body below the level of the cut. This type of partial paralysis is termed "paraplegia" in reference to the fact that the paralysis (i.e., "plegia") is in effect beyond (i.e., "para") the cut.

Parasympathetic (par "ə sim "pə thet'ik) **nervous system** or **parasympathetic division** (of the autonomic nervous system). The parasympathetic division of the autonomic nervous system, which is, in turn, part of the peripheral nervous system. Parasympethic nerve fibers release acetylcholine (ACh) at their neuromuscular junctions (i.e., synapses) with the membranes of targeted smooth muscle or gland cells. These axons arise either from the brain [exiting the central nervous system (CNS) as components of cranial nerves] or from the very caudalmost (lowermost, hindmost) portion of the spinal cord, the sacral segments of the cord. As a result of these origins, the parasympathetic nervous system is also referred to as the craniosacral nervous system. The term "parasympathetic" is also at least partly anatomical. "Para-" means beyond. Some of the system, the part controlling the head and upper trunk, originates from the brain, that is, from a CNS region rostral (superior) to the uppermost end of the central beginnings of the sympathetic nervous system (SNS). The rest of the parasympathetic nervous system begins with axons from the spinal cord's sacral segments, which are caudal (inferior) to the lowermost end of the central origins of the SNS. Thus the system has origins both above and below (i.e., beyond [in both directions]) those of the SNS, so it is para_sympathetic. The axons that leave the brain or spinal cord within the parasympathetic division have no handy nearby ganglia to reach

but must travel almost the total distance to the organ that they innervate, although they do terminate, finally, at a ganglion. Hence the parasympathetic ganglia are widely scattered throughout the body. From the ganglion, a short axon runs the rest of the distance to the targeted smooth muscle or gland. The first axon in the series (the preganglionic axon), the long one from the CNS to the ganglion, is covered with myelin. The second axon, the one from the ganglion to the organ innervated (the postganglionic axon), lacks a myelin sheath. The second axon releases ACh (acetylcholine) to muscarinic-action motor end plates. This muscarinic action can be inhibited (blocked) by the drug atropine. The parasympathetic division of the autonomic nervous system promotes bodily relaxation following periods of stress. In this regard, its function is almost the direct opposite of that of the sympathetic division. The parasympathetic nervous system causes (1) constriction of the pupil in response to bright light (the pupillary reflex), (2) slowing down of the heartbeat, (3) activation of gastrointestinal functions, (4) perspiration for most parts of the body (the exceptions being the palms, soles, and forehead), (5) dilation of blood vessels in the skin, (6) constriction of the bronchi (causing calm, slow breathing), (7) stimulation of the pancreas, (8) activation of the gall bladder, (9) contracting of the bladder, (10) stimulation of intestinal motility, (11) stimulation of the gonads during sexual intercourse (e.g., leading to penile erection), and (12) secretion of tears. If the parasympathetic system is dominant, however, the situation is not as happy as its "relaxation" role would lead us to believe. For example, excessive churning by the stomach and an oversecretion of digestive enzymes might lead to the erosion of parts of the stomach wall after the work of digesting food has ended. The result would be the formation of stomach ulcers. In this connection, please refer to the definition of **parasympathetic rebound**. See also: **autonomic nervous system; peripheral nervous system; sympathetic nervous system.**

Parasympathetic (par "ə sim "pə thet'ik) **rebound**. A sudden return of parasympathetic nervous system functioning following an overly long period of time during which the sympathetic nervous system's "fight-or-flight" reaction has prevailed. Many "psychosomatic" (stress-related) disorders exhibit a pattern of overzealous parasympathetic action. For example, the formation of a gastric or duodenal ulcer is due to the parasympathetic nervous system's digestive activity (smooth muscle churning and hydrochloric acid secretion) when the stomach is not packed with food. The walls of the gastrointestinal tract are attacked as a result. As another example, voodoo death may be due to heart stoppage, an overly enthusiastic parasympathetic slow-down of the heartbeat resulting in a fatal cessation of all heart action. The natural "fight-or-flight" reaction is normally short-lived. The wild animal either escapes from danger or is killed; there is seldom any in-between result. Human civilization provides us with plenty of reasons to experience chronic emergency reactions, lasting far longer than normal. The long-denied parasympathetic nervous system then bounds back into action, whether or not we are prepared for it. Hence, our stress-related disorders tend to have parasympathetic, rather than sympathetic, looks to them. See also: **general adaptation syndrome; parasympathetic nervous system; stress.**

Parathormone (par˝ə thôr′mōn). The hormone secreted by the parathyroid glands, four small endocrine glands that are attached to the thyroid gland. Parathormone regulates calcium and phosphate levels in the blood, which directly affect the state of activation of the autonomic nervous system. See also: **parathyroid glands**.

Parathyroid (par˝ə thī ′roid) **glands**. These endocrine glands are four small, pea-shaped organs attached to the thyroid gland. The parathyroid glands secrete the hormone parathormone. Excess parathormone leads to lethargy, poor muscle coordination, a shock-like state, and perhaps death, since the inadequate levels of phosphate lead to a breakdown of the circulatory system. Too little parathormone results in an excessively-low level of calcium, which causes the nervous system to be hypersensitive and results in tetany, convulsions, and death. See also: **endocrine system; parathormone.**

Paraventricular (par ˝ə ven trik′yoo lər)

nucleus **(PVN)**. A nucleus (collection of neuronal cell bodies) in the hypothalamus. If the neural transmitter norepinephrine or an endorphin is injected into this nucleus, the animal will increase its food intake. The paraventricular nucleus synthesizes the antidiuretic hormone (ADH) and sends it via portal blood vessels to the posterior pituitary (the neurohypophysis).

Parent surrogate. Someone who represents a disabled child when the parent or guardian is not available or is not willing to advocate for the child during the preparation of an IEP (individualized educational plan) or in other dealings with school personnel.

Parietal (pə rī ′ə təl) **lobe**. The word "parietal" means "wall" in Latin. If the side or lateral view of the cerebral cortex resembles a fist in a boxing glove, the parietal lobe is analogous to the back of the hand. The general senses (i.e., those senses with receptors all over the body, such as temperature, touch, pain, and kinesthesis) are represented in this lobe, in the postcentral gyrus. Other parietal lobe functions, such as orientation in space and maze-solving ability, may, in most people, be specializations of the right parietal lobe only.

Parieto-occipital (pə rī˝i tō-ok˝sip′i təl) **fissure**. A long, deep groove visible on the midline or medial surface of the cerebral cortex. It runs roughly in a vertical direction. Its superior end is somewhat below the upper edge of the brain, but it serves as an effective border the rest of the way, separating the parietal lobe from the occipital lobe. It has an intersection with the calacarine fissure, which is horizontally situated. The calacarine fissure subdivides the medial aspect of the occipital lobe into two gyri, the dorsally placed cuneus and the ventrally positioned lingual gyrus. See also: **medial; calcarine fissure.**

Parkinson's disease or **Parkinsonism**. A neuromuscular disorder involving intention tremor, the inability to complete an intended act due to a seizure of the hand and fingers just before the act can take place. Other symptoms include slow movements and muscular rigidity. In Parkinson's patients, the nerve pathway from the midbrain's substantia nigra to two of the basal ganglia of the cerebrum, viz., the caudate nucleus and the putamen, is deteriorated. These axons release the neurotransmitter dopamine at their endings; the patient accordingly has a shortage of dopamine in the forebrain. Traditionally, Parkinsonism has been treated by the administration of *l*-DOPA, an amino acid which is a precursor of dopamine. The *l*-DOPA crosses the blood-brain barrier, and the brain cells metabolize the amino acid into dopamine. See also: **blood-brain barrier; dopamine; schizophrenia.**

Parks-Weber-Dimitri (pärks′-web′ər-dimē′ trē) **disease**. See: **Sturge-Weber syndrome.**

Partially-sighted. Visual acuity falling between 20/70 and 20/200 in the best eye even with corrective lenses.

Partial reinforcement schedule. Partial reinforcement means the reinforcement of some, but not all, of the correct operant responses of a given type (e.g., disk-pecking by a pigeon in a Skinner box). A partial reinforcement schedule is an arrangement whereby those reinforcements are provided. Examples of such a schedule are the **fixed interval schedule of reinforcement** (FI), the **fixed ratio schedule of reinforcement** (FR), the **variable interval schedule of reinforcement** (VI), and the **variable ratio schedule of reinforcement** (VR) (see definitions).

Partial seizure. A seizure that does not involve the entire cerebral cortex. See also: **seizure.**

Parvocellular (pär″vō sel′yoo lər) (from Latin "parvum" ="small"). A term referring to the X cells, relatively small-sized ganglion cells in the retina (ganglion cells being the retinal cells whose axons are the optic nerve fibers), and to the neurons in four layers of the lateral geniculate nucleus to which these optic nerve fibers run. The parvocellular pathway is thought by some to be the same as the sustained visual pathway. See also: **sustained visual pathway; X cells.**

Passive-aggressive personality disorder. A personality disorder whereby the individual fears to express feelings of anger or displeasure openly. Negative feelings are covertly expressed (in an aggressive manner) so that blame or repercussions will not occur. For example, an individual who consistently knocks over furniture when angry would be considered passive-aggressive.

Patellar tendon reflex. The clonic or phasic stretch reflex evoked by striking at the patellar tendon which is located just below the knee. This is often done during a medical examination by using a rubber hammer. The patellar tendon reflex is better known as the knee-jerk reflex. See also: **stretch reflex.**

Pathognomonic (path″og nom′ik) (from Greek "pathognomonikos", meaning "skilled in diagnostics"). Presenting the indications of a given type of disease, especially its typical symptoms.

Pathological drug use. Exaggerated drug abuse, such as repeatedly ingesting the same drug for days.

Pathophobia (path″ə fō′bē ə). Fear of disease. See also: **phobias.**

Pavlovian conditioning. Another name for **classical** or **respondent conditioning.**

PCPA (parachlorophenylalanine) (par″ə klôr″ō fen ″əl al′ə nēn). A drug that blocks the synthesis of the neurotransmitter serotonin. Experiments show that animals given PCPA become viciously aggressive. The inference is that aggressiveness may be the result of a low level of brain serotonin activity. See also: **serotonin.**

Pediatric neuropsychology. The practice of neuropsychology with children who display pediatric neurological diseases or syndromes. The treatment of such problems involves a thorough diagnostic assessment and treatment prescriptions that address the medical and behavioral symptoms.

Pedophilia. A psychosexual disorder whereby the patient is sexually attracted to children and sexual congress with a prepubertal child provides the patient with more sexual gratification than sex with other partners. Most pedophiles are men under the age of 40 with dependent personalities who are sexually frustrated and immature.

Peer group. The age-appropriate social group to which an individual belongs. One's peer group provides a social support network especially during the adolescent years. Peer groups are important influences in determining one's actions and behaviors.

Peptide. A compound consisting of a chain of two

or more amino acids. Some of the neuro-transmitters are peptides, namely the endor-phins, the enkephalins, CCK (cholecystokinin), and neurotensin. Some of the neuromodulators are peptides. In many cases, a peptide is released along with another neurotransmitter from the same synaptic bouton. Dopamine-releasing boutons will also release either CCK or neurotensin, for example.

Percentile ranks. A percentile rank for a given raw score shows the percentage of the examinees whose raw score was the same or lower. For example, if only 14% of the group who took the test with you scored higher than you did, you would have chalked up a respectable percentile rank of 86th. If however, 86% of the scores were better than yours, your percentile rank would be 14th.

Perception. Making use of the sensory messages we receive from our receptors and sensory nerve cells to recognize objects and relationships between them in the world around us. I may <u>sense</u> low-frequency, high wavelength visible light, but I <u>perceive</u> a red stop light.

Perceptual constancy. The learned ability to perceive an unchanging object despite passing variations in the retinal image provided by the object. Brightness constancy allows one to retain the impression of the object's reflected light in relation to the background illumination, even when the object passes through shadowed and well-lit areas. Size constancy allows one to retain a single size judgment about an object, even when its position varies from close up (enlarging the retinal image) to far off (reducing the retinal image). Shape constancy permits the viewer to have a single impression of an object's shape, even when shifting the view of it from directly in front to off to the side, which changes the shape of the object's image in the retina. Finally, color constancy permits the object to have a constant color for the viewer, even when he or she is looking through a color filter. Newborns tested for perceptual constancies fail to show them; therefore, the ability to perceive a constant environment is learned in infancy.

Perceptual defense. The failure to perceive clear stimuli that are well over the absolute threshold because the stimuli are frightening or threatening or because they may be unwelcome demonstrations of our own weaknesses or shortcomings (i.e., things that would cause us to be ashamed of ourselves). The perceptual defense concept is an extension of Freud's concept of repression, which applies to failures of memory. Perceptual defense is considered a dubious concept, however, because apparent instances of perceptual defense are much more readily explained by response suppression, the unwillingness to say something that might put one in a bad light. See also: **absolute threshold; subliminal perception**.

Perceptual illusions. Illusions that surprise or startle the normal observer, due to the action of misleading stimulus cues that create inaccurate perceptions. An example would be the illusion of induced movement, which involves the sensation of moving when sitting in a stationary vehicle. One seems to be moving backward because there is no point of reference to indicate that one is staying put. Looking at the ground may help to establish a frame of reference and correct the mistaken perception. This sort of illusion contrasts with physical illusions, which are quite common and do not elicit reactions of surprise. See also: **physical illusion**.

Perceptual-motor functioning. The combination of sensory information with controlled action. A perceptual-motor task might, for example, require hand-eye coordination, as in moving one's finger to follow a moving object that is being tracked by the eyes.

Perceptual skills. The abilities of selectively attending to external stimuli, organizing these external stimuli, and interpreting them.

Perforant path. A tract of axons terminating in the granular-cell layer of the hippocampus. See also: **hippocampus.**

Performance IQ. A component of the intelligence quotient (IQ) on the Wechsler series of intelligence tests. It consists of the following subtests: Object Assembly, Picture Arrangement, Picture Completion, Block Design, Digit Symbol (Coding), and, optionally, Mazes.

Performance standard. A standard that is developed in order for comparisons to be made. Individuals can be rated in terms of relative standing against a group performance in terms of average standing.

Performance tests. Tests (especially IQ tests) that

do not involve a verbal language component.

Periaqueductal (per″ē ak″wə duk′təl) **gray matter**. See: **central gray matter.**

Perimetry. A technique for mapping the visual sensitivity of all parts of the retina. "Dynamic perimetry" involves sliding small targets along guiding metal hoops into the visual field and on through to the opposite end of the field. "Static perimetry" involves the flashing of small test lights to various small areas of the retina by means of an automated program. The test stimuli may be small colored objects used to map the color-discriminating zones of the retina. They may be small spots of white light, of varying intensity, used to map the brightness sensitivity of each small retinal area.

Perinatal (per″i nāt′l). During birth.

Peripheral. Toward the outside. The antonym of "peripheral" is "central." The peripheral nervous system, for example, is outside the centrally located skull and backbone, the bony coverings of the central nervous system.

Peripheral nervous system. The peripheral nervous system and the central nervous system (CNS) are the two major divisions of the nervous system. The peripheral nervous system consists largely of afferent neurons that send messages to the CNS (i.e., the brain and spinal cord) and efferent neurons that send messages from the brain or spinal cord to the muscles or glands. The muscles and glands in general are called the effectors. As a mnemonic device, to help you keep "afferent" and "efferent" straight, the efferent neurons communicate with the effectors. What the peripheral nervous system has that the central nervous system lacks is the neurilemma. Within the peripheral nervous system are various nerves and ganglia. The peripheral nervous system is made up of two main divisions: the autonomic nervous system (ANS) and the somatic (or skeletal) nervous system. In its turn, the ANS is composed of two main parts, the sympathetic nervous system (SNS) and the parasympathetic nervous system. See also: **autonomic nervous system; central nervous system; parasympathetic nervous system; somatic nervous system; sympathetic nervous system.**

Peripheral vision. The type of vision provided by the peripheral areas of the retina. Compared to central or foveal vision, peripheral vision is insensitive to color differences, poor in the resolution of details, and superior in sensitivity to faint light. This reflects the arrangement of the rods and cones on the surface of the retina. The central fovea has only cones; these receptors are specialized for acuity and color discrimination. The periphery of the eye has relatively more rods, at least to the extent that its high sensitivity, poor acuity, and lack of color discrimination are consistent with the properties of the rods. In many dyslexics, however, peripheral vision does permit some resolution of visual detail and the correct recognition of the color of a visual stimulus.

Peristaltic (per ″i stôl′tik) **contractions (peristalsis)**. Pulselike contractions of the smooth muscles lining the gastrointestinal tract that function to move food down the tract.

Permastore. A term sometimes used to refer to relatively-permanent long-term memories. The memory of addition facts, for example, would represent permastore memory.

Permissive parenting. Parental behavior that involves exercising little or no disciplinary control, being inconsistent in expectations from children, making few or no demands, and showing unconditional warmth and love toward the children.

Perseveration (per sev ″ə rā′shən). The compulsory, irrational continued repetition of a response when it is not reinforced. This behavior may result from injury to the anterior part of the cingulate gyrus. See also: **cingulate cortex.**

Persona. According to Jung, our public self, or the mask we wear in public to represent ourselves.

Personal fable. Elkind's terminology for adolescents who have the mistaken notion that they are invulnerable because they are extremely important.

Personality. The collection of relatively long-lasting behavioral characteristics and predispositions that determine the relationships between the individual and her or his social environment. The homeostatic stability of the individual is one major factor in determining the stability of one's interpersonal adjustments.

Personality disorder. A long-lasting maladaptive pattern of thinking, feeling, or behaving that interferes with everyday social and personal functioning and often will diminish in intensity after age 40. Examples of personality disorders are **paranoid personality disorder, affective personality disorder, schizoid personality disorder, schizotypal personality disorder, explosive personality disorder, anankastic personality disorder, histrionic personality disorder, asthenic personality disorder,** and **antisocial personality disorder** (see definitions).

Personality trait. A psychological characteristic of an individual (e.g., introversion or extroversion) that greatly impacts one's behaviors, thinking processes, and feelings. Certainly one's physical health can have an impact on the development of certain personality traits. For example, individuals who must be medicated can have unpleasant side effects such as depression, a short temper, hyperactive inattentiveness, and so on.

Personal unconscious. Jung's level of the unconscious where repressed thoughts and forgotten experiences are stored.

Pervasive developmental disorder. A classification of a childhood behavior disorder replacing the earlier term "childhood schizophrenia." There is a marked impairment of social and communication skills, combined with very few interests and activities, along with unusual reactions to sensory stimuli.

Pervasive language deficit. The presence in one individual of several language-related problems, such as the combination of poor spelling, poor reading, articulation difficulty, a lack of word fluency, and so on. Whether some people can have extremely severe dyslexia (which would entail such widespread language deficits) and still not be classifiable as "garden-variety poor readers" (simply poor learners in anything) is controversial.

Petit mal seizure. A mild form of epileptic seizure (involving the entire cerebral cortex) without overt convulsions. Consciousness may be lost, however. See also: **epilepsy; grand mal seizure**.

PET scan. Acronym for **positron emission tomography**, a technique that is a modification of the CAT scan, and that is used to identify areas of high and of low activity in the brain. The subject is given an injection of glucose containing a radioactive atom (the "label"). The idea is that (1) neurons will take up glucose before other body cells do and (2) active neurons will take up glucose before inactive neurons do. The PET scan may be taken while the subject is engaged in some sample behavioral task or undergoes some sort of emotional arousal. This would permit a researcher to identify areas of the cortex that become active during the emotional arousal or behavior. Various types of individuals (e.g., dyslexic subtypes) may be given reading materials while the PET scan is taken. The procedure yields pictures of brain slices, like the CAT scan; but, unlike the results of a CAT scan, active and inactive areas of the brain appear clearly in the pictures. See also: **CAT scan; positron emission tomography.**

Phagocytes (fag′ə sīts). Cells, such as some white blood cells, that ingest dead tissues or foreign chemicals. Among the neuroglia, the microglia, astrocytes, and Schwann cells are able to act as phagocytes when needed.

Phagocytosis (fag″ə sī tō′sis). The ingesting, by phagocyte cells, of decayed tissues or foreign chemical substances.

Phantom limb. The perception of stimulation affecting a part of the body that has been amputated. For instance, a person who has had a foot amputated feels itching in the toes of the missing foot. This experience is due to irritation of the leg stump, stimulating afferent neurons that had once been attached to the toes. The feeling is referred to the missing toes instead of to the end of the stump. This phenomenon was part of the evidence reviewed by Johannes Müller when he stated the **law of specific nerve energies** (see definition).

Pharmacology (fär″mə kol′ə jē). The study of drugs and their effects on the functioning of the body. A branch of this science is psychopharmacology, which is concerned with the behavioral effects of drugs.

Phasic (often used as a synonym for "clonic"). Involving actual muscular activity or muscle-twitching, as opposed to "tonic", which involves a buildup of muscle-tone without overt motion. In the description of the behaviors that take place during REM-sleep, the fine muscle activity (that of the outer eye muscles and the middle ear muscles) and the gross body movements of myoclonus are phasic events; periods of eye-muscle inactivity within the REM stage of sleep would be an example of tonic activity; so would the overall drop in muscle tone of the anti-gravity muscles. See also: **tonic**; **REM sleep; stage 1 sleep (ascending); myoclonus.**

Phencyclidine (fen sīʼkli dēn) **(PCP)**. A strongly hallucinogenic drug. It may lead to paranoid aggressiveness and destructive behavior.

Phenothiazines (fēˮnō thīʼə zēnzˮ). A group of neuroleptic drugs, one of which is chlorpromazine, each of which binds with both the D_1 and the D_2 types of dopamine receptors. See also: **chlorpromazine; dopamine; neuroleptic drug; schizophrenia.**

Phenylalanine (fenˮəl alʼə nēn, fēˮnəl-). An amino acid available in food. Its metabolism normally produces tyrosine, another amino acid. Tyrosine itself is available in some foods. In turn, the metabolism of tyrosine produces the amino acid *l*-DOPA, which is not available from the diet. The metabolizing of *l*-DOPA results in the production of dopamine (DA), a chemical neurotransmitter. In turn, some neurons convert DA into norepinephrine (norEp), another neurotransmitter. DA and norEp also occur as hormones in the adrenal medulla gland. The adrenal medulla can metabolize norEp into epinephrine (commonly known as adrenalin). All the compounds mentioned, phenylalanine included, are catecholamines. See also: **catecholamines; phenylketonuria.**

Phenylketonuria (fenˮəl kēˮtə no͞oʼrē ə, fēˮnəl-) **(PKU)**. An autosomal recessive disorder in which the individual is unable to metabolize appropriately the amino acid phenylalanine (i.e., into the amino acid tyrosine). The problem is that the enzyme that is needed to guide this metabolic step is missing. As a result, the patient's urine will contain unusually high levels of unmetabolized phenylalanine and also a phenyl ketone compound that results from the incorrect metabolism, namely phenylpyruvic acid. The result can be mental retardation due to the chemical poisoning of neurons in the cerebral cortex. If the condition is detected in the newborn, a physician will prescribe a diet free of phenylalanine. This diet is low in proteins and includes large amounts of fruits and vegetables. This avoids the development of any retardation.

The individual must stick to that diet for life. If this regimen is not followed, the individual will develop seizures and tremors and suffer mental retardation. See also: **phenylalanine; phenylpyruvic oligophrenia.**

Phenylpyruvic oligophrenia (fenˮəl pī ro͞oʼvik, fēˮnəl- olˮi gō frēʼnē ə). An old name for phenylketonuria. It refers to the abnormal breakdown product, phenylpyruvic acid, formed as the result of the incorrect metabolism of the amino acid phenylalanine. This is due to the absence of a necessary enzyme. That absence is the result of a genetic disorder. See also: **phenylketonuria.**

Pheromones (ferʼə mōnzˮ). Chemicals which are released by some animals in order to communicate with other animals of their species via their sense of smell. Queen bees, for example, release odors that are different from those of other bees. Ants release pheromones in laying down a trail between a food source and the colony. The term refers to "social hormones."

Phi phenomenon. A perceptual illusion of apparent movement. The observer is seated in a dark room. A stationary light is flashed on, and, later, it is turned off. Promptly, at another position, a second light is turned on. The observer sees one moving light, starting from the position of the first light, going through space to the location of the second light. This effect is used in advertising signs in which symbols or other objects seem to move in space, depending on the spacing and the timing of various stationary lights going on and off.

Philosophical behaviorism. A sophisticated variety of twentieth-century materialism. Materialism is one type of answer given by some philosophers to the <u>mind-brain problem</u>. Advocates of this form of materialism contend that, when we describe the facts of conscious awareness, we are making a kind of mistake in our use of language. We are using nouns or verbs where we should be using adverbs. For example, if we say "That interview experience was horrible--I hated every minute of it," we are not describing an action called "hating" or an experience that had a "horrible" nature. Rather we are talking about listening to questions <u>uncomfortably</u> and answering those questions with difficulty. Only the spoken questions and answers were real and their reality was of a physical sort. The adverb and the adverbial phrase (i.e., "uncomfortably" and "with difficulty") further describe those physical realities. It is only when we are unclear about this sort of distinction that we attribute reality to feelings; i.e., we are making what Ryle has called a "category mistake." See also: **materialism; mind-brain problem; monism.**

Phobias or **phobic disorders.** Disorders which involve an intense fear of certain objects, persons, or events that ordinarily do not produce such an effect with others under normal circumstances. Anxiety is the primary symptom in all phobias. There are three main divisions of phobias according to the DSM III-R: simple phobias or abnormal fears of specific objects; an intense fear of venturing outside the home to such populated places as supermarkets or theaters; and social phobias, or anxiety-provoking situations caused by abnormal fears of being judged or scrutinized by others (e.g., in a classroom or in a restaurant). It is estimated that up to 6 people per 1,000 suffer from some type of phobic disorder. Behavioral therapy has been shown to be effective in dealing with certain phobias. Dynamic psychotherapy and antianxiety drugs have also been used successfully with some phobics. Examples of types of phobia include: **acrophobia, agoraphobia, arachnophobia, astraphobia, claustrophobia, hemophobia, nyctophobia, pathophobia,** and **zoophobia** (see definitions).

Phocomelia (fō″kō mē′lē ə, mē′lyə). An innate deformity in which the normally proximal parts of the hands and feet are absent, so that the digits and outer limbs are directly connected to the torso like a seal's flippers. This is often a teratogenic reaction to the drug thalidomide, which was taken to relieve morning sickness by pregnant women in the period before the drug's side effects were understood. See also: **teratogenic.**

Phonatory disorders. Structural or functional problems involving the vocal apparatus. These may include inflammation of the vocal cords, the development of polyps on the vocal cords, etc. See also: **resonance disorders.**

Phoneme (fō′nēm″). An individual speech sound

that characterizes our spoken language. While our language includes 26 graphemes, there are as many as 44 phonemes. For example, the "sh" in "ship" represents a single phoneme. See also: **grapheme; morpheme.**

Phonological dyslexia (fō″fə loj′i kəl dis lek′sē ə). This type of dyslexia is a developmental analog to Boder's dysphonetic dyslexic, Coltheart's acquired dyslexic, and Doering and Hoshko's phonological deficit type; it is marked by problems in interpretation or execution of the phoneme-grapheme correspondence match.

Phonological process disorder. Consistent production of incorrect speech sounds on the part of a preschool child. This may be due to the child's applying an incorrect rule, such as dropping all final consonants instead of only some final consonants. The purpose of teaching children with phonological process errors is to have them learn the correct rule. It is more useful to work on a child's pattern of errors than to try to train the child to make the correct speech sounds one at a time.

Phonological processing. This cognitive task is important to reading, as Liberman and Shankweiler have demonstrated that dyslexics can (1) lack awareness of phonology rules and concepts, (2) lack proficiency in accessing phonological representations in memory, and/or (3) lack proficiency in accurately using these rules and concepts. Mann has shown that good and poor readers differ in the rates at which they acquire phonological processing skills.

Phonological (fō″nə loj′i kəl) **rules.** The specific statement of the speech sounds that are used in a given language and how these sounds are combined to form words.

Phonology (fə nol′ə jē). The study of speech sounds and the development of the ability to form sounds that convey meaning.

Phosphenes (fos′fēnz ″). Visual experiences resulting from mechanical stimulation of the retina (e.g., by applying pressure on a closed eyelid). See also: **law of specific nerve energies.**

Phosphoinositide (fos″fō i nō′si tīd). A chemical that acts as a second messenger, affecting the excitability of a neuron less dramatically but in a longer-lasting manner than the after-effect of a neurotransmitter. Often a second messenger is triggered by a neuromodulator. The lithium ion blocks the synthesis of phosphoinositide. See also: **cyclic AMP; lithium; neuromodulator; second messenger.**

Photopic (from Greek "phot" = "light"; "opic" = vision). The type of vision that we have in broad daylight under strong illumination. The cones are the retinal receptors responsible for photopic vision. This type of vision results from the breakdown of the cone photopigments erythrolabe, chlorolabe, and cyanolabe. In faint light, this type of vision is superseded by scotopic (rod) vision, because the cone photopigments are less light-sensitive than the rod photopigment rhodopsin. See also: **chlorolabe; cones; cyanolabe; erythrolabe; photopigment; Purkinje effect; scotopic.**

Photopigments. Chemicals that break down in the presence of light. The photopigment in the rods, rhodopsin, is extremely sensitive, undergoing a chemical change even in the presence of weak light stimulation. Rhodopsin is not very selective for wavelength and can be affected by short-, medium-, and long-wavelength light stimuli. That makes the pigment ideal for scotopic vision (night vision) and of little or no use in color discrimination. The three cone pigments are each selective for wavelength; erythrolabe tends to break down in the presence of long-wavelength (red) light but holds up under moderate stimulation from medium-wavelength (green) and short-wavelength (blue) light. Similarly, chorolabe is best broken down (affected chemically) by green light, while cyanolabe is susceptible to chemical change under the impact of blue light.

Phototherapy (fō″tō ther′ə pē). A treatment for seasonal affective disorder. Some people are really down in the dumps during the shortened days of the winter season. Phototherapy involves exposing them to a full-spectrum bright light. See also: **seasonal affective disorder.**

Phylogenetic (fī ″lō je net′ik). An adjective meaning "dealing with the evolution of the various species of animals." The word is sometimes used the same way as the word "evolutionary." See also: **phylogeny.**

Phylogeny (fī loj′ə nē). The evolutionary development, flourishing, and extinction of biological species over eons of time.

Physical dependence theory. The view that drug addiction should be attributed to the need of addicts to avoid or escape withdrawal symptoms. See also: **positive incentive theory of addiction.**

Physical dependence. The condition of drug users who experience painful withdrawal symptoms when they stop taking the drug.

Physical development. The growth of the body. This growth is most rapid in the first year of life, becoming slower year by year until adolescence. Physical development is mostly controlled by the genes. Girls develop at a faster rate than boys.

Physical illusion. An illusion that is the result of distorted stimulus information reaching the sense receptors. An example would be the bent appearance of a straight stick that is partly under water. This appearance of bending is due to the fact that the water acts like a prism, bending the light rays reflected from the stick. The light rays from the part of the stick that is above the water are not bent. The illusion is not surprising to the normal observer because it is a readily explained phenomenon. Such is not the case with perceptual illusions, which do surprise us when we experience them. See also: **perceptual illusions.**

Physical prompting/fading. A teaching method involving the manual manipulation of the student to get the correct behavior going, then doing less and less manual coaching from one time to the next, until the student winds up doing the action with no help. See also: **fading.**

Physiological chemistry. See: **biochemistry.**

Physiological psychology. A specialty within the science of psychology. Psychology is concerned with the explanation of mental, behavioral, and emotional events that occur in living organisms. Physiological psychology is concerned with the attempt to account for such events by referring to the nervous system, the chemical neuro-transmitters, the sense organs, the hormones, and/or the muscles of behaving organisms. Synonymous terms are "behavioral neuro-science," "biological psychology," and "biopsychology."

Physiology. A specialty within the science of Biology, the science of life. Physiology is concerned with the explanation of the workings or functions of the various organs of the body.

Pia mater (pī′ə mā′tər, pē′ə mä′tûr). The

innermost of the three membranes (meninges) that surround the brain and spinal cord. The pia mater (literally, "holy mother", although secondary translations of the words "pia" and "mater" probably are more accurate, to wit, "fine material"). The pia mater is thin and soft enough to move into the grooves (sulci) of the cerebral cortex and cerebellum. Between the pia mater and the middle meninx, the arachnoid, which follows the gyri (folds) but cannot penetrate the sulci, is the subarachnoid space, which is filled with cerebrospinal fluid. The pia mater and arachnoid together are collectively called the leptomeninx ("thin membrane").

Pica (pī′kə). A craving for eating nonfood objects such as chalk, wood, nails, and so on. It may be observed in pregnant women as well as in some cases of hysteria or psychosis.

Pick's disease. A form of dementia, the gradual loss of mental abilities. The patient experiences memory losses, language deficits and depression. Pick's is distinguishable from Alzheimer's disease only after postmortem examination of the brain. In the Pick's patient, there is evident degeneration of the frontal and temporal lobes of the cerebral cortex, with sparing of the parietal and occipital lobes. The neuritic plaques and neurofibrillary tangles that occur in Alzheimer's cases are <u>not</u> to be found in the brains of Pick's disease patients.

Piloerection (pī″lō i rek′shən). The erection of the hairs, which involves sympathetic commands to smooth muscles attached to the bases of the hair follicles. In hairless skin, the response produces "gooseflesh" or "goose pimples." See also: **gooseflesh.**

Pineal (pin′ē əl) **gland.** A pine-cone-shaped endocrine gland, located at the roof of the diencephalon, which secretes the hormone melatonin. Melatonin, in conjunction with the day-night changes of illumination, seems to be one of the Zeitgebers controlling our circadian rhythms. Increased light levels inhibit the pineal gland's secretion of melatonin. This hormone prepares our bodies for sleep by lowering our temperatures and reducing our general activity levels. In this way, increased light levels promote increased activity, that is, waking up in the morning. Of historical interest, the philosopher Descartes nominated the pineal body of the brain as the place where sensory messages along afferent nerves become ideas in the mind and where decisions of the will are implemented into activity by the initiation of commands sent via efferent nerves to the muscles. In other words, the pineal body was supposed to be the place of interaction of the mind and the body. Descartes granted the pineal body this honor due to its central location on the midline of the body, under the cerebral cortex and above the brainstem. See also: **circadian rhythms; endocrine system; entrainment; melatonin; Zeitgeber.**

Pinna (from Latin for "feather," since the outer ear resembles a feather at the side of the head). See: **auricle.**

Pioneer growth cones. The beginnings of growth into a given region of the developing nervous system.

Pitch. The subjective impression of how low or high a tone sounds. The aspect of the sound stimulus that corresponds most directly with pitch judgment is the frequency of the sound wave. In general, the higher the frequency, the higher the pitch will be. The human ear senses sounds ranging from a frequency of 20 Hertz (Hz) to 20,000 Hz. Pitch discrimination has been explained by two main theories: (1) the place-resonance theory and (2) the frequency (or telephone) theory. The place theory states that it is the place (on the basilar membrane) that resonates the most to the sound stimulus which encodes the pitch of that sound; the code is maintained by afferent neurons that ultimately communicate with the place in the auditory cortex that represents that particular pitch. The frequency theory states that it is the number of times the hair cells in the organ of Corti fire impulses that reports the pitch of the sound; if the sound has a pitch of 80 cycles per second (i.e., 80 Hz), then 80 impulses per second will travel along the auditory nerve toward the brain. See also: **basilar membrane; frequency theory of hearing; hearing; Hertz; organ of Corti; place-resonance theory of hearing; sound; telephone theory of hearing; tonotopic arrangement.**

Pituitary (pi tōo′i ter″ē) **gland.** Located at the base of the hypothalamus, the pituitary is actually two glands: the anterior pituitary, or adenohypophysis, which is the master gland of the endocrine system, and the posterior pituitary, or neurohypophysis. See also: **anterior pituitary gland; endocrine system; posterior pituitary gland.**

Pituitary stalk (or **infundibulum**). The stemlike structure connecting the hypothalamus to the pituitary gland. It contains the axons running from neurosecretory cells to the adenohypophysis and the portal blood vessels running from neurosecretory cells to the neurohypophysis. See also: **adenohypophysis; neurohypophysis; neurosecretory cells; pituitary gland.**

PKU. See: **phenylketonuria.**

Placebo (plə sē′bō) (from Latin "I shall please"). A physiologically inactive medicine-like object (e.g., a pill or a teaspoon of fluid) that can be used on the control subjects in a drug experiment. The experimental subjects are those who are given the real drug. This procedure is used to make sure that all the subjects, control and experimental, expect that they are getting the same treatment. The procedure is called "single-blind control." In order to make it a double-blind procedure, the scoring of the behavior of the subjects is done by an experimenter who is unaware of which treatment (placebo or drug) was given to which subject.

Place coding. The view originally stated by Helmholtz that sensory information is interpreted according to the position in the cerebral cortex of the incoming nerve impulses. For example, we hear because nerve impulses carried toward the brain along the auditory nerve cause activity in the auditory areas of the cortex. See also: **labeled-line theory; law of specific nerve energies; place-resonance theory of hearing; trichromatic theory of color vision.**

Placenta. The organ which provides nourishment to the fetus during prenatal development. It is attached to the uterus of the mother.

Place-resonance theory of hearing or **place theory of hearing.** Helmholtz's explanation of our ability to judge the pitch of a sound holds that the basilar membrane, which varies in width along its length, will provide maximum vibration at the position that matches the vibration of a stimulating sound wave in frequency (the physical phenomenon of

sympathetic vibration or resonance). Each location on the basilar membrane is connected to its own special region of the auditory part of the cerebral cortex. Each of these local cortical areas is selectively active for its own special pitch experience. The theory is valid for higher pitches that yield precise resonance vibrations. Low bass notes, though, can make the whole basilar membrane vibrate, and their pitches are probably decoded by the mechanism described in Rutherford's telephone theory of hearing. See also: **basilar membrane; telephone theory of hearing; volley theory of hearing.**

Planes of sectioning. To prepare brain or spinal cord material for microscopic study, it is often necessary to make microscope slides of it. The central nervous system material must be chemically fixated (i.e., hardened). It is then thinly-sliced in a machine called a microtome. The angle of slicing has to be specified if one is to understand the material on the slide. That angle is the plane of sectioning. Since we inhabit a three-dimensional world, we can specify any position in space by a set of three measurements, one in each of three planes (dimensions), each of which is perpendicular to (at a right angle with) either of the other two. We are familiar with measures of length, width, and thickness, for example. These are analogous to the three planes used as references for slicing anatomical material by microtome. See also: **frontal; histological techniques; horizontal; microtome; sagittal.**

Planum temporale (plā′num tem″pər al′ā). A flattened portion of temporal lobe of the cerebral cortex. Ordinarily, it is larger in the left temporal lobe than in the right (i.e., asymmetrical), but in most dyslexics, the left and right plana temporales are of the same size (i.e., symmetrical).

Plateau phase. [1] The stage of sexual activity with the maximum arousal, in which the erectile tissues of the male's penis and the female's vagina are engorged with blood, in preparation for orgasm. [2] That stage during a fever when the body actively sustains a high temperature.

Play audiometry (ō″dē om′e trē). This is the use of pure tones or speech sounds in establishing rapport situations. For example, a child might be asked to wave or clap when she or he hears a tone through a set of headphones.

Pleiotropism (plī ō trō'piz əm). The influence of a single gene on more than one hereditary trait.

Plethysmography (pleth ″iz mog'rə fē). The measurement of changes in blood volume in a given part of the body. Finger plethysmography measures circulation in the extremities. A finger plethysmograph placed around the penis can measure the presence or absence of an erection.

Pneumoencephalogram (noo ̄″ mō en sef'ə lə gram ″, nyoo-). A method for increasing the visibility of the interior of the brain in order to make a diagnosis. The cerebrospinal fluid is drained from the lumen (hollow interior) of the central nervous system and replaced with air by way of a lumbar puncture. The air-filled ventricles are opaque to X-rays. An X-ray photograph taken of the brain could identify blocked passages in the lumen, displacements of ventricles (which occurs in subdural hematomas), or enlargement of ventricles (which occurs in hydrocephalus or schizophrenia).

POAH. The preoptic area/anterior hypothalamus. The area contains thermoreceptors and it also receives neural inputs from thermoreceptors located in other parts of the body.

Poikilotherms (poi kil'ə thûrmz). Animals such as fish, amphibians, and reptiles that are not able to regulate body temperature by reflex action. These creatures are also known as cold-blooded animals. Poikilotherms are restricted to habitats with fairly uniform temperatures. When some fish find themselves in sun-warmed waters, they swim to lower depths. Reptiles such as rattlesnakes coil themselves up and take shelter under rocks during the cold nights and crawl out into the open during the warm days. See also: **homoiotherms**.

Polarization. [1] The electrical condition of a resting neuron. When the neuron is electrically stable, and no voltage changes are occurring anywhere on its membrane, the neuron exhibits a voltage difference between the outer and interior surfaces of its cell membrane. This represents a chemical difference between two watery solutions, the extracellular fluid outside the neuron and the cytoplasm within the neuron. Of special interest here is the axoplasm, which is

the cytoplasm of the axon. Only the axon, of the three major parts of a neuron, can carry a true nerve impulse. The voltage difference between the axoplasm relative to the external fluid may be in the range from -30 to -90 millivolts. Thus, at rest, the charge is positive on the outside and negative on the inside, by a fraction of a volt. In order to keep it straight, think of the old song lyric, "I'm laughing on the outside, crying on the inside." In other words, the resting axon exhibits a positive external picture but conceals a negative state inside. [2] A shift in attitudes by members of a particular social group toward more extreme positions (e.g., a shift in drug acceptance attitudes by some teenage groups during the 1960s).

Poliomyelitis (pō″lē ō mī″ə lī'tis) (or **infantile paralysis**). A paralysis brought on by virus-caused damage to the motor neurons of the spinal cord.

Polydipsia (pol″ē dip'sē ə) (from Greek "poly" = many; "dipsia" =drinks). Excessive drinking of water (or of alcoholic beverages).

Polygamy (pə lig'ə mē) (from Greek "poly" = many; "gamos" = spouses). Engaging in sexual behavior with many partners. There are two main forms, polyandry (pol″ē an'drē), in which one female mates with many males, and polygyny (pə lij'i nē), in which one male mates with many females. Polyandry is rare but is shown by at least one species of bird, the jacana, and exists in a few human societies. Polygyny occurs in some birds (e.g., ostriches) and some mammals (e.g., deer and macaque monkeys), as well as in some human societies. See also: **monogamy**.

Polygenic (pol ″ē jen'ik) **inheritance**. The process of gene interactions before birth as they combine to produce certain traits in individuals (e.g., eye and hair color, and weight). The combining of genes has been described as a symphonic ensemble: each gene contributes uniquely to the overall finished product, which is different from each gene or instrument alone.

Polygraphy (pə lig'rə fē) or **polygraph examination**). A forensic psychologist, L. Keeler, devised the polygraph shortly after World War I. The name "polygraph" literally means "many writings." It is commonly known as the "lie detector." Four pens simultaneously record each of four physiological indicators, namely, heartbeat, blood pressure, galvanic skin response (palmar sweating), and breathing rate. The galvanic skin response results from sympathetic nervous system activity. The assumption behind lie detecting is that the attempt to deceive will arouse the sympathetic nervous system. The sympathetic neural activity is expected to produce rapid heartrate, rapid and shallow breathing, sweaty palms, and high blood pressure. Polygraphy is one of the applications of **psychophysiology** (see definition). Research has shown that the results of a polygraph examination include too many errors in both directions (false positives that label an innocent person "guilty" and false negatives that label a guilty individual as "innocent"). See also: **galvanic skin response; psychophysiology; sympathetic nervous system.**

Polypeptide (pol″ē pep′tīd″). A chain of at least ten amino acids. Those hormones which are not steroids are polypeptides. One polypeptide is believed to function as a sleep-inducing hormone. See also: **endocrine system; hormones.**

Polyps. Growths on the vocal cords that lead to hoarseness and low pitch, or tumorous membranes appearing in various body organs, such as the nose, the throat, the intestines, etc.

Pons (ponz) (from Latin "pons" = "bridge"). The portion of the brain that is connected to the medulla behind, to the midbrain in front, and to the cerebellum above. It is named after its most conspicuous feature, namely, the band of white matter that sweeps around the sides of the pons on the way into the cerebellum. The pons is thereby given the look of an upside-down suspension bridge having "cables" of white matter.

Population. The entire set of subjects, objects, or events that is observed and/or measured in a scientific study. If an experiment or survey is done on all the patients in a given hospital, and statements about the conclusions drawn from the study are applied only to those persons, the entire population has been tested and inferential statistics are irrelevant. Usually, however, the researcher wishes to generalize from a sample of observations to a wider population, most members of which have not been studied. In this

instance, the procedures of inferential statistics are required. Only when the statistical testing yields a finding of statistical significance is the researcher correct in making general statements about the entire population on the basis of the sample that was studied. See also: **inferential statistics; sample.**

Population heterozygosity (het″ər ō zī gos′i tē). The variation in the genetic equipment of a species. This variance accounts for individual differences. It assures that, when the environment is greatly changed, at least a few members of the species will be adapted for survival and reproduction under the new conditions. See also: **natural selection; population homozygosity.**

Population homozygosity (hō″mō zī gos′i tē). The common genetic material of a species. This genetic equipment makes the species unique, differentiating it from all other forms of animal life. See also: **natural selection; population heterozygosity.**

Positive feedback. The opposite of negative feedback. With positive feedback, a part of the outcome of a process is fed back to the beginning of the process, so that the process is led to continue in the same direction, instead of correcting itself. It is as if a warm temperature affected an imbalanced thermostat such that the furnace becomes even hotter. Thus, the process becomes a "vicious circle", and there is a runaway loss of control as things get worse and worse. An example of positive feedback in the field of learning disabilities is the Matthew effect. See also: **Matthew effect; negative feedback.**

Positive incentive theory of addiction. This is the view that the chief reason for drug addiction is the pleasurable effect of taking in drugs. This would be the opposite view from that of the **physical dependence theory** (see definition).

Positive reinforcement. The action of giving a learning organism a positive reinforcer. Positive reinforcement is an event, the giving of a kind of stimulus. See also: **operant conditioning; positive reinforcer.**

Positive reinforcer. A stimulus that, when given to the organism directly after the organism has made an operant response, results in an increased probability that the response will be repeated. Such a stimulus is one that the organism will strive to obtain and keep, one that may be called rewarding. See also: **operant conditioning; positive reinforcement.**

Positive symptoms (of schizophrenia). Such overt signs of schizophrenia as hallucinations, delusions, incoherent speech, and outbursts of aggression.

Positive transference. In a clinical or therapeutic relationship, the development of positive or warm feelings toward the therapist.

Positron (poz'i tron˝) **emission tomography** (tə mog'rə fē). The method for making visible the rates of metabolic activity in various places in the brain due to the high or low accumulations of radioactively-labeled glucose in the form of 2-deoxyglucose (2-DG). See also; **PET scan.**

Posterior. Toward the back, or at the back end.

Posterior chamber. The larger part of the eyeball which is behind the iris and lens. The posterior chamber is filled with a jelly-like, clear substance, the vitreous humor.

Posterior columns. Another term for the dorsal columns, which are the gracile and cuneate tracts of the spinal cord. The adjective "posterior" fits the case of upright, bipedal humans, because dorsal parts of the anatomy are "superior" in four-legged animals. The word "dorsal" can be applied correctly for both bipeds and quadrupeds. See also: **dorsal columns; cuneate tract; gracile tract.**

Posterior parietal (pə rī'ə təl) **cortex** (kôr'teks'). The posterior portion of the parietal lobe of the cerebral cortex. It is related to one's spatial localization ability. It receives information from the senses of vision, audition, and somesthesis.

Posterior pituitary (pi to͞o'i ter˝ē) **gland** (also called the **posterior lobe of the pituitary gland** or **neurohypophysis**). The hormones of this gland are manufactured by specialized neurons called neurosecretory cells. These neurons are to be found in the supraoptic and paraventricular nuclei of the hypothalamus. The hormones, after being made, are sent along the axons of these neurons. The axons run the length of the infundibulum, which is a stalk that attaches the pituitary body to the floor of the hypothalamus. The hormones are released into the posterior lobe for storage. The gland will release the hormones on receiving nerve impulses via the very same axons that transported them! The three main hormones of the posterior pituitary are (1) oxytocin, which prepares the mammary glands of females to release milk and also plays a role in parturition (childbirth) and the transporting of sperm cells in the uterus; (2) vasopressin, which raises blood pressure in peripheral capillaries and arterioles by causing the smooth muscles to constrict them; vasopressin is also known as the antidiuretic hormone (ADH), because it restricts the rate of urine formation and slows down the rate of urinating, and, consistent with its role of helping to preserve the body's water supply, it helps trigger the osmotic type of thirst; and (3) somatostatin, which inhibits the release of the growth hormone from the anterior pituitary. Incidentally, oxytocin may be the social psychologist's favorite hormone. It is connected with such emotionally charged, socially relevant situations as grooming, sexual activity, and social companionship. See also: **antidiuretic hormone; endocrine system; osmotic thirst; oxytocin; pituitary gland; somatostatin.**

Posterior ventral nucleus of the thalamus (PVNT). A collection of nerve cell bodies in the thalamus. The PVNT receives the axons of the medial lemniscus, the ventral spinothalamic tract, and the lateral spinothalamic tract. In turn, it sends radiation fibers via the internal capsule to the somatosensory cortex or postcentral gyrus (namely, Brodmann's areas 1, 2, and 3, at the rostral edge of the parietal lobe). The PVNT also relays taste-sense messages to the cerebral cortex. The primary gustatory area is adjacent to the area of the postcentral gyrus serving as the terminal for the general senses (touch, temperature, etc.) from the face. See also: **lateral spinothalamic tract; medial lemniscus; parietal lobe; somatosensory system; thalamus; ventral spinothalamic tract.**

Postnatal. After birth.

Postpartum (pōst˝pär'tum) **depression.** A type of depression in women which occurs in varying degrees of severity after they have given birth.

Postsynaptic inhibition. Inhibitory changes on the cell membrane of a neuron's cell body and/or dendrites that reduce reactivity to excitatory inputs to the neuron. See also: **inhibitory post-**

synaptic potential (IPSP).

Posttraumatic (pōs˝trô mat'ik, -trou-) **amnesia**. A loss of memory resulting from closed-head injury. Retrograde amnesia is conspicuously present, but some anterograde amnesia may also take place. See also: **anterograde amnesia; retrograde amnesia.**

Posttraumatic (pōs˝trô mat'ik, -trou-) **stress disorder**. This phenomenon has in the past been referred to as shell shock or battle fatigue. It involves the re-experiencing by victims of identified environmental shocks (traumas), of the pain and fear that accompanied the trauma. This is an intense reaction to a severe, anxiety-provoking trauma, such as rape, fire, war, etc. It is manifested in recurring nightmares related to the trauma. Physical manifestations include sweating, breathing problems, heart palpitations, and dizziness. Other psychological symptoms of posttraumatic stress disorder include paranoia, emotional lability, anger, and a loss of the ability to love and trust other people. When a stimulus or initiating event cannot be identified, a panic attack is identified. See also: **panic attack.**

Postural rehabilitation. The basic aim of the Doman-Delacato approach to correcting learning disabilities. The individual restarts his or her development of crawling, walking, and running.

Power motive. The psychological need to obtain influence or recognition by controlling other individuals.

Practical intelligence. The kind of intelligence reflected in living successfully. Practical intelligence is not necessarily exhibited in academic tests.

Pragmatics (prag mat'iks). The rules for the use of a language to achieve specific communication goals. Examples include requesting help, expressing pleasure or displeasure, commenting on environmental events, asking questions, and answering questions.

Prandial (pran'dē əl) **drinking**. Drinking water along with a meal. The water is consumed in brief gulps right after swallowing, so that it can wash down the food. This is a symptom displayed by laboratory animals with bilateral damage to the lateral hypothalamus. See also: **lateral hypothalamus.**

Precocial (pri kō'shəl). The characteristic of newly hatched birds, in some species, to be able to fend for themselves by pecking at the food bits scattered on the ground before them, walking to the mother bird, and so on. The opposite term is "altricial." Precocial birds include the young of chickens, ducks, and geese. Altricial birds are tree-dwellers, such as songbirds. See also: **altricial.**

Precocious puberty. The premature appearance of secondary sexual characteristics in children much earlier than the expected age of puberty.

Predatory aggression. One of the seven varieties of aggression in Moyer's classification scheme for mammalian aggression. This is the organized set of responses used in the stalking and killing of prey for food. Predatory aggression is also known as quiet-biting attack. The lateral hypothalamus is involved in organizing predatory aggression. [The term "quiet biting" provides a cue for a useful mnemonic device. The initials QB also stand for the quarterback of a football team. The QB will sometimes throw a lateral pass. Thus, we can remember that QB aggression is connected with the lateral hypothalamus, not the medial hypothalamus!] This form of aggression also requires the activity of the amygdaloid nucleus. Other brain areas that participate are the midbrain's periaqueductal gray (central gray) matter and ventral tegmental area. See also: **lateral hypothalamus; central gray; aggression; amygdaloid nucleus.**

Predictive animal model. A model of a human disorder that may not resemble all aspects of the condition in human beings, but which helps to predict some aspects of it.

Predispositional theory of schizophrenia. The view that people who are genetically predisposed to schizophrenia are much more likely than others to succumb to schizophrenia in reaction to environmental stress.

Prefrontal lobotomy. See: **lobotomy.**

Prehension (pri hen'shən). The grasping skills that are achieved by fine motor development. See also: **fine motor skills.**

Prejudice. The development of unfair attitudes, beliefs, behaviors, and/or feelings toward an individual, group, institution, environmental situation, and so on because of impaired cognitive reasoning. Prejudicial beliefs (e.g., disliking someone because of their religious affliation or denying a physically disabled individual a job he or she could adequately perform) can result in unfair prejudicial behaviors that ultimately have a negative impact on the overall cohesiveness of a society.

Premature ejaculation. The inability to delay ejaculation of spermatic fluid from the penis. This may interfere with the male's ability to share the timing of the orgasm with his partner. The cause of the problem is usually psychological.

Premotor cortex. An area of the frontal lobe anterior to the precentral gyrus. It corresponds to Brodmann area 6. From this part of the frontal lobe arise many of the short-axon motor pathways which comprise the extrapyramidal motor system. These neurons interact with the neurons of the basal ganglia. Since numerous synapses are involved, this line to the striped muscles can be called the "local," while the pyramidal tract is the "express." The premotor cortex seems to be involved in the planning of a movement (whether or not the movement is actually carried out). See also: **basal ganglia; extrapyramidal motor fibers; pyramidal tract; supplementary motor cortex.**

Prenatal. Existing before birth.

Prenatal development. Physical (and some feel psychological) development of the fetus from conception to birth.

Preoptic (prē op′tik) **area.** A region of the hypothalamus (near the anterior hypothalamus) which is involved in the control of body temperature. It is also thought to participate in the release of gonadotropic hormones from the anterior pituitary gland. See also: **POAH.**

Prereferral intervention. The educational strategy of providing students at risk for school failure with alternative modes of instruction and/or assistance from consultants, team teaching, and so on in the effort to identify just what the regular curriculum can do to provide an effective learning situation for such students.

Pressure. An external or internal stressor that pushes one to actions beyond comfortable levels, usually in relation to pursuit of some goal (e.g., one's job, an educational degree, etc.). Some pressures are positive, as when they assist us in achieving a goal (e.g., receiving a good grade in a physiological psychology course after pressure

from the instructor to improve study habits). Negative pressures, on the other hand, can result in physical or psychological harm (e.g., peer pressure to abuse drugs). Pressures that cause prolonged stress can weaken the body's immune system, resulting in illness. See also: **general adaptation syndrome; stress; stressor.**

Prestriate cortex. The area of the occipital lobe immediately surrounding the primary visual cortex. The prestriate cortex is area 18 in the Brodmann numbering system. See also: **Brodmann numbering system; cerebral cortex; occipital lobe; primary visual cortex.**

Presymptomatic (prē″simp tə mat′ik) **test.** A test of whether someone is at risk for a late-appearing disease. Huntington's disease, for example, strikes people when they are middle-aged. It is genetically caused. Researchers have found a genetic marker called G8 on chromosome 4, the chromosome that carries the gene for the disease. The G8 gene has four alleles or forms. If relatives with Huntington's have all exhibited only one of the four forms of G8, that form of G8 is the genetic marker indicating that its possessor is set up for Huntington's. As another example, people at risk for schizophrenia have trouble making pursuit eye movements. Tracking people's eye movements during a visual pursuit task would be a way of giving them a presymptomatic test for schizophrenia.

Presynaptic facilitation (prē″sin ap′tik fə sil″i tā′shən). A process promoting the phenomena of sensitization and classical conditioning.

Presynaptic inhibition (prē″sin ap′tik in″i bish′ən). The production of an inhibitory effect by the release of an excitatory neurotransmitter. In a synapse between neuron A and neuron B, for example, neuron A sends out an axon terminal that can release an excitatory neurotransmitter. A small neuron, C, sends its axon to the axon terminal of A. Cell C's axon releases an excitatory neurotransmitter, which produces a partial excitation of A. Some of the vesicles in A's terminal bouton release their excitatory neurotransmitter molecules onto cell B's receptor sites, but the effect on cell B is not excitatory enough to start an impulse in that neuron. Along comes a nerve impulse in cell A. It causes the release of its neurotransmitter from its own terminal, but the supply has been depleted such that the usual excitation of cell B by cell A cannot take place. This process can be likened to the stopping of a raging prairie fire by burning off a strip of grass before the prairie fire comes along. The fire will come to a stop at the edge of the burned grass because it has no available fuel. See also: **autoreceptors; axoaxonic synapses; excitatory synapse; inhibitory synapse; neurotransmitter; receptor sites; Renshaw cell; synaptic bouton; synaptic vesicles.**

Prevalence. The number of individuals in a population who currently exhibit a particular characteristic. See also: **incidence**.

Primacy effect. This term refers to the old adage, "first impressions are the most lasting." The information one receives about another individual during initial contacts has a greater psychological impact than subsequent information. We hope that the primacy effect for this dictionary is a most positive one!

Primary drive. The behavioral motive associated with a biological need. Examples of such needs are those for oxygen, food, water, and sex. An example of a primary drive is the one for food, namely, hunger. Primary drives are unlearned. They are also called physiological drives. Most of our motives, however, are acquired from our experience rather than inborn; such motives are called psychogenic needs, psychological needs, or acquired drives.

Primary effect. See: **primacy effect.**

Primary erectile (i rek′til, -tīl) **dysfunction**. The long-term inability to achieve (and/or maintain) a penile erection for a period long enough to allow for satisfactory sexual intercourse.

Primary motor cortex. The precentral gyrus, which is bounded rostrally by the precentral sulcus and caudally by the central sulcus. Its Brodmann numeral is 4; the fifth cortical layer (that of the giant pyramidal cells) is much more highly developed than anywhere else in the cerebral cortex. From these giant pyramidal cells (the Betz cells) arise the long axons of the pyramidal tract, the "express" line to the striped muscles of the extremities. See also: **Betz cells; Brodmann numbering system; cerebral cortex; frontal lobe; premotor cortex; pyramidal tract.**

Primary orgasmic (ôr gaz′mik) **dysfunction**. The long-term inability on the part of a female to achieve an orgasm.

Primary prevention. Programs which emphasize preventative planning in the mental health area (e.g., like taking a vacation after writing this dictionary!)

Primary reinforcer (or **unconditioned reinforcer**). A reinforcing stimulus that does not have to be set up by a process of classical conditioning. Usually, a primary reinforcer will satisfy (reduce the level of) a physiological drive. In addition, though, some primary reinforcers are not drive-reducers but are inherently hedonic (i.e., reinforcing in and of themselves); examples of the latter would be, e.g., the opportunity to do a jigsaw puzzle, or to arrange a bouquet of flowers.

Primary sensory cortex. That cortical area of a sensory neural pathway which receives neural inputs from a thalamic relay nucleus. Such areas are well-known for the senses of vision, audition, and somesthesis; the senses of taste and of balance also seem to have primary cortical areas. The granular layers of primary sensory areas are enhanced, while the pyramidal layers are underdeveloped. See also: **cerebral cortex.**

Primary visual cortex (also known as the **striate cortex**). That part of the cerebral cortex which receives the axons of the geniculocalcarine tract (i.e., the input from the lateral geniculate nucleus of the thalamus). It is Brodmann's area 17, visual area V1 of the occipital lobe, and more precisely, it is found both dorsal and ventral to the calcarine fissure on the medial surface of the occipital lobe. See also: **calcarine cortex; calcarine fissure; cerebral cortex; geniculocalcarine tract; lateral geniculate nucleus; occipital lobe; thalamus; visual cortex.**

Priming. The "coaxing" or "inducing" of a rat to press a lever for an electrical reinforcing stimulus to the brain (via an implanted electrode) by presenting a few "free" stimulations. See also: **self-stimulation of the brain.**

Principle of equipotentiality. See **equipotentiality.**

Principle of mass action. The concept suggested

by Karl Lashley in the 1920s that the neural programs for complex tasks are stored throughout the cerebral cortex. A more modern variant is the view of A. R. Damasio that linguistic concepts (as well as the words for them) are to be found in various places in the cortex.

Proactive. The kind of antisocial behavior that is performed out of spite or because the individual has a high operant level for that behavior. The opposite term is "reactive," which refers to the sort of antisocial act for which there are recognizable causes in the way others have treated the individual.

Proactive interference. The cognitive phenomenon by which old material in long-term memory interferes with new information held in short-term memory (e.g., in learning a new language, one's native language can interfere with the acquisition of new grammar structures and vocabulary).

Problem representation. The process of problem identification which pinpoints the nature of the problem. This is an important first step when problem solving.

Procedural memory. A part of the long-term memory that includes the encoding of the skills needed to perform specific tasks. It may take a long time to acquire such knowledge and get it into long-term memory, but, once stored, this type of knowledge will be well-retained and hard to lose. It is also called implicit memory because it is used without the individual being aware of it. See also: **declarative memory; semantic memory.**

Proceptivity (prō″sep tiv′i tē). The tendency on the part of a female mammal to approach the male and solicit sexual contact. See also: **attractivity; estrus; receptivity.**

Process schizophrenia. A course of development that a schizophrenic illness may take in a patient with the initial symptoms appearing at an early age, and with a steadily evolving and ever-worsening condition following.

Procion (prō′sē ən) **yellow stain** or **procion brown stain.** Procion stains enter all parts of the neuron and produce a bright fluorescence. These stains, like the Golgi stain, highlight an entire neuron. See also: **Golgi stain.**

Profound mental retardation. Mental retardation indicated by a measured IQ of 25 or below; also, to qualify for this label, the individual should be unable to live independently. Such individuals constitute the least able 1% or 2% of the mentally retarded population. See also: **mental retardation.**

Progesterone (prō jes′tə rōn ″). One of the female sex hormones secreted by the corpus luteum. The formation of the corpus luteum in the ovary, with the subsequent release of progesterone, is stimulated by the anterior pituitary hormone LH. When progesterone, circulating in the blood, arrives at the hypothalamus of the brain, it inhibits the production and release of LH from the pituitary. This type of self-controlling activity is an example of the negative feedback principle. If the egg has been fertilized, progesterone prepares the wall of the uterus for the implantation of the fertilized egg, or zygote. This hormone helps to prepare the breasts for lactation (milk-secretion). Progesterone also prevents the further formation of egg cells (ovulation) during pregnancy. See also: **estrous cycle; luteinizing hormone; steroid hormone.**

Progestins. A group of gonadal hormones, of which progesterone is the principal member.

Progression index. A mathematical ratio devised by Stephan and others in order to estimate the relative intelligence of various mammalian species. It consists of the ratio of neocortex (volume) in the animal's brain to the expected amount of neocortex in the typical comparison mammal. Some examples of the progression index are 3.2 for humans (relative to standard primates) and slightly more than 1 for chimpanzees in relation to the same standard. See also: **A/S ratio; encephalization quotient.**

Projection (in neuroanatomy). [1] A band of axons in the central nervous system linking a structure A on one side of the midline to another structure B on the same side of the midline. This amounts to a vertical connection between separate levels of the nervous system. An example would be the projection of locations on the basilar membrane of the cochlea (the hearing organ) onto the dorsal cochlear nucleus of the medulla. [2] A projection could even be a long-distance connection that may be broken up by synapses between neurons along the way, for which case the restriction to one side of the midline need not apply. One example would be the projection of the receptors for light touch on the fingers of the left hand onto the postcentral gyrus of the right cerebral hemisphere. Another example would be the projection of points on the left nasal retina to small regions of the right primary visual cortex.

Projection (in the psychology of personality). One of the defense mechanisms listed by Sigmund Freud. The individual has anxiety- or shame-provoking feelings that are not only denied or repressed; they are attributed to another person or to a group of people. The paranoid's hostility and aggressiveness may be the result of projected feelings of hostility, enabling the individual to accept his or her own violent tendencies as justifiable and legitimate counters against the "hostile acts" of others. See also: **defense mechanism**.

Proliferation (prō lif ″ə rā′ shən). The production of new cells. Neurons in the brain multiply in layers lining the cerebral ventricles. These new nerve cells migrate toward the outer regions of the brain. Thus, newer neurons have to travel past older ones as they migrate to their permanent destination. See also: **migration**; **cerebral ventricles**.

Proprioceptor (prō ″prē ō sep′tər). A sense receptor that senses either the position, the motion, or the muscular tension of a part of the body. The receptors for the kinesthetic senses such as the **Golgi tendon organ** and the **muscle spindle** are examples of proprioceptors. So too are the **semicircular canals** and the **otolith organs** of the inner ear, because, after all, the head is a part of the body. See the definition of each of these types of proprioceptor. See also: **kinesthesis**.

Prosopagnosia (pros″ō pag nō′zē ə, -zhə). The inability to recognize faces despite having other visual perceptual skills intact. Prosopagnosia (according to detailed evidence collected by Damasio and his colleagues) seems to be the result of bilateral damage to the (left and right) occipital lobe (parts of Brodmann's areas 18 and 19) as well as parts of the temporal lobe (Brodmann areas 20, 21, and 37). Earlier, the symptom was attributed to unilateral damage to the right cerebral hemisphere.

Prospective memory. Our long-term memory "work list." This type of memory involves knowing what to do and then doing it. An example of prospective memory would involve remembering to buy a relative a birthday card. Sometimes this type of memory is tricky, because we constantly have to remind ourselves what needs to be done inasmuch as frequent environmental distractions often postpone items on our "work list."

Prostaglandin E1 (pros ″tə glan′din). Prostaglandins are fatty compounds, over a dozen in number, that are physiologically active. Prostaglandin E_1 in particular causes neurons in the preoptic area of the hypothalamus to increase body temperature at the onset of an infection. The chemical is therefore responsible for developing a fever when one is ill. See also: **preoptic area.**

Prosthesis (pros thē′sis). Any artificial device used to makeup for a missing or malfunctioning sense organ. An example for the benefit of the blind would be the Optacon. The implantation of electrodes in the cochlea of a deaf person would be another example. See also: **assistive technology**; **Optacon**.

Protanopia (prō tə nō′pē ə). A type of color blindness (dichromatism) in which the red receptors are not working (i.e., red objects appear black). Vision for the short- wavelength colors is not affected; blue things look blue. For middle wavelengths, green objects are seen as yellow. See also: **dichromats**.

Protein. A basic component of the diet (along with fats and carbohydrates). Proteins are complex chemicals that consist of combinations of hundreds of amino acid molecules. They are necessary materials for building the individual body cells.

Prototype. A cognitive or behavioral model which contains the most salient or typical features of that model. For example, Skinner's operant conditioning model can be considered a prototype of behavioral models.

Proxemics (prok sē′miks). The systematic study of the human use of space and, in particular, the uses of interpersonal spacing in a variety of social settings.

Proximal. Close (approximate) to the attachment of a part or to the point of origin of a part; or, close to the midline of the body or to the torso.

Proximal segment. That part of a severed axon which remains attached to the neuron's cell body. See also: **retrograde degeneration.**

Proximodistal (prok″si mō dis′təl) **principle**. A rule of embryological development which states that parts of the body near the midline will grow and develop more rapidly than the extremities of the body. See also: **cephalocaudal principle**.

Pseudohermaphrodite (so͞o″dō hûr maf′rə dīt) (also called **intersex**). An individual who at birth possesses some male and some female characteristics. Nearly all pseudohermaphrodites are infertile. Most are raised as females. See also: **hermaphrodite**.

Psilocin (sī′lō sin, sil′ə-). A hallucinogen obtained from a species of mushroom that is found in Mexico. See also: **hallucinogens; psilocybin.**

Psilocybin (sī″lō sī′bin, sil″ə). A hallucinogen found in certain Mexican mushrooms. The psilocybin molecule is more complex than that of psilocin. See also: **hallucinogens; psilocin.**

Psychedelics (sī ″kə del′iks). Hallucinogenic drugs; these are also known as psychotogenic or psychotomimetic drugs. See also: **hallucinogens; psychoactive drugs.**

Psychiatry. A medical speciality concerned with the diagnosis and treatment of behavioral, emotional, and mental disorders. Unlike clinical psychologists, who have similar professional tasks, psychiatrists are legally permitted to prescribe and administer drugs, perform surgery on the brain, and deliver electroconvulsive shock therapy.

Psychoactive drugs. Any drug is a chemical that affects the body's functions, that is, the chemical has a physiological impact on the organism. A psychoactive drug has an impact on the behavior, the emotional adjustment, the sensory perceptions, or the personality of an individual. There are five general categories of psychoactive drugs: (1) depressants, such as the barbiturates and ethyl alcohol; (2) stimulants, such as the amphetamines, cocaine, and caffeine; (3) opiates, such as opium, morphine, heroin, and methadone; (4) psychedelics (hallucinogens), such as LSD, mescaline, and marijuana; and (5) antipsychotics, such as the tricyclic anti-depressants, the MAO inhibitors, and the neuroleptic drugs. As a mnemonic device to aid recall of these five categories, you could use the following acrostic: Does Santa open people's attics? If you are inclined to cynicism and are skeptical about Santa Claus, you might prefer to use this alternative: Does Santa offer people acid?

Psychoanalysis. See: **psychotherapy.**

Psychobiology. See: **physiological psychology.**

Psychodynamic (sī″kō dī nam′ik) **model**. The view that every behavior disorder is a symptom of an underlying personality disorder.

Psychogenic (sī″kō jen′ik) **amnesia**. A memory disorder that arrives suddenly and prevents the person from accessing important personal memories.

Psycholinguistic (sī″kō ling gwis′tik) **deficiency**. First studied in detail in 1961 when the ITPA (Illinois Test of Psycholinguistic Abilities) was developed, this refers to such weaknesses as the inability to use phonics to decode words from printed symbols and a failure to outgrow early language habits. (In other words, the speaker-hearer is unable to integrate the grammatical and, in particular, the phonological knowledge he or she possesses.)

Psycholinguistics (sī ″kō ling gwis′tiks). A branch of linguistics, the scientific study of language, it merges psychological concepts with language science in order to explain the development of language and the universal features shared by all languages. Largely developed by one innovative scientist, Noam Chomsky, psycholinguistics is concerned with the mental structures and operations that make language possible. The concepts of surface structure and deep structure are essential aspects of this point of view.

Psychological dependence. The compulsion to take drugs in the absence in the user of any apparent physical dependence on the drug.

Psychological trauma. A psychological injury or shock caused by an accident, violence, abuse, neglect, separation, or tension. See also: **stress**.

Psychology. The science of human and animal behavior and of human mental processes. Psychology as a science is quite compatible with the physiological study of the functions of the organs of the body. One's own physical well-being is closely connected to one's cognitive and emotional processes.

Psychometrics (sī ˝kō met′riks). A specialty within psychology concerned with measuring cognitive or personality processes, usually by testing.

Psychomotor. A term for actions that combine cognitive and physical movement processes, such as handwriting, playing baseball, or playing a musical instrument.

Psychomotor seizure or **psychomotor attack**. An epileptic seizure during which the person produces simple stereotyped movements, such as doing and undoing the same button.

Psychopath. An individual who lacks the ability to judge the difference between right and wrong and feels little if any guilt about destructive or unsatisfactory behavior.

Psychopathic personality disorder. See: **antisocial personality disorder.**

Psychopathology (sī˝kō pə thol′ə jē). The study of mental/emotional disorders.

Psychopharmacology (sī˝kō fär˝mə kol′ə jē). Pharmacology is the science of drugs, their physical and chemical attributes, and their impact on bodily functions. Psychopharmacology is a subdivision of both pharmacology and physiological psychology. It is concerned with the study of psychoactive drugs and their effects on behavior and mental processes. See also: **pharmacology;   physiological   psychology; psychoactive drugs.**

Psychophysical   observations.   These   are observations made by human subjects of various sensory stimuli (e.g., visual, auditory, or kinesthetic stimuli) which are recorded for study. Theories are often based upon psychophysical observations before technological tools can be used to secure confirming or disconfirming evidence. The trichromatic (Young-Helmholz) theory of color vision, for example, was originally based on psychophysical observations of different colors.

Psychophysical parallelism. An answer offered by some philosophers to the mind-body problem. Psychophysical parallelism is a type of dualism, the idea that there are two kinds of reality at bottom, one being mental and the other physical. The question of how events taking place in the one can cause events to take place in the other is solved by a clean stroke. The parallelist says that

events in the one reality run parallel to events in the other, but that neither the mental nor the physical world can influence the other. In Gottfried Leibniz' version of parallelism, the world is constructed of sealed, independent units called monads, which run out a predetermined sequence of events. Leibniz therefore had a metaphysical   view   of   psychophysical parallelism, that it was a description of ultimate reality. Baruch (or "Benedict"--what's the difference, they both mean "Blessed", one in Hebrew, one in Latin) Spinoza argued that the physical and the mental reality were sealed-up, separate entities only because of the limited scope of human awareness. In essence, the universe is one thing, but all we can know are two small aspects of it, the physical and the mental. Spinoza therefore was a monist in his metaphysics (believing that reality was single) but supported parallelism in epistemology (the mind and the material have to be experienced separately). The Spinoza view has been called the double-aspect theory, because it refers to the two knowable aspects of one very complex universe. See also: **mind-brain   problem; dualism.**

Psychophysics. An area of psychological research which involves the relationship of a physical variable (e.g., light intensity) to a subjective variable (e.g., experienced level of brightness of light). Particular approaches to measurement were developed originally in order to solve psychophysical problems (e.g., the method of limits, the method of constant stimuli, the method of average error, among others). Some of the psychophysical methods, with appropriate modification, have been used to measure attitudes. Traditional psychophysics has been challenged by a newer approach, signal detection theory, which considers the habitual and motivational factors that enter into a perceptual judgment. While somewhat useful, the new approach has not completely replaced the older methods.

Psychophysiological disorders. Physical disorders which are exacerbated by psychological stressors such as anxiety or depression. Although many cases of ulcers, headaches, asthma, and allergies have a physical cause, psychological factors can affect the onset and duration of attacks related to the physical problem.

Psychophysiology (sī˝kō fiz˝ē ol′ə jē). The study of the relationships between mental life, motivation, and the emotions on the one hand and physiological events (such as the EEG, evoked responses, galvanic skin response, respiratory rate, heartbeat, blood pressure, skin temperature) on the other. Applications of psychophysiology include polygraphy, biofeedback, and the use of Transcendental Meditation (or the Relaxation Response) to relieve psychosomatic (stress-related) disorders.

Psychosis (sī kō′sis). A mental/emotional /behavioral disorder that is severe enough to require that the patient be institutionalized for his or her own protection and that of society in general.

Psychosomatic (sī ˝kō sō mat′ik) **disorders**. Illnesses involving physical damage to body tissues as the result of emotional reactions to stress. These include some cases of ulcers, asthma, colitis, and high blood pressure. The patient's life history and personality are important factors in the length and severity of the disorder. See also: **stress**.

Psychosurgery. Destruction of a part of the brain in order to repair or remove an emotional or adjustment problem affecting an individual. This is to be done only after the patient has failed to respond to psychotherapy, behavior therapy, or treatment with psychoactive drugs and where the condition presents a serious risk to the life of the patient and/or other persons. One example of such surgery is the Mark-Ervin procedure, which involves the specific destruction of a small portion of the amygdaloid nucleus, which is used to remedy outbursts of destructive aggression. An early and unfortunate example was prefrontal lobotomy. See also: **amygdaloid nucleus; lobotomy.**

Psychotherapy (including **psychoanalysis**). Treatments of behavior disorders and mental/emotional problems, developed by Sigmund Freud and others. Psychotherapy is based on the belief that causation resides with the individual; thus therapy sessions involve only the afflicted person. In Freudian psychoanalysis, problems are thought to stem from childhood conflicts that are usually of a sexual nature. Psychoanalysis centers on the process of free association whereby the therapist assists the individual in bringing to the forefront (i.e., full awareness) those unpleasant thoughts or feelings believed to induce the psychological problems. This technique is not as popular today as in previous decades because treatments now center on more inclusive therapies, such as the ecological approach. Also, most therapists do not believe that a majority of psychological problems stem from childhood sexual conflict. See also: **ecological model.**

Psychotogenic (sī kot ˝ō jen′ik) drugs. See: **hallucinogens**.

Psychotomimetic (sī kot˝ō mi met′ik) **drugs**. See: **hallucinogens**.

P-type dyslexia (dis lek′sē ə). The condition of a dyslexic whose reading problems primarily involve visual perception, according to Bakker and Licht. The P-type dyslexic uses primarily the right hemisphere (a developmental fixation, because after the good reader learns the fundamentals of language, he or she uses primarily the left hemisphere). Although reading accurately, a P-type dyslexic will read very slowly.

Puberty. The beginnings of sexual maturation, occurring around age 11-1/2 in boys and 10-1/2 in girls. Sexual maturity in boys involves the growth of the testes followed by the growth of the penis and pubic hair. Development of facial hair and the deepening of the voice are the final pubertal changes in young men. Sexual maturity in girls involves the development of the breasts and pubic hair and the onset of menarche (first menstrual period). This developmental time frame is generally referred to as adolescence, with individuals varying in the age of onset of pubertal changes. Associated with puberty, too, is the adolescent growth spurt. Correlating psychological changes during this time present a challenge for parents. Adolescents are frequently moody, "feeling their oats," argumentative, difficult to reason with, and so on. We're certain that the college students reading this dictionary never experienced these feelings (ahem!).

Pulsatile hormone release. The tendency of endocrine glands to release their hormones in bursts several times a day, with each spurt lasting several minutes.

Punch-drunk syndrome. The set of mental

problems resulting from the experiencing of repeated concussions.

Punishment. Providing an aversive stimulus (i.e., an unwanted object or situation) to an organism when the organism makes an operant response, usually resulting in a decrease in the chances that the response will be repeated in the same environment. (In a few cases, punishment is accomplished by the removal of a positive reinforcer, although this variety is more rarely used.) The concept of punishment is often confused with the idea of negative reinforcement. What the two ideas have in common is aversive stimulation of the organism and some sort of tie-in to the consequences of responding. But punishment involves the presentation of the undesirable stimulus, whereas negative reinforcement involves the removal of that stimulus (with a subsequent increase in response probability, which occurs in all instances of reinforcement). See also: **negative reinforcement; negative reinforcer; operant conditioning.**

Pupil. Analogous to the aperture of a camera, it admits light into the eye. The pupil is kept nearly closed in brightly lit settings and is widened where the light is dim.

Pupillary (pyo͞o′pi ler ″ē) **reflex**. This is the constriction of the pupil of the eye in response to bright light (analogous to closing the aperture of a camera when taking a picture outdoors on a sunny day). The parasympathetic nervous system acts to conserve the sensitive resources of the retinal receptors, guarding against an "overexposure." The circular muscles contract, filling in the outer space of the pupil and thus causing the pupil to shrink. See also: **circular muscles**.

Pure-tone air conduction test. An audiometric test using pure tones of different frequency presented by earphones. Hearing losses from both sensorineural and conduction factors contribute to the readings. When coupled with the pure tone bone conduction test, various combinations of results on these two tests can show whether the hearing loss is conductive, sensorineural, or mixed. See also: **conductive hearing loss; mixed hearing loss; pure-tone bone conduction test; sensorineural impairments.**

Pure-tone audiometric screening. A brief screening test with pure frequency tones performed to determine if more auditory testing is advisable.

Pure-tone bone conduction test. A bone conduction test using pure tones as test stimuli. See also: **bone conduction test; pure-tone air conduction test.**

Purkinje (pûr kin′jē, -jə) **cells**. Named for the Czech physiologist Johannes Purkinje, these are multipolar neurons of the cerebellum. A Purkinje cell has very bushy dendrites and an axon that leaves the cerebellum in order to communicate with the cerebral cortex. There are 7,000,000 Purkinje cells in the human brain. The axon endings of these neurons are, in all cases, inhibitory. The dendritic tree of one Purkinje cell has over 100,000 dendritic spines and provides up to 200,000 synaptic links with other cerebellar neurons.

Purkinje (pûr kin′jē, -jə) **effect** or **Purkinje shift** or **Purkinje phenomenon**. A change in the relative brightness of the colors as the lighting changes from broad daylight to the very dim light of evening. In bright light, yellow is subjectively the brightest color; if all colors of the spectrum are presented with the same illumination, yellow seems to be receiving more illumination than other colors. Yellow flowers are the brightest things to be seen in a garden at noon, but the green grass is the brightest part of the same scene at dusk. The cones are the most reactive to lights at a wavelength of about 550 nanometers (nm), whereas the rods are maximally sensitive to light at a wavelength of around 500 nm. The color associated with a wavelength of 550 nm is yellow, and the color of light at the 500 nm wavelength is green. The cones (less sensitive than rods but capable of providing acute vision and color discrimination) provide photopic (daylight) vision while the rods provide scotopic (dim light) vision. See also: **cones; photopic; rods; scotopic.**

Purkinje (pûr kin′jē, -jə) **fibers**. A set of specialized muscle fibers in the heart. The Purkinje fibers rapidly carry electrical impulses from the atrioventricular node to all parts of the heart's ventricles. The ventricles, in turn, respond by contracting.

Pursuit eye movements. Eye movements that occur when the eyes are visually tracking a moving target.

Putamen (pyo͞o tā′min) (from Latin "putamen" = "shell"). One of the forebrain basal ganglia, situated close to the globus pallidus, which it surrounds on three sides. With the globus pallidus, the putamen makes up the lentiform ("lens-shaped") nucleus. These two nuclei are separated by the narrow internal capsule from a third nucleus of the basal ganglia group. That third nucleus is the caudate nucleus. All three of them comprise the corpus striatum. See also: **basal ganglia; caudate nucleus; corpus striatum; globus pallidus.**

Pyloric sphincter (pī lôr ′ik sfingk′tər). A ring of muscles that are so placed that they can close the opening between the stomach and the duodenum, the first portion of the small intestine.

Pyramid. A swelling in the side of the medulla, marking the place where most of the pyramidal tract crosses to the opposite side (i.e., decussates) and forms the contralaterally situated dorsolateral tract of the spinal cord. See also: **decussation; dorsolateral tract; medulla; pyramidal tract.**

Pyramidal cell layer. A layer of nerve cell bodies in the hippocampus.

Pyramidal tract or **corticospinal** (kôr ″ti kō spī′nəl) **tract** -The primary motor pathway. Its axons originate from the Betz cells in Brodmann's area 4, which is the precentral gyrus in the frontal lobe of the cerebral cortex. In the precentral gyrus, the parts of the body are mapped upside down. Thus an axon controlling the motion of the little toe, in this "express train" route of the motor system, can be very long. Picture the tallest basketball player around today. This axon, which is so thin it cannot be seen with the naked eye, runs down the man's head and down his back until it reaches the very bottom of the spinal cord, where it finally ends. A synapse there provides a direct connection to the muscles of the little toe; that second axon will also be a long one. Note that there is only one synapse separating the muscles from the precentral gyrus neurons; now, that's quick service! After the pyramidal tract escapes the forebrain, it travels in a caudal direction along the floor of the midbrain, forming the cerebral peduncles. It is also visible in the medulla, because it produces bulges in the left and right sides of the medulla known as the pyramids. Whether the pyramidal tract gets its name from the giant pyramidal cells (the Betz cells) or from the pyramids of the medulla is a moot point. We have two good reasons for the name. As it leaves the medulla (entering the spinal cord), the pyramidal tract splits. Most of the axons decussate, joining the contralateral (opposite) side of the spinal cord as the dorsolateral tract. This controls movements of the extremities-- arms, legs, hands, feet, fingers, and toes. The remaining, uncrossed, axons stay on the ipsilateral (same) side of the spinal cord to form the ventromedial tract. This tract is involved in movements of the trunk. See also: **cerebral cortex; contralateral; decussation; dorsolateral tract; frontal lobe; ipsilateral; medulla; midbrain; spinal cord; ventromedial tract.**

Pyrogen (pī′rō jen″). A chemical that can induce fever.

Pyromania (pī ″rō mā′nē ə, -man′yə). An impulse control disorder in which the individual derives pleasure from deliberately setting fires, provided this occurs on more than one occasion.

Q

Q-sort. An analysis of multiple test scores in which people are placed into various categories and correlation coefficients are calculated between these groups and other variables. The object of such research may be to verify the validity of a subtyping system, for example, investigating possible varieties of dyslexia.

Quadrantanopia (kwod″rant ən ō′pē ə) (from Latin "quadrans" = "one-fourth", "quadrant" = a 90-degree arc, which is a quarter of a circle; from Greek "an" = 'without"; "opia" = "vision"). Loss of vision from one-half of either the left or the right visual half-field; the loss may occur in the upper or lower half of either the right or the left visual field. For example, a lesion destroying half of the visual cortex on the left side of the brain may lead to a blind area over a quarter of the entire visual field, on the right side of the visual field. See also: **hemianopia.**

Quadriplegia (kwod″ri plē′jē ə, -jə) (from Latin "quattuor" = "four"; from Greek "plegia" = "paralysis"). The loss of muscular control and sensation from all four limbs caused by a severing of the spinal cord above the level of the neurons sending motor axons to the arms. See also: **hemiplegia; paralysis; paraplegia.**

Quiet-biting attack. See **predatory aggression**.

Quinolinic (kwin″ə lin′ik) **acid**. A chemical with a molecular resemblance to the excitatory neurotransmitter glutamate, a metabolic product of glutamic acid. Quinolinic acid destroys the receptor sites for glutamate, probably by overstimulating them. See also: **glutamate; neurotransmitter; receptor sites.**

R

Rabies (rā′bēz). A brain disease stimulated by a virus. The part of the brain involved is the temporal lobe of the cortex along with the amygdala, which lies below the temporal lobe. The patient becomes viciously aggressive, indicating that some of the brain's mechanisms of restraint against aggression have been damaged. Some regions of the amygdala may have the opposite action, normally turning rage on instead of restraining it. See also: **Klüver-Bucy syndrome**.

Radial arm maze. A maze for testing the spatial localization ability of laboratory rats. The starting platform leads to multiple paths (the "radial arms").

Radial glia (glī′ə, glē′ə). A type of central nervous system neuroglia, perhaps the embryonic form of astroglia. These glial cells have very long branches on which developing neuroblast cells travel to reach the positions they will occupy in the mature central nervous system as neurons. After the brain has formed, these radial cells are, some suggest, modified into ordinary astrocytes. See also: **astrocytes; neuroglia.**

Radial muscles. Smooth muscles inserted into the outer rim of structures surrounding the pupil. Contraction of the radial muscles causes the pupils to dilate. This action, which is taken in dim light, is mediated by the sympathetic nervous system. See also: **circular muscles; pupil; pupillary reflex.**

Radiation. The tendency for organisms to settle into all corners of the environment to which they are well adapted. The increase in population density of a successful species, together with competition for limited environmental resources, provides a pressure that forces the group members to disperse into whatever spaces are still available. See also: **natural selection; phylogeny.**

Rape. A forced sexual assault on a nonconsenting individual, usually committed by a man on a woman. Statutory rape, though, is a variety of rape in which the sexual initiative is taken with a consenting partner when that partner is either younger than the legal age of consent or, if old enough to consent, lacks the intelligence or understanding to give meaningful consent. A rape is usually committed by an antisocial individual whose sex drive is gratified by the victimization and brutalization of others. It is estimated that as many as 20% of female college students have been victims of attempted rape. Most rapists fall within the age range of 15 to 25.

Raphé nuclei (rā′fē nōō′klē ī, nyōō′-) (from Greek "rhaphe" = "seam"). Nuclei along the midline of the body that are found in the midbrain. The left and right midbrain look like two halves of an object that have their sides stitched together; the raphe nuclei comprise the "stitches." These nuclei contain serotinergic axons (i.e., axons that release serotonin at their endings), which are considered responsible for slow-wave sleep (ordinary sleep, which may be fairly deep but involves only slow eye movements and during which some muscle tone remains in the skeletal muscles). See also: **slow-wave sleep; serotonin.**

Rapid eye movement sleep. See: REM sleep.

Rapid Golgi stain. See: **Golgi stain.**

Rapid smoking. A widely-used aversion therapy for smoking (one employed as a last resort) which involves requiring the individual to smoke continuously, puffing every 6 to 10 seconds. The purpose of this treatment is to make the smoker miserable and create an aversion to the habit of smoking. This technique is moderately effective when conducted under the direction of a trained behavior therapist. See also: **aversion therapy.**

Rational-emotive therapy. One type of cognitive therapy, developed by Albert Ellis. This approach to psychotherapy aims at restructuring the cognitive world of the patient in order to make it more reasonable and sound than her or his present view of the world. The patient is directed to identify irrational thoughts and cognitions in order to change them. Later in therapy, the patient is enabled to take steps to achieve goals that were earlier perceived to be unattainable. For example, if a student fails a test in physiological psychology, he or she might believe that the subject cannot be understood. Rational-emotive therapy can show the student that such a course can be mastered by, among other things, the use of this dictionary. See also: **cognitive therapy.**

Rationalization. One of the defense mechanisms catalogued by Freud. The individual justifies an irrational action, feeling, or motive to her- or himself by providing what seems to be a reasonable explanation for it. The excessive use of this defense interferes with the individual's chances of behaving normally and reaching maturity in her or his social relationships. See also: **defense mechanism.**

Ratliff's laws of lateral inhibition. These are the area law, the intensity law, and the proximity law. For a full description of these laws, in context, please refer to **lateral inhibition.**

Raw score. A simple total score, such as the number of test items correctly answered. The raw score has very little meaning in the absence of any allowance for the ease or difficulty of the test items.

Raynaud's (rā nōz') **disease.** A condition due to abnormal spasms of smooth muscles lining the blood vessels in the extremities. This spasm may be a reaction to cold that would not occur in a normal individual. Psychological stress may help bring on the symptoms (the activity of the sympathetic nervous system leading to constriction of peripheral blood vessels). Many more females than males present with this complaint. The finger(s) and/or toe(s) affected may become pale, cold, and numb. The condition is difficult to treat by standard medical procedures. If gangrene threatens, the doctor may resort to sympathectomy, that is, the surgical removal of the entire sympathetic nervous system. Fortunately, there is some evidence that biofeedback can be used to alleviate the problem. See also: **biofeedback.**

Reaction formation. One of the defense mechanisms identified by Sigmund Freud. In reaction formation, an unacceptable memory or motivation is disguised from oneself by a rigid overemphasis of its opposite. For example, a mother who regrets having had children becomes overprotective, concealing hostile motivation under a mask of caring concern. A reactive motivation can be differentiated from a genuine one in that the reactive one is both single-minded and exaggerated, often being exhibited at the wrong time and place, with greater intensity and enthusiasm than is appropriate under the circumstances. See also: **defense mechanism.**

Reactive. The kind of antisocial behavior that follows a history of having been neglected, having been treated unfairly, or having been subjected to cruelty. See also: **proactive.**

Reactive schizophrenia (skit sə frē' nē ə, -fre n'ē ə). A development pattern for schizophrenia in which the onset of the symptoms is sudden and the condition becomes very severe in a short time. See also: **process schizophrenia.**

Rebound (of REM sleep). After several nights of sleep during which the person is awakened after an attempt to begin REM sleep (i.e., a period of REM deprivation), the sleep record of the individual on the next few nights of sleep will include much longer-than-usual periods of REM sleep. This emphatic return of REM sleep at the earliest opportunity is known as REM rebound.

Recapitulation (rē″kə pich″ə lā'shən, rē″kə pit ″yoo-). Doing something over again. In the cliche "ontogeny recapitulates phylogeny", the human embryo starts out resembling a fish, then somewhat resembles an amphibian, still later a reptile, then a smaller mammal, and looks like a recognizable human being only rather late during gestation.

Receptive. Having to do with the comprehension of speech, i.e., the auditory perception of spoken language.

Receptive aphasia (ə fā'zhə) or **Wernicke's** (ver'ni kēz) **aphasia** or **sensory aphasia.** A selective loss of language ability. The patient speaks fluently, with good rhythm. The trouble is that the words spoken do not make sense. The receptive aphasic has a deficit at the semantic level; the chief problem is understanding speech. Traditionally, this syndrome has been thought to result from damage to Wernicke's area in the posterior part of the superior temporal gyrus of the cerebral cortex. Not all receptive aphasics have the same symptoms. Some have anomia, the inability to name objects. Others may be unable to form sentences, although they are able to name objects. It seems that there is remarkable specificity of function in the cortical regions devoted to language. Some investigators express skepticism about the traditional explanation of this syndrome, doubting that damage precisely restricted to Wernicke's area of the cerebral cortex can produce a lasting aphasia, and thereby implying that either subcortical damage or injury to a larger cortical region is necessary for permanent damage to occur to linguistic behavior.

Receptive field. Each nerve cell (except for actual sense receptors) in a sensory pathway from the receptors to the cerebral cortex is affected by only some receptors. The set of receptor cells affecting a given sensory neuron constitute the receptive field of that neuron. The field may have a characteristic shape describing the patch of receptor surface (e.g., the circular shape of a small retinal region) filled in by the receptors that belong to the field.

Receptive field (of a higher-order sensory neuron). The receptive field of a neuron in a sensory pathway headed toward the brain is that portion of the surface of the relevant sense organ that can change the voltage (either up or down) on the membrane of the neuron in question. Take, for example, a ganglion cell in the retina of the eye. Not all the cones and rods in that retina will alter the excitability of that ganglion cell. Those few rod and cone receptor cells that, when excited, can make this particular ganglion cell's excitability increase (or decrease) constitute the receptive field of that ganglion cell. For another example, take a touch-sense specialized neuron in the post-central gyrus of the cerebral cortex. The activity of this neuron, let us say, indicates that the right index finger has touched an object. Then, the sense-receptors for touch in the skin of the right index finger make up the receptive field of that cortical neuron. (Note that there is a class of sensory neurons that cannot, by definition, have a receptive field. This is the case where the receptors are modified neurons, such as the rods and cones of the eye or the olfactory receptors of the nose. Since rods and cones have to be the components of another neuron's receptive field, they themselves are not in a position to have receptive fields of their own.) See also: **center (of a receptive field); surround (of a receptive field).**

Receptive language. The ability to receive and understand language communications by hearing with comprehension, reading, or interpreting gestures. See also: **expressive language.**

Receptivity. The tendency of a female mammal to respond favorably to sexual advances from a male and accept copulation. See also: **attractivity; estrus; proceptivity.**

Receptor binding autoradiography. A procedure in which neurotransmitter molecules are given radioactive markers. When the transmitter binds to its receptor sites, the latter can be located from the radioactivity. See also: **neurotransmitter; receptor sites.**

Receptors. [1] Sense organs. [2] Cells that are specialized for the detection and assessment of physical energy. The visual receptors, for example, are the rods and the cones. The basic function of a receptor is transduction, which is the conversion of one form of physical energy to another. In our example, the visual receptors contain photopigments that break down when exposed to light. In turn, an electrical pulse, the generator potential, occurs. This starts a chain of events leading to nerve impulses arriving at the visual cortex. Light energy from the visual stimulus is thus transformed into the electro-chemical energy used by neurons.

Receptor sites. Places on the surface of the postsynaptic membrane (the membrane of the receiving neuron at the synapse) that are form-fitted to the molecular shape of the matching chemical neurotransmitter. This "lock-and-key" mechanism for receptor sites prevents the "wrong" neurotransmitter from activating the synapse. Only the correctly-fitted chemical can squeeze into the receptor site to do its excitatory or inhibitory work.

Recessive gene. The one form of a gene (i.e., an allele) for a given hereditary trait that will not be expressed if it is paired with the other, dominant, allele. For example, if eye color is the trait in question, the allele for blue eyes is recessive and the allele for brown eyes is dominant. An individual with one allele of each type, that is, an individual heterozygous for eye color, will exhibit brown eyes, the dominant trait. The gene for blue eye color is not expressed. See also: **allele; dominant gene; heterozygous.**

Reciprocal inhibition. [1] This is one of the

features that makes reflex action possible in the human nervous system. The factors that lead to the excitation of one member of a pair of antagonistic muscles also excite interneurons that in turn lead to the inhibition of the antagonist. For example, the biceps muscle's contraction will flex the arm (i.e., bring the arm back to the main part of the body) and the contraction of the antagonistic muscle, the triceps, will extend the arm (i.e., fling the arm out away from the body). A motor command to contract the triceps is normally accompanied by an inhibition of the motor neurons connected to the biceps. This is reciprocal: A motor command to contract the biceps is accompanied by an inhibitory message to the neurons that work the triceps. The autonomic nervous system's two divisions have such a reciprocally inhibitory relationship. One group of the smooth muscles and glands, for example, are commanded to go into action by the sympathetic nervous system. Simultaneously, inhibitory commands are sent to the parasympathetic nervous system. Of course, there is reciprocity: When a parasympathetic function is taking place, the sympathetic division is being inhibited. Another term for "reciprocal inhibition" is "Sherrington's inhibition." [2] The autonomic nervous system's arrangement for reciprocal inhibition has been employed by behavior therapists such as Wolpe to replace stressful anxiety (mediated by sympathetic nervous system activity) with calm relaxation (presumably with the aid of the parasympathetic nervous system). Desensitization techniques are instances of reciprocal inhibition in this sense of the term. See also: **desensitization techniques.**

Reciprocal innervation (in ″ər vā′shən). The arrangement of motor nerve connections that makes **reciprocal inhibition** (see definition) possible.

Reciprocal synapses. Synapses in which message transmission can move from each neuron to the other; the membrane of each neuron has both presynaptic features (e.g., the capacity to release neurotransmitter molecules) and postsynaptic aspects (e.g., receptor sites to accept neurotransmitter molecules). See also: **synapse.**

Recording. One of the three chief methods for investigating the relationship between the brain and behavior. The other two are ablation and stimulation. The best known approach to recording is the electroencephalogram, which uses from 8 to 19 electrodes, depending on the electrode-placement convention selected. Each electrode is the size and shape of a quarter, with each one positioned to record the summed voltage of thousands of cerebral neurons. The opposite extreme is single-unit recording, in which a microelectrode records the ups and downs of electrical charge from a single neuron. Variations on the recording theme include the **CAT scan, PET scan, MRI, MANSCAN,** and **SQUID** techniques (see definitions). See also: **ablation; stimulation.**

Recurrent collateral. A side branch of a long axon that communicates with the dendrites of the very same neuron.

Recurrent collateral inhibition. The inhibition of a neuron as the direct result of its own nerve impulses, since the axon terminals of the recurrent collateral branch of the axon provide inhibitory postsynaptic potentials to the neuron's own cell membrane. Sometimes the axon collaterals affect small intermediary cells, such as Renshaw cells, that send the inhibitory messages to the neuron. See also: **axon collateral; Renshaw cell.**

Recurrent-items delayed matching-to-sample task. A task in which the subject is shown one object (such as a red triangle) which serves as the "sample"; the subject is later presented a choice between the red triangle and a green square, the "non-sample." After a delay (for a specified interval), they are given a second trial in which they are again shown the sample (one of the same two objects) and later required to choose between the same two stimuli, and so on for further trials. A correct selection of the sample results in a reward. Since the same two objects (e.g., a red triangle and a green square) are presented on each task, the subject has to recall the one object that was the sample on the most recent trial. This provides sufficient difficulty for monkeys with prefrontal lesions that their problem-solving is disrupted. These same monkeys can perform correctly if new items are always given. See also: **delayed matching-to-sample task; frontal lobe.**

Recurring-items delayed nonmatching-to-sample task. A task in which the subject is shown one object (e.g., a red triangle), which is thereby defined as the "sample." Later, after a lapse of time, the subject is presented with a pair of items (e.g., the red triangle and a green square) and, in this task, can earn a reward by selecting the stimulus other than the sample (i.e., the green square). Similar trials are then given with the same interval between the sample presentation and the opportunity to make a choice. Since the same two items are presented on each task, the monkey must remember the most recent occasion that one of the two stimuli served as the sample. As in recurring-items delayed matching-to-sample, this task is impaired by lesions to the prefrontal cortex. See also: **delayed matching-to-sample task; delayed nonmatching-to-sample task; recurring-items delayed matching-to-sample task; frontal lobe.**

Red nucleus. One of the more caudal of the basal ganglia, located in the midbrain tegmentum, just dorsal to the ventral tegmental area and the substantia nigra. The name is due to a red pigment in the cell bodies of the neurons comprising the red nucleus. See also: **basal ganglia; extrapyramidal motor fibers; substantia nigra; ventral tegmental area.**

Reduction of path. Although there are 127,000,000 retinal receptors, there are only 1,000,000 retinal ganglion cells. This looks as if, for every 127 channels of communication to the brain, only one is allowed to arrive at its destination. Actually, information is being encoded and rechanneled into a smaller number of paths.

Reference memory. A memory of general principles (such as the rules of a game). Reference memory is less likely than working memory to suffer the effects of amnesia.

Reflex. A fixed relationship between a given environmental stimulus and a particular response, so that the response is made automatically. Some reflexes are unlearned ("unconditioned reflexes") and can be used as a basis for establishing learned (or "conditioned") reflexes. Whether they are learned or unlearned, reflexive actions are often referred to as involuntary behaviors. Ironically, reflexes often involve reactions of the so-called voluntary muscles. For example, a puff of air to the eye causes a blinking reaction of the eyelid. As

another example, a sharp blow to the patellar tendon just below the knee forces a thrust of the leg forward, due to the activation of an extensor muscle called the quadriceps femoris. The latter is known as the knee jerk reflex, which is one of the stretch reflexes. See also: **reflex arc.**

Reflex arc. A description of the route taken by nerve impulses, beginning at the receptor and ending at the muscle fiber, in carrying out a reflexive behavior. Each level of action is represented by only one cell. Since real reflexive activities involve a number of cells at each level, the reflex arc is merely a model of the neurological organization of a reflexive act. Every reflex arc begins with an afferent neuron. There is at least one synapse with a second neuron. Every reflex arc is completed by an efferent neuron. The afferent neuron in a spinal cord reflex arc enters the cord by way of the dorsal root; the efferent neuron leaves the cord via the ventral root. The reflex arc is the most elementary organization of a behavior possible. The simplest reflex arcs are the two-neuron, or monosynaptic, reflex arcs (e.g., the stretch reflexes) and the three-neuron, or disynaptic, reflex arcs (e.g., those that inhibit the antagonistic extensor muscles in pain-flexion reflexes). In a three-neuron arc, the middle neuron is an interneuron which is contained entirely within the gray butterfly of the spinal cord and runs from the dorsal horn to the ventral horn. See also: **reflex.**

Reflex audiometry (ô dē om′e trē). These are techniques used with very young children or mentally handicapped individuals in order to assess hearing ability. Two reflex responses would be the Moro reflex (movement of body parts, including the head when a sound is heard) and the orienting response (turning body parts, especially the head, toward the speech source when a sound is heard). See also: **Moro reflex.**

Refraction (ri frak′shan). The bending of light rays when they pass from one transparent medium into another. This property of light allows for focusing of the image by the cornea and the lens.

Refractory (ri frak′t(ə)rē) **period** (in the sexual act). After the resolution stage of the sexual act, the male temporarily cannot be aroused again. The period of time in which arousal cannot take place is called the refractory period.

Refreezing. A concept related to brainwashing. Refreezing is the process of reinforcing new attitudes and beliefs. See also: **brainwashing; sensory deprivation.**

Refreshable Braille or **paperless Braille**. A system in which pins are either raised or lowered electromechanically to provide readable touch-sense messages for the blind. See also: **MIT Braille Embosser; Optacon.**

Regional cerebral blood flow (rCBF). The measurement of high and low rates of blood flow through parts of the brain. Typically, the patient inhales a trace of the rare gas xenon (a radioactive isotope). The xenon circulates throughout the blood, and its activity is monitored by radiation detectors. Cortical blood flow will vary according to metabolic demands placed on various areas by cognitive processes. Different patterns of rCBF have been observed in schizophrenics, brain-damaged persons, stutterers, and individuals showing alexia without agraphia.

Regression (in visual activity). An eye movement that goes in the reverse direction (right to left) during reading.

Regression (in personality psychology). A Freudian defense mechanism in which the individual acts more childish and immature than he or she should, considering his or her age. This relatively immature conduct provides the individual with a defense against anxiety or shame, but at a price. The cost is that the person has to resort to such childish behaviors as throwing temper tantrums. See also: **defense mechanism.**

Rehabilitation. The retraining or the reorganizing of a skill in an individual who has lost that skill due to injury or disease.

Rehearsal. Reviewing (by repeating material in memory) as a means of assisting the process of consolidation of short-term memories into long-term memories.

Reinforcement. The event that strengthens a conditioned response. In classical conditioning, the presentation of the unconditioned stimulus provides reinforcement for learning by following the presentation of the conditioned stimulus. In operant conditioning, it is the presentation of a desirable situation (positive reinforcement) or

the removal of an undesirable situation (negative reinforcement) directly after the organism has emitted the operant response which is being conditioned. The result is an increased rate of responding. See also: **classical conditioning; negative reinforcement; operant conditioning; positive reinforcement; punishment.**

Related services. Services offered by specialists to supplement the education of exceptional children. These specialists may be employed in a number of professions, such as speech/language pathology, audiology, optometry, physical therapy, occupational therapy, and psychology.

Relative adaptive fitness. The set of physical and behavioral traits of a particular species of animal that affects its ability to compete and survive in one or more environments. Relative fitness is applied at all levels - the individual, the group, and the entire species. See also: **multiple causality; natural selection; phylogeny.**

Relative refractory (ri frak′t(ə)rē) **period**. A time period of one-half millisecond just after the absolute refractory period. A very strong stimulus, well above the normal threshold value, can lead to a new nerve impulse in the axon. The required strength for the stimulus to be effective goes down steadily until it reaches the normal threshold value at the end of the relative refractory period. The significance of this fact is that the nervous system can use impulse frequency (number of impulses per second) as a measure of stimulus strength. Of course, impulse strength cannot be used to measure stimulus strength, due to the all-or-none law. See also: **absolute refractory period; all-or-none law; nerve impulse.**

Relaxation Response. H. Benson consolidated the basic therapeutic ideas of Transcendental Meditation (TM) into a simple formula for shifting one's autonomic nervous system away from sympathetic nervous system "fight-or-flight" functioning toward parasympathetic nervous system satisfaction-relaxation functioning. The practice of a learned set of behaviors, a discipline, is needed because we do not have a simple reflex for turning on the parasympathetic nervous system functions. The individual sits down in a quiet environment, letting the soles of the feet rest on the floor. He or she thinks repeatedly of the word "One," which operates like a TM-type mantra and has the advantage of enforcing regularly spaced exhalations. Note the resemblance of the word "one" to "Om", the word chanted by Tibetan Buddhist lamas. "Om" (as does "one") leads to regularly-spaced exhaling. All the attention should be focused on the word "one" or "Om", to the exclusion of other concerns. The person relaxes all the muscles, starting from the feet and working up the body, until totally relaxed. This, however, has to be done without striving (as in the Beatles' song, "Let it be"). The procedure should be kept up for 10 to 20 minutes and performed twice a day. It is claimed that the Relaxation Response is therapeutic for stress-related physical disorders, emotional disorders, and drug or other addictions. See also: **autonomic nervous system; biofeedback; parasympathetic nervous system; psychophysiology; stress; sympathetic nervous system; Transcendental Meditation.**

Releasing hormone or **releasing factor**. A hormone formed in neurosecretory cells of the hypothalamus. There are several different kinds of releasing hormones, each being specific for the release of a given tropic hormone from the anterior pituitary gland. The releasing hormone travels in the bloodstream by way of portal blood vessels in the infundibulum (the stalk that attaches the pituitary body to the hypothalamus) to the anterior pituitary. See also: **anterior pituitary gland; hypothalamus; neurosecretory cells**.

Reliability. That test is reliable which measures the same object or phenomenon consistently, even under varying conditions.

Reliability measurements. The test constructor does not know what exactly are the sources of error in a test, or, obviously, she or he would never have let them enter into it. Test reliability has to be computed indirectly, by one of three different strategies: (1) Test-retest correlation: Give the test to a group of subjects, wait a while (allowing enough time for normal forgetting of test items to occur) and give the same test again to the same subjects. Compute the correlation coefficient between the first set of scores and the second. (2) Parallel, or alternate, forms: Construct a second test containing the same kind of test items as the original and based on the same theory as the original. Give both forms of the test to the same subjects. Compute the correlation coefficient for the two forms of the test. (3) Internal reliability: If the test were to be split in half, the total score for the items in one half of the test could be correlated with the total for the items in the remaining half. (3a) Spearman's split-half reliability coefficient: Take all the odd-numbered test items and treat them as one form of the test; do likewise for all the even-numbered test times. Compute the correlation between these two halves. Since cutting a test's length lowers its reliability, a correction factor is applied to that correlation, so that the reliability coefficient is increased appropriately. (3b) Kuder-Richardson internal consistency coefficient: Use the formula devised by Kuder and Richardson to take an average of all possible split-half coefficients the test can yield. There are more ways to divide a test in half than just to take the odd-numbered and even-numbered items. The Kuder-Richardson method does not require us to know which is the best way to subdivide the test.

REM sleep (also known as **paradoxical sleep** or **ascending stage 1 sleep**). REM stands for rapid eye movements. This stage of sleep appears toward the end of each of the 90-minute cycles of sleep stages. The EEG pattern for REM sleep is similar to that of stage 1 sleep. Since REM sleep both follows and precedes stage 2 sleep, as it follows the conclusion of one 90-minute sleep cycle and initiates the next 90-minute cycle, REM sleep is numbered stage 1. It is distinguishable from the "falling-asleep" (descending) kind of stage 1 sleep by the presence of rapid eye movements and a widespread loss of muscle tone in the skeletal muscles. The term for falling-to-sleep stage 1 is descending stage 1, whereas stage-REM sleep is called ascending stage 1. REM-sleep is regarded as the stage of sleep in which most dreaming occurs. Why is it called "paradoxical"? Because it shows the active brain EEG (the stage-1 EEG has high-frequency, low-voltage waves, as does the EEG for the waking, active brain) simultaneously with the greatest muscle flaccidity (least muscle tone) of all the sleep stages. Paradoxically, it seems to be the shallowest and one of the deepest sleep stages all rolled into one! In infants, REM sleep time takes up half of the total sleep duration. It has been hypothesized that this type of sleep is needed for brain development and for learning. One effect of the deprivation of REM sleep seems to be an impairment of memory consolidation. Better established, however, is the phenomenon of "REM rebound." During the several (perhaps as many as a month's) nights of sleep following a REM deprivation, more than the usual amount of the total sleep period is spent in REM sleep. REM deprivation has led to the relief of depression in patients with severe clinical depression. Presumably, this is because the onset of REM sleep is accompanied by a decrease in brain levels of the neurotransmitters serotonin and norepinephrine. A depressed mood has been hypothesized to correlate with decreased brain levels of serotonin and/or norepinephrine. Therefore, a patient who is deprived of REM sleep will have elevated levels of these neurotransmitters in the brain. This is just what is accomplished by most of the antidepressant drugs! See also: **sleep.**

Renin (rē nin). A hormone released by the kidneys in response to a lowering of neural signals from the baroceptors (pressure sensors) of the heart or to a rise in the level of the antidiuretic hormone (vasopressin) in the blood. The released renin forms angiotensin I which is metabolically converted to angiotensin II. Angiotensin II leads to a constriction of the blood vessels in order to compensate for the lowered blood pressure. See also: **angiotensin II; antidiuretic hormone; hypovolemic thirst.**

Renshaw cell. A small inhibitory neuron found in the ventral (motor) horns of the spinal cord. Renshaw cells respond to excitatory inputs by inhibiting the motor neurons that have just sent the excitatory impulses. See also: **excitation; inhibition; pre-synaptic inhibition.**

Repetition priming. After showing a subject with amnesia a list of words, a neuropsychologist may test the subject's memory for the words by presenting the subject a few letters from each of the words and ask the subject to supply the entire word from the few letters (the "priming cues"). Such subjects often do well at this task, indicating that the word list has been stored in

their implicit memories. See also: **implicit memory.**

Replacement injection. The injection of a hormone in order to make up for the disease, or the surgical removal, of the endocrine gland that would normally provide the hormone.

Representative sample. A sample of individuals from a larger population that, in important attributes, resembles the entire population. In research, one is usually unable to measure the entire population of interest due to limitations of time and money. The next best thing is to take a representative sample from the population (i.e., one that resembles the larger population, having about the same mean score and the same variability of scores around the mean) and measure that sample. Techniques for obtaining representative samples include stratified sampling and random sampling. In random sampling, every member of the population is given an equal chance to be selected for the sample. See also: **population; sample.**

Repression. The selective loss of painful memories; motivated forgetting. Repression is the basic Freudian defense mechanism, since the other defense mechanisms cannot be put into effect without a modicum of repression taking place. Repression may be a forerunner of somatization symptoms such as tics or headaches. It may help cause psychasthenia (neurasthenia), because energy may be diverted from ongoing normal daily activities in the effort to maintain repression. See also: **defense mechanism.**

Reserpine. A drug for the treatment of mania. It lowers the levels of dopamine, norepinephrine, and serotonin (the monoamine neurotransmitters) by causing them to leak from the synaptic vesicles holding transmitters within the synaptic boutons.

Residual type of schizophrenia. A type of schizophrenia in which the patient retains contact with reality, even though the patient may have inappropriate emotional reactions and perform irrational actions.

Resistance phase. This is the second of three stages of Hans Selye's general adaptation syndrome of the body's reaction to an environmental stressor(s). During this phase, the body is actively coping with a stressor. For example, white corpuscles might be sent to the site of an infection in order to combat invading bacteria. If this stage is unsuccessful, it is followed by a third stage, referred to as exhaustion. See also: **exhaustion; general adaptation syndrome.**

Resolution stage. The stage of the sexual response that follows orgasm. Here, the body settles back into its normal (unaroused) state. Men enter a refractory period (in which sexual arousal is not possible) at the onset of the resolution stage.

Resonance disorders. Structural or functional disturbances of the vocal equipment such that the resonance and tone of the voice is affected. These problems may involve a head cold, a cleft palate, a nasal obstruction that may lead to either hypo- or hypernasality of the tone of voice. See also: **phonatory disorders.**

Resonance (rez′ə nəns) **theory of hearing.** See: **place-resonance theory of hearing.**

Response chunking. The combining of the sensorimotor programs for individual responses into more complex programs for skillful motor patterns. The concept of chunking was introduced in the study of the memory of verbal items, but it is equally valid for the procedural memory of motor skills.

Resting potential. The voltage difference between the outer and inner surfaces of the axon membrane that prevails when no impulse occurs. Typically, the exterior (the extracellular fluid) is 70 millivolts positive relative to the interior (the axoplasm). The resting potential represents the potential energy stored up, available for use during the passage of a nerve impulse down the axon.

Restless legs. A variety of insomnia in which the inability to relax the legs is the main problem in keeping the person awake.

Retention. The aspect of memory involving storage of learned information. Retention can be considered the opposite of forgetting.

Reticular (ri tik′yoo lər) **formation.** A patchwork of gray and white matter found throughout the brain stem, that is, the medulla, pons, and midbrain. The midbrain portion of this formation is called the ascending reticular arousal system. Some nuclei within the pons portion of the reticular formation help regulate the waking-sleeping-dreaming cycle.

Retina. The third coating of the eyeball just inside the second coat, the choroid. The retina contains light-sensitive chemicals, which are found in the endings of two types of receptor cells, the rods and the cones. The rods and the cones are our primary visual receptors.

Retinal (ret′n əl). One of the components of a visual pigment in the rods or the cones. It is added to an opsin, which gives the pigment its functional characteristic and enables it to be broadly receptive (rhodopsin), sensitive to red light (erythrolabe), sensitive to green light (chlorolabe), or sensitive to blue light (cyanolabe). It is the 11-cis-retinal form that adds to the opsin. When light decomposes the pigment, the pigment breaks down into all-trans-retinal and opsin. Unfortunately, the all-trans-retinal form cannot combine with the opsin again. We must consume more vitamin A to reconstitute the visual pigments. The ending "-al" indicates that retinal is a kind of chemical compound called an aldehyde. See also: **opsin; retinol.**

Retinal disparity (also called **binocular parallax** or **binocular disparity**). The fact that the two eyes receive slightly different visual images accounts for much of our ability to judge distances in depth (the front-to-back dimension), even though the retinal image is only a two-dimensional (up-down and left-right) one. Alternately wink either eye. In the case of a solid (three-dimensional) object situated to one side, you may see around the object with one eye, but not the other. This enables you to be quite confident that the thing is solid and not flat, despite its two-dimensional retinal image. See also: **depth perception.**

Retinal ganglion cells. See: **ganglion cells.**

Retinal perimetry. The testing of the peripheral boundaries of the retinal areas capable of recognizing a particular color. This has been extended in optometry to include the measurement of light sensitivity throughout the retina. This testing may be kinetic (a hand moves the stimulus in and out of range), or static (a machine automatically delivers the stimulus).

Retinene (ret′n ēn, -in). See: **retinal.**

Retinex (ret′n eks) **theory of color.** This is a theory of color vision developed by Land (of Polaroid Land camera fame). The retinex theory proposes that color is perceived through an interactive effect of retinal and cortical activities. Wavelengths of light are compared in the cerebral cortex and from that processing a determination is made for the color(s) perceived. See also: **color vision; opponent-process theory of color vision; trichromatic theory of color vision**.

Retinohypothalamic (ret'n ō hī″pō thə lam'ik) **tract**. The set of axons running from some retinal ganglion cells to the suprachiasmatic nucleus of the hypothalamus. See also: **ganglion cells; suprachiasmatic nucleus.**

Retinol (ret'n ôl). Vitamin A. This vitamin is used in the metabolic buildup of the visual pigments in the retina. The "-ol" at the end indicates that the compound is a kind of alcohol (having an -OH group). See also: **opsin; retinal.**

Retinopathy of prematurity (ROP). A visual problem affecting premature infants who weigh less than 3 pounds at birth. An abnormal growth of blood vessels within the eyeball leads to bleeding and scarring on the retinal surface. In most cases these vessels degenerate and the eye heals completely by the time the baby is 1 year old. Some victims may have lazy eye or myopia. In the most severe cases, a detached retina may result. The term "retinopathy of prematurity" has replaced an earlier one, "retrolental fibroplasia."

Retinotopic arrangement. The correspondence between the light-dark pattern on the retina and the pattern of active and resting neurons in the visual cortex. The latter is often referred to as a "map" of the retina. As many as 16 such maps have been found in the brain, with each map being used for a different aspect of visual perception.

Retrieval. That aspect of memory involving gaining access to stored memories and expressing them in speech or in other actions, such as writing or pointing.

Retrieval failure. A type of memory failure which occurs when relevant retrieval cues are not present. One might forget the name of a teacher at home (retrieval failure) but suddenly remember the teacher's name if driving by the school where the teacher works.

Retrograde amnesia (ret'rō grād am nē'zhə). Literally, backward-going loss of memory. There is a forgetting of events that occurred prior to

brain damage. A head injury is often followed by retrograde amnesia. This form of amnesia is also one of the symptoms in Korsakoff's syndrome.

Retrograde axonal (ret'rō grād ak'sən l, ak son'l, ak sō'nəl) **transport**. The transporting of materials along the axon in the reverse of the usual direction. In retrograde transport, bits of presynaptic membrane are sent from the terminal boutons back to the cell body. See also: **axonal transport.**

Retrograde (ret'rō grād) **degeneration**. A phenomenon of spreading destruction following the cutting of an axon. Degeneration of both the axon proper and the myelin sheath (if present) occurs following the cut. The destruction moves gradually (1) toward the cell body and (2) toward the end brush. The degenerative changes that occur in the direction toward the cell body are called retrograde degeneration. In the central nervous system, retrograde degeneration continues unchecked until the cell body itself is involved and the entire neuron is destroyed. In the peripheral nervous system, the retrograde degeneration travels for a few internodes in the direction of the cell body but then stops, after which regeneration begins. See also: **Wallerian degeneration.**

Retrograde transneuronal degeneration. The degeneration of a neuron whose axon terminals contact only degenerated neurons at their synapses. The neuron dies "because", in anthropomorphic terms, "it has no further reason for living."

Retrolental fibroplasia (ret″rō len'təl fī″brō plā'zhə, -zē ə). A condition, seen in premature infants, in which an opaque fibrous membrane covers the posterior side of the lens of the eye. It is not necessarily the result of excessive oxygen, as had been thought until recently. "Retrolental fibroplasia" is an obsolete term, as the condition is now regarded as a type of retinopathy of prematurity. See also: **retinopathy of prematurity**.

Return sweep. A smooth, quick right-to-left-eye movement from the end of one line of print to the start of the next.

Reuptake. The deactivation of a neurotransmitter in the synapse after it has transmitted the message may occur in several ways, one of which is reuptake. In this case, the transmitter crosses the presynaptic membrane, going back into the axon terminal that earlier had released it. It later is transported back into a synaptic vesicle for use when the next nerve impulse reaches that axon terminal.

Reverse staircase. A continuous series of backward saccades (regressions) and fixations. See also: **erratic eye movements; staircase.**

Reverse tolerance. The increase in sensitivity to a psychoactive drug after having ingested the drug. It therefore takes less and less of the drug to produce the same effect. An example of a drug having such an action is marijuana.

Rey-Osterrieth Complex Figure Test. A test of visuospatial ability involving the memory of, and the re-drawing of, complex formal patterns. The Rey test is sometimes used in a neuropsychological test battery.

Rheobase (rē′ō bās). A type of threshold value, the rheobase is that strength of electric current needed to excite a nerve impulse when the stimulus is left on for an unlimited time (in other words, the duration of the electrical pulse is equal to infinity). Of course, for shorter times, the required current strength has to be greater than the rheobase. See also: **chronaxie; strength-duration curve.**

Rheumatic (roo mat′ik) **fever**. A disease usually attacking children after they have been infected by streptococcus bacteria. Symptoms include joint pain, fever, and frequently heart disease that may take the form of myocarditis, endocarditis, or pericarditis (inflammation of the heart wall, inflammation of the interior heart lining, and inflammation of the membrane surrounding the heart, respectively). The individual may have to be on antibiotics for an indefinite period.

Rheumatoid arthritis (roo′mə toid ärth rī′tis). The most common form of arthritis in school-age children. Symptoms include aching in the joints, stiffness, and fatigue. Treatment with steroid hormones may produce side effects that are worse than those of the disease.

Rh genes. A set of eight alleles of the gene for Rh blood type. Four of the alleles lead to an Rh negative type and four to an Rh positive type.

Rh incompatibility. A fetal condition that occurs when the mother has Rh-negative blood while the fetus has Rh-positive blood. The mother develops antibodies that attack the fetus, often resulting in partial or complete deafness. In many cases, athetosis (a movement disorder) develops. See also: **athetosis**.

Rhinencephalon (rī″nen sef′ə lon) (from Greek "rhin" = "nose"; "encephalon" = "brain"). A part of the forebrain. It includes the olfactory bulbs, which receive the olfactory nerves from the nose, as well as areas of the "old cortex" to which the olfactory bulbs send axons. In humans, however, what were once the higher parts of the olfactory system have become areas concerned with emotion. Directly emerging from the olfactory bulb is the olfactory tract. From then on, though, the parts of the rhinencephalon may be more concerned with feelings than smells. They include the anterior perforated substance, the pyriform area, the hippocampus, the fornix, and so on. The rhinencephalon, then, includes most of the telencephalon's limbic system.

Rhodopsin (rō dop′sin). The photopigment of the rods which is highly sensitive to light, in comparison with the somewhat less sensitive (and more selective) photopigments of the cones. See also: **photopigments; rods.**

Rigidity cerebral palsy. A form of cerebral palsy in which there is muscular hypertonicity producing such extreme stiffness that voluntary activity is impeded. See also: **cerebral palsy; hypertonicity**.

Rods. Visual receptor cells found in the retina. They are sensitive to faint light and can yield information about shades of gray, but not information about color.

Rooting reflex. The newborn infant's reflexive turning of its head toward an object touching its cheek. Directly after this, the neonate's mouth makes grasping movements. This reflex prepares the neonate to seek and take in milk from the mother's breasts.

Rostral (ros′trəl) (from the Latin "rostrum," the prow or beak of a ship). Toward the head of a biped or quadruped. A synonym is "cranial," toward the head. The antonym is "caudal." In a biped, where the head is above the rest of the body, "rostral" is synonymous with "superior," but in a quadruped, where the head is in front of other body parts, "rostral" means the same thing as "anterior." There is, however, a special exception for the human (two-legged) creature's brain. Since the central nervous system bends forward sharply where the spinal cord merges with the brain, the human brain is oriented the same way as is the four-footed creature's brain. Thus in all animals, vision and smell monitor the world directly in front of the organism. As a result, for the human brain, "rostral" is the same as "anterior."

Rotary pursuit task. A task assigned to a human subject, possibly in a neuropsychological examination. The subject is required to hold a rod (called a stylus) on a small circle marked out on a turntable. The turntable is rotated at a speed of 72 revolutions per minute and the number of times the subject's stylus slips off the disk is recorded automatically. Time-on-target is another available measure, with an electrical timer connected to the circuitry. Patients with bilateral damage to the hippocampus can improve at this task but fail to recall having practiced it. This is because the damage to the hippocampus prevents short-term memories from consolidating into long-term memories, when they are episodic memories. But the learning of skills is not prevented by injury to the hippocampus -- it is procedural memory. See also: **consolidation; episodic memories; hippocampus; long-term memory; procedural memory; short-term memory.**

Round window. The membrane between the inner ear and the middle ear that permits the fluid pressures within the cochlear canals to be absorbed. The round window is located just below the oval window, which admits sound waves into the cochlear canals from the ossicles of the middle ear. See also: **cochlea; inner ear; middle ear; ossicles; outer ear; oval window.**

Rubella (roo bel′ə) or **German measles**. A viral disease communicated from person to person. If a pregnant woman is infected, there is a high probability that the infant will have severe disabilities, one of which can be impaired vision.

Ruffini corpuscle. A type of encapsulated sensory receptor for the sense of touch, in the dendritic zone of some of the unipolar afferent neurons. This receptor is especially useful during sustained, long-lasting tactile stimulation.

S

Saccade (sə käd′). A quick, jerky movement of the eyes used to inspect a row of fixed visual stimuli such as letters in a line of print. The lowest time of fixation (stoppage of movement between saccades) is 0.25 second.

Saccharin elation effect. A phenomenon observed in non-deprived experimental rats that have been given access to saccharin-sweetened water. After the saccharin-flavored water has been made unavailable, the rats display an even greater preference for saccharin-flavored water over tap water than earlier when the sweetened water is once again available.

Saccule (sak′yŏŏl). The otolith organ (for the sense of balance in the inner ear) that monitors up-and-down linear accelerations. The mnemonic word "huvs" allows us to remember which otolith organ goes with which direction: "horizontal-utricle; vertical-saccule." See also: **labyrinthine sense organs; otolith organs; utricle.**

Sacral (sā′krəl, sak′rəl). Pertaining to the sacrum, which is the second lowest of the vertebrae. There are five pairs of sacral spinal nerves, which emerge from five sacral segments of the spinal cord. See also: **sacrum; spinal cord; spinal nerves.**

Sacrum (sā′krum, sak′rum). The second-lowest of the vertebrae, the bones of the spine. Because it is the outcome of a fusion of five vertebrae in the evolutionary history of the species, the sacrum is quite long for a single vertebra. See also: **sacral; spinal cord; spinal nerves.**

Sadomasochism (sā″dō mas′ə kiz″əm, -maz′-, sad″ō-). The pathological desire to obtain sexual gratification through aggressive, harmful, and pain-causing behaviors. In sadism, there is a desire to inflict physical restraint and pain on one's sexual partners. In masochism, there is a desire to receive pain from and be physically restrained by one's sexual partners. Some individuals exhibit both these tendencies.

Sagittal (saj′i təl). One of the three planes of reference for microtomic sectioning of central nervous system tissue, which is done to prepare microscope slides. Each of these planes is perpendicular to the other two. The word "sagitta" means "arrow" in Latin. It refers to the long, thin look of an arrow. The sagittal section divides an organism into left and right parts. A midsagittal cut precisely down the middle, splitting the body into left and right halves, is in the midsagittal or median plane. This cutting plane allows an observer to have a full view of the tissue from the side. The sagittal plane can never be cross-sectional, regardless of whether the sectioned organism is a two-legged (bipedal) animal or a four-legged (quadrupedal) one. In the case of a two-legged creature, a properly wielded, well-sharpened tomahawk could provide such a cut. See also: **planes of sectioning; medial.**

Saint Vitus' (vī′təs iz) **dance**. See: Sydenham's chorea.

Salicylate. The fever-reducing (i.e., antipyretic) component of aspirin.

Saltatory (sal′tə tôr″ē) **propagation** (from Latin "saltus" = 'leap"). The way in which a nerve impulse spreads down the axon when that axon is covered by a myelin sheath. In an ordinary nerve impulse traveling down an unmyelinated axon, the exchange of cations $Na+$ (the sodium ion entering the axon) and $K+$ (the potassium ion leaving the axon) occurs at every little step down the axon. Myelin, being a lipid, blocks the passage of the cations, except where the myelin sheath is very thin, namely, at the nodes. Ion exchanges, therefore, occur only at successive nodes (which are a millimeter apart, and that is a relatively long distance), allowing the impulse to get all the way to the axon terminal in the same time that it would travel a much shorter distance along an unmyelinated axon.

Sample. The subset of the population of measurements that has actually been studied. All the members of a population may not be available due to the limitations of cost and time. In research, the scientist attempts to obtain a representative sample, that is, a sample that, when measured, yields data similar to those that would have been obtained from the whole population. See also: **inferential statistics; population; representative sample.**

Saralasin. A chemical that acts as a blocking agent on angiotensin II receptors. See also: **angiotensin II; receptor sites.**

Saturation. The vividness of a color. This is a subjective perception that is correlated with the uniformity of the light waves entering the eye. If only one wavelength is involved, the color will be extremely pure (i.e., highly saturated). If other wavelengths are mixed in, the purity of the color will be reduced. An example of poor saturation is the color pink, which results from an admixture of so many wavelengths to the red wavelength that the color impression is shifted toward white. White, in turn, is the color experience obtained from a combination of all the wavelengths. See also: additive color mixing.

Scapegoat. An individual (or group) who is habitually selected as the target of displaced aggression.

Scatter diagram or **scatter plot**. A graph representing the scores of a group of persons, for example, on each of two behavioral measures, such as grade point average and IQ. One of the measures is represented along the abscissa (the X-axis, or horizontal baseline); the other is mapped by the ordinate (the Y-axis or vertical dimension). Points are plotted according to each person's two scores, so that each point represents the results obtained from one person. If the points tend to group themselves in linear fashion, a strong correlation between the two behavioral variables is indicated. If high scores on one variable tend to go with high scores on the other, it would be a positive correlation. If high scores on one variable tend to occur along with low scores on the other, the correlation is negative. If the points do not form a linear array, but are scattered widely all over the space between the X and Y axes, the correlation approaches zero, that is, there is little or no correlation (either positive or negative) between the two behavioral measures. See also: **correlation.**

Scatter plot. See: **scatter diagram.**

Schedule-induced polydipsia. A feeding schedule of one food pellet every minute leads to an experimental subject consuming large amounts of water between pellet deliveries.

Schedules of reinforcement. Rules for determining the delivery or administration of a reinforcer. Schedules can be fixed or variable, depending on time factors or numbers of correct responses. The most common schedules are the **fixed interval schedule of reinforcement, and**

variable interval schedule of reinforcement, which are dependent on time factors, and the **fixed ratio schedule of reinforcement** and **variable ratio schedule of reinforcement,** which are dependent on numbers of correct responses (see definitions).

Schema (skē'mə) (plural, "schemata" (skē mä' tə) or **scheme**. A generalized idea about persons, events, or objects that are encountered more than once. For example, you have a schema of what a birthday party should be that would include birthday presents, singing, a cake with candles, and so on. Schemas help us to organize our long-term memories. A schema is a conceptual framework for organizing information.

Schizoid (skit'soid ʺ) **personality disorder**. A person with this disorder tends to be unresponsive, "cold," aloof and withdrawn, preferring isolation to bonding with people. These individuals often lack humor.

Schizophrenia (skit ʺsə frē'nē ə, -fren'ē ə) (from Greek "schiz" = "split"; "phrenia" = "mind"). A severe mental/emotional disorder that qualifies as a psychosis in that the patient's beliefs are delusional (not in contact with reality) and many of the patient's perceptions are hallucinations (false perceptions unrelated to sensory events). Depending on the specific type of schizophrenia, the patient may indulge in silly actions and talk gibberish, may be prone to commit acts of aggression against other people, or may show catatonic postural aberrations. The positive symptoms of schizophrenia are those that are more overt and more likely to have an impact on others. The negative symptoms include withdrawal and unresponsiveness. Schizophrenia should not be confused with the dissociational neurosis known as **multiple personality disorder** (see definition). Schizophrenia is a young person's psychosis, setting in before the age of 45; once established, the condition will last at least 6 months. Currently the drug clozapine is recommended as one that counteracts the positive symptoms of schizophrenia. Clozapine does not involve a risk of inducing the motor disorder tardive dyskinesia, which may result from the regular use of chlorpromazine or haloperidol. Like the other two drugs, clozapine is an antagonist of the neurotransmitter dopamine, which is believed to be overly active in the forebrain of schizophrenics. The clozapine treatment can be a costly one, as weekly blood tests are necessary. There is also a risk of the patients incurring the blood disease agranulocytosis; this is a life-threatening condition involving a low count of white blood cells. See also: **accumbens; antagonist; chlorpromazine; clozapine; dopamine; haloperidol; neuroleptic drug; tardive dyskinesia.**

Schizophrenics (skit″sə fren′iks). Studies of the brains of schizophrenics have yielded several facts about how they differ from the brains of normal persons. For one thing, the lateral ventricles take up much more space within the telencephalon of the schizophrenic brain, leaving less volume to be filled by the neurons of the cerebral cortex. Again, the schizophrenic brain has an unusually high number of receptor sites for the neurotransmitter dopamine (consistent with the dopamine theory of schizophrenia). Recent magnetic resonance imaging (MRI) studies have shown that the volume of gray matter in three specific regions of the left temporal lobe is reduced significantly (by from 13% to 19%). See also: **cerebral cortex; cerebral ventricles; dopamine hypothesis; MRI; receptor sites; schizophrenia; telencephalon; temporal lobe.**

Schizotypal (skit″sō tī ′pəl) **personality disorder**. A personality disorder not severe enough to be labeled schizophrenic but with very similar symptoms, including eccentricities in thought, speech, and perception, as well as abnormal fantasies and bizarre delusions.

School phobia. Intense fear on the part of a child of any aspect of the school environment--teachers, classrooms, peers, and so on. The child may develop psychosomatic symptoms when it is time to go to school. See also: **phobias; psychosomatic disorders.**

School psychology. A specialty of applied psychology that deals with the measurement and treatment of academic or emotional/behavioral problems of children in school.

Schwann (shwän) **cells**. The neuroglia of the peripheral nervous system. The Schwann cell is one internode in length (about 1 millimeter), and these cells lock into one another (i.e., they interdigitate, like the fingers when one folds the hands), forming the neurilemma sheath. In some cases, the Schwann cells roll themselves around an axon, producing layers of Schwann cell membrane, Schwann cell cytoplasm, and extracellular fluid. In this way, a myelin sheath is formed. If the peripheral neuron does have a myelin sheath, the neurilemma sheath composed of interdigitated Schwann cells is outside of the myelin sheath. After an axon is damaged, Schwann cells multiply. Some break free of the neurilemma and become freely moving phagocytes, clearing up the chemically degenerated nerve and myelin remnants. The empty neurilemma sheaths serve as tunnels, guiding the regenerating axons back along the way to their pre-injury terminals. See also: **neurilemma; neuroglia; retrograde degeneration; Wallerian degeneration.**

Sclera (sklēr′ə). The tough, white membrane surrounding the eyeball.

Scoliosis (skō″lē ō′sis). An S-shaped curvature of the spine due to weakness of the trunk muscles. It may be corrected with a brace or surgery.

Scopolamine (skō pol′ə mēn ″). A depressant drug familiarly known as "truth serum" due to its use in law enforcement to elicit confessions from suspects. Scopolamine blocks acetylcholine synapses and also interferes with memory.

Scotoma (skə tō′mə)(from Greek "skotoma" = "darkening"). A blind spot in the visual field observed in individuals who have suffered lesions of the primary visual cortex. The area of the blind spot would ordinarily be part of the receptive field of the now-missing occipital lobe neurons. The individual performs a compensatory "filling-in" of the missing part of the visual field; this phenomenon is called "completion." See also: **blind spot; completion; primary visual cortex; occipital lobe.**

Scotopic (skō top′ik) (from Greek "scot" = "dark"; "opic" refers to vision). The type of vision that is characteristic of the rods and that results from the breakdown of the rod photopigment rhodopsin in the presence of light. Scotopic vision is typically night vision; the photopic (daylight) vision of the cones dominates the way we see under high illumination. See also: **photopic; photopigment; rhodopsin; rods.**

Scotopic (skō top′ik) **sensitivity syndrome (SSS)**. This is Helen Irlen's conception of a dyslexic's underlying problem, that is, a painful sensitivity to light and difficulties perceiving certain wavelengths and black-white contrast. This diagnosis is often given to dyslexic children by practitioners of the Irlen Institute. Children with SSS are given colored lenses, which are claimed to alleviate this reading problem.

Scratch reflex. A reflexive alternate extension and flexion of a limb in response to an irritating stimulus applied to the skin. This reflex has the properties of an oscillator, because its rhythmic pace is controlled by the network of neurons in a nearby part of the spinal cord, rather than by the properties of the irritant. See also: **oscillator.**

Screening. The testing of a large number of people with a fast and easy test. The idea is to look for indications of which few of those being tested are at risk for a learning disability. Those who are identified as being at risk can be given more thorough and precise examination to determine the nature of the problem, its severity, and the most advisable therapeutic/instructional approach for each at-risk individual.

Scrotum. The double sac holding the male gonads, the testes. The descent of the scrotum (its leaving the abdominal cavity and appearing on the body's exterior) is one of the events marking the arrival of puberty in the human male. See also: **puberty.**

Seasonal affective disorder (SAD). A type of depression which returns every winter.

Secondary drives. More commonly known as psychogenic motives in modern psychology. Secondary drives do not, like primary drives, correspond to definite biological needs. For example, the primary drive of hunger corresponds to the body's need for food. It is questionable whether the word "drive" is appropriate for psychogenic motives, such as a need for obtaining additional real estate. The word "secondary" (implying that these psychogenic motives are based on learning) is a reasonable one.

Secondary erectile (i rek'til, -tīl) **dysfunction.** A temporary inability in a male to achieve or maintain an erection of the penis. The criterion for the diagnosis is that the failure happens in at least one-fourth of the attempts. See also: **primary erectile dysfunction.**

Secondary orgasmic (ôr gaz'mik) **dysfunction** or **situational orgasmic dysfunction.** A temporary

inability in a female to achieve orgasm, or her need to make particular responses in order to be able to have an orgasm. It is considered "temporary" if she has experienced orgasm at some time in the past. See also: **primary orgasmic dysfunction.**

Secondary punisher or **conditioned aversive stimulus.** A stimulus that is neutral in relation to an operant response made by an organism but, through pairing with an aversive stimulus, acquires punishment value. This is demonstrated when the stimulus is presented directly after the response is emitted and the result is a decrease in the rate of responding; that is, a lowered probability of emitting the operant has occurred. See also: **aversive conditioning; punishment.**

Secondary reinforcer or **conditioned reinforcer.** A stimulus that was originally non-rewarding but, after having been presented (to the behaving organism) just prior to a primary reinforcer during operant conditioning, is now able to reinforce an operant response when presented by itself. This ability to reinforce a response is demonstrated by an increase in the rate of responding by the organism. The classical example of a secondary reinforcer is the click of an automatic feeding device after a rat presses a lever projecting from the wall of a Skinner box. When the rat has been conditioned to press the lever at a high rate, the feeder is emptied but still plugged in. The animal's lever-pressing will be extinguished much more slowly than if the automatic feeder had been unplugged. The more rapid extinction in the case of the unplugged feeder demonstrates the power of the click to sustain responding, that is, to maintain an increased rate, when the primary reinforcer (the food pellet) is not provided. See also: **extinction; operant conditioning.**

Secondary sensory cortex. That cortical area (in each of several sensory neural pathways) that receives inputs from the corresponding primary sensory cortex, but is not targetted by axons from the pathways of the other senses. The primary sensory areas are those areas that serve as terminals for the sensory pathways from lower brain areas and, ultimately, from the sense organs at the beginnings of those pathways.

Secondary sex characteristics. Features not including the actual organs of reproduction that are typical of the members of either of the sexes.

Male secondary characteristics, e.g., include a deep voice and facial hair.

Secondary somatosensory area. The secondary sensory area for the somesthetic senses in which touch-related memories may be stored. It is situated at the ventral end of the primary somatosensory area, i.e., at the base of the postcentral gyrus. See also: **parietal lobe; somesthesis.**

Second messenger. A chemical in a postsynaptic neuron that, when activated, alters the permeability of the cell's membrane to sodium, potassium, or chloride ions. The excitatory or inhibitory effect is slower than that of a neurotransmitter, but it is longer-lasting. Examples of such chemicals are cyclic AMP and phosphoinositide. Neuromodulators usually are the factors that get the second messenger into action. See also: **cyclic AMP; neuromodulator; phosphoinositide.**

Secretin (si krē′tin). A hormone involved in the process of digestion.

Sedatives or **hypnotics**. Depressive drugs that produce calm and relaxation; in larger doses sedatives/hypnotics produce sleep. See also: **barbiturates; opiates.**

Seeing-Eye Dogs. See: **Guide dogs.**

Seizure. An impairment of consciousness which may or may not involve disruption of muscular control. See also: **epilepsy; grand mal seizure; petit mal seizure.**

Selective attention. The perception of a very few stimuli among the whole complex of environmental stimuli affecting the senses at the same time. This selective process is aided by such stimulus factors as loudness and brightness and such personal factors as reference to oneself and/or one's associates. This process helps preserve a small part of the information in the sensory store for retention in the short-term memory. Disorders in the selective attention process are involved in the psychosis called schizophrenia.

Self-concept. The set of beliefs a person holds about his or her own nature.

Self-efficacy. A set of personal beliefs about one's own ability to plan and carry out actions to attain one's goals.

Self-monitoring. The process of checking one's own behavior by recording the frequency and duration of the various responses one makes. This practice allows one to modify one's own activities as needed in order to present a good appearance in social situations.

Self-perception. A set of beliefs and attitudes about oneself that is partly the product of other people's attitudes toward the individual.

Self-reference effect. Relating environmental stimuli and events to one's own frame of reference. This has been shown to be the most effective way to store information in long-term memory. For example, you might remember a friend's birthday more if it is close in time to your own.

Self-report measures. A research technique that involves asking people questions about some of their own behaviors.

Self-stimulation of the brain. The reinforcement of a conditioned operant response (such as pressing a lever in a Skinner box) by the delivery (via a chronically embedded electrode) of an electrical stimulus to one of the "pleasure areas" of the brain. The medial forebrain bundle, the septum, and some of the nuclei in the hypothalamus have been found to be such areas. See also: **medial forebrain bundle; operant conditioning; positive reinforcement.**

Self-stimulatory behaviors. Bizarre activities seemingly unrelated to the external environment, such as mouthing, biting, or licking parts of one's own body; intense scratching; banging one's head against solid objects; rocking back and forth; and so on. Requests to stop doing these things are usually futile. Profoundly retarded children may demonstrate some of these behaviors. Autistic children may also exhibit them. See also: **autism; profound mental retardation**.

Semantic memory. A part of long-term memory that is extremely stable, semantic memory is the storage of information about general facts and rules belonging to the world, to mathematics, to the language, and so on. This kind of memory is not tied to facts about one's own personal life story.

Semantics (si man′tiks). The study of word meanings and the types of definition a word may have, viz., denotation or connotation.

Semicircular canals. Part of the vestibular sense organ in the inner ear, the three semicircular canals monitor the rotation of the head. Each semicircular canal is positioned in a plane that is at right angles to the planes of the two others.

One semicircular canal is responsive to rotary acceleration in the front-to-back plane, another to rotary acceleration in the right-to-left plane, and the third to horizontal rotations. See also: **labyrinthine sense organs; otolith organs; vestibular senses.**

Seminal vesicles. Two small sacs in males, situated posterior to the bladder. Each seminal vesicle is connected to a vas deferens, which carries seminal fluid, i.e., the sperm, to the penis for ejaculation. In the vesicles, the sperm is stored while awaiting ejaculation.

Senility. A general term for the disabilities of aging, including loss of memory and confused perceptions. This term is becoming obsolete, because such problems seem to be related to specific diseases that are more likely to affect older persons than younger ones. These diseases include **Alzheimer's disease, Pick's disease** and **Creutzfeldt-Jakob disease** (see definitions). See also: **gerontology.**

Sensation. The raw experience of a sensory stimulus (e.g., an auditory tone, visual flickering lights, or the heat of a hot-water bottle). Sensory experiences generally last less than 1 second and then higher-order cognitive processes become involved for stimulus interpretation.

Sensitive period. A time during the early development of an organism during which major permanent changes can occur. This term is sometimes used as a substitute for "critical period," with the implication that the permanence of the developmental change is more relative and less fixed than the word "critical" would imply. See also: **critical period.**

Sensitivity. The ability to detect faint stimuli. In vision, this is a property of those photoreceptor cells known as rods.

Sensitization (sen″si ti zā′shən). The enhancement of an unconditioned reflex by the application of an extra, neutral stimulus to a different sense organ from the one getting the unconditioned stimulation. An example is the sensitization of tail withdrawal in the sea snail Aplysia californica. This takes place when an electric shock is applied to the tail (the unconditioned stimulus). The tail withdrawal response is intensified by adding a mild touch to the animal's mantle at the time the shock is applied to the tail. See also: **Aplysia californica; dishabitua-**tion; habituation; model systems approach.

Sensorineural impairments. Hearing problems which result from problems in the **inner ear** (see definition).

Sensory aphasia. See: **receptive aphasia**; **Wernicke's aphasia.**

Sensory area. The region of the cerebral cortex onto which the nerve impulses for a given sense are projected. The amount of cortical area committed to a sense is only partially dependent on the size of the sense organ projecting to it; another factor is the fineness of detail (i.e., the resolution) of the sensory information required for the organism's behavior. For example, the cortical region representing touch sensations from a mouse's whiskers is unusually large; this is also true for the area covering touch sensations from a pig's snout and for the area covering auditory sensations in the cerebral cortex of the bat. In primates, visual areas take in the entire occipital lobe as well as some of the neighboring areas in the temporal and parietal lobes.

Sensory deprivation. The condition of being denied normal levels of stimulation to the sense organs. A volunteer subject may be blindfolded, given earplugs, required to wear gloves, have cardboard cuffs on the forearms that extend past the fingertips, and required to remain lying down on a cot in an enclosed space with the only sound being the noise of the air-conditioner. Research on this subject was originally stimulated by reports that the Chinese Communists were "brainwashing" American prisoners during the Korean war. See also: **brainwashing.**

Sensory evoked potential. A voltage change observed in the EEG (electroencephalogram) immediately following the delivery of a sensory stimulus to the subject. See also: **average evoked response.**

Sensory extinction. A tendency (observed in brain-damaged individuals) to respond more strongly and more rapidly to stimuli on the same side of the body as the injury. This is due to the tendency for most information channels (both sensory and motor) between the brain and the rest of the body to be crossed (i.e., contralateral). See also: **unilateral neglect.**

Sensory feedback. Response-produced sensations that are used to control further responses. See also: **gamma efferents; muscle spindle.**

Sensory memory. The perception of environmental stimuli in raw form before major information processing occurs (less than 2 seconds). Sensory memory allows us to keep an accurate record of environmental stimulation for brief periods of time while we select important or relevant information for further processing. Iconic (visual) memory (up to 1/2 second) is visual sensory memory, and echoic memory (up to 2 seconds) is auditory sensory memory. Sensory memory for touch involves pleasure and pain sensations. In the framework of memory theory, the sensory memories are said to comprise the sensory register or sensory store. The process of selective attention passes a small part of the sensory information on to the short-term memory. See also: **selective attention; short-term memory.**

Sensory neglect. See: **unilateral neglect.**

Sensory neurons. See: **afferent.**

Sensory projection areas. Areas of the cerebral cortex which receive input from sensory nerve pathways after sensory stimulation or sensation. See also: **sensation.**

Sensory register. See: **sensory memory.**

Sensory store. See: **sensory memory.**

Sequencing or **sequential processing**. The cognitive ability to understand a sequence of events and to comprehend the relationships between the first and last events in the sequence. The Digit Span subtest from the WISC-R, which requires the testee to repeat number sequences both forward and backward, is one way to investigate sequencing ability.

Sequencing problems. Some dyslexics display problems in some aspect of letter, word, and narrative sequential processing. Mattis, for example, reported a group of dyslexics with sequencing disorders that involved difficulties with the concepts of before-behind and left-right.

Serial Arm Movements and Copying Test. A neuropsychological test for apraxia. See also: **apraxia.**

Serial model. An information-flow model in which messages can follow only one path.

Serotinergic (ser″ō ti nûr′jik). An adjective referring to axons that release the neurotransmitter serotonin at their terminals. See also: **neurotransmitter; serotonin.**

Serotonin (ser″ə tō′nin) [also called **5-hydroxy-**

tryptamine (hī drok″sē trip′tə mēn″) or **5-HT**]. Serotonin belongs to the indole amine group of chemicals. It is metabolized from the indole amine amino acid known as tryptophan, in two steps, the intermediary product being 5-hydroxytryptophan. Serotonin is largely released from the median raphé of the midbrain and brings on slow-wave (NREM) sleep; it is sometimes called the sleep hormone. The hallucinogen LSD is also an indole amine; the hallucinations may be due to a combination of two types of interactions between LSD and the serotonin receptor sites. Namely, LSD may block some serotonin receptor sites, denying them to serotonin molecules, and it may mimic serotonin at other receptor sites. The result would be night dreams while being awake, hence, the hallucinations. See also: **5-hydroxytryptophan; indole amines; slow-wave sleep; tryptophan.**

Set point. The particular level at which homeostatic functioning maintains some biological variable in an individual. For example, according to the set point theory of hunger and satiation, an individual maintains weight at a given value, the set point, and one's eating behavior is prevented from allowing one's weight to deviate very much from that value.

Severely emotionally disturbed. A condition primarily involving severe cognitive and/or behavioral disturbances very probably comp-licated by physical and/or sensory disabilities. Such a child requires extra remedial/ psychological services in comparison to mildly or moderately disabled children.

Severe mental retardation. Mental retardation indicated by measured IQ in the 25-39 range, with the individual being unable to live independently.

Sex chromosome abnormalities. The most common deviations from the normal set of two X chromosomes for females and one X and one Y chromosome for males are the XXY in males (Klinefelter's syndrome), the XYY in males, the X0 (just one chromosome) in females (Turner's syndrome), and the XXX in females. See also: **X0; XXX; XXY; XYY.**

Sex differences. It has frequently been reported that, in certain types of learning disabilities, males outnumber females in prevalence distribution ratios of 3:1 to 5:1. Reasons for this have generally centered on (1) excessive testosterone in male fetuses, (2) less-well-developed left-hemispheric language functioning on the part of males, and (3) greater bihemispheric verbal and spatial processing skills on the part of females. Recent evidence challenges these ratios and suggests that prevalence rates are comparatively equal for both males and females.

Sex-role stereotyping or **sex-typed behavior**. The approval or disapproval of a child's behavior because it matches or fails to match, respectively, an adult's preconceived notions of gender-appropriate activity. Sex-role stereotyping can get in the way of a little girl's aspirations to become an astronaut, for example. See also: **gender roles**.

Sexual deviation. Any type of sexual activity involving one or more of the following: (1) having intercourse with a nonconsenting partner; (2) being sexually excited by material objects (e.g., shoes, undergarments, or even dead bodies) in preference to people; (3) requiring oneself or one's sex partner to undergo pain or humiliation.

Sexual dysfunction. An inability to be satisfied by sexual activity; it may be accompanied by erectile dysfunction (in men) or orgasmic dysfunction (in women). Today such words as "impotent" and "frigid" are not used by most therapists because of their negative and sweeping implications. See also: **erectile disorder; female sexual arousal disorder; primary erectile dysfunction; primary orgasmic dysfunction; secondary erectile dysfunction; secondary orgasmic dysfunction**.

Sexually dimorphic nuclei. Two nuclei (collections of nerve-cell bodies) located in the preoptic area of the hypothalamus that are larger in size among males than among females. See also: **preoptic area; hypothalamus.**

Sexually transmitted disease (STD). A disease transmitted by sexual contact. Examples include AIDS, chlamydia, genital herpes, gonorrhea, hepatitis B, and syphilis. The infecting agent (whether bacterium or virus) requires the moist medium of seminal fluid or blood: this agent cannot survive in dry air. For this reason, some STDs can be spread by the use of contaminated hypodermic needles as well as by sexual congress. Behaviors that present a serious risk of contagion are: (1) sharing drug needles and sy-

ringes; (2) anal sex, with or without a condom; (3) vaginal oral sex with a partner who takes drugs intravenously or practices anal sex; (4) sex with unknown partners; and (5) unprotected sex. Safe alternatives include: (1) abstention from sex; (2) having sex with one, known partner; (3) having protected sex; and (4) refusing to get involved with drugs.

Sexual selection. Individuals who leave many offspring are those who are most likely to pass their own traits on to future generations. Evolutionary selection pressure favors those who can ward off competitors and can attract mates more effectively than others of the same species and gender. See also: **natural selection; phylogeny; relative adaptive fitness**.

Shadowing. A research method used with dichotic listening. The subject is required to keep track of the message being delivered into one ear, which requires the ability to avoid being confused by the stream of information sent to the second ear. See also: **dichotic listening.**

Sham drinking. A research technique used on experimental animals in which an opening (called a fistula) is cut into the esophagus, the stomach, or the duodenum. When the animal drinks water, the water escapes from the fistula before it can reach the bloodstream. This ineffective drinking is labeled "sham drinking." See also: **sham feeding.**

Sham feeding. A research technique used on experimental animals in research on hunger and satiation. A fistula (opening) is made in the esophagus or stomach, so that food is lost directly after being eaten and is never digested. This technique is useful in conjunction with another plan, that of using various preloads (i.e., giving various amounts of nutrition to the subject before the sham feeding occurs). Sometimes an animal is tested when preloaded with a good amount of food, sometimes after having been food-deprived for a long time, and so on. See also: **sham drinking.**

Sham lesion. As a control procedure in some experiments in physiological psychology, the experimenter will go through the motions of preparing a control subject for the experimental surgery, including administering anesthesia, providing antibiotics, shaving off the hair, cutting the scalp, opening the skull, perhaps even cutting the dura mater, but then closing the scalp without performing any electrode implantation or brain lesion at all. The intent is to make sure that the cause of postoperative changes in behavior in experimental subjects is the manipulation of the brain and not the necessary (but incidental) procedures that go with it.

Shape constancy. The tendency to view an object as the same shape regardless of the angle or distance from which it is viewed.

Shaping. The way to use operant conditioning in order to train the organism in a new skill. At first, the organism is rewarded when the response is merely a correct orientation or posture. Then, reinforcement is withheld until a performance closer to the desired skill is given. After that improved response has been well practiced, reinforcement is withheld until a still better response is made, and so on. Another term for "shaping" is "successive approximations." The behavior is gradually shaped from an amorphous lump into a precise skill. Skinner described the process of shaping as analogous to the work of a skillful potter shaping a lump of clay.

Sherrington's inhibition. See: **reciprocal inhibition.**

Short-term memory (STM). Information storage for up to 30 seconds at a time. Generally, we can hold about seven items (plus or minus two) in short-term memory. Information is encoded either automatically or through rehearsal strategies and most often is encoded acoustically. For retention for more than a minute or so, the STM has to be converted to long-term memory (LTM). The hippocampus (a structure in the limbic system of the brain) is necessary for the process of consolidation into LTM. The consolidation mechanism has been tentatively identified as long-term potentiation. See **glutamate; hippocampus; long-term memory; long-term potentiation; sensory memory.**

Short-term memory deficit. There is some evidence to show that some dyslexics are slower than proficient readers in retrieving information from short-term memory, and this slowness hampers comprehension of textual material.

Shuttle box. A chamber in which an experimental animal is trained in an active avoidance response. The floor consists of metal grids that can be electrified in order to deliver a painful electric shock to the subject's feet. The floor grid is divided into two parts, so that only one side is electrified at a time. A low hurdle is placed at the division between the two parts of the floor. On a light and/or buzzer signal, the animal can go over the hurdle to avoid the oncoming shock. There are two varieties of shuttle box: (1) The two-way shuttle box uses either grid as a shock grid, so that the well-trained animal runs in alternate directions on consecutive trials. (2) The one-way shuttle box uses only one electrified area and one safe area. Between trials, the experimenter has to return the animal to the shockable side.

Sickle-cell anemia. A genetic disorder in which the red blood corpuscles have shriveled-up, sickle-like shapes. Symptoms include swollen stomach, eye jaundice, poor appetite, and shortened life span. The condition affects 10% of the American black population. Its high prevalence has been explained by its accompanying trait, a strong resistance against malaria. Thus the gene for the sickle-cell trait had survival value in tropical Africa for the ancestors of the individuals who suffer from sickle-cell anemia today.

Signal averaging. A method of clarifying the "real" EEG response (the so-called "signal" in communication theory) by reducing random variability (the "noise", in communication theory). This is done by averaging the results of a number of trials in which the same stimulus is presented to the subject.

Signal detection theory. A system of psychophysics that goes beyond the measurement of sensory thresholds to include the motivational and learned components of perception. The theory permits the manipulation of these nonsensory factors so as to produce a more complete description of the perceiving organism than can be provided by traditional psychophysical methods.

Significance, statistical. See: **statistical significance.**

Signing English. A type of communication approach (especially with individuals with severe hearing impairments) whereby signs are used for the express purpose of language communication. American Sign Language (ASL) is one type of signing English system that can be expressed via a complex set of finger motions. For example, the letter "O" can be finger-spelled by clenching one's fist and shaping the letter "O" with the thumb and first finger. See also: **American Sign Language.**

Simple cell. A kind of feature detector. Neurons in the primary visual cortex (Brodmann's area 17 in the occipital lobe; visual area V1) have linear receptive fields. They best respond to linear visual stimuli (i.e., lines, slots, or edges). The simple cell responds only to a very small part of the visual field; the stimulus must be in that particular place or the neuron will not respond. Furthermore, the line must have the correct slant, the one for which the simple cell is specialized. Some simple cells may respond only to lines at a thirty-degree angle, some only to verticals, and so on. See also: **Brodmann numbering system; feature detectors; occipital lobe; primary visual cortex; receptive field; V1.**

Simple phobia. A neurosis involving a persistent and irrational fear of a given type of object or situation. The most common examples involve animals, for example, fear of snakes. Other examples include such specific fears as those of blood, tissue injuries, closed spaces (claustrophobia), heights (acrophobia), and flying. The intensity of the fear is in direct proportion to the closeness of the patient to the phobic object.

Simple-systems approach. The attempt to clarify the workings of complex learning, memory, and/or other cognitive processes by obtaining basic principles from the examination of simple neural systems. See also: **model systems approach.**

Simultaneous information processing. Refers to our processing perceptual inputs at high and low levels at the same time, using both bottom-up and top-down channels of information flow.

Simultaneous masking. Presenting both the target stimuli and the interfering stimuli at the same time. This requires only a background screen and a single presentation screen, so that the most simple kind of tachistoscope, the one-field tachistoscope, can be used. See also: **masking in visual research; tachistoscope.**

Single-source/divergent circuits. A pattern of neuronal connections in which one neuron sends messages to many receiving neurons. This is also called multiplication of path. See also:

multiplication of path.

Single-unit recording or **single-cell recording.** A recording technique for the study of the brain in which a single neuron is under observation. The use of a microelectrode (an electrode so small that the width of the tip is only 1 micron, one-millionth of a meter) as the recording electrode allows the registration of voltage change in a single neuron (unit). Data from this method do not constitute the average responses of many neurons; it is a necessary technique for learning what individual cells are capable of doing. See also: **recording.**

Sinistral. [1] Pertaining to the left. [2] Favoring the left hand or the left foot, as in left-handedness and left-footedness. [3] Situated on the left side.

Situational causes of behavior. Those causes of behavior that arise from factors in the environment of the behaving organism.

Situational orgasmic (ôr gaz'mik) **dysfunction.** Another name for secondary orgasmic dysfunction, or the inability of a woman to achieve orgasm even though she has had orgasms in the past. See also: **primary orgasmic dysfunction; secondary orgasmic dysfunction.**

Situationism. The theoretical position which holds that our behaviors result solely from external stimulation. See also: **operant conditioning.**

Size constancy. The perception of an object as the same size regardless of the angle or distance from which it is viewed.

Skeletal muscles. Muscles that control movements of body parts in relation to the outer environment. These muscles are usually attached by tendons to the bones, hence the name "skeletal." There is one small exception. The "skeletal" external eye muscles are attached to the eyeballs. See also: **striped muscles.**

Skeletal nervous system. See: **somatic nervous system.**

Skewed distribution. An asymmetrical frequency distribution that is clearly different from the bell-shaped normal curve. In a frequency distribution, the X-axis (abscissa) shows the size of a measurement and the Y-axis (ordinate) shows the number of cases (i.e., the frequency) scoring each value of the measurement. A skewed distribution is asymmetrical, with most of the measurements coming at either the low end of the range of scores or the high end. When a test is too easy to discriminate well between grades of A+, A, and A-, most measurements are chalked up at the right (the higher numbers of the X-axis). Middle and low scores trail downward into a long tail pointing to the left. The type of skew is indicated by the direction in which the single tail points. The example above is negatively-skewed or skewed to the left. These are the same because negative numbers are found to the left of zero. When the test is so hard that it is difficult to sort out who should get grades of E (F), E+ (F+), or D-, with most measures piling up on the left side, there is one long tail pointing to the right, to the higher numbers. In this example, the curve is positively-skewed or skewed to the right. Remember this: the tail points in the direction of skew. In a skewed distribution, the mode is found on the side where most scores occur. The median turns up more toward the middle of the range of scores. Finally, the mean is found almost in the tail; the mean is sensitive to extreme score values, so one very high score can outweigh a number of moderately low scores. All in all, for skewed distributions, the median is the preferred measure of central tendency. See also: **normal curve.**

Skin. The largest sense organ. A six-foot tall person has 21 square feet of skin. The skin serves as a protective covering for our body fluids. It also allows us to maintain body temperature. The cutaneous senses provided by receptors in the skin include pain, warmth, cold, deep pressure, and light touch. The sensitivity of these vary over the different areas of the body. The lips and the fingertips provide the maximum sensitivity to touch stimulation, while the skin of the back provides the lowest sensitivity to touch. See also: **skin senses**.

Skin conductance level (SCL). The steady, background level of skin conductance (electrically, the conductance of a substance is the reciprocal of its electrical resistance) in a given situation. The conductance is measured in units called mhos; electrical resistance is measured in ohms.

Skin conductance response (SCR). A measure (in mho units) of the change in skin conductance as the result of stimulation. See also: **galvanic skin response (GSR); skin conductance level (SCL).**

Skinner box. An apparatus for the conditioning of a simple operant response. For a small mammal such as a rat, an enclosed chamber is provided with a food cup and a movable lever. Pressing the lever results in the delivery of a food pellet to the food cup. The device is named for its inventor, B.F. Skinner.

Skin senses. Senses with receptors in the skin; these include warmth, cold, deep pressure, light touch, and pain. See also: **skin**.

Sleep. A set of behaviors involving relatively little muscular activity and relatively high thresholds for arousal by stimuli from the external environment, consuming about one-third of our daily lives (i.e., 8 hours out of every 24). The two main varieties of sleep are slow-wave sleep and REM sleep. Some researchers credit a rhythmic interplay among three brain stem nuclei [the locus coeruleus (a nucleus in the pons whose cells are norepinephrinergic), the giant-celled nucleus of the pontine reticular formation (nucleus reticularis gigantocellularis), the neurons of which are acetylcholinergic, and the serotoninergic neurons of the midbrain raphé nucleus] with the control of our waking/slow-wave sleep/REM-sleep cycle. Dreaming occurs mainly during REM sleep. We all have dreams; we differ in the ability to recall the dreams we have had. The stages of sleep succeed one another in a 90-minute cycle, at least during the first part of an 8-hour sleep session. When we first fall asleep we go into stage 1 sleep, which is characterized by a low-voltage and high-frequency electro-encephalogram (i.e., fast-wave sleep). The fast waves of stage 1 sleep greatly resemble the beta waves of the waking EEG. Next comes stage 2 sleep, where the stage 1 EEG is interrupted by high negative voltage deflections (called K complexes) and by occasional slower changes between positive and negative voltage (the sleep spindles). Stage 2 sleep is followed in turn by stage 3, during which the stage 2 record is modified by the appearance of delta waves (voltage changes that have the very low-frequency rate of 1/2 to 4 cycles per second). Stage 3 as well as its successor, stage 4, make up slow-wave sleep. Stage 4 sleep is distinguished from stage 3 only by having the delta waves take up 50% or more of the EEG record. After stage 4, the staircase is climbed up instead of descended; the sleeper goes to stage 3, then stage 2, and then stage 1. This second stage 1 has new features, however. The sleeper shows rapid eye movements that may run between up and down, right and left, or a combination. The sleeper also has a nearly total loss of muscle tone in the antigravity muscles. Nevertheless, muscle twitches of the limbs (gross body movements) do take place (due to disinhibition of one member of a pair of antagonistic muscles). Additionally, the autonomic functions become uneven, including more rapid but irregular breathing, a more rapid but irregular pulse, penile and clitoral erection, and so on. Ascending stage 1 sleep is the name assigned to this stage in order to distinguish it from the falling-asleep kind of stage 1, which is called descending stage 1. Ascending stage 1 has also been called paradoxical sleep because the highly active eye movement and EEG seem to be inconsistent with the great relaxation of the striped muscles. Still another name for this stage is the dreaming stage, as most dreams are reported following awakenings from ascending stage 1 sleep. The most common name for this ascending stage 1 type of sleep has become REM sleep. As the night of sleep goes on, the 90-minute cycles start to leave out stage 4 sleep and the extra time is taken up by additional REM sleep. The functional reasons for this temporal pattern remain unknown. The total amount of sleep that a person needs depends on a number of variables, such as life stressors being experienced, personality traits, environmental interference, age, and health. The function of sleep is controversial, as is the more detailed question of the need for both slow-wave sleep and REM sleep. The sleep deprivation of experimental animals has produced enlargement of the adrenal glands, ulcers, and other symptoms of severe stress. See also: **REM sleep; slow-wave sleep; stage 1 sleep (ascending); stage 1 sleep (descending); stage 2 sleep; stage 3 sleep; stage 4 sleep.**

Sleep apnea. See **apnea; sleep; sleep disorders**.

Sleep disorders. Sleep disorders fall into five main categories: (1) disorders of excessive sleep, such as narcolepsy; (2) disorders involving an inability to fall asleep or to maintain sleep, such as insomnia; (3) disorders related to subjective mental/emotional disturbances, such as night-

mares (intense frightening dreams that produce awakening) and night terrors (experiences producing a panic reaction, with attempts to escape and, often, screaming); (4) disorders involving muscular activities that can bring harm to the sleeper or to other people (e.g., sleepwalking); and (5) sleep apnea, which is a lack of breathing during sleep. Apnea, obviously, can be life threatening. The pharynx may collapse during REM sleep, as in obstructive sleep apnea, or a brain disorder may lead to a failure of the respiratory muscles of the ribs and diaphragm to operate properly, as in central sleep apnea. In apnea, there are frequent awakenings forced by oxygen deprivation. The breathing stoppages may last 20 seconds or longer. The individual wakes up just long enough to take in air and goes right back to sleep. This cycle may be repeated hundreds of times a night. The individual may be unaware of the apnea and complain of tiredness throughout the day. Some hypothesize that sleep apnea is the cause of mysterious crib deaths of otherwise healthy babies, sudden infant death syndrome (SIDS). See also: **apnea; narcolepsy; sudden infant death syndrome.**

Sleep spindles. EEG wave forms that appear during Stage 2 sleep. They are made up of brief bursts of 12 to 15 Hz waves, which would make them comparable to very fast alpha or very slow beta waves. See also: **stage 2 sleep; electroencephalogram.**

Sleep-wake schedule disorder. Most often, a job-related problem that forces the individual to accept an altered sleep-wake cycle by having to sleep during the day and work at night.

Slow-twitch muscle. A kind of striped muscle that resists fatigue at the cost of producing less vigorous contractions than other muscles. Slow twitch muscles tend to be red muscles, provided with muscle hemoglobin and fat. The slow-twitch muscles are used in standing or walking. See also: **fast-twitch muscle.**

Slow-wave sleep. A deep type of sleep involving an EEG record of brain activity typified by delta waves which have a frequency of 1/2 to 4 cycles per second. Delta waves are the slowest of all the identified EEG frequency ranges. Sometimes slow-wave sleep is subdivided into stage 3 sleep (during which the EEG shows less than 50% delta waves) and stage 4 sleep (during which more than 50% of the EEG record consists of delta waves). Sleeptalking and sleepwalking occur during delta sleep, because the sleeper is far from waking (i.e., has high arousal thresholds) and has some muscle tone (enabling such activities to take place). Despite the presence of sleepwalking or sleeptalking, we do not tend to report bizarre, irrational dreams after awakening from this form of sleep, although more rational-seeming dream thoughts may be reported. See also: **raphé nuclei; REM sleep; serotonin; sleep.**

Smooth muscle. The kind of muscle lining the visceral organs and blood vessels. The smooth muscles are controlled by the autonomic nervous system. They are formed into sheets rather than spindle-shaped bundles. The smooth muscles do not have the horizontal stripes that have given the name "striate" or "striped" to skeletal muscles. See also: **autonomic nervous system**.

Snellen chart. A chart used to measure visual acuity consisting of rows of letters or E's. Charts using just the letter E contain arrangements of this letter in a variety of positions so that the individual must verbalize or use fingers to show which direction the E is located. Verbal identification of letters is made with Snellen charts using the alphabet. There are eight rows on Snellen charts, each corresponding to distances of 15, 20, 30, 40, 50, 70, 100, and 200 feet. Individuals are usually tested at 20 feet. If a person can distinguish letters in the 20-foot row, he or she is said to have 20/20 central vision in the eye(s) tested.

Social acceptance. The overall level of acceptance by other people of one's persona. Social acceptance is based on many physiological and psychological factors, including one's height, weight, athletic prowess, language skills, familial background, job, and physical attractiveness.

Social aggression. Aggressive acts against another member of the same species, and, almost always, of the same sex. The apparent cause of such aggression is the attempt by the aggressor to move up in the social hierarchy of his or her animal group. See also: **aggression.**

Social cognition. One's social understanding and knowledge of the social environment, including oneself.

Social influences. The environmental influences (e.g., family, peer group, and type of schooling) that affect our social perceptions, attitudes, feelings, cognitions, and behaviors.

Socialization. The process by which children (or adult immigrants) acquire the customs, language, values, and rules of the society to which they belong.

Social maladjustment. Refers to youngsters whose acts may deviate from established societal rules but whose behavior does conform to the rules of their own peer group.

Social-perceptual problems. There are several researchers who have found that dyslexics lack social skills that are largely dependent on one's ability accurately to perceive and interpret social situations and contexts. For example, it has been frequently noted that some dyslexics inaccurately perceive body language cues such as facial expressions and therefore act and react inappropriately.

Social phobia. Persistent fear of being placed where one can be scrutinized critically by other people. There may be a specific fear (e.g., of public speaking), but in other cases there is a more general fear of almost all social encounters. Ordinary anxiety about doing one's best is not the point; rather the social fear has to be disabling enough to interfere with one's ability to function normally. Such physical symptoms as sweating, rapid heart rate, and difficulty in breathing may be present. This condition is distinct from the **panic disorder** with **agoraphobia** (see definitions). See also: **phobias.**

Social psychology. The science of the behavior and mental processes of individuals in social situations. Physiological factors have an impact on some social behaviors, as is especially evident when life-threatening diseases create social situations that involve people in role conflicts.

Sociobiology. A biologically based model of human social behavior (chiefly developed by the work of E.O. Wilson and R. Dawkins, among others) which seeks to account for various social behaviors by evolutionary pressures to survive; this results in the genetic inheritance of a tendency to perform such behaviors. For example, altruistic self-sacrifice is said to be inherited, because the genes of protected relatives outnumber the similar genes of the individual who dies by sacrificing life that others may live. This hypothesis predicts that altruistic self-sacrifice would be far more likely to occur on behalf of close relatives than distant ones, or more likely to occur for relatives than for strangers.

Socioeconomic status. One's position in society, which is partly the result of financial circumstances (the "economic") and partly the result of one's relationships with others in the same society (the "social"). This concept is considered to be more sociologically accurate than the older concept of "social class."

Sociological model. A model of deviant behavior that contains the assumption that the child's social environment causes and maintains her or his deviant behavior.

Sociopathic (sō˝sē ō path′ik) **personality disorder.** See: **antisocial personality disorder.**

Sodium amytal test. See: **Wada test.**

Sodium-potassium pump. The metabolic process that keeps most of the sodium ions outside the axon and most of the potassium ions inside the axon. Neither the electrostatic force that attracts positive ions to the negatively charged axoplasm (the cytoplasm of the axon) nor the ion concentration gradient (which causes ions to diffuse throughout a solution until their concentration is uniform) are available for use, particularly when the pump is most needed, that is, right after a nerve impulse. The nerve impulse has left excess sodium in the axoplasm and excess potassium outside the axon. Yet the outside is positive and the interior is negative, as in a normal resting state. Therefore, the energy stores of adenosine triphosphate in the mitochondria must be tapped in order to drag the excess sodium ions out to the extracellular fluid and the excess potassium ions back inside the axon. See also **absolute refractory period; adenosine triphosphate; axon; mitochondria; nerve impulse; relative refractory period.**

Soft signs. Very slight abnormalities of behavior that are observed and recorded in the course of a neurological examination. In addition to the actual neurological exam, there are other ways in which soft signs may reveal themselves, such as in psychological test performance, in overt behavior, or in expressions of emotion. Examples of soft signs are speech disturbances, awkward gait, hyperactivity, poor balance, lack of coordination, low muscle tone, and incorrect responses

to two-point threshold testing (i.e., being given two tactile stimuli simultaneously). Often, losses of auditory and visual skills may serve as soft signs. Soft signs are also known as equivocal signs.

Solipsism (sol′ip siz˝əm) (literally, "self-alone" ism). One of the logically possible answers to the mind-body problem. It results from the basic stance of monism, that there is only type of real existence, along with the decision that the one type of reality is mental. It follows that all physical things are either sensations or memories of past sensations. Therefore, "you" are no more real than any other figment of "my" imagination. This position creates a very unstable world of changing impressions without permanence. The only permanent and sustained object is "my own self." Few philosophers or scientists have argued this position very forcefully. After all, what would be the point? Who would the believing solipsist have to convince? See also: **mentalism; mind-brain problem; monism.**

Somatic nervous system or **somatic division (of the peripheral nervous system).** That part of the peripheral nervous system which is connected to the striped muscles (also known as the voluntary or skeletal muscles). Its motor end plates (which are analogous to synapses in the case of neuron-to-neuron connections) are activated by the chemical neurotransmitter acetylcholine (ACh). These end-plates depend on the nicotinic action of ACh and they can be deactivated by the drug curare.

Somatization (sō˝mə ti zā′shən, sō mat˝i-) **disorder.** Recurrent complaints about bodily problems, involving the seeking of medical help, but for which there is no genuine physical malady. Complaints are vague but are described in exaggerated form. The condition begins in the teens and is almost always found in female patients.

Somatoform (sō mat′ə fôrm) **disorders.** Psychological problems that are given physical expression. One example is **hypochondriasis** (see definition), wherein the person reports a physical disorder that cannot be confirmed by objective medical examination. Other somatoform disorders include conversion disorder, in which anesthesia and/or paralysis are reported. The function of sensation or movement is apparently lost from a physically intact body part. The patient seems to face the paralysis or anesthesia with unconcern, a calm attitude that seems very inappropriate. The undifferentiated somatoform disorder is much more common than somatization disorder, but it is less of a problematic condition. Somatoform disorders apparently affect males and females in equal numbers.

Somatosensory (sō mat″ō sen′s(ə)rē). A synonym for **somesthetic** (see definition).

Somatosensory homunculus (sō mat″ō sen′s (ə)rē hō mung′kyōō lus) ("homunculus" from "homo", ="man" and "unculus" = "little", = Latin for "dwarf"). The representation of the primary somatosensory cortex in the likeness of a distorted human figure lying upside down along the postcentral gyrus of the parietal lobe with its toes anchored in the longitudinal fissure. Each body part of the figure corresponds to the small area of somatosensory cortex receiving sensations of deep pressure or light touch from the organism's corresponding body structure. Areas that are richly innervated for touch (such as the fingers and the lips) are drawn disproportionately large in the somatosensory homunculus. The left cortical hemisphere's postcentral gyrus maps the right side of the body, while the right side somatosensory homunculus refers to the left side of the body. See also: **motor homunculus; parietal lobe; somesthetic area.**

Somatosensory system (also called **general body senses** or **somesthesia**). That sensory system which receives information from all parts of the body rather than from specialized sense organs in the head. The somatosensory system deals with such sensations as light touch, deep pressure, warmth, cold, pain, and kinesthesis (i.e., movement sensations from the muscles, tendons, and joints). The touch receptors (at the endings of afferent unipolar neurons) send messages into the spinal cord. Some touch information travels directly up the spinal cord to arrive at nuclei in the medulla of the brain. The axons emerging from those nuclei cross the midline and run up through most of the brain to the thalamus. Other touch sense messages arrive at synapses soon after reaching the spinal cord. The second-order neurons send axons directly across the spinal cord. These axons travel all the way up to the thalamus. From the thalamus, new axons are di-

rected toward the somatosensory cortex, which is the postcentral gyrus of the parietal lobe. Vast differences exist in the touch sensitivity of different sections of the skin. A common test is the "two-point threshold," in which either two points or one point of a compass are (is) placed on the skin. On the fingertip, which is the most sensitive, there are 700 touch receptors for every 2 square millimeters of skin surface. On the back, which has the lowest two-point sensitivity, the compass points could be spread several inches apart and the individual would still not be sure of whether he or she was feeling one point or two. See also: **anterolateral system; dorsal column medial lemniscal pathway; parietal lobe; somesthetic.**

Somatostatin (sō mat″ō stat′in). This hormone, which is released by the posterior pituitary body (neurohypophysis), is the growth-hormone-release-inhibiting hormone, which blocks the release of somatotropin from the anterior pituitary. It also blocks the release of the thyroid-stimulating hormone from the anterior pituitary but does allow prolactin to be released from the anterior pituitary. This combination of effects allows a nursing mother to avoid a hyperthyroid condition. It also blocks the secretion of insulin. See also: **insulin; posterior pituitary; somatotropin; thyroid.**

Somatotopic (sō mat ″ō top′ik, -tō′pik) **arrangement**. Arranged according to the relative positions of the various parts of the body. This term could apply to the motor and to the somatosensory homunculus. See also: **motor homunculus; somatosensory homunculus.**

Somatotropin (sō mat″ō trō′pin) or **somatotropic** (sō mat″ō trop′ik, trō′pik) **hormone (SH)** or **growth hormone (GH)**. Somatotropin is released by the master gland (the anterior pituitary). It causes growth of body tissues. See also: **growth hormone (GH).**

Somatotypes. This is Sheldon's conceptualization of three body types; <u>endomorphic</u> (round and soft bodies with large abdomens), <u>mesomorphic</u> (strong upright bodies with strong muscles and bones), and <u>ectomorphic</u> (thin, small-framed, frail bodies), which are believed to impact personality development. Sheldon believed that endomorphs are very sociable and love food and people (<u>viscerotonic</u>); mesomorphs are risk-taking adventuresome types who love physical activities (somatotonic); and ectomorphs are restrained, quiet, self-conscious, and private individuals (cerebrotonic). These types have not been extensively verified or confirmed. See also: **stereotype.**

Somesthesia (sō"mes thē'zhə, -zē ə). A collective name for all the general body senses. See also: **cerebral cortex; parietal lobe; somesthetic; somesthetic area.**

Somesthetic (sō"mes thet'ik). Pertaining to the general body senses. Some of our senses use receptors that are not found in specialized organs set into the head but are scattered all over our bodies. These general body senses include light touch, deep pressure, the movement sense (kinesthesis), warmth, cold, and pain.

Somesthetic (sō"mes thet'ik) **area** or **somatosensory** (sō"mat ō sen's(ə)rē) **area.** The region of the parietal lobe in the cerebral cortex where the terminals of the sensory pathways for somesthesia are found. See also: **cerebral cortex; parietal lobe; somesthesia; somesthetic.**

Somnambulism (som nam'byōo liz əm) (from Latin "somnus" = "sleep" and "ambulare" = "to walk"). Sleepwalking.

Sone. A unit of perceived loudness which is measured at 1,000 Hertz (Hz) at 40 decibels (dB) above the listener's threshold for sound stimuli.

Sonic Guide. A device resembling a pair of eyeglasses used by a blind person. The device emits high-frequency sounds (too high-pitched to be sensed by human hearing) which are bounced off obstacles and reflected back to the Sonic Guide. The wearer is given information about the distance, direction, and the surface hardness of the obstacle. The device detects objects about eight feet away. Another device constructed along the same lines is called the Sonic Pathfinder. See also: **Sonic Pathfinder.**

Sonic Pathfinder. An ultrasound-emitting device resembling a pair of eyeglasses to be worn by a blind person. Another version is known as the Sonic Guide. See also: **Sonic Guide.**

Sound. [1] The physical stimulus for our sense of hearing. Sound energy takes the form of waves of molecules that are alternately compressed and rarefied (spread apart). Accordingly, sound has to travel through a physical medium, such as air or water. This is not the case with light, which is a form of electromagnetic energy and can travel through a vacuum. Astronauts, who were only 6 feet apart on the airless moon, had to talk to one another by radio. According to this first definition, a sound is present when a tree crashes to the forest floor and nobody is around to hear it. [2] The subjective experience or sensation resulting from sound waves stimulating the ears. According to this second definition, when a tree crashes down and nobody is around, there is no sound. Sound waves are specified by their frequency (in cycles per second, or Hertz), which is the main determinant of the high or low pitch of sound; by their amplitude, which is the main determinant of a sound's loudness; and by their timbre, which refers to the combination of overtones added to the basic sound frequency. See also: **amplitude; Fourier analysis; harmonics; hearing; Hertz (Hz); pitch; timbre.**

Sound localization. The perception of the location of the origin of a sound, that is, knowing where a sound is coming from, in what direction the sound source is located, and how far away it is. See also: **binaural cue; monaural cue; superior olivary nucleus.**

Spafford-Grosser lower peripheral brightness sensitivity hypothesis or **higher light-brightness threshold hypothesis.** The hypothesis that, in some individuals with dyslexia, the peripheral retina (defined as between 30 and 60 degrees of visual angle from the fovea) has lower brightness sensitivity (i.e., resulting in higher light detection thresholds) than this region of the retina has in individuals who are proficient readers. See also: **Grosser-Spafford anomalous receptor hypothesis; Grosser-Spafford reduced contrast sensitivity hypothesis.**

Spafford-Grosser visual dysphonetic subtype. See: **Visual-dysphonetic dyslexic subtype.**

Span of perception. The visual range (scored in number of character-spaces) providing either word-length or word-identification data to the reader during a fixation.

Span of recognition. What the reader sees during a fixation; this may vary from half a word to about one full word.

Spasticity (spas tis'i tē). A type of cerebral palsy in which voluntary muscular movements are interrupted by muscle spasms, with two opposed muscles contracting (as in a charley horse), and temporary paralyses. See also: **spastic paralysis**.

Spastic paralysis. The inability to move a part of the body voluntarily because the muscles required for the motion have excessive muscle tone. Reflexes and muscle tremors are possible. The axons running directly to the muscles are undamaged, since they are responsible for the muscle tone. Consequently, there must be an injury either to the dorsal (sensory) spinal cord or to some motor area or pathway in the brain. In the case of damage to brain motor pathways, the initial result is a temporary flaccid paralysis (little or no muscle tone), after which the spastic paralysis sets in. See also: **paralysis; spasticity; tabes dorsalis.**

Spatial ability. A right hemispheric cognitive ability which involves the interpretation of visual and somesthetic inputs so as to relate the positions of one's own body parts to the locations of environmental stimuli.

Spatial localization. Finding an object's position in three-dimensional (or two-dimensional) visual space.

Spatial summation. The additivity of excitatory and/or inhibitory synaptic effects on a postsynaptic membrane as the result of the simultaneous activation of several synapses at one local area of the membrane of a neuron's dendrite or cell body. This results in the increased amplitude of the positive or negative voltage on the postsynaptic membrane. Such summation can only occur in the case of **graded potentials** (see definition).

Special education. A type of instruction offered to children whose needs cannot be met by routine educational methods in regular classrooms.

Special education technology. Any technological tool useful in helping a disabled or special-needs student learn, especially if the tool is expressly designed for such use. See also: **assistive technology.**

Species-common behaviors. Responses that are carried out in the identical manner by all the members of an animal species.

Species-specific behaviors. Responses that are performed by the members of a given species but not by members of related species (e.g., species belonging to the same genus). For example, two species of birds may resemble one another in physical appearance, but they may construct

nests of different architectures or they may have different songs.

Spectrophotofluorimetry (spek″trō fō″tō floo rim′ e trē, -flô-). A technique employing fluorescence-labelling to identify the presence of, and to determine the concentration of, monoamines in a sample of tissue. See also: **catecholamines; indole amines.**

Speech. The production of the various sounds used in spoken language by means of the larynx and other organs.

Speech audiometry. A technique which assesses an individual's detection and understanding of speech.

Speech detection. The lowest level in decibel units at which an individual can detect speech sounds but without complete understanding.

Speech Plus Talking Calculator. A hand-held calculator with a speech synthesizer built in. It has a 24-word vocabulary. The device, although, cheap, is not very extensive.

Speech reading. A technique used to teach hearing-impaired individuals how best to use visual information to understand what is being said. Speech reading is a more accurate description than lip reading, because lip reading involves only the use of visual cues from the physical movements of the lips. See also: **lip reading**.

Speech reception threshold (SRT). The lowest intensity at which the subject can repeat two-syllable words correctly at least 50% of the time. This defines the decibel (dB) level at which an individual is able to understand speech. Frequently, individuals are given lists of two-syllable words to test each ear. The SRT would be considered the dB level at which the individual could understand at least half of the words.

Sphenoid (sfē′noid″). A winged, compound bone at the base of the skull.

Sphenoid (sfē′noid″) **wing malfunction**. This is hypothesized by some chiropractors to prevent normal eye movements and cause dyslexia. The sphenoid is a bone of the skull. The wing is an outflung projection of the sphenoid bone.

Spike potential. The peak of the action potential in an axon, when the interior axoplasm loses its negative charge (about -75 millivolts) and temporarily receives a positive charge (of about +40 millivolts) due to the inrush of positive sodium ions. This is the condition of maximum depolarization, during which a nerve impulse takes place. See also: **all-or-none law; depolarization; nerve impulse; resting potential.**

Spina bifida (spī˝nə bif˝i də). A congenital defect in which parts of the spine fail to come together, allowing the spinal cord and its meninges (outer membranes) to protrude into a sac on the back. The result may be paraplegia or the loss of bladder and bowel control. Spina bifida is estimated to be the second most common birth defect, with only trisomy 21 (Down's syndrome) being more prevalent. In many cases of spina bifida, hydrocephalus is also present.

Spinal accessory nerve. The eleventh pair of cranial nerves. This nerve has motor functions; it controls our head movements. Its parasympathetic component joins the vagus nerve. Part of its somatic nervous system component joins the glossopharyngeal nerve in innervating the pharynx. Some of the somatic motor fibers innervate the neck muscles. See also: **cranial nerves.**

Spinal cord. The lower portion of the central nervous system (CNS). Part of the spinal cord's functioning is carrying messages between the main part of the body and the brain, the latter being the upper part of the CNS. Some reflexes of locomotion and posture may be mediated by the spinal cord without the need for communication to the brain. The exterior of the spinal cord is white matter, while the inner part, shaped like a butterfly or a capital "H," is gray matter.

Spinal muscular atrophy. An inherited recessive autosomal disorder in which the trunk muscles grow progressively weaker and undergo atrophy. Bone may be lost because of disuse of muscles and joints near the bone. There is a delay in the acquisition of motor skills. Physical therapy is very important for such patients. Children with this problem will lack muscular strength but can have normal intelligence. The child can be educated normally if no muscular skills are required of him or her.

Spinal nerves. The peripheral nerves that, along with the cranial nerves, enter and/or leave the central nervous system. The spinal nerves are arranged in pairs, one left and one right. They emerge from the spinal cord at 31 levels, called spinal cord segments, so there are 31 pairs of spinal nerves. In rostral to caudal order, from the head to the legs, the 31 spinal nerves are designated thus: 8 cervical, 12 thoracic, 5 lumbar, 5 sacral, and 1 coccygeal. The numbers from this list, 8-12-5-5-1, constitute the neural formula. The vertebrae of the spinal column do not match up perfectly with these, being only 26 in number. There are 7 (not 8, only 7!) cervical vertebrae, 12 thoracic vertebrae, and 5 lumbar vertebrae. The long sacrum (1 vertebra with five pairs of exit-holes for nerves) follows. Lastly, there is the tailbone, which is called the coccyx. The vertebral formula is 7-12-5-1-1.

Spinal shock. After a transection of the spinal cord, the individual loses all voluntary movements, all sensation below the level of the cut, and all spinal reflexes. After several weeks, the spinal reflexes reappear. Even a partial injury to the spinal cord leads to spinal shock, although it is not as severe. The severity of spinal shock and the speed of recovery from it are related to the loss of input to the motor neurons controlling the reflexive responses involved. In this respect, the spinal shock phenomenon resembles **diaschisis** (see definition).

Spindle afferent neurons. The sensory neurons sending axons from the muscle spindle sense organ to the spinal cord by way of the dorsal roots of the spinal nerves. See also: **gamma efferents; muscle spindle.**

Spindle cell or **fusiform cell).** A small spindle-shaped neuron. Many of these are found in the sixth and deepest layer of the human cerebral cortex. They are responsible for the name given to that layer, viz., the fusiform layer. See also: **cerebral cortex.**

Spinoreticular (spī˝nō ri tik´ yoo lər) **tract.** One of the three components of the anterolateral tract which carries sensory messages of pain and temperature (as well as crude touch information) and which has its second-order axons run from the dorsal horns across the midline and then rostrally toward the opposite side of the brain. The spinoreticular tract synapses in the brain stem reticular formation. From the reticular formation, in turn, axons carrying pain information project to the intralaminar and parafascicular nuclei of the thalamus. See also: **anterolateral system.**

Spinotectal (spī˝nō tek´təl) **tract.** One of the

three components of the anterolateral tract that carries sensory messages of pain and temperature, as well as some rudimentary light-touch afferents. The second-order axons arise in the dorsal horns of the gray H and immediately cross the midline before turning rostrally toward the brain. These axons terminate in the midbrain tectum. See also: **anterolateral system; tectum.**

Spinothalamic tract. See **lateral spinothalamic tract** and **ventral spinothalamic tract.**

Spiral ganglion (spī'rəl gang'glē ən). A set of bipolar neurons lying near the inner ear, named for that spiral-shaped organ, the cochlea. The axons from these bipolar cells comprise the acoustic branch of the auditory vestibular nerve. The axons terminate in two nuclei of the medulla, namely, the dorsal and the ventral cochlear nuclei. See also: **acoustic nerve; cochlea; ganglion.**

Spiroperidol (spī''rə per'i dôl). A neuroleptic drug of the butyrophenone family of drugs. See also: **butyrophenones; haloperidol; neuroleptic drug.**

Splanchnic (splangk'nik) **nerve** (from Greek "splanchna" = "the viscera"). A nerve issuing from the thoracic and lumbar region of the spinal cord and the sympathetic nervous system that runs to the digestive organs. It has been hypothesized to convey sensory information about the food content in the stomach.

Splenium (splē'nē um) (from Greek "splenion" = "bandage"). The posterior (caudal) portion of the corpus callosum. It links the left and right occipital lobes to one another. The splenium also links the posterior portions of the left and right parietal and temporal lobes of the cerebral cortex. See also: **cerebral cortex; corpus callosum.**

Split-brain surgery. A severance of the corpus callosum (which links the left and right cerebral hemispheres to one another), usually prescribed to prevent the spreading of epileptic bursts of neural activation. The term "split-brain" is a misnomer, since only the cerebral hemispheres are separated; lower parts of the brain are not involved in the surgery. See also: **chimeric faces; commissure; corpus callosum; tachistoscope.**

Split-half reliability. An approach to the statistical computation of an index for a test's reliability. The test is subdivided into equivalent halves

(such as the even-numbered test items and the odd-numbered test items). The scores on the two halves are correlated. The obtained correlation coefficient must then be corrected, because the test was artificially shortened, thereby lowering the reliability. The correlation between the test halves, after correction, is the split-half reliability coefficient. See also: **reliability.**

Spontaneous drinking. Drinking water when there is neither a hypovolemic or an osmotic basis for thirst.

Spontaneous recovery. A phenomenon that is brought to light by interrupting extinction training. The conditioned response has been unreinforced and the rate of the operant response (or, in classical conditioning, the amplitude of the respondent response) has decreased. After the extinction training is resumed, following the break, the response is made at a greater rate or amplitude than the level reached before the interruption. Since nothing was done by way of reconditioning or remotivating the organism, this recovery seems to be a spontaneous one.

Spontaneous remission. In medicine and psychotherapy, a recovery from an illness or dysfunction without benefit of any therapeutic procedure.

Spoonerism. A transposition of the parts of two or more words, named for Professor Spooner of Oxford University. The professor was being introduced to Queen Victoria by the dean of his college. Ever polite, the good professor began by saying, "My queer dean." In cases where this occurs very frequently, such a partial loss of language ability may be a sign of pathology in an area of the cerebral cortex involved with language functions. See also: **soft signs.**

SQUID (superconducting quantum interference device). High-temperature superconducting sensors are arranged to fit around the head in a caplike manner in order to detect variations in magnetic fields generated by brain activity.

Stabilized retinal image. A visual image kept in the same position on the retina despite the movement of the eye. This can be accomplished by mounting a microprojector on a contact lens so that projection is always targeted on the same retinal spot.

Stage 1 sleep (ascending). A sleep stage similar to the first stage of sleep (descending stage 1 sleep), going by the low-voltage, high-frequency EEG shown by the subject. It is reached after the subject has passed through stage 2 sleep. Ascending stage 1 sleep is not like descending stage 1 sleep, in that it is accompanied by a loss of tone in the larger skeletal muscles and the frequent occurrence of rapid eye movements. Ascending stage 1 sleep is also called stage REM sleep. Another name for it is paradoxical sleep, because the skeletal muscles have very little tone (typical of full relaxation) even though the EEG is typical of an active brain. See also: **sleep**.

Stage 1 sleep (descending). The first stage of sleep, with a low-voltage, high-frequency EEG.

Stage 2 sleep. The sleep stage which follows descending stage 1 sleep, during the first ninety-minute sleep cycle, and which follows stage REM sleep in the following cycles. In stage 2 sleep, the EEG resembles that of stage 1 but shows two kinds of interruptions: (1) large negative deflections (K-complexes) and (2) sleep spindles (slow waves briefly interpolated among the prevailing fast waves).

Stage 3 sleep. The first of two stages of deep sleep (or "delta sleep"). The stage 2 EEG is gradually replaced by an EEG with low-frequency and high-voltage waves called delta waves. Delta waves are the slowest of all EEG waves; they range in frequency from 1/2 cycles to 4 cycles per second. Stage 3 is different from stage 4 in that the delta waves take up less than 50% of the EEG record.

Stage 4 sleep. The stage of deep sleep marked by delta waves consuming more than 50% of the EEG record. Such events as sleepwalking, tooth grinding, and sleeptalking occur here, because the skeletal muscles have sufficient muscle tone to allow these events to happen.

Stages of learning. The steps that a student goes through in the process of learning. In order of occurrence, they are (1) acquisition, (2) proficiency, (3) generalization, (4) maintenance, and (5) application.

Staircase. A continuous series of saccades (short eye movements) alternating with fixations (brief stoppages of eye movement). A graphic picture of a series of saccades and fixations resembles the outline of a staircase. In good readers, the staircase runs left to right. Rayner and Pirozzolo

report that some dyslexics, those whose problem is primarily visual-perceptual, show backward staircases that go from right to left.

Standard deviation. An index of the variability of a set of scores. Unlike the range, the simplest indicator of variability, the standard deviation accounts for every single score in the set. This is because the computation of the standard deviation begins by systematically subtracting the mean from each score.

Standard error of estimate. This is the standard deviation (square root of the variance) of the errors in predictions made from a test. It is equal to the product of the standard deviation of the criterion scores times the square root of the quantity 1 minus r^2, where r is the correlation between the test scores and the criterion measures (i.e., r is the validity coefficient for this test). The lower that correlation, the greater will be the standard error of estimate. This explains why it is not advisable to make predictions from scores on a low-validity test, that is, a test having a low correlation with the criterion.

Standard error of measurement. If one examinee were to take the same test many times, the scores would yield a variance statistic, the square root of which is called the standard error of measurement. This standard error is equal to the product of the square root of the observed variance times the square root of the quantity one minus the test's reliability coefficient.

Standardization group or **norm group**. This is a large and representative sample of the population for whom a test is intended.

Standardized tests. These tests are administered to a large sample, the norm group, of those types of people for whom the test is intended. The statistical data describing the performance of the norm group, or standardization group, are known as norms.

Standard scores. These are computed from raw scores by the following process. Begin with an individual's raw score, X. Let M be the arithmetic mean of all the raw scores. Subtract the mean from X. This is the right order, because if the raw score is above the mean, the difference will be positive, and, if the raw score is less than the mean score, the difference will be negative. Now divide this positive or negative difference score by s, the standard deviation of the raw scores. The results will be a conversion from X, the raw score in test points, to z, the standard score in standard deviation units. A standard score of +1, for example, is exactly 1 standard deviation higher than the mean. The process is akin to obtaining the number of feet equivalent to 72 inches, which you would divide by 12, because that is the size of 1 foot in inch units. Another analogy is the conversion of 537 cents to its equivalent in dollars. The key step is dividing by the size of 1 dollar in cents, namely 100, to obtain the answer of $5.37. The beauty of using standard scores is that it enables you to compare results from radically dissimilar tests, once you have converted the raw scores from each test to standard scores.

Stanford-Binet Intelligence Test. An intelligence test containing assorted tasks which have been assigned mental age values according to the average age of the children able to do the tasks. In the original form of the Stanford-Binet, the values of those tasks a child could perform were averaged to obtain the child's mental age; the mental age divided by the true or chronological age produced an intelligence quotient. The current form of the test uses the more modern practice of placing the examinee's performance on a percentile scale, with a 50th percentile performance interpreted as an IQ of 100.

Stanines (stā′nīnz ˝). The term comes from "standard nine" scale. The stanine scale is a modified scale of standard scores, with the mean set at 5 (instead of zero, as it is for the z-scale) and the standard deviation at nearly 2 (while the standard deviation is 1 on the z-scale). The widths of stanines 2 through 8 are equal, but, at the extremes, stanines 1 and 9 are very wide. Stanine values represent ranges rather than specific points.

Stapedius (stə pē′dē us). A muscle of the middle ear. The stapedius is attached to the stapes, one of the three small auditory bones (ossicles). Its function is to dampen down the vibrations of the stapes when the sound stimulus is high in both intensity and frequency, since the very high and very fast vibrating could shatter the bone or tear the oval window membrane to which the stapes is attached. Since the brain sends the command to slow down and tone down the ac-

tivity, there is no loss of information about the true intensity and frequency of the stimulation. The facial nerve's chorda tympani sends motor fibers to the stapedius. See also: **middle ear; stapes; tensor tympani.**

Stapes (stā′pēz) or **stirrup**. The third of a chain of three small bones (the malleus or hammer and the incus or anvil being the first two, respectively) of the middle ear. These three auditory ossicles mechanically relay the sound wave vibrations of the eardrum, which is the final structure of the outer ear. The stapes is attached to the oval window, the membrane at the beginning of the inner ear. See also: **middle ear; ossicles.**

Startle reflex. The complex reaction to a sudden loud noise, during which the eyes bulge, the hair stands on end, the arms and legs fling apart, the fingers spread, and the back arches.

State-dependent learning. In many instances of learning, it has been shown that one can readily recall what one has learned well when tested under the same conditions as those that had been present when the learning occurred; whereas, if the learning and the testing occur under very different conditions, recall is quite poor. Learning that shows that kind of sensitivity to the prevailing situation is considered to be "state-dependent."

Static phase. The second and terminal phase of hypothalamic hyperphagia. After destruction of the left and right ventral medial nuclei of the hypothalamus of a laboratory rat, the animal eats and overeats until it has tripled its starting weight. That weight-gaining phase is the initial, dynamic phase of the hyperphagic syndrome. After having tripled its weight, the animal maintains weight at that higher level; it is now in the static phase of hyperphagia. The set point for normal weight seems to have been adjusted to a much higher level. See also: **dynamic phase; hypothalamic hyperphagia; set point; ventromedial hypothalamus.**

Statistical significance. The decision, arrived at as the result of an inferential statistics test applied to research data, that the probability of the obtained data resulting from chance factors alone is so small that it may be safely dismissed. The purpose of applying such a test to research data from a sample of subjects is to learn whether the research results may be reasonably generalized to the entire population from which the sample was taken. The probability that the result could have been due to chance alone has to be acceptably low. If an experimental outcome could have come about by chance once out of 20 times (i.e., p = 0.05), or less frequently than that, the outcome is considered statistically-significant. Technically, this is known as the rejection of the null hypothesis. Psychologists who set the significance level at .05 (i.e., 5%) are willing to accept as true a statement about a measured difference or correlation that could be incorrect (because the measurements may have been due to chance) only 5 times in every 100 research studies. Generalization from the sample data to the entire population is considered permissible, once the null hypothesis has been rejected. See also: **inferential statistics; population; representative sample; sample.**

Status. The social group memberships or positions that one assumes or is given. One's physiological, genetic, maturational, or other biological condition may decisively affect what status one can attain. For example, mentally retarded persons may have no access to most of the higher-status jobs in the society. As a second example, mentally ill persons may lose high-status jobs after the onset of the illness.

Stepping reflex. A reflex seen in babies. When the infant is held in a vertical posture with the feet allowed to touch, just barely, a flat surface, the baby will begin to make small stepping motions. A similar reflex can be seen in adult laboratory animals. When a blindfolded cat is brought to the edge of a table so that its foreleg barely brushes it, the cat will lift the forelimb and attempt to place it on the tabletop.

Stereognosis (ster˝ē og nō'sis). The identification of objects by use of the tactile sense. See also: **astereognosis.**

Stereopsis (ster˝ē op'sis). Seeing the world stereoscopically, that is, in three dimensions.

Stereoscopic (ster˝ē ō skop'ik) **depth perception**. Seeing objects in three dimensions, the third one being depth (near versus far), due to the comparison in the brain of the nerve impulses coming from the slightly differing images on the left and the right retina.

Stereotaxic (ster˝e ō tak'sik) **atlas**. A book of illustrations of the brain of an animal, presented in continuously-arranged serial sections, with horizontal and vertical coordinates and with distances specified to scale. The atlas is used as a guide for the neuroscientist who is doing neurosurgical work with the stereotaxic instrument. See also: **stereotaxic instrument.**

Stereotaxic (ster˝e ō tak'sik) **instrument**. A device providing access to any three dimensionally specified point in the brain of an experimental animal so that the tip of an electrode will contact specified nerve cells. The inserted electrode can be given a high-voltage direct current which will destroy that part of the brain, if one is using the ablation method. Alternatively, after placement, the electrode can be permanently implanted so that it can be used for the stimulation or the recording method. In the case of stimulation research, a high- frequency, alternating current of low voltage can be used to stimulate the brain cells without harming them. Of course, with the recording method, the current flow in the electrode comes from voltage changes initiated by the brain neurons themselves. The stereotaxic instrument has been compared to a machinist's drill press, which allows the machinist to make a hole at a given location inside a three-dimensional solid object. The experimenter is provided with books of illustrations of the brain of the animal, with metric distances from the outside to specified tracts and nuclei of the brain along each of the three spatial dimensions. Such books are known as stereotaxic atlases. See also: **ablation; recording; stereotaxic atlas; stimulation**.

Stereotype. A set of traits believed to be shared by all members of a certain category (e.g., all twins look alike) or social group (e.g., all 1-year olds speak in words or phrases). Most stereotypes are not valid because there are exceptions to just about every rule.

Stereotypic (ster˝ē ə tip'ik) **behavior**. See: **self-stimulatory behaviors**.

Sterility. A lack of the ability to reproduce. In females, this is an inability to conceive. In males, this is the failure to produce sperm with sufficient motility to fertilize the ovum.

Steroid (stēr'oid˝, ster'-) **hormones**. The hormones of the testes, ovaries, and adrenal cortex. All the other hormones are polypeptides. Steroids participate in metabolism, the control of blood pressure, and various stages of sexual behavior. Steroid chemicals are made up of four linked rings of carbon atoms, three hexagonal and one pentagonal; they are chemically related to cholesterol. Compounds other than hormones also belong to this chemical family; one such is vitamin D. See also: **adrenal cortex**; **endocrine system**; **gonads**; **hormone**.

Stimulants. Drugs that speed up metabolism, causing increased heartbeat, increased blood pressure, and greater muscular tension. These drugs usually produce an elevation of mood. Stimulants are often used to treat hyperactivity in children. These drugs can be habit-forming, and the abuse of stimulants may lead to various physical and mental disorders.

Stimulation. Until recently, one of the three chief ways of exploring brain-behavior relationships, the other two being ablation and recording. Stimulation uses the logic of addition. If, during an ongoing behavior, a part of the organism's brain is energized by means of a current sent to an implanted electrode, an observable change may occur in behavior. This new action is attributed to the stimulated part of the brain. There is a logical difficulty with this technique; the neurons in the area stimulated are, in real life, never simultaneously active. The stimulation applies a condition to the organism that is not duplicated during normal day-to-day activities. The method is useful as a means of finding out what the stimulated neurons can do, but it does not tell us what those neurons usually do. Injecting chemical neurotransmitters in liquid form (instead of delivering electrical jolts) can partially improve on the logic of the stimulation technique, since only neurons with receptor sites of the same chemically reactive type will be energized at the same time; neighboring neurons will remain quiescent, because they will not react to the chemical stimulus.

Stimulus discrimination. A learning process by which the organism keeps responding to one stimulus but stops responding to other stimuli.

Stimulus generalization. The tendency to respond not only in the presence of the conditioned stimulus or discriminative stimulus used in training (and, therefore, one that has been experienced by the organism as a stimulus that pre-

cedes reinforcement), but also to respond to other stimuli that have some resemblance to that stimulus. This tendency is a natural one and does not require training in order for it to be demonstrated.

Stimulus motive. An unlearned motive, such as curiosity, which is triggered by external stimuli as opposed to internal stimulation.

Stirrup. See: **stapes**.

Stoma (stō′mə). An opening at the base of the neck surgically created to allow air to reach the lungs of a person who has had a laryngectomy. See also: **laryngectomy**.

Storage. The first (more obvious) step in remembering what one has learned. See also: **retrieval**.

Strabismus (strə biz′mus). A failure of the two optic axes to direct themselves on the same object, due to lack of eye muscle coordination. Divergent strabismus finds one eye deviating outward. In convergent strabismus, the deviating eye turns inward. In concomitant strabismus, both eyes move freely, but they maintain a false relationship to one another.

Strain studies. These are genetic studies of behavioral factors (e.g., weight) using animals which are inbred in order to avoid unnecessary risks to humans and to produce animal strains which are genetically similar.

Strength-duration curve. Manipulating the time (duration) of a stimulating pulse of electricity, along with the strength (volts) of the electrical stimulation, allows the plotting of points showing how strong the stimulus has to be (in order to trigger a nerve impulse) for each duration. Electrical strength is measured along the Y-axis (ordinate), and the time value is represented on the X-axis (abscissa). At the left of the graph, for very brief durations, the required strengths are quite high. This graph is called the strength-duration curve. The function (graphed line) curves downward and eventually, at the right of the graph, it levels off, showing that at very long durations the applied electricity must have at least a certain minimum strength if there is going to be a nerve impulse. That minimum electrical strength is the rheobase. At a point on the curve where the current requirement is equal to two times the rheobase, a time is identified called the chronaxie. Either the strength-duration curve or the chronaxie can be used as an indication of the excitability of the measured tissue [which might be a sense receptor, an axon, a nerve (a bundle of axons), a muscle bundle (a collection of muscle fibers), or a muscle fiber]. See also: **chronaxie; rheobase.**

Strephosymbolia (stref´ō sim bol´ē ə). The word itself means "twisted symbols" in Greek. Orton coined this term as a way to describe how he thought dyslexics read; that is, distorted, with sometimes reversed, sometimes upside-down retinal images of words and letters caused by a malfunctioning in the brain. Strephosymbolia is due, Orton stated, to incomplete hemispheric dominance. With the two cerebral hemispheres competing rather than cooperating with one another, dyslexics perceive unstable and reversed visual images.

Stress. A psychological and physiological reaction resulting from any threat to the life or well-being of the organism, ranging from negative emotions through nearly fatal injuries. Stress generates the general adaptation syndrome (GAS), which was first described by Hans Selye. Physical stressors (agents of stress) include, for example, extremes of temperature; the cutting, crushing, burning, or freezing of body tissues; the ingestion of toxic substances; or the body's infection by bacteria or viruses. The endocrine system responds to stress with increases in the output of such hormones as cortisol (from the adrenal cortex), epinephrine (from the adrenal medulla), and growth hormone (from the anterior pituitary). The hypothalamus contains neurosecretory cells that are like neurons but release hormones rather than regular neurotransmitters at their axon endings. The axons run into the anterior lobe of the pituitary gland, that is, the master gland. There they release CRH, the cortico-tropin-releasing hormone. CRH causes the master gland to release ACTH, the adreno-corticotropic hormone. ACTH in turn is the command hormone that stimulates the adrenal cortex to secrete the steroid hormone cortisol into the bloodstream. The neurosecretory cells are triggered by norepinephrine from the axon endings of neurons whose cell bodies lie in the locus coeruleus of the pons. The stress reaction normally is self-limiting; as cortisol is carried by the bloodstream to the hypothalamus, it affects cortisol receptor sites on the membranes of neurosecre-

tory cells, cutting off the further release of CRH. When one successfully completes a stressful task, the hormone levels are reduced the next time the individual encounters the task. Sometimes the self-limiting feature of the stress reaction fails. If the individual continually exposes himself or herself to a stressor, the stress reaction may be inadequate to improve the individual's condition. Civilized society provides situations that are stress-inducing without being life-threatening. The human body has not evolved as quickly as human social relationships, and it responds to modern stresses with prehistoric defenses. When the emergency "fight-or-flight" reaction and the activation response phase of the GAS are unduly prolonged, they (the components of the emergency reaction and the activation response) may become quickly fatigued and a wrongly timed onrush of parasympathetic nervous system activity may occur. For example, a burst of digestive tract commands may produce gastrointestinal tract peristalsis (churning of smooth muscles) and the release of hydrochloric acid from the stomach walls into an empty stomach. Because the only thing around to be digested is the lining of the gastrointestinal tract, ulcers develop. In the case of voodoo curses leading to death, the parasympathetic nervous system overdoes the command to relax the heart, stopping it altogether. See also: **adrenal cortex; autonomic nervous system; biofeedback; emergency reaction; general adaptation syndrome; parasympathetic nervous system; parasympathetic rebound; psychophysiology; Relaxation Response; sympathetic nervous system; Transcendental Meditation.**

Stress inoculation. A procedure that attempts to forestall some effects of stress by giving advance warning, advice, and reassurance.

Stress inoculation therapy. A type of cognitive therapy which directs patients to use "positive self-talk" to reduce psychological stress. For example, the college student who has anxiety attacks when taking exams in physiological psychology can learn a pattern of self-talk such as the following: "I took excellent notes and have studied hard. I have also read the Grosser/Spafford dictionary from cover to cover to reinforce my learning. I will do just fine." See also: **cognitive therapy.**

Stress management. Stressful situations, upsetting thoughts, and unreinforced (ineffective) behaviors require management in order to avoid stress-related physical disorders. Such management is possible by resorting to the following: (1) exercise, (2) meditation, (3) relaxation, (4) improved organizational techniques, (5) slowing down, (6) getting adequate sleep, and (7) striking the proper balance among work, play, family, and the community.

Stretch reflex. The automatic contraction of a muscle that either has been extended by the application of a stimulus or has simply been contracting too slowly. The knee-jerk, or patellar tendon reflex, is one example of a stretch reflex. In a medical examination, the doctor swings a rubber hammer onto the patellar tendon, which stretches the quadriceps femoris, an extensor muscle that runs along the length of the thigh. The muscle spindle sense organs within this muscle are stimulated by the stretching and send afferent nerve impulses to the spinal cord. There the afferents synapse with efferent neurons that fire impulses to the quadriceps muscle, which contracts, jerking the lower leg upward. The maintenance of a standing posture, counteracting the force of gravity, involves the activity of numerous stretch reflexes. These reflexes maintain a sufficiently high level of muscle tone in the striate muscles to enable them to serve as supports. See also: **alpha efferents; extrafusal fiber; gamma efferents; intrafusal fiber; muscle spindle organ; reflex arc.**

Striate (strī′āt) **cortex** or **striate area.** A name for Brodmann's area 17 of the occipital lobe, the primary visual cortex. See also: **cerebral cortex; visual cortex.**

Striate (strī′āt) **muscles.** See: **skeletal muscles; striped muscles.**

Stridor. Harsh, noisy breathing due to obstructions in the air passages. See also: **dyspnea.**

Striped muscles. A name for the skeletal muscles based on the horizontal stripes running across a striped-muscle bundle. The individual muscle cell, the muscle fiber, has the horizontal stripes. The fibers are lined up alongside one another in a muscle bundle, so the entire bundle presents the striped appearance. See also: **skeletal muscles.**

Stroboscopic (strō″bə skop′ik) **motion.** The visual illusion of movement which is used in making "motion pictures" seem to move. A rapid series of still pictures is flashed on in quick succession. The gap between two consecutive "still shots" is covered up by visual persistence, the lingering aftereffect of visual stimulation. See also: **phi phenomenon; physical illusion; visual persistence.**

Stroke or **cerebrovascular** (ser″ə brō vas′kyə lər, sə rē″brō-) **accident.** Damage to the brain caused by a blood clot or other obstruction that impedes blood flow, causing some brain cells to die from oxygen deprivation.

Stroop test. A task requiring divided attention on the part of the subject. A list of color names is presented to the subject. The name of a color is typed in ink of another color, and the subject is required to name the color of the ink.

Sturge-Weber syndrome (also called **Sturge-Kalischer disease, Parks-Weber-Dimitri disease, Sturge-Weber-Dimitri disease,** and **Sturge-Weber-Krabbe disease**). A disease characterized by a unilateral port-wine-colored stain on the face, this was first described by Sturge in 1879. These patients have vascular lesions and abnormal blood-flow patterns and exhibit such symptoms as seizures, glaucoma, mental retardation, and behavior problems. The treatment aims at reversing the more serious problems, namely, the glaucoma, the seizures, and the vascular irregularities.

Stuttering. See: **disfluency.**

Subcutaneously (SC). By one avenue for the injection of a chemical agent into the body, namely, through the skin. See also: **intramuscularly (IM); intraperitoneally (IP); intravenously (IV).**

Subfornical (sub fôr′ni kəl) **organ.** A hypothalamic region situated next to the third ventricle, which puts it in a good position to monitor the water content of the extracellular fluid, blood, and cerebrospinal fluid. This kind of information provides the basis for hypovolemic thirst. See also: **hypovolemic thirst.**

Subject. The term for an organism (person or animal) whose behavior is examined in psychological research. A subject is a participant other than the experimenter(s)/researcher(s) in a research study.

Sublimation. One of Sigmund Freud's defense mechanisms. Conflicting drives are not only repressed, but they are converted into acceptable forms. For example, a person covering up inner hostile urges becomes a literary critic. The concept of this particular defense mechanism is not accepted by all clinicians; a major defect is that the "sublimated achievements" of the defensive individual have not succeeded in changing the repressed material, which is still there in any case. See also: **defense mechanism**.

Subliminal (sub lim′i nəl) **perception** (once known as "subception," a term which has become obsolete). Perception of a stimulus that is either too weak, too brief, or too well concealed to be detected or recognized by normal sense receptors. The reality of this phenomenon has been challenged, usually successfully. For example, the claims of advocates of the power of subliminal advertising have been refuted in experimental tests. See also: **absolute threshold; extrasensory perception**.

Subluxation (sub″luk sā′shən). A partial dislocation of a bone. This is said by some chiropractors to lead to dyslexia. See also: **sphenoid wing malfunction**.

Subplate cell. A temporary neuron that takes shape in a layer just underneath the developing cerebral cortex. It (along with other subplate cells) acts as a guide for subcortical cell axons growing upward to the cortex and for cortical axons growing down through the subplate layer to subcortical synapses. These axons follow axons of the subplate cells that connect to the cortex above the subplate and the subcortical brain below it. After the more mature subcortical-cortical connections have developed, the subplate neurons die off.

Substance P. A chemical neurotransmitter used by the afferent neurons that relay pain messages to the central nervous system.

Substantia nigra (sub stan′shə, -shē ə nī′grə) (from Latin "substantia" = "substance"; "nigra" = "black"). A nucleus in the midbrain tegmentum, ventral even to the ventral tegmental area, which is part of the basal ganglia system for motor coordination and the control of movement. The name is due to the presence of melanin (our skin-tanning chemical) in the cell bodies of the neurons comprising this nucleus. The

neurotransmitter dopamine is synthesized in these cell bodies and sent along the axons that run to the caudate nucleus and the putamen, two parts of the corpus striatum and two of the basal ganglia of the forebrain. A malfunctioning of the substantia nigra and/or its axons is implicated in the neuromuscular disorder called Parkinson's disease. See also: **basal ganglia; corpus striatum; dopamine; nigrostriatal pathway; Parkinson's disease.**

Substitution. A disorder of articulation in which one sound of a language is replaced by another sound from that language. See also: **articulation disorder**.

Subthalamic (sub″thə lam′ik) **nucleus**. One of the more caudal of the basal ganglia, situated near the borderline between the thalamus and midbrain. Like the rest of the extrapyramidal motor system, this nucleus plays a part in the planning of movements. See also: **basal ganglia; extrapyramidal motor fibers; supplementary motor cortex.**

Subtractive color mixing. The process of combining different color crayons (or coats of paint) in order to produce new hues. Subtractive mixing involves the principle that a pigment absorbs all wavelengths except the one (or few) that it reflects to the perceiver. When red and green paints are overlaid, only poorly saturated parts of the red and green light are able to be reflected; thus the nonspectral color brown is produced when red and green are combined. When all colors of paint are laid over one another at the same place, the result is the perception of black, because no wavelengths are reflected from the object. This is very different from the effects of **additive color mixing** (see definition).

Subtyping. Research has shown that dyslexics display diverse symptomatologies, with possible clusters of individuals evincing enough within-group homogeneity to warrant classification into subtypes. The present authors have suggested three dyslexic subtype groups.

Sucking reflex. The reflexive sucking by an infant of objects touching its lips.

Sudden infant death syndrome (SIDS). Crib death; the unexplained death of a seemingly healthy infant. SIDS accounts for the majority of deaths among infants aged less than 1 year. Various theories have been suggested by different types of practitioners. Psychologists tend to blame SIDS on sleep apnea, the inability to breathe while sleeping. Some attribute the apnea to the immaturity of the respiration pathways in the brain stem. The most effective medical advice at this writing is to make sure that the baby sleeps on its back, not its belly. The reason that sleeping on the back favors survival may be that this position permits freer breathing than does the other, the belly-down position. High-risk signs for SIDS include: (1) a teenage mother who smokes; (2) premature birth; (3) the baby's cries are unusually high-pitched and shrill; (4) the baby snores, holds its breath, and awakens frequently; (5) the baby usually breathes through the open mouth; and (6) the baby is passive when face-down on a pillow and moves very little when asleep. There are baby monitors for high-risk infants; these devices can awaken the caretaker when the baby's breathing has stopped. See also: **apnea**; **sleep disorders**.

Sulcus (sul′kus, sool′-) [plural = sulci (sul′sī)]. A groove or inward fold in the cerebellum or the cerebral cortex. The upward folds or convolutions between the sulci are the gyri (singular = gyrus). When a sulcus is especially long and deep, it is called a fissure.

Superior. [1] Above or higher than. [2] At the top end.

Superior colliculus (kə lik′yoo lus). A hill-shaped structure atop the midbrain. Some optic nerve fibers bypass the lateral geniculate nucleus and arrive at the superior colliculus instead. The one visual function it is known to have in the human nervous system is blindsight, which is a phenomenon whereby a person can locate an object by vision and reach for it successfully without the awareness that he or she is able to see. See: **blindsight**.

Superior olivary nucleus (ol′i ver ē noo′klē əs, nyoo′-). A collection of nerve cell bodies in the medulla situated just above the olive-shaped inferior olivary nucleus. Nerve fibers are sent to the right and left superior olivary nuclei from the medulla's ventral cochlear nuclei. The output from the two superior olivary nuclei, traveling over the left and right lateral lemniscus, arrives at the left and right nucleus of the lateral lemniscus. Sound localization (knowing what side of the body the sound stimulus is coming from)

based on a loudness difference between the ear nearest to the sound source and the other ear is perceived by a pathway through the lateral part of the superior olivary nucleus. Sound localization based on the time of arrival of a single sound wave at each ear (i.e., the phase difference cue) is processed through the medial part of the superior olivary nucleus. Very small-headed animals (e.g., mice) cannot use the latter (phase-difference) cue, since one side of the sound wave cannot affect the second ear when the head is less wide than the sound's wavelength. Accordingly, mice have only a lateral-type superior olivary nucleus, and they and other very small-headed animals must use only high-frequency sounds for the localization of a sound's source. Mnemonic device: LLLL, the lateral (superior olivary nucleus) localizes by [differences in] loudness, in little heads.

Supplementary motor cortex. A part of the frontal lobe, which is active when a movement is being planned (even if the movement is not actually carried out). It is located in the superior (uppermost) regions of Brodmann's areas 6 and 8; part of it is within the longitudinal fissure. See also: **basal ganglia**; **extrapyramidal motor fibers**; **premotor cortex**; **subthalamic nucleus**.

Supported employment. Support provided by occupational trainers and coaches that offers job training and employment in integrated settings to disabled persons.

Suprachiasmatic nucleus (soo″prə kī az mat′ik noo′klē əs, nyoo-) (SCN). A collection of nerve cell bodies located just above the optic chiasma in the hypothalamus, the SCN is involved in the regulation of our circadian rhythms. Information about the relative light or darkness of the external world reaches the SCN from the eye by way of a small branch of the optic nerve. Metabolic activity in the SCN varies in rate; much protein synthesis occurs in SCN neurons in the daylight hours, and the activity is greatly reduced during the night. This activity cycle is an example of a physical or chemical process that can be used to control body functions that occur once a day, that is, the circadian rhythms. Such an example is called a Zeitgeber ("time-giver" in German). See also: **circadian rhythms**; **entrainment**; **Zeitgeber**.

Supraoptic nucleus (soo″prə op′tik noo′klē əs,

nyo͞o-). A set of nerve cell bodies found just above the optic chiasma of the hypothalamus. The supraoptic nucleus neurons release the antidiuretic hormone (ADH), which is transported along the axons of those neurons to the neurohypophysis (posterior lobe of the pituitary gland). ADH promotes the retention of urinary water, slowing down urine production and conserving the internal water resources of the body. See also: **antidiuretic hormone**.

Surface dyslexia (dis lek′sē ə). Surface, or semantic, dyslexia has been described as an inability to recognize whole words rapidly and accurately, although phonetically regular words can be decoded. This suggests some phonemic synthesis ability. The misreading of irregularly spelled words has been seen to result from an overapplication of phonics principles (e.g., "precise" is pronounced "priest"). Neurological damage has been postulated to cause this problem.

Surface structure. The spoken or written form of a sentence. Psycholinguists argue that it is only in their surface structures that the various languages differ. According to this theoretical view, the underlying basis of the sentence, the deep structure, is common to all languages.

Surround (of a receptive field). The outermost circle of the circular receptive field of a bipolar or ganglion cell in the retina. The stimulus is from the surround of a bipolar neuron when the receptor communicates to a horizontal cell that relays the message to the bipolar cell. See also: **center (of a receptive field)**; **horizontal cell**; **receptive field**.

Suspensory ligament (sus pen′sə rē lig′ə ment). The relaxation of the ciliary muscle allows this ligament, attached to the upper and lower ends of the human lens, to snap the lens into an elongated, only slightly-bulged, shape.

Sustained visual pathway. A neural pathway from the eye to the brain which is activated at the onset of the visual stimulus and continues to be active while the stimulus remains. The input to it is mainly derived from activation of cone receptors.

Sweep test. A popular hearing screening test which is done with a portable audiometer. Tones between 20 and 25 decibels are presented at frequencies of 500 Hertz (Hz), 1,000 Hz, 2,000 Hz,

and 6,000 Hz. Individuals who have difficulty detecting sounds at these frequencies are referred for more extensive hearing tests.

Sydenham's chorea (sīd′n hamz kə rē′ə). A mild form of motor disorder involving rapid twitching of the muscles. This condition, which mainly affects young people, is sometimes called St. Vitus' dance. See also: **chorea**; **Huntington's chorea**.

Symbolization (sim″bə li zā′shən). The internal representation of sensory perceptions in memory, comprehension, and communication. The symbols used may be iconic (i.e., visual), linguistic, echoic (i.e., auditory), musical, and so on.

Sympathectomy (sim″pə thek′tə mē). The surgical removal of the two chains of sympathetic ganglia that lie on either side of the spinal cord. Because this operation would remove all sympathetic nervous system functions, it is used as a last resort. For example, if Raynaud's disease has progressed to the point where the involved fingers or toes get gangrene, the surgery may be undertaken. See also: **Raynaud's disease; sympathetic nervous system**.

Sympathetic (sim″pə thet′ik) **nervous system (SNS)** or **sympathetic division of the autonomic nervous system**. Short neurons from the brain and the thoracic and lumbar (middle) segments of the spinal cord arrive at one or another of a chain of vertically aligned ganglia. The alternate name for the sympathetic nervous system is the thoracicolumbar system. There are two sympathetic chains of ganglia, running parallel to (but clearly outside of) the spinal cord, one on the left side and one on the right. The short axons from the central nervous system to the ganglionic chain are provided with myelin sheaths. After synapsing within the ganglia, the sympathetic pathway is continued, as nerve fibers (having their cell bodies in the ganglia) run for long distances to their respective endings upon smooth muscles or glands. These longer, unmyelinated axons from the ganglionic chains would seem paradoxical, since a myelin sheath speeds up the passage of the nerve impulse along the axon, and yet the shorter fibers have such a sheath while the longer fibers lack one. The sympathetic nervous system terminals release the chemical neurotransmitter norepinephrine (norEp) at the neuromuscular junction. The parts of the SNS tend to work all at once; hence, the name "sympathetic," implying the "togetherness" of all the members of the system. The SNS is called upon to organize and execute "emergency reactions" when the organism is forced into a type of behavior that can be classified as "fight or flight." The sympathetic nervous system (1) activates the adrenal medulla gland, so that it releases its hormones (i.e., norepinephrine and epinephrine); (2) controls the dilation of the pupils of the eyes; (3) speeds up the heartbeat; (4) relaxes the gastrointestinal tract smooth muscles; (5) inhibits the tear glands; (6) constricts the small blood vessels of the skin; (7) inhibits the pancreas; (8) relaxes the bladder; (9) stimulates ejaculation of seminal fluid from the penis; (10) dilates the coronary arteries; (11) dilates the bronchi; and (12) promotes perspiration of the forehead, the palms, and the soles. Indirectly, due to the release of epinephrine from the adrenal medulla, the level of blood sugar is increased. With more oxygen and glucose being rushed to the skeletal muscles, the latter are greatly increased in strength. Additionally, the increase in norEp results in activation of the stress-resisting functions of the adrenal cortex gland. Signs of sympathetic activity can betray the fact that a person is under the influence of strong emotion. Having a rapid heart rate while resting, showing sweat at the forehead and the palms when the temperature is moderately cool, and showing constricted pupils when the lighting is not very strong are all instances of sympathetic nervous system activation, implying that a "fight- or flight"-related emotion is present. See also: **adrenal gland; adrenal medulla; autonomic nervous system; emergency reaction; endocrine system; epinephrine; hormones; norepinephrine; peripheral nervous system.**

Symptom substitution. The appearance of a new symptom which replaces an earlier one that had been eliminated as a result of therapy.

Synapse (sin'aps). The place where one neuron communicates with another. The communication across a synapse is much slower than the rate at which the nerve impulse travels down the axon. The synapse is like a one-way street, since one neuron is sending a message and the other neuron is receiving the message. Synapses can have

either of two functions, excitation or inhibition. An excitatory synapse, when activated by the sending (or presynaptic) neuron, causes the membrane of the receiving (or postsynaptic) neuron to be depolarized, making it easier for a nerve impulse to be started in that neuron. The activation of an inhibitory synapse causes a hyperpolarization of the postsynaptic membrane. Almost all synaptic activity involves the movement of a small quantity of chemical neurotransmitter from the presynaptic membrane to the postsynaptic membrane. See also: **depolarization; hyperpolarization; polarization.**

Synaptic bouton (sin ap'tik boo ton'). The knob-like structure at the end of each of the telodendria at the end of an axon. The bouton is also called an end bulb, synaptic knob, or end foot. Within the bouton are stored the synaptic vesicles. The membrane of the bouton is the presynaptic (sending) membrane at a synapse; the neurotransmitter is released into the small gap between the neurons from this membrane.

Synaptic cleft or **synaptic space**. The very narrow gap between the presynaptic and postsynaptic membranes. The molecules of neurotransmitters cross the gap from the presynaptic membrane and travel to receptor sites on the postsynaptic membrane.

Synaptic transmission theory. A theory of information processing whereby neurons in the central nervous system communicate information across synapses, the narrow spaces between neurons, via chemical neurotransmitters. This mode of communication is analogous to a locomotive racing along fixed tracks to its destination. The synaptic transmission theory can be considered the "dry" theory of information processing. See also: **information processing; volume transmission theory**.

Synaptic vesicles (ves'i kəls). Small containers of chemical neurotransmitter(s) within the synaptic boutons. When the nerve impulse arrives, the vesicles migrate to the presynaptic membrane. Catalyzed by the calcium ion, a process of vesicle rupture ensues, with small amounts of neurotransmitters getting released into the synaptic cleft. With some neurotransmitters, the unused quantity of transmitter reenters the bouton (reuptake) and migrates to the vesicles after reaching the interior of the bouton.

Syndrome (sin'drōm). The collection of symptoms comprising a single disease entity or disorder.

Synergistic (sin″ûr jis'tik). Refers to any two muscles whose contraction leads to the same movement of a joint. See also: **synergy.**

Synergy (sin'ûr jē). The situation in which the combination of two factors having like effects on a phenomenon is more powerful than doubling the amount of just one of these factors. It is often expressed as "2 + 2 = 5." An example of synergy is the effect on hypovolemic thirst of low blood pressure messages from the baroceptors together with the release of the kidney hormone angiotensin II. See also: **angiotensin II; baroceptor.**

Syntax. The set of rules in a language describing how words should be formed into sentences.

Syntonics (sin ton'iks). A system (advocated by some optometrists) used for treating learning disabilities by hypothetically expanding the visual field with red and blue lights.

Syphilis (sif'i lis). A bacterial infection resulting from sexual activity that, after some years of dormancy, attacks brain and spinal cord tissues. If untreated, the disease may be fatal.

Systematic desensitization. A method of behavior therapy used for phobias. The object of the fear is first presented faintly and far away, while the subject is deeply relaxed. Gradually the presence of the object is strengthened (i.e., its image is made clearer and it is brought closer). Finally, the patient is completely accepting and feels quite comfortable with the object.

T

Tabes dorsalis (tā′bēz dôr sal′is, -sā′lis) (from Latin "tabes" = "wasting away"). A neuromuscular disorder resulting from the destruction of the dorsal root neurons, which provide touch and kinesthetic inputs to the spinal cord. It is usually caused by the bacterium involved in the sexually transmitted disease syphilis. The symptoms include reduced sensation from lower parts of the body, impaired reflexes of the lower limbs, difficulty in walking, and loss of control of the bowels and bladder.

Tachistoscope (tə kis″tə skōp′ik). A type of slide projector which allows visual stimuli such as pictures, numerals, letters, or words to be flashed for brief times (measurable in milliseconds). The word "tachistoscopically" means "by the use of a tachistoscope."

Tachistoscopic (tə kis′tə skop″ik) **presentation**. The projection of a visual stimulus for a specified fraction of a second. The precise control of projection times may be accomplished by optical or electronic means or by a combination of the two.

Tachycardia (tak″i kär′dē ə) (from the Greek "tachys" = ʻrapid"; "kardia" = "heart"). Faster-than-normal heart rate.

Tactile-kinesthetic (tak′til-kin″es thet′ik) **techniques**. These techniques are based on the VAKT (visual-auditory-kinesthetic-tactual) method outlined first by Fernald. Typically, a student will be taught to see a word, hear the word, feel the word (e.g., by tracing it in sand or using sandpaper letters), and say (and hear) the word as it is traced in order to reinforce learning through more than just the visual/auditory mode.

Talented. Gifted; or, having a superior ability in a particular area, such as music, art, or mathematics. See also: **giftedness**.

Talking Books. Books on tape; along with large-print books, talking books are the primary forms of literary instruction for the visually impaired.

Talking Programs. Computer programs using digitized speech which may originate from a speech synthesizer or from a computer disc.

Tangle. A group of entangled, degenerated axon and dendrite fibers observed in the brains of deceased Alzheimer's disease patients. Tangles are believed to be the relics of destroyed neurons.

See also: **Alzheimer's disease**.

Tardive dyskinesia. A Parkinson's disease-like set of symptoms that develop in schizophrenic patients who have been given neuroleptic drugs on a daily basis for many years. The presumed cause of this syndrome is the anti-dopamine activity of such drugs and the dependence of the basal ganglia on the unrestricted activity of dopamine-releasing neurons. See also: **accumbens; basal ganglia; chlorpromazine; clozapine; l-DOPA; dopamine; haloperidol; neuroleptic drug; neuroleptic-induced Parkinsonism; Parkinson's disease; schizophrenia; substantia nigra; ventral tegmental area.**

Task analysis. The breakdown of a complex skill into its simplest components so that each component can be taught. This is done in order to make learning easier.

Task commitment. One of Renzulli's three criteria for giftedness. An individual shows that he or she is task-committed by voluntarily taking on difficult assignments in the area in which he or she is gifted. The other two criteria are above-average ability and creativity.

Taste. A chemical sense, with most receptors on the tongue and others on the linings of the mouth. There are four primary taste qualities: sweet, the receptors for which are found at the tip of the tongue, in the front; salty and sour, both of which have receptors along the sides of the tongue, in back of the "sweet" receptors; and bitter, which has its receptors at the back of the tongue. The receptors are housed in structures called taste buds. See also: **taste buds**.

Taste blindness. A sometimes hereditary loss of the ability to detect specific tastes. For instance, there is an inherited trait, which is recessive, for the inability to taste the chemical phenylthiocarbamide (PTC). This substance tastes bitter to most people, and those who are taste-blind to PTC are able to taste other bitter substances. See also: **miraculin; taste.**

Taste buds. The structures containing the receptors for taste that are found on the papillae of the tongue as well as on the linings of the mouth. When you look in the mirror and stick out your tongue, the papillae are those upright, bumpy things you can detect. Adults have approximately 10,000 taste buds, and each taste bud holds 50 receptors. The receptors are short-lived hair cells and are constantly being replaced, about every seven days. Chemical reactions take place between the taste buds and the food that result in nerve impulses that are sent via the seventh and ninth cranial nerves ultimately to the parietal lobe of the cerebral cortex.

Tay-Sachs (tā'saks') **disease**. A genetic disorder that can lead to early death. It most commonly attacks Jewish individuals of eastern European descent.

T cell. A type of leukocyte (white blood corpuscle) that develops in the thymus organ.

TDD (also called a **TTY**). Telecommunication Device for the Deaf. The device permits deaf people to communicate by telephone. They type on a keyboard instead of speaking and read incoming messages that are being printed on the screen of a rectangular glass monitor.

Tectorial (tek tôr'ē əl) **membrane**. The membrane in the cochlea that rests upon the hairs of the hair cells. The hair cells are the receptors for hearing. See also: **basilar membrane; cochlea; hair cells; hearing.**

Tectum (tek'tum) (from Latin "tectum" = "deck" or "covering"). The roof of the midbrain. On it are the four landmarks, the hillock-shaped bumps known as the two superior colliculi and the two inferior colliculi. The superior colliculi are related to visual functions and the inferior colliculi are involved in auditory functioning. See also: **inferior colliculus; superior colliculus**.

Tegmentum (teg men'tum) (from Latin "tegmentum" = "roof" or "covering"; we guess that a tectum covers a tegmentum, though!). The medium-height portion of the midbrain. It is ventral to the **tectum** or roof of the midbrain and dorsal to the cerebral peduncles which form the floor of the midbrain. Within the tegmentum are the **ascending reticular arousal system**, the **central gray matter**, the most superior (or rostral) of the **raphe nuclei**, the **red nucleus**, the **ventral tegmental area**, and the **substantia nigra**. (See definitions of terms in boldface.)

Telecommunication Device for the Deaf (TDD). See **TDD**.

Telegraphic speech. Using sentences that contain only essential nouns and verbs, omitting articles,

prepositions, and adverbs. This may be one of the symptoms of Broca's aphasia.

Telencephalon (tel″en sef'ə lon″) (from Greek "tel" = "end"; "encephalon" = "brain"). The front end of the brain. The telencephalon is in front of and above the diencephalon. The telencephalon (which is the same part of the brain as the cerebrum) includes the cerebral hemispheres, the limbic system (except for the hypothalamus, of course), the basal ganglia, and the olfactory bulbs. Within the telencephalon are two large cavities, the lateral ventricles, which contain cerebrospinal fluid. See also: **basal ganglia; cerebral cortex; cerebral ventricles; diencephalon; limbic system.**

Telephone theory of hearing. A theory of auditory pitch perception proposed by the physicist Ernest Rutherford. The number of cycles per second (c.p.s.) in the frequency of the sound stimulus is matched by the number of nerve impulses per second in the auditory nerve. The mechanism is feasible for only the low frequencies (from 15 c.p.s., the lowest pitch we can detect, to 1,000 c.p.s. at the most), because the absolute refractory period follows each and every single nerve impulse. See also: **basilar membrane; place-resonance theory of hearing; volley theory of hearing.**

Telodendria (tel″ō den'drē ə). The tiny end-branches at the opposite end of the axon from the cell body. Each end-branch terminates in a synaptic bouton, or end bulb.

Temperament. The inborn emotional tone and quality of a person's behavior. One's temperament has been called the sum total of the innate aspects of one's personality.

Temporal (tem'pər əl) **bone**. A compound bone at the side of the skull.

Temporal hemiretina (tem'pər əl hem″i ret'n ə). The half of the retina nearest the temple (i.e., the lateral half). It sends ipsilateral optic nerve fibers to the visual areas of the brain on the same side of the body's midline as the eye. See also: **ipsilateral; retina.**

Temporal (tem'pər əl) **lobe**. The most ventral of the four lobes of the cerebral cortex. It is located directly in front of (rostral to) the occipital lobe. The temporal lobe lies near the temporal bone of the skull and, therefore, the temple of the head. The outer (lateral) aspect of either cerebral hemisphere resembles a fist in a boxing glove. The temporal lobe would be like the thumb of the boxing glove in that analogy. A long and deep horizontal groove, the fissure of Sylvius, or lateral fissure, separates the temporal lobe from the frontal and parietal lobes that are dorsal to it. The temporal lobe does not completely take up the ventral surface of the cortex, because the posterior part of that ventral surface belongs to the occipital lobe. The temporal lobe is associated with visual, auditory, language, and long-term memory storage functions.

Temporal stem. A tract of axons in the medial temporal lobe just dorsal to the hippocampus. Destruction of the temporal stem may lead to a type of memory loss called medial-temporal-lobe amnesia.

Temporal summation. The additivity of a series of excitatory or inhibitory synaptic effects on a postsynaptic membrane resulting from a quick succession of nerve impulses in the axon of the presynaptic neuron. The result is that the postsynaptic or receiving membrane shows an increased amplitude of a positive or negative voltage. Such summation can only occur in the case of **graded potentials** (see definition).

Tensor tympani (ten′sər tim′pə nē). A muscle in the middle ear attached to the hammer (malleus), the first of the three auditory ossicles. The hammer is attached to the inner surface of the eardrum, or tympanic membrane. The function of the muscle is to dampen the vibrations of the hammer when the sound stimulation is of both high intensity and high frequency. Very rapid and very forceful blows by the hammer on the anvil, the second ossicle, could cause these small bones to shatter. Since the command to dampen the action comes from the brain, the information about the sound frequency and the sound intensity is not lost. The motor nerve fibers to this muscle come from the fifth cranial nerve, the trigeminal. See also: **middle ear**; **ossicles**.

Teratogenesis (ter″ə tō jen′ə sis) (from Greek "teratos" = "monster"; "genesis" = "production"). The development of deformed infants, during the gestation period, caused by the mother's use of some drug, such as thalidomide or ethyl alcohol. See also: **phocomelia**; **teratogenic**; **thalidomide**.

Teratogenic (ter ″ə tō jen′ik) ("teratos" = "monster" in Greek; "genic" refers to "forming"). Refers to environmental influences which correlate highly with the onset of certain handicapping conditions. Drugs, alcohol, smoking, and food deprivation are teratogenic. See also: **teratogenesis**.

Terminal buttons. See: **synaptic bouton**.

Test anxiety. A syndrome exhibited by 30% of all students and occurring in all socioeconomic groups. Females exhibit more anxiety in testing situations than do males. The psychological symptoms include negative thoughts about personal abilities and performance, feelings of inadequacy and ineffectiveness, a sense of personal failure, and feelings of being poorly regarded by others. Reactions involving the autonomic nervous system include rapid heartbeat, sweaty palms and underarms, and an upset stomach. This problem has been treated by behavior modification techniques, skills training, training in the strategy of test taking, and cognitive-behavioral methods.

Testes (tes′tēz). The male sex glands, or gonads. The testes secrete a set of steroid hormones called androgens, one of which is testosterone. The androgens are responsible for the appearance of the male secondary sexual characteristics, including the dropping outside the abdomen of the testicles, the lowering of the voice, and the increased hair growth in the pectoral and pelvic regions.

Testicular (tes tik′yoo lər) **feminization** (also called **androgen insensitivity**). The appearance of female gender in a person with the XY chromosome pair. The body does not have the ability to bind the androgens to the genes in the cell nuclei. As a result, the cells do not react to the androgens. At puberty, there is no menstruation, since the body possesses the abdominal testes and no ovary or uterus. The pubic hair fails to develop. In other respects, the person is a normal female. Surgery can remove the internal testes to avoid the risk of future illness.

Testosterone (tes tos′tə rōn″). The male hormone which is secreted by the testes, the male gonads. On occasion, the ovaries, the female gonads, also secrete testosterone. Like the other sex hormones, testosterone is a steroid. Testosterone determines the gender of a developing infant. If there is enough testosterone present during the third and fourth months of pregnancy, the infant will be a male; otherwise, the infant will be female. In healthy men aged 18 to 60, the range of testosterone level in the blood is from 350 to 1,000 nanograms per 100 milliliters of blood. After the age of 60, testosterone levels fall, although, even in their eighties, many men exhibit normal testosterone levels. In adults, the level of testosterone has been linked to the amount of aggressive violence that an individual exhibits. Violence is greatest among males between the ages of 15 and 25. In these years, testosterone levels reach their highest values. In both male and female prisoners, violent crime is correlated with increased testosterone; prisoners tend to have more violent personalities when they have high testosterone levels. It would be a mistake, however, to draw a causal inference from these correlational data. See also: **endocrine system; gonads; hormones; steroid hormones**.

Test-retest reliability. This is a technique for measuring the reliability of a test, whereby the test is given a second time to a group of examinees. The scores on the first administration of the test are correlated with the scores on the second testing. The resulting correlation coefficient is the test-retest reliability coefficient for the test.

Texture gradient. A monocular (requiring only one eye) visual cue which assists us in determining the distance and depth of objects in the environment. Objects in distant places have smoother and less textured appearances.

Thalamus (thal′ə mus). A structure in the forebrain dorsal to the hypothalamus. The thalamus, which is pillow-shaped ("thalamus" is the word for "bridal chamber" in Greek), surrounds an opening called the third ventricle, which is filled with cerebrospinal fluid. The left and right thalami are so close to the midline that they resemble two footballs side by side. Above and around the thalamus are the cerebral hemispheres. The thalamus serves as a way-station for pathways running from lower parts of the brain to the cerebral cortex. Many nuclei within the thalamus are called relay nuclei, because they send axons to the sensory projection areas of the cortex. For instance, the lateral geniculate nucleus sends its axons to the visual occipital lobe of the cortex. As another example, the medial genicu-

late nucleus communicates to the auditory region in the temporal lobe. Again, the posterior ventral nucleus of the thalamus sends nerve fibers to the postcentral gyrus of the parietal lobe, bearing information concerning the various body senses, such as deep pressure, light touch, warmth, cold, pain, and kinesthesis.

Thalidomide (thə lid′ə mīd). A drug once used to relieve morning sickness that can produce congenital deformities in the gestating fetus when taken by a pregnant woman. See also: **phocomelia; teratogenesis; teratogenic**.

Thanatologist (than″ə tol′ə jist). One who studies death and dying. Thanatological research has demonstrated five basic emotional reactions of people who are dying: (1) denial and isolation, (2) anger, (3) bargaining, (4) depression, and (5) acceptance. Subsequent research has shown that not all terminally ill persons display all five of these emotions, and these emotions are not necessarily displayed in precisely this order.

THC (tetrahydrocannabinol) (tet″rə hī″drō kə nab′i nôl). The active ingredient in marijuana. This is one of the **hallucinogens** (see definition). See also: **anandamide; marijuana**.

Theories of forgetting. Some major theories about the forgetting of information from long-term memory include **decay, interference, retrieval failure**, and **motivated forgetting** (see definitions). Senile dementias (such as Alzheimer's disease), head traumas, cancer, strokes, viruses, and other pathological factors can also cause forgetting.

Theories of hearing. See: **hearing, theories of**.

Theory. A series of organized facts and hypotheses which attempt to explain a known or unknown phenomenon and that allow for the prediction of new facts or events related to phenomenon; sound theories provide starting points for new research endeavors in order to confirm, disconfirm, or revise underlying premises and assumptions.

Theta (thā′tə) **waves**. A very slow up-and-down rhythm of voltage changes in the EEG. Theta waves have a frequency of from 5 through 7 cycles per second. This is not as slow as the delta waves of sleep stages 3 and 4, but it is the slowest kind of brain wave we can have while we are awake. The stage of relaxation that accompanies theta waves is reportedly superior to that which accompanies alpha waves. Achieving a theta wave EEG shows that someone really knows how to take it easy! See also: **electroencephalogram.**

Thigmotropism (thig mot′rə piz ″əm) (from Greek "thigma" = "touch"; "tropos" = "turning"; "ismos" = "condition"). The tendency to stay near vertical walls, to attempt to have tactile stimulation over most of one's skin receptors. For instance, rodents placed in a strange area will tend to hug the walls rather than venture out into the open.

Thirst drive. One of the primary drives. The stimuli for thirst are (1) the fluid levels outside the cells and (2) the concentration of materials dissolved in the cytoplasm within cells. Different mechanisms deal with the two sources of thirst, although, in real life rather than contrived laboratory conditions, both kinds of thirst stimuli occur together. Situational factors such as the foods we eat, the emotional states we are in, and social circumstances can influence the level of the thirst drive. See also: **intracellular thirst; volemic thirst.**

Thoracic (thô ras′ik). Pertaining to the thorax or chest. There are 12 pairs of thoracic spinal nerves leaving from 12 thoracic segments of the spinal cord. See also: **spinal cord; spinal nerves.**

Threshold. [1] The degree of depolarization needed for a neuron to produce an action potential. This is the point at which brief stimulation initiates a rapid and large flow of ions across the neuronal cell membrane. [2] The minimum intensity of physical energy needed to produce a sensation. The minimum amount of physical energy required to produce this sensory experience is called the <u>absolute threshold</u>. Some interesting sensory thresholds are: a candle flame can be seen 50 kilometers, or 30 miles, away on clear late evening; one can hear the tick of a watch from 20 feet, or 6 meters, away in a quiet room; and one can taste 1 gram, or .0356 ounce, of salt in 500 liters, or 529 quarts, of water. These are the absolute thresholds at which the various stimuli mentioned (i.e., candle flame, watch and salt) initiate a sensory experience (i.e., sight, hearing and taste). It should be added that not all sensory thresholds are examples of the absolute threshold. For example, there is the <u>differ-</u>

<u>ence threshold</u>, which is the least amount of a change or difference in stimulation that can be detected as being a difference. In the measurement of a difference threshold, the two stimuli being compared need to be well above the subject's absolute threshold.

Threshold of hearing. The least value of sound intensity that will let the subject sense a sound stimulus; the point at which hearing begins. See also: **absolute threshold.**

Thyroid (thī′roid″) **gland.** An endocrine gland located just above the larynx (the voice box). It secretes **thyroxine** (see definition). Overactivity of the thyroid leads to restlessness, inattention, irritability, and very fast speech which is hard to decipher because new words begin before the preceding words are completed. Individuals with overactivity of the thyroid are said to be hyperthyroid. Underactivity of the thyroid is accompanied by lethargy, sluggishness, weakness, and slow, soft speech. Such persons are described as hypothyroid. An individual born with an underfunctioning or absent thyroid gland is at risk of developing cretinism, which involves shortness of height, a receding forehead and protruding tongue, and mental retardation. The stage moron of vaudeville days was modeled on the typical cretin. Nowadays, prenatal tests can detect the problem early enough to prevent such development. The individual can take supplemental thyroxine treatments and avoid this problem. A less serious thyroid problem, enlargement of the thyroid (goiter), is due to a shortage of iodine in the blood. Iodine is one of the ingredients of thyroxine. In attempting to capture whatever traces of iodine might be present in the blood, the thyroid cells enlarge.

Thyroid- (thī′roid″) **stimulating hormone (TSH).** A tropic hormone of the anterior pituitary (or master gland) which, on reaching the thyroid gland via the bloodstream, stimulates it to release its hormone thyroxine. See also: **tropic hormone.**

Thyrotropic (thī″rə trop′ik, -trō′pik) **hormone (TH).** See: **thyroid-stimulating hormone.**

Thyrotropin (thī rot′rə pin, thī′rə trō′pin). See: **thyroid-stimulating hormone.**

Thyrotropin-releasing hormone (TRH). A hormone manufactured by neurosecretory cells of the hypothalamus. The axons of these cells run along the infundibulum to the master gland, the anterior pituitary. TRH stimulates the release of TSH from the anterior pituitary. See also: **anterior pituitary; hypothalamus; infundibulum; neurosecretory cells; thyroid-stimulating hormone.**

Thyroxine (thī rok'sin). A hormone of the thyroid gland. Thyroxine causes the body cells to step up their rate of metabolism. It helps maintain body temperature at the normal value of 98.6 degrees Fahrenheit. Thyroxine also helps maintain muscle tone and metabolic rate. A shortage of thyroxine will lead to lethargy, temperature change, and reduced muscle tone. See also: **endocrine system; thyroid gland; thyroid-stimulating hormone.**

Timbre (tam'bər, tim'bər). The quality or texture of a sound created by the harmonics (overtones) added to the basic or fundamental note. When a note is produced on a musical instrument, some but not all of the whole number multiples of the note's frequency are added. The particular set of overtones gives the instrument its distinctive sound. This is why you can tell which of the orchestra's instruments is playing; each instrument has its own timbre, that is, its unique set of overtones. Music synthesizers can be set to produce, electronically, the timbre of any standard instrument. See also: **harmonics; sound.**

Time out. A technique of punishment for undesirable behavior in which the individual is removed from a pleasant, reinforcing situation. See also: **punishment; reinforcement.**

Tip-of-the-tongue phenomenon. The sensation of knowing you can produce a word or phrase but of not being able to recall it when needed. Even when we cannot recall a specific word or phrase, we do have knowledge of how the word(s) sound(s). Trying to remember the name of a person to whom one has just been introduced can result in the tip-of-the-tongue experience. One might remember the first letter or letters of the name and "just know" that, if given time, one can come up with the name.

Token economy. Tokens (such as stamps, poker chips, etc.) are given to an individual (usually in an institutional setting such as a hospital, school, or prison) as reinforcers following good behavior. The tokens are exchanged for desirable objects or privileges at some later time.

Token test. A test for language loss (aphasia) in which the subject is required to manipulate tokens of various shapes and colors.

Tolerance. One of the hallmarks of drug addiction. The individual becomes less and less sensitive to the drug and must take an ever-higher dosage of the drug simply to obtain the same effect. Strongly addictive drugs such as opiates, amphetamines, and barbiturates produce tolerance effects. Strangely, marijuana use results in "reverse tolerance," whereby it requires less and less of the drug to produce the same effect. See also: **opponent-process theory of drug-withdrawal symptoms**.

Tonic. Having to do with muscle tone changes, without actual movement of a part of the body taking place. Postural reflexes that supply muscle tone to our limb flexors and extensors simultaneously turn our limbs into structural supports so that we can remain standing. Tonic responses during REM sleep include the overall loss of tone in the larger, anti-gravity muscles and the temporary quieting of the rapid eye movements between REM-bursts.

Tonic phase. The first phase of a grand mal seizure in an epileptic patient. All the muscles contract and the limbs are extended stiffly. Air is forced from the lungs. Consciousness is lost completely. The posture is quite rigid and stiff. This phase lasts for 15 seconds, when it is succeeded by the clonic phase. The clonic phase involves the familiar thrashing and convulsive movements, the falling down, and the tongue-biting that most people would think of as the typical grand mal syndrome. See also: **epilepsy; clonic phase; grand mal seizure.**

Tonotopic (ton"ō top'ik, tō"nə-) **arrangement**. In the primary auditory cortex, the activity of the neurons in a spatially continuous manner matches the frequencies of the sound stimuli. It is as if a musical staff had been used to guide the development of the auditory cortex, with tuned neurons standing in for the lines and the spaces of the staff. This even holds true vertically; each cell of a column of cells responds to the same frequency of sound. The exact location of the map on the cortex varies from one individual to another, but each individual has his or her own tonotopic map. See also: **retinotopic arrange-**

ment.

Top-down processing. The use of higher mental processes to decode individual perceptual details. See also: **bottom-up processing; top-down reading models.**

Top-down reading models. These models stress the importance of scripts, that is, inferences and knowledge schemata that contribute to one's ability to formulate hypotheses about information processed. See also: **bottom-up reading models; top-down processing.**

Topographic-gradient hypothesis. A view of neurological development which holds that nerve-cell growth is the resultant of cell positioning with regard to various chemical gradients rather than the product of a mechanism for producing point-to-point connections.

Torticollis (tôr″ti kol′is) (from Latin "tortus" = "twisted"; "collis" = "of the neck") or **wryneck**. The torticollis patient presents a stiff neck, with the head drawn to one side in such a way that the chin points across to the other side. The muscles are much more tense on one side of the neck than on the other. The condition can be in-born or acquired. Biofeedback training may help to reduce the spastic activity of the malfunctioning neck muscles. See also: **biofeedback.**

Total Communication. A philosophy of instruction advocating the use of all available modes of communicating that can assist in mutual understanding between teacher and learner. For the deaf student, Total Communication calls for a mixture of sign language and speechreading techniques instead of relying on only one of the two. For the severely visually impaired, Total Communication would be consistent with the use of visual (large type, high contrast), auditory, and tactile stimuli instead of only one of the three.

Total habilitation. This occurs when a disabled person is living in the same kind of environment in which he or she would have lived in the absence of any disability.

Totipotential cells. Cells that have the potential to develop into any kind of tissue.

Trabecula (trə bek′yoo lə). Connective tissue within the arachnoid membrane, which is the middle of three membranes surrounding the central nervous system. See also: **arachnoid; meninges.**

Tracking. Continuous eye movement following the movement of a visual stimulus through the visual field.

Tract. See: **fasciculus.**

Trainable mentally retarded (TMR). A term used for students with moderate mental retardation. They can take instruction in basic self-help skills and unskilled vocational procedures. They need supervision as adults. The IQ range is from 20 to 55. See also: **moderate mental retardation.**

Transcendental (tran″ sen dent′l) **Meditation (TM)**. A self-treatment discipline which has been recommended as therapeutic for emotional problems, psychosomatic disorders, and addictions. Some would suggest that the useful aspect of TM is the systematic and slow buildup of parasympathetic nervous system activity together with the inhibition of sympathetic nervous system "fight-or-flight" activity. H. Benson claims to have distilled the practical essence of TM into a simple set of procedures called the Relaxation Response. In TM, the individual concentrates as much attention as he or she can muster upon a private word or "mantra" while relaxing the voluntary muscles. See also: **autonomic nervous system; biofeedback; parasympathetic nervous system; psychophysiology; Relaxation Response; stress; sympathetic nervous system.**

Transcerebral dialysis (tran ″ser′ə brəl, -sə rē′brəl dī al′i sis). A technique for recording moment-to-moment fluctuations of brain chemistry in an active laboratory animal. A cannula with a part of its walls semipermeable is implanted in the brain and connected to an automatic chromatograph so that brain chemicals can diffuse from the brain into the cannula and then be measured.

Transcutaneous (trans″kyoo tā′nē əs) **electrical nerve stimulation (TENS)**. A method for providing relief from pain which involves passing a low-voltage electrical shock to the legs, arms, or back. See also: **gate control theory of pain.**

Transdisciplinary (tranz″dis′i plin er″ ē) **approach**. A model of education and treatment for special-needs children that integrates goals and objectives from various professions. Each child targeted for this approach would benefit simultaneously from various services. Among the transdisciplinary team members might be a special educator, physical therapist, occupational therapist, speech/language pathologist, psychologist, pediatric nurse, nutritionist, optometrist, ophthalmologist, neurologist, audiologist, dentist, orthopedist, and social worker. See also: **collaborative consultation.**

Transduction. The conversion of one form of energy into another. An electric heater converts electrical energy to heat energy; light on photographic film causes the chemical change of silver bromide to metallic silver; the kinetic energy it took to run to the store to buy this book could have caused metabolic (chemical energy) changes to occur in the body (e.g., speed up digestion). These are examples of transduction, which is the physical process whereby one form of energy is converted into another. For example, when light strikes a photopigment, a chemical reaction takes place. Thus light (electromagnetic) energy is converted into chemical energy. As another example, taste receptors on the tongue specialized for sweet encounter a substance containing the chemical sucrose. A voltage change known as a generator potential occurs in the receptor. Here we have chemical energy undergoing a transduction into electrical energy. In fact, it is thanks to transduction that we are able to have so many different kinds of sense receptors and be attuned to many different aspects of the world around us.

Transformational grammar. See: **universal grammar.**

Transient (tran'shənt, -zhənt, -zē ənt) **system deficit.** It has been hypothesized that dyslexics display a deficit in the transient system visual pathway from the eye to the cerebral cortex.

Transient (tran'shənt, -zhənt, -zē ənt) **visual pathway.** A pathway in the visual nervous system, receiving both rod and cone input, which is activated only at the onset or offset of visual stimulation, but which is capable of inhibiting the sustained visual pathway during the continued presence of the stimulus.

Transneuronal (tranz″noo rō′nəl) **degeneration.** The degeneration of a neuron resulting from the prior destruction of a neuron to which it sends its axon terminals.

Transplant. Removal of a section of tissue or a complete organ and replacing it with another. A tissue that is removed from one part of the body

(e.g., the thigh) and transplanted to another part of the body (e.g., the face) in the same person is called an autograft. Autografts cannot be rejected by the individual's immune system. Even blood transfusions are considered a type of tissue graft. Organ and limb grafts can only be successful if the blood vessels of the transplanted part are rapidly joined to the blood vessels of the receiving person. The psychological effects of receiving organ and tissue parts from deceased individuals may necessitate counseling.

Transsexual. An individual who has a strong urge to be a member of the opposite sex. The early development of such urges is taken as an indication that hereditary factors play a major role in establishing them.

Transverse section. See: **cross-section.**

Transvestism. The situation in which an individual dresses in clothing appropriate to the other sex in order to achieve sexual gratification.

Traumatic (trə mat′ik, trô-, trou-) **brain injury.** An injury to the brain due to the impact of an external force or to an internal event such as a stroke or aneurysm. Such an injury often leads to an impairment of cognitive functioning, physical functioning, behavioral functioning, and/or emotional functioning. See also: **stroke.**

Tremor. Repetitive motions interfering with smooth motor performance. They may be due to a brain disorder or to psychological stress. Brain damage-caused tremor is a variety of cerebral palsy, usually involving shakiness in an extremity. This shaking tendency is sometimes controlled, but it will appear as soon as the patient attempts a specific voluntary movement.

Triangular theory of love. Sternberg's view that love has three major components: intimacy, passion, and decision-commitment. See also: **decision-commitment; intimacy.**

Triangulation. An application of electroencephalography using bipolar electrodes. Each of two brain areas suspected of being abnormal is electrically compared with a normally-functioning area.

Triarchic (trī ärk′ik) **theory of intelligence.** Sternberg's contention that there are three main parts of general intelligence: **componential intelligence, contextual intelligence,** and **experiential intelligence.** (see definitions).

Trichotillomania (trik″ō til″ə mā′nē ə) (from

Greek "thrix" = "hair"; "tillein" = "to pull"). A type of compulsive behavior, namely, hair pulling. The individual pulls his or her own hair out from various body parts, including even eyelashes and pubic hairs! The drug clomipramine is effective in reducing this symptom. Biochemically, clomipramine blocks the reuptake of serotonin into the presynaptic membrane, thereby allowing more serotonin to be available at the synapses. This in turn suggests that the obsessive-compulsive disorder may be due to a shortage of serotonin in the brain.

Trichromatic (trī˝krō mat′ik) **theory of color vision.** Beginning with the observation by Young that light waves of only three widely separated values of wavelength could be mixed in various amounts to reproduce all the colors of the visible light spectrum, Helmholtz drew the inference that the light receptors in the human retina come in three sets, one for red (long wavelengths), one for green (intermediate wavelengths), and one for blue (short wavelengths). The trichromatic theory is also known as the Young-Helmholtz theory of color vision. Its earliest known strength was its value in the classification of the three varieties of partial color blindness, protanopia (vision lacking the first, i.e., red, photoreceptor), deuteranopia (vision without the services of the second, or green photoreceptor), and the rare tritanopia (vision lacking blue reception). It was corroborated by biochemist George A. Wald's discovery of the three cone photopigments, namely, erythrolabe, chorolabe, and cyanolabe. See also: **photopigments.**

Trichromats (trī ′krō mats˝). Most trichromats are individuals having normal color vision. Anyone who requires three primary colors to produce any color is defined as a trichromat. There are some trichromats who mix the primary colors in a nontypical way, however. They are known as anomalous trichromats. One kind of anomalous trichromat is the protanomalous; a protanomalous trichromat requires an extra amount of red to mix with green in order to obtain yellow. The second kind of anomalous trichromat is the deuteranomalous; a deuteranomalous trichromat needs more than the usual amount of green in order to mix it with red to obtain yellow. See also: **additive color mixing;**

color vision; photopigments; trichromatic theory of color vision.

Tricyclic (trī sī′klik, trī sik′lik) **antidepressants.** This is a family of drugs that have proven effective in alleviating severe chronic depression. The tricyclics (one of which is imipramine) interfere with the deactivation of norepinephrine (norEp) at the synapse. After norEp has delivered its message, it must be cleared away from the synapse so that activity there may be meaningful for communication, not simply "noise." One way that norEp is cleared is by reuptake, whereby this chemical crosses the presynaptic membrane to be stored for future reuse at the same synapse. Another way is for the enzyme COMT to break up the norEp molecule into nonstimulating fractions. Neuropsychiatrists have theorized that the mood disorders are related to the abnormal activity of catecholamine neurotransmitters in the cerebral cortex. Depression, they believe, is due to the underactivity of norEp, perhaps because the chemical is not available in sufficient quantities. The tricyclic drugs do two things to increase the availability of norEp at synapses: (1) They block reuptake, leaving the little norEp which is present around to restimulate its receptor sites. (2) They also block the action of the enzyme COMT, again allowing the small number of norEp molecules to remain intact and operative. See also: **COMT.**

Trigeminal (trī jem′i nəl) **nerve.** The fifth cranial nerve. This is a mixed-function nerve, with both sensory and motor components. The name implies that it has multiple connections to the brain ("three origins"). Touch, temperature, and pain sensations from the head are picked up by the afferent fibers of the trigeminal. These include sensations from the skin around the face, nose, and mouth areas. Motor fibers supply the jaws and can initiate chewing movements. See also: **cranial nerves.**

Triglycerides (trī glis′ə rīdz˝) (also called **neutral fats**). These are chemical compounds of various fatty acids and glycerol. Triglycerides are the fatty materials stored up in the adipose tissues during the absorption phase of metabolism (i.e., right after eating a meal). The adipose tissues are modified connective tissue which includes lipocytes (fat cells). Sometime following the last previous meal, the body enters the fasting stage of metabolism. The hormone glucagon induces the conversion of the stored triglycerides into free fatty acids and glycerol. The glycerol is sent to the liver, converted into glucose there, and then released into the bloodstream. This glucose is now available to the body's tissues, which burn it as fuel. See also: **absorption phase; fasting phase; glucagon; glucose; lipocytes.**

Trigram (trī′gram″). A set of three consecutive letters that may be tachistoscopically presented as a test of visual perception.

Triplegia (trī plē′jē ə, -jə). The paralysis of three of an individual's four limbs.

Tritanopia (trī″tə nō′pē ə). A rare form of color blindness (dichromatism) in which the individual cannot distinguish between blue and yellow.

Trochlear (trok′lē ər) **nerve**. The fourth of the pairs of cranial nerves, the trochlear, is attached to one of the six external eye muscles that move the eyeball, namely, the superior oblique muscle. See also: **cranial nerves**.

Trophic (trō′fik) **factor**. A chemical that promotes the survival and activity of certain neurons. Examples of such factors are **nerve growth factor** and **brain-derived neurotrophic factor** (see definitions).

Tropic (trō′pik) **hormone**. A hormone released from the anterior pituitary gland that specifically influences another endocrine gland to begin to release, or to stop releasing, one of its hormones. Examples of tropic hormones include the thyrotropic hormone (TH), which stimulates the thyroid to release its hormone, thyroxine; ACTH (adrenocorticotropic hormone), which stimulates the release of cortisol from the adrenal cortex; and FSH (follicle-stimulating hormone) and LH (luteinizing hormone), which stimulate particular responses from the gonads. See also: **anterior pituitary glands**.

Tryptophan (trip′tə fan″). An amino acid, obtained from the diet (primarily from two sources: (1) milk or cheese, and (2) poultry, such as chicken or turkey meat), belonging to the indole amine chemical group. Tryptophan is metabolized into the neurotransmitter serotonin in only two steps. First, a hydroxy group (-OH) is added to the indole ring at the "5" position, resulting in 5-hydroxytryptophan. This is a nondietary amino acid; it is a precursor (chemical forerun-

ner) of serotonin. The amino acid structure of 5-hydroxytryptophan allows it to pass the blood-brain barrier. The brain neurons are then able to convert it into the amine form, 5-hydroxytryptamine, which is serotonin (5-HT). See also: **indole amines; 5-hydroxytryptophan; serotonin.**

TTY. Teletypewriter and printer for the hearing impaired. Also called a **TDD**. See also: **TDD**.

Tuberculosis (too bûr″kyə lō′sis, tyoo-). An infectious bacterial disease that may be acquired by contact with an infected person. The lungs are the organs that are chiefly attacked by the bacteria.

Tuberous sclerosis (too′bər əs skli rō′sis). A genetic disease, autosomal dominant, discovered by Bournville in 1880. Tuberous sclerosis strikes in 1 out of every 150,000 live births. It affects the central nervous system and the viscera. Many patients have damage to the kidneys, the heart, the lungs, and the bones. All show skin lesions (resembling acne) by the age of 35. Psychological symptoms include signs of schizophrenia and epilepsy. Psychiatric intervention is required in order to deal with hyperactivity, destructiveness, and aggression.

Tunnel vision. A visual symptom (which may result from glaucoma) in which vision is restricted to a small circle directly around the center of the visual scene.

Turnover. The amount of a neurotransmitter that is released and resynthesized by the presynaptic neurons (i.e., the neurons that release that transmitter into the synaptic cleft). See also: **5-HIAA.**

Twin studies. Research conducted with identical and fraternal twins in order to determine the influences of heredity and the environment on behavior, learning, and social adjustment. In the case of identical twins, when each member of the pair gets a different treatment, a later difference in behavior cannot be attributed to hereditary causes, because the "experimental" twin has the same heredity as the "control" twin. This concept of using a hereditary difference of zero is called a co-twin control.

Tympanic (tim pan′ik) **membrane**. This is also known as the eardrum. The tympanic membrane is the boundary between the outer and middle ear. Sound is transmitted through the auricle (outer ear) to the tympanic membrane, where sound waves vibrate before being sent to the middle ear bones.

Type A behavior or **Type A personality**. The tendency of an individual to be impatient, competitive, readily frustrated, quick to anger, cynical, and often aggressive. Type A persons seem always to be rushing from one activity to another. They tend to speak rapidly, work quickly, and react to any disagreement with irritation and hostility. This behavior pattern is theorized to be a strong factor in proneness to heart attack. See also: **Type B behavior**.

Type B behavior or **Type B personality**. The tendency of an individual to be noncompetitive and nonaggressive, showing patience when things are difficult. This behavior pattern theoretically lowers the chances of a future heart attack. See also: **Type A behavior**.

Tyrosine (tī´rə sēn ˝). An amino acid of the catecholamine family. Tyrosine may be obtained from the diet, but it is usually the first stage in the metabolism of the amino acid phenylalanine (which is more prevalent in most diets). In turn, tyrosine is the precursor of the nondietary amino acid *l*-DOPA, and *l*-DOPA is the precursor of the neurotransmitter dopamine. The blood-brain barrier can be crossed by amino acids, but not by amines. Therefore, *l*-DOPA crosses the barrier and then the brain neurons can metabolize it into dopamine. In its turn, dopamine can be transformed into norepinephrine. At the end of this long metabolic chain, some norepinephrine is converted into the hormone epinephrine. See also: **blood-brain barrier; catecholamines; *l*-DOPA; dopamine; epinephrine; norepinephrine.**

U

UFONIC Speech System. A speech synthesizer, produced by Jostens Learning Corporation, which can be added to a microcomputer. This would allow visually impaired people to benefit from working with computer technology.

Ulcer. An open sore or lesion of the skin or a mucous membrane of the body. An ulcer on the lining of the stomach or intestine can be the result of emotional stress. See also: **general adaptation syndrome; parasympathetic rebound; psychosomatic disorders; stress.**

Ultradian (əl trā′dē ən) **rhythms.** Cyclic bodily functions occurring more often than once a day. The once-a-day type of rhythm is called circadian (meaning "around a day"). "Ultra" means "more than [once]"; therefore, an ultradian rhythm refers to the kind of activity that repeats itself more often than once a day. Examples are the eating of several meals, the repeating 90-minute cycles of sleep stages, the release of some hormones, and intervals of activity and rest. See also: **circadian rhythms.**

Ultrasonography (ul″trə sə nog′rə fē) or **ultrasound.** The use of sound waves to scan the interior of the body, a procedure developed in the 1970s. It involves transducer-generated sound waves directed into the body. The resulting sound "echoes" are different, depending on the tissue being scanned. The sound waves are then converted to visual images on an oscilloscope. This technique is useful for the examination of several medical conditions, including the assessment of internal hemorrhaging in normal and hydrocephalic children. This technique is also used during pregnancy to describe aspects of the developing fetus.

Unconditional positive regard. The demonstration by a teacher or psychotherapist of absolute and unqualified respect for the student or client. One objective of requiring the helper to have this attitude is the development of "unconditional positive self-regard" on the part of the person being helped.

Unconditioned reflex. A reflex which is genetically programmed. It is a type of reflex that is not acquired through learning. See also: **classical conditioning; unconditioned response; unconditioned stimulus.**

Unconditioned response (UR). The response part of an unconditioned reflex. This response to the unconditioned stimulus (US) is made automatically; it does not have to be established by special training. See also: **classical conditioning; unconditioned reflex; unconditioned stimulus.**

Unconditioned stimulus (US). The stimulus part of an unconditioned reflex. The presentation of the US automatically elicits the response, because its ability to do so does not require training. Following the presentation of a conditioned stimulus and the appearance of the conditioned response, the appearance of the US serves as a reinforcement for the conditioned reflex. See also: **classical conditioning; unconditioned reflex; unconditioned response.**

Unconscious. According to Freud, our unconscious level of awareness includes the ideas, thoughts, and feelings of which we are not normally aware. Typically, these are thoughts which are psychologically painful (e.g., forgetting a dirty trick we played on someone years ago) and are relegated to an unconscious state of awareness.

Underachiever. A child whose academic performance is below the level that would be expected on the basis of that child's IQ or other evidence of general aptitude.

Undifferentiated schizophrenia (skit″sə frē′nē ə, -fren′ē ə). A type of schizophrenic that is defined by the characteristic delusions, hallucinations, and disorganized thinking patterns, yet does not include symptoms associated with the other schizophrenic subtypes. See also: **catatonic schizophrenia; disorganized schizophrenia; paranoid schizophrenic type.**

Unilateral neglect. A syndrome that appears after brain damage to the somatosensory area (in the parietal lobe) on one side of the cerebral cortex. The individual acts as if the opposite side of the body does not exist. For instance, after damage to the right parietal lobe, a man might fail to shave the left side of his face. See also: **parietal lobe; sensory extinction.**

Unipolar affective disorder. The types of mood disorder in which the patient suffers from either mania or depression but does not experience the opposite extreme mood. This is in contrast with bipolar affective disorder. See also: **bipolar disorder.**

Unipolar neuron. The second-rarest type of neuron in the human body. These occur only at the dorsal root ganglia of the spinal cord; there are 62 such ganglia, 31 on each side. The term refers to the fact that this type of neuron has a cell body that meets a fiber only at one location (i.e., "pole"). The fiber is technically a "dendrite" from its origin near the sense receptors that connect to it all the way up to the cell body and an "axon" during its continuation from the cell body into the spinal cord. This means that all unipolar cells are sensory in function. The anatomist Bodian has proposed a more consistent naming scheme for unipolar cell fibers. According to Bodian, the tiny receptor-linked branches at the peripheral extremity should be called the unipolar cell's "dendritic zone." This releases the entire main portion of the fiber, both before and after the position of the cell body, to be labeled as the "axon". This better reflects the fact that the main part of the fiber is cylindrical, like an axon, and that it carries true nerve impulses, also like an axon.

Universal grammar. Noam Chomsky believes that there is an underlying grammar structure which is present in all languages. He attributes it to the inborn structure of the human cerebral cortex.

Chomsky has a theory for describing the grammatical and logical structure of language which is called transformational grammar. The transformational grammar is a set of rules to generate a surface structure (e.g., active and passive voice) from the more basic deep structure (e.g., basic logic of what's being said). Supposedly, these transformational rules hold for all languages, so that the various languages can differ from one another only in surface structure. See also: **psycholinguistics; surface structure.**

Unstable ocular dominance. This is a theory which links the loss of binocular coordination or unstable ocular dominance to the visual-perceptual problems of dyslexics. Research has generally not favored this explanation, although it may apply to one subtype of dyslexic.

Utricle (yōō′tri kəl). One of the otolith organs in the sense of balance organ of the inner ear, the utricle monitors linear accelerations in the horizontal direction. As an example, we become aware of the linear acceleration when hurled forward after stepping on the brake in a fast-moving car. Which of the two otolith organs covers which direction can be recalled from the mnemonic device "huvs", an acrostic for "horizontal, utricle; vertical, saccule." See also: **labyrinthine sense organs; otolith organs; saccule.**

V

V1. Refers to the primary visual cortex, where visual processing begins.

V2. Refers to the secondary visual cortex, which involves the second stage of visual processing.

V3. Refers to the area of the visual cortex involved in spatial perception.

V4. Refers to the area of the visual cortex involved in processing colors.

Vagina (və jī ′nə). The hollow structure in the female that accommodates the penis during sexual activity.

Vagus (vā′gus) **nerve**. The tenth pair of cranial nerves. The vagus nerve is of mixed function. It receives interoceptive sensations concerning glucose levels, high or low pressure on the walls of gastrointestinal organs, carbon dioxide content of the blood, blood pressure, and so on. The vagus also picks up exteroceptive sensations from the neck. It sends parasympathetic messages to the head, the thorax, and the upper abdomen. It commands the excitation of the smooth muscles within blood vessels as a part of the parasympathetic nervous system; for example, it would constrict vessels feeding into the striate muscles of the arms and legs and relax the smooth muscles lining blood vessels to the digestive organs so that these vessels are dilated. In fact, the alternate name of the parasympathetic division, the craniosacral, owes the "cranio-" part of the name to the vagus and its running mate, the spinal accessory nerve. See also: **cranial nerves**.

VAK method. See: **Visual-auditory-kinesthetic method**.

Validity. This is the degree to which a test measures that which it is designed to measure. It is expressed as a correlation coefficient computed between the test and some criterion measurement of the behavior or ability that is meant to be measured. NOTE: A test with low reliability can never have high validity, but a test with high reliability may or may not be valid. Content validity refers to whether or not a test appropriately samples skills or knowledge from a particular subject area (e.g., does a particular reading test really measure reading skills per se?). Criterion-referenced validity is a measure of how a test fares against other independent measures which

are designed to measure similar skills or knowledge. Concurrent validity is a type of criterion-related validity which correlates similar measurements in order to determine the strength of the theoretical relationship. For example, the math section on the Wide Range Achievement Test-Revised could be correlated with the Test of Mathematical Abilities (TOMA) in a concurrent validity study. Predictive validity is a type of criterion-related validity which looks at the ability of an assessment measure to predict some criterion of success at a future point in time (e.g., the predictive validity of IQ tests). Construct validity is the degree to which a test measures some hypothetical construct, such as creativity. Age-differentiation validity is a type of construct validity which looks at the degree to which test scores show increases or decreases in performance with age increases or decreases (e.g., IQ scores do increase in some groups with age). Convergent/discriminant validity occurs when an assessment measure's construct correlates with constructs the assessment purports to measure (e.g., correlating the simultaneous and sequential scales on the Kaufman-ABC Scales with the Das-Kirby-Jarman Successive-Simultaneous Battery). See also: **construct validity; content validity; criterion-referenced validity.**

Variability. The extent to which the individual scores in a given set of scores differ from one another. This is statistically measured in several ways, the most obvious being the range, which is the difference between the highest and the lowest score. The most useful measure of variability in psychological testing is the **standard deviation** (see definition).

Variable interval schedule of reinforcement (VI). A schedule for the reinforcement of some but not all of the correct responses emitted by an organism. After a time (the length of which varies as determined by control equipment), the first response made is reinforced. Since intervals between the reinforcements are varied, although on a repeating cycle, the organism works at a stable rate, behaving just fast enough to pick off the two reinforcements separated by the shortest interval in the cycle. An example would be trying to dial an individual whose phone often is busy.

Variable ratio schedule of reinforcement (VR). A schedule for arranging the reinforcement of only some correct responses made by the organism. The controls are arranged so that a reinforcement is made after a number of responses have been made. That number is not fixed but is variable, because it is set up by the way the control equipment is arranged. The organism is forced to work at a high rate (since there is an element of "piece work," as with a fixed ratio schedule) and at a steady rate (since the reinforcement cannot be predicted). An example would be the way people work at the slot machines in a gambling casino, steadily feeding coins and pulling the handle.

Variance in subtyping. Because of the plethora of explanations concerning the nature and causes of dyslexia, there has been a great deal of variance regarding a standard classification system, that is, many different classification schemes have been suggested. The current authors suggest three subtypes: auditory-linguistic dyslexia, visual-dysphonetic dyslexia, and a mixed subtype (with both visual and linguistic deficits). See also: **auditory-linguistic dyslexia; dyslexia; learning disability; visual-dysphonetic dyslexia.**

Vas deferens (vas″def′ər ənz, -ə renz″) (from Latin "vas" = "vessel"; "defero" = "I carry away"). The duct that transports the sperm from the testes to the urethra. The name of this duct is, in English, the main part of an answer to the question "How unlike are the male and female genitalia?" (The answer: "There is a vas(t) difference.").

Vasoconstriction (vas″ō kən strik′shən, vāz″-). Constriction of the capillaries that supply the skin, due to the activity of the sympathetic nervous system in response to excessive cold stimulation.

Vasodilation (vas″ō dī lā′shən, vāz″-). Dilating of the capillaries supplying the skin, due to the action of the parasympathetic nervous system in response to excessive heat stimulation.

Vasopressin (vas″ō pres′in). See: **antidiuretic hormone.**

Ventral (ven′trəl) (from Latin "venter" = "belly button"). Toward the anatomical belly. The na-

vel, or belly-button, is a ventral structure in any animal, whether biped (two-legged) or quadruped (four-legged). The antonym of "ventral" is "dorsal". A ventral structure can be considered anterior, in the case of a biped, or inferior, in the case of a quadruped. The belly is on the underside of a dog (the inferior side) and on the front side (the anterior side) of a human. One special and important exception is the human brain. Where the spinal cord attaches to the medulla of the brain, the central nervous system is bent forward at a 90-degree angle, so that the brain is oriented the same way as that of a quadruped. The result is that the eyes and the nose face forward to monitor the part of the environment that the creature is facing. As a result, in the case of the human brain, the word "ventral" is usually synonymous with the word "inferior."

Ventral corticospinal (ven′trəl kôr″ti kō spī″nəl) **tract.** See: **ventromedial tract.**

Ventral funiculus (ven′trəl fə nik′yo͞o lus, fyoo-) (from Latin "funiculus" = little cable). One of the three large collections of white matter found in either the right or left side of a cross-section of the spinal cord. The ventral funiculus is bounded by the midline, the ventral edge of the spinal cord, and the ventral horn of the gray butterfly. Smaller collections of myelinated axons, called tracts or fasciculi, run through the ventral funiculus. Some of them travel rostrad, toward higher parts of the central nervous system, while some travel caudad, toward lower parts of the spinal cord. An example of a forward-going, rostrally directed, tract in this funiculus would be the ventral spinothalamic tract, which carries nerve impulses that convey information about light touch to the posterior ventral nucleus of the thalamus. An example of a downward-directed, caudad, tract using this funiculus would be the ventromedial tract, otherwise known as the ventral corticospinal tract, which carries motor messages from Brodmann's area 4 (in the precentral gyrus of the frontal lobe) toward the muscles of the trunk. See also: **cross-section; funiculus; gray butterfly; spinal cord; ventral horn; ventral spinothalamic tract; ventromedial tract.**

Ventral (ven′trəl) **horn.** The horn-like extensions of the inner gray matter of the spinal cord (one on the left, one on the right) that point toward the ventral surface of the spinal cord, as seen in a cross-section of the spinal cord. The ventral horns do not reach the outer surface of the cord. In the ventral horns are the multi-fibered ventral horn motoneurons, motor neurons with dendrites aimed in many directions. The axons of ventral horn motoneurons collect into a tight bundle, the ventral root, and travel to the nearest spinal nerve, which they join.

Ventral (ven′trəl) posterior nucleus. See: **posterior ventral nucleus of the thalamus.**

Ventral (ven′trəl) root. The ventral branch of a spinal nerve formed as the nerve approaches the spinal cord. (The rest of the nerve joins the dorsal root.) In the ventral root, the axons are outward-bound, toward the muscles and glands (i.e., they are efferent fibers). The cell bodies of the neurons to which these axons belong are in the ventral horn of the spinal cord's gray butterfly.

Ventral spinothalamic (spī′nō thə lam′ik) tract. A collection of axons running through the ventral funiculus of the spinal cord carrying nerve impulses related to light-touch stimuli. The cell bodies from which these axons arise are found in the dorsal horns of the spinal cord's gray butterfly. The axons immediately cross the midline, so that the ventral spinothalamic tract axons are contralateral; they run up the side of the spinal cord opposite to the side of the body getting stimulated. These axons finally terminate in the posterior ventral nucleus of the thalamus. See also: **contralateral; dorsal horn; gray butterfly; posterior ventral nucleus of the thalamus; spinal cord; tract; ventral funiculus.**

Ventral tegmental (ven′trəl teg men′təl) area (VTA). A part of the midbrain tegmentum containing nerve cell bodies. These neurons synthesize dopamine, which is released at their axon endings. The axons from the VTA reach the nucleus accumbens, which is at the septum. Thus the VTA communicates with the limbic system, of which the septum is a part. See also: **accumbens; dopamine; limbic system.**

Ventricular (ven trik′yoo lər) zone. In neurological development, the section of the developing neural tube next to the ventricle.

Ventromedial cortico-brainstem-spinal (ven″trō mē′dē əl kôr′ti kō-) pathway. The relatively indirect motor pathway with short axons and numerous synapses between the cerebral cortex and the musculature (think of it as the "local" train).

Ventromedial corticospinal (ven″trō mē′dē əl kôr″ti kō spī′nəl) pathway. The direct motor pathway running from the primary motor cortex to the musculature, with only one axon required to reach the ventral horn motoneurons controlling the muscles. This pathway can be thought of as the "express" train. See also: **primary motor cortex; pyramidal tract; ventral horn motoneuron.**

Ventromedial hypothalamus (ven″trō mē′dē əl hī″pō thal′ə mus) (VMH). The area of the hypothalamus that is necessary for an animal to feel satiated after a meal and cease eating behavior. Other parts of this region are necessary for the restraint of aggressive behavior. See also **aggression; hypothalamic hyperphagia.**

Ventromedial (ven″trō mē′dē əl) tract (also known as the **ventral corticospinal tract**). This is the smaller of the two spinal cord extensions of the brain's pyramidal motor pathway. The axons destined for this tract do not decussate (i.e., cross over to the other side of the midline) but remain on the ipsilateral side (i.e., the same side that they started from) as the ventromedial tract continues down the spinal cord. The axons of the ventromedial tract control trunk movements. See also: **decussation; dorsolateral tract; pyramidal tract.**

Verbal-deficit hypothesis. This hypothesis suggests that some of the more severe reading problems are caused by linguistic disorders which can be subtle in nature and result from language coding problems and poor facility in processing verbally coded information.

Verbal IQ. Half of the Wechsler Intelligence Test series contains verbal tests, whereas the other half contains performance tests. These produce the verbal IQ and the performance IQ, respectively. The two are averaged to yield the full-scale IQ. Subtests contributing to the verbal IQ are: Information, Comprehension, Arithmetic, Similarities, Digit Span, and Vocabulary.

Verbal-performance discrepancy. This refers to a statistically significant difference between one's verbal IQ score and one's performance IQ score. There has been widespread debate regarding whether or not a verbal-performance discrepancy (difference) can differentially define dyslexic and proficient readers. One of the present authors, Spafford, has found that such differences can be of diagnostic utility.

Vergence (vûr′jens). The movement of a single eye. Convergence refers to the movement of both eyes so that the lines of sight converge, allowing the close scrutiny of a nearby object. When control of eye movement has been disrupted, the separate control of each eye's movement becomes an issue, hence, "vergence."

Versabraille system. A system for storing Braille material on a cassette tape. The information on the tape is sent to a microcomputer in Braille or in print to a monitor screen.

Vertigo (vûr′ti gō). An inner ear symptom in which people feel light-headed, dizzy, and nauseated. It is due to the malfunctioning of the vestibular organs of the sense of balance (the semicircular canals and/or the otolith organs). See also: **vestibular senses.**

Vesicle (ves′i kel). A small, spherical container for a fixed amount of chemical neurotransmitter. The vesicles are found within the synaptic boutons at the ends of axons. When a nerve impulse arrives, the vesicles migrate to the presynaptic membrane of the bouton and then are ruptured, so that their contents are released into the synaptic cleft. See also: **axon; neurotransmitter; synapse.**

Vestibular (ve stib′ye ler) **nerve.** The vestibular branch of the auditory vestibular nerve, cranial nerve VIII. The cell bodies for this nerve are bipolar cells found in the vestibular ganglion, which is near the inner ear, and named for the sense organ for the balance senses, the vestibular apparatus. The axons from these bipolar neurons travel with the eighth cranial nerve most of the way to the medulla, where they separate from the acoustic nerve axons and terminate in the various vestibular nuclei. See also: **auditory vestibular nerve; bipolar neuron; ganglion; labyrinthine sense organs; nucleus (part of the gray matter); vestibular nuclei; vestibular senses.**

Vestibular nuclei (ve stib′ye ler nōō′klē ī, nyōō-). Collections of nerve cell bodies in the medulla that receive the endings of the vestibular nerve, the vestibular branch of the auditory vestibular (eighth) cranial nerve. Some axons

from the vestibular nuclei run to other nuclei that control the position and muscle tone of the neck muscles. Other axons from vestibular nuclei run to the nuclei of the three cranial nerves (III, IV, and VI) that control eye movements. The latter type of connection is what allows the vestibulo-ocular reflex to occur. See also: **vestibular nerve; vestibular senses; vestibulo-ocular reflex.**

Vestibular (ve stib′ye ler) **sacs.** These are two sacs located in the inner ear which are involved in gravity sensations and in forward, backward, and vertical movements in space. The sacs, known as the utricle and the saccule, are filled with a jelly-like fluid. This fluid contains millions of minute crystals which bend vestibular hair bundles when starting the sensory message. Even when you remain motionless, the crystals bend hair bundles because of a gravitational pull, providing a sense of head position at all times.

Vestibular (ve stib′ye ler) **senses** (from Latin "vestibule" = "entrance hall"). The senses of the inner ear other than hearing. They constitute our sense of balance or equilibrium and provide awareness of the position of the head. The semicircular canals monitor rotary accelerations of the head in any direction; there are three semicircular canals, each positioned at right angles to the two others. The two otolith organs or vestibular sacs report linear accelerations, one (the saccule) covering vertical changes of speed and the other (the utricle) dealing with horizontal accelerations. They are often called, collectively, the sense of balance. Birds and fish, in particular, need their vestibular senses to tell them where they are going when they cannot see well. See also: **labyrinthine sense organs; saccule; semicircular canals; utricle.**

Vestibulo-ocular (ve stib′yoo lō-ok′yoo ler) **reflex.** A rapid adjusting response of the external eye muscles to a change in the position of the head. This allows the visual world to be stabilized for the observer. It insures that the spatial coordinates from the vestibular apparatus will be integrated with changes of visual information on spatial position. Any damage to the sense organs or neurons sufficient to impair this reflex would make things difficult for you. Whenever you ran or jogged, all you could see would be blurred motions! See also: **nystagmus.**

Vibro-tactile aid. A device used by hearing-disabled persons which converts sounds to tactile vibrations.

Vicarious desensitization. A desensitization technique whereby clients observe models or videotapes of individuals engaged in performing anxiety-provoking actions. See also: **desensitization techniques; reciprocal inhibition.**

Vicarious punishment. In observation learning, the effect of punishment works on the learner, even though the punishment is delivered only to the model. See also: **observational learning; punishment.**

Vicarious reinforcement. In observational learning, the effect of reinforcement acts on the learner, even though the reinforced behavior is performed by a model and the reinforcement is delivered only to the model, not to the learner. See also: **observational learning; reinforcement.**

Video Digitizer. A device, used in some computers, that converts video images into computer graphics for digital storage on electronic media such as disks or tapes.

Video Disk. A system for the storage of graphics, text, video, and audio information; it can be used for high-quality still pictures and moving pictures. The messages are accessed through the use of a video disk player.

Viewscan. A print enlarger for use by the visually impaired. A small video camera tracks lines of print and displays the printed lines, magnified, on the screen of a monitor which is watched by the user.

Viral infections. Infections caused by viruses which can lead to sensory impairments. Mumps and measles, for example, are viral infections, severe cases of which can possibly lead to hearing or visual impairments.

Viscera (vis′ər ə). The internal organs of the thorax and abdomen that are primarily regulated by the autonomic nervous system.

Visual acuity. The ability of the individual's eyes and visual nervous system to resolve fine detail, as measured in a controlled manner. See also: **cones; Snellen chart; sustained visual pathway.**

Visual agnosia (ag nō′zhə). The failure to recognize visual stimuli, even though the visual re-ceptors are intact. One variety of visual agnosia is prosopagnosia. See also: **prosopagnosia.**

Visual-Auditory-Kinesthetic Method (VAK). A remediation system for the learning-disabled, which combines sight, sound, movement, and auditory sensations, so that words and letters are learned by way of several sensory channels.

Visual axis. The line traced by a horizontal beam of light passing directly through the pupil and the lens until it reaches the part of the retina known as the fovea.

Visual cortex (kôr′teks ˝). That portion of the cerebral cortex serving as the terminal of the neural pathway from the retina, which begins with the optic nerve. The primary visual cortex (designated Brodmann's area 17, or V1 for primary visual area) is found at the posterior tip of the occipital lobe in each cerebral hemisphere. Many aspects of visual functioning are carried out in other cortical regions. Visual tasks of one kind or another have been found to be performed by the entire occipital lobe as well as parts of the adjoining lobes, the temporal and the parietal lobes.

Visual dyslexia (dis lek′sē ə). Myklebust has provided a succinct explanation for this type of dyslexia; and visual dyslexia, simply stated, is the inability to obtain meaning from print because of visual-perceptual deficiencies or deficits.

Visual-dysphonetic dyslexia (vizh ′o͞o əl-dis˝fō net′ik dis lek′sē ə) (VDD). A subtype of dyslexia inferred by Spafford and Grosser from research data involving impaired contrast sensitivity, keen peripheral vision, peripheral color-detection ability, low peripheral brightness sensitivity, and so on, on the part of dyslexics who have poor ability at phonetic interpretation of words. The VDD subtype is unique in that neural dysfunctioning is thought to occur at the sensory level as opposed to the higher-order processing levels involved in the visual-perceptual subtypes in most subtype listings.

Visual field. The area in which visual objects may be seen while the eye is in a fixed position. The extent of the area is expressed in degrees of visual angle. Usually the upper, lower, nasal, and temporal boundaries of the visual field are specified. The positions of tested points within the visual field are often reported in quadrants, viz., the upper nasal, upper temporal, lower nasal, and lower temporal quadrants. See also: **hemianopia; quadrantanopia.**

Visual grating. A type of visual stimulus used by optometrists and by vision researchers. It consists of a set of parallel lines, usually black and white. The alternating lines are equally thick. The lines may vary in black-white contrast. The gratings may also be varied in spatial frequency, that is, in the rate of alternating black and white, with a low frequency meaning that the lines are thick. The higher the spatial frequency, the thinner the lines. Spatial frequency is specified in cycles per degree. A cycle is a full black-white change. A degree is a unit of measure for visual angle. See also: **visual persistence.**

Visualizing. A type of cognitive strategy one can use in order to better remember concepts or important information. For example, one can better remember the contents of a room if at first one can visualize exactly what the room looks like.

Visual-motor deficit. Psychologists have frequently used measures of visual-motor performance (for example, using the hands to reproduce printed pictures) as indicators of potential reading problems. The Bender Visual-Motor Gestalt Test (BVMGT), which requires the reproduction of two- and three-dimensional designs, has been the most frequently used assessment tool, with current research showing no clear predictive value for this instrument.

Visual-motor model of dyslexia. Getman has devised a visuomotor model of dyslexia whereby visual development is tied to reading and learning, with intervention strategies tied to practice in general coordination, balance, eye-hand coordination, visual memory, and form recognition. This model has been criticized for overemphasizing the role of vision in learning to read.

Visual perception. The use of visual sensations to identify and recognize objects in the environment. Research on visual-perceptual measures, such as the Frostig Developmental Test of Visual Perception (DTVP), has yielded inconclusive results as to the usefulness of these measures in assessing reading performance.

Visual persistence. The visual nervous system continues to respond to a light stimulus for a brief time after the light is turned off. The activity that persists following the removal of the stimulus is called visual persistence. Visual gratings (sets of parallel lines) are often used as stimuli in visual persistence research. Black-white contrast and spatial frequency are the two major factors in determining the length of the visual persistence of a visual grating. See also: **visual grating.**

Visual-spatial subtype. This is a dyslexic subtype identified by Pirozzolo and others which can be described as involving impairment in visual-discrimination ability, analysis, and memory.

Visual spectrum. That range of wavelengths of electromagnetic energy to which the eye is sensitive (i.e., the visible light spectrum). The visual spectrum is not the same for all species of animals. For example, bees see in the ultraviolet wavelengths to which humans are blind. Snakes can see in the infrared wavelengths that humans can sense only as heat. Recent research has shown that many fish (which, like humans and snakes, are vertebrates) can see in the ultraviolet wavelengths.

Vitreous humor (vit′rē əs hyoo′mər). This gel fills the posterior chamber of the eyeball. It may remind one of a clear, transparent serving of gelatin dessert.

VOCA. See: **Voice Output Communication Aid and Synthetic Speech.**

Vocal nodules. Calluses that grow on the edges of the vocal cords. They may impart a breathy quality to the voice and detract from the loudness of the voice.

Vocomotor skills. The control skills used in the operation of the tongue, jaws, and lips in speech-production.

Voice disorder. Any disturbance of the speaking voice (involving pitch, loudness, or quality. Quality involves nasality, breathiness, harshness, and/or hoarseness). The disorder may arise from the mistreatment of the vocal apparatus or from tissue damage in the vocal tract.

Voice Output Communication Aid (and Synthetic speech) (VOCA). A communication device that produces electronic speech sounds. It can aid those with damage to the vocal cords.

Voiced sounds. All speech sounds that make use of vibrations of the vocal cords.

Volemic (vō lē′mik) **thirst** (also called **hypovolemic thirst** or **extracellular thirst**). A condition capable of arousing the thirst drive, it consists of a loss of water from the fluid surrounding the body cells. It may be brought on by diarrhea, vomiting, or the consumption of ethyl alcohol. This kind of thirst can be quenched by drinking slightly salty water. See also: **hypovolemic thirst; intracellular thirst.**

Volley theory of hearing. A theory authored by Wever to overcome the limitations of Rutherford's telephone theory of hearing. By allotting portions of the auditory nerve to four separate squads, each firing impulses in a separate rhythm from the others, the auditory nerve is not limited to an expected ceiling of 1,000 nerve impulses per second (the ceiling for a single auditory axon) but can deliver (as a whole) as many as 4,000 impulses per second. Thus the volley theory fills a needed gap between the low frequencies of 15 to 1,000 cycles per second (c.p.s.) (accounted for by the telephone theory) and the high frequencies (4,000 to 20,000+ c.p.s.) covered by Helmholtz' place-resonance theory. The modern scientist who sorted out the roles of the three independently proposed mechanisms was Georg von Békésy. See also: **basilar membrane; place-resonance theory of hearing; telephone theory of hearing.**

Voltage-gated ion channels. Passageways for ions through a neuron's cell membrane that are opened or closed in response to changes of the membrane potential.

Volume transmission theory. This theory of the central neural processing of information holds that neurons release, at their axon endings, chemical neurotransmitters that diffuse over the extracellular space. This means that the transmitter molecules are not necessarily detected by nearby neural membranes; instead, they may have reached the receptor sites on neural membranes quite a distance away from the neurons that released the transmitter. That type of neurotransmitter is referred to as a neuromodulator. The mechanism is quite similar to the action of hormones that are released by endocrine glands and travel for a distance in the bloodstream until they reach receptors that respond to them. This volume transmission theory can be called the "wet" theory of information transmission. See also: **cyclic AMP; information processing; neuro-modulator; synaptic transmission theory.**

Vomeronasal (vō″mər ō nā′zəl) **organs**. A special group of olfactory sense receptors, connected to the hypothalamus, which are found in reptiles and lower mammals but which are absent in primates. In snakes the vomeronasal organs detect the scent of prey, whereas in rodents they pick up the odors of potential mates.

Von Recklinghausen's (von rek′ling hou zenz) **disease**. See: **neurofibromatosis**.

VOTRAX Personal Speech System. A speech synthesizer, made by Votrax, Inc., that can be added to a personal computer. See also: **talking programs.**

Voyeurism (vwä′yûr iz″əm, voi′-). The condition, also called Peeping Tom phenomenon, of obtaining sexual gratification after viewing the at-least-partially naked bodies of other people, or people who are engaged in the sex act, without their knowledge or permission. The voyeur may masturbate while watching. In extreme cases, this may be the only form of sexual behavior for the voyeur.

W

Wada test. A procedure used to identify the separate functions of each cortical hemisphere in a neurological patient. The barbiturate drug sodium amytal is injected into one of the two carotid arteries. The cortical hemisphere on that side where the injection occurs will be temporarily put out of action. Behaviors (including language) that are now performed by the patient are partially controlled by the only functioning hemisphere, the one on the side opposite to that of the injection. One may wonder why this method has not been used to clear up all the questions about separate hemispheric functioning. The answer is that the Wada test is used only with patients needing diagnosis and treatment, because it does involve some risk to the individual getting the injection. See also: **barbiturates; cerebral cortex; neurology**.

Waking consciousness. This is the state of our conscious awareness while we are awake, attentive, and alert. During this time, our conscious awareness involves such processes as thinking, feeling, and perceiving the environment around us. There are also altered states of consciousness, or instances when our consciousness drifts into other states (e.g., daydreaming). See also: **altered states of consciousness**.

Wallerian (wä lir′ē ən) **degeneration.** When an axon is severed, a gradual process of degeneration sets in. Slowly, the neural material of the axon, as well as the myelin (if present), breaks down. This destruction moves slowly toward the cell body in retrograde degeneration and also in the direction from the cut toward the end brush. The degeneration that proceeds from the site of injury toward the end brush is known as Wallerian degeneration. The broken-down remnants of axon and myelin sheath are cleared off by phagocytes. In the peripheral nervous system, freely moving Schwann cells act as phagocytes. In the central nervous system, microglia and astroglia perform the phagocyte duty. An alternative name for Wallerian degeneration is anterograde degeneration. See also: **retrograde degeneration.**

W cells. A set of retinal ganglion cells that are neither parvocellular nor magnocellular. They are most likely to be related to the maintenance of the visual tracking action of eye movements.

Weber's law. The psychophysical principle that holds for the difference threshold, Weber's law serves as a rule for the expected values of measurements of sensory difference thresholds. It specifies that the difference threshold (or just noticeable difference) has a constant ratio to the stimulation that is already present, before anything is either added or subtracted. This is written out as delta-S /S = k, where delta-S is the just noticeable difference and k is a constant. The value of the ratio (or of the constant, which it equals) varies according to the sense modality and the task required. An example would be the Weber fraction for the judgment of weight, which is 1/10. For a 50-pound weight, a 5-pound increase or decrease is required for a change to be just noticeable, while for a 50-gram weight, only a 5-gram change is needed before the change can be noticed.

Wechsler (wek′slər) **Intelligence Scales (WAIS = Wechsler Adult Intelligence Scale; WISC = Wechsler Intelligence Scale for Children-III).** The most highly regarded individually administered tests of intelligence. Standard scores (based on the normal curve) are translated into the entrenched traditional statistic, viz., the IQ (intelligence quotient). In addition to a full-scale IQ, the Wechsler Intelligence Scales yield a verbal IQ and a performance IQ. The average IQ score of the entire population is 100, with approximately 95% of the population falling between IQ scores of 70 and 130.

Weigert (wī′gûrt) **stain.** A staining technique for the central nervous system which uses hematoxylin and chromium salts that are deposited on the myelin sheaths around axons, rendering them blue-black. This allows myelin-covered axons of undamaged neurons to be traced from their cell bodies to their synaptic endings by the microscopic examination of brain sections mounted on glass slides.

Wernicke-Korsakoff syndrome. A combination of two syndromes, one milder and one much more grave. Wernicke's syndrome is caused by a deficiency of vitamin B-1 (thiamin), which leads to unsteadiness, profound fatigue, double vision, and lowered emotionality. Without thiamin, brain neurons are impaired in their ability to utilize glucose and oxygen. When still more neurons are killed, the individual's condition worsens, changing from Wernicke's syndrome to Korsakoff's syndrome, which involves severe memory disturbances (including the loss of long-term memory) and hallucinations. See also: **Korsakoff's syndrome; Wernicke's syndrome.**

Wernicke's aphasia (ver'ni kēz ə fā'zhə) (also called **sensory aphasia** or **receptive aphasia**). A speech-production deficit supposedly resulting from a lesion damaging part of the left superior temporal gyrus with accompanying impairment of speech comprehension. The person with Wernicke's aphasia appears to be fluent and grammatical, but the output is nonsensical and characterized by paraphasic errors, with substitutions of incorrect words like "grable" for "table." See also: **receptive aphasia.**

Wernicke's syndrome. A condition of some elderly persons in which there is loss of memory, disorientation, and confabulation. See also: **confabulation; Wernicke-Korsakoff synd-rome.**

White matter. Areas of the central nervous system that are mostly comprised of myelin- covered axons. The glistening white is the color of the lipid substance, myelin, not that of the actual nerve tissue. See also: **gray matter.**

Wisconsin Card-Sorting Test. A neuropsychological test in which the patient is required to give up previously correct strategies when sorting cards into piles. Sorting can be done by means of the shapes of the figures on the cards, the color of the figures, or the number of figures. Patients with damage to the frontal lobes will persist in an old strategy long after the need to switch strategy should have become obvious to them.

Withdrawal reflex. The flexion reflex in response to painful stimulation of one of the extremities. The message to the flexor muscle is directly relayed from the dorsal horn cells to the ventral horn cells, making this a one-synapse (monosynaptic) reflex arc (like a stretch reflex). At the same time, however, the extensor muscle that is the antagonist of the activated flexor must be inhibited. This requires a three-neuron arc (i.e., a reflex arc with two synapses): the dorsal horn cells signal inhibitory interneurons to hyperpolarize the motor neurons leading to the extensor.

Withdrawal symptoms. [1] Physical withdrawal. One of the criteria that define drug addiction. The symptoms that an individual undergoes when quitting a drug "cold turkey" are the withdrawal symptoms. They are thought (by adherents of the opponent-process theory) to be the opposite symptoms from those provided by the drug. [2] Psychological withdrawal. A coping mechanism whereby one avoids unpleasant or aversive situations or circumstances that would produce a high level of stress. See also: **opponent-process theory of drug-withdrawal symptoms.**

Wolffian (wool'fē ən) **ducts.** Structures in the developing fetus that are the precursors of mature male genitalia. See also: **Mullerian ducts.**

Word blindness. W. P. Morgan, an ophthalmologist from England, first used the term "congenital word blindness" (which is also referred to as developmental alexia) to describe an inability to read despite apparently normal intelligence.

Word-superiority effect. In attempting to recognize individual letters, people perform better when the letter is part of a word than when the letter is part of a meaningless string of letters. This difference is referred to as the word-superiority effect.

Working memory. The term refers to the concept that, prior to retrieval from long-term memory, the information must first be channeled to the short-term memory. See also: **short-term memory.**

Wryneck (rī'nek"). See also: **torticollis.**

X

X0 or **Turner's syndrome** or **gonadal dysgenesis** (go nad' əl dis jen'ə sis). A sex chromosome abnormality that occurs 5 times in every 100,000 live female births. These individuals are short and have webbed necks, arms positioned so that they rotate outward too much, a wide chest, and amenorrhea (absent or suppressed menstruation). They lack ovaries. Psychologically, they exhibit defective information processing and have poor spatial judgment. It has been suggested that there is abnormal functioning of the right parietal lobe in such patients, an inference drawn from the psychological symptoms just described. See also: **sex chromosome abnormalities.**

X cells. A group of retinal ganglion cells related to the parvocellular visual pathway(s). These cells monitor information regarding color and fine detail. X cells have concentric on-fields and off-fields. See also: **receptive field; off-responses; on-responses.**

X chromosome (krō'mə sōm"). The chromosome which determines the female gender. Normally, women have two X chromosomes. A gene has been found on the X chromosome that is very similar to the TDF (testis-determining factor) gene, which sets in motion a sequence of events which lead to maleness. However, the precise nature of this gene has yet to be determined.

XXX. A sex chromosomal abnormality in which the female has an extra X chromosome, this occurs in 6 out of every 10,000 live female births. There are deficits in auditory processing and in receptive language. However, cognitive ability varies widely, as these individuals range from low average to superior in general intelligence. Although they seem to be normal females, XXX cases often prove to be sterile. See also: **sex chromosome abnormalities.**

XXY or **Klinefelter's syndrome.** This male chromosome abnormality occurs in 1 out of 700 live male births. The patients appear to be normal males who are rather nonmasculine in general appearance and are often tall. Some have cognitive deficits in language. Hormonal therapy can assist in the appropriate physical development. See also: **sex chromosome abnormalities.**

XYY. A male chromosomal abnormality related to a severe behavior disorder. At one time, possession of this abnormality was used as a defense for those charged with violent crimes. It was later established that the condition is more likely to be linked to white-collar criminal activity than to assaultive behavior, so the defense is no longer available. See also: **sex chromosome abnormalities.**

Y

Y cells. A group of retinal ganglion cells that participate in the magnocellular visual pathway(s). These cells register information regarding movement and depth.

Y chromosome. The chromosome which determines maleness. A gene called the testis-determining factor (TDF) is located on the Y chromosome, and this one gene is thought to be the predisposing factor for the male sex. Normally, men have one X and one Y chromosome. Accordingly, in the formation of his own sperm cells, a father can contribute either an X or a Y chromosome to the offspring.

Yerkes-Dodson law. The model of the relationship between motivational level and efficiency of performance. When efficiency is measured at ever-increasing levels of motivation, it increases initially, comes to a peak, and decreases thereafter. This means that there is an optimal level of arousal for good performance; motivation can be too low or too high for the best work. Other psychologists have extended this relationship by replacing the motivation variable with anxiety level and with muscular tension level. Again, in both of these instances, a moderate tension level leads to the best performance. The model also covers a second variable, the complexity of the task. The more complex the task, the lower is the optimal arousal level for peak performance. For a very simple task, for example, the optimal value of the arousal can be quite high.

Young-Helmholtz theory or **trichromoatic theory of color vision** (from Greek "treis" = "three"; "chroma" = "color"). The hypothesis that color perception occurs by means of the response rates of three different types of visual cone receptors, each kind maximally sensitive to different wavelengths.

Z

Zeigarnik (zī gär′nik) **effect**. The phenomenon of having a better memory for interrupted tasks than for completed tasks.

Zeitgeber (tsīt′gə bər) (from German for "time-giver"). Any physical or chemical event that resets the organism's biological clock. For example, the ups and downs of illumination throughout the 24-hour day control our circadian rhythms, the activities that we do just once a day. Any clue that helps people adapt to the 24-hour daily cycle qualifies as a Zeitgeber. This includes watches and clocks, as well as the internal cues that accompany mealtime, the positioning of the sun in the sky, and the outdoor temperature. See also: **circadian rhythms; entrainment; melatonin; pineal gland; suprachiasmatic nucleus.**

Zero reject. In the context of Public Law 94-142 of the United States of America, the Individuals with Disabilities Education Act, this is the requirement that a free and appropriate education be provided for any child with special needs. No handicapped child is to be rejected.

Z-lens. An optical system designed by E. Zaidel that allows a visual stimulus to be projected to just one visual field (the right one or the left one). Previously, such a selection of either visual field required rapid tachistoscopic projection of the figure, usually for a fraction of a second. The Z-lens allows the subject to inspect the image for minutes, if necessary, with no risk of having the image move into the other visual hemifield. With split-brained patients (those with a severed corpus callosum), the Z-lens allows a researcher to investigate the unique functions of either the left or the right cerebral hemisphere. This is because the left visual field is represented in the right hemisphere and the right visual field is represented in the left hemisphere.

Zoophobia (zō″ə fō′bē ə). Unreasoning fear of animals. See also: **phobias**.

Zygote (zī ′gōt″). A fertilized egg (i.e., an ovum that has been successfully penetrated by a sperm cell). Its cell nuclei contain the complete plans for the assembly of the fully adult organism.